Psychodynamic Technique in the Treatment of the Eating Disorders

Psychodynamic Technique in the Treatment of the Eating Disorders

Edited by

C. Philip Wilson, M.D.,
Charles C. Hogan, M.D.,
and Ira L. Mintz, M.D.

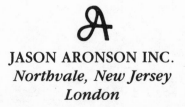

JASON ARONSON INC.
Northvale, New Jersey
London

Production Editors: *Gloria L. Jordan* and *Leslie Block*

Editorial Director: *Muriel Jorgensen*

This book was set in 10-point Garamond by Lind Graphics of Upper Saddle River, New Jersey, and printed and bound by Haddon Craftsmen of Scranton, Pennsylvania.

Library of Congress Cataloging-in-Publication Data

Wilson, C. Philip.
   Psychodynamic technique in the treatment of the eating disorders / C. Philip Wilson, Charles C. Hogan, and Ira L. Mintz.
    p. cm.
   Includes bibliographical references and index.
   ISBN 0-87668-622-6
   1. Eating disorders—Treatment—Case studies. 2. Psychodynamic psychotherapy—Case studies. I. Hogan, Charles C. II. Mintz, Ira L. III Title.
   [DNLM: 1. Eating Disorders—psychology. 2. Eating Disorders--therapy.   WM 175 W747p]
RC552.E18W56 1991
616.85'26—dc20
DNLM/DLC
for Library of Congress   91-17197

Manufactured in the United States of America. Jason Aronson Inc. offers books and cassettes. For information and catalog write to Jason Aronson Inc., 230 Livingston Street, Northvale, New Jersey 07647.

Contents

Contributors

Barton J. Blinder, M.D., PH.D.
Clinical Professor and Director, Eating Disorders Programs and Research Studies, Department of Psychiatry and Human Behavior, College of Medicine, University of California, Irvine; Member, Southern California Psychoanalytic Institute.

Kenneth D. Cohen, M.D.
Training and Supervising Analyst, Institute of the Philadelphia Association for Psychoanalysis; Clinical Associate Professor of Psychiatry, University of Pennsylvania School of Medicine.

John Hitchcock, M.D.
Past Director and member of the faculty of the Pittsburgh Psychoanalytic Institute; Supervising Analyst for Child and Adolescent Analysis.

Charles C. Hogan, M.D.
Assistant Clinical Professor of Psychiatry, Albert Einstein College of Medicine; Lecturer, Columbia University College of Physicians and Surgeons; Faculty, Columbia University Center for Psychoanalytic Training and Research.

Charles R. Keith, M.D.
Associate Professor of Psychiatry and Training Director, Division of Child and Adolescent Psychiatry, Department of Psychiatry, Duke University Medical Center; Training Analyst and Supervising Child Analyst, University of North Carolina, Duke Psychoanalytic Training Program.

Ira L. Mintz, M.D.

Associate Clinical Professor of Psychiatry, New Jersey College of Medicine; Supervising Child Psychoanalyst, Columbia University Psychoanalytic Training Center; former President of the New Jersey Psychoanalytic Society.

Cecil Mushatt, M.D.

Associate Professor of Psychiatry, Boston University School of Medicine; senior staff member in Psychiatry, The University Hospital, Boston University Medical Center; Board of Consultation in Psychiatry, Beth Israel Hospital, Boston; Lecturer in Psychiatry, Harvard Medical School, retired.

Howard S. Rudominer, M.D.

Faculty, The Psychoanalytic Institute, New York University Medical Center; Clinical Assistant Professor of Psychiatry, State University of New York, Health Science Center at Brooklyn (formerly Downstate Medical Center); Clinical Instructor, Department of Psychiatry, New York University Medical Center.

Christina Sekaer, M.D.

Assistant Clinical Professor of Psychiatry, Columbia University College of Physicians and Surgeons; Associate Attending Psychiatrist, St. Luke's–Roosevelt Hospital Center, New York.

C. Philip Wilson, M.D.

Chairman of the Psychosomatic Discussion Groups of the American Psychoanalytic Association and the Psychoanalytic Association of New York, Inc.; Assistant Clinical Professor of Psychiatry, Columbia University College of Physicians and Surgeons; Faculty, Columbia University Center for Psychoanalytic Training and Research; Senior Attending Psychiatrist and Lecturer in Psychosomatics, St. Luke's–Roosevelt Hospital Center; Faculty and Lecturer in Eating Disorders, The Psychoanalytic Institute, New York University Medical Center.

Preface

The fat phobias manifested in the eating disorders, such as anorexia, bulimia, and obesity, are deeply rooted in unresolved sadomastic, oral-phase conflicts, whose developmental impact on the psyche has been so overwhelming that these patients are in an ambivalent state in which they actually do not know whether they are "living to eat or eating to live." They repetitiously obsess about diets and food. This volume details techniques of interpretation that can resolve these patient's stubborn defenses against the acknowledgment of their underlying conflicts. The contributors provide a clinically documented understanding of the psychodynamic structure of the various personality disorders that are masked by eating-disorder symptoms. They explore the structure of the ego and superego and the nature of the object relations in a wide range of diagnostic categories, including neurotic compulsive eating, restrictor and bulimic anorexia nervosa, obesity, and rumination. Special therapeutic problems are detailed, such as the analysis of severe regressive symptomatology, the use of medication, hospitalization, countertransference, and the treatment of an eating disorder in a child with an alimentary congenital defect. A particular focus is on preverbal and early verbal communication, separation-individuation, the underlying impulse disorder, part-object relations, and projective identification. In case after case the authors demonstrate that a psychotherapeutic approach that focuses on the underlying neurotic conflicts can result in normal eating and psychic health.

Acknowledgment

We would like to express our appreciation to the founder of the Psycho-somatic Discussion Group of the Psychoanalytic Association of New York, Inc., Dr. Melitta Sperling, for her pioneering research, teaching, and publications. We also owe a great debt to Drs. Max Schur and Otto Sperling, our teachers at the Downstate Psychoanalytic Institute, and to Drs. George Daniels and Aaron Karush of the Center for Psychoanalytic Training and Research of Columbia College of Physicians and Surgeons.

Seminal to our research have been the contributions of the Melitta Sperling Memorial Lecturers: Drs. Norman Atkins, L. Bryce Boyer, Harold P. Blum, Lawrence Deutsch, James Herzog, Stanislaw Kasl, Peter H. Knapp, Cecil Mushatt, George Pollock, Morton Reiser, Samuel Ritvo, Robert A. Savitt, Albert Solnit, C. Philip Wilson and Eleanor Galenson.

The contributors to this volume have had their work greatly enriched and stimulated by their involvement in two psychosomatic research units, both composed of psychoanalytically trained psychiatrists specializing in the treatment of psychosomatic disorders. The first is the Psychosomatic Discussion Group of the Psychoanalytic Association of New York, Inc. This long-standing group was led by Dr. Melitta Sperling from 1960 until her death in 1973; since that time, the chairman has been Dr. C. Philip Wilson. The second research unit is the Psychosomatic Discussion Group of the American Psychoanalytic Association, which has been chaired by Dr. Wilson since its inception in 1983. In these long-term research groups there has been the unique opportunity to review, study, and discuss the analyses of numerous psychosomatic cases. Thus a rich cross-fertilization has resulted from the deliberations of some fifty psychoanalysts from the major psychoanalytic centers of the United States. Particularly important has been the presentation of the psychodynamic treatment of the mother, the father, the siblings, and the spouses of these patients, which has provided an in-depth understanding of family psychopathology.

We are indebted to the many members of the psychosomatic research groups, particularly Drs. Norman Atkins, Leonard Barkin, Stephen L. Bennett, Barton J. Blinder, L. Bryce Boyer, Sylvia Brody, Anna Burton, Kenneth D. Cohen, Lawrence Deutsch, Gerald Freiman, Eleanor Galenson, David Goldman, Remi G. Gonzalez, Henry Haberfeld, Charles C. Hogan, Jennifer Hunt, Doris M. Hunter, Mary J. Jensen, Ceceilia Karol, Charles R. Keith, Edward Leader, Ronald Levin, Deborah S. Link, Charles McGann, Jack Miller, Burness E. Moore, Muriel Gold Morris, Donald Moss, Cecil Mushatt, Mary Roberts, Sam Rubin, Howard S. Rudominer, Charles A. Sarnoff, Anita Schmukler, Henry Schneer, Harvey J. Schwartz, Howard L. Schwartz, Robert Schwartz, Christina Sekaer, Noah Shaw, Charles Stone, Jacob Stump, Pietro Castel-Nuovo Tedesco, Howard K. Welsh, and Barbara Young.

Many of the chapters and hypotheses in this volume were originally presented in the form of lectures, electives, symposiums, and papers at the Departments of Psychiatry of St. Luke's–Roosevelt Hospital Center; the Albert Einstein College of Medicine; Saint Barnabas Medical Center; Hackensack (New Jersey) Hospital Medical Center; the Downstate Psychoanalytic Institute; the Department of Psychiatry, State University of New York, Downstate; the Department of Psychiatry, Brookdale Hospital Center; the Center for Psychoanalytic Training and Research of the Columbia University College of Physicians and Surgeons; the Psychoanalytic Institute, New York University Medical Center; and the Department of Psychiatry, New York University Medical Center.

We are in debt to the staffs, students, and faculties of these institutions, especially Drs. John M. Cotton, Maurice Friend, John Frosch, Stanley Heller, Byram Karasu, Sylvan Keiser, Clarice Kestenbaum, Sandor Lorand, David M. MacDonald, Helen C. Meyers, John W. Rosenberger, Nathaniel Ross, John A. Sours, and Theodore Van Itallie.

Our work has also been enriched by the many discussants of psychosomatic papers that we have given throughout the United States, particularly Drs. Norman Atkins, Stanley Friedman, Raymond Gehl, Daniel L. Goldstein, Ronald Levin, Norman Oberman, Frank H. Parcells, Sherwin S. Radin, Howard Schlossman, and Frederick Shevin.

Drs. Richard Galdston, Athol Hughes, Murray Jackson, Naama Kushnir, and Muriel Gold Morris focused and clarified our psychosomatic research in their excellent book reviews of our anorexia and psychosomatic volumes.

Finally, we want to express our gratitude to our wives for the support and work they have contributed to the preparation of this book.

Introduction

Although symptoms such as anorexia nervosa or obesity are phenomenologically similar, eating-disorder patients themselves differ widely in genetic makeup, psychodynamics, and type of character disorder, ranging from hysterical and obsessive-compulsive to borderline and near-psychotic. Constitutional, environmental, and emotional factors are expressed in a complex interaction for which the symptoms are the final common pathway.

For psychoanalysts it is axiomatic that symptom complexes (of which eating disorders are one of many components) are multidetermined and overdetermined. We recognize the importance of the family history and associated genetic vulnerabilities. Likewise, somatic compliance is significant. Thus, phase-specific events, such as trauma or infection, may sensitize or damage an organ system, predisposing it for the development of psychosomatic symptoms. For example, maternal illness may interfere with normal breastfeeding and the mother–infant relationship, predisposing the child for the development of an eating disorder later in life.

However, the question is not which factor—genetic, environmental, immunologic, traumatic, infectious, or emotional (neurosis)—is paramount, but whether interference in the operation of one of these factors results in the significant amelioration or long-term cessation, that is, "cure," of the eating disorder symptom. We have found that the analytic therapy of the underlying personality disorder leads to a resolution or marked diminution of symptoms.

In Chapter 1, Wilson emphasizes that restrictor and bulimic anorexia nervosa can be considered specific pathological outcomes of unresolved oedipal conflicts in patients whose preoedipal relationship to the parents predisposed them to these particular reactions under precipitating circumstances. He notes that fat phobia should replace anorexia nervosa, since these patients do not suffer from lack of appetite but from the opposite, a fear of being overwhelmed by their impulses, including voraciousness, and that the basic analytic task is the analysis of the underlying personality disorder (Wilson and Mintz 1989). While the underlying conflicts masked by the fear-of-being-fat complex are similar, the restrictor, part of whose ego structure resembles that of the compulsive neurotic, overcontrols the impulse to gorge and impulses of other kinds because of punitive archaic superego demands and intact ego controls. The bulimic, whose ego structure is an admixture of hysterical and compulsive traits, is unable to contain the impulses to gorge as well as other impulse gratifications because the defective ego is unable to carry out the punitive strictures of an archaic punitive superego.

An etiologic family psychological profile was detailed that was characterized by parental perfectionism, overcontrol, and overemphasis on dieting and fears of being fat. The parents of bulimics evidence a greater incidence of neurotic conflict and addictive behavior. In most adolescent cases, the mother and/or father need conjoint therapy to change their pathological relationship to their child. While some cases can be analyzed with classical technique, with many patients the initial technique focuses on dyadic material. Most patients are seen face to face with early interpretation of manifestations of their impulse disorder. Only when there has been a modification of the archaic superego with ego maturation and a shift from part-object relationships can triadic oedipal material be interpreted.

In this early phase, an effective technique with restrictor anorexics is to interpret defenses (rationalization, denial, and so on) that mask masochistic behavior, whereas with bulimics the multiple functions of the patient's gorging, vomiting, and laxative use are interpreted as acting-out defenses against the experiencing of affects such as guilt, anxiety, depression, anger, or sexual feelings.

The therapist is in charge of treatment. Hospitalization is reserved for real emergencies. Medication is usually contraindicated if psychoanalysis is feasible.

In Chapter 2, Wilson focuses on "Personality Structure and Psychoanalytic Treatment of Obesity." Drawing on a wide spectrum of obese patients, including six analytic cases, he offers a psychoanalytic explanation and treatment of obesity. He compares obese patients to restrictor and bulimia anorexics and points out that patients complaining of obesity are also obsessed with an overdetermined "fear-of-being-fat" complex and concerns about dieting. Whereas the ego of the restrictor anorexic evidences intact impulse control capacities, resulting in overcontrol of impulses, the obese patient's ego is defective in its capacity to control not only oral impulses, but impulses of other kinds, and the superego is not as perfectionistic and controlling as that of the anorexic.

Obesity as a symptom complex is found in a variety of character disorders. Wilson stresses that whatever the diagnosis, obesity is an indication of an impulse disorder. The obese patient is aware of being fat and does not have the same body-image distortion as the anorexic. Wilson attributes this fact to the less strict superego and the defective ego functioning of the obese. He offers a clinical example of an obese young man in analysis to illustrate the interrelation of the psychodynamics of the patient's underlying impulse disorder, manifestations of which were obesity, a habit of nail-biting, and addictions to cigarettes and alcohol.

In the treatment of obesity, Wilson emphasizes the importance of understanding the impulse disorders, the addictive personality structure, and the habit disorders of childhood. The ego makes use of the same defenses in its struggles with a childhood habit or a childhood impulse disorder as it does later on in efforts to cope with eating disorders. Thus the defenses of denial, splitting, displacement, externalization, and conscious withholding and lying are deeply ingrained in the ego structure of the obese. When addicted patients interrupt their habits, they may gain weight and become obese; conversely, obese patients, while losing weight, may turn to addictions to relieve their conflicts with other impulse gratifications. The good humor and joking of the obese is a façade that masks conflicts, anxiety, and depression. In spite of the complexity of parental behaviors, the developmental conflicts, and identifications that have to be taken into account, the family psychodynamics in obesity differ from those of anorexic patients. Wilson cites cases where the analysis of the patient's narcissistic impulsivity resulted in an organized sense of time and a resolution of the underlying personality disorder, obesity, and other symptoms.

In Chapter 3, Mintz emphasizes that the conscious fear of being fat can cover up the unconscious need to be fat: that the unconscious meaning of being fat varies with different people, but within a range of relatively specific conflicts. The intensity of that fear depends upon, first, the unconscious nature of the conflicts defended against; second, the ability of the ego to contain its impulses; third, the capacity to tolerate anxiety; and finally, the amount of guilt that the conflict generates. He adds that in many patients it is not always the fatness or weight per se that is feared, but the process of eating that is frightening. The patient then displaces this fear onto the weight gain.

Mintz presents vivid clinical examples of the fear of being fat in normal, obese, starving, and gorging individuals. In each case, he shows that the conscious fear of being fat represented an attempted unconscious resolution of conflicts primarily over aggressive, sexual, and dependency problems. In the first case, obesity served as a protective wall that preserved external objects in the face of the patient's unconscious explosiveness and simultaneously protected the patient from realistic and projected external aggressive attack. The second patient used obesity as a multidetermined symbol to express the reliving of an unresolved pregnancy conflict, an attempt to kill her unborn child with toxemia, punishment for this wish, denial of her father's death, and a rebirth fantasy. In another patient, obesity was used to defy the patient's mother while maintaining a symbiotic attachment to her, and to avoid sexual involvement. In the fourth case, a young boy starved himself, expressing his flight from an unconscious identification with a pregnant woman and his need to deny unconscious cannibalistic impulses to destroy his hated sister, to eat her, and to blow up with a pregnancy. In the fifth case, Mintz found that major determinants in a woman patient's bulimic episodes reflected an unconscious pregenital impulse to merge with her father and to act out a preoedipal and an oedipal fantasy. The induction of vomiting represented a symbolic rage, and the vomiting itself was an outpouring of aggression and unconscious orgastic experience.

In Chapter 4, Hogan presents an interesting and compelling thesis that the significant increase in the number of cases of anorexic eating disorders is due primarily to changing attitudes toward sexuality in our society. He feels that the most dramatic impact of such changes is on the adolescent population. Hogan presents histories of two women with anorexia, one an ascetic restrictor and the other a sexually acting out bulimic. Despite their different personalities and behavior, each eventually revealed severely impaired capacities for sexual pleasure and sexual sensation. At puberty both women encountered not only an intensely conflicted relationship with their own aggressive and sexual impulses, but equal difficulties in regard to peer pressure, peer temptation, media stimulation, and society's general erotic stimula.

Hogan observes that the greatest societal change in the Western and Japanese worlds (where the greatest increase in anorexia has occurred) in the last two generations has been the radical revision of society's ostensible social mores. He suggests that those outside pressures and temptations lead to a premature eruption of neurotic or at times psychotic symptoms in a group of vulnerable, predisposed women and men. He speculates that three decades ago such young people had more time to mature sexually before yielding to, or rejecting, peer and societal demands for erotic activity. Other neurotic symptoms might have appeared at a later date, but such precipitous self-destructive symptomatic activity would not have been necessary.

Hogan goes on in Chapter 5 to address the problem of gender identity in both restrictor and bulimic anorexic women. Repeated split-off episodic intervals of masculine behavior and fantasy in each of four patients illustrate the need for early interpretation. Such behavior in transference and life circumstance occurs as a response to the perceived vulnerability and humiliation of femininity and sexual excitement. One patient's history also includes a brief description of the dynamics of her kleptomania to illustrate the masculine and phallic fantasies coincident with this common anorexic symptom.

Hogan discusses one of the exceptions to the observation that one interprets the masochistic and aggressive pregenital fantasies and defenses early and awaits the later emergence of oedipal concerns before offering interpretations of genital identifications. When the fantasies of sexual identification are on an almost-conscious level (preconscious), it is advisable to provide transference interpretations early in the analysis. In these patients there is an amalgam of pregenital fantasies of identification with the primal part-object (breast, mother) and the oedipal object (phallus, father). It is the task of the analyst to decide the level to interpret at any given stage of the therapy.

In Chapter 6, Hogan demonstrates that unmodified classical psychoanalysis has a most important role as a treatment choice with many anorexic women. He presents the history of a restrictor anorexic who also suffered from migraine headaches. There is a detailed review of the treatment, which was successful in eliminating both the anorexia and the migraine. The evolution of this patient's treatment demonstrates the amalgam of oedipal concerns and pregenital regressions that are characteristic of patients with eating disorders. The ubiquitous intense adolescent oedipal struggle is clearly illustrated. Such cases demonstrate that the major problems in patients with psychosomatic symptoms such as anorexia or migraine lie not in the remission of symptoms but in the resolution of the underlying personality disorder.

In Chapter 7, Mintz had the unusual opportunity to read the patient's diary sixteen months after the initial phase of treatment and learned about her reactions to her treatment. In Chapter 7 he correlates on a session-by-session basis her response to specific sessions. Certain fascinating, dynamic, technical, and therapeutic implications were evident from reading the diary that were not clearly manifested during the treatment sessions.

The patient's understanding of the purpose of her starving was either conscious or certainly very close to conscious awareness. Nevertheless, she initially was coerced into the consultation against her will, claiming that there was nothing wrong with her. Many of Mintz's patients seen in consultation and treatment arrive under these same conditions. Nevertheless, early exploration with these patients reveals that they occasionally volunteer some peripheral awareness that the starving is set off by conflict and that it decreases anxiety or, more frequently, they acknowledge this fact with little surprise when it is suggested. Similarly, bulimic patients volunteer or acknowledge that the gorging is precipitated by conflicts and that it decreases the anxiety. Like the anorexic patients who return to the starving, they return to the gorging.

Subsequently, such understanding is almost never voluntarily recalled, explored further, or again utilized in the service of attempting to control or avoid future tension or conflict. An open discussion of the past distressing experience is not initiated. Without the analyst's reintroducing the issue, the patient will ignore it or repress the previously acknowledged relationship between an external or internal conflict, the development of anxiety, feelings of being overwhelmed or starving, and the subsequent easing of the conflict. The same sequence exists where binging substitutes for starving. Thus, the therapist is confronted with a paradox. A patient under pressure to eat normally either starves or secretly binges while seeming to have some awareness of the cause of her behavior, yet does not voluntarily reveal her understanding. Moreover, she frequently acts as if she is unaware of it and behaves as if there is nothing wrong with her. Concomitantly, pointing out the dynamic relationship between crisis, starving, and decreasing anxiety is often accepted, without much surprise. This resistance to using understanding is profound.

A second feature of considerable interest was the intensity of this patient's turmoil. While it was not surprising that conflict produces anxiety, the intensity and the extent of the anxiety and tension were more profound and devastating than was anticipated. There are poignant references in the diary to the sense of anguish and agitation as the patient attempted to confront powerful issues. In order to decrease her perceived intolerable turmoil, the patient experienced the overwhelming need to starve, to run, and to engage in typical anorexic behavior. This behavior then caused the anxiety to recede.

A third element noted was the change in attitude toward the treatment and her relationship toward the analyst. She arrived for a consultation feeling coerced by her parents, volunteering that she did not wish to be there, and stating that there was nothing wrong with her. By the third session however, she wanted to continue the treatment, thought that she might be able to get well, and had developed a therapeutic alliance. This striking turnabout had not been revealed to the analyst.

The preoccupation with "the other" at the expense of the self, a typical anorexic character trait, was explored during a starvation crisis. The patient's need to starve, with no endpoint in sight, with focus upon its effect upon "the other" (person) without thoughts of consequence to the self, could produce an illusive sense of satisfaction leading to an unrecognized moribund condition.

A 30 percent loss of body weight revealed no evidence, either from her behavior in treatment or from her reflections in the diary, that her thinking capacity or the depth of her emotional experience was in any manner compromised. Her thinking, when she chose to verbalize, was astute, cogent, and incisive, while her range of emotional feelings was broad and intense. This finding correlates with the intact cognitive functioning that has been detailed by analytic clinicians in other emaciated anorexics and negates the psychiatric dictum that all patients who starve require nutritional supplements prior to being able to utilize analytic types of treatment.

In Chapter 8, Rudominer offers us a provocative case history of the treatment of a male bulimic patient. He notes that male bulimic and anorexic patients are a minority. This patient was in preparatory treatment for eleven months and then in traditional psychoanalysis for two and one-half years. When he terminated, he had been symptom-free for at least six months, had married, and had made significant career choices. This productive, positive outcome of the therapy was maintained three years later.

Rudominer notes that, although there was complete remission of symptoms, the patient terminated prematurely. He felt that there were feminine identifications and homosexual transferential issues that had not been worked through. These observations illustrate a most important issue in the treatment of eating disorders: We are not satisfied with just the remission of overt symptoms, although that is always important, but rather in the resolution of the underlying neurotic and personality problems. Herein is the solution to the pathological conflict behind symptom formation.

In Chapter 9, Cohen presents the history of a 40-year-old bulimic patient who was successfully treated with classical psychoanalysis. There were no parameters to traditional treatment. The symptom complex had had a duration of twenty-five years. Cohen presents a carefully detailed evaluation of the analysis. The symptom of bulimia was a multidetermined regressive defense against the oedipal triumph that was couched in oral-cannibalistic terms. Similar mechanisms were utilized in the effort to overcome penis envy. The patient worked well in analysis, achieving structural change and a resolution of her long-standing bulimic symptoms.

The importance of aggression in the early development of children with eating disorders is explored by Hitchcock in Chapter 10 which contains a wealth of clinical, dynamic, and therapeutic understanding about the anorexic-bulimic syndrome in young children. Not only did Hitchcock gather information from the analyses of three young girls, ages 4, 6, and 9, but he had the rare opportunity to observe the setting in which the illness crystallized and unfolded during the analysis of other symptoms for which the children were being treated. Thus, we are able to observe highlights from the detailed data on the anorexic-bulimic illness, in which the relationship to parents and the early developmental stages are virtually current, not requiring later reconstruction, with possible accompanying misperceptions or inaccuracies.

Most prominent was Hitchcock's consistent analysis of the denial and reaction formation defenses against aggression in all three of the children. These interpretations, along with the developing transference and its interpretation, contributed to the destabilizing situation in which the anorexic-bulimic illnesses emerged. Of additional interest was the clinical similarity of the manifestations of the aggressive conflict in the three children. This extended into detailed aspects of oral-aggressive symbolic behavior. Two of the children, both with perpetual smiling, reflected during play an animal-like opening of their mouths, with their lips drawn and their teeth bared, when catching a ball. As the aggressive conflict was exposed, the smile of one of the two gradually was replaced by a hostile grimace. When the aggression of the third child was analyzed and emerged, there developed a tightening of the lips and clenched teeth.

The findings suggest that with eating disorders, disturbances in aggression are evident during all stages of development, including infancy, with interference in all subphases of the separation-individuation process. These early clinical data lend additional validity to the analytic conclusions that the anorexic-bulimic illness usually present in adolescence has an earlier underlying historical background and should not be viewed as solely a current problem in eating.

In Chapter 11, Sekaer details the psychodynamic treatment of a $5\frac{1}{2}$-year-old tube-fed child, a girl born with a congenital defect, esophageal fistula, who, following successful reparative surgery, refused to eat. Analytic psychotherapy of the girl and her parents resulted in normal eating. This case is a unique opportunity for the exploration of oral-drive development, body image pathology, the therapist as a new object, and the crucial importance of the conjoint psychotherapy of the parents to get them to leave eating up to their daughter.

In Chapter 12, Keith presents the complex problems in the case of a neurotic woman who *developed* bulimic symptoms in the second year of analysis. He explores the ego functioning and the transference and the complications of the patient's seeking out and obtaining antidepressant medication at the urging of her mother as well as the interruption and resumption of analysis. Keith focuses on the important therapeutic issues encountered in these impulsive acting-out patients.

Mushatt's Chapter 13 emphasizes the limitations of viewing anorexia nervosa (fat phobia) primarily in terms of oedipal sexual conflicts. Anorexia may be precipitated by and expressive of conflicts from all levels of development. Bodily functions such as not eating (anorexia) or overeating (obesity) can express the separation-individuation process, the loss-destruction-restitution conflict. In his clinical vignettes, Mushatt underscores the anorexics' fears of their voraciousness and insatiability and the intensity of their narcissism.

In Chapter 14, Mintz presents a review of the presence of animal symbolism in the analytic literature and in extensive case material. The focus, however, is upon anorexic and bulimic conflict where a preponderance of sharp-toothed animals is clinically evident. The preoccupation with teeth in these patients is striking. Rats, gerbils, sharks, piranhas, snakes, maggots, pigs, eels, spiders, wolves, and finally dragons and vampires abound in fantasy, play, behavior, reading, and dreams. This preoccupation with teeth is a reflection of aggressive conflict during infancy and childhood, with the resulting incorporation of these destructive, biting, ambivalently cathected introjects. These early animal identifications are evident in the later clinical picture of anorexia and bulimia, where the animals and their symbolic representations reemerge and reflect the patient's unconscious identification with these tooth-bearing animals, the hypercathexis of the teeth, and deeply regressed cannibalistic fantasies.

While bulimic gorging and anorexic starving are symptomatic and preoccupy the patient, the impulse to bite and the inhibition against it play a major role in the intrapsychic conflict. This is revealed in the projections of these impulses onto rats and other prominent tooth-bearing animals and their symbolic representations. On occasion the liberation of the introjects emerges in dreams or fantasies, with rats pouring out of the patient's mouth. Symbolic representations are common in the frequent aggressive use of the knife, a condensation of jaws full of thirty-two "knife-teeth," with the patient's fantasies of stabbing the hated object. Destructive sucking with a denial of use of the teeth is a modification of these carnivorous impulses. The 10-year-old boy whose sole nutrition was derived from sucking milk shakes was the same patient whose carnivorous impulses, preoccupations, and overt cannibalistic fantasies were most prominent.

Finally, the interrelationship between destructive sucking and destructive eating is most clearly represented by the vampire fantasy, which reveals a fusion of biting and sucking. This may help clarify the increased coexistence of asthma and anorexia, where the violent sucking in of the "air-milk mother" is an expression of aggression toward the ambivalently cathected introject.

A series of clinical vignettes are presented in Chapter 15. These illustrate a prominent feature of anorexic or bulimic illness and attempt to clarify the underlying meaning of the behavior.

In the first, "The Relationship between Anorexia-Bulimia and Exercise," Mintz utilizes a unique chance experience to analyze the interrelationship between exercise and the onset of bulimia. An athletic adolescent girl suffers a broken elbow and, a year later, a broken ankle and is unable to exercise. Both fractures are followed by the development of bulimia, which clears as the patient recovers the ability to exercise. The underlying dynamic factors behind this circumstance are analyzed and compared to the anorexic features often seen in compulsive runners.

In "Gum-Chewing in Anorexia Nervosa and Bulimia: A Bulimic Equivalent," Mintz attempts to clarify the reason for gum chewing in anorexia. In certain circumstances, a patient will chew 125 sticks of gum daily, making it a major portion of nutritional intake. Reasons by the patient for this excessive chewing are many: "enjoyment of the sweet taste," "like eating candy as a child," "a relationship to mother," "like eating all the time and keeping my mouth busy," "an alternative to gorging." Unconsciously, however, it appears to be related to the ambivalent relationship to people, where the aggressive need to destroy the object is fused with the dependent need to preserve it. Gum is the only substance that can be chewed endlessly and yet be preserved.

In "The Unconscious Meaning of Laxative Use in Anorexia and Bulimia," the third vignette, the prodigious use of large doses of 50 to 100 laxatives is analyzed. Gorging usually predisposes the patient to vomiting or to laxative use. It is often rationalized as the need to avoid getting fat or to rid oneself of constipation, but this rationalization does not explain the use of 25 to 50 times the normal dosage. Two clinical cases are presented to clarify the unconscious meaning of this self-destructive behavior. The clinical data illustrate that the stool represents unconscious, fantasied, significant people in the patient's life, and the laxative usage is a reflection of the patient's attitude toward them.

In the fourth vignette, "Living on the Edge," Mintz describes the secondary gain derived from an anorexic patient's ego attitude. In treatment for three years and no longer emaciated, the patient stated that emaciation, a previously sought-after goal, was now disgusting. What she now enjoyed was "being on the edge." By that she meant that while she no longer looked skeletal, she was close enough to it that people perceived that it would not take much to reproduce the earlier emaciation; therefore, people should treat her thoughtfully and carefully in order not to feel responsible for making her sick again. Ultimately, she was led to recognize that this attitude gratified still-unresolved regressive, aggressive, sexual, and dependency conflicts of a lesser magnitude. It thus represented a change, a less intense need to evoke sympathy derived from more intense symptomatology.

In "An Anorexic Perspective on Toothbrush Swallowing in Anorexia and Bulimia," Mintz describes a 15-year-old bulimic girl who swallowed four toothbrushes during the course of bulimic gorging and vomiting. Both conscious and unconscious motivations are discussed. The patient suggested that the toothbrush swallowing occurred because she experienced increased pressure from her parents to stop gorging and vomiting. Clinical material presented reveals the unconscious meaning of the toothbrush swallowing, integrated into the general nature of her conflicts and the typical methods of ego resolution for these conflicts. The need to clean out unacceptable unconscious impulses was reflected in the symptomatic act. The consequence of pressured removal of symptoms is also illustrated.

In the vignette "Menstruating in Anorexia as a Defense against Self-Destructive Acting Out," Mintz cites a 22-year-old woman whose anorexic conflict became increasingly expressed by binging and laxative use. During her course of treatment, as she came to terms with her inner repulsion and unwillingness to menstruate, she was gradually able to begin menstruating. In the process, it became clear to her that when she regressed she was also able to modify or completely interrupt her period. She became convinced of her control over her periods. It was within this context that during a subsequent distressing conflict, when she decided not to act out destructively by binging and laxative use, she contemplated sexual acting out. Although it was pointed out that in the past this behavior precipitated a severe depression, was undaunted in her resolve. In the next day's session, however, she consciously decided against it. Issues involving menstruation played a role in the resolution of the self-destructive behavior.

In the seventh vignette, "Binging Inside and Outside as the Displacement of Dependency Conflict," Mintz illustrates a bulimic patient's increasing awareness of her mother's bulimic equivalent. Both the patient and her mother would respond to stress with bulimia. Gradual recognition of the meaning and purpose of her own bulimic behavior enabled the patient to see her mother's modified form of bulimia. When the mother did not binge with food in response to increased anxiety, the patient recognized a bulimic equivalent in her specific acting-out behavior as an alternate resolution to dependency conflict.

In Chapter 16, Blinder suggests a formulation to bridge the gap between psychodevelopmental events and neurobiologic determinants in patients manifesting rumination. Rumination, an uncommon disorder occurring from infancy through adult life, consists of regurgitating and then reswallowing partially digested food. It may result in considerable morbidity in infants and young children. Adult ruminators may have a benign course with embarrassing involuntary reflux or may have an associated eating disorder (bulimia or anorexia nervosa) or depression.

Biologic theories of etiology associate rumination with gastroesophageal reflux, hiatus hernia, and delayed gastric emptying. Psychological theories have focused on infants who have severe failure to thrive and often appear depressed. Frequently noted were severe dysynchrony between mother and infant and maternal psychopathology consisting of anxiety, depression, and the inability to nurture the child adequately. Behavioral theory discusses the self-reinforcing aspect of the ruminatory behavior.

Theories of neuropeptide and opioid regulation posit central and peripheral deficits of endorphinergic neurotransmission and receptor sensitivity. There may be an endorphinergic deficit that appears in response to disruption of attachment, resulting in the appearance of rumination.

Therapy approaches include biologic treatment of reflux, psychological treatment of the infant–mother dysynchrony (with the use of substitute caretakers), and behavioral treatment, consisting of both aversive stimuli and positive reinforcement. Rumination may also be considered an affective disorder variant. Since it may have either a biological- or a psychological-predominant context, a multidisciplinary approach to diagnosis and treatment, using various modalities, is imperative to treat this disorder comprehensively.

In Chapter 17, the Epilogue, Wilson reviews short- and long-term results of therapy, emphasizing the importance of the resolution of the fear-of-being-fat body image pathology. Case material is presented to demonstrate that while there are many successfully analyzed cases, if eating-disorder symptoms clear before there has been sufficient change in the underlying neurosis and the object relations, equivalents may emerge that include self-destructive acting out; an alternate addictive disorder such as obesity, alcoholism, or drug addiction; alternate psychosomatic symptom formation; neurotic symptom formation or severe regressive (psychotic) symptom formation.

C. Philip Wilson, M.D.
Charles C. Hogan, M.D.
Ira L. Mintz, M.D.

PART I

The Fear of
Being Fat

1

Ego Functioning and Technique

C. Philip Wilson, M.D.

Eating disorders are symptom complexes that occur in a variety of character disorders: hysterical, obsessive-compulsive, borderline, and, in some cases, conditions close to the psychoses. The major problem is that the eating-disordered patients do not readily seek treatment, and if they do, they want a resolution of the symptom itself rather than a comprehensive approach to the underlying personality disorder, which can be provided only by psychodynamic treatment (Sperling 1967, 1978, Wilson 1971a, 1982a, 1986a, 1988a,b, 1985, Wilson and Mintz 1989, Wilson et al. 1985).

Eating disorders make their appearance within a range of developmental phases (Blinder et al. 1988, Blitzer et al. 1961, A. Freud 1946, Sours 1980, Wilson and Mintz 1989, Wilson et al. 1985). If an eating disorder appears as a symptom in a neurotic patient, it may often be resolved in the course of the analysis of the patient's nuclear conflicts and may not be a problem in the initial phase of treatment. The focus of this chapter will be largely on the complex and difficult initial phase of analysis of restrictor and bulimic anorexia nervosa in cases where the eating disorder is a major presenting symptom.

THE FEAR-OF-BEING-FAT COMPLEX

An understanding of "the fear-of-being-fat complex" is necessary for the treatment of the eating disorders. Fear of being fat can occur for realistic medical or personal reasons. However, the conscious fear of being fat can cover up the unconscious need to be fat. The unconscious meaning of being fat varies with different people, such as in an adolescent girl or boy. It is overdetermined. The intensity of this fear depends upon the number and intensity of conflicts defended against, the individual's developmental phase, the ability of the ego to contain its impulses, the capacity to tolerate anxiety, and the amount of guilt that the conflicts generate.

The skeptic may posit some degree of orality in any unconscious conflict. Why postulate a fear-of-being-fat complex? The answer to this question lies in the analysis of the body-image disturbance in anorexia nervosa.

Briefly, the fear-of-being-fat complex is defined as that cluster of orally rooted unconscious conflicts whose most clear-cut conscious manifestation is a psychotic-like anorexic body image characterized by an irrational fear of being fat and an obsessive overconcern with being thin. A similar fear-of-being-fat complex is seen in the other eating disorders such as obesity (Savitt 1980) but with variations in the body-image pathology because of differences in the structure of the ego and superego.

At a recent panel of the American Psychoanalytic Association I reported on my experience with a wide spectrum of obese patients, including six analytic cases offering a psychoanalytic exploration and treatment of obesity (Wilson 1988d). I compared obese patients to restrictor and bulimic anorexics and pointed out that patients complaining of obesity were also obsessed with an overdetermined fear-of-being-fat complex and with concerns about dieting. However, whereas the ego of the restrictor anorexic evidences intact impulse control capacities, resulting in overcontrol of impulses, the obese patient's ego is defective in its capacity to control not only oral impulses, but impulses of many other kinds, and the superego is not as perfectionistic and controlling as that of the anorexic. Whatever the diagnosis, obesity is an indication of an impulse disorder. The obese patient is aware of being fat and does not have the same body-image distortion as the anorexic, because of the less strict superego and the defective ego functioning of the obese.

Scrutiny of certain nonanorexic patients in analysis showed a less intensely cathected but clear-cut fear-of-being-fat body-image disturbance, and normal women who were questioned showed that they also had the fear. Male homosexuals and men with severe latent homosexual conflicts, as a result of their unconscious feminine identification, also have the fear-of-being-fat body-image disturbance, while other men do not evidence this pathology (Mintz 1988, Wilson 1980c, 1982a, Wilson et al. 1985).

TECHNIQUE OF TREATMENT

Analytic technique has to be adapted to the varying defenses of the ego. Eating-disorder patients deny conflict and neurosis, act out, rationalize, withhold, and lie. Technique varies according to the ego structure and the degree of regression encountered. Interpretations are determined by multiple factors such as the transference and the quality of the patient's object relations. A crucial consideration is the split in the patient's ego and the degree to which this split is comprehended by the self-observing functions of the patient's ego. The patient must come to understand the split-off primitive, impulse-dominated part of the eating disorder ego and its modes of functioning.

RESTRICTOR AND BULIMIC ANOREXICS AND THE-FEAR-OF-BEING-FAT-COMPLEX

While there is a heterogeneous range of anorexic patients with great dynamic, structural, and genetic variability under the coating of a relatively uniform symptomatology, in recent years restrictor anorexics have come to be differentiated from bulimics on the basis of ego structure (Wilson 1980c, 1982a, 1985b, 1986a, 1988a,b, Wilson and Mintz 1982, 1989, Wilson et al. 1985). Restrictor anorexics evidence a deliberate refusal to eat and a tenacious pursuit of thinness, often to the point of emaciation and occasionally death. Bulimic anorexics attempt to starve themselves but are unable to control an irresistible urge to gorge, often put on weight, and frequently try to gain control by repeated vomiting. Both groups of patients have a fear of being fat.

Even in the most disturbed cases of anorexia there is a split in the ego, with areas of relatively intact ego functioning and some capacity for a transference relationship.

Thomä's (1967) delineation of anorexia nervosa, concurred with by Wilson and colleagues (1985), includes both the restrictor and the bulimics: (1) the age of onset is usually puberty; (2) the patients are predominantly female (although male cases have been reported by Carlat [1991], Falstein and colleagues [1956], Wilson, Hogan, and Mintz [1985], and Sours [1980]); (3) the reduction in nutritional intake is psychically determined; (4) when spontaneous or self-induced vomiting occurs, the diagnosis of bulimia is made; (5) amenorrhea (which is psychically caused) generally appears either before or, more rarely, after the beginning of the weight loss; (6) constipation, sometimes an excuse for excessive consumption of laxatives, speeds up weight loss; (7) the physical effects of undernourishment are present and in severe cases death may ensue. Wilson, Hogan, and Mintz (1985) added three further observations: (8) there is commonly a tendency toward hyperactivity and exercise, which may be extreme; (9) in females there is often a disproportionate loss of breast tissue early in the disease; and (10) the symptom complex is often accompanied by or alternates with other psychosomatic symptoms (or psychogenic equivalents such as depressions, phobias, or periods of self-destructive acting out that may include impulsive sexual behavior, stealing, or accident-prone behavior. I have detailed (Wilson 1988b) the replacement of bulimia by psychosomatic asthma and, in another patient, by a neurotic character development characterized by "bitchy" behavior; Mintz (1989) and Silverman (1989) have detailed the analysis of anorexia and asthma in two adolescent girls.

Wilson and colleagues (1985) have found that with successful psychodynamic treatment, almost all the physical signs and symptoms of restrictor and bulimic anorexia nervosa return to normal except for irreversible tooth and gum damage in some bulimics caused by gorging and vomiting. However, if significant psychosexual conflicts have not been resolved, menstruation may not resume, even though the patient's weight returns to normal limits.

To my knowledge, there has been no in-depth *psychoanalytic* exploration of the fear of being fat. Bruch (1978) observes that the fear of being fat in anorexic girls has many different meanings, such as sensitivity to criticism, fear of growing up, fear of loss of control, and fear of superconformity. However, Bruch does not use the structural hypothesis or the concept of the unconscious in her formulations.

In a book written for the lay public, *Fat Is a Feminine Issue* (1978), Orbach mentions some psychological meanings of the fear of being fat without giving their deeper psychodynamic causes. She concludes that compulsive eating is an individual protest against the inequality of the sexes but does not substantiate her hypothesis with clinical analytic data, since her experience lies with group therapy. Intimately related to the fear of being fat is the wish to be thin, which has been noted in anorexics by many researchers, among them Bruch (1973) and Sperling (1978). Bruch observes that "thin fat people" have the same conflicts as obese patients and that millions of young women in our culture are obsessed with being thin. She also notes (1978) that often the mothers of anorexics are overly preoccupied with weight and diet. Crisp (1980) states that anorexia nervosa is a fat phobia but does not connect it with unconscious conflicts.

Boskind-White and White (1983) found a fear of being fat in 2,000 bulimic cases but also did not link it to unconscious conflicts. Sperling (1983, 1985) emphasizes the etiologic role that parental attitudes about food and dieting play in predisposing a child to develop anorexic symptoms. She discusses unconscious conflicts and eating conflicts but does *not* connect them to the fear of being fat in anorexic patients.

Dally (1969), who, like Bruch, Orbach, Crisp, and Boskind-Lodahl

White, is not a Freudian psychoanalyst, also describes anorexia nervosa as a fat phobia without, of course, including the multiple etiologic unconscious conflicts.

These patients do not suffer from lack of hunger but from the opposite—insatiable hunger (Bruch 1978, Crisp 1980, Sours 1980, Sperling 1978, 1983, 1985, Thomä 1967, Wilson, Hogan, and Mintz 1985). Names have powerful conscious and unconscious meanings; to use a word that implies a lack of appetite when the true state is the opposite is unscientific and misleading.

The defenses of the ego in these patients—denial, displacement, externalization, and projection—are the same as in the traditional phobias, and indeed many anorexics are phobic. The major difference is in the nature of the phobic object, which in the usual phobia is not ingested (incorporated). However, the psychodynamics of restrictor and bulimic anorexia nervosa, with their phobic fears of being fat and obsessive thoughts of being thin, are similar to those of the phobias. Common to both are suicidal conflicts when patients are forced to face and master the phobia. The potentially suicidal nature of anorexics' attempts to rid themselves of the internalized object by self-starvation or by binging, vomiting, and laxative use can lead to death, however, whereas the patient with a traditional phobia is not bringing about total self-destruction. As I have pointed out previously (Wilson 1983d):

> Wurmser (1980), an authority on addictions, emphasizes the phobic core of addictions with claustrophobia seen as the primary phobia. He sees the use of drugs as counterphobic and he notes that another impersonal agent, food, can be used as a problem solver. Wurmser's formulations confirm my hypothesis that anorexia nervosa is a food phobia. In anorexic families the mother and/or father's fear-of-being-fat syndrome from the earliest years causes a continuous displacement and projection of conflicts onto food and the eating process which profoundly warps and distorts this aspect of the child's reality. In fat-phobic patients, conflict in the oral phase results in a displacement and projection of conflicts with the mother (breast) onto food and the eating process. Traditional phobias develop at later maturational phases when the ego is more mature, there is a choice of phobic objects, and the object relationships with parents are more advanced. However, in both types of phobia, aggressive and libidinal drives, fantasies, and conflicts are split off and projected onto the phobic object.
>
> The retention of "anorexia nervosa" as a diagnostic term seems likely at present, but its gradual replacement by "phobic fear of being fat" or "fat phobia" seems inevitable. Howard L. Schwartz (1980) uses the term "fat phobia" in his confirmatory discussion of my research. For the purposes of this book, readers will gain a deeper psychodynamic understanding of these patients if they substitute "phobic fear of being fat" or "fat phobia" for "anorexia nervosa." [p. 26]

ORAL-PHASE SYMBOLS

Air, fire, water, sand, and stone are universal symbols of the oral phase. The interpretation of conflicts they mask, which if unresolved contribute to pathology at each maturational and libidinal phase, is essential for the analytic treatment of the oedipal and preoedipal psychopathology of which eating-disorder symptoms are a manifestation. Air symbols, which Mintz (1989b) describes particularly in asthmatics, involve inhalation and the internalized image of the air mother; water, Niederland (1956, 1957) emphasizes, involves representations of mother's milk, the breast, and the uterus; and fire, Arlow (1955) notes, masks oral devouring impulses.

However, although all the oral symbols and the conflicts they mask are involved in primal repression, stone is its basic symbol. It is likewise the core symbol of that most primitive defense of the ego, projective identification, which covers oral-incorporative, cannibalistic conflicts.

My research on early psychic structure demonstrates that stone, which can symbolize both the breast of the mother and the tooth of the infant, is the earliest symbol used by the ego and that the symbol is precipitated out in the process of weaning with the repression of oral-sadistic impulses. In this process the first significant internalized representations of the good and bad mother and the good and bad self are set up in the ego. Recent research (Sarnoff 1970, 1988, 1989) concludes that it is only in the first half of the third year of life that symbols with unconscious meanings appear and that the child becomes capable of producing true symbols. He suggested (Sarnoff (1972) that stone be termed a protosymbol.

I have come to the conclusion that stone is the most primitive symbol because it has qualities of hardness, persistence in time and space, and tactile definiteness which makes it most readily available for organized kinesthetic visual and tactile projection by the primitive ego. Boyer 1974, Bychowski 1972, Niederland 1972, Sarnoff 1968, 1972 and other researchers in dream symbols are in agreement with and have confirmed this hypothesis.

In contrast to stone, the symbols sand, water, fire, and air are inconstant in space, time, shape, consistency, and color, thus requiring further ego maturation and more developed ego functioning for their symbolization. Therefore, although the drive aspects of these symbols are more primitive ontogenetically and philogenetically (such as sucking of the breast [sand] or the wish for mother's milk [water]) than the drive aspect of stone symbolism (cannibalistic incorporation of the breast), the symbolisms of sand, water, fire, and air are not utilized by the ego until the second year at the earliest.

Stone symbolism dreams (Wilson 1963, 1965, 1967a, 1971a, 1981, 1989b, Wilson et al. 1985) appear only in the terminal phase of analysis of patients with severe preoedipal psychopathology such as an eating disorder. The appearance of stone dreams reflects analytic progress as the patient is working through sadomasochistic oral-incorporative material. Since there is a strong resistance to facing such conflicts, which date from preverbal and early verbal developmental stages, the analyst has to inform the patient of the meanings of the stone symbols. The following case is illustrative.

Claire, a 16-year-old bulimic anorexic high school student in her third year of analysis, had put on weight and resumed menstruating but still had not resolved her fear of boys and heterosexuality. She reported the following dream: "A man was a vampire in a house with me and another woman. He wanted to kill us or at least to suck our blood. My sister and father were there. Then we were driving somewhere on vacation."

In her associations, Claire said that she had a déjà vu feeling about the dream. It reminded her of a repetitive dream she had had since childhood of a stone cottage with a beautiful lake to the right of it. Another repetitive dream was of trying to escape from a stone castle by a lake. There was a terrifying mushroom cloud: an atomic explosion. The patient associated it to eating normally. She had trouble going to sleep and was upset that the analyst was leaving her for his summer vacation. She recalled as a 3-year-old child seeing her mother bathe her baby sister. She always used to be afraid of the dark and wanted all the lights on.

Oral-incorporative conflicts are basic and etiologic in anorexia. This patient's bulimia had been preceded by a period of restrictor anorexia in which she lost 30 pounds. Prior to the onset of her eating disorder she had been a vegetarian, as was her mother. At this phase of analysis she was eating more normally, and in particular could now eat meat.

I informed her that the stone element in the dream symbolized her teeth and oral desires. Claire thought of how she liked *red* meat and chewing bones and stated that she must be afraid of biting and being bitten. A further interpretation was made that she projected her devouring impulses onto men and me in the transference when threatened by separation. She had previously dreamt that I had become a monster who was going to attack her. In Claire's fantasy, the dream and mushroom cloud represented a birth—her sister's birth, which had been a traumatic event since it brought about her first major separation from her mother. The stone symbolism also masked oral-incorporative impulses directed at the baby sister as well as an identification with the baby.

In another case, a restrictor anorexic was phobic about water and had never learned to swim. She had a repetitive dream of a *marble* swimming pool with a monster in the water that swallowed and devoured those who dared to swim in the pool. Analysis of the multiple conflicts masked by this dream led to her basic terror of devouring and being devoured. The marble symbolized her teeth, those of her mother, and other objects.

In classical psychoanalytic technique, therapists have been analyzing the Isakower phenomenon (Isakower 1938) when it appears in the course of an analysis. Isakower traced the sensory phenomena described by certain patients when they fall asleep. "The tactile sensation is of something crumpled, sandy and dry and is experienced in the mouth and at the same time on the skin of the whole body" (p. 333). In a series of communications I have suggested that sand is the symbol of thirst and of the Isakower phenomenon and have tried to bring the psychopathology of oral-phase thirst into connection with the eating disorders, the habits, the addictions, and preoedipal psychopathology.

Sand symbolizes the dry mouth and the thirst of the infant between feedings (Wilson 1980a, 1983c, 1985a, 1986a, 1988a, 1989b, 1990b). Sand, antithetically, symbolizes the depriving mother, the withdrawn nipple and breast, the total loss of mother's milk, of human kindness and tenderness and love. Thus the developing capacity to control oral sucking impulses results in asceticism and the defense of altruistic surrender (A. Freud 1946, 1974, Kaplan 1984); whereas a healthy superego structure evidences altruism, pathological altruism (masochism) is characteristic of eating disorder cases and other patients with severe preoedipal psychopathology.[1] Stone symbolism develops in connection with the process of teething in the 6th to 12th month (Wilson 1967, 1971, Wilson 1989b). Oral-incorporative conflicts, the wish to devour and to be devoured, are repressed and stone comes to symbolize the primitive object relation with the mother. Basic trust, reliability, and object constancy are symbolized by stone.

The mother's ambivalent feelings about her infant can cause a displacement of conflict onto fluids (breast and milk and bottle-feeding) and (later) onto food. As Fliess (1956) and I (1967) have emphasized, these oral conflicts persist and can be expressed in the form of symptoms at each subsequent libidinal and developmental phase. Stone, which is the most universal and plastic of all symbols, symbolizes impulse control, whether it represents teeth, the baby, the mother, the breast, teeth, bladder, feces, vagina, or phallus.

While the sucking impulses symbolized by sand are more primitive, stone is the earliest symbol conceptualized and integrated into the ego. It is a symbol of primal repression and develops in the process of teething (Wilson 1963, 1965, 1967, 1971b, 1980a, 1982a, 1989b, 1990a and b).

The etiology of the eating disorders is rooted in the mother's and/or father's ambivalent feelings about the infant. This conflict is displaced onto fluids, breast, milk, and bottle-feeding, and in the teething phase onto food. Sand symbols reflect fusion conflicts and stone those of aggression.

Oral-phase conflicts result in an ambivalent relationship to the mother. These unresolved conflicts influence each subsequent maturational phase so that anal, oedipal, and later developmental conflicts are also unresolved. Wurmser (1980), an authority on addictions, emphasizes the phobic core of addictions and sees claustrophobia as the primary phobia. He sees the use of drugs as counterphobic and he notes that another impersonal agent, food, can be used as a problem solver. Wurmser's formulations confirm my hypothesis that anorexia nervosa is a food phobia. In anorexic families, the mother's and/or father's fear-of-being-fat complex from the earliest years causes a continuous displacement and projection of conflicts onto fluids and food and the eating process, profoundly warping and distorting this aspect of the child's reality. In fat-phobic patients, conflicts in the oral phase result in a displacement and projection of conflicts with the mother

---

[1] At appropriate times, such as when dreams containing sand symbolism occur or when the patient is severely depressed or complaining of insomnia, the therapist should ask about thirst and dry mouth and should explain the meanings of sand symbols.

(breast) onto fluids and food and the drinking and eating processes. Traditional phobias develop at later maturational phases when the ego is more mature, there is a choice of phobic objects, and the object relationships with parents are more advanced. However, in both types of phobia, aggressive and libidinal drives, fantasies, and conflicts are split off and projected onto the phobic object.

EATING DISORDER DEPRESSIONS AND THEIR CAUSES

The vicissitudes of the analysis of depressed affects in eating disorders can be viewed in terms of what Greenacre (1958) described as pathological weeping. In the analysis of certain restrictor and bulimic anorexics and addictive patients (Wilson 1980a) confirmed Greenacre's findings that pathological "stream" weeping can be a substitute for an expression of fantasies of male urination displaced upward to the eye and the lachrymal system, as well as her finding of an extreme body–phallus identification. As analysis makes these conflicts conscious, they are worked through in the transference neurosis; pathological weeping, of which silent tearing is one example, is replaced by normal crying and sobbing with appropriate affects. With many patients, crying has an exhibitionistic aspect; they have learned to act out emotions, a behavior that has to be analyzed. Hogan in his research on ulcerative colitis (in press) emphasizes the underlying depression.

As the conflicts underlying eating-disorder and other psychosomatic symptoms are analyzed, a variety of affects emerge, particularly those of depression (Wilson 1985a,b,c,1986, Wilson et al. 1985). It is the analysis of affects, particularly depressive affects, that is crucial to therapeutic success. However, as these affects emerge, various psychic shifts occur which result in eating disorders being replaced by other symptoms.

The components of these depressions are overdetermined and are caused by unresolved oedipal and preoedipal conflicts. Among the important determinants are unhappiness because of failure to achieve the perfectionistic goals required by the archaic superego; neurotic guilt inflicted by the archaic superego, which legislates against the expression of libidinal or aggressive impulses and fantasies; failure to achieve mature object relations; unhappiness and anger because of a failure to actualize magical narcissistic fantasies; adaptive failures; and unhappiness because of failure to achieve normal separation-individuation from parents or parent surrogates.

THE ANALYSIS OF DEPRESSIVE AFFECTS

Emerging depression is described by Mintz (1983a), who notes that some patients become depressed *after* they begin to eat. "The self-destructive conscience that dictated suffering by starvation shifts to an alternative form of criticism, suffering by feeling worthless and depressed" (p. 95). In the bulimic anorexic, the ego cannot maintain the attempt at self-starvation. The patient submits to the impulse to gorge and then tries to expiate by vomiting. When this habit is interrupted, intense depression surfaces.

Mintz also describes here the analysis of a severely regressed bulimic anorexic, noting conflict about separation from the analyst as his summer vacation approached. This conflict prompted self-destructive discharge of aggressive impulses alternating with feelings of depression and anorexic symptoms (binging and vomiting). From the analysis of a 45-year-old man suffering from anorexia nervosa and bulimia, Mintz (1983b) reports, "On occasion, he felt depressed, which substituted for his self-destructive starving. The depressed feelings frightened him and threw him back into his preoccupation with eating. Eruptions of anger were substituted for by bursts of bulimia. A new symptom related to his perceived loss of control over his aggression" (p. 294). In this case the anorexia (and bulimia) appeared to be a substitute for depression and indeed alternated with depressive moods.

Freiman (1983) describes the emergence of depression in a bulimic anorexic in the initial phase of analysis: "For some time in a state of mild depression, the predominant theme of her sessions was that of self-devaluations and self-reproaches. She referred to herself as a sick, helpless individual. She felt her boss, father, mother, and analyst thought of her as an inferior being" (p. 261). At first the patient responded to genetic and transference interpretations with denial, but then the masochistic defensive system that masked her anger (rage) gave way. Depression was replaced by aggressive thoughts, fantasies, and affects.

Mintz (1983a) also describes graphically the vicissitudes of depressed emotions in an adolescent girl. Thelma typically felt that she was both fat and ugly. When she ate, she felt fat in her stomach and thighs. (Most anorexics are particularly concerned with the belly and thighs.) She also stated that her face, arms, wrists, fingers, back, and toes were fat. All these body parts have symbolic meanings.

As she provided details of her gorging, she acknowledged that it seemed to happen when she was upset and that the upset feeling disappeared during the bulimic attack. It was pointed out that if she could think about what upset her, she might not have to gorge. One month later Thelma reported that she had gone for three weeks without gorging, until the previous night, when she had binged and vomited. When she had defended her older brother's choice of a college, her mother had yelled at her and hit her across the face. The mother had become enraged, called her stupid, and told her to get out of the house. Thelma had run upstairs sobbing, overwhelmed by the feeling that no one cared for her. Later that night she had eaten all the food in the refrigerator, felt stuffed, vomited, and then had eaten again and felt sick. The dorsum of her hand had bled from the violent thrust into her throat. She admitted that the gorging episode had eliminated the previous depression and sense of panic. Now she hated herself for her eating and vomiting. She had hated her mother and then felt guilty, but after the vomiting she had felt "purged" and relieved. The vomiting seemed to serve both as a somatic eruption of anger and as a punishment. The patient remained in treatment and eventually was able to resolve her conflicts.

Similarly, Hogan (1983a) comments, "In each of the five patients presented here (a mixture of restrictor and bulimic anorexics), as the above defenses and impulses were reluctantly acknowledged and understood, there were temporary rather severe depressions. These depressions frequently followed the relinquishment of the major anorexic (bulimic) symptomatology" (p. 145). In a previous work (Wilson 1983c), I give an example of emerging depression in a bulimic anorexic at a point in analysis when she was controlling her binging and facing her unresolved symbiotic need for her mother and the analyst in the transference. My emphasis is on the repression of emotions in the restrictor and bulimic anorexic family. The parents are intolerant of libidinal and aggressive manifestations and of depression in their children. They do not promote normal separation-individuation, that is, the developing ego's capacity to tolerate depression.

Bulimic anorexics evidence manic-depressive-like mood swings when they give in to or control impulse gratification: that is, binge eat or drink or smoke or act out in defiance of the totally controlling internalized mother imago; they experience elation, omnipotence, and ecstasy, whereas when they control their impulses by dieting and self-imposed asceticism, they feel depression, hopelessness, and despair.

PARENTAL PSYCHOPATHOLOGY

Aside from the inconclusive constitutional, genetic research in anorexia nervosa (Altschuler and Weiner 1985, Pope and Hudson 1984), the solution to the question of why one child develops anorexia and another does not is to be found in the study of the parent–child relationship.[2] In my research on the psychological profile of the families of patients with anorexia nervosa (1980b, 1982a,b, 1986a,b,c, 1988a,b,c,d, Wilson et al. 1985), I found that in 100 families of anorexics, there was a psychological profile that appeared to have been etiologic in establishing in early childhood a personality disorder that manifested itself later in the symptoms of anorexia nervosa.

Four of the components of this profile—(1) perfectionism which results

---

[2]I recently detailed a comparable psychosomatic family psychological profile in over 300 cases of asthma, ulcerative colitis, migraine, psoriasis, and other symptoms (Wilson 1989a). There are, of course, exceptions to the profile, and in a considerable number of cases a patient manifests two or more psychosomatic symptoms, a situation that points to the underlying personality disorder. Our psychosomatic volume details the analysis of two patients with anorexia and asthma (Mintz 1989, Silverman 1989) and traces the "choice" of two different psychosomatic symptoms in the same patient—ulcerative colitis and anorexia—to parental psychopathology (Wilson 1989a).

in overcontrolling behavior; bulimic parents, although they are perfectionistic, evidence more marital discord, divorce, neurotic conflict, and addictive behavior; (2) repression of emotions, libidinal or aggressive; (3) infantilizing decision-making for the anorexic-prone child; and (4) dieting and fears of being fat—correlate with attitudes and behavior noted by Bruch (1978) and Minuchin (1978) in their descriptions of over 100 anorexic families. The last two features of the profile are (5) exhibitionistic parental sexual and toilet behavior whose significance is completely denied and (6) the selection of one child for the development of anorexia and treating that child differently from other siblings.

Basically parents of restrictor and bulimic anorexics are quite concerned about the health and well-being of their children and will make great efforts to help them get well. In most adolescent cases we ask the parents to do conjoint counseling with a colleague to gain an understanding of family pathology.

EXCEPTIONS TO THE FAMILY PSYCHOLOGICAL PROFILE

Hogan (1983a) confirmed the difference in character structure of the restrictor and the bulimic anorexic but questioned the relevance of the family psychological profile in the eating disorders. He noted a restrictor anorexic who grew up with alcoholic parents. Sperling (1983) reported the analysis of a restrictor anorexic whose mother was psychotic. I have also seen exceptions to this profile. One restrictor anorexic came from a family in which the parents and siblings were all obese. Another restrictor's family included a father who was an alcoholic gambler. Of course, the number of cases we have seen is limited and the complexities of early development are multiple. Moreover, in some families one child may be a restrictor and another bulimic. Nevertheless, in the great majority of cases the family psychological profile is applicable. In many adolescent cases, conjoint or individual therapy of the psychosomatic parents that focuses on aspects of the family psychological profile is essential for therapeutic success.

It remains for future research, particularly more analyses of the parents of these "exceptions," to determine whether the etiologic factor has been the parents' unconscious selection of a particular child to develop the predisposition for psychosomatic symptoms, or whether the "exception" evidences differences in genetic, constitutional endowment and/or differences in preverbal and early verbal psychological development.

SOUL MURDER IN THE PSYCHOSOMATIC AND EATING DISORDERS

Shengold (1978) defines "soul murder" as a person's "dramatic designation for a certain category of traumatic experiences, those instances of repetitive and chronic overstimulation alternating with emotional deprivation that are deliberately brought about by another individual" (p. 533). I noted (1978) that psychosomatic symptoms often mask "soul murder," and I cited an anorexic patient's parents who forbade any expression of aggression. A routine discipline at mealtimes was face-slapping. Shengold traces the cause of "soul murder" in his patients to actual experiences of torture, seduction, and rape; in our studies of psychosomatic patients we have found cases of aggressive and sexual physical abuse (incest and rape). Most often somatization was caused by the repetitive impact of the parental attitudes and behavior that we describe in the psychological profile. There has been overparenting rather than underparenting.

However, the hypermorality of the psychosomatic parents can lead to traumatic physical punishment under the guise of moral discipline. For example, the father of an adolescent boy with ulcerative colitis cried in my office, saying that he caused the son's colitis because he beat his son when he misbehaved, just the way his father had beaten him. While this was a psychodynamic oversimplification by the father, the beatings of the son were an important aspect of the father's total infantilizing control of his child. The degree of "soul murder" can limit the potential for analytic results. It is important for the parents to do conjoint therapy.

INCEST AND CHILD AND SPOUSE ABUSE IN THE EATING DISORDERS

In our original research (Wilson et al. 1985, Wilson and Mintz 1989) we found few cases of aggressive and sexual abuse, rape, or incest in the eating disorder or psychosomatic families. Recent psychiatric research has found a significant incidence of sexual abuse and incest in the eating disorders (i.e., Bulik 1978, Bulik et al. 1989, Goldfarb 1987, Morrison 1989, Oppenheimer et al. 1985, Russell 1983). Moreover, psychoanalytic research has uncovered a significant number of cases of abuse and incest. Confidentiality is an extremely sensitive issue where analysis resolves such problems. One male bulimic patient uncovered in his analysis repressed memories of a two-year period from ages 12 to 14 when he had had sexual relations with his sister, one year older than he. His starving and gorging symptoms developed as he broke up this incestuous relationship. One colleague reported a case of anorexia developing after the patient had incestuous relations with her father. Another reported a 16-year-old bulimic whose gorging and vomiting developed after her perverse uncle forced her to fellate him. In a supervised case of the analysis of the mother of two anorexic daughters, it became clear that one component of the daughters' fears of sexuality and men was their prolonged childhood-witnessing of wife abuse. Their father, a hypermoral Baptist, lectured and hit his wife for any mistakes. The wife, a lawyer, gave all her money to her husband and related to him in an extremely masochistic way. The husband, a CPA, would first lecture his wife on her stupid mistakes and then slap her or knock her down. She, equally hypermoral, was so humiliated that she told no one about the abuse. After her husband died of a heart attack, following a two-year period of mourning, she met and married a business-man, and within six months he was berating and beating her. She became aware of her masochistic way of relating to men, divorced her husband, and came to analysis. Analysis revealed that she had recapitulated with her husbands her submissive relationship with her mother, who would yell at her and slap her.

Other cases involved serious addictions, particularly parental, most frequently an alcoholic father. The addicted parents were physically and sexually abusive. The pathological role of a sadistic "Nanny" in a bulimic anorexic case is detailed in the case of Elaine (p. 51, this volume).

EGO STRUCTURE

While the restrictor anorexic is capable of controlling the impulse to eat, the bulimic patient is not, consuming tremendous quantities of food. The patient gorges, then becomes so frightened of gaining weight that she feels forced to vomit to regurgitate her caloric intake.

The clinical and psychodynamic relevance of gorging deserves some consideration because it offers an additional perspective on the patient's feelings, psychodynamics, and personality structure. The starving patient is able to contain the unconscious impulse to gorge because of intact ego and punitive superego controls. The bulimic patient has a comparably strict archaic superego but ineffective ego controls that are unable to regulate the impulse to eat (Wilson 1986, 1988a,b, Wilson et al. 1985). This defect in self-control is so threatening to the patient that the slightest gain in weight produces panic, exercising, starving, and vomiting. The bulimic patient who is unable to control eating is also unable to control other impulses, so that one sees sexual promiscuity, delinquency, stealing, lying, and running away more frequently in the bulimic than in the starving anorexic patient. This defect in ego controls arises in part from identifying with the parents, who not infrequently argue and act out destructively more often than the parents of the starving anorexics.

The role of unconscious pregnancy fantasies in the genesis of this illness is almost universally recognized by psychoanalytic authors. The anorexic patient fears and denies these fantasies.

AMENORRHEA IN ANOREXIA NERVOSA AND BULIMIA

The amenorrhea in anorexia nervosa and bulimia is a primary rather than a secondary symptom. Thomä (1967) and other analysts (Sperling 1978, Wilson et al. 1985) believe that amenorrhea in anorexia nervosa and bulimia is primarily psychological rather than endocrinological. During

World War II, 60 to 70 percent of the women capable of menstruation developed amenorrhea *immediately* after they were captured and interned by the Japanese in Hong Kong (Sydenham 1946). In most cases the amenorrhea precedes or occurs simultaneously with the anorexia. There are multiple conflicts underlying amenorrhea (Mintz 1983).

While body weight and starvation are factors in amenorrhea, the emotional (unconscious) causes of amenorrhea are central in the eating disorders. Savitt (1980) emphasized unconscious conflicts in the amenorrhea of the obese, and my colleagues and I have seen amenorrheic neurotic patients whose menses returned when unconscious psychosexual conflicts were resolved.

Nonanalytic researchers (Frisch 1977, Frisch and McArthur 1974, and Frisch and Revelle 1970) postulate a critical body weight below which anorexic women become amenorrheic. Falk and Halmi (1982), after a research study of forty anorexic patients, emphasized that whereas 15 patients resumed their menses when weight became normal, twelve patients continued to be amenorrheic when they achieved similar normal weight levels. They found that patients with continuing amenorrhea, both of normal and low weights, had significantly more anorectic attitudes and behaviors than the menstruating patients.

Wennik-Kaplan (in press) found that in one hundred patients in psychodynamic treatment by a wide range of therapists, fifty patients regained their menses with weight gain but fifty with similar weight gain did not. Using a Maternal Identification Scale, a test based on psychoanalytic theory, Wennik-Kaplan found that the fifty nonmenstruating patients had significantly more unresolved unconscious conflicts than those who regained their menses.

Wilson and colleagues (1985), along with Sperling (1978), do not agree with Bruch (1962, 1965, 1970, 1978), Crisp (1965, 1967, 1968, 1980), Dally (1969), and Selvini Palazzoli (1978) that a psychoanalytic approach to these patients should be avoided. Our experience agrees with Mushatt (1975), Blitzer and colleagues (1961), Jessner and Abse (1960), Lorand (1943), Masserman (1941), Fischer (1989), Sperling (1953, 1968, 1978), Thomä (1967), Waller and colleagues (1940), Sours (1980), Mogul (1980), Risen (1982), Ritvo (1984), H. J. Schwartz (1986, 1988), and many others that psychoanalytic investigation is of the utmost importance in understanding this illness as well as determining the treatment of choice in most cases.

DYNAMIC, GENETIC, ECONOMIC, STRUCTURAL, AND ADAPTIVE ASPECTS OF EGO FUNCTIONING IN RESTRICTOR AND BULIMIC ANOREXICS[3]

In psychodynamic terms, the metapsychology of this complex is rooted in unresolved oral-phase conflicts that result in an ambivalent relationship

---

[3] I am indebted to Dr. Howard J. Schwartz (1983, 1985), who restated my findings in a metapsychological framework upon which I have elaborated in these formulations.

with the caretaker. Fixation to this phase of development, with its accompanying fears of object loss, is caused by maternal and/or paternal overcontrol and overemphasis on food and eating functions as a symbol of love. This unresolved conflict influences each subsequent maturational phase so that anal, oedipal, and later developmental conflicts also are unresolved.

The unresolved preoedipal fixation on the mother has contributed to the difficulty in psychosexual development and the intensity of the oedipal development. As Sperling (1978) noted, anorexia nervosa can be considered a specific pathological outcome of unresolved oedipal conflicts in patients whose preoedipal relationship to the mother has predisposed them to this reaction under precipitating circumstances.

The genetic influences on this complex are parental conflicts about weight and food specifically, and about aggressive and libidinal expression generally. In addition, the parents tend to be compulsive, moralistic, and perfectionistic, significantly denying the impact on the developing child of their exhibitionistic, toilet, bedroom, and other behavior. Other genetic factors are cultural, societal, and general medical influences, as well as secondary identifications with people who share the fear-of-being-fat complex.

From an economic point of view, the unremitting pressure in bulimic and restrictor anorexics of repressed, unsublimated, aggressive, and libidinal drives, conflicts, and fantasies is a central issue. In the bulimic anorexic, the attempt to control drive derivatives is manifested by the fear-of-being-fat complex but defective ego functioning results in a giving in to voraciousness as well as to impulse gratifications of other kinds. The intense guilt inflicted by the archaic superego causes attempts at undoing by self-induced vomiting and laxative use as well as other masochistic behavior. In the restrictor anorexic, the same feared drive eruptions are masked by the fear-of-being-fat complex but intact ego controls result in total impulse control brought about by the restrictor's archaic superego. The terror of loss of control (i.e., of becoming fat) comprises the conscious fear of overeating and the unconscious fear of incorporating body parts, smearing or eating feces, bleeding to death, mutilating or being mutilated, or masturbating and/or becoming nymphomaniacal, which could result in orgasmic pleasure. In the restrictor anorexic, these feared drive eruptions are masked by the fear-of-being-fat complex and held totally in check by the terror of retaliatory punishment from the archaic, sadistic superego.

From a structural point of view, ego considerations are central. In the preoedipal years the ego of the bulimic anorexia-prone (fat-phobic) child becomes split. One part develops in a pseudonormal fashion: cognitive functions, the self-observing part of the ego, adaptive capacities, and other ego functions appear to operate normally. While the restrictor anorexics in childhood are often described as "perfect" and have excellent records in school, the bulimic anorexics evidence more disobedience and rebellion at home and school. In adolescence there is more antisocial behavior, sexual promiscuity, and addiction. The ego represses, denies, displaces, externalizes, and projects conflicts onto the fear-of-being-fat complex. Conflicts can be displaced onto habits such as thumb-sucking, enuresis, encopresis, nail-biting, head-banging, and hair-pulling. There may be a concomitant displacement and projection of conflict onto actual phobic objects. Anorexia nervosa may alternate with other psychosomatic disease syndromes, such as ulcerative colitis (Sperling 1978), migraine (Hogan 1983), and asthma (Mintz 1983). This split in the ego manifests itself in the intense, psychotic-like denial of the displaced wishes, conflicts, and fantasies. In other words, the split-off neurotic part of the personality is denied in the fear-of-being-fat complex.

From an adaptive point of view, conflicts at each maturational and libidinal phase are denied, displaced, and projected onto the fear of being fat. Conflicts in separation-individuation (Mushatt 1975) are paramount and are denied by the parents and developing child. Normal adaptive conflict is avoided and denied. Many parents of anorexics rear them in an unreal, overprotected world. Perfectionistic parents impair the ego's decision-making functions with their infantilizing intrusions into every aspect of their child's life. A focus of analysis is on the pregenital object relations (Hogan 1983a) that have been caused by the unresolved parental relationships and the conflicts in separation-individuation.

Unlike Sperling (1978), I, along with Hogan and Mintz (Wilson et al. 1985), include males under the diagnostic category of anorexia nervosa. Mintz shows (1983b) that male anorexics have oedipal and preoedipal fixations and unresolved problems in separation-individuation, severe latent homosexual conflicts and a feminine identification, and the same fear-of-being-fat complex seen in the females, which is caused by an identification with the mother's and/or father's fear-of-being-fat complex. Whether the psychodynamics are primarily oedipal or preoedipal depends upon the quantity of preoedipal psychopathology, the degree of impairment of ego functioning, and the capacities for object relations. For research on object relations in anorexics, see Aronson (1986). Table 1–1 is a simplified diagram of the differences in ego structure in restrictor and bulimic anorexics.

BODY IMAGE

For lasting analytic results, the pathological fear-of-being-fat body image must be resolved. Some bulimics and a few restrictor anorexics do not have a clear-cut body image disturbance nor do they have the conviction that they look beautiful when thin. They are, however, preoccupied with fears of being fat and with dieting. These patients seem to have a preponderance of oedipal psychopathology.

Freud (1923) stated that the ego is first and foremost a body ego, the projection of a surface. The surface of the mother's breast—and by extension her figure—is projected in one's body image. The fear of being fat reflects the terror of oral sadistic incorporation of the breast, mother, and later other objects. The average expectable environment of a female in our culture offers the fear of being fat as a normative value that reinforces the developing girl's body image conflicts. The intensity and irrationality of the fear of being fat points to its primitive ontogenetic source; analysis reveals its primary process roots. A graphic example is the anorexic's ambivalent all-or-nothing fear of being totally fat or totally thin, which can result in psychosomatic suicide by starvation.

Freud emphasized the importance of the perception of pain for the development of a normal body image. Because of parental psychopathol-

TABLE 1–1. Differences in Ego Structure of the Restrictor and Bulimic Anorexic

Pseudonormal ego of the restrictor resembles compulsive neurotic	Pseudonormal ego of the bulimic is a mixture of compulsive and hysterical neurotic complexes

Pseudonormal ego with varying degrees of ego functioning, capacities for object relations, adaptations, self-observing functions, reality testing

Fear of the archaic sadistic superego causes conflicts from every maturational and libidinal phase to be denied, split off, externalized, and projected onto.

Split-off fear-of-being-fat part of ego

obsession with being thin

dieting

symptoms of restrictor or bulimic anorexia nervosa

The ego of the restrictor has intact impulse control capacities so they overcontrol oral impulses (starve themselves) and impulses of many other kinds.	The ego of the bulimic is defective in its capacities to control impulses so that it is periodically overwhelmed not only by voraciousness but by impulses of many other kinds. Gorging and impulse gratification occur, followed by attempts to expiate by vomiting, the use of laxatives, and masochistic behavior.

ogy, the anorexia-prone child is overindulged and the ego does not develop sufficient capacity to delay impulse gratification. Parental oral conflicts disturb the important role of the mouth and hand (Hoffer 1950) in differentiating the self from the nonself. Preoedipal and oedipal primal-scene experiences, and other overstimulating parent–child sensory interactions whose significance is completely denied, severely distort the significant role of visual perception of the face and genitals (Greenacre 1958) in the development of a normal body image. The strict superego of the mother and/or father limits and warps the normal autoerotic and playful body investigations that build up early self and object representations (Jacobson 1964) and that aid in differentiation of self and nonself (Fenichel 1945). The parents' need to control and retain the child as an infantile object prevents normal separation-individuation. Their intolerance of aggressive and libidinal drive manifestations also prevents normal separation-individuation in the anal phase. The histories of my cases confirm Sours's (1974) observations that the child's development from 16 to 25 months—Mahler and Furer's rapprochement phase (1972)—are entirely lacking. The oppositional behavior and negativism commonly seen from 24 to 36 months (Mahler and Furer 1968) are likewise absent. The histories of some bulimic anorexics evidence oppositional behavior and negativism, but manifestations of assertive behavior in these families are ego alien.

The preoedipal component of the body–phallus identification is foremost; overt homosexuality is infrequent among female anorexics. For nonanorexic women, parallel but less intensely cathected developmental body image conflicts underlie the fear of being fat. Preoedipal penis envy

TABLE 1–2. The Fear-of-Being-Fat Complex in Restrictor Anorexia, Bulimic Anorexia, and Obesity; Obsession with Being Thin; To Diet

Restrictor Anorexia	Bulimic Anorexia	Obesity
Strict archaic superego conflicts, terror of being fat, leading to self-starvation and possible death; controlling ego structure	Less strict but perfectionistic superego. Patients can't control their impulses and they give in to urges to gorge and other impulses. The strict superego, however, inflicts guilt and they try to expiate, undo by self-induced vomiting and/or the use of laxatives.	A demanding but less perfectionistic superego than restrictor or bulimic anorexics.
Ego Structure	Ego Structure	Ego Structure
Restrictor anorexic ego structure, perfectionistic, rigid, controlling	Controlling but inconsistent in its ability to totally control impulses	Not controlling, gives in to impulse gratification, not only oral drives but impulses of many kinds

and pregnancy fears, as well as the maternal ego ideal, are particularly important in the fear-of-being-fat body image disturbance.

The wish to deny time and aging in the anorexic body image is startling, but there are comparable conflicts in most women. For instance, one woman executive, because of her narcissistic investment in looking young and beautiful, avoided pointing out to subordinates that she had twenty years of business experience.

The female body image conflicts manifested in the fear of being fat are heightened during adolescence, when earlier developmental conflicts are recapitulated with the added libidinal and aggressive manifestations of puberty. Parental intolerance of the latter makes adolescence the prime time for the emergence of anorexia. Females must undergo more complicated physical and emotional changes than males (Blum 1976, Freud 1932, Ritvo 1976, 1984). They are subject to the combined pressure of the maternal ego ideal, greater dependency needs, and oedipal and preoedipal penis envy, all of which contribute to the universal female fear of being fat. Social, cultural, and medical factors can also contribute to an overemphasis on the importance of dieting and a thin figure.

Anorexics often are admired and envied by their friends, who unconsciously have a similar, but less intensely cathected, body image and the fantasy of being thin. Thus, at all maturational phases the developing girl has potential secondary identifications with women and men who fear being fat. Ritvo (1984) relates adolescent female body-image pathology to eating disorder conflicts.

RESOLUTION OF THE BODY IMAGE

Clinical experience repeatedly demonstrates that the oral-incorporative (cannibalistic) and fusion (sucking) conflicts are the most primitive and that the ego's defenses against acknowledging these conflicts must be analyzed and worked through for a resolution of the fear-of-being-fat, obsession-with-being-thin body image. Thus the fear of being fat masks a terror of cannibalizing and fusing with the object, that is, becoming fat. The severely regressed, acting-out suicidal bulimic Elaine (whose treatment I discuss later in this chapter (Wilson et al. 1985), when talking of visiting her sister, of whom she was bitterly jealous, made a slip of the tongue, saying that she "ate her sister" instead of saying she "visited" her. This slip occurred as a result of many analytic interpretations that resulted in the patient's trying to interrupt her frantic gorging, vomiting, laxative habits that partially acted out and covered up primitive cannibalistic and fusion conflicts.

The terror of the oral sucking impulses is likewise strongly defended against. The fear is of becoming a baby: babies are fat, they suck and suck. Eating-disordered patients express this primitive regression in their symptoms and behavior but deny it vehemently. The obese often joke about their eating, but this joking is a defense. If the therapist concurs that they are impulsive and babyish, they may become enraged or terminate treatment. Their understanding of the pervasiveness, ramifications, and different manifestations of their impulse disorder has to emerge in the analytic process. The obese "elephant symbolism" man's (Wilson and Mintz 1989) developing insight into his regressive babyish wishes and behavior was first expressed in an increasing anxiety and fear of bums, derelicts, and beggars encountered on the streets. As his insight into these conflicts deepened, he revealed eating behavior that he had concealed. With feelings of humiliation and shame, he "confessed" that at night he would wake from a deep sleep and, jealous of his year-old baby son, would go down to the kitchen and eat the zweiback (hard toast) given to the baby for teething on. Another obese patient ruefully began burping during a session. Associating to his indigestion, he said that at lunch prior to the session, which he resented because it shortened his lunch hour, he debated whether to order a pastrami or a chicken salad sandwich, and he ordered and ate both sandwiches. Genetic memories emerged of having eaten a whole box of chocolate chip cookies and being yelled at by his mother. Laughing, he said, "I guess I am confusing you with my mother." This type of incident demonstrates why these patients need to control their eating and drinking themselves. With the vicissitudes of analysis and insight, *the actual weight may go up or down; it is the patients' insight into their conflicts that is the central therapeutic problem.*

CLINICAL MATERIAL

I have worked analytically with five restrictor and fifteen bulimic cases (Wilson et al. 1985) and I have seen many more in consultation and supervision. Also I have analyzed four parents of anorexic patients (three mothers and one father) and have seen many more in conjoint psychotherapy. In one case developing anorexia nervosa in a 12-year-old girl was resolved in the course of the analysis of her mother. There is a heterogeneous range of restrictor and bulimic anorexic cases with a wide variety of ego structures and defenses. Technique varies greatly with the individual case and the level of regression. Freiman (1983) presents the analysis of a bulimic anorexic conducted using the couch throughout the treatment. On the other hand, Mintz (Wilson et al. 1985) in the analysis of a more regressed bulimic, used the phone, visited the hospital for therapeutic sessions, and saw the patient face to face for the first phase of analysis.

The technique of therapy advocated is intensive psychotherapy or analysis, with concurrent psychotherapy of parents, if necessary, with a different therapist. If the same therapist treats both the anorexic and the parents, the anorexic will tend to mistrust the therapist, who becomes identified too closely with the judging parents. In some cases, the mother and/or father needs intensive therapy. Where the anorexic patient refuses or resists treatment, preliminary therapy of the parent(s) can lead to a healthy treatment motivation. Modified classical or traditional psychoanalytic treatment methods are often used. For example, even though the patient may be seen three or four times a week, the couch may not be used until late in therapy. If the only practical arrangement is psychotherapy, much can be accomplished at two times a week, although three sessions are better. It is useful therapeutically for the adolescent patient to pay some part of the fee if possible. Even with adult anorexics, the analyst must keep in mind the patient's unresolved symbiotic conflicts and the possibility of conjoint treatment.

The interpretations cited in the following cases exemplify various interpretations that were applied systematically as the defenses of the ego (denial, rationalization, belief in magic, acting out, etc.) unfolded. At times, because of space limitations, there has been a condensation of multiple interpretations.

RESTRICTOR ANOREXIC CASE MATERIAL

There is a wide spectrum of restrictor anorexic cases, ranging from those tending toward the neurotic category to those evidencing more regressed psychopathology.[4]

An Adolescent Restrictor and Her Family

In the following case, restrictor anorexic symptoms were resolved and the underlying personality disorder was analyzed. The parents were in conjoint therapy with colleagues. Time will reveal whether the therapy process was sufficient for a resolution of the patient's neurosis or whether further symptom development will occur, requiring resumption of treatment.

The R. family came for consultation about their 17-year-old daughter Sally, who recently had became anorexic and lost 30 pounds. Sally's history was typical of the majority of restrictor anorexics. A "good" girl, she was obsessed with proper behavior, studying, and social achievement. Her idealistic father, although successful in business, always wished that he had been a physician. A workaholic, he delegated the care of his children to his wife, who divided her time between a social-work career and her family. She was overconcerned with ladylike and proper behavior for her daughter.

Sally's brother, Robert, two years her senior, was an easygoing adolescent boy who had a succession of girlfriends, smoked, drank, and enjoyed parties, dancing, and rock music. Although the mother apathetically chided him for his poor performance in school, most of her attention was focused on her daughter. She did everything she could for Sally, helping her with her studies and barraging her with advice and criticism.

The R.s followed a strict routine: meals were on time, television was rationed to one hour a day, and the major form of relaxation for the parents

---

[4]Some aspects of these cases were published previously (Wilson et al. 1985).

was intellectual discussion and serious reading. They never quarreled in front of their children and, in general, they shared the same ethical, social, and political views.

Memories of having witnessed parental intercourse (primal scene) emerged in the course of Sally's analysis. At age 3 she woke up screaming from a nightmare and, in order to quiet her, her mother had her sleep the rest of the night in the parents' bed. It was then that Sally heard the heavy breathing of intercourse, which she fantasied was an attack by her father on her mother. Other occasions of witnessing parental intercourse, at ages 4 and 6, increased Sally's fear of sexuality. There were no operable locks on the doors in the R.s home. Sally observed parental nudity and toilet activities, and she became inhibited and afraid of boys.

Analysis

Many conflicts were displaced onto and masked by Sally's anorectic symptoms. Therapy focused on showing Sally the nature of her strict conscience, which demanded perfect behavior in herself and others. In treatment she was hypercritical; memories and dreams revealed that she had developed this attitude by identifying with her mother's perfectionism.

Examples of Interpretations

In the early sessions Sally came on time, sat quietly, and talked only about eating or not eating. I confronted her with her denial and displacement and pointed out that she had other conflicts as well. She answered sharply, "I don't even want to go to the school dance." My interpretation was that, because she felt she should have no conflict, she avoided anything that upset her and that, as she had mentioned before, going to a dance meant choosing a dress and having to go with a date who was not popular. Sally replied that she guessed she would go with him, even though he did not dance very well. I commented that she demanded that she and the boy be perfect in everything.

The next session, which was after the dance, Sally announced that she was starting a new diet and was not going to have any lunch. The interpretation was made that the dance must have upset her, that since she could not control her emotions, she could control eating. She replied angrily, "You are so stupid; I am just dieting." I said that she felt she could avoid all conflict by not eating. Sally then said that actually she felt very depressed, that she had suicidal thoughts and ideas of stopping all eating after the dance, and that she had been jealous of her friend Jane, whose date was handsomer than hers. My interpretation was that she paid a price if she tried to avoid feeling lonely, suicidal, and bitter (depressed) by not eating and socializing. She replied that "maybe you [are] right; Billy called to ask me to a rock concert and I decided to go."

Both Mr. and Mrs. R. were referred for psychotherapy. Mrs. R. came to understand that she was treating Sally differently from Robert and that she had been pressuring her daughter to carry out certain of her own unfulfilled aspirations. The R.s moderated their overconcern with dieting and weight loss and their need to control Sally. They learned how to tolerate the emerging rebellious, depressed, critical adolescent behavior that Sally manifested when her anorectic symptoms subsided. The parents also took some vacations without their children for the first time and began to quarrel in front of their children. Operable locks on the bedroom and bathroom doors were installed, and Sally was given privacy.

As is typical of such patients, Sally was bothered by her mother's changed attitudes and behavior. For example, at one session she remained silent and then, depressed and crying, she said, "My mother does not love me anymore; she doesn't even ask me about my eating." The interpretation was offered that her mother realized now that Sally had other problems than eating and that eating was up to her.

Sally's restrictor anorectic symptoms cleared up in six weeks. She resumed eating, achieved normal weight levels, and began to menstruate again. Two years of analysis were required to resolve her underlying personality disorder.

DISCUSSION OF RESTRICTOR FAT PHOBICS

Since these regressed patients usually are negativistic and withholding, it is best, if possible, to obtain information from concerned relatives, and any, previous therapist, with hospitalized patients, the hospital staff. Usually anorexics deny their illness and will not ask for financial aid for therapy. The therapist often has to explain the need for therapy and discuss fees and other arrangements with concerned third parties.

The problem of developing a therapeutic relation with severely regressed patients was discussed by Boyer and Giovacchini (1990), to the extent that such a relation recapitulates positive aspects of normative processes in the infant–caretaker relationship and provides opportunity for the development of a new object relationship, a developmental thrust that can be differentiated from the transference neurosis. I agree with Boyer and Giovacchini that:

A corrective emotional experience takes place, one that is based on the emotional availability of the analyst and the constancy of the therapeutic environment rather than the therapist's manipulation. To a degree that has been underrecognized in our literature, the optimal availability of analysts is based on their emotional sensitivity and their security and responsiveness to a wide range of emotions. Stated otherwise, the analyst must be able to tolerate emotionally the patient's need to regress to very primitive psychological, even psychosomatic states, including in some cases those in which the fantasies are *in* the soma. It is in this type of atmosphere that a therapeutic alliance can develop within which appropriate interpretations will be effective. In Emde's

(1988b, p. 29) words, "If the process goes well, the analytic relationship becomes fortified by a new executive sense of "we" and an analytic "we-ego."

Freud's (1910) "countertransference" came to be considered as the repetition of the analyst's irrational, unconscious, previously acquired attitudes, now directed toward the patient. Today, most analysts would consider this view to be Racker's (1953) countertransference neurosis. The literature on countertransference is vast and burgeoning; the most comprehensive review in English is that of Langs (1976). Hann-Kende (1933) may have been the first to have suggested that the countertransference could be turned to purposes beneficial to therapy. Today, countertransference is viewed generally as the analyst's total emotional response to his patient's needs (Little 1957). [p. 14]

The restrictor anorexic crisis, which is documented below by the case of Frances, gives us the most clear-cut opportunity to study a state of regression to a very primitive psychological state, a psychosomatic state when fantasies are in the soma. The process that many analysts seem not to have understood is that a most intense pregenital transference has already developed at the start of analysis. After the first consultation, these patients often are confused, may try the wrong door. A powerful deep emotional experience has occurred. The patients sense that the analyst is a person (a new object) who will accept them and their total personality, including their unconscious and, most important, their aggression.

Let me give you an example of what I am describing. In this situation the therapist may be likened to an American interviewing a Jew in Communist Moscow, before perestroika, who wants to emigrate to the United States but who can't talk or must lie or withhold because he knows that the room has been bugged by the K.G.B. The patient similarly is terrified of his archaic, sadistic punitive superego, his unconscious secret police. When I made the interpretation to Frances (described later) that her strict conscience disapproved of her own and of the intern's aggression, that it disapproved of all aggression, I was implying that I did approve of aggression and that I would accept her impulses in all their manifestations. A positive therapeutic alliance and positive transference developed at that time, remaining essentially positive for fifteen years.

The following two severely regressed eating-disorder cases recapitulate clinical material that was in part presented in Wilson and colleagues 1985, but here I offer an amplified discussion of the clinical issues. Confidentiality prevents me from presenting other comparable cases in such detail.

FROM ANOREXIC HOSPITAL CRISIS TO HEALTH

This patient was first seen in the hospital in a dangerously emaciated state. In the terminal phase of analysis, when her fat-phobic neurosis had been largely resolved, she had become pregnant, delivered a healthy baby, graduated from college summa cum laude, and published a successful novel. This case is presented in some detail because of the twenty-year follow-up and because the analytic resolution of the severe regression reveals the basic psychopathology, the defenses of the ego, and the technique of interpretation more clearly than is the situation with less regressed patients.

Frances, a 25-year-old woman, was seen in consultation in the hospital. She was under combined psychiatric and medical treatment that included Thorazine and nutritional supplements. The history revealed that the restrictor anorexia of four months' duration had developed after Frances terminated an affair, during which she had not used any contraceptives. She manifested symptoms of insomnia, fasting, amenorrhea, and difficulties in concentration while working. She had gone for office psychotherapy for three months prior to hospitalization. She had liked the psychiatrist, but symptomatically had gone downhill. She had developed suicidal fears of killing herself with a razor and had refused to eat anything but a little ice cream. When seen on the ward, she was being tube-fed per the nasal passage. The parents were seen together in consultation and, at the analyst's request, wrote up their observations on their daughter.

Patient's History

Frances was the elder of two girls. Following a normal pregnancy, the mother had been unable to nurse Frances because of a fever of unknown origin. Frances was described as a "good baby," but she began hair-pulling at age 2, which continued until age 3. A psychiatric consultation at that time yielded no specific therapeutic recommendations. At first Frances had been a good eater, but then became difficult, forcing her mother to devise games to feed her. She was phobic about new situations such as getting haircuts, meeting strangers, entering stores, and taking train rides. Fire engines and ambulance sirens frightened her. She showed an early musical talent. A school phobia had appeared when she started kindergarten; the mother had stayed in school with her until she adjusted. At age 5 Frances reacted to the birth of her sister by hiding and crying. Analysis revealed later that she had not been prepared for the birth. From that time on, she had multiple phobias of fires, ambulances, hospitals, and doctors. She had been an excellent student. The mother ambivalently described her as a "complex, fearful, but basically cheerful child."

In the latency years she had shown strong tomboy wishes, rejected frilly, feminine clothes, and insisted on boys' clothes. She had played all contact sports, including touch football, and had been extremely competitive with boys. Throughout childhood, Frances had not been a big eater. During her college years she had been 30 pounds underweight.

In high school Frances had had few friends and had not been close to any of her teachers, nor had she had any dates or crushes on boys. She had no memory of masturbation. She had been conscientious about her studies, getting up at 4:30 A.M. to review her homework. She had excelled in sports and had enjoyed music and art. She had chosen a women's college to avoid problems of dating. Scholastically, she had done well and had gone on to graduate school, where she began to date.

The father was a compulsive professional man who said that he "could not stand children." The mother was also compulsive[5] and was a strict disciplinarian at home. When provoked, she would slap the children on the face.

The Technique of Interpretation of Life-Threatening Projective Identification in the Crisis Self-Starvation of Restrictor Anorexia Nervosa

When first seen in the hospital, Frances was walking around the locked ward pushing an intravenous apparatus. With typical anorexic denial of conflict, she did not reply to questions. I introduced myself and informed her that her parents had asked me to see her because I was an anorexic specialist. She made no reply and tried not to look at me. I told her that in our work we would find out why she felt forced to starve herself to death. She again made no reply.

The next day when I came in to see her, she thrust her arm at me, and angrily said, "Look what those interns did to me!" The intravenous needle had come out and her arm was black and blue and swollen from repeated attempts to reinsert the needle. The nurse and residents reported to me that Frances had resisted their attempts to reinsert the needle. I interpreted to the patient that her conscience was so strict that she could not admit to anger, that she fought with the staff but had to deny it. She burst out, "The nurses and interns are fascists!" I stated that I knew that the staff members were concerned with her health and that anyone who tried to control her made her angry but her conscience did not permit anger.

Her associations were to childhood; she had a "funny" memory that at 8 years of age she had cut her sister with some scissors. I asked her if she could remember her sister's reaction or what had caused the incident. Frances could not recall anything more. I told her that her conscience was so strict that she could not remember her sister's anger or her own, just as she disapproved of her own and the intern's aggression.

Giving Responsibility to a Regressed Patient

At a conference with the attending physician I informed him that Frances was developing a positive therapeutic relation. I asked him if he could delay on hyperalimentation because Frances's weight was nearly half-normal. He said he could wait for a week. Then I met with the hospital staff

---

[5]Her parents did individual psychotherapy with colleagues to achieve an understanding of their pathological relationship to their daughter that continued into her adult years.

and explained that I wanted all attempts to encourage Frances to eat stopped because I wanted to make the patient responsible for her eating.

Confrontational, Educational Interpretations Focused on the Healthy but Silent Part of the Anorexic Ego

At the next session I told Frances that as soon as she put on enough weight, she could leave the hospital and come to my office for analytic therapy, that behind her anorexic symptoms she had conflicts about men, marriage, pregnancy, and childbirth. She made no reply to my statement but said she did not want her boyfriend to see her because he upset her. I said that her way of dealing with conflict was to avoid it: food upset her, so she didn't eat; her boyfriend bothered her, so she avoided him; I talked about issues that angered her, and she ignored me. Frances said she would see her boyfriend, but he had pushed her too hard to get married. I pointed out that she had begun dieting when she was dating him because she was afraid of getting pregnant. Frances said that she avoided reading about pregnancy in adolescence and that she used to think that pregnancy came from kissing.

In her previous supportive psychotherapy the therapist had sent the bills to her father. I gave her the bill; this starved, emaciated patient took over full responsibility for payment.

Early Acting Out

Frances began to eat and gain weight. She called me to ask permission to leave the hospital to do special exercises. I interpreted that she was denying how ill she had made herself. The next day the nurses told me she was fasting and losing weight again. She reported a dream of being given the intravenous feeding again, but she would not associate to it. Interpretations were made that she was angry with me for not letting her do anything she wanted, that she hoped to defeat me by being fed intravenously again.

Dreams Indicating Progress, and a Positive Relationship

In the next session she reported that she had had a fight with her boyfriend, that he was too demanding. I interpreted to her that she wanted to control her boyfriend and me totally. She reported dreams of skiing and of having her periods again. She began to eat and put on more weight.

The foregoing emergency phase of therapy lasted three weeks; in the subsequent three weeks of hospital therapy, she evidenced a developing positive transference. The content of her sessions largely involved her conflicts with her boyfriend and her work. I continued to interpret her wishes to deny conflict and anger with me because of my confronting her with her neurosis. She stopped fasting, intravenous feeding was not necessary, and she put on enough weight so that she could be discharged for office analytic treatment.

Therapy after Leaving the Hospital

After discharge from the hospital, Frances immediately began analysis. However, from the start, the therapeutic approach in the hospital had been basically analytic. My contacts with relatives were confined to the initial interview. For further problems the relatives were referred to another therapist. The issue of discharge arose in our sessions.

Making the Patient Responsible for Decisions

I had been careful, when stating that I felt Frances was ready for discharge, to ask for her opinion about it. She had tried to evade the issue and make me totally responsible. I told her that she could control her eating if she chose to. Later she accused me of being hard-hearted because I had released such a weak, helpless patient. I again interpreted that she had had conscious control and that, if she had told me she did not feel ready to leave the hospital, I would not have discharged her.

Risk-Taking to Frighten the Analyst

Soon after starting outpatient treatment, while riding home on the subway at 1 A.M., Frances became embroiled in an argument with two intoxicated men who wanted her to join them for a drink and threatened to beat her up if she did not. She was terrified when she left the subway car at her station. She revealed in analysis that her friends and relatives had often warned her against taking the subway alone at such hours but that she denied realistic dangers in this and other situations.

The Question of Dangerous Regression in the Transference: The Return of Childhood Pathology

Frances's massive denial of internal and external conflict was persistently interpreted. A transference meaning of this incident was interpreted—that she wanted to frighten me and force me to rehospitalize her for protection from her impulsive behavior. Frances and her relatives had been forewarned that symptomatic improvement might occur quickly but that long-term analysis was necessary. Frances quickly regained her normal weight and her menstrual periods. Her acute symptoms cleared, and she went back to work and resumed her social life.

It was at this time, six weeks after discharge, that the basic analytic task began. I will discuss aspects of the analysis, which was terminated successfully at the end of the third year. Severe regressive psychosomatic symptoms do not necessarily recur in the analysis of these patients because of the new object relationship that develops, which has to be carefully distinguished from the transference neurosis relationship.

Brief episodes of anorexia and hair-pulling occurred during the first year and were analyzed in the context of the transference neurosis. These symptoms were provoked by separations from me on weekends and holidays, and interpretations focused on the wish to make me anxious and to control me as she had her parents.

Frances did not go over to a phase of bulimia, as is frequently the case with restrictors. Her extreme ambivalence appeared during the first year as a frequent strong wish to stop therapy and deny illness. Another symptom was a fear of being alone and a need to keep the light on all night; this was resolved by the end of the first year.

As with other anorexics, Frances's dreams reflected both oedipal and preoedipal conflicts, and the defense of denial had to be interpreted repeatedly in order for her ego to face the latent conflicts reflected in dreams. There was also a strong resistance to interpreting any of her own dreams, which reflected her need to control affects.

A repetitive anxiety dream was of being under water and not being able to get to the surface, which masked oedipal-phase fears of childbirth dating from the birth of her younger sister when she was 5. A regressive preoedipal fantasy of being the baby in utero was also expressed in the dream, as were conflicts about showing emotions (that is, crying). In her childhood struggle with her implacable parents, Frances had cried repeatedly when her desires were frustrated. For a time she had had the nickname of "crybaby."

Changes in the Manifest Content of Dreams

In the course of analysis, the progressive development of a more benevolent superego, a stronger ego, and a stronger self-observing function of the ego was reflected in change in the manifest content of her dreams. Early dreams of being raped and attacked gave way to dreams of observing a rape or burglary followed by dreams of being a hostage held by criminals who would probably release her. Then frank dreams of mother, father, and the analyst dying reflected a shift from masochistic to sadistic fantasies. Finally, in the terminal phase, dreams of pregnancy, marriage, and intercourse appeared.

Sadomasochistic, Oral-Incorporative Dreams

Dreams of rabid black dogs reflected oral- and anal-phase sadomasochistic conflicts. At the height of the working through of these conflicts in the transference neurosis, Frances dreamed of being assaulted and robbed. In her associations, she said that she had seen a macabre off-Broadway play in which women had whole hands chopped off and tongues cut out. She had vomited at a scene in which a man was chopped up and served for dinner. This oral-incorporative material was related to Frances's occasional aversion to red meat, and its analysis led to more relaxed behavior in the transference and in her object relations. Although such material is indicative of oedipal conflicts, in analysis it must be approached first from the point of view of preoedipal material. For the full analysis of the anorexic fat-phobic oral-incorporative, cannibalistic and fusion conflicts and fantasies have to be uncovered and analyzed.

Identification with the Aggressor Emerges

Frances dreamed of "slugging" her roommate in the face. This reflected her identification with mother, who had often slapped her in the face for disobedience at the dinner table. She had a taboo against really "beating" anyone at tennis until she came to see that beating had a literal and sadistic meaning for her. Typical of anorexics' parents, her parents, and particularly her mother, were extremely controlling and never argued in front of the children. Decisions and rules were inflexible.

Anorexics have less than normal opportunities to play one parent off against the other or to turn to one parent for support and love when working through conflicts toward the other parent. Again typically, the mother did all the cooking, even though she weakly suggested that the daughters learn to cook.

The parents were very strict about sweets. While she was in the hospital, Frances asked for ice cream, which had been strictly rationed by the parents. Yet when friends brought her this special food, she would not eat it. It was easy to see that the anorexia reversed an earlier battle that the parents had won: by starving herself, Frances brought about the offer of any food, in any quantity, at any time, from everyone.

Manifestations of Extreme Ambivalence

Frances's ambivalence was reflected in her having one foot off the couch for the first year of analysis and in recurrent wishes to stop treatment. Denial was a pervasive defense, with many ramifications in her speech. A minimizing mannerism of speech was, "I just did not feel like doing it"; analysis revealed this to mean that she would not do it under any circumstances. "It was perfectly all right" meant that it was boring. Frances's tense readiness to run from the analytic room was a way of avoiding both her unconscious hostility toward the analyst (mother) and her fantasied projected retaliation from the analyst (mother and father).

Analysis revealed a strong latent homosexual conflict. Both consciously and unconsciously, Frances had wanted to be a boy. In latency she had fantasied extensively about an adventurous boy with whom she identified. In adolescence she had denied her femininity and did not date. She had chosen a women's college in order to avoid men. Her anorexic symptoms had developed in adult life because of a delayed adolescent struggle in her three "affairs," and because of preoedipal and oedipal seduction by the father, who when she was a child, had bathed her and toweled her off, up until early adolescence.

All-or-Nothing Ego Functioning

All-or-nothing ego functioning has to be interpreted in terms of decision making, delay in impulse gratification, demands of the ego ideal and superego, sublimations, adaptations, sexual and aggressive conflicts, and object relations. For example, hyperactivity was manifested in Frances's increasing preoccupation with bicycling. She belonged to a bicycle club that arranged strenuous overnight trips. Prior to hospitalization, as her weight plummeted, she became more and more hyperactive. The all-or-nothing quality of this behavior is characteristic of anorexic patients. Later in analysis, after Frances had mastered her anorexia, her conflicts in sublimation still reflected this problem. For example, for a time she resisted spending some pleasurable hours swimming because she could no longer achieve her adolescent goal of being an Olympic swimmer.

The all-or-nothing problem involved other areas of psychic life as well. Frances either saw her family for long visits, or did not see them at all.

There was no return to severe regressive restrictor anorexic self-starvation. In situations of separation, there was an increase in fat phobia and restricted eating as well as revival of a mild amount of hair-pulling. On Mondays, for example, the patient was usually quiet and withholding, and I would point out the increase in her need to control. Genetic material emerged about the early feeding relation to the mother.

Early Mother–Child Eating Conflicts: The Airplane Hangar Dream

After a week's winter vacation break, Frances came to her session and was particularly quiet. Asked about dreams, she said she had had a dream the night before about an airplane hangar and an airplane. After a period of silence, she added that she had also pulled out some of her hair, which felt painful but good. An interpretation was made that she hurt herself by hair-pulling rather than facing anger and that she wished to hurt me for deserting her when I canceled for a week. The patient laughed and said that the airplane dream reminded her of a game her mother used to play to get her to eat. In the patient's memory back to age 2 or 3, her mother very patiently would pretend that the patient's mouth was an airplane hangar. Mother would say, "Here comes the airplane; open the hangar doors." Frances would clamp her jaws down even more firmly shut, but her mother would be endlessly patient and persistent until she finally opened her mouth and ate. The interpretation was again made that the patient was angry at me for leaving her, that she wanted me to be like her mother and never leave her, that I'd be endlessly patient with her and just get her to eat, and that I should never leave her.

The good feeling (actually she was secretly elated) that she felt in inflicting pain on herself in the hair-pulling had multiple causes, among them a secret delight in having protected the object (me in the transference, mother in childhood) from destruction. It also represented pleasure at not having to submit totally to the *archaic superego that forbids any aggression toward the self or the object*.[6] The elation also resulted from her being able by this masochistic behavior to maintain an ego ideal of being pure and noble. Later in analysis, oedipal meanings of the hair-pulling habit emerged. It masked masochistic sexual and birth fantasies as well as castration conflicts.

In the transference the tendency to make interpretations into fiats that are manifestations of projective identifications in these patients had to be interpreted as well as their meaning in terms of all-or-nothing behavior. Frances's handling of money reflected this ambivalence. She saved money frugally for the first years of treatment, spending very little on herself; however, impulses to do the opposite emerged in the form of not being able to make purchases because she wanted only the best. While she was compulsively choosing a new apartment over a period of months, her fantasies and dreams of the perfect dwelling place emerged.

At termination, Frances showed marked structural change, with a stronger ego, a more benevolent superego, and a capacity for whole-object relations and healthy sublimations.

Long-term Results of Analysis

Ten years after her first therapy, the patient returned for more analysis. She had married and achieved success in her career but had conflicts about having a child. The analysis of oedipal-phase pregnancy fears of being mutilated in childbirth was a crucial aspect of her further therapy. Also important was the further analysis of her compulsions, which resulted in her being able to relax during pregnancy and to modify her work patterns. She gave birth to a healthy son.

The second analysis revealed that her fear-of-being-fat body image had been resolved. She no longer used food in neurotic ways and "never felt better than when she was pregnant." Twenty-year follow-up showed healthy functioning in personal relations, motherhood, career, and marriage.

---

[6]This elated euphoric affect is experienced whenever eating-disorder patients feel they can (usually suddenly) get free of the internalized punitive mother imago, as when they impulsively go on an unplanned vacation or jump up and leave a family group who are socializing to "go for a jog."

EGO FUNCTIONING IN SEVERE STARVATION

The clinical material in the cases of both Sally and Frances, where the weight was often below two-thirds normal, as well as Mintz's similar case (1983c) and other cases my colleagues and I have supervised and analyzed, demonstrates that ego functioning (reality testing, cognitive functioning, etc.) is intact and in some cases even heightened.

TECHNIQUE WITH RESTRICTOR FAT PHOBICS

The analytic technique with restrictor fat phobics in the first phase of treatment is to interpret manifestations in the patient's behavior, dreams, and verbalizations of the masochism which is caused by the patient's archaic superego.

The direct confrontation of Frances with her suicidal behavior is an interpretation that is used only in cases of severe regression. Where there is no serious situation, the defenses of the ego determine the interpretation. Early in treatment I do suggest to the patient that he or she seems to have an overly strict conscience, a comment that sets the stage for a positive transference. The early interpretation of Frances's denial of suicidal behavior (masochism) parallels the technique of Sperling (1978), Wilson and colleagues (1985), and Wilson and Mintz (1989) with psychosomatic patients and correlates with the therapeutic technique used in the therapy of schizophrenic, borderline, and character disorders by Boyer (1975), Boyer and Giovacchini (1980), Kernberg (1975), Volkan (1976), and Wilson (1971a).

First one interprets the patient's masochism—his or her archaic superego and the guilt experienced upon admitting to any conflicts. Next, one interprets defenses against facing masochistic behavior; then, when the ego is healthier, defenses against aggressive impulses are interpreted. These interpretations are inexact; frequently patients' associations do not confirm them. These patients have an archaic, punitive superego and a relatively weak ego. The analyst provides auxiliary ego strength and a rational superego (Boyer 1975, 1980, Wilson 1971a). Interpretation should be made in a firm, consistent manner (Boyer 1975, 1980). The analyst needs to have authority.

Early in treatment patients do not usually offer useful associative verbal material, as is also the case in the analyses of children and patients with character disorders (Boyer and Giovacchini 1980). That Frances reported the dreams was a sign of positive transference; previously she had been silent and negativistic. The dreams of skiing and menstruating seemed to be indicators of a positive therapeutic alliance. At this stage of treatment, the analyst uses construction and reconstruction to respond to patients' silences. An example was my telling Frances that behind her fat phobia were fears of men, marriage, pregnancy, and childbirth. Like other psychosomatic patients, Frances developed an early strong positive transference and gave up some of her symptoms before she had any in-depth understanding of her conflicts. To facilitate this process, in the analysis of patients' masochism, the analyst must let patients know that they can express their emotions and conflicts in therapy.

Frances had received joint psychiatric and medical treatment, which had resulted in a splitting of the transference, anger on Frances's part at being controlled, and subsequent self-starvation and resistance to medical treatment. When I was able to stop the forced medical treatment, the transference became concentrated on me. In this process, I studied my countertransference and counterreactions to Frances's negativistic behavior. I realized that if she resisted further, treatment would be interrupted to save her life, since her weight had dropped to near half-normal. Instead of worrying about Frances's dying, which was the affective state she wanted to induce in me, I interpreted her masochism and suicidal impulses.

In discussing the problem of how far the analyst should go in interpreting intense denial, Anna Freud (1968) refers to Bond, in treating an anorexic girl, countering her fantastic denial of self-destruction (extreme emaciation) by telling her that she would die. As with other anorexics, the effects of the self-starvation did not impair Frances's ego functioning. On the contrary, often when patients' masochistic impulses are most intense and the results of their behavior most pathological and self-destructive, the split-off, silent, rational part of the ego is ready for a confrontation and the potential for a positive transference is heightened. Alcoholics Anonymous (1979) believes that some addicts have to experience "the gutter" before they will face what they are doing to themselves and battle their addiction. The psychological situation is similar to that seen in patients who have made a serious attempt at suicide. The analytic consultant brings out to patients, in the context of their life history and personal psychodynamics, that the problem is to discover in therapy why they want to kill themselves. Frequently, in this approach, suicidal patients can be released from the hospital for analysis with no recurrence of serious suicidal behavior. Frances evidenced a positive transference throughout her analysis and did not resume any life-threatening fasting.

Like all regressed restrictor fat phobics (anorexics), Frances overcontrolled her impulses; she did not smoke, drink, or indulge in substance abuse. The expression of aggression was ego alien—she was a good, conforming girl. Analysis recovered memories of a phase of guilty masturbation at age 12. Her areas of successful adaptive functioning were schoolwork and athletics. In sports, however, her guilt at fantasies of "beating people" kept her from winning important matches. Her habits were hypernormal. She was always punctual; she planned her day carefully; her language was polite; her affects, both aggressive and libidinal, were under strict control. The ego structure was in part similar to that of a compulsive neurotic. Like other anorexics, she had a split ego. She had to be confronted with manifestations of denied, split-off, aggressive and libidinal fantasies, impulses, and conflicts. Analysis of the many dreams she reported was fruitful, but she resisted interpreting them herself. However, she was basically cooperative and trusting throughout her treatment. She did not lie; she withheld thoughts and feelings. Silence was an analytic problem at times. Acting out and acting in were limited and amenable to analysis. Her parents' behavior—overconscientious, moralistic, overcontrolling, presenting a united parental authority—dovetailed with the psychological profile of other anorexic families.

A BULIMIC ANOREXIC CASE: MARTHA

The patient was a 21-year-old single woman living with her family and working as an editorial assistant in a publishing firm. She had been gorging and vomiting for six years. Overweight since early childhood, she went on a Weight Watchers diet at age 15, shortly after her first menstrual period, and lost 30 pounds. Then a friend taught her how to vomit and she had been dieting, gorging, and vomiting ever since, up to five times a day. She was on a perpetual diet of salads, cottage cheese, and diet food. When she gorged she consumed prodigious quantities of rich food, candy, ice cream, cereals, and spaghetti, until she felt she would burst. Then, overwhelmed with guilt and intense fat phobia, she would vomit repeatedly. She also used laxatives and exercise (jogging up to twenty miles a day at times) to get rid of her "fat." Her parents, who were referred for conjoint therapy, were of Irish-Catholic background. The mother, a church-going housewife who was 10 to 15 pounds overweight, chronically complained of being too fat and unsuccessfully went on and off diets. The father was a controlling, perfectionistic, workaholic insurance executive whose only "vice" was cigarette smoking. The patient, Martha, was their only child and the center of their attention. Martha was inhibited sexually until her teens, when she had many dates, permitting herself some necking and petting. She developed a phobia about travel and found that the boys she liked took other girls out. Her periods were irregular, and prior to consultation she had been amenorrheic for six months.

In the fifteenth session of her analysis she was late to her session for the first time. Her associations were that she missed the bus because she had been enjoying a conversation with a friend. She thought about not being efficient and not allowing time to get to appointments. She also did not take care of things. She had lost her bag when she went skiing. She procrastinated on filing her medical health insurance forms. She realized that she did not do the things she should do. Her car needed to be taken in for an oil change, but she did not do it. She knew she would wait until her parents and others became impatient with her. The interpretation was made that chores and details of living are not exciting, that one part of her wanted immediate pleasure and resented tasks, and that it was more fun to talk to a friend than to come for her sessions.

Her associations were to childhood: her father was a perfectionist who would create chores for her. He would store up anger when she did not do them and then he would explode. "Even now when I'm an adult," she said, "he yells at me." The interpretation was made that she was angry with me, fearing that I was a perfectionist like her father but that she kept her anger to herself, having a secret valve for it: her binging. The patient said, "It's funny I don't think about what I'm doing when I binge." The interpretation was made that her strict conscience did not let her know about things that she was angry about and that she felt she had to get rid of conflicts by binging. At this point, for the first time, she became upset and cried. She said that she had never realized before how unhappy she was.

In subsequent sessions her associations and dreams unfolded aspects of her neurosis, her dependence on her parents, her agoraphobia, and various age-appropriate realities that she avoided, such as having a bank account and checkbook. A number of dreams revealed her wish to be back in high school, to remain a teenager with no adult responsibilities. She talked about age and time; she hated the idea of anyone growing old; she refused to accept the possibility of her parents ever dying. As she faced more and more of her conflicts, she also began to exert will power to interrupt her binging. The frequency of her binging decreased from five times a day to every other day. *The underlying depression that is masked by fat-phobic symptoms began to emerge.* She cried in sessions and expressed hopeless feelings. She wondered if anything could be done for her and asked if analysis would be forever. She had suicidal ideas and was aware of wishes not to come to sessions. She wanted medication to relieve her depressed feelings. As a result of confrontational interpretations, she acknowledged that she gorged when she was depressed and that her upset feelings disappeared when she gorged. Repeated interpretation emphasized that if she could think about what upset her, she might not have to gorge.

She remembered that as a girl she used to be called "princess" by her father, that she was his favorite, and she knew she could get anything she wanted from him. Feelings of hopelessness emerged as she thought about the fact that she did not have many friends, and those few she had, she felt, used her. She talked of not wanting to grow up. She ignored the idea of people dying; her parents were ageless to her. Recently she had refused to go to the funeral of her cousin's grandmother. Her family was angry with her but told the others she was sick with the flu. Although she was 21, she thought of herself as a little girl and dreaded the idea of her next birthday.

With further maturation of ego capacities to face and tolerate conflicts and affects, particularly depression, binging frequency decreased to once or twice a month. Four years of further analysis resolved the underlying personality disorder.

CHRONIC ANOREXIA WITH BULIMIA AND VOMITING: ELAINE

The following case report highlights the ego structure and the technical problems in the analysis of a bulimic who for many months kept her weight at a very low level, a level that many therapists (Bruch 1973, Thomä 1967) would insist requires mandatory hospitalization and emergency medical treatment.

Elaine, a 28-year-old woman, came for consultation after undergoing a long and expensive hospitalization with behavioral modification treatment that failed to resolve her anorexia.

Patient's History

Elaine's family were Irish Catholics. The younger of two girls, Elaine had been a model child, bright and precocious. Her sister had been blue-eyed, slender, and tall, whereas Elaine had been brown-eyed, chubby, and short. As an adult, Elaine thought of herself as "dumpy and fat," despite her awareness that men were very attracted to her. Elaine, who was five feet, two inches, always envied her tall, slender sister. During her anorexia, she felt she looked beautiful at a very thin weight.

Elaine had been weaned from the breast at $1\frac{1}{2}$ years and bowel-trained before her second year. Throughout childhood she had been so severely constipated that at times she had been given laxatives. Severe nail-biting and cuticle-chewing dated back to her earliest years. She was phobic about heights and closed spaces. During adolescence, when agitated, Elaine would bite her toenails and toe cuticles, causing serious toe infections. In late adolescence, because of shame at the appearance of her hands, she stopped nail-biting but became a chain smoker. As an adult, she was proud of her long, curved fingernails.

Elaine did well in school but had anxiety about taking exams. Talented and educated in music, she went into the business world on graduation from college but could not get beyond the secretarial level.

Inhibited and repressed sexually in childhood, she developed crushes on boys following the onset of her menses at age 12. For several years she had sexual experiences without using any contraceptives. She was terrified of pregnancy but finally started using the pill in late adolescence.

Elaine's mother was a 60-year-old housewife from a conservative midwestern family who devoted her time to her husband, home, and daughters. She was in good health but was a chain-smoker, preoccupied with fears of being fat and going on and off diets, although she was actually never more than 10 pounds overweight.

Elaine's father had been an American success story: a child of Irish immigrants, he built a small construction company into a statewide business. He had been a hard-working man who doted on his daughter but was away on business much of the time. He had been in good health except for infrequent headaches, probably migraines. A heavy smoker, he died of lung cancer when Elaine was 22.

Depression and Restrictor Anorexia Nervosa Preceding the Development of Bulimic Anorexia Nervosa

Following her father's death, Elaine became anxious and depressed. She bitterly mourned her father and cried frequently. For six weeks she felt hopeless, feeling that the world was empty. Then she experienced strong and repeated wishes and fantasies *that mother had died instead of father.* She tried to suppress and repress anxiety and depression by starving herself. She began dieting and within three weeks lost one-third of her body weight. Unable to continue dieting because of ineffective ego controls, she gave in to impulses to gorge, and the bulimic cycle of attempts at self-control and dieting followed by vomiting and laxative use ensued.

Regression Following Behavior Modification Therapy

Underneath Elaine's compliant manner of relating to the analyst was a mistrust, suspicion, and hostility characteristic of patients who have undergone behavior modification therapy (Bruch 1974). In spite of my attempts to interpret her ego's defenses against admitting to negative feelings about me, Elaine denied these but soon forced her weight down even more. She revealed that she had used hidden lead weights to fool the hospital staff into thinking that behavior modification had been successful.

After leaving the hospital, Elaine became almost a recluse in her apartment—not looking for work, seeing few people except her mother. She spent most of her time fasting, gorging, vomiting, and taking laxatives. She said she would rather kill herself than go back into the hospital, since she felt her lengthy and expensive hospitalizations had been worthless and a "rip-off." Her medical treatment was with an internist, who prescribed dietary supplements.

Analysis of Residual Negative Transference from Previous Therapy

In the early sessions I interpreted Elaine's defenses against admitting to her anger toward and mistrust of her previous analyst, the hospital doctors, and me. She began to come out of her isolation and consider work and socializing.

After my vacation break Elaine said that she resented resuming treatment, since she had done well at business school and had met a nice man who took her dancing. Away from sessions, she felt free; in them, she felt strangled. She hated treatment. I interpreted her displacement; it was not the "treatment" she hated, but me. She left the office visibly angry and did not come to her next session. In the next hour she talked of how much she wanted praise; she had not come to the last hour because she was angry at me for not praising her.

Technique of Interpretation of Suicidal Behavior

In a subsequent session she said she had been to her internist and, although her lab tests were better, her potassium was still low. I interpreted to her some of her denial of suicidal behavior. I said that through her habits she vitiated her internist's careful diet advice and the absorption of food and medication, that she denied making him and me medically concerned about her, and that neither the internist nor I would be surprised if she made herself so sick that she forced hospitalization. The patient was angry at this interpretation but then ruefully said that she realized she enjoyed making people anxious about her.

In the next session Elaine reported that 15 and 8 years before, and once in the hospital, she had a repetitive dream of a wall cracking. The wall was in the family's old apartment, which had 16-foot ceilings. The room in the dream was the one Elaine and her sister had shared until the latter had gone away to boarding school. Her sister was never in the dream. Elaine feared that someone would come in to get her through the glass window. As an adult, she had feared that someone would come onto her terrace and get her. As an adolescent, she had had growing pains and her mother had elevated her legs. The cracking reminded her of a mirror cracking. The interpretation was made that she felt she should be punished for having hostile thoughts about her sister. Elaine cried and said, "Cracked must mean crazy, murderous thoughts I had about my sister as a little girl."

Interpretations of Various Manifestations of the Impulse Disorder

In the next hour Elaine resumed her cigarette smoking, which she had interrupted in sessions to try to uncover the impulses and fantasies it masked. I interpreted to her that she must be afraid that if she did not smoke she would return to nail-biting, that as a little girl she had felt guilty and miserable at having anger toward her sister and had taken it out on herself in her habit. Elaine burst into tears and said that her sister could be so mean; she would tease Elaine, but Elaine never would fight back.

In the next hour she talked of visiting her mother: "Mother is bored to tears, says her teeth hurt, she is always going to give up cigarettes, she is always complaining about stupid little things; I wish she would die and get it over with. Mother's friend just had a breast removed for cancer."

Elaine became silent and tense. I interpreted to her that she tried to control thoughts and feelings magically by not talking and by cigarette smoking and her anorexic habits. Elaine said that it was all the same—the nail-biting, cigarettes, and anorexia were a "mish-mosh." The interpretation was made that she had to have conscious control—by putting her fingers and cigarettes in her mouth, her fingers down her throat to vomit, and laxatives in her mouth to control her bowels—but tried to make a mystery of her habits. Elaine's reply was: "Until ten years of age I had to sleep with light coming through the door of my room. I must have been afraid to be alone."

Pseudo-Insight

In another session she was silent for twenty minutes and her need to control was again interpreted. Crying angrily, she burst out: "The whole thing is mother. I am torturing her and can't stop, it is so stupid. I am getting back at her for all the things that weren't her fault. I blame her for everything. I feel sorry for her, she is my victim. She doesn't know that I wind her around my little finger. I wonder if she does know. I tell her, don't give me things, but she does anyway. Everything ended when father died; he was the generator. Mother has done nothing since. You don't understand what I feel when I am cynical and bitter; everyone is divorced and bitter, few people are happy. I gave up graduate school because I could not be the best. I think if my mother died, all my symptoms would clear up."

When she finished this outburst, she was sobbing. The interpretation was made that, by hanging onto her habits, she wished to wrap the analyst, as well as her mother, around her little finger and that she preferred the humiliation of her habits to the anxiety, guilt, anger, and fear of her neurosis, which she thought she hid from people. Furthermore, her symptoms and neurosis would not magically clear up if her mother died. She stopped sobbing and said that she realized she wanted a magical, quick cure, a big insight, and that she was impatient with the time that analysis took for results.

Emerging Insight into Projective Identification

In a crucial session, Elaine reported thoughts and memories of her father. Once she had had a fight with him after defying his curfew. She had said, "Why don't you hit me so that you will show your interest?" The night before the session she had interrupted her laxative taking. She recalled her severe constipation in childhood. Her thoughts turned to a baby-sitter who used to beat her and her sister if they misbehaved. Mother caught the sitter punishing them and fired her. Elaine recalled that mother once had slapped her face for making a critical remark. Then Elaine said, "There are times when you move, Doctor, or you lean forward, that I think you are going to hit me; then I think, but you are my analyst. That sitter we had, I hated her so much. She had two faces, one real sweet and the other a son of a bitch. She told me such weird things."

The analyst has to distinguish carefully between counterreactions and countertransference in the analysis of these patients. The analyst experiences all the conscious reactions to the patient's provocative behavior and acting in and acting out that one experiences with a rebellious child, except that the eating-disordered patient is not a child and is far more provocative, deceptive, and manipulative (Wilson 1986, 1987, Wilson et al. 1985). Compulsive therapists often have difficulty confronting counterreactions to these patients, and this interferes with their capacity to analyze these patients.

Informing Patient of Counterreaction
(Not Countertransference)

In my counterreactions to Elaine's stubborn acting in and acting out, which included routinely coming to her sessions fifteen to twenty minutes late, I felt like shouting at her and shaking her. I felt that I was reacting to her as one would to a stubborn, negativistic, provocative 3-year-old child. I also noted that she repeatedly provoked wishes in me to spank her or throw her out. The interpretation was made that, in analysis, she was recreating the battle for control that she had had with her nurse and parents. I told her of some of the hostile feelings and fantasies she had stirred up in me.

I told the patient of my counterreactions at this one point in analysis only because she revealed her projective identifications, which had been going on for a long time, and because I felt she was ready for the interpretation. It is not therapeutically useful to routinely inform patients of counterreactions. On the other hand, any analyst who cannot face and study his or her counterreactions (which must be differentiated from countertransference, which is unconscious) should not attempt to treat these provocative patients.

Following the interpretation, Elaine was silent and then said, "You know, my father was so controlled when he was angry, but he was shouting at me from underneath." In the next session she reported a dream: "I was shouting at me." Her thoughts were of perfectionistic demands on herself and others. An interpretation was made of her identification with her father's excessive self-control. Her associations were to her father's illness, how thin and weak he had become; she left the session crying. This dream reflected also the patient's insight into an internalized object representation of a critical mother.

Resolution of Fear-of-Being-Fat Body Image

At the end of this phase of analysis, Elaine was putting on weight, her severe regression had lifted, and—most important—her body image had changed. She now hated both her own figure and the figures of other anorexic women. This change occurred before the oedipal aspects of her neurosis were analyzed. Her nightmare of the cracked wall reflected conflicts about uncontrollable rage, but oedipal sexual fears about the female crack, the vagina, did not emerge until later. She had resumed her periods but resisted exploring her psychosexual fears for another year, at which time she recalled sadomasochistic fantasies she had had about a scar on her aunt's abdomen.

The changes in Elaine seemed to result from the analysis of her defenses against admitting to emotions and conflicts, particularly in the transference, with the liberation of anger and depression in sessions. It has been my experience (Wilson 1971a, 1983a,b,c, 1985a,b,c, 1987, 1988a, 1989c) and that of others (Boyer 1980, Kernberg 1971, Sperling 1953) that the occurrence of a "psychotic transference"[7] in the analysis of such patients is not unusual and that, although the relative strengths or weaknesses of the

---

[7]The psychotic transference-projective identification, which is an area of major current research.

ego are important, the relationship with the analyst is the most potent force in the reconstruction or construction of the ego and the resolution of transference psychosis.

THE DEGREE OF ACTUAL CHILD ABUSE BY PARENTS AND CARETAKERS

The degree of actual physical abuse in many psychosomatic and eating-disorder cases has not been understood until recently. Elaine was unconsciously afraid of my beating her and wanted me to beat her. For example, a patient with multiple psychosomatic symptoms, including anorexia nervosa, developed a hive on her tongue the night before her session. Her associations were to sticking her tongue out at people as a child, and transference interpretation of her wish to stick her tongue out at me resulted in a clearing of the hive. In her childhood history there were repeated memories of mother losing her temper, slapping the patient, knocking her down, and pulling her hair. Phases of silence, obvious fear, and anxiety when the patient was terrified of me were difficult therapeutic problems. The analyst *must* keep in mind the question of actual sexual or physical abuse in terms of the repressed sadomasochistic fantasies and the archaic superego. In the case of Frances, could her outburst about the fascist medical residents who mutilated her arms, inserting intravenous needles, have masked early assaultive punishment by her mother or other caretaker? This material did not clearly emerge in the analysis.

The turning point in Elaine's therapy occurred when she told me of her fear that I would hit her. I then revealed to her my counterreactions and she *dreamed of shouting at herself,* which was an indication of her growing insight into her strict superego and her projective identifications. In Giovacchini's (1980) words, "Such patients re-create a psychoanalytic ambience that is an approximate reproduction of the infantile environment . . . the analyst has to realize this state of affairs and be at times more intuitive, live with the patient's anger and complaints, and study his counterreactions and countertransference" (p. 475). Patience is essential in the analysis of addictive patients, whose habits, at their most primitive level, mask preverbal conflicts and traumas. Impulsive, psychotic, and psychosomatic patients, all of whom have preoedipal conflicts, have the means to communicate the impact and effects of their early preverbal traumas (Wilson 1968a, 1971a, 1983, 1985a, Wilson and Mintz 1989).

Gradually, basic changes were occurring in Elaine's body image and in her attitudes toward her symptoms. She noted with surprise that she had thought herself to be beautiful when she was extremely thin. Repeated interpretation of the unconscious reasons for inflicting such narcissistic mortification on herself was necessary (Eidelberg 1957, 1959). Frequently the narcissistic mortification is experienced by anorexics and psychosomatic patients as *feeling humiliated.*

EGO STRUCTURE AND TRANSFERENCE INTERPRETATION

Analytic technique has to be adapted to the defenses of the ego. The bulimic patients utilize acting out, rationalization, denial, withholding, and lying more intensely and persistently than do the restrictors. In many cases, once the restrictor's anorexic crisis subsides, the course of analysis is in some ways similar to that of a compulsive neurotic. There are many varieties of ego structure in these patients. Analytic technique varies with the patient, the degree of regression encountered, and the individual style and experience of the analyst.

While some restrictor and bulimic anorexics can be analyzed along more classical lines with the couch being used from the beginning (Wilson et al. 1985, Wilson and Mintz 1989), most often the patient is seen face to face in the first dyadic phase of treatment. During this phase of treatment, as Blos emphasized in discussing the technique of analysis of adolescents (1987), every type of "parameter," such as educational approaches, suggestion, and advice, may be used, but always in a dynamic context. Of course, the patients' reactions to such parameters have to be analyzed later during the triadic oedipal phase.

The technique of interpretation is also determined by multiple factors such as the transference and the quality of object relationships. A crucial consideration is the split in the anorexic's ego and the extent to which this split is comprehended by the self-observing functions of the patient's ego. The first phase of analysis involves making the healthier part of the patient's ego aware of the split-off, primitive, impulse-dominated part of the ego and its modes of functioning.

Typical defenses and character qualities of the anorexic are (1) denial and splitting, (2) belief in magic, (3) feelings of omnipotence, (4) demand that things and people be all perfect—the alternative is to be worthless, (5) need to control, (6) displacement and projection, (7) intense ambivalence, (8) masochistic perfectionism, particularly relating to conflicts around aggression, (9) a pathological ego ideal of beautiful peace and love, and (10) a fantasy of a perfect, conflict-free mother–child symbiosis.

Only when the patient's archaic superego has been modified and when the ego has matured so that there is a capacity to face and tolerate libidinal and aggressive conflicts, and when there has been a shift from part-object relations toward whole-object relations, can the analyst begin to interpret triadic oedipal material.

Both the restrictor and bulimic anorexic make extensive use of the defense of projective identification (Bion 1956, Boyer and Giovacchini 1980, Carpinacci et al. 1963, Carter and Rinsley 1977, Cesio 1963, 1973, Giovacchini 1975, Grinberg 1972, 1976, 1979, Hughes 1984, M. Klein 1955, Ogden 1978, Perestrello 1963, Rosenfeld and Mordo 1973, Searles 1965). As Wilson and colleagues (1983d, 1985) demonstrated, the anorexic projects unacceptable aspects of the personality—impulses, self-images, superego introjects—onto other people, particularly the analyst, with a resulting identification based on these projected self-elements. The extreme psychotic-like denial of conflict of the anorexic is caused by primitive projective identification onto others of archaic, destructive superego introjects.

THE DEFENSE OF DENIAL IN THE EATING DISORDERS

Eating-disordered patients make extreme use of the defense of denial and related defenses of fragmentation splitting (Wilson 1983d), and suppression (Werman 1983). Sperling (1978) noted that part of the anorexic's conflicts are conscious. These patients make use of the defense of suppression (Werman 1983), which usually serves to oppose superego prohibitions and demands. Self-starvation and/or gorging and purging are utilized by the ego as forms of suppression, and Werman notes that self-hypnosis or the use of stimulants (i.e., addictions) are suppressive processes. I have noted that anorexia nervosa is a food phobia and that it is closely related to the addictions.

Silence is a difficult defense in many anorexic cases. An illustrative case was that of a restrictor anorexic.

Joshua, a chronic anorexic 60-year-old rabbi, denied conflicts and was silent for a week. Each day he would wait in the therapy room of the hospital, pull out the therapist's chair, give him a pad and pencil, and politely listen while the therapist constructed aspects of his life from the voluminous case record to show him his masochism. For example, his wife had left him, and his synagogue had ousted him because he was too moral. On the seventh day, in response to this line of interpretation, he started scratching his forearm, to which the therapist called attention, making the interpretation that he made Joshua angry but that Joshua took out this anger on himself by scratching. For the first time, his attitude of polite listening changed to one of excited interest, and he told the therapist a dream about a man who had been burned to death as a martyr. For a time he flooded sessions with undoing dreams in which he was successful in situations where he had failed in real life.

This type of case could be used by certain clinicians (e.g., see Nemiah 1976) to demonstrate alexithymia and, indeed, this man had been diagnosed as schizophrenic and had been given drug and electroshock treatment, to no avail. His dreams demonstrated typical magical undoing, a pregenital defense of anorexic patients.[8]

With these regressed cases, in the first phase of the treatment the transference is handled along the principles set forward by Kernberg (1975) and by Boyer (1980) in regard to borderline cases:

1. The negative transference is interpreted only in the present.
2. The patient's typical defensive constellations are interpreted as they enter the transference.

---

[8]Silverman (1989) discusses problems of technique in the analysis of a 12-year-old girl who was silent for the first four months of therapy.

3. Limits are set in order to block acting out in the transference.
4. Less primitively determined aspects of the positive transference are not interpreted early, although primitive splitting is systematically interpreted.
5. Patients' distortions are clarified.
6. The highly distorted and at times psychotic transference is worked through first in order to reach the transferences related to actual childhood experiences.

The early interpretation of the denial of suicidal behavior (masochism) parallels the technique with psychosomatic patients (Wilson and Mintz 1989) and correlates with the therapeutic technique used in the therapy of schizophrenic, borderline, and character disorders by Boyer and Giovacchini (1980), Kernberg (1975), and Volkan (1976). (1) In the first phase of treatment these patients usually do not free-associate, as also happens in the analyses of children and of patients with character disorders (Boyer and Giovacchini 1980). (2) The therapist takes an active stance, frequently using construction and reconstruction. (3) Behavioral responses can be interpreted. (4) Dreams have to be used in the context of the patient's psychodynamics. (5) First one interprets the masochism of these patients— their archaic superego and the guilt they experience in admitting any conflict. (6) Next one interprets defenses against facing masochistic behavior; then, when the ego is healthier, one interprets defenses against aggressive impulses. (7) Such interpretations are inexact and frequently are not confirmed by the patients' associations. (8) For these patients who have an archaic, punitive superego and a relatively weak ego, the analyst provides auxiliary ego strength and a rational superego (Boyer 1980, Wilson 1971a, 1982a, 1988a). (9) Interpretations should be made in a firm, consistent manner (Boyer 1980). (10) With such patients, the analyst needs to have authority. (11) The all-or-nothing ego functioning is interpreted early in treatment, since it pervades the patients' ego functioning. They are totally good or totally bad, totally successful or a complete failure, totally and contentedly loved or totally unloved or hated. They are totally beautiful and perfect in the appearance of their face and figure but also in their manners and behavior, or they are a mess and ugly (fat) and humiliated for their imagined nasty or incorrect behavior. They are totally independent or totally dependent.

TECHNIQUE OF INTERPRETATION OF EMERGING SADOMASOCHISTIC IMPULSES AND FANTASIES

Unlike patients with an oedipal neurosis and more intact ego and superego functioning, the eating-disordered and psychosomatic patient usually is unable to integrate and synthesize emerging sadomasochistic material. The analyst has to emphasize that, for example, suicidal and homicidal impulses and fantasies are not going to go away, that they are an aspect of everyone's mental functioning. The patient can develop new and healthier ways to express such impulses, but the fantasies and impulses will never completely disappear. This extreme conflict in facing and tolerating their sadomasochism, particularly their aggression and sadism, causes many patients to terminate therapy abruptly, just when ostensibly therapeutic gains, symptom improvement, and progress have been achieved.

Because anorexic patients, in their projective identifications, can pick up almost imperceptible nuances in the tone of voice, facial expression, movements, and even feelings of the analyst, they provoke counterreactions and intense countertransferences (Sperling 1967, Wilson 1987, Wilson et al. 1985).[9]

A crucial aspect of technique in the analysis of eating disorders is demonstrating to these patients early in treatment their need for immediate gratification (the impulse disorder, i.e., the primary narcissism; Sperling 1967, 1978, Wilson et al. 1983d, 1985). Thus the patient is shown that the symptoms are manifestations of a split-off, impulsive part of the ego, the fear-of-being-fat complex.

Do eating-disorder starvation and emaciation impair cognitive functioning and the capacity for insight? Current behavioral and cognitive treatments of the eating disorders are based on the concept that *weight must be restored* before psychological insight can be achieved. In both of these hospitalized cases, Frances and Elaine, in Mintz's patient Jeanette (1983c), and in consultation cases the weight was down below two-thirds normal yet there was no evidence of impaired cognitive functioning or capacity for insight. The crucial issue in such situations is the nature of the transference.

THE PURPOSE OF HOSPITALIZATION

Most if not all major treatment centers for the eating disorders insist on immediate hospitalization of adolescent and adult eating-disordered patients, with periods of in-hospital treatment ranging from three months to two years. They emphasize restoration of normal weight in restrictors and binging control in bulimics before psychotherapy is attempted. My view and that of my colleagues (Wilson 1985c) is that hospitalization should be reserved for acute, severe regressive behavior, where either medical or psychological reasons indicate that the patient is in danger of dying or becoming severely ill from marked emaciation, convulsions from electrolyte imbalance, cardiac arrhythmias, or severe depression with suicidal impulses or psychosis. Selvini Palazzoli (1978) emphasized the importance of attempting to treat the patient out of the hospital whenever possible and

---

[9]Unresolved perfectionism of the analyst (Abend 1986) can be a particular countertransference problem.

in spite of marked weight loss. She pointed out that therapists might contemplate hospitalizing patients for their own peace of mind—to avoid the stress of outpatient treatment.

The period of hospitalization should be as short as possible. The goal is to provide massive support systems to carry the patient through the severe regression and to restore a reasonable modicum of health so that the patient is able to function safely outside the hospital. Treatment would include correcting any electrolyte imbalance or other blood chemistries; resolving severe depression, suicidal danger, and psychosis; and improving body weight to a level that is no longer dangerous and that can be worked with in treatment. This general approach also applies to the treatment of psychosomatic diseases such as asthma and ulcerative colitis (Wilson and Mintz 1989). This attitude is beneficial to the patient and cuts down on hospital costs. It also tends to emphasize to the patient that the primary goal of the treatment is not weight gain but the resolution of the conflicts that have led to the development of the eating disorder.

None of the analysts at the panel of the American Psychoanalytic Association on anorexia nervosa and bulimia in 1985—P. Castelnuovo-Tedesco, Barton J. Blinder, C. Philip Wilson, John Hitchcock, Mark Gehrie, or Stephen Risen—advocated an emphasis on early weight gain and binging control, nor has the issue been brought up by any analyst in the many case presentations and publications of the psychosomatic discussion groups of the American Psychoanalytic Association.

Thus, psychoanalytic eating-disorder specialists (H. J. Schwartz 1986, 1988, Sperling 1978, Wilson et al. 1985) as well as the members of the discussion group of the American Psychoanalytic Association,[10] more than fifty psychoanalytically trained psychiatrists, do not agree with an emphasis on early weight gain in restrictors and early binging control in bulimics. For the psychoanalyst, weight gain or binging control is not the crucial issue unless there is a threat to the patient's life. The crucial issue is the development of a transference relationship with the therapist.

OEDIPAL OR PREOEDIPAL INTERPRETATION

A taxing problem in the therapy of anorexics is that while the patient's communications and associations reflect both oedipal and preoedipal themes, until the restrictor and/or bulimic anorexic symptoms and related pregenital conflicts are resolved and patients can accept their neurosis, the analyst usually has to focus exclusively on the preoedipal data.

The dreams in the following case highlight the complexities of this problem.

---

[10]As consultant for the Ameican Psychiatric Association's Eating Disorders Guidelines (Wilson 1992), I emphasized that except for medical crises, the primary goal of therapy is the analysis of the underlying conflicts, not early weight gain or binging control.

Janet, a 28-year-old anorexic married woman, reported two dreams. In the first a great serpent was slithering up and down a flight of stairs. In the second she was trying to get rid of a scabbed wound on the inside of her knee.

The night before, she had had intercourse with her husband on top. She usually preferred the superior position herself because it gave her control. Her associations were to gaining weight, to her breasts hurting, and to wanting her periods. Except for her amenorrhea, her anorexic symptoms had been resolved and her body image was undergoing healthy changes. She no longer felt that to be thin was beautiful, and at times she had an almost visceral wish to be pregnant. The previous evening she had indeed felt that her husband was a snake because he had been critical of her. She felt that, like her father, he got away with everything. She resented his playing billiards while she stayed at home. Although she had felt sexy before intercourse, during the act she had not communicated well and had not been orgastic.

Thinking of the dream, she recalled an early childhood memory of her mother killing a large snake she had found in a drain. She felt that her husband was clumsy making love, that she was more imaginative. She liked the top position because by writhing up and down and moving her nipples across his chest she could tease and excite him. She recalled her father saying that her mother was "positively toothsome." He loved her plump figure and never wanted her to lose weight. Before analysis, she had felt that his attitude was horrible; now she thought it was nice. Her thought was that she must have believed that, like the snake, the penis could bite, and she must have been afraid of being bitten. To the dream image of a scabbed wound on the knee she associated a mutilated organ, the vagina.

Despite emerging oedipal wishes to be pregnant and to identify with her feminine mother, the crucial association was to her fear of a penis with teeth. A frequent pregenital fantasy of anorexics is that the vagina is a wound inflicted by a penis with teeth. In Janet's two dreams, the serpent represented the penis with teeth, and the scabbed wound represented a displacement to the knee of the fantasy of the wounded, bitten vagina. Anorexic patients deny, suppress, and repress their oral-incorporative impulses and fantasies, projecting them onto food.

Janet had a body-phallus-snake identification. It was she who was slithering up and down stairs in the dream. She was very proud of her lithe figure, did exercises daily, and went to a health club. As a child, she had loved ballet classes. She had begun to realize that she would feel narcissistically wounded if she lost her perfect figure through pregnancy and childbirth.

In the analysis of snake dreams, one frequently finds that the ontogenetic source of the snake image is a primitive gestalt of the shaft of the male organ devoid of testicles. This gestalt is established before the child's ego has advanced to a stage where it can cognitively integrate perceptual and kinesthetic data (Wilson 1967). Janet's preoedipal identifications with the phallic breast-mother and the pregenital phallic father were fused with later oedipal fantasies and identifications. Although the scabbed-wound dream image is a typical oedipal castration dream element, this dream was interpreted in the context of the preoedipal fear of being bitten by a penis with teeth.

THE "LITTLE PERSON" PHENOMENON

Volkan (1976) described an anorexic patient with a split-off, archaic part of her ego—a "little person." He related this pathological ego structure to the "little man" phenomenon described by Kramer (1974) and Niederland (1956, 1965). In my experience, all psychosomatic patients, including anorexics, have a split-off, archaic primitive ego which is narcissistic, insatiable, and impulsive. This is what we subsume under the term "impulse disorder." A conscious manifestation of this split-off ego is represented by the fear-of-being-fat complex.

Susan, a bulimic anorexic high school student, brought in a series of dreams containing images of an innocent, wide-eyed little girl that reminded her of current sentimental oil paintings that depicted an innocent, raggedly dressed child with tears in her enormous eyes. Susan was beginning to understand that these paintings showed how she tried to come across to people and to me. After these dreams were analyzed, she had a dream of a little prince whom she wanted to be her "little person"—the archaic, split-off ego. The little prince was narcissistic, omnipotent, and magical. That he was male was a reflection of her secret wish to be a boy. For her, males were aggressive and magical while females were innocent, passive, and masochistic. The split-off part of her ego was filled with murderous rage and hatred.

THE DEFENSES OF THE EGO IN CONNECTION WITH CHILDHOOD HABITS AND ADOLESCENT OR ADULT RESTRICTOR OR BULIMIC ANOREXIA NERVOSA

To understand and treat restrictor and bulimic anorexics, it is necessary to understand the impulse disorders, the addictive personality structure (Wilson et al. 1985, Wurmser 1980), and the habits of childhood that are frequently the developmental forerunners of restrictor and bulimic anorexia nervosa. Both are food phobias, that is, addictions. In other patients I have noted the frequent occurrence of thumb-sucking, nose-picking, nail-biting, cuticle-chewing and -eating, hair-pulling and -eating, and other childhood impulse disorders such as encopresis and enuresis. There need not be a history of a childhood habit but rather might be one of model behavior. However, therapy uncovers isolated episodes or phases of rebelliousness.[11] The ego utilizes similar defenses with habits to those it uses later in trying to cope with restrictor or bulimic anorexia nervosa or the other eating disorders. Thus the defenses of denial, splitting, displacement, externalization, suppression (Werman 1983), withholding, and lying are deeply ingrained in the ego structure. In some cases we see a chaotic ego structure, as when as childhood habit coexists with restrictor or bulimic anorexia nervosa and an addiction.

Usually this fear of being fat becomes heightened in adolescence, when restrictor or bulimic anorexia nervosa most often occurs. The fear of giving in to a habit, of not being able to control it, is the forerunner of the fear of being fat. When a habit or addiction is interrupted, patients are afraid of overeating and becoming fat but also are afraid of losing control in other ways, such as losing their temper or acting out.

COMPULSIVE AND/OR HYSTERICAL CHARACTER STRUCTURE IN ANOREXIA NERVOSA

One has to keep in mind the split in the ego. I noted (Wilson et al. 1983, 1985) that from a structural point of view, ego considerations are central. In the preoedipal years, the ego of the anorexia-prone child becomes split. One part develops in a pseudonormal fashion; cognitive functions, the self-observing functions of the ego, adaptive capacities, and other ego functions appear to operate normally. The ego suppresses (Werman 1983), represses, denies, displaces, externalizes, and projects conflicts onto the fear-of-being-fat complex. *The pseudonormal part of the ego of the abstaining (restrictor) anorexic evidences many of the characteristics seen in compulsion neuroses.* The word "restrictor," which describes a holding onto, a suppression and repression of drive derivatives, conflicts, and affects, expresses in itself an anal-retentive behavior pattern. The term "abstaining" also has a compulsive meaning. To not indulge, to abstain from impulse gratification, to not enjoy is typically compulsive.

A recent article reviewing the literature on obsessive-compulsive neurosis and anorexia nervosa (Hecht et al. 1983) notes that Rahman, Richardson, and Ripley in 1939 had already described obsessive-compulsive symptoms in nine anorexic cases. In the same year, Palmer and Jones classified anorexia nervosa as a subtype of obsessive-compulsive neurosis. Schutze (1980) noted the common aspects of anorexia nervosa and obsessive-compulsive personality and, along with others, Dubois (1949) and Palmer and Jones (1939), underscored the premorbid anacastic personality structure of anorexic patients. However, none of these authors distin-

---

[11]Such episodes of aggressive behavior may have been repressed by the ego. They may be isolated behavioral episodes whose significance is denied. This was illustrated by the recovered memory of the hospitalized restrictor of cutting her sister with scissors.

guishes between the ego functioning of the restrictor and the bulimic anorexic, including them both under the rubric of anorexia nervosa (Hecht et al. 1983).

My findings on the different ego structures of restrictor and bulimic anorexics seem to be confirmed by Strober (1981, 1983) in nonanalytic studies of a large number of anorexic female patients (130 females in one study) who were treated in hospital-based programs, which included individual and group psychotherapy, family therapy, and social skill development. The major thrust of treatment was to restore normal weight, an approach that seems to involve aspects of behavior modification and that differs from our psychodynamic methods of treatment (Wilson et al. 1985). Challenging the notion of anorexia nervosa as a unitary behavioral phenomenon are several recent studies (Beaumont 1977, Casper et al. 1980, Garfinkel et al. 1980, Strober 1981) that present evidence of replicable familial genetic, clinical, and personality differences between anorexics with bulimia and those who fast without episodes of overeating. Thus, although data are as yet scarce, the hypothesis that anorexics separate into more or less distinct patient groupings seems valid (Strober 1983). Strober's type 1 and 2 anorexics, who would be termed abstainers (restrictors), evidence obsessionality, whereas his type 3 patients, the bulimics, present "a distinctive profile of low ego strength, impulsivity, proneness to addictive behaviors, and more turbulent interpersonal dynamics."

The ego structure and functioning of the bulimic anorexic evidences a mixture of compulsive and hysterical characteristics. The bulimic ego is notable for its characteristic impulsivity. The premorbid personality structure and functioning show anacastic characteristics and obsessive-compulsive traits, but there is more of an admixture of hysterical features to the personality and early evidence of impulsivity is more frequent. I am referring here to the ego functioning of the pseudonormal part of the bulimic ego, since both the restrictor and bulimic split off conflict on the fear-of-being-fat complex.

PROGNOSTIC DIFFERENCES IN RESTRICTOR AND BULIMIC ANOREXICS

Many bulimic anorexics, those who would diagnostically be termed neurotic, give an appearance of healthier (pseudonormal) ego functioning than the restrictor anorexic. Since they evidence an admixture of hysterical traits, their emotions are under less repression. They develop a seemingly good therapeutic alliance. (Wilson 1987, Wilson et al. 1985), along with Bruch (1973), feel that the prognosis is poorer for the chronic bulimic, however. Hogan (1983b) sees little difference. In general, because of the lesser degree of acting out and the stronger ego, the prognosis would appear better for the restrictor anorexic; however, in some bulimic cases where the symptoms are of recent development and limited to gorging and vomiting, the prognosis may be favorable because there is a readiness for the expression of affect. It is still felt by many analysts that the hysterical neurotic is easier to analyze than the compulsive neurotic. However, the degree of preoedipal psychopathology is the limiting factor in both the hysterical and compulsive neurotic and the bulimic and restrictor anorexic.

THE USE OF MEDICATION

Ceasar (1988) feels that medication (antidepressants) and analysis should be used in bulimics who suffer from major affective disorders. In the case example he cites, the patient stopped binging at the end of three years, achieved structural change and insight, but did not achieve full separation from her parents. He feels that analysis should be used with bulimic anorexics with oedipal conflict and those fixated at the phallic-narcissistic dyadic phase. We feel that an application of the new techniques for the interpretation and working through of preverbal and early verbal regressions should be tried before medication is used.

Some of our cases had major affective disorders and borderline psychopathology but were analyzable without the use of medication. Barkin (1985) reported a severely depressed suicidal borderline bulimic anorexic who in the course of therapy was hospitalized, several times attempted suicide, and was repeatedly given antidepressants and shock treatment. The patient has for the first time developed a viable transference relation and her most serious symptom, self-mutilation, has cleared, along with a moderation in her depression. Free of medication and other nonanalytic modalities of treatment, she has finally developed a therapeutic alliance. Similar diagnostically borderline or psychotic cases have been reported to our psychosomatic discussion group and in our publications (Levin 1990, Miller 1989, Mintz 1983c, Wilson 1983e, Wilson et al. 1985).

Patients who diagnostically were borderline or even psychotic have been successfully treated analytically. For example, the severely regressed anorexic whose treatment Mintz detailed in 1983 resolved her eating disorder, achieved structural change, married, and had two healthy children. A ten-year follow-up confirms this successful result.

Walsh (1988), in his comprehensive article on pharmacotherapy of eating disorders, concluded that because of the limited number of controlled studies of pharmacological treatment, medication can play at most a secondary role as one component of the comprehensive treatment strategy. In regard to bulimia, he notes that at least for some patients with normal-weight bulimia, antidepressant medication has significant therapeutic effect. He notes that the clinician cannot rely on the presence of depression as an indication of which patients will respond to antidepressant medication. He concludes his article by emphasizing, however, that *very little is known about the long-term outcome of drug treatment or how best to combine drug treatment with other forms of therapy. He emphasizes that all the controlled studies of antidepressant medication are of relatively short duration and there is no knowledge of how long patients who respond to medication need to remain on it or of what the relapse rate is when the drug is discontinued.*

Walsh, in his research, carefully screened patients for their ability to comply with a tyramine-free diet and therefore he has not had a serious hypertensive reaction because of patient noncompliance. He notes, however, that other side effects of phenelzine, such as possible hypertension and sleep disturbance, are major impediments to the use of MAOs in many patients.

Of course, Walsh is addressing only symptom resolution by medication, not the underlying personality disorder (neurosis) or such problems as psychosomatic and eating disorder equivalents. Keller and colleagues (in press), in a clinical psychiatric study, conclude that the long-term course of bulimia nervosa is marked by chronicity and relapse.

New drugs are being tried out, the most recent being fluoxetine (Prozac). However, its widespread use is questioned by some because of recent research showing that intense, violent, prolonged suicidal preoccupation developed for the first time in six depressed patients (Teicher et al. 1990).

Whatever genetic, constitutional factors there are in the eating disorders (Altschuler and Wiener 1985, Pope and Hudson 1984, Sims 1990, Stunkard et al. 1990, Van Itallie 1986, Walsh 1988), they do not preclude psychoanalytic treatment. Some of our cases would have been diagnosed as "endogenous depression"; however, they were analyzable. A parallel may be with asthmatic patients, some of whom have a constitutional genetic allergic predisposition and can be successfully analyzed. After analysis they may still test positively for allergies, but they no longer experience asthmatic attacks in conflictual situations (Deutsch 1987, Sperling 1978, Wilson 1980b, Wilson and Mintz 1989). Brenner (1988) recently emphasized that depression, including endogenous depression, is a symptom, a compromise formation, of clusters of unconscious conflicts.

I have (1) explored the psychodynamics and etiology of the bulimic anorexic's depression, (2) outlined our psychoanalytic technique with bulimics and documented the psychoanalytic resolution of depressed affects in the course of treatment, and (3) described in detail the dangers, risks, and consequences of the use of medication (Wilson 1985c). The treatment of bulimics has to be guided by the psychodynamic diagnosis of the individual case and the presenting clinical situation (Wilson 1983c, Wilson et al. 1985). The presenting situation can be one of alcoholism, drug addiction, and/or a suicidal crisis. Obviously, if the patient is acutely suicidal, his life must be preserved and if an antidepressant drug can alter the patient's behavior, it, like other medication and total parenteral nutrition, may have to be used. However, if analytic psychotherapy or analysis is feasible, the patient will have to be weaned from the drug, to which he or she may have developed a psychological addiction.

Bulimic depression is caused by multiple preoedipal and oedipal conflicts. A crucial goal of the psychotherapy of bulimia is to strengthen the patients so that they can face and tolerate both realistic and neurotic depression. Like restrictors, bulimic anorexics are obsessed with fantasies of remaining young forever and being free of any conflict, realistic or neurotic. They do not want to grow up. They deny the conflicts they manifest, such as their dependency on their parents or parent surrogates. They vehemently deny the masochistic nature of their symptoms and their character structure. It is the aim of a psychodynamic treatment to analyze their defenses against experiencing painful emotions, particularly depressed feelings. It is an advance in therapy when they become depressed and cry. To relieve depression by medication prevents the analysis of this most important aspect of their neurosis.

Moreover, bulimic anorexics experience hyperactive states. In these anxiety conditions, they gorge and vomit endlessly but also will disobey monoamine oxidase dietary restrictions, inducing dangerous side effects, and may ingest dangerous amounts of prescribed medication.[12] Supervised cases have attempted suicide with aspirin, acetaminophen, ipecac, imipramine, and amitriptyline. One colleague's case experienced a resolution of bulimic symptoms following the administration of phenelazine but developed a toxic manic psychosis, became noncommunicative, and acted out sexually. Dangerous overdosage with laxatives is a manifestation of the either-or nature of their ego functioning (Sperling 1978, Wilson et al. 1983, 1985). Bulimics and restrictors, for example, resort to extremes of exercise to relieve anxiety and take off weight. Because of unresolved oral conflicts, the bulimic patient believes in magical solutions to problems, is intolerant of delay, and is ambivalent about such a lengthy learning process as analytic therapy. The temporary removal of symptoms can eventuate in premature termination of treatment.

The crucial therapeutic force is the transference neurosis. Patients must reexperience in the transference the dyadic relationship with the mother and must understand depression and rage at not being able to control the therapist as they did the mother. Likewise, later in therapy, the triadic Oedipus complex emerges and can be analyzed in the transference neurosis. If the patient is on medication, the transference loses its intensity and the therapist's interpretations become diluted and intellectual. From the ego and psychodynamic point of view, a paradox emerges. Only those bulimics who are well motivated and have stronger egos can be medicated without the risk of alternate symptom development or acting out; however, it is just such healthier patients who have the most favorable psychotherapeutic prognosis.

In those situations where the use of medication, particularly antidepressants, is necessary—in medical crises or when the patient cannot be motivated for psychotherapy, in treatment stalemates, or where cost and

---

[12] Of course, internists, pediatricians, and other specialists work with us to monitor the patient's health and we are constantly aware that these self-destructive patients may force us to interrupt dynamic therapy and intervene for life-saving purposes.

therapist availability are problems—the use of drugs is a trade-off with potentially disadvantageous consequences. Therapeutic stalemates can occur in cases of chronic bulimia, where there has been a long-term resistance to insight and change in analytic therapy.

While medication in some intractable cases may facilitate therapy, we have found that even in severe regressed states, knowledgeable interpretations have resolved the impasses. Mintz's (Wilson et al. 1985) detailing of the analysis of such a severely regressed hospitalized bulimic and Wilson's and colleagues' analysis of an emaciated bulimic's repeated provocative, brinksmanshiplike, suicidal use of laxatives document the effectiveness of our technique in these crisis situations.

Before one resorts to medication, then, consultation and/or supervision are advisable. In cases seen in consultation and supervision and in cases presented to the psychosomatic groups of the Psychoanalytic Association of New York and the American Psychoanalytic Association, such therapeutic impasses have been resolved by (1) a deeper psychodynamic understanding, (2) a review of the countertransference conflicts of the therapist, and (3) an exploration of the often subtle treatment sabotage on the part of the parents, who frequently are unable to accept self-assertive behavior by the enmeshed bulimic anorexic. It must be kept in mind that at best medication may make the patient more amenable to dynamic therapy but it cannot change the underlying impulsive, masochistic personality disorder.

Antidepressants and analysis are routinely being used with bulimics by some therapists. There are no reports on their results. If medication is being considered, should the analyst prescribe and monitor the drug or should he/she refer the patient to a psychopharmacologist, preferably one who has been analyzed? In cases where the analyst refers the patient for medication, in order to prevent a split transference the analyst should know and discuss the clinical situation thoroughly with the psychopharmacologist. In Chapter 12 of this volume, Dr. Keith details some of the complications of the use of medication. In certain supervised cases patients repeatedly used medication themselves in defiance of the analyst as a form of acting out, which had to be analyzed.

SUMMARY

This chapter focuses largely on the psychodynamic treatment of anorexia. Restrictor and bulimic anorexia nervosa can be considered specific pathological outcomes of unresolved oedipal conflicts in patients whose preoedipal relationship to the mother predisposed them to these particular reactions under precipitating circumstances.

The term *fat phobia* should replace *anorexia nervosa,* since these patients do not suffer from lack of appetite but rather the opposite, a fear of being overwhelmed by their impulses, including voraciousness. The basic therapeutic task is the analysis of the underlying personality disorder (Wilson and Mintz 1989). While the underlying conflicts masked by the fear-of-being-fat complex are similar, the restrictor, part of whose ego structure resembles that of the compulsive neurotic, overcontrols the impulse to gorge as well as impulses of other kinds because of punitive archaic superego demands and intact ego controls. Bulimics, whose ego structure is an admixture of hysterical and compulsive traits, are unable to contain the impulse to gorge as well as other impulse gratifications because their defective ego is unable to carry out the punitive strictures of their archaic superego. The strict superego, however, involves guilt, and they try to expiate by self-induced vomiting and/or the use of laxatives. Obese patients, in contrast, have a less demanding superego and give in to impulse gratifications, not only oral but impulses of many kinds.

An anorexic etiologic family psychological profile was detailed that was characterized by parental perfectionism, overcontrol, and overemphasis on dieting and fears of being fat. The parents of bulimics evidenced a greater incidence of neurotic conflict and addictive behavior. In most adolescent cases, the mother and/or father need conjoint therapy to change their pathological relationship to their child. While some cases can be analyzed with classical technique, in most patients the initial technique involves focusing on dyadic material. Patients are seen face to face with early interpretation of manifestations of their impulse disorder. Only when there has been a modification of the archaic superego with ego maturation and a shift from part-object relationships can triadic oedipal material be interpreted. Recently developed techniques that enable therapists to interpret and resolve severe regressions (primitive mental states) were presented. These include new research on oral-phase dream symbols, such as sand and stone, xerostomia, and projective identification.

In this early phase, effective technique with restrictor anorexics is to interpret defenses (rationalization, denial, etc.) that mask masochistic behavior, whereas with bulimics the multiple functions of the patient's gorging, vomiting, and laxative use are interpreted as acting out defenses against the experiencing of affects such as guilt, anxiety, depression, anger, or sexual feelings.

The analyst is in charge of treatment, with hospitalization reserved for true emergencies. Medication is contraindicated if psychoanalysis is feasible. Psychoanalysis or analytic psychotherapy are the treatments of choice for restrictor and bulimic anorexics.

REFERENCES

Abend, S. M. (1986). Countertransference, empathy, and the analytic ideal: the impact of life stresses on analytic capability. *Psychoanalytic Quarterly* 5:563–575.

Alcoholics Anonymous (1979). Personal communication from a recovering alcoholic.

Altschuler, K. Z., and Weiner, M. F. (1985). Anorexia nervosa and depression: a dissenting view. *American Journal of Psychiatry* 142:328–332.

Arlow, J. A. (1955). Notes on oral symbolism. *Psychoanalytic Quarterly* 34:63–74.

Aronson, J. A. (1986). The level of object relations and severity of symptoms in the normal weight bulimic patient. *International Journal of Eating Disorders* 5:669–681.

Barkin, L. (1985). Analytic treatment of a severely regressed suicidal bulimic anorexic. Psychosomatic Discussion Group of the American Psychoanalytic Association, New York, December 18.

Beaumont, P. J. V. (1977). Further categorization of anorexia nervosa patients. *American Journal of Psychiatry* 11:223–226.

Bion, W. R. (1956). Development of schizophrenic thought. *International Journal of Psycho-Analysis* 37:334–346.

Blakeslee, S. (1989). A dry mouth can mean more than just discomfort for many. *New York Times,* August 13, 1989, Section B, pp. 12–13.

Blinder, B. J., Chaitin, B. F., and Goldstein, R. (1988). *The Eating Disorders.* Jamaica, NY: S. P. Scientific Books.

Blitzer, J. R., Rollins, N., and Blackwell, A. (1961). Children who starve themselves: anorexia nervosa. *Psychosomatic Medicine* 23:369–383.

Blos, P. (1987). Keynote Address on Treatment of Adolescents. Meeting of the Association for Adolescent Analysis, Miami, FL, April 4.

Blum, H. P. (1976). Masochism, the ego ideal, and the psychology of women. *Journal of the American Psychoanalytic Association* 249(Suppl):157–191.

Boskind-White, M., and White, W. C. (1983). *Bulimarexia: The Binge Purge Cycle.* New York: Norton.

Boyer, L. B. (1974). Personal letter, June 16, 1974.

_____ (1975). Treatment of characterological and schizophrenic disorders. In *Tactics and Techniques in Psychoanalytic Therapy,* ed. P. L. Giovacchini, A. Flarsheim, and L. B. Boyer, pp. 341–373. New York: Jason Aronson.

_____ (1980). Work with a borderline patient. In *Psychoanalytic Treatment of Schizophrenic, Borderline, and Characterological Disorders,* ed. L. B. Boyer and P. L. Giovacchini, pp. 171–208. New York: Jason Aronson.

Boyer, L. B., and Giovacchini, P. L. (1980). *Psychoanalytic Treatment of Schizophrenic, Borderline, and Characterological Disorders.* 2nd rev. ed. New York: Jason Aronson.

_____ (1990). *Master Clinicians: On Treating the Regressed Patient.* Northvale, NJ: Jason Aronson.

Brenner, C. (1988). Reflections on the psychoanalytic treatment of depression: Annual Freud Lecture of the Psychoanalytic Association of New York, New York, May 16.

Brotman, A. W., Herzog, D. G., and Woods, S. E. (1984). Anti-depressant treatment of bulimia: the relationship between binging and depressive symptomatology. *Journal of Clinical Psychiatry* 45:7–9.

Bruch, H. (1962). Perceptual and conceptual disturbances in anorexia nervosa. *Psychosomatic Medicine* 24:187–194.

_____ (1965). Anorexia nervosa and its differential diagnosis. *Journal of Nervous and Mental Diseases* 141:555–556.

_____ (1970). Psychotherapy in primary anorexia nervosa. *Journal of Nervous and Mental Diseases* 105:51–67.

_____ (1973). *Eating Disorders: Obesity, Anorexia Nervosa, and the Person Within.* New York: Basic Books.

_____ (1974). Perils of behavior modification in the treatment of anorexia nervosa. *Journal of the American Medical Association* 230:1409–1422.

_____ (1978). *The Golden Cage: The Enigma of Anorexia Nervosa.* Cambridge, MA: Harvard University Press.

Bulik, C. (1978). Drug and alcohol abuse by bulimic women and their families. *American Journal of Psychiatry* 114:1604–1606.

Bulik, C., Sullivan, P., and Rorty, M. (1989). Childhood sexual abuse in women with bulimia. *Journal of Clinical Psychiatry* 50:460–464.

Bychowski, G. (1972). Discussion of C. P. Wilson's paper: "Further Reflections on Stone as the Earliest Ontogenetic and Philogenetic Symbol." Presented at the New Jersey Psychoanalytic Society, Hackensack, NJ, January 13.

Carlat, D. (1991). Review of *Bulimia Nervosa in Males*. *American Journal of Psychiatry* 148:831-843.

Carpinnaci, J. A., Liberman, E., and Schlossberg, N. (1963). Perturbaciones de la comunicación y neurosis de contratransferencia. *Revista de Psicoanálisis* 20:63-69.

Carter, L., and Rinsley, D. B. (1977). Vicissitudes of empathy in a borderline patient. *International Review of Psycho-Analysis* 4:317-326.

Casper, R. C., Eckert, E. G., Halmi, K. A., et al. (1980). Bulimia: its incidence and clinical importance in anorexia nervosa. *Archives of General Psychiatry* 37:1030-1036.

Ceasar, M. N. (1988). Anorexia nervosa and bulimia. Panel of the American Psychoanalytic Association on Anorexia Nervosa, Theory, and Therapy. *Journal of the American Psychoanalytic Association* 36:155-156.

Cesio, F. T. (1963). La comunicación extraverbal en psicoanálisis: transferencia, contratransferencia e interpretación. *Revista de Psicoanálisis* 20:124-127.

_____ (1973). Los fundamentos de la contratransferencia: el yo ideal y las identificaciones directas. *Revista de Psicoanálisis* 30:5-16.

Crisp, A. H. (1965). Clinical and therapeutic aspects of anorexia nervosa: a study of 30 cases. *Journal of Psychosomatic Research* 9:67.

_____ (1967). Anorexia nervosa. *Hospital Medicine* 1:713-718.

_____ (1968). Primary anorexia nervosa. *Gut* 9:370-372.

_____ (1980). *Anorexia Nervosa: Let Me Be.* New York: Academic Press.

Dally, P. J. (1969). *Anorexia Nervosa.* New York: Grune and Stratton.

Deutsch, L. (1987). Reflections on the psychoanalytic treatment of patients with bronchial asthma. *Psychoanalytic Study of the Child* 42:231-232. New Haven, CT: Yale University Press.

Dubois, F. A. (1979). Compulsion neurosis with cachexia. *American Journal of Psychiatry* 50:106-115.

Eidelberg, L. (1957). An introduction to the study of narcissistic mortification. *Psychiatric Quarterly* 31:657-658.

_____ (1959). A second contribution to the study of the narcissistic mortification. *Psychiatric Quarterly* 33:363-466.

Emde, R. (1988a). Development terminable and interminable. II. Innate and motivational factors from infancy. *International Journal of Psycho-Analysis* 69:23-41.

_____ (1988b). Development terminable and interminable. II. Recent psychoanalytic theory and therapeutic considerations. *International Journal of Psycho-Analysis* 69:283-296.

Falk, J. R., and Halmi, K. A. (1982). Amenorrhea in anorexia nervosa: examination of the clinical body weight hypothesis. *Biological Psychiatry* 17:799-806.

Falstein, E. I., Feinstein, S. C., and Judas, I. (1956). Anorexia nervosa in the male child. *American Journal of Orthopsychiatry* 26:751-772.

Fenichel, O. (1945). Anorexia. In *The Collected Papers of Otto Fenichel,* ed. H. Fenichel, pp. 296-304. New York: Norton, 1954.

Fine, B. D., and Moore, B. D., eds. (1990). *Glossary of the American Psychoanalytic Association: Psychoanalytic Terms and Concepts.* 3rd ed. New York: International Universities Press.

Fischer, N. (1989). Anorexia nervosa and unresolved rapprochement conflicts: a case study. *International Journal of Psycho-Analysis* 70:43-54.

Fleiss, R. (1956). *Erogeneity and Libido.* New York: International Universities Press.

Freiman, G. V. (1983). Psychoanalysis: the case of Carol. In *Fear of Being Fat: The Treatment of Anorexia Nervosa and Bulimia,* rev. ed., ed. C. P. Wilson, C. C. Hogan, and I. L. Mintz, pp. 255-262. New York: Jason Aronson, 1985.

Freud, A. (1946). The psychoanalytic study of infantile feeding disturbance. In *Writings,* vol. 4. New York: International Universities Press.

_____ (1968). *Indications for Child Analysis and Other Papers, 1945-1956.* In *Writings,* vol. 4. p. 391. New York: International Universities Press.

_____ (1974). *The Ego and the Mechanisms of Defense.* New York: International Universities Press.

Freud, S. (1910). The future prospects for psychoanalytic therapy. *Standard Edition* 11:141-151.

74   C. Philip Wilson, M.D.

_____ (1918). From the history of an infantile neurosis. *Standard Edition* 17:7–122.
_____ (1923). The ego and the id. *Standard Edition* 19:13–66.
_____ (1932). New introductory lectures in psychoanalysis. *Standard Edition* 22:1–193.
Frisch, R. E. (1977). Food intake, fatness, and reproductive ability. In *Anorexia Nervosa,* ed. R. Vigersky, pp. 149–161. New York: Raven Press.
Frisch, R. E., and McArthur, J. W. (1974). Menstrual cycles: fatness as a determinant of minimum weight for height necessary for their maintenance or onset. *Science* 185:949–951.
Frisch, R. E., and Revelle, R. (1970). Height and weight at menarche and a hypothesis of critical body weights and adolescent events. *Science* 169:397–399.
Garfinkel, P. E., Moldofsky, H., and Garner, D. M. (1980). The heterogeneity of anorexia nervosa. Bulimia as a distinct syndrome. *Archives of General Psychiatry* 26:57–63.
Giovacchini, P. L. (1975). Self-projections in the narcissistic transference. *International Journal of Psychoanalytic Psychotherapy* 4:142–166.
Goldfarb, L. (1987). Sexual abuse antecedent to anorexia nervosa, bulimia, and compulsive overeating: three case reports. *International Journal of Eating Disorders* 6:675–860.
Greenacre, P. (1958). Early physical determinants in the development of the sense of identity. *Journal of the American Psychoanalytic Association* 6:612–627.
Grinberg, L. (1972). *Prácticas Psicoanalíticas Comparades en las Psicocis.* Buenos Aires: Editorial Paidos.
_____ (1976). *Teoría de la Identificación.* Buenos Aires: Editorial Paidos.
_____ (1979). Countertransference and projective counteridentification. *Contemporary Psychoanalysis* 15:226–247.
Hann-Kende, F. (1933). On the role of transference and countertransference in psychoanalysis. In *Psychoanalysis and the Occult,* ed. G. Devereux, pp. 158–167. New York: International Universities Press.
Hecht, H. M., Fichter, M., and Postpischil, F. (1983). Obsessive-compulsive neurosis and anorexia nervosa. *International Journal of Eating Disorders* 2:69–77.
Hoffer, W. (1950). Development of the body ego. *Psychoanalytic Study of the Child* 5:18–23. New York: International Universities Press.
Hogan, C. C. (1983a). Object relations. In *Fear of Being Fat: The Treatment of Anorexia Nervosa and Bulimia,* rev. ed., ed. C. P. Wilson, C. C. Hogan, and I. L. Mintz, pp. 129–149. New York: Jason Aronson, 1985.
_____ (1983b). Psychoanalytic treatment of an anorexic woman. Psychosomatic Discussion Group, Meeting of the American Psychoanalytic Association, Philadelphia, April 17.
_____ (1989). Inflammatory disease of the colon. In *Psychosomatic Symptoms: Psychodynamic Treatment of the Underlying Personality Disorder,* ed. C. P. Wilson and I. L. Mintz, pp. 367–399. Northvale, NJ: Jason Aronson.
_____ (In Press). *Psychosomatics and Inflammatory Disease of the Colon.* Madison, CT: International Universities Press.
Hughes, A. (1984). Book review of *Fear of Being Fat: The Treatment of Anorexia Nervosa and Bulimia,* ed. C. P. Wilson, C. C. Hogan, and I. L. Mintz. *International Journal of Psychoanalytic Psychotherapy* 65:498–499.
Illowsky, B. P., and Kirch, D. G. (1988). Polydypsia and hyponathemia in psychiatric patients. *American Journal of Psychiatry* 145:675–683.
Isakower, O. (1938). On the psychopathology of phenomena associated with falling asleep. *International Journal of Psycho-Analysis* 19:331–345.
Jacobson, E. (1964). *The Self and the Object World.* New York: International Universities Press.
Jessner, L., and Abse, D. W. (1960). Regressive forces in anorexia nervosa. *British Journal of Medical Psychology* 33:301–311.
Kanzer, M. (1958). Image formation during free association. *Psychoanalytic Quarterly* 15:419–434.
Kaplan, R. (1984). Of empathy or altruistic surrender. *Dynamic Psychotherapy* 2:123–131.
Keller, M. B., Laver, D. W., Herzog, D. G., et al. (in press). High rates of chronicity and rapidity of relapse in patients with bulimia nervosa and depression. *Archives of General Psychiatry.*

Kernberg, O. F. (1975). *Borderline Conditions and Pathological Narcissism.* New York: Jason Aronson.

Klein, M. (1955). On identification. In *New Directions in Psychoanalysis,* ed. M. Klein, P. Heimann, and M. Money-Kyle, pp. 309–345. London: Basic Books.

Kramer, S. (1974). A discussion of Sours's paper on "The Anorexia Nervosa Syndrome." *International Journal of Psycho-Analysis* 55:577–579.

Langs, R. (1976). *The Therapeutic Interaction.* Vol. 2. New York: Jason Aronson.

Levin, R. (1990). The analytic treatment of a severely regressed anorexia patient. Discussion Group of the American Psychoanalytic Association on Psychoanalytic Considerations about Patients with Organic Illness or Major Physical Handicaps, Miami, FL, December 7.

Lewin, B. (1950a). *The Psychoanalysis of Elation.* New York: Norton.

———— (1950b). Sleep, the mouth, and the dream screen. *Psychoanalytic Quarterly* 15:419–434.

Little, M. (1957). "R"—the analyst's total response to his patient's needs. In *Transference Neuroses and Transference Psychoses,* pp. 51–80. New York: Jason Aronson.

Lorand, S. (1943). Anorexia nervosa: report of a case. *Psychosomatic Medicine* 5:282–292.

Mahler, M. S., and Furer, M. (1968). *On Human Symbiosis and the Vicissitudes of Individuation.* New York: International Universities Press.

———— (1972). On the first three subphases of the separation-individuation process. *International Journal of Psycho-Analysis* 53:333–338.

Masserman, J. H. (1941). Psychodynamics in anorexia nervosa and neurotic vomiting. *Psychoanalytic Quarterly* 10:211–242.

Miller, J. A. (1989). Incest, anorexia, and multiple psychosomatic symptoms in a young woman. Psychosomatic Discussion Group of the American Psychoanalytic Association, New York, December 15.

Mintz, I. L. (1971). The anniversary reaction: a response to the unconscious sense of time. *Journal of the American Psychoanalytic Association* 19:720–734.

———— (1980). Multideterminism in asthmatic disease. *International Journal of Psychoanalytic Psychotherapy* 8:593–600.

———— (1983a). The clinical picture of anorexia nervosa and bulimia. In *Fear of Being Fat: The Treatment of Anorexia Nervosa and Bulimia,* rev. ed., ed. C. P. Wilson, C. C. Hogan, and I. L. Mintz, pp. 83–113. New York: Jason Aronson, 1985.

———— (1983b). Anorexia nervosa and bulimia in males. In *Fear of Being Fat: The Treatment of Anorexia Nervosa and Bulimia,* rev. ed., ed. C. P. Wilson, C. C. Hogan, and I. L. Mintz, pp. 263–303. New York: Jason Aronson, 1985.

———— (1983c). The psychoanalytic therapy of severe anorexia: the case of Jeanette. In *Fear of Being Fat: The Treatment of Anorexia Nervosa and Bulimia,* rev. ed., ed. C. P. Wilson, C. C. Hogan, and I. L. Mintz, pp. 217–244. New York: Jason Aronson, 1985.

———— (1988). The fear of being fat in normal, obese, starving, and gorging individuals. Panel Report: Compulsive Eating, Obesity, and Related Phenomena. *Journal of the American Psychoanalytic Association* 1:165–166.

———— (1989a). Treatment of a case of anorexia and severe asthma. In *Psychosomatic Symptoms: Psychodynamic Treatment of the Underlying Personality Disorder,* ed. C. P. Wilson and I. L. Mintz, pp. 251–307. Northvale, NJ: Jason Aronson.

———— (1989b). Air symbolism in asthma. In *Psychosomatic Symptoms: Psychodynamic Treatment of the Underlying Personality Disorder,* ed. C. P. Wilson and I. L. Mintz, pp. 211–249. Northvale, NJ: Jason Aronson.

Minuchin, S., Rosman, B. L., and Baker, L. (1978). *Psychosomatic Families: Anorexia Nervosa in Context.* Cambridge, MA: Harvard University Press.

Mogul, S. L. (1980). Asceticism and anorexia nervosa. *Psychoanalytic Study of the Child* 35:155–175. New Haven, CT: Yale University Press.

Moore, B. E., and Fine, B. D. (1990). Anorexia nervosa. In *Psychoanalytic Terms and Concepts,* ed. American Psychoanalytic Association, pp. 23–24. New Haven, CT: Yale University Press.

Moran, M. G. (1980). The analysis of a superobese woman. Discussion Group on Psychoanalytic Considerations about Patients with Organic illness or Major Physical Handicaps, P.

Castelnuovo-Tedseco, Chairman. Meeting of the American Psychoanalytic Association, New York, December 14.

Morrison, J. (1989). Childhood sexual histories of women with somatization disorder. *American Journal of Psychiatry* 146:239–246.

Mushatt, C. (1975). Mind-body environment: toward understanding the impact of loss of psyche and soma. *Psychoanalytic Quarterly* 44:81–106.

Nemiah, J. C. (1976). Alexithymia: a view of the psychosomatic process. In *Modern Trends in Psychosomatic Medicine,* vol. 3, ed. O. W. Hill, pp. 430–439. New York: Appleton-Century-Crofts.

Niederland, W. G. (1956). Clinical observations on the "little man" phenomenon. *Psychoanalytic Study of the Child* 11:381–395. New York: International Universities Press.

———— (1965). Narcissistic ego impairment in patients with early physical malformations. *Psychoanalytic Study of the Child* 20:518–534. New York: International Universities Press.

———— (1972). Discussion of C. P. Wilson's paper: "Further Reflections on Stone as the Earliest Ontogenetic and Philogenetic Symbol." New Jersey Psychoanalytic Society, January 13.

Ogden, T. H. (1978). A developmental view of identifications resulting from maternal impingements. *International Journal of Psychoanalytic Psychotherapy* 7:486–504.

Oppenheimer, R., Howells, K., Palmer, R., et al. (1985). Adverse sexual experience in childhood and clinical eating disorders: a preliminary description. *Journal of Psychiatric Research* 19:357–361.

Orbach, S. (1978). *Fat is a Feminist Issue.* New York: Berkeley Publishing.

Palmer, H. E., and Jones, M. S. (1939). Anorexia nervosa as a manifestation of compulsion neurosis: a study of psychogenic factors. *Archives of Neurology and Psychiatry* 41:856–859.

Perestrello, M. (1963). Un caso de intensa identificação projectiva. *Journal Bresileiro de Psiquiatria* 12:425–441.

Pope, H. G., and Hudson, J. T. (1984). *New Hope for Binge Eaters. Advances in the Understanding and Treatment of Bulimia.* New York: Harper & Row.

Porder, M. S. (1987). Projective identification: an alternative hypothesis. *Psychoanalytic Quarterly* 46:431–451.

Post, S. L. (1988). Panel on compulsive eating: obesity and related phenomena. American Psychoanalytic Association.

Racker, H. (1953). A contribution to the problem of countertransference. *International Journal of Psycho-Analysis* 34:313–324.

Rahman, L., Richardson, H. B., and Ripley, H. S. (1939). Anorexia nervosa with psychiatric observations. *Psychosomatic Medicine* 1:3.

Reiser, L. W. (1988). Panel Report: Compulsive eating: obesity and related phenomena. *Journal of the American Psychoanalytic Association* 1:163–171.

Risen, S. E. (1982). The psychoanalytic treatment of an adolescent with anorexia nervosa. *Psychoanalytic Study of the Child* 37:433–459. New Haven, CT: Yale University Press.

———— (1988). Panel Report: Anorexia nervosa: theory and therapy, a new look at an old problem. *Journal of the American Psychoanalytic Association* 1:153–162.

Ritvo, S. (1976). Adolescent to woman. *Journal of the American Psychoanalytic Association* 24(Suppl):127–137.

———— (1984). The image and uses of the body in psychic conflict: with special reference to eating disorders in adolescence. *Psychoanalytic Study of the Child* 39:449–470. New Haven, CT: Yale University Press.

Rosenfeld, D., and Mordo, E. (1973). Fusión, confusión, simbiosis e identificación. *Revista de Psicoanálisis* 30:413–423.

Russell, D. (1983). The incidence and prevalence of intrafamilial and extrafamilial sexual abuse of female children. *Child Abuse Neglect* 7:133–146.

Sarnoff, C. (1968). Personal communication. Letter, October 14.

———— (1970). Symbols and symptoms: phytophobia in a two-year-old girl. *Psychoanalytic Quarterly* 39:550–562.

———— (1972). Personal communication. Letter, February 14, discussing protosymbols.

———— (1988). *Psychotherapeutic Strategies in Late Latency through Early Adolescence.* Northvale, NJ: Jason Aronson.

—— (1989). Early psychic stress and psychosomatic disease. In *Psychosomatic Symptoms: Psychodynamic Treatment of the Underlying Personality Disorder,* ed. C. P. Wilson and I. L. Mintz, pp. 83–103. Northvale, NJ: Jason Aronson.

Savitt, R. A. (1980). Discussion of C. P. Wilson's paper: "The Fear of Being Fat in Female Psychology and Anorexia Nervosa." *Bulletin of the Psychoanalytic Association of New York* 17:8–9.

Schutze, G. (1980). *Anorexia Nervosa.* Bern: Huber.

Schwartz, H. J. (1986). Bulimia: psychoanalytic perspectives. *Journal of the American Psychoanalytic Association* 34:439–462.

—— (1988). *Bulimia: Psychoanalytic Theory and Treatment.* New York: International Universities Press.

Searles, H. F. (1965). *Collected Papers on Schizophrenia and Related Subjects.* New York: International Universities Press.

Selvini Palazzoli, M. (1978). *Self-Starvation: From Individual to Family Therapy in the Treatment of Anorexia Nervosa.* New York: Jason Aronson.

Shengold, L. L. (1978). The problem of the soul murder. *Journal of the American Psychoanalytic Association* 23:8–10.

Silverman, M. (1989). Power, control, and the threat to die. In *Psychosomatic Symptoms: Psychodynamic Treatment of the Underlying Personality Disorder,* ed. C. P. Wilson and I. L. Mintz, pp. 351–364. Northvale, NJ: Jason Aronson.

Sims, E. A. H. (1990). Destiny rides again as twins overeat. *New England Journal of Medicine* 322:1522–1523.

Sours, J. A. (1974). The anorexia nervosa syndrome. *International Journal of Psycho-Analysis* 55:567–576.

—— (1980). *Starving to Death in a Sea of Objects: The Anorexia Nervosa Syndrome.* New York: Jason Aronson.

Sperling, M. (1953). Food allergies and conversion hysteria. *Psychoanalytic Quarterly* 22:525–538.

—— (1967). Transference neurosis in patients with psychosomatic disorders. *Psychoanalytic Quarterly* 36:342–355.

—— (1968). Trichotillomania, trichophagy, and cyclic vomiting: a contribution to the psychopathology of female sexuality. *International Journal of Psycho-Analysis* 49:683–690.

—— (1978). *Psychosomatic Disorders in Childhood.* New York: Jason Aronson.

—— (1983, 1985). Anorexia nervosa: a revision of classification, concepts, and treatment. In *Fear of Being Fat: The Treatment of Anorexia Nervosa and Bulimia,* ed. C. P. Wilson, C. C. Hogan, and I. L. Mintz, p. 73. New York: Jason Aronson.

Spitz, R. A. (1955). The primal cavity: a contribution to the genesis of perception and its role for psychoanalytic theory. *Psychoanalytic Study of the Child* 10:215–240. New York: International Universities Press.

Strober, M. (1981). The significance of bulimia in juvenile anorexia nervosa: an exploration of possible etiologic factors. *International Journal of Eating Disorders* 1:28–43.

—— (1983). An empirically derived typology of anorexia nervosa. In *Anorexia Nervosa: Recent Developments in Research,* ed. P. L. Darby, T. E. Garfinkel, and D. M. Garner, pp. 185–196. New York: Alan R. Liss.

Stunkard, A. J., Harris, J. R., Pedersen, N., et al. (1990). The body mass index of twins who have been reared apart. *American Journal of Psychiatry* 322:1483–1487.

Sydenham, A. (1946). Amenorrhea at Stanley Camp, Hong Kong, during internment. *British Medical Journal* 2:159–165.

Teicher, H. T., Glock, E., and Cole, J. O. (1990). Emergence of intense suicidal preoccupation during fluoxetine treatment. *American Journal of Psychiatry* 147:207–210.

Thomä, H. (1967). *Anorexia Nervosa.* New York: International Universities Press.

Van Itallie, T. B. (1986). Bad news and good news about obesity. *New England Journal of Medicine* 314:239–240.

Volkan, V. D. (1976). *Primitive Internalized Object Relations: A Clinical Study of Schizophrenic, Borderline, and Narcissistic Patients.* New York: International Universities Press.

Waller, J. V., Kaufman, M. R., and Deutsch, F. (1940). Anorexia nervosa: a psychosomatic entity. *Psychosomatic Medicine* 2:4–16.

78   C. Philip Wilson, M.D.

Walsh, B. J., Stewart, J. W., Weight, L., et al. (1982). Treatment of bulimia with monoamine oxidase inhibitors. *American Journal of Psychiatry* 193:1629–1630.
Walsh, B. T. (1988). Pharmacotherapy of eating disorders. In *The Eating Disorders: Medical and Psychological Basis of Diagnosis and Treatment,* ed. B. J. Blinder, B. F. Chaitin, and R. Goldstein, pp. 469–476. Jamaica, NY: S. P. Scientific Books.
Wennik-Kaplan, R. (in press). *The Question of Psychogenecity in Anorexia Nervosa: A Study of Maternal Identification Conflict.* Ann Arbor, MI: University Microfilms, Inc.
Werman, D. S. (1983). Suppression as a defense. *Journal of the American Psychoanalytic Association* 31(Suppl):405–415.
Wilson, C. P. (1963). *The earliest symbol: stone.* Paper presented at the Spring Meeting of the American Psychoanalytic Association, Chicago, IL.
—— (1965). *The earliest symbol: stone. Bulletin of the Psychoanalytic Association of New York* 6:18–21.
—— (1967a). Stone as a symbol of teeth. *Psychoanalytic Quarterly* 36:83–84.
—— (1967b). Symbolism of the umbrella. *Psychoanalytic Quarterly* 38:519.
—— (1968a). Psychosomatic asthma and acting out. *International Journal of Psycho-Analysis* 49:330–333.
—— (1968b). Discussion of R. Little's paper on xerostomia. Meeting of the American Psychoanalytic Association, New York, December 20.
—— (1969). *The symbolism of sand.* Paper presented at the Annual Meeting of the American Psychoanalytic Association, Miami, FL, December 18.
—— (1970). Theoretical and clinical considerations in the early phase of treatment with patients suffering from severe psychosomatic symptoms. *Bulletin of the Philadelphia Psychoanalytic Association* 20:71–74.
—— (1971a). On the limits of the effectiveness of psychoanalysis: early ego and somatic disturbances. *Journal of the American Psychoanalytic Association* 19:552–564.
—— (1971b). *The earliest ontogenetic and philogenetic symbol, stone.* Paper presented at meeting of the New Jersey Psychoanalytic Association.
—— (1978). Discussion of L. Shengold's paper, "The Problem of Soul Murder." *Bulletin of the Psychoanalytic Association of New York* 23:9.
—— (1980a). Sand, the primary symbol of smoking addictions and the Isakower phenomenon. *Bulletin of the Psychoanalytic Association of New York* 14:45–55.
—— (1980b). The family psychological profile of anorexia nervosa patients. *Journal of the Medical Society of New Jersey* 77:341–343.
—— (1980c). On the fear of being fat in female psychology and anorexia nervosa. *Bulletin of the Psychoanalytic Association of New York* 17:8–9.
—— (1981). Sand symbolism: the primary dream representation of the Isakower phenomenon and smoking addictions. In *Clinical Psychoanalysis,* ed. S. Orgel and B. D. Fine, pp. 45–55. New York: Jason Aronson.
—— (1982a). The fear of being fat and anorexia nervosa. *International Journal of Psychoanalytic Psychotherapy* 9:233–255.
—— (1982b). Abstaining and bulimic anorexics, two sides of the same coin (with Ira L. Mintz). In *Primary Care, the Nutrition Volume,* ed. W. Steffee, vol. 9, pp. 517–530. Philadelphia: Saunders.
—— (1983a). Psychodynamic and/or psychopharmacological treatment of bulimic anorexia nervosa. In *Fear of Being Fat: The Treatment of Anorexia Nervosa and Bulimia,* rev. ed., ed. C. P. Wilson, C. C. Hogan, and I. L. Mintz, pp. 345–362. New York: Jason Aronson, 1985.
—— (1983b). Fat phobia as a diagnostic term to replace a medical misnomer: anorexia nervosa. Meeting of the American Academy of Child Psychiatry, San Francisco, October.
—— (1983c). Dream interpretation. In *Fear of Being Fat: The Treatment of Anorexia Nervosa and Bulimia,* rev. ed., ed. C. P. Wilson, C. C. Hogan, and I. L. Mintz, pp. 245–254. New York: Jason Aronson, 1985.
—— (1983d). The fear of being fat in the psychology of women. In *Fear of Being Fat: The Treatment of Anorexia Nervosa and Bulimia,* rev. ed., ed. C. P. Wilson, C. C. Hogan, and I. L. Mintz, pp. 12–13. New York: Jason Aronson, 1985.

_____ (1983e). Contrasts in the analysis of bulimic and abstaining anorexics. In *Fear of Being Fat: The Treatment of Anorexia Nervosa and Bulimia,* rev. ed., ed. C. P. Wilson, C. C. Hogan, and I. L. Mintz, pp. 169–193. New York: Jason Aronson, 1985.

_____ (1985a). The psychoanalytic treatment of anorexia nervosa and bulimia. Panel on Anorexia Nervosa and Bulimia, Pietro Castelnuovo-Tedesco, Chairman. Spring Meeting of the American Psychoanalytic Association, Denver, May 19.

_____ (1985b). Obesity: personality structure and psychoanalytic treatment. Panel on Compulsive Eating: Obesity and Related Phenomena, Pietro Castelnuovo-Tedesco, Chairman. Winter Meeting of the American Psychoanalytic Association, New York, December 11.

_____ (1985c). Psychodynamic and/or psychopharmacologic treatment of bulimic anorexia nervosa. In *Fear of Being Fat: The Treatment of Anorexia Nervosa and Bulimia,* rev. ed., ed. C. P. Wilson, C. C. Hogan, and I. L. Mintz, pp. 345–354. New York: Jason Aronson.

_____ (1985d). The treatment of bulimic depression. Paper presented at Grand Grounds, Department of Psychiatry, St. Luke's-Roosevelt Hospital, New York, March 6.

_____ (1986a). The psychoanalytic psychotherapy of bulimic anorexia nervosa. In *Adolescent Psychiatry,* ed. S. Feinstein, pp. 274–314. Chicago: University of Chicago Press.

_____ (1986b). A discussion of E. Levin's paper: "Bulimia as a Masturbatory Equivalent." *Jefferson Journal of Psychiatry* 3:24–35 and 4:77–87.

_____ (1986c). Letter in response to J. M. Jonas's paper: "The Biological Basis and Treatment of Bulimia." *Jefferson Journal of Psychiatry* 4:78–85.

_____ (1987). Panel on Transference and Countertransference in Anorexia Nervosa. Scientific Meeting of the Psychoanalytic Association of New York, November 19.

_____ (1988a). The psychoanalytic treatment of anorexia nervosa and bulimia. In *The Eating Disorders,* ed. B. J. Blinder, B. F. Chaitin, and R. Goldstein, pp. 433–446. Jamaica, NY: S. P. Scientific Books.

_____ (1988b). Bulimic equivalents. In *Bulimia: Psychoanalytic Treatment and Theory,* ed. H. J. Schwartz, pp. 489–522. New York: International Universities Press.

_____ (1988c). Psychoanalytic treatment of anorexia nervosa and bulimia. Panel Report. *Journal of the American Psychoanalytic Association* 1:163–171.

_____ (1988d). Obesity: personality structure and psychoanalytic treatment. Panel Report. *Journal of the American Psychoanalytic Association* 1:163–171.

_____ (1988e). Letter with the assistance of C. C. Hogan and I. L. Mintz as consultants to the committee preparing Treatment Reports of the American Psychiatric Association, sent to Byram Karasu, Chairman, concerning anorexia nervosa and bulimia

_____ (1989a). Family psychopathology. In *Psychosomatic Symptoms: Psychodynamic Treatment of the Underlying Personality Disorder,* ed. C. P. Wilson and I. L. Mintz, pp. 63–92. Northvale, NJ: Jason Aronson.

_____ (1989b). Dream interpretation. In *Psychosomatic Symptoms: Psychodynamic Treatment of the Underlying Personality Disorder,* ed. C. P. Wilson and I. L. Mintz, pp. 140–142. Northvale, NJ: Jason Aronson.

_____ (1989c). Elephant symbolism. In *Psychosomatic Symptoms: Psychodynamic Treatment of the Underlying Personality Disorder,* ed. C. P. Wilson and I. L. Mintz, pp. 188–192. Northvale, NJ: Jason Aronson.

_____ (1989d). Countertransference. In *Psychosomatic Symptoms: Psychodynamic Treatment of the Underlying Personality Disorder,* ed. C. P. Wilson and I. L. Mintz, pp. 117–122. Northvale, NJ: Jason Aronson.

_____ (1990a). *The psychoanalytic treatment of psychosomatic disorders.* Paper presented as the 16th Melitta Sperling Lecture of the Psychoanalytic Association of New York. Lenox Hill Hospital, New York, March 19.

_____ (1990b). On beginning analysis with an eating disorder. In *On Beginning Analysis,* ed. T. J. Jacobs and A. Rothstein, pp. 243–260. Madison, CT: International Universities Press.

_____ (1990c). The psychodynamic treatment of anorexia nervosa and bulimia. Grand Rounds of the Department of Endocrinology, St. Luke's–Roosevelt Hospital Center, St. Luke's Hospital, New York, October 24.

_____ (1990d). Reconstruction as a technique of interpretation in severely regressed anorexic cases. Case presentation at Arden House Retreat of the Faculty of the Center for Psychoanalytic Training and Research, Columbia University, College of Physicians and Surgeons, Harrison, NY, October 28.

—— (1992). Consultant to the taskforce for the American Psychiatric Association's proposed guidelines for the treatment of eating disorders.

Wilson, C. P., Hogan, C. C., and Mintz, I. L. (1985). *Fear of Being Fat: The Treatment of Anorexia Nervosa and Bulimia*. Rev. ed. New York: Jason Aronson.

Wilson, C. P., and Mintz, I. L. (1989). *Psychosomatic Symptoms: Psychodynamic Treatment of the Underlying Personality Disorder*. Northvale, NJ: Jason Aronson.

Wurmser, L. (1980). Phobic core in the addictions and in the paranoid process. *International Journal of Psychoanalytic Psychotherapy* 8:311–355.

2

Personality Structure and Psychoanalytic Treatment of Obesity

C. Philip Wilson, M.D.

Psychoanalytic research (Wilson and Mintz 1989) demonstrates that obesity is a symptom manifestation of an underlying personality disorder. Because of the ineffective and inconsistent ego functioning of psychosomatic patients, abrupt changes in behavior such as acting out, neurotic symptoms, or different manifestations of psychosomatic disease can be caused by changes in the level of stress or patterns of defense, in shifting intensity of drives and shifting unconscious conflicts and fantasies, and in alternating levels of ego integration and regression as well as changes in object relations (Mintz 1980, Wilson and Mintz 1989). For example, the case that will be discussed later evidenced a phobic neurosis, addictions, obesity, and hypertension. In every case, any of the various genetic, biochemical, neurologic, endocrinologic, and sociologic factors contribute to the unconscious "choice" of a symptom complex such as obesity (L. Deutsch 1980, 1988, Reiser 1988, Wilson and Mintz 1989). Effective psychoanalytic treatment of the underlying personality disorder can lead to a long-term cessation or cure of a psychosomatic symptom such as obesity. The problem may be analogous to certain cases of asthma where there are clear-cut genetic constitutional factors that result in allergies; however, after successful analysis there may still be positive allergic test findings but the patient no longer gets asthma when exposed to the allergies (Wilson 1989b).[1]

It should be kept in mind that underneath the genial, kind, cooperative, often joking façade of most overweight people there is the same guilt, ambivalence, impulsivity, and wish for a magical cure that we find in the anorexic patients. Most obese patients do not come for the analysis of their obesity but for neurotic conflicts such as depression and phobias.

While there is a wide range of dynamic and structural variability among obese patients, their ego structure can be differentiated from that of the restrictor and bulimic anorexics. The ego structure of the obese patient is defective in its capacity to control not only oral impulses but impulses and conflicts of many other kinds. The obese superego structure is not as perfectionistic and controlling as that of the restrictor and bulimic anorexics. In each case I found an identification with pathological narcissistic parental behavior patterns that manifested themselves in denied split-off defects in impulse control.

In recently published research on eating disorders (Wilson 1983, 1985, Wilson and Mintz 1982, Wilson et al. 1985), I have noted that there is a widespread fear of being fat in our culture. In certain individuals, who have an ego structure that in some respects resembles that of a compulsive neurotic, a phobic avoidance of food develops, resulting in self-starvation. Such patients are then diagnosed as restrictor anorexics. Others, who have a different ego structure, attempt starvation but cannot control their voraciousness. They give in to the impulse to gorge and try to reestablish control by vomiting and using laxatives. These patients are diagnosed as bulimic anorexics. As I noted in my research on the fear of being fat in female psychology, patients complaining of obesity are also obsessed with fears of being fat and concerns with dieting (Wilson 1988, Wilson et al. 1985). Savitt (1979) emphasized that the fear-of-being-fat complex with all its characteristic psychodynamic conflicts is found in obese patients. Like anorexics, obese female patients may suffer from emotionally caused hypothalmic amenorrhea. The obese ego attempts to master conflict by instinctual gratification rather than the instinctual overcontrol manifested by anorexics. Furthermore, the obese do not try to expiate their guilt by drastic self-starvation, vomiting, or using laxatives as do the typical anorexics; instead they mobilize a massive psychoticlike denial of responsibility for giving in to their impulses. Although certain aspects of behavior of the obese are extremely primitive, omnipotent, and childlike, these individuals enlist the onlookers' sympathy with the spoken or unspoken complaint: "I can't help it. I can't control myself." Because of their

---

[1]Sims (1990), in a recent editorial in *The New England Journal of Medicine,* emphasized that environmental factors augmented by heritable tendencies are important but that they are potentially reversible.

ineffective ego, the endless attempts of the obese to diet really are most often gestures or tokens of self-control.

Obesity is a symptom complex that is found in a variety of character disorders: hysterical, obsessive-compulsive, borderline, and conditions close to psychoses. Whatever the psychiatric and psychodynamic diagnosis, obesity is an indication of an underlying impulse disorder.

LITERATURE REVIEW AND PSYCHODYNAMICS

A variety of psychodynamics and unconscious conflicts have been described in obese patients (Boyer 1980, Bruch 1973b, Bychowski 1950, Friedman 1978, Hecht 1955, Richardson 1946, Rochlin 1953): exhibitionism (Bychowski 1959), denial of femininity, renunciation of oedipal rivalry, or protection against masculine aggression (Bychowski 1950), fantasied incorporation of the phallus (Bychowski 1950, Richardson 1946, Wulff 1932), eating as an attempt to regain the lost object (Wulff 1932), upward displacement of masturbatory drives (Arlow 1953, Friedman 1978), cannibalism (Heilbrunn 1955), eating as a defense against boredom (Greenson 1953), eating as a defense against depression (F. Deutsch 1933, Sachs 1977), eating as a substitute for maternal love (Bruch 1947, Bruch and Touraine 1940, Bychowski 1950, Conrad 1952), the anniversary reaction related to overeating (Mintz 1971), shift from other psychosomatic symptom complexes to obesity (Garma 1968, Wilson 1981), dreams and dreaming in relation to early trauma (Dowling 1982), the significance of the analysis of metaphor in an obese patient (Voth 1970), and an obese patient as an example of "unwanted patients" (Eigen 1977). Giovacchini (1975) noted that a disturbance in the early object relationship with the mother in an obese patient affected later parental functioning. Conrad (1952) described the association of obesity with the body as phallus in certain cases.

> The obese individual often equates his large body with a large phallus. In the case of the female the obese body represents the illusory penis, thus fulfilling her primary penis envy. In addition, obesity (equals phallus) becomes a reaction-formation (secondary penis envy) against her feminine masochism. In the case of the obese male, the important motive force behind the body-phallus equation is the small-penis complex; obesity is an attempt to create the illusion of possessing a larger penis. [p. 18]

Friedman (1978) notes extra fat representing a fantasied penis. In discussing my fear-of-being-fat paper, Friedman cited a novel, *Final Payments* (1978) by Mary Gordon, in which a woman has incestuous conflicts about exhibiting her breasts to her father; in self-punishment, she destroys the beauty of her breasts by overeating, eventually becoming depressed and bulimic. Friedman's confirmatory case material included a woman who at age 9 had fellated a 12-year-old boy, who ejaculated in her mouth. She fantasied that the seeds remained inside her, and in adolescence she awaited every period with the anxiety that she might be pregnant. Her weight shifted radically. Her fear of being fat concealed a wish to become pregnant by her brother, and she made herself sexually unattractive with excess body fat. The masturbation fantasy of another woman analysand was that she was in a Nazi brothel where the soldiers liked only fat women so that all sorts of tempting foods were made available. To eat and become fat meant to be sexually out of control, a prostitute.

The fear of being fat and obesity cover anal-phase conflicts (Oliner 1988). Kaplan (1976) feels that, in latency, there is a greater tendency in girls toward oral and tactile contact than in boys. Ritvo (1976) attributes the probably universal feminine attitude of concealment of menarche and all sexual feelings and fantasies to the more powerful repression of the pregenital, and particularly anal, strivings in the girl rather than the boy. While obesity can be used as a defense against sexual conflicts, I have found it can also gratify forbidden anal and urinary impulses and fantasies. Many obese patients perspire profusely, soil or wet themselves a little, or are grossly enuretic or encopretic.

In discussing the fear of being fat in female psychology, I summarized the conflicts displaced onto the eating function (1978, 1979, 1980b, 1983, 1985): sexual conflicts, fears of oral and anal and urinary impulses, fears of regression, conflicts in separation-individuation, and a superego prohibition against facing any of these conflicts. Conflicts from every developmental and maturational level (oedipal or preoedipal) are denied, split off, and externalized in the fear-of-being-fat complex and eating or not eating (Wilson 1980b, 1982, 1983, 1985).

I have analyzed six obese patients (Wilson 1983, 1985, 1988) and treated many more in psychotherapy, supervised the treatment of still others, and seen a wide spectrum of cases in consultation. Rand and Stunkard (1977, 1978, in press) and Wadden and Stunkard (1989), in a study of eighty-four patients, report analytic results that compare very favorably with those of other therapies.

BODY IMAGE OF THE OBESE

Whatever the weight level of obese patients, like anorexics they suffer from a phobic fear of being fat and an obsession with being thin. The routine psychotic like subjective conviction of anorexics that they look fat when in reality they are thin or even emaciated does not occur in obese patients. However, overweight individuals are aware of being fat; they certainly do not perceive themselves as very thin.

This difference in body image is caused by the less strict superego and the less controlling ego structure of the obese. Obese patients are disturbed about their obesity; those who say they are not bothered by being overweight are using extreme denial and rationalization in the face of what they secretly feel is an insoluble problem. As a female patient said of her obese diabetic father's refusal to adhere to a diet, "If we confront him with his eating, he'll become a crazy man."

FAMILY PSYCHODYNAMICS IN OBESITY

Unlike the families of restrictor and bulimic anorexic patients who demonstrate the typical behavior patterns and attitudes that I have described in the anorexic family psychological profile (Wilson 1980, 1982, 1989a, Wilson et al. 1985), there is no characteristic cluster of parental attitudes in the families of the obese.

In over 100 families of anorexics I found a psychological profile, an acronym for which is P R I D E S. P equals *Perfectionism,* R equals *Repression* of emotions, I equals *Infantilizing* decision-making for the child, D equals *Dieting* and fears of being fat, E equals *Exhibitionistic* sexual and toilet behavior whose significance is denied, S equals *Selection* of a child for the development of anorexia because of parental conflicts. In bulimic families there is more marital discord, divorce, and neurotic and addictive behavior than in the restrictor families.

The parental family attitudes in obese cases did not correlate with this anorexic family psychological profile. There was not the same degree of perfectionism. The repression of emotions was less. Rather than expressing infantilizing decision-making for the child, there was a gross neglect of certain normal parenting roles. Dieting and fears of being fat were concerns of the parents but were not intense parental obsessions. Sexual and toilet exhibitionism did occur, but the degree and intensity of the parental denial of such behavior was less because the parental superego structure was not as perfectionistic. The selection of a child for the development of obesity occurs by process of parental neglect rather than overconcern. Of course, many other families of obese individuals have to be investigated psycho-analytically. I have seen families in which the anorexic daughter has been "unconsciously chosen" by the mother, while the obese son has been neglected. There is a complex range of parental behaviors and complicated developmental conflicts and identifications in the child that have to be taken into consideration.

THE MUSH MAN

The following is necessarily condensed material from an obese patient whom I have termed the Mush Man (Wilson and Mintz 1989) to delineate the ego structure, the underlying impulse disorder, the treatment process, and psychodynamics.

An obese young man in analysis described an ego state of feeling as though he were "moving through mush" when he was preoccupied with conflicts in relation to his impulses and to time. He suffered from a severe impulse disorder and symptoms of anxiety hysteria, phobias of bridges, fears of new situations, and fears of blindness. An only child, he had been spoiled by his doting mother and received little help in growing up from his narcissistic father, who avoided parental roles, insisting, for example, that his son call him by his first name. The impulse disorder was manifested by nail-biting and cuticle-chewing that dated from the age of 2; masturbation with sadomasochistic fantasies in childhood, adolescence, and adulthood; obesity and hypertension that began in adolescence, increased while he was away at college, and continued into adulthood. In addition, he was addicted to cigarettes and alcohol.

The following clinical material reveals the interrelated psychodynamics of the patient's behavior, nail-biting and cuticle-chewing, and his impulse disorder, obesity.

Confirmatory Session

The patient was ten minutes late and said that he had bitten his left thumbnail and cuticle the previous evening until "it bled." He reported a series of three dreams:

Dream 1

"I had a finger and fingernail that were disfigured as if I had a fungus disease. My father was in the dream and I saw that he had a similar fungus-infected finger. The whole of my nail and father's came off; underneath it was a regular normal nail. The infected fungus finger looked like an animal. This disfigured thing had a life of its own."

Dream 2

"My crotch felt like it had a rash; it felt chafed and soft, porcine, and pig-like, like the groin of a big fat homosexual. I had a penis, all shriveled and white. There were no testicles."

Dream 3

"My Timex watch came apart. There was a three-dimensional engineering drawing of all the parts arranged in my hand."

Day Residue and Associations

The previous evening the patient had been angry with his girlfriend, who was at a business dinner, and at his analyst, who was leaving the following week for summer vacation. He associated to chewing his thumb and developing a headache, thinking of being deserted by his girlfriend and his analyst. He became angry at chewing on himself and had gone out and bought a melon, which he ate before going to bed. The second, groin-rash, shriveled-penis dream made him think that he felt like a sexual blob, a mass, that he did not have his father's genital equipment. As a teenager he had become so fat that his thighs chafed and he developed thigh and groin rashes. Today he has stretch marks on his chest and thighs like a woman who has been pregnant. In adolescence he had a 40-inch waist and weighed 225 pounds. Now, as a result of analysis, he has a 24-inch waist and weighs 173 pounds, runs two miles a day, and plays squash. The watch-coming-apart dream he associated to destroying time and reality by his habits, addictions, and overeating.

An interpretation was made of the wish to be a fat, passive female to avoid anger with his girlfriend and analyst for leaving him.

We can see in this material the struggle this patient was engaged in to develop his ego's capacity to control his impulses. His unpleasant ego state, the feeling that he was "moving through mush," occurred at times when he was preoccupied with conflicts in relation to time and his impulses. The dreams reported here occurred when the patient had achieved some control of his impulses and had brought his weight down to normal by a "healthful diet," which meant eating regularly but not in great quantities. He also had developed healthful exercise patterns, jogging, swimming, and playing squash. His wishes to eat and to become obese are reflected in the porcine homosexual dream. His wishes to continue his habits of nail-biting and flesh-chewing appear in the animal-under-the-nail dream, and his desires to resume his former passive addictive way of life are graphically depicted in the watch-that-came-apart-in-his-hand dream. The ego of the dreamer was beset both day and night with struggles to defend itself against the eruption of uncontrollable impulses to act out. The watch that came apart in his hand expressed an unconscious wish to destroy time by his overeating (obesity) and other habits. The references to homosexuality reflected his growing insight into the passive (feminine) way he related to women, who for him were females with phalluses. There were many other meanings to these dreams, including conflicts about masturbation: the watch (time) coming apart in his hand. This patient was an expert masturbator and had given up the habit since he wanted to expend his sexual energy on real objects; however, the dream reflected residual wishes to masturbate. Another oedipal aspect of the dreams was his negative oedipal development, his identification with his passive dependent mother.

The analysis of sand symbols (Wilson 1968, 1971, 1981, 1982, 1986, 1988, Wilson and Mintz 1989; see also Chapter 1 of this volume) in the dreams of obese patients is of great importance. Spitz (1955) emphasized that infants feel *thirst, but not hunger,* in the hallucinatory state. My research demonstrates that sand can be used as a pregenital symbol in which repressed oral and anal conflicts are represented. Sand symbolizes oral-phase thirst and hunger and/or the formless stool of the infant. Antithetically, it depicts asceticism, an ego capacity that is deficient in the obese patient, unlike the restrictor anorexic, who is capable of total impulse control, that is, self-starvation.

In a typical obese patient's sand dream, the dreamer is on the beach at the seashore. For example, an obese alcoholic woman in analysis who had temporarily curbed her heavy drinking dreamt that she was on a beach near her childhood home with B. (her passive lover). There were a lot of rocks on the beach. Analysis of this typical dream revealed that the sandy beach symbolized her repressed wishes for fellatio, as well as for alcohol (the water in the dream), and cigarettes. This woman, like other obese analysands, was unconsciously always searching for a breast-phallus. Her thirst (xerostomia, or dry mouth syndrome) was intense. The rocks in the dream symbolized her teeth and masked her cannibalistic conflicts (Wilson 1967, Wilson and Mintz 1989). The analysis of sadomasochistic oral-incorporative conflicts is crucial in the therapy of obese patients.

In these patients, a resolution of their pathological ego functioning was effected and they developed an organized sense of time as their deep-seated impulse disorder yielded to analysis.

THE RELATIONSHIP OF OBESITY TO ADDICTIONS AND CHILDHOOD HABITS

To treat obese patients effectively, it is necessary to understand the impulse disorders, the addictive personality structure (Wilson 1981, Wurmser 1980) and the habits of childhood that are frequently the developmental forerunners of obesity. I have emphasized that obesity is an addiction (Wilson 1988, p. 36) and noted the frequent occurrence of childhood thumb-sucking, nail-biting, cuticle-chewing and -eating, head-banging, hair-pulling and -eating, and other impulse disorders such as encopresis and enuresis. Some patients report no habits and a childhood history of excessive good behavior. Therapy, however, uncovers isolated episodes or phases of rebelliousness. The ego makes use of the same defenses in its struggles with a childhood habit or impulse disorder as it does later in efforts to cope with eating disorders. Thus the defenses of denial, splitting, displacement and externalization, and conscious with-holding and lying are deeply ingrained in the ego structure of the obese.

EGO STATES AND THE FEAR-OF-BEING-FAT COMPLEX

Alcoholics' fear of being fat is masked by their fear of drinking, smokers' fear of being fat is covered by their fear of smoking, and addicts' fear of being fat is hidden by their fear of addiction. It is well known that when addicted patients begin to interrupt their habits, they may gain weight and become obese; conversely, the obese individual while losing weight may turn to addictions to relieve the conflicts with their impulses. In children and adults a preoccupation with a habit—encopresis, enuresis, thumb-sucking, nail-biting, head-banging, hair-pulling, and so on—masks the fear-of-being-fat complex. In the case of the mush patient, his impulse disorder, his fear-of-being-fat complex, was embedded in his ego state of mush.

In Savitt's (1979) discussion of my fear-of-being-fat paper, he observed that obese patients could manifest all the psychodynamic preoedipal and oedipal conflicts that the anorexic displaces onto her fear-of-being-fat complex. He noted that the obese female suffers from an intense fear of being fat and that she may manifest emotionally caused amenorrhea with underlying fears of pregnancy.

Post (1988) and Reiser (1988) questioned the application of my fear-of-being-fat complex hypothesis to obesity, noting that in the cases they had seen they noted a fear of being thin. In my fat phobic formulations the fear of being thin is one aspect of a structural conflict. In the obese body image the ego ideal is to be thin, which has multiple psychodynamic meanings, a most important one being the wish to be in control of impulse gratification. To be thin means to be in perfect control. Thus there is a wish to be thin and overdetermined unconscious conflicts (fears) of being thin; at the same time, there is a conscious fear of being fat: a fat phobia caused by the multiple unconscious conflicts that I have detailed (Wilson 1981, 1983, 1985).

PERSONALITY CHARACTERISTICS OF THE OBESE

The compulsive obese person like the mush patient resorts to wit, sarcasm, irony, and subtle barbs. The hysterical obese individual jokes, kids, teases, and can be contagiously funny, boisterous, and playful. The compulsive obese want to be thought of as gourmets and are experts on the best restaurants and the finest wines. They are gregarious, trying to relieve their guilt and justify their voraciousness by getting others to eat with them. Their friends join them in eating, secretly rationalizing to themselves that no matter how much they eat, it is nothing compared to the amount consumed by their obese friends.

Many obese people evidence a perpetual good humor and often ridicule themselves and their eating behavior. This stereotypical jolliness is a façade (Castelnuovo-Tedesco and Schiebel 1979) that masks depression, anxiety, and conflict. Typical character qualities of the obese are insatiability, impatience, ambivalence, and a belief in magic. Upon any success, they experience feelings of omnipotence, which are quickly replaced by despair and fears of poverty (starvation) with any frustration or failure.

TECHNIQUE IN THE DYADIC PHASE

The following problems and techniques of interpretation are used in the first dyadic phase of treatment. (1) These patients usually do not free-associate, as also happens in the analyses of children and of patients with character disorders (Boyer and Giovacchini 1980). (2) The therapist therefore takes an active stance, frequently using construction and reconstruction. (3) Behavioral responses can be interpreted. (4) Dreams have to be used in the context of the patient's psychodynamics. (5) First one interprets the masochism of these patients—their archaic superego and the guilt they experience in admitting any conflict. (6) Next one interprets defenses against facing masochistic behavior; then, when the ego is healthier, one interprets defenses against aggressive impulses. (7) Such interpretations are inexact and frequently are not confirmed by the patients' associations. (8) For these patients who have an archaic, punitive superego and a relatively weak ego, the analyst provides auxiliary ego strength and a rational superego (Boyer 1980, Wilson 1971, 1982, 1989d). (9) Interpretations should be made in a firm, consistent manner (Boyer 1980). (10) With such patients, the analyst needs to have authority.

Most obese patients consciously are not guilty but are anxious. They have layered defenses against feeling guilt. Unconsciously they see everyone, including the therapist, as a potentially critical parental figure. This is an aspect of projective identification that I have detailed (Wilson 1989c). Successfully analyzing the defenses against feeling guilt is a major advance. It is only when this is done that these patients' communications shift from pseudo-free association to valid analytic free association.

The defense of denial in the obese is multilayered and connected with other defenses: self-ridicule, good humor, joking, and kidding are all defenses that ward off criticism from other people. When these defenses are analyzed, depression emerges but also irritability, contentiousness, and defiance, which are actually manifestations of projective identifications. Obese patients feel guilty about their self-indulgence. If they feel exposed, they can become angry, hostile, and paranoid. In this situation they confuse people who question their behavior with the early critical parents of childhood.

Because obese patients, in their projective identifications, can pick up almost imperceptible nuances in the tone of voice, facial expression, movements, and even feelings of the analyst, they provoke intense countertransference reactions (Sperling 1967, Wilson et al. 1985, Wilson and Mintz 1989).

As with children and other patients with severe preoedipal pathology, in obese patients the analyst in addition to being a transference object is a new and different object who promotes healthy maturation (Wilson 1971, 1989d).

Another special technique is to demonstrate to the patient early in treatment his or her need for immediate gratification (the impulse disorder, i.e., the primary narcissism). See Hogan 1985, Sperling 1967, 1978, Wilson and colleagues 1985. Thus the patient is shown that the symptoms are manifestations of a split-off, impulsive part of the ego (i.e., the fear-of-being-fat complex). If the ego's defenses against the acknowledgement of this primitive aspect of his or her personality are not interpreted in the patient's dreams, associations, body language, enactments, treatment behavior, and object relations from the beginning of therapy, acting out, particularly sudden termination, may occur.

A useful acronym for the technique of interpretation in the initial phase of therapy is M A D: M equals *Masochism,* A equals *Aggression,* D equals *Dyadic transference.*

In most cases, the analyst can begin to interpret triadic oedipal material only when the patient's archaic superego has been modified, when the ego has matured so that there is a capacity to tolerate libidinal and aggressive conflicts, and when there has been a shift from part-object relations toward whole-object relations.

It is important that the psychiatrist be in charge of the treatment process (Sperling 1978, Wilson et al. 1985). A split transference with the medical specialist can vitiate treatment. Hospitalization should be reserved for true emergencies.

As with other psychosomatic symptoms, when overeating subsides, acting out increases. Patience is essential in the analysis of obese patients, whose habits, at their most primitive level, mask preverbal conflicts and traumas. Impulsive, psychotic, and psychosomatic patients, all of whom have preoedipal conflicts, have the means to communicate the impact and effects of their early preverbal traumas (Wilson 1971, 1981).

The therapist must be intuitive about when to confront patients regarding their withholding of relevant information about eating or other addictive behavior. One should not ask about it constantly or demand that the habit be given up. Instead, the therapist should point out the reason for interrupting a habit (i.e., to uncover fantasies and conflicts that it masks). The obese want and believe in magical control and want to stop the habit without analyzing it. The defensive purposes of habits, which in these patients mask suicidal and homicidal impulses and conflicts, have to be repeatedly interpreted. If the therapist does not actively confront patients with the meanings of their symptoms and habits that serve defenses purposes, these symptoms and habits will become more intense, and the patients' negative transference will be split off and expressed in exacerbations of symptoms and habits while the patient is manifesting pseudo-respect and compliant behavior in verbal communications.

DIETS, WEIGHT PROGRAMS, OVEREATERS ANONYMOUS, AND OTHER THERAPIES

In most cases, as with anorexic patients (Wilson et al. 1985), we leave eating up to the patient. It is only when patients develop insight into the many conflicts that are displaced onto their fear of being fat and their impulse disorder that they will begin to change their eating habits as well as other aspects of their behavior. We do not prescribe diets, nor do we have the patient working with diet specialists.

Savitt (1970) described a technique with an obese patient who acted out, gaining 100 pounds by the second year of analysis. He confronted the patient with the choice of hospitalization or referral to a diet specialist while continuing analysis. Savitt noted that his confrontation, which had a successful result, was adequately prepared for and was presented in a nonpunitive way within the framework of a well-established and continually tested positive transference. Its purpose was to break through a defense of intellectualization of the analytic process. He emphasizes, as do my colleagues and I, that an early prohibition of eating may lead to the patient's terminating treatment. In any case, the ineffective ego of the obese is unable to comply with prohibitions or diets. Most such patients have been on and off diets for years with no lasting effect. If a patient coming for analysis is in Overeaters Anonymous or some other diet program or is working with a diet specialist, the analyst has to develop a positive transference and, by interpretations, wean the patient from involvement with these other modalities of treatment.

Obese patients may also act out in a state of anger and frustration with the analyst and the slowness of the analytic process and join Overeaters Anonymous or go to a diet specialist. In this case, the analyst should interpret the transference situation and its genetic derivatives. Unless the analysis is advanced with a strong therapeutic alliance, he should not prohibit such behavior but interpret its psychodynamic meanings.

COUNTERREACTIONS AND COUNTERTRANSFERENCES

Many analysts' counterreactions and countertransferences to superobese patients as described by Rowland (1985, 1988) apply to obese patients in general. Rowland noted that there is a kind of fascination aroused by such huge persons that recalls one's own childhood relationships with adults and brings forth a coexistent urge to understand and a feeling of helplessness. The prospect of a person twice as large as oneself, or of the 50- to 60-pound overweight person whose impulses, voraciousness, and general insatiability are so out of control, calls forth certain primitive responses that may be pro- or contratherapeutic, depending on how one deals with them.

For example, in my supervised cases it was useful for the therapist to interrupt special parameters such as pulling out a chair every day for the patient or avoiding any mention of or questions about the unpleasant body odors of analysands. When these parameters were given up, the obese patients talked about the secondary gain of being overweight, of intimidating people as their narcissistic parents had done with them. Exploration of body odors led to the sadistic pleasure of defying mother and society (the analyst) by soiling and wetting, and the patient acknowledging that being obese gratified wishes to belch, fart, and soil under the guise of "I can't help it because I am so fat."

Rowland noted that cheerfulness as a character trait was a prominent feature in all four of his cases. However, it quickly became apparent that a kind of paranoid touchiness lay just below the surface and could be reactivated. The physician is then faced with not only a person who outweighs him by 200 pounds, but also the choice of stirring up the troubled waters or supporting the cheerful denial. I would agree with Rowland that a primitive response of fearfulness on the therapist's part often underlies the therapist's mode of relating to the patient. Thus the therapist can feel that the patient is stronger and his or her anger is to be avoided; that the patient eats as much as he or she wants and this regressive pull is to be avoided since it masks even more frightening processes such as psychosis; that the patient is bigger (smarter, more sexual) and will overpower the therapist. There can be an opposite attitude: that the patient is beneath consideration and contempt—the therapist should not waste his time. This is a very frequent counterreaction and can, of course, be the result of failed attempts at treatment.

I would also agree with Rowland's emphasizing that there are certain kinds of countertransference reactions one encounters in dealing with startling clinical procedures, acute schizophrenia, suicide, prolonged starvation (Rowland 1972), terminal illness, and severe marital discord. Although the treatment is difficult from the patient's vantage point, the therapist's overcoming his or her own reluctance to work is often the primary task.

Another problem Rowland emphasizes is overcoming undue respect for one's elders. If the size factor overawes the therapist, he is then a child questioning his parents' loss of control, sexuality, anger, fearfulness, and so on. The verbosity of the obese may force the therapist into an overly combative or passive response.

In discussing his first case, Rowland noted that losing weight and undertaking a more conventional lifestyle involved an enormous amount of suffering for the patient, as well as considerable discomfort for the therapist. The patient became depressed, suicidal, and extremely anxious and began to hate the analyst, himself, and his family because he had lost pleasure in a major sustaining force over 30 years—eating. Rowland, in agreement with Stunkard (1957), emphasized that all patients experience a severe depressive mood when, in the course of therapy, they give up overeating, an event that Stunkard termed "the dieting depression." I would concur with this clinical finding but emphasize that the dieting depression is only one aspect of the multidetermined and multifaceted depression (and other symptoms) that these patients have to face and resolve during the resolution of the underlying impulse disorder.

From the viewpoint of psychotherapy I would agree with Rowland that the question of confronting the eating and weight problem early on should be carefully considered (Adler and Myerson 1973). With some patients, in whom recent, acutely reactive overweight is the problem, this can sometimes be done with quickly effective psychotherapeutic results. Here Rowland emphasizes that one would find solid object relationships, an effective work life, readily available affects, a positive transference, and a more mature character structure. Basically, individual evaluation is crucial, as in anorexic states (Rowland 1972). In Rowland's four cases, physical symptoms, which were present throughout, were somewhat neglected in favor of understanding personal relationships. Generally it was the experience of all the members of the obesity panel (Reiser 1988) that these patients will take care of the obesity in their own way, in their own time, if other factors can be resolved. Realistic discussion of weight, diet, and exercise is a termination issue rather than an opening one, as is discussed by Hilda Bruch (1957). Most obese patients use discussions of diets and calories as a resistance; like anorexics, they often are experts on the current and past medical and nutritional literature and most often have tried medical and nutritional treatments to no avail.

In my experience, the superobese present problems in regard to office and waiting room arrangements that should be faced directly. Larger chairs, a larger analytic couch, and more space in the office and waiting room are required for the treatment of the obese. For example, a supervised therapist delayed for weeks putting the patient on the couch for analysis because he was afraid that the couch would collapse under the weight of the 375-pound patient. He resolved this dilemma by purchasing a new couch. The therapist must be aware of reactions to those obese who are dirty: partially incontinent of urine and feces as well as not too well bathed. At a preoedipal level the therapist's unconscious reaction can be envy and jealousy of the obese, who are carrying out their unconscious wishes to eat, wet, and soil as well as the regressive wish that they be babied. At the oedipal level, for the therapist the patient's tremendous body is a fantasied phallus (Conrad 1965) and also symbolizes the macho ideal of omnipotent defiance of the prohibiting early parents. The huge patient also represents the preoedipal baby. The tremendous body of the obese can represent to the therapist the pregnant maternal imago perceived in preoedipal as well as oedipal terms.

As with anorexics, the patience of the analyst will be tried to the limit (Wilson et al. 1985). Bychowski's (1950) analysis of a 250-pound woman, Rowland's (1985) psychoanalytic psychotherapy of the superobese, along with other analyses of obese analysands (Wilson and Mintz 1989, Savitt 1970) reflect successful outcomes.

As with anorexics in the preliminary phase of treatment, we acquaint the patient with his or her impulse disorder, of which obesity is only one manifestation. The fear-of-being-fat complex itself should be understood in terms of an impulse disorder. We can achieve insight into the various conflicts that are masked and hidden by the fear of being fat by approaching it as one approaches any other unconsciously caused symptom complex.

SUMMARY

There is a wide diagnostic spectrum of patients suffering from obesity. The obese individual's ego structure can be differentiated from that of the restrictor and bulimic anorexics. These patients evidence an identification with pathological narcissistic parental behavior patterns, one manifestation of which is a defect in impulse control. Psychoanalysis, utilizing techniques similar to those of Kernberg (1975) and Boyer and Giovacchini (1980), can result in healthy ego functioning, a resolution of the obese patient's fear-of-being-fat complex, and the underlying personality disorder.

REFERENCES

Adler, G., and Myerson, P. G., eds. (1973). *Confrontation in Psychotherapy.* New York: Science House.

Arlow, J. A. (1953). Masturbation and symptom formation. *Journal of the American Psychoanalytic Association* 1:45–58.

Boyer, L. B. (1980). Working with a borderline patient. In *Psychoanalytic Treatment of Schizophrenic, Borderline, and Characterological Disorders,* ed. L. B. Boyer and P. L. Giovacchini, pp. 171–208. New York: Jason Aronson.

Boyer, L. B., and Giovacchini, P. L. (1980). *Psychoanalytic Treatment of Schizophrenic, Borderline, and Characterological Disorders.* 2nd rev. ed. New York: Jason Aronson.

Bruch, H. (1947). Psychological aspects of obesity. *Psychiatry* 10:373–381.

———— (1957). *The Importance of Overweight.* New York: Norton.

———— (1973a). Anorexia nervosa. In *American Handbook of Psychiatry,* 2nd ed., vol. 2, ed. M. F. Reiser, p. 791. New York: Basic Books, 1975.

———— (1973b). *Eating Disorders: Obesity, Anorexia Nervosa, and the Person Within.* New York: Basic Books.

Bruch, H., and Touraine, G. (1940). Obesity in childhood: the family frame of obese children. *Psychosomatic Medicine* 2:141–206.

Bychowski, G. (1950). On neurotic obesity. *Psychoanalytic Review* 37:301–319.

Castelnuovo-Tedesco, P., and Schiebel, S. (1979). Studies of super-obesity: I. Psychological characteristics of super-obese patients. *International Journal of Psychiatry* 7:465–480.

Conrad, S. (1965). Phallic aspects of obesity. *Bulletin of the Philadelphia Association for Psychoanalysis* 15:207–233.

Deutsch, F. (1933). Studies in pathogenesis: biological and psychological aspects. *Psychoanalytic Quarterly* 2:225–243.

Deutsch, L. (1980). Psychosomatic medicine from a psychoanalytic viewpoint. *Journal of the American Psychoanalytic Association* 28:653–703.

———— (1988). A psychoanalytic perspective on recent biological contributions, in panel on compulsive eating, obesity and related phenomena, reported by L. W. Reiser. *Journal of the American Psychoanalytic Association* 36:167–168.

Dowling, S. (1982). Dreams and dreaming in relation to trauma in childhood. *International Journal of Psycho-Analysis* 63:157–166.

Eigen, M. (1977). On working with "unwanted" patients. *International Journal of Psycho-Analysis* 58:109–121.

Friedman, S. (1978). A discussion of Wilson's paper on "The Fear of Being Fat and Anorexia Nervosa" at the meeting of the New Jersey Psychoanalytic Society, Hackensack, NJ, October 13.

Garma, A. (1968). The psychosomatic shift through obesity, migraine, peptic ulcer, and myocardial infarction in a homosexual. *International Journal of Psycho-Analysis* 49:241–245.

96   C. Philip Wilson, M.D.

Giovacchini, P. L. (1975). Self-projections in the narcissistic transference. *International Journal of Psychoanalytic Psychotherapy* 4:142–166.
Greenson, R. (1953). On boredom. *Journal of the American Psychoanalytic Association* 1:7–21.
Hecht, M. B. (1955). Obesity in women: a psychiatric study. *Psychoanalytic Quarterly* 29:203–231.
Heilbrunn, G. (1955). The basic fear. *Journal of the American Psychoanalytic Association* 3:447–466.
Hogan, C. C. (1985). Transference. In *Fear of Being Fat: The Treatment of Anorexia Nervosa and Bulimia*, rev. ed., ed. C. P. Wilson, C. C. Hogan, and I. L. Mintz, pp. 153–168. New York: Jason Aronson.
Kaplan, E. B. (1976). Panel on the psychology of women: latency and early adolescence, reported by E. Galenson. *Journal of the American Psychoanalytic Association* 24:155.
Mintz, I. L. (1971). The anniversary reaction: a response to the unconscious sense of time. *Journal of the American Psychoanalytic Association* 19:720–735.
——— (1980). Multideterminism in asthmatic disease. *International Journal of Psychoanalytic Psychotherapy* 8:593–600.
Oliner, M. M. (1988). Anal components in overeating. In *Bulimia: Psychoanalytic Treatment and Theory*, ed. H. J. Schwartz, pp. 227–253. Madison, CT: International Universities Press.
Rand, C. S. W., and Stunkard, A. J. (1977). Psychoanalysis and obesity. *Journal of the American Academy of Psychoanalysis* 5:459–499.
——— (1978). Obesity and psychoanalysis. *American Journal of Psychiatry* 135:547–551.
——— (in press). Obesity and psychoanalysis: treatment and four-year follow-up. *American Journal of Psychiatry*.
Reiser, L. W. (1988). Panel report: compulsive eating, obesity, and related phenomena. *Journal of the American Psychoanalytic Association* 1:163–171.
Richardson, M. B. (1946). Obesity and neurosis: a case report. *Psychiatric Quarterly* 20:400–424.
Ritvo, S. (1976). Presentation to the panel on the psychology of women: late adolescence and early adulthood, reported by E. Galenson. *Journal of the American Psychoanalytic Association* 24:638.
Rochlin, G. (1953). Disorder of depression and elation. Abstract in the *Bulletin of the American Psychoanalytic Association* 8:241.
Rowland, C. V., Jr. (1972). Diagnosis and treatment of anorexic states. *Postgraduate Medicine* 51:159–162.
——— (1985). Panel on Compulsive Eating, Obesity, and Related Phenomena. Meeting of the American Psychoanalytic Association, New York, December 21.
Sachs, O. (1977). Discussion of C. P. Wilson's paper on "The Fear of Being Fat in Anorexia Nervosa." *Bulletin of the Psychoanalytic Association of New York* 17:8–9.
Savitt, R. A. (1970). Panel on Addiction and Habituation, reporter. *Journal of the American Psychoanalytic Association* 18:209–218.
——— (1979). Discussion of C. P. Wilson's paper on "The Fear of Being Fat in Female Psychology and Anorexia Nervosa." *Bulletin of the Psychoanalytic Association of New York* 17:8–9.
Sims, E. H. (1990). Destiny rides again as twins overeat. *New England Journal of Medicine* 322:1522–1524.
Sperling, M. (1967). Transference neurosis in patients with psychosomatic disorders. *Psychoanalytic Quarterly* 36:342–355.
——— (1978). Anorexia nervosa (Part 4). In *Psychosomatic Disorders in Childhood*, ed. O. Sperling, pp. 129–173. New York: Jason Aronson.
Spitz, R. A. (1955). The primal cavity: a contribution to the genesis of perception and its role in psychoanalytic theory. *Psychoanalytic Study of the Child* 10:215–240. New York: International Universities Press.
Stunkard, A. J. (1957). The dieting depression. *American Journal of Medicine* 23:77.
Voth, H. M. (1970). The analysis of metaphor. *Journal of the American Psychoanalytic Association* 15:599–621.

Wadden, T. A., and Stunkard, A. J. (1989). Obesity: etiology and treatment. In *Psychosomatic Medicine: Theory, Physiology and Practice,* ed. S. Chevon, pp. 707–762. Madison, CT: International Universities Press.

Wilson, C. P. (1967). Stone as a symbol of teeth. *Psychoanalytic Quarterly* 36:418–425.

———— (1968). Discussion of Little's paper on "Xerostomia" at the meeting of the American Psychoanalytic Association, New York, December 21.

———— (1971). On the limits of the effectiveness of psychoanalysis: early ego and somatic disturbances. *Journal of the American Psychoanalytic Association* 19:552–564.

———— (1978). The psychoanalytic treatment of hospitalized anorexia nervosa patients. Panel discussion on anorexia nervosa. *Bulletin of the Psychoanalytic Association of New York* 15:5–7.

———— (1980). On the fear of being fat in female psychology and anorexia nervosa. *Bulletin of the Psychoanalytic Association of New York* 17:8–9.

———— (1981). Sand symbolism: the primary dream representation of the Isakower phenomenon and smoking addictions. In *Clinical Psychoanalysis,* ed. S. Orgel and B. D. Fine, pp. 45–55. New York: Jason Aronson.

———— (1982). The fear of being fat and anorexia nervosa. *International Journal of Psychoanalytic Psychotherapy* 9:233–255.

———— (1983). *The fear of being fat and obesity.* Paper presented at a meeting of the Psychosomatic Discussion Group of the Psychoanalytic Association of New York, Inc., October 12.

———— (1985). Obesity: personality structure and psychoanalytic treatment. Panel on Compulsive Eating and Related Phenomena. Meeting of the American Psychoanalytic Association, New York, December 11.

———— (1986). The psychoanalytic psychotherapy of bulimic anorexia nervosa. In *Adolescent Psychiatry,* ed. S. Feinstein, pp. 274–314. Chicago: University of Chicago Press.

———— (1988). Obesity: personality structure and psychoanalytic treatment. Panel report. *Journal of the American Psychoanalytic Association* 1:163–171.

———— (1989a). Family psychopathology. In *Psychosomatic Symptoms: Psychodynamic Treatment of the Underlying Personality Disorder,* ed. C. P. Wilson and I. L. Mintz, pp. 63–82. Northvale, NJ: Jason Aronson.

———— (1989b). Overstimulation in bronchial asthma. In *Psychosomatic Symptoms: Psychodynamic Treatment of the Underlying Personality Disorder,* ed. C. P. Wilson and I. L. Mintz, pp. 330–331. Northvale, NJ: Jason Aronson.

———— (1989c). Projective identification. In *Psychosomatic Symptoms: Psychodynamic Treatment of the Underlying Personality Disorder,* ed. C. P. Wilson and I. L. Mintz, pp. 105–132. Northvale, NJ: Jason Aronson.

———— (1989d). Epilogue: psychotherapeutic techniques. In *Psychosomatic Symptoms: Psychodynamic Treatment of the Underlying Personality Disorder,* ed. C. P. Wilson and I. L. Mintz, pp. 432–343. Northvale, NJ: Jason Aronson.

———— (1990a). On beginning analysis with a patient with an eating disorder. In *On Beginning Analysis,* ed. T. J. Jacobs and A. Rothstein, pp. 241–276. Madison, CT: International Universities Press.

———— (1990b). *Obesity, personality structure, and psychoanalytic treatment.* Paper presented at the Sixth Annual Symposium of the Detroit Psychiatric Institute and the Michigan Psychoanalytic Institute. Detroit, November 6.

Wilson, C. P., Hogan, C. C., and Mintz, I. L. (1985). *Fear of Being Fat: The Treatment of Anorexia Nervosa and Bulimia.* Rev. ed. New York: Jason Aronson.

Wilson, C. P., and Mintz, I. L. (1982). Abstaining and bulimic anorexics: two sides of the same coin. *Primary Care* 9:459–472.

———— (1989). *Psychosomatic Symptoms: Psychodynamic Treatment of the Underlying Personality Disorder.* Northvale, NJ: Jason Aronson.

Wulff, M. (1932). An interesting oral symptom-complex and its relation to addiction. *International Zeitschrift fur Psychoanalysis* 18:281–302.

Wurmser, L. (1980). Phobic core in the addictions and the paranoid process. *International Journal of Psychoanalytic Psychotherapy* 8:331–335.

3

The Fear of Being Fat in Normal, Obese, Starving, and Gorging Individuals

Ira L. Mintz, M.D.

It will come as no surprise that the conscious fear of being fat can cover up the unconscious need to be fat. The unconscious meaning of being fat can vary with the individual but lies within a range of relatively specific conflicts. The intensity of this fear depends upon the unconscious nature of the conflicts defended against, the ability of the ego to contain its impulses, the capacity to tolerate anxiety, and the amount of guilt that the conflict generates. It is not always the fatness or weight per se that is feared, but the process of eating that is frightening. The patient displaces the fear onto the weight gain. Similarly, those patients who are obsessed with becoming thin are as concerned with the behavior by which they become thin, as with the actual thinness itself.

THE RELATIVELY NORMAL GROUP

In relatively normal people, obesity has a different meaning today sociologically than it did in the past. It was once associated with regalness.

99

The Queen of Hawaii, because of obesity, had to be hoisted onto the deck of Captain Cook's ship in a cargo net; amply filled burghers were able to throw their weight about and attest to their financial means in avoiding hunger or the wasting ravages of tuberculosis or malignancy; the Rubens's paintings of somewhat rotund figures were physically appealing to the people of that time and were accepted as a prototypes necessary to health and beauty.

Today, the idea of "to be thin is in" is attested to by fashion models, ballerinas, and the slender, healthy middle-aged people seen in the media. Thinness has become a conscious cultural norm, achieved by many of us without obvious evidence of clear-cut conflict. Within this broad group, however, are many subclinical anorexics, often related to family members who are either overtly obese or anorexic.

THE OBESE GROUP

To blow up in size and become fat, viewed from the aspect of an impulse, may mean to "blow up" with repressed rage, often under a character structure of lighthearted, agreeable cheerfulness. To be fat may mean to blow up with a pregnancy, to give in to unstably defended sexual impulses. To be fat as a defense can be associated with a wall of obesity, a protection against the realistic and projected aggressive and sexual assaults from a frightening, external world. To be fat can represent a repressed, infantile position wherein the person is still cared for by mother and preoccupied with sucking at the breast.

Case 1

A 32-year-old married woman, 75 pounds overweight, entered treatment because of symptoms of anxiety, depression, obesity, and frigidity. During the treatment, a great deal of repressed anger toward her parents, husband, and children surfaced. At one point she acknowledged feeling like a hand grenade and associated her weight to a wall of fat that prevented her explosiveness from damaging those around her. Well into the treatment, she reported the following dream:

I am inside a castle with thick, high walls, feeling very frightened, insecure, and small. I look out beyond the walls and see you mounted on a horse with a lance on your arm. You ride over the drawbridge into the castle toward me, and I'm very frightened.

She associated my approach on horseback to a physical and then sexual assault and recognized that her obesity was represented in the dream by the thick-walled castle. Additional associations related to her current fears of exploitation and feelings of helplessness reaching back into childhood experience. It was additionally relevant that on that day, the patient had around her neck a large pendant closely resembling a British coat of arms, further completing her unconscious identification with the protective castle. Her comment in the third session that "analysis would strip everything from my bones" had multiple meanings from the view of impulse, defense, and transference.

Case 2

A 36-year-old woman, the mother of four children, entered analysis for symptoms of chronic obesity, after three years of therapy with two previous therapists (Mintz 1971). In the initial interview she described feeling depressed during the past week and also having the inexplicable need for continually calling her husband at work to see if he was well. She spoke about her strong attachment to her father, who had died when she was 14 years of age. When I inquired as to when that had occurred, she answered that her father had died on the eleventh of October; the date of her first visit was October 9. She seemed to be reliving the earlier experience on the anniversary of her father's death, twenty-two years earlier. The depression and anxiety over her husband's welfare were displacements of the earlier trauma when the father lapsed into a moribund condition one week before he died of carcinoma of the stomach.

Exploration in subsequent hours revealed that the patient became pregnant before marriage at the age of 18. She felt extremely guilty about her precipitous marriage, although this guilt had never been a conscious preoccupation. Her husband had repeatedly assured her that they would have married anyway. She said that when her father was dying, he told the priest he wanted all his children to bring honor to his name and never to do anything to disgrace him. With great guilt, she felt that if her father been alive when she became pregnant, she would have been forced to kill herself: it was better that he died rather than witness this disgrace.

The obesity began with her first pregnancy and was tied to her fantasy that obesity leads to toxemia and a possible abortion. She had been obese ever since, with her weight fluctuating in a significant cycle. The due date of her first baby was between October 12 and 15, very close to the anniversary of her father's death. The patient suddenly realized that she embarked on a crash diet every fall and lost some weight, but invariably went off the diet around February, which was the time of her original conception. She was able to date the point of a previous crash diet because the rapid weight loss had produced a colic from a kinked ureter and she was forced to see a urologist. What became evident was that the cyclic weight changes corresponded with the time sequences of her first pregnancy: her weight gain corresponded to the beginning of the pregnancy, and the weight loss to the delivery. There was also more than a suggestion that the pregnancy contained a rebirth fantasy of the lost father. The baby's due date corresponded to the date of the father's death, almost to the day. The patient voiced the wish to be reborn without unhappiness. She said that during the cyclic losses of weight she could never drop below what her father's weight had been, and that she named the baby for the father.

The weight gain had multiple determinants. In relation to the unborn child, initially to become obese was to court toxemia in the hope of a fantasied abortion. Later the cyclic weight gain in part reflected a reliving of the pregnancy act out of guilt for the fantasied abortion. With respect to the father, the obesity perpetuated her unresolved guilt over the pregnancy and the shame it would cause in her father's eyes. It also represented her identification with her father, the obesity symbolizing an unconscious attempt to undo his wasted, cachectic moribund state. This conflict was then displaced to her husband, a fact evident in the anxiety attacks about his well-being on the anniversary of her father's death. Finally the cyclical obesity unconsciously stood for her attempt at a rebirth of her lost father.

Case 3

A 24-year-old woman was seen in treatment for her obesity. Five feet tall, she had gained 90 pounds. Plagued by obesity since the age of 14, she had been in four weight-reducing programs including hospitalization. Any accomplished weight reduction was followed by unacceptable weight gain. Following the latest gain, her shame at her appearance resulted in a need to quit a lucrative position, remain unemployed, shun social contacts, and behave like a recluse while living at home for a period of six months.

It became apparent that she harbored hostility toward many people, but especially toward her mother, who was a concerned but very controlling, dominating, and infantilizing figure. The patient had always been a good and obedient girl, similar to the prototype of a preanorexic child. Her thoughtfulness and obedience arose in great part out of a need to obey and to please in order to court approval as well as to repress aggression. She had never opened her mouth to assert herself, express some manifestation of healthy adolescent rebellion, or express anger. While the need to express herself was strong, she could only "open her mouth" to eat and to destroy food.

Rather early, the patient became aware that one component in her need to be obese was to defy and aggravate her mother. She recognized how effective a weapon her obesity was. She could safely open her mouth to eat and thereby provoke and upset her mother without risking condemnation and attack, because this was a weight problem, not rebellion. She was sick, not hostile, an unconscious equation slavishly adhered to by anorexics and bulimics. She also became aware that characterologically her long-standing need to please and be concerned with the other person was at the expense of her own legitimate self-interest. She could therefore act self-destructively without conscious awareness of the nature of her self-damaging behavior. She was too focused on the effect upon "the other." Torturing her mother was most important.

Another major determinant in her obesity was a need to deal with sexual anxiety by flight into unattractiveness. She feared close relationships because her need to be compliant left her feeling helpless in the face of sexually demanding men. The unappealing wall of fat turned them off in the same fashion as the starving anorexic's skeleton would. Uncovering these anxieties liberated an endless series of wild, promiscuous dreams. She also remembered past sexual fantasies and adolescent sexual and drug-related experiences that terrified her—and were all replaced by her obesity and withdrawal.

With this patient, the need to be fat had to do with unresolved aggressive, sexual, and dependency conflict. Interestingly, the patient's weight reduction, accompanied by insight, was accomplished by relatively little effort and almost no preoccupation with food or diet. She was concerned with sexual, aggressive, and dependency fantasies instead, in marked contrast to her previous unsuccessful attempts at weight reduction.

ANOREXIA

In anorexia and bulimia, unconscious conflicts underlying the fear of being fat are essentially similar to those in obesity, but they are dealt with differently, reflecting different aspects of ego functioning (Mintz and Wilson 1982). Wilson (1985) has made dynamic differentiation of the two syndromes. He notes that the anorexic has a relatively intact ego structure able to contain the impulse disorder and deny the impulse to eat. The bulimic's defenses against the impulse to gorge has been eroded by a less-intact ego structure whose defenses have not fully developed characterologically, or have been eroded by the repetitive impulses to eat, or both. Clinically one sees more impulse-ridden parents among the bulimics, while the anorexics usually have parents whose impulses are better contained. Although the conflicts are similar, the clinical picture varies.

In the anorexic, the fear of being fat can also be viewed as the need to be thin. Difficulty in relationships with people sets off feelings of helplessness, resentment, rage, frustration, sexual anxiety, wishes to be little and cared for, separation anxiety, guilt, and the need for punishment (Mintz 1985a). Unwilling to face the conflict because of fear that she cannot cope, she displaces the conflict onto food, the impulses to eat representing unconscious symbolic resolution of the displaced conflict. When she cannot control relations with people, she attempts to control food. The impulse to eat sets off the fear of being fat, dealt with by starving. Anorexics usually have elements of obsessional character structure utilizing isolation, intellectualization, displacement, and miniaturization of conflict similar to their compulsive rituals. Some anorexic patients have severe compulsive rituals. It is rare to find an anorexic who does not report that whenever upset, she thinks about food and starving in ritualistic fashion. As she becomes increasingly preoccupied with food and the fear of being fat, the original difficulty subsides and is often forgotten.

Case 4

A 10-year-old anorexic boy in treatment because of a 25-pound weight loss began to subsist solely on McDonald's milk shakes (Mintz 1985b). Prominent themes emerging in the beginning of treatment were related to aggression, his wish to be weak and a baby, and his conflict over sexual identification. Prior to the development of anorexic symptoms, he had complained to his mother that it seemed he was fat as she was while his siblings were thin like his father. Anorexic symptomatology crystalized after he saw his pregnant aunt. Then he reported feeling fat and fearing that he would get fatter. Identifying with his aunt, following his cousin's birth, the patient began to starve and was hospitalized prior to my seeing him.

In the beginning of treatment, increasing hatred of his younger sister gradually emerged. As the treatment progressed and his trust increased, he described having fantasies for the previous two years of killing his sister by plunging a knife into her chest. Early in treatment his thin, emaciated state was interpreted as a need to be little and weak, a baby drinking only milk, out of fear that if he were strong he might hurt his hated sister. He began to assert himself with his provocative sister but reported the fear, "If I hit her in the stomach where she might have a cut, I might hurt something inside." This interchange followed considerable discussion about his aunt's pregnancy and how his sister used to irritate him when she was little. As his aggression emerged, his fear of putting on weight subsided, but he ate not a mouthful of food, nor a drop of water: just milk shakes at 7 P.M. every night. If they were not available at 7 P.M., he starved for the next twenty-four hours.

In time a prominent cannibalistic theme emerged, initially displaced onto different animals, especially rats, sharks, and lizards. A fantasied pet dragon would protect him from people who might attempt to harm him. He asked his parents for a pet iguana but was fascinated by a komodo lizard, which was 15 feet long and ate deer. He became absorbed by a series of rat movies in which the boy and the rats were friends and the rats killed and ate people who opposed him. He spent hours in the library learning about sharks and their feeding frenzies with associative linkage to cutting fish open to get at the eggs. A series of dreams emerged in which he was being killed with an ax or sawed up, ultimately leading to dreams in which "cannibals cut off people's heads and put them in a big pot and boil and eat them." Another dream: ". . . on an island and we watch cannibals chasing someone and throw a spear at him . . . pull him apart and roast the parts of his body over the fire on a spit."

This boy's fear of being fat and his need to starve arose out of multiple conflicts: repressed aggression and denial of oral destructiveness which ultimately led to cannibalistic fantasies, the need to be weak and infantile to avoid aggression and conflicts over psychosexual identification, and fears of becoming fat and pregnant. Although these conflicts are not unusual, I have not seen another patient who regressed to the point of living totally on milk shakes. Other patients curtail the quantity or modify the type of food. They will also control how, when, and where they eat. But they do not stop eating all food but milk. Usually anorexic patients are satisfied by the control over their food choice, weight level, and decreased use of their teeth. Most have difficulty eating red meat, because of the need to use their teeth, and its unconscious connection to human flesh requires its renunciation. This boy needed to renounce all use of his teeth. The preoccupation with the teeth took precedence over controlling weight. He actually gained weight on the milk shakes and did not appear distressed by it.

In searching for an explanation, I remember being struck by his intense immersion in fantasy and behavior related to ripping voraciousness. He identified with the boy in the rat movies and became totally absorbed in their destructive orgies. His involvement in the movie *Jaws* resulted in his going to the library and reading all the details of shark behavior, especially their feeding frenzies. This behavior contributed to a hypercathexis of his teeth.

Cannibalistic dreams had been present since the age of 7, often three to four weekly. It is not clear whether there were actual dreams of his cannibalizing or whether the cannibalistic dreams spawned his fantasies of it. That material never emerged directly. Only the disclaimers were volunteered. The denials were so explicit and detailed that it was clear the patient was absorbed with killing, cooking, and eating people, at a level very close to consciousness. It is also possible that his memory of his sister climbing into the clothes dryer and shutting the door could have been a distortion of a wish to have her return to the prebirth cavity or a cooking fantasy in the oven. What was most striking was the intense involvement with teeth and cannibalism, which may have accounted for the regressive inability to use his teeth.

BULIMIA

Case 5

Alma was a 17-year-old bulimic patient with a three-year history of gorging and vomiting, sometimes ten times a day. In the first consultation she stated; "Eating is my way to get out of things. If I have work to do and I can't do it, I go downstairs and eat. . . . Then I vomit. . . . Vomiting is the only thing I'm good at. No, I am good at a lot of things, but it's my evil side. When I gorge, I eat everything, even my father's dinner." It became clear in later sessions that eating her father's dinner when he arrived home late had a number of causal factors. The father was affectionate with her and attached to her, while she felt that her mother was extremely critical and punitive toward her and partial to her brother, doting upon him and infantilizing him. After describing how she ate her father's meal, she spoke about how affectionate he was and how she loved to spend time with him.

The best time of all was when they ate alone together, just the two of them. This affectionate relationship with her father, coupled with the rejection by her mother, facilitated an identification with the father. Eating brought them the closest, and eating his food symbolized her identifying and merging with him. Gorging served to unconsciously facilitate fusing with the father while consciously resulting in her fear of becoming fat.

Alma many times described her fear of obesity from gorging. She felt that the only way she could control her weight was by vomiting. On one occasion in a reflective moment, she mentioned that vomiting was letting all her feelings pour out of her. I added that the feelings came out without the words, so that she could not get into trouble. Another time she associated putting her finger down her throat in order to vomit as a sexual assault upon her body. She noted that occasionally she scratched her uvula with her fingernail and it bled, further confirming her view that it represented a sexual assault. The subsequent convulsive vomiting may well have represented a symbolic orgiastic response as well as an outpouring of unexpressed rage against the exploitation.

This gorging and vomiting alternated with extremely self-destructive behavior so characteristic of bulimics. The patient was in the habit of promiscuously picking up sexual partners who would hurt her physically during sexual activity.

SUMMARY

Clinical examples related to the fear of being fat were presented in normal, obese, starving, and gorging individuals. In each case, the conscious fear of being fat represented an attempted unconscious resolution of a series of conflicts related primarily to aspects of aggressive, sexual, and dependency problems.

In the first case, the obesity served as a protective wall in which external objects were preserved in the face of the patient's unconscious explosiveness on the one hand and simultaneously the obesity protected the patient from realistic and projected external sexual and aggressive attack. The second case used the obesity to symbolize the reliving of an unresolved pregnancy conflict, an attempt to kill her unborn child with toxemia, punishment for the wish, a denial of her father's death, and a rebirth fantasy.

In the third, the obesity was used to defy her mother, to maintain a symbiotic attachment to her, and to avoid sexual involvement. The 10-year-old boy in the fourth case starved in his flight from an unconscious identification with a pregnant woman and needed to deny unconscious cannibalistic impulses to destroy his hated sister as well as to eat her and blow up with a pregnancy. In the fifth case, major determinants in the bulemic episodes reflected an unconscious pregenital impulse to merge with the father and to act out an oedipal fantasy; the induction of vomiting represented a symbolic rape, and the vomiting itself, an outpouring of aggression and unconscious orgastic experience.

REFERENCES

Mintz, I. (1971). The anniversary reaction: a response to the unconscious sense of time. *Journal of the American Psychoanalytic Association* 19:389–398.

——— (1985a). The clinical picture of anorexia nervosa and bulimia. In *Fear of Being Fat: The Treatment of Anorexia Nervosa and Bulimia,* rev. ed., ed. C. P. Wilson, C. C. Hogan, I. L. Mintz, pp. 83–113. New York: Jason Aronson.

——— (1985b). Anorexia nervosa and bulimia in males. In *Fear of Being Fat: The Treatment of Anorexia and Bulimia,* rev. ed., ed. C. P. Wilson, C. C. Hogan, I. L. Mintz, pp. 263–303. New York: Jason Aronson.

Mintz, I. L., and Wilson, C. P. (1982). Abstaining and bulimic anorexics: two sides of the same coin. In *Primary Care,* ed. W. Steffee and S. Krey, 9:459–472. Philadelphia: Saunders.

Wilson, C. P. (1985). Contrasts in the analysis of bulimic and abstaining anorexics. In *Fear of Being Fat: The Treatment of Anorexia Nervosa and Bulimia,* rev. ed., ed. C. P. Wilson, C. C. Hogan, and I. L. Mintz, pp. 169–193. New York: Jason Aronson.

PART II

Developmental Issues

4

The Adolescent Crisis in Anorexia Nervosa

Charles C. Hogan, M.D.

Since anorexia nervosa was first described by Morton in 1689, there has been almost universal agreement that it is primarily a disease of women and usually develops during puberty and adolescence. While occasional cases do appear in earlier years or in later adult life, the vast majority are precipitated in adolescence with a reasonable minority of cases beginning in the early twenties.

In the last decade countless authors have noted that the incidence of both abstaining anorexia nervosa and bulimic anorexia has increased enormously. A statistical appraisal of the magnitude of this increase is impossible to document, but the clinical observations of psychiatrists, pediatricians, and other professional observers leave no doubt about an increase of sizable proportions. When we note a marked increase in other allied eating disorders as well, we recognize that we are dealing with a formidable problem.

It is my thesis that a phenomenal increase in the number of cases of eating disorders of an anorexic nature is due primarily to changing attitudes

111

toward sexuality in our society. The most dramatic impact of that change has been on the adolescent population.

The expectations and demands for sexual expression and participation have placed profound social pressure on all adolescents. In a particular group of young women with a specific neurotic (or occasionally psychotic) character structure, these demands are more than they can tolerate and symptoms make an early appearance.

At puberty such external stimulation and expectation give rise to overwhelming unconscious internal conflict. In all probability, the unconscious (and to some extent conscious) guilt over drives and appetites, with their accompanying unconscious fantasies, have always caused conflicts to the adolescent in every age and every society (Deutsch 1944, p. 129). In the middle-class Western world, the change in attitudes and morality in the past two decades has been enormous. Outside social pressures and temptations from the media, the adult world, and the adolescent's peers are no longer under the control of the family. Conflict leading to devastating symptoms is inevitable in a group of predisposed children.

Such a conflict over sexual and aggressive drives naturally gives rise to symptoms involving the external manifestations of their budding adult sexuality. The body image and menstrual activity are severely affected.

I believe that in the past, the more leisurely acknowledgment of sexual needs and opportunities led to a less acutely precocious neurotic resolution of conflicts. The neurosis was there, but the manifestations and symptoms came later and were of a less devastating character. Helene Deutsch (1944, pp. 129–130) was correct when she speculated: "Young people of both sexes are tormented by a feeling of insecurity, uncertainty, and inner restlessness throughout adolescence. The straight line of development to adjust itself and master reality are over and over again interrupted by the rising tide of sexuality." I also agree with her observations that a period of time, acclimation, fantasy, experiment, and development are a necessity for the asymptomatic evolution of adult sexuality in some groups of adolescents.

However, social reality is a part of contemporary reality and only time will tell what happens with this hideously destructive syndrome as future generations adapt to the changing lifestyles of our society.

Some professionals have considered other determinants as primary reasons for increased incidence of eating disorders. However, speculation on the effects of the skinny fashion model considers only the most superficial manifestations of underlying changes. Ritvo's (1986) tribute to psychoanalysis may have some relevance, but it is obviously a secondary consideration. He speculated:

> The eating disorders, with their depressive and obsessional clinical features, are in vogue today much as conversion hysteria was in vogue in the 1880s and 1890s. It is an indication of how extensively the psychoanalytic paradigm has pervaded our culture that conversion hysteria is too disingenuous a condition

to pass the sophisticated scrutiny of a generation which takes unconscious conflict for granted.

This etiological explanation is superficial; whatever sophistication is involved probably concerns a sexually "sophisticated" social milieu rather than the intellectual sophistication of today's generation. Unfortunately, emotional sophistication seems to lag far behind intellectual sophistication in the individual anorexic patient that we see today.

CLINICAL MATERIAL

The impact is sexual, and while preoedipal conflicts play a profound part in the predisposition to anorexia and bulimia, the most repressed and profound disturbances are in the sexual (oedipal) areas of unconscious development.

The most dramatic and devastating symptoms involve self-starvation of some sort, but there are less dramatic primary symptoms involving suppression, repression, and denial of the subjective experience of sexuality. The retreat from an adult sexual body image and the loss of menses are only a small part of the picture. Regardless of whether a patient goes through the motions of sexual activity or retreats to an ascetic, withdrawn existence, there is a profound inhibition of sexual sensation. *Every* patient that I have seen has been totally devoid of orgasm with sexual intercourse. I have seen a number of female patients with partial or total anesthesia of the vaginal canal. One patient in analysis, after recovering from such anesthesia, developed a depersonalization in the Jacobson (1959) sense, experiencing the vaginal canal and the inserted penis as in a space outside her body but between herself and her sexual partner. More typical states of depersonalization and derealization involving the entire self during sexual activity are commonplace phenomena in abstaining and bulimic anorexic patients (Hogan 1985a).

As I shall illustrate, early sexual activity is not infrequent in patients with eating disorders, and sexual acting out is not uncommon in bulimic patients, but when it does occur, it is merely going through the motions. In the patient's attempt to present herself as "normal," the early history and analytic hours frequently contain denials of frigidity as well as exhibitionistic descriptions of superb sexual performance. It is only as one gets into the psychoanalysis of genital sensation that the actual state of inhibition and denial becomes recognizable. (Such observations should certainly cause one to question statistical studies based on limited interviews or questionnaires. There is a great difference between the initial case history and what one discovers about a patient's subjective life after a year or two of analysis.)

Two abbreviated case histories will contribute to our understanding of this adolescent crisis. One patient was an abstaining anorexic, the other a binging bulimic patient. Both had severe body-image problems and both were amenorrheic. The histories and other details of the two adolescents are disguised to preserve anonymity. However, the symptoms, dynamics, family dynamics and conflict, and evolving changes remain faithful to the material presented by these patients during the psychoanalysis. Both have resolved their conflicts and have remained symptom-free for a number of years. One is married and has children.

CASE HISTORY: LOUISE

When Louise came to see me, I faced an attractive but very emaciated 15-year-old girl with an expressionless face and rather hollow orbital sockets enclosing apparently fearful eyes. She was 5 feet, 4 inches tall and weighed 89 pounds. This quietly determined girl had been starving herself for one year. She had had her last menstrual period sixteen months before her interview. Her irregular menstrual history extended back to the early part of her twelfth year.

Like many abstaining anorexics, Louise did not believe that she needed treatment. She claimed to be happy with her current status, except for one reservation: she felt she was too fat and was afraid of putting on weight. She had the usual almost delusional preoccupation with her self-image and saw her emaciated, pathetic figure in the mirror as disgustingly fat.

She did agree to treatment because her parents wanted her to get help. As consultations went on and she realized that she was not facing coercion or instruction, she became a willing and interested participant. However, like most psychosomatic patients, she consciously and unconsciously needed to feel in control. In the early months there was a great deal of lying. Free and spontaneous associations did not make their appearance for two years. The guarded thoughts followed consciously preconceived directions that she felt were expected by the analyst (superego projections, unconscious fragmented internalized parental imagos) (Hogan 1985b).

Family background revealed a somewhat depressed mother who had given up her own career for marriage and family. This mother had had her own bouts with overweight and had placed great emphasis on a healthful diet and avoidance of "junk foods." Mother and Louise both agreed that they had understood each other "completely" until the previous two or three years. There was a sister two years Louise's junior, who had been terribly "devoted" to Louise until the onset of the anorexia. According to the parents, Louise had been an "ideal" older sibling. This picture contrasted somewhat with material that emerged later. Nevertheless, it was acknowledged that the younger child's birth had occasioned a period of evening vomiting by the patient.

During her early latency years Louise had indulged in some covert sadistic behavior toward her sibling and her pets that was unknown to the parents.

The father had been indulgent toward the two girls when he was home, but business activities had forced him away from the family for extended periods. While the mother and father led a superficially agreeable and uneventful life together, there was ample evidence of underlying friction. The socially ambitious mother felt ill-used and deprived by the more passive, retiring husband. The family was religious, with rather strict moral values, but here there was a note of hypocrisy. After a time in treatment, Louise admitted to herself the implications of rather obvious evidence that her mother was involved in some outside sexual activity. She also acknowledged evidence of sexual dissatisfaction between the parents.

It is worth repeating that once Louise reached puberty, she rejected with embarrassment her father's interest, which she had previously coveted. He had been physically affectionate with both daughters, but she now felt angry and humiliated at any attempts on his part to hug or kiss her (Hogan 1985a, Sperling 1978).

In contrast to her grade school experience of close relationships with classmates and a moderately active social life, she became more and more reserved after entering high school. Her grades remained excellent and she related unusually well to her teachers, but she stayed apart from her peers. She and her mother spent a great deal of time together, but the relationship was no longer ostensibly satisfying. She devoted herself to endless jogging and dance activities.

After the onset of Louise's self-starvation, her mother was obviously concerned over her daughter's attempts to destroy herself and could not relate to her newfound stubborn opposition. At various times mother would try to beg, intimidate, or force the child to eat. She would frequently enlist the father's help, but to no avail. Breakfast and dinner deteriorated into bitter four-way battles. The controlling wills of mother and daughter became a focus for comments by father and sister. Mother's concern about behavior and health was matched by daughter's anger over feelings of being coerced and misunderstood. Lunch at school was a relief for Louise. There she could accompany a diet soft drink with a single piece of lettuce.

Louise rapidly established a guarded and somewhat trusting relationship with me. She switched her rather intense, defiant, childlike dependence on her mother to a dependence on her perception of the analyst. Her submission to her own conscience and to her perception of mother covered the resentful rage toward the mother's protective control and the guilt that she was able to induce. As is usual in psychoanalysis, when she stood up to mother and mother's dictates, the crisis at home worsened and the analyst took the blame. Fortunately, the parents' threats to terminate analysis never materialized.

In the early part of the analysis, interpretations followed the usual preoedipal material relating to control, self-destruction, conscience, and underlying aggression, all of which have been amply discussed in this volume and our earlier work (Wilson et al. 1985). In the transference the analyst suffered the repeated onslaughts of self-destructive rage directed at the projected introjects (Hogan 1985c). After the first year we began to examine material relating to her libidinal development. As time went on, her sadomasochistic fantasy life with all of the accompanying terror and remorse became available.

In this chapter, I will focus on the social and personal concerns as well as the behavior of this postpubescent adolescent.

As is usually the case, she assured me of her "normal" development and stated that she had been "delighted" with the onset of menstruation and breast development. As one might expect, as analysis progressed she began to volunteer reservations that seemed to amend or contradict her earlier assertions. There was the usual split between what she had internalized of mother's ostensible enthusiasm about her daughter's entry into adult life and her own anger, disgust, and humiliation associated with her sexual impulses and their bodily manifestations. She verbalized what she felt mother wanted her to feel, and for some time denied her own needs and conflicts. When during the analysis she recognized this split and tried to talk about intimate personal feelings, she was exquisitely humiliated and often disgusted with the idea of disclosing this material to herself, the analyst, or anyone else. (See Deutsch 1944 and Mintz 1985.)

There was particularly intense embarrassment connected with close emotional or physical contact with her father. This was later dramatized by her paralyzing humiliation as she tried to and finally did expose transference feelings and fantasies which led to the usual concerns of an oedipal nature.

Humiliation at the disclosure of personal sensual experience and fantasy is, of course, common to every patient in analysis, but it is particularly acute and overwhelming to patients with eating disorders and other illnesses with marked pregenital conflicts. It is defended against with various manifestations of denial, including splitting and fragmentation. In the transference, projective identification is provocatively employed in the early part of treatment to avoid acknowledgment of primitive libidinal and aggressive concerns. There is such shame over personal responsibility for such impulses and fantasies that denial by projection is necessary. This profound inhibition was evident in her behavior.

In high school she had begun to date occasionally but did not know what to do when a male friend tried to kiss her, fondle her, or even hold her hand. She wanted to be popular, but in her personal relationships with men she would find herself feeling superior, aloof, and distant, looking down on such "childish" and "animal-like behavior." She gave lip service to her sexual sophistication and interest in sexual activities, but after some time admitted to her feelings of detachment whenever such material came up in gossip with her few friends or in the media and entertainment world. It was not until she was well into treatment that she became aware of the anxiety and embarrassment associated with her own sexual impulses and curiosity. At this time she became aware of her aversion toward any real gratification of such needs. She had withdrawn from other social contacts and protected herself by establishing a close intellectual relationship with a studious young man who seemed to be equally disinterested in physical closeness.

She had become an ardent feminist. She defended her disgust with men and sexuality on the grounds of social rationalizations which always contained a kernel of truth. Unfortunately, these defenses came after the onset of the crisis. They existed in an environment that was, for her, an intensely sexual one.

As treatment evolved, she was able, with difficulty, to volunteer her humiliation and terror associated with bodily and genital responses to physical intimacy. She indicated her intense embarrassment at alluding to the subject of masturbation, despite the fact that at that time she had no conscious memory of ever having attempted such an activity. As an aside, I might add that it is terribly important to investigate the details of the where, how, when, and how much of any and all sensual experiences in these patients.

She was then able to relate her fear of being fat to her hatred of an adult female body, which was intimately associated with her fear of and hatred for her own sexual impulses and her masochistic fantasies of sexual life and pregnancy. This type of material is discussed in detail in other chapters of this volume (see also Deutsch 1944).

As this biography was revealed and her memory expanded and deepened, she recognized her fondness for those seemingly rich pastures of earlier childhood when she was not faced with the anticipation of seemingly humiliating and disruptive social pressures and temptations. She became aware of conscious wishes for a return to that remembered security where responsibility could be delegated to parental protection. She wished to submit to the idealized fragments of her superego introjects.

It was a long time before Louise became confident enough to contemplate handling her own impulses, sensations, and fantasies in a realistic manner consistent with her values and long-term wishes. However, earlier, as she began to recognize the nature of her fear of being fat and to feel the self-destructive nature of her aggression toward the parental introjects, she had tentatively begun to allow herself a little more reasonable nourishment. The fear of losing control of her appetites, herself, and her environment diminished and her menstrual periods returned, at first irregular, as before. However, she finally established the usual expected regularity of a healthy young woman.

I have neglected the description of the various defensive measures in the dynamic interplay of the transference, the difficulties with her own sexual identity, and the unconscious fantasy life.

What I should like to emphasize is the overtly sexual world in which this patient found herself. Already in latency she was intellectually acquainted with the "facts of life" and had been exposed to all sorts of sexual behavior, normal and perverse, on television and in popular literature. At puberty her newly experienced libidinal interests unconsciously and to some extent consciously erupted in an outside world of permission, temptation, and demand. To her, this life of seeming chaotic inner turmoil and the confusing environmental sexual stimulation contrasted sharply with the rather rigid, controlling, and verbally moralistic atmosphere of her home. A crisis was in the making. With all the outside sexual stimulation, she faced the tremendous difficulty of resolving her intense adolescent oedipal concerns (Hogan 1985a,b, Sperling 1978).

She found ways to withdraw and retreat from outside sexual sensation, but a split and fragmentation were necessary for her to maintain a superficial intellectual sexual sophistication while denying the guilt, humiliation, and terror associated with her own drives and fantasies. It was as though successive new walls were constructed to separate herself from this internal world as well as the world of outside temptation. An illusion of some type of control over both was necessary.

I do feel that in our patients of thirty years ago we saw adolescents fumbling through a world in which subject and peers recognized their anxiety, and preparatory playacting of necking and petting was not accompanied by the implied and explicit demands by partners and society to perform immediately. Fantasy life usually superseded any serious overt activity.

CASE HISTORY: MARGIE

Margie presented a seemingly contrasting pattern of behavior but nourished similar unconscious conflicts.

She was 17 when I first saw her in consultation. She was an outgoing if somewhat disorganized, attractive young woman. Her attractiveness would have been enhanced if she had not been trying so hard to destroy her feminine figure. Her thin, boyish frame of 5 foot 6 inches tilted the scales at about 90 pounds. Unlike Louise, she had come for treatment at her own request.

At the age of 14 Margie had given up her menstrual periods but was, of course, unaware of her unconscious need to interrupt the physical process. Shortly after this, at the suggestion of a friend, she had begun to control her weight by self-induced vomiting after meals. Like Louise, she was terrified of being fat and, no matter how emaciated she became, she appeared too fat to herself. The semi-delusional fear had been progressive after the discovery of self-induced vomiting.

Rapidly she discovered other apparent advantages in the practice of placing her hand in her mouth and eliciting a vomiting reflex with her finger. She was able to angrily indulge her previously restrained appetite by binging. Frequently she would go on a drinking spree and then evacuate her stomach contents by the same procedure. Such attacks on herself were soon accompanied by large doses of laxatives, which she felt helped keep her stomach down and which she thought prevented intestinal distention. By the time she came to see me, her body chemistry was further complicated by frequent self-abuse with diuretics. Despite her evident pride in her fantasied control over her body, she was ashamed and disgusted by all of these activities, which she could not control.

As we know, in high schools, boarding schools, and colleges, vomiting is currently a common means of weight control. While this is not a particularly attractive or healthful habit, it would appear that some adolescents are able to utilize such a practice without proceeding to extreme bulimia or anorexia. Such unpredisposed individuals are able to try it for a while and then abandon the activity in deference to esthetic and hygienic considerations. Others, like Margie, have discovered a group of symptoms that are fired by overdetermined displacements and compromise formations combining primitive cannibalistic and anal-destructive fantasies with less primitive guilt-ridden masturbatory displacements. This patient came to treatment rather desperately looking for some other means of control but felt unable to stop the binging and vomiting without help.

Margie, however, did not want to gain weight. Like many such patients, the smallest protruberance of her abdomen would elicit fears of appearing pregnant and she would run for laxatives in the hope of eliminating the bulge. When a woman attains this degree of emaciation, a very small amount of food or intestinal gas will produce a noticeable abdominal swelling, which brings on a wave of terror.

Margie's background had some resemblance to that of Louise. Her mother had been a somewhat disorganized but hearty, ambitious professional woman who had curtailed some of her activities when the children arrived. The first child was a boy, two years older than Margie. After Margie there was a sister, two years her junior. The mother, while less depressed than Louise's mother, gave evidence of depressive episodes and psychosomatic symptoms as she curtailed her professional activities. Despite her mild personal disorganization, with conscious good intentions she governed her family with the same efficiency that she manifested in her professional endeavors. She carefully supervised their behavior and food consumption. Vitamins followed always-finished servings of nourishing, well-cooked meals. Both daughters were slightly overweight during their latency years. At the time I treated Margie, the older brother seemed to have handled the situation well and there was no ostensible evidence of a serious neurotic disability. However, he had been defiant and rebellious during childhood. Margie and her sister had both seemed models of decorum and cooperation during these early years; both ended up suffering from postpubertal eating disorders. My patient was bulimic, and her younger sister was an abstaining anorexic.

Margie's father was an intellectual businessman who retired easily from family conflict, deferring family decisions to his wife. He did enjoy participating in athletic activities with his children and was proud of their athletic achievements. Like Louise's father, he fell into the pattern of frequent absences from the family and was somewhat passive in his relationship with his wife. He was particularly close to both daughters when present at family activities. He had an inclination to share marital dissatisfactions with his daughters, or at least with Margie.

As has been noted by Wilson and colleagues (1985) as well as Sours (1974), Bruch (1973), and others, such characteristics are exceedingly common in the personalities of fathers of anorexics. These authors and others, such as Sperling (1978) and Selvini Palazzoli (1978), have pointed up the conflict over control that occurs between mother and daughter in these families. For the purposes of this chapter we will oversimplify the scenario and note that the daughter seems content to ostensibly surrender the arbitration and control of her feelings, opinions, and impulses to her mother and later to her developing judgmental and somewhat primitive superego (internalized part-objects). Usually shortly after puberty, but at times later in life, she faces a crisis of potentially disruptive impulses and feelings. The denied, suppressed, and repressed anger at and defiance of the parents, particularly the mother, threatens to emerge but is in conflict with her punitive superego. She cannot tolerate the overt verbalization of hate toward her loved object. She becomes intensely sensitive to any hostile thoughts, feelings, or actions that she might entertain. Coping seems overwhelming. Such patients at first usually insist on idealizing their closeness to mother and exaggerate their deference to her in most matters. At the same time, the defiance is acted out in a refusal to eat or in binging and vomiting. Such eating disabilities often appear to the parents as little more than idiotic stubbornness. Actually they are manifestations of complicated compromise formations, combining the unconscious aggressive and sexual impulses with unconscious self-punishment.

While the family constellations were similar, Margie did differ from Louise in important ways. Margie had shown some early defiance toward the family. She had been enuretic until the age of 4. Later, during latency she had occasional uncontrollable episodes of urinary urgency. While this defiance was unconscious, the conscious innocence and anxiety anticipated helplessness and anxiety at puberty. Her strict superego demanded continuous superlative performance, but she did allow breakthroughs of aggressive and inhibited sexual impulses.

Secretly, however, she too had frequently tortured small animals and enjoyed physical domination of her younger sister during her latency years. She had been involved in some early childhood sexual experimentation with her older brother. Also, through latency Margie had a history of conscious masturbation, which is common in bulimics but less common in abstaining anorexics such as Louise.

During Margie's late prepubertal years she had tolerated some social forms of rebellion in herself. She had been provocative with some adults but not her parents. It is notable that she almost always provoked retaliation and punishment; she could not allow herself to "get away with it." At the time of menarche she ostentatiously and almost defiantly told many of the parents' friends. This exhibitionistic behavior is most unusual in young women at the onset of puberty.

Shortly after puberty her behavior deviated abruptly from the pattern we witnessed in Louise. Margie began to actually pursue dates. She was eager to know about the sexual experience of her peers. As analysis progressed, she was able to admit to attempts to seduce friends in those early adolescent years. She began sexual activity early, but it is important to note that it was only activity. She was acting out angry, defiant, rebellious needs which were intimately connected with intense curiosity about adult sexual behavior in the media and literature. She enjoyed taking the lead with the man and displaying what she felt was her superior knowledge and performance. She was involved in activity with profound unconscious conflictual implications and equally complicated social complications, involving frequent rejections and on one occasion a venereal infection. The self-punishment continued.

Margie was still the performer in other endeavors as well. She was a good student and an accomplished athlete but derived little pleasure from either activity. There was an almost total repression of sensual sexual pleasure. This reflected an obvious denial and repression of an intense oedipal conflict.

As Margie developed this biography in psychoanalysis, it became clear that this young woman's defiance of the moral dictates of her conscience was a matter of behavioral bravado. While she talked freely of her sexual activities in general behavioral terms, she avoided any discussion of sexual sensation. When it did finally begin to come to light in her experience and in the transference, such verbalizations were accompanied by exquisite humiliation and for a long time were consciously avoided. There was absolutely no genital excitement or response in all of this sexual activity, which she considered quite exotic. While she did experience some anticipatory excitement, the actual sexual experience was always an anxious, self-conscious performance, which was occasionally accompanied by episodes of depersonalization (Hogan 1985a).

Confusions about sexual identity are fairly obviously demonstrated in her behavior. The details of her envy and masculine identifications are unimportant for the purposes of this chapter.

With Margie we find a young woman who was as terrified of her own sexual impulses and needs as was Louise. For her own dynamic reasons, Margie had chosen a different way to cope with similar internal sexual conflicts. In her attempts to overcome the demands of conscience, she produced another set of conflicts that required unconscious self-punishment for the attempted indulgence of the aggressive and sexual impulses that she could not enjoy in the first place. The anatomical, physiological, social, and consciously administered self-punishments that these patients indulge in their denial of guilt are well-documented.

The actual anatomy of the adolescent crisis varies from patient to patient. Battles between parent and child, physiological debilitation, attempted self-destruction in response to perceived coercion, and other desperate maneuvers are commonplace in these young women.

CONCLUSION

As I have noted, the societal changes in contemporary Western and Japanese civilization have been precipitating factors accounting for the huge increase in middle-class adolescent patients with eating disorders.

Helene Deutsch (1944) wisely observed:

> Psychoanalysis has never denied that the social milieu is of the utmost importance, that it creates problems and determines how they are to be solved. . . . While social milieu on one hand and biological factors on the other have determining importance in relation to psychological manifestations . . . they cannot be reduced to biologic or sociological influences. There is a constant interplay of these factors. [p. x]

Deutch's first volume of *The Psychology of Women* (1944) was a brilliant and intuitive discussion of the vicissitudes of sexual development in a young woman. There she emphasizes the complexity of, and the time necessary for, the healthy resolution of conflict in the sexual evolution of the woman. She also notes the neurotic conflicts that can develop in some women with precocious interruptions in this evolution. She observes that "The 'primitive woman' who yields happily and without conflict to her sexual desires is as unknown to me as the 'primitive man.' . . . Experience teaches us that manifestations of a too great sexual freedom are not found where there is harmonious femininity" (p. 196).

In addition, she notes the following:

> The need for sublimated eroticism is so inherent in the feminine psyche that young girls who deny the necessity of a platonic love ideal and prematurely engage in sexual activity usually react to it with feelings of emptiness and disappointment. . . . Normally women strictly subordinate sensuality to the condition of love or longing for love. Sexual fantasy and the yearning for fulfillment can for a long time be more satisfactory than realization. [p. 186]

To many of today's adolescents, this sublimated eroticism is abruptly interrupted by environmental sexual pressures. The possibility of a platonic love ideal is severely compromised.

In light of our immediate discussion of eating disorders it is important to add that "the unresolved preoedipal fixations to the mother contribute . . . to the intensity of the oedipal conflict in these girls" (Sperling 1978, p. 166) and that anorexic women "defended themselves against intense adolescent oedipal attachments to the father that seemed to be the outgrowth of equally intense infantile attachments" (Hogan 1985a, p. 24). We can now understand with a little greater clarity the vulnerability of this particular segment of female society. Sperling has specifically pointed out that the "*essential* in the genesis of anorexia nervosa in adolescent girls is the revival or persistence of an intense, positive oedipal conflict during puberty and adolescence" (p. 165). Such conflicts of puberty and adolescence were certainly part and parcel of the two cases presented here, as well as of virtually all of the other patients with eating disorders that I have observed.

With such young women, a period of "sublimated eroticism" (Deutsch 1944, p. 196) is an absolute necessity to the resolution of oedipal anxieties. "Sexual fantasy and a yearning for fulfillment" with an idealized potential male partner allow a young woman with intense unconscious attachments to her father to disengage herself more leisurely and adjust to the realities of contemporary masculine companionship. The onslaught of the highly sexualized adolescent world of the last two decades is too much for such a vulnerable group to handle. Deutsch notes (p. 383) "how much woman's role in society depends upon the environment." She also states that "the cornerstones of . . . fundamental feminine characteristics are laid down during adolescence" (p. 130).

The cornerstones, or foundations, of my own conclusions are as follows.

First, in the major disturbances of young women with eating disorders, sexual conflict and inhibition are among the most prominent, if less dramatic aspects of the symptom complex. The more dramatic symptoms—suppression of menstruation, desire to return to a prepubertal body image, binging and vomiting, and self-punishment—are all compromise formations and displacements intimately related to infantile sexual fantasies and conflicts and infantile pregnancy fantasies and conflicts (oedipal concerns).

Second, as is discussed elsewhere in this book, there has been a tremendous increase in the incidence of eating disorders in the last twenty years.

Third, the clearest and most obvious change in the environment of the adolescent girl during this period has been her exposure to radical changes in sexual mores, overt sexual activity as displayed by the media, and pressure and temptation from her peers to become involved in sexual activity.

My fourth and most important cornerstone concerns the superego formation of this group of women. It is this superego that must handle drives and possible environmental gratifications. In all cases of anorexia and bulimia that I have analyzed there has first been a premature and lasting identification with numerous conflicting imagos of the parents, primarily the mother. These girls have internalized contradictory directions and taboos, and the contradictions have led to marked confusion in both sexual and aggressive spheres of fantasy and activity. The premature, somewhat chaotic superego formation has led to special difficulties in handling oedipal problems in infancy, latency, and adolescence. The chaos and fragmentation are denied by a reliance on the "good" internalized maternal imagos and an unusually involved reliance on the contemporary maternal figure. This intense dependency on parental control also extends to and is projected on companions and environment as such individuals enter adolescence.

When these women are pressured by their unconscious needs and fantasies on one hand, and a seductive, highly sexualized environment on the other, their superego handles the conflict with a number of mechanisms. It can exert obsessive reaction formations and control, resulting in a withdrawal to a somewhat ascetic existence, as we often see in the abstaining anorexic such as Louise. At the other end of the spectrum there may be an uncompromising capitulation to perceived contemporary values and activities, as is common in many counterphobic acting-out bulimics.

Most commonly we see a little of both, often alternately, as described in Chapter 6 of this volume. There is an intense need to lean for strength either on an internalized idealized conscience or on conflicting environmental stimuli which are enveloped with the projected internalized maternal imagos. When there is such an identification with a perceived environment and acting out does occur, frequently a temporary pleasure or elation comes from the illusion of a pleasing, acceptable performance. This elation is related to the reunion of the superego with the primitive ego (Lewin 1950) rather than to more mature libidinal gratifications. This reunion with unconscious internalized part-objects serves the function of denying and repressing more mature sexual experiences. The primitive reunion denies and represses oedipal needs and concerns.

To put these same conflicts in another context, we can observe that with their pregenital fixations the ability of this group to perceive themselves as separate from their objects is severely compromised. Their identification with others manifests itself in an inadequate sense of self or independence. The outside social scene is the recipient of the projection of the parental imagos. The demands of that society are experienced consciously and unconsciously in terms of repressed infantile needs and terrors. There is either a withdrawal or an attempted identification in which conformity, performance, and exhibitionism are acted out.

Such a state of affairs was clearly demonstrated by both Louise and Margie. In each, the impact of the social milieu was not apparent until the patient was well into psychoanalysis. Louise handled her need for the illusion of control by withdrawal and the search for an unthreatening contemporary adolescent love object. Margie threw herself defiantly into the perceived demanding sexual fracas with action, exhibitionism, and her usual good performance. Both succeeded in repressing and denying their sensual sexual desires with all of the accompanying oedipal concerns; both succeeded in punishing themselves for their conflicted impulses.

In patients with profound pregenital concerns, the impulses against which the superego relentlessly battles are denied and repressed early in life. In the unconscious they still retain that special quality of a demand for instant gratification. I have previously noted the following:

> The need for such primitive splitting, reversals, and denials rests on the unconscious need for immediate gratification. The impulse has not been modified and represented in the free associations [or life experience] as a wish by a mature superego, but instead has remained as a denied [unconscious] need for immediate action and gratification. [Hogan 1985b, p. 145]

The unconscious compromise formations and their oral displacements are displayed clearly in the realm of consciousness in the binging or in the reaction formations of self-starvation. In less dramatic ways we see such conflicts in other forms of acting out or in the reaction formations of asceticism.

For both Louise and Margie, on an unconscious level of psychic activity the erotic temptations and pressures of the environment were placing demands on unconscious impulses which demanded gratification. Such impulses, entwined as they were in conflict, yielded to self-destructive compromise gratifications and these vulnerable girls succumbed to illness.

The radical changes in sexual behavior, along with the freely available sexual stimulation in the media, are hailed by some observers as sexual liberation, and that may well be. Certainly the vast majority of young women are able to handle the usual adolescent conflicts without regression to anorexia or bulimia. They can, as women have in the past, integrate their own sexual interests and needs with their own conscience and maintain a reasonably integrated vision of themselves.

Parenthetically, one hopes that society itself will achieve a greater integration of its collective impulsivity with its collective conscience. A fundamentalist counterrevolution would be as fragmenting to the social structure as the severe chaotic superego is to the unhappy anorexic woman.

Yet it is a possible presumption that in generations past a young woman was able more leisurely to acquaint herself with objects of temptation and demand. Gratification was partially achieved through adolescent fantasy. With such a process of maturation, a less self-destructive, neurotic resolution of conflicts was a possible adult adjustment. It is always an error to indulge in speculations on "what would have happened if." However, I am allowing myself just such an indulgence.

I think that, without contemporary stimulation, demand, and temptation, some of our abstaining anorexics might well have gone on to obsessional neuroses or obsessional character structures. In a similar vein, some of our bulimics might have gone on to hysterical configurations in their adult lives. The sexual inhibitions would, of course, have still had to be handled either by less destructive defenses, resolution with a more leisurely life experience, or by psychoanalysis, but such a dramatic and self-destructive immediate solution to conflict might not have been necessary.

There are, of course, a few young women who have succumbed to this disease in every generation, at least since Morton's observations in 1689. It seems obvious that some will get ill in any adolescent environment. It must also be emphasized that the vast majority of young women do not succumb to illness but maintain a reasonably healthy, if conflicted, relationship with reality in our present-day adolescent society.

I have attempted to demonstrate that the dramatic symptomatology of anorexia and bulimia are superficial but profoundly self-destructive compromise formations which involve pregenital regressions. Such behaviors, which involve defensive sadomachochistic acting out, are available to this group of perhaps genetically predisposed patients because of conflicts over their early relationships with the primary object or its surrogate. The cause can be incidental exposure to early trauma, or conflicts with or defects in, this relationship with the primary object.

As development proceeds, from the psychoanalytic perspective, we find

deeper and denied problems over what the patient perceives as an inability
to control the primitive aggressive and sexual impulses in the phantasied
oedipal spheres of relationships. This is more immediately experienced in
the reflection of such conflicts in the relationships with one's peers.

SUMMARY

A proposition is presented that the leading precipitating factors causing
the vast increase in abstaining and bulimic anorexics today are the rapidly
and dramatically changing sexual codes of conduct in contemporary
adolescent society.

The abbreviated case histories presented here are intended to illustrate
the overwhelming influence of peer pressure, peer temptations, and media
exposure in a certain group of predisposed women in their adolescent
years. I believe that such factors lead to a premature eruption of neurotic
(or at times psychotic) conflict in this unhappy group of vulnerable
women, giving rise to symptomatic abstaining or bulimic anorexia nervosa.

In this chapter I have indulged in some perhaps loose speculation of
"what would have happened if." Such speculation may lead one to the
conclusion that, in past generations, more leisurely and less dramatic
self-destructive neurotic resolution of conflict might have been possible.

REFERENCES

Bruch, H. (1973). *Eating Disorders: Obesity, Anorexia Nervosa, and the Person Within.* New
    York: Basic Books.
Deutsch, H. (1944). *The Psychology of Women: A Psychoanalytic Interpretation.* Vol. I. New
    York: Grune & Stratton.
Hogan, C. (1985a). Psychodynamics. In *Fear of Being Fat: The Treatment of Anorexia
    Nervosa and Bulimia,* rev. ed., ed. C. P. Wilson, C. C. Hogan, and I. L. Mintz, pp. 115–128.
    New York: Jason Aronson.
_____ (1985b). Object relations. In *Fear of Being Fat: The Treatment of Anorexia Nervosa
    and Bulimia,* rev. ed., ed. C. P. Wilson, C. C. Hogan, and I. L. Mintz, pp. 129–149. New
    York: Jason Aronson.
_____ (1985c). Transference. In *Fear of Being Fat: The Treatment of Anorexia Nervosa and
    Bulimia,* rev. ed., ed. C. P. Wilson, C. C. Hogan, and I. L. Mintz, pp. 153–168. New York:
    Jason Aronson.
_____ (1985d). Technical problems. In *Fear of Being Fat: The Treatment of Anorexia
    Nervosa and Bulimia,* rev. ed., ed. C. P. Wilson, C. C. Hogan, and I. L. Mintz, pp. 197–216.
    New York: Jason Aronson.
Jacobson, E. (1959). Depersonalization. *Journal of the American Psychoanalytic Association*
    7:581–610.
Lewin, B. (1950). *The Psychoanalysis of Elation.* New York: Norton.
Mintz, I. (1985). The relationship between self-starvation and amenorrhea. In *Fear of Being
    Fat: The Treatment of Anorexia Nervosa and Bulimia,* rev. ed., ed. C. P. Wilson, C. C.
    Hogan, and I. L. Mintz, pp. 335–344. New York: Jason Aronson.
Morton, R. (1689). *Pathisologica or a Treatise on Consumption.* London: Smith and
    Walford.

Ritvo, S. (1986). *Eating disorders and female adolescent development with special reference to distortions in the body image.* Winter Meeting, American Psychoanalytic Association, Seminar on Psychoanalytic Treatment of Patients with Psychosomatic Disorders, New York, December 17.

Selvini Palazzoli, M. (1978). *Self-Starvation: From Individual to Family Therapy in the Treatment of Anorexia Nervosa.* New York: Jason Aronson.

Sours, J. (1974). The anorexia nervosa syndrome. *International Journal of Psycho-Analysis* 55:567–576.

Sperling, M. (1978). Anorexia nervosa (Part 4). In *Psychosomatic Disorders in Childhood,* ed. O. Sperling, pp. 129–173. New York: Jason Aronson.

Wilson, C. P., Hogan, C. C., and Mintz, I. L. (1985). *Fear of Being Fat: The Treatment of Anorexia Nervosa and Bulimia.* Rev. ed. New York: Jason Aronson.

5

Sexual Identifications in Anorexia Nervosa

Charles C. Hogan, M.D.

Some patients with eating disorders use fantasies of masculine identification in their defensive maneuvers against the perceived inferiority, humiliation, and vulnerability of their feminine position and their feminine needs. The most prominent aspects of the clinical material presented in this chapter illustrate split-off ego states that are almost conscious self-presentations involving masculine identifications in the contexts of both the transference and life experience.

Fantasies of identification may be discernible as rather obvious ego states such as those demonstrated in the major clinical presentations in this chapter or as more subtle threads of masculine fantasy participating in character traits, in personality configurations, or as part of symptom complexes.

In this chapter the term *identification* is used in the sense that Freud used it, to refer generally to those processes that internalize previous external regulations. I do not subscribe to the more formal separations of authors, such as Schafer (1968, pp. 16, 21), who differentiate terms such as *introjection* from terms such as *assimilation.* Clinically the amalgams make such differentiation impossible.

I want to correct here what I feel was an error in an earlier publication of mine (1985d, p. 209). It may be worthwhile to speculate briefly on what may have contributed to such an error. In the first edition (1983), as well as the 1985 edition, I stated, "Of four anorexic analysands who shoplifted in a manner reminiscent of kleptomania, only one evidenced over-whelming phallic connections." I was relieved that I had included the word "overwhelming." It saved me from what I feel would have been a tremendous oversight. Nevertheless, I do believe that there was a scotoma that altered somewhat my perceptions in those earlier cases.

Since treating those cases (some go back thirty years), and after much broader experience with a larger patient population, I have seen the symptom of stealing or kleptomania in a number of them. It is a common symptom in bulimic anorexics and a not-uncommon one in abstaining anorexics. In all of my more recent patients the phallic content of the associated fantasies of acquisition, internalization, and control has been clear. I shall illustrate this in one patient, Amelia, who also demonstrated the more dramatic split-off masculine ego state.

I refer to this correction because I feel that with patients with eating disorders, discerning observers are so impressed with the acting out, the oral envy, and the angry conflicts over primitive entitlement that they are wont to neglect the more repressed but equally important phallic and oedipal concerns. The neglect of sexuality is very common in the literature on eating disorders. One of many examples was noted by Sperling (1978, p. 136) in her review of the work of Selvini Palazzoli (1978). She concluded, "There is hardly any mention of sexual conflicts, masturbation, and sexual identifications."

It is easy to identify in patients with primitive defenses the protestations of victimization by the primary object and the primitive battle over separation from this object. These omnipresent, often fragmented, inter-nalized maternal imagos were of cardinal interest to me in those early studies and they, of course, continue to interest me. This interest perhaps allowed the exclusion of more subtle dynamic problems of gender identity and available oedipal concerns. It is, after all, the fears and anger involving these conflicts from which the ego flees as it establishes and utilizes available dyadic defenses. In any event, these patients did well nevertheless and are without symptoms years later.

In the following examples the recognition and interpretation of defen-sive fantasies of masculine identification might easily be neglected in light of the primitive pregenital nature and content of their presentation. In all of the major examples there is splitting and at times fragmentation. The primitive rage is easy to interpret as a reaction to primitive fantasies of entitlement. The important, more mature conflicts over gender and oe-dipal concerns could easily be overlooked to the detriment of the analysis of a patient. The psychoanalysis of the underlying oedipal material would certainly be prolonged.

REVIEW OF SEXUALITY AND ITS PREGENITAL DETERMINANTS IN EATING DISORDERS

An intense conflict over emerging adult sexuality seems to be universally present in eating disorders. Sperling (1978, p. 165) felt that the "dynamic factor . . . essential in the genesis of anorexia nervosa in adolescent girls is the revival or persistence of an intense positive oedipal conflict during puberty and adolescence." I have agreed (Hogan 1985b, p. 29); all of my patients "defended themselves against intense oedipal attachments to the father which seemed to be the outgrowth of equally intense infantile attachments." In addition I have noted (1985a, p. 123, and elsewhere) the repression of sexual response in abstaining and bulimic anorexics: "None of my anorexic patients were orgastic in intercourse. Anna and Betty, although vaginally anesthetic when they began treatment, feigned interest in sexual activity and regularly acted it out. . . . Deborah, who was a virgin, could not remember ever achieving an orgastic response from her frequent masturbatory activity."

The various pregenital regressive maneuvers and the primitive object relations of such patients in life experience and in the transference were well documented in an earlier volume (Wilson et al. 1985). Multiple facets of the flight from adult sexuality and the accompanying defenses have been described (Fenichel 1945a, Gero 1953, Hogan 1985a, Masserman 1941, Mintz 1985c, Moulton 1942, Sperling 1953, 1968, 1978, Thomä 1967, Waller et al. 1940, Wilson, 1985a,b, and many others).

On the deepest level, the manner in which this regression can involve conflict around primitive sadistic and masochistic concerns on the most primitive cannibalistic oral and anal levels has been noted by such authors as Fenichel (1945a), Sperling (1953, 1968, 1978), Selvini Palazzoli (1978), Volkan (1965, 1976), Thomä (1967), Masterson (1977), Hogan (1985a,b,c,d), Wilson (1985a,b), Mintz (1985b), and Ritvo (1986).

The mechanisms involved in these defensive maneuvers involving splitting and fragmentation, both dependent on internalization of part-objects and the subsequent projection of these onto contemporary object perceptions, have been described by Volkan (1965, 1976), Thomä (1967), and Hogan (1985b,c,d).

Psychoanalytic authors have devoted a great deal of interest to the primitive defense mechanisms cited above, but as Sperling (1978) and Hogan (1985 and elsewhere in this volume) have observed, the precipitating situation involves coping with conflicts over sexual drives, their accompanying fantasies, and outside stimulation. This is reflected in specific conflicts over sexual identity.

Some important cautionary observations have been made about the treatment of these patients by Wilson and colleagues (1985) as well as by other psychoanalysts. In general, these observers have noted that one should avoid interpreting sexual and oedipal material until the more primitive defenses have been interpreted and analyzed.

The more mature but strictly repressed and denied triadic phallic and oedipal material is so amalgamated with the preoedipal fantasies that it can at times disorganize and fragment the patient's ego to the point of panic and rejection of treatment on one hand, or total emotional withdrawal (so-called alexithymia) on the other hand. Usually it is important for such patients to have some understanding of the genesis of these primitive components of their fantasy life in order to deal with their infantile sexual and oedipal wishes.

In our other publications, as well as in studies by other psychoanalysts, a roughly hewn hierarchy of interpretation has been presented. First the analyst clarifies with the patient his or her feelings of shame, guilt, and fear surrounding any angry impulses. In short, one interprets the superego and its masochistic derivatives of aggression in these early phases of psychoanalysis. Then, as these self-destructive aspects of personality become clear, the underlying anger with its oral sadistic fantasies are available for study in the life experience of the patient and in the transference relationship. In turn, as such defenses are consciously acknowledged, the accompanying, and underlying phallic and oedipal concerns make their appearance and can be handled.

By this time the primary symptoms have usually cleared, but the transference neurosis is there to be analyzed.

Such a neat hierarchy of interpretations is not always appropriate. A rule has no meaning unless one notes its exceptions. Especially in a complicated procedure such as psychoanalysis, there are no universal solutions. Thus it is frequently advisable to interpret problems of sexual identity and oedipal interests early in treatment, when such material is presented in the transference or in life experiences.

CLINICAL MATERIAL ON PROBLEMS OF SEXUAL IDENTITY

Since the presentation of my observations in *Fear of Being Fat* in 1983 and 1985, I have completed the further analysis and psychoanalytic psychotherapy with a number of other young women with eating disorders. Several of these had problems with kleptomania, and the content of their fantasies about the stolen articles generally involved phallic determinants. With the exception of one case, Amelia, I will not focus on kleptomania since I would like to direct our interest to a wider view of the problems of sexual identity in anorexic patients.

In the following pages, four rather unique patients are discussed: Amelia, Beth, Claire, and Daphne. All of these women presented a clearly discernible split in their personality configurations early in treatment, exposing delineated, identifiable fantasies of masculine identification. I shall not go into detail about Daphne since she is just beginning her second year of psychoanalysis. However, I will go into particular detail with Amelia, inasmuch as she was also a kleptomaniac and some of the phallic dynamics of her stealing will be of particular interest to the reader.

We have noted that one common finding in the family backgrounds of patients with eating disorders is a passive and/or frequently absent father (Bruch 1970, 1973, Hogan 1985a,b, Sours 1974, Sperling 1978, Wilson 1985b). In all of these four cases the women have had fathers who seemed to show some modification of this pattern. This difference accounts for the demonstrable dramatic presentation of disturbances in sexual identity early in treatment. The fathers of all four were passive and unusually affectionate toward their daughters in infancy, latency, and adolescence. Each would revert frequently to a (perhaps defensive) form of angry, authoritative, and contemptuous behavior pattern toward their wives and occasionally toward their daughters. One father's rages verged on paranoia. Such regression to rage has not been common in the fathers of other anorexic patients whom I have observed.

As I have indicated (Hogan 1985d, p. 215), "The vast majority [of patients with eating disorders] are clearly utilizing defensive regressions from a traditional oedipal conflict with an accompanying transference neurosis. . . ." As one is dealing with problems in sexual identity (Hogan 1985b), the pregenital defenses such as splitting and fragmentation are utilized in the presentations of gender conflict.

Amelia

She was a 26-year-old bulimic patient who had been an abstaining anorexic since the age of 17. Binging and bulimia became evident at college in her early twenties, at which time she also began "acting out." The acting out included repeated episodes of stealing.

Early in treatment she recognized certain defined periods in which she would give up the bulimia and return to abstinence to control weight. At such times she was physically and professionally very active, felt confident, and was able to deny needs for excessive social contact, excessive use of alcohol, and cigarettes. Also during these intervals she had little interest in more than casual contacts with men.

With a dramatic change in personality, she would abruptly go into other periods. She would become seriously involved in an aggressive, dependent relationship with a man and retreat to a binging, bulimic existence dominated by smoking, drinking, social activity, late hours, and a retreat from her professional and athletic life. At such times she felt like "a mess." During such episodes she acted out masochistic and sadistic impulses.

In the transference, the controlled periods of abstinence were accompanied by a rather superior, contemptuous attitude, when she had few dreams and withheld information in an almost provocative manner. She would proclaim her health in all areas except for her dissatisfaction with her weight. As a matter of fact, she appeared to function quite well in most of her activities but was obviously hyperactive. During such periods, she enjoyed competing with, and arguing with, her professional colleagues. She would often make disparaging comments about males and their abilities, contradicted at other moments with discussions of the pathetic inferiority of most females.

Very early in treatment I interpreted her "confidence" and "health" as defensive and noted that her posture reminded me of her descriptions of her father, who was aloof and contemptuous of her mother and was a competitive achiever in business and athletics. It was not long before she agreed, describing her own contempt for her disorganized, alcoholic, controlling mother. As the rage emerged toward the mother, a flood of other material became available. Such controlled behavior did get her father's approval, but she could use it to provoke him to rage when she combined it with too much moral superiority. She had a conscious envy of his apparent power and reserve, which contrasted with mother's contradictory commands and defensiveness. For example, her father did not drink or smoke; her mother did both.

Analytic material led to deeper feelings of phallic envy and disgust with the female body in much the same way described by Mintz (1985c, p. 341): "While on one level the weight loss represented the loss of feminine curves and conflict over feminine identity, on a deeper level it seemed to symbolize the loss of multiple penises . . . which stemmed from unresolved penis envy."

In her bulimic periods she was sporadically obsessed with her conscious anger and envy of the man she was going with, her ambivalence toward him as a mother surrogate, and her contempt for her own identification with mother. She frequently felt the male was taking advantage of her sexually, socially, and personally. There was no feeling of controlled superiority at these times. Her anger was in response to her fear of potential humiliation and to her vulnerability.

I can perhaps illustrate some of the more subtle manifestations of Amelia's conflict over sexual identity. I return to my original speculations over kleptomania in these patients.

During a bulimic period, when Amelia was involved with this desirable young man, she indulged in stealing an object (under potentially dangerous circumstances) from a department store. When I questioned her, she first associated to a battle with her controlling, disorganized mother, who was pushing the romance. She regretted her self-indulgence in taking gifts from her. She resented the dependency and, with little logic, described the elation that she felt when taking what she wanted herself and not depending on mother. This short period of elation was not unlike the more prolonged controlled periods of confidence already described.

The following hour she brought in a dream:

She was with her mother, and her mother was berating her for not taking proper medical care of her mouth. (The patient described a pathological condition or deformity that was something like a cleft palate.) She defended herself by pointing out that she was seeing a doctor. Mother roughly accused her of leaving the doctor whom she had recommended and of not using the

remedial appliance prescribed to keep the defect closed. The patient replied
with an angry diatribe about how mother allowed the condition to occur in
the first place and reiterated her own certainty that her present physician
could cure this defect. Then each retreated from the other in silent, smolder-
ing, stubborn rages (as was characteristic of the two since the patient's
adolescence).

Associations first went to braces on her teeth during latency and then to
transference material. Her mother actually hated the psychoanalyst and
continually tried to interfere with treatment. Amelia had some kindly
associations to her somewhat overbearing yet passive father for allowing
her to maintain the analysis. She referred to the stolen item as she recalled
that the father did "take what he wanted." She had always alternated
between respecting his integrity and questioning his honesty.

She also associated to reconstruction work that had been completed on
her boyfriend's teeth and what a good job had been done. She went on to
her ambivalent feelings toward this man, who was having difficulties with
his career but who came from a prominent family. She speculated on how
both aspects played a part in her interest in him. She despised herself for
wanting his family's social status to enhance her own image. She was also
ashamed of the pleasure and superiority she experienced when he talked of
his career difficulties. The masculine and phallic connections are obvious
and were volunteered or acknowledged.

I should note that the stolen article was a scarf that she intended to wear
to a family gathering of her boyfriend. She felt that it was just the thing to
complete her outfit, where "something had been missing." The scarf,
incidentally, was green, which she spontaneously associated with envy.

I will not emphasize her numerous associations to her envy of her father,
of the analyst, and of her male friend. The symbolization and displacement
of her perceived castration are obvious. Her revulsion at the identification
with her "crazy" (castrated) mother was at times conscious. The stolen
scarf temporarily seemed to fill all the gaps. She did not question the phallic
interpretation of this pilfered symbol.

Briefly I note the progress of Amelia's analysis only because, even during
periods of her most "masculine" control, she occasionally volunteered a
fragmentary perception of libidinal interest in her father. Describing the
provocative battle with him, she associated to similar rituals in her early
childhood with some understanding of the excitement involved. Some
mild early interpretation of oedipal interests was almost demanded. As one
might anticipate, these sadomasochistic battles represented rather intense
genital interest in the father on a deeper oedipal level which emerged at a
later date.

However, as with the other three patients, at the earlier stage and level
of treatment, there was a regression to an apparent splitting between rather
clearly demarcated contradictory personality patterns. In all of these
young women there was a fantasied "masculine" personality which represented power and control, as opposed to the patient's "feminine" self
which experienced painful fantasies of humiliation and vulnerability.

Beth

In this case of a 19-year-old abstaining anorexic, there was the usual need to control the analysis early in treatment. She avoided free association and all references to bodily or sexual sensations other than feelings of being fat.

It was clear that when any sense of vulnerability or humiliation seemed to be overwhelming, she would become defensive. At a particularly disturbing point in the analysis, this usually ostensibly cooperative, submissive patient became transformed into what seemed to be a different personality. She became overbearingly angry. With almost paranoid accusations she raised her voice to vindictive sarcasm. She swore at me and derided treatment. It was such a startling transformation that with its first appearance I had no idea how to interpret the situation and had some temporary doubt about my diagnostic impressions. At this time and in later episodes she would often sit up on the couch and stare me straight in the eye.

As this dramatic change continued into the second session, I interpreted that she sounded exactly like the occasionally angry father whom she had described. In his rages he would talk of blood and violence, thus intimidating the wife and frightening the children. I went further and suggested that such a show of anger and contempt might make her feel strong and powerful. After the second such interpretation, she agreed and produced confirmatory information.

Beth said that it gave her a feeling of power and control that she attributed to her father. As time went on, she said that when she was able to "cross the barrier" and really get angry, she felt confident and almost invulnerable. The shame and humiliation that precipitated such a split just disappeared. She volunteered that at these times the reality of outside justification became unimportant, but the feeling of power and omnipotence was all that counted. In most cases, however, she needed a modicum of outside justification for the rage. This material became available as she repeated such a behavioral transformation many times.

Dreams revealed a clear body-phallus identification, but I shall not trace the further subtle elaborations of her envy and fear of the father, his penis, and his rages. We finally discovered that this split-off fragment of powerful action did date from a battle between the parents which roughly coincided with the birth of a sibling. The memory of this battle probably screened a primal scene experience. As she improved in analysis, her total personality took on some of this aggressive, assertive quality, but in a far more controlled way. She became a personally ambitious achiever who was able to succeed without great inhibition.

Claire

She was a 21-year-old bulimic who had been through hospitalizations, drug treatment, supportive psychotherapy, and more. In all of the information I received from earlier records, there was no evidence of behavior other than a quiet obedience to prescribed rituals. The only defiance was in her symptoms.

Her father was an almost paranoid businessman who showed contempt for his (probably anorexic) wife but who had lavished affection on and idealized his daughters in their earlier years. He remained overtly physically affectionate toward them during adolescence but did assert a rather authoritative, judgmental control. The mother exerted her only control in a masochistic, guilt-provoking manner which could be quite devastating.

Claire herself demonstrated mild paranoid traits in her quiet suspicions of others' motives. Beneath her obsequiousness she revealed rather extreme feelings (even for an anorexic) of unchallengeable superiority in intellectual and academic ability, as well as, with certain reservations, beauty. This mild grandiosity alternated with periods of feeling worthless, stupid, and ugly when facing unknown competition or when feeling envious of someone she admired or respected. Such material was available, but socially she retreated into herself, trying to avoid feelings of shame and anger associated with competition. There was nothing in her contrite behavior to prepare me for the following.

After my first long absence (a summer vacation), I returned to find a surprisingly angry, haughty, imperious woman, well-dressed in a tailored outfit, who entered the room with her head held high. She stared at me with an unblinking gaze. This was in contrast to the casually, often sloppily dressed, shy creature of the previous year, who had averted her eyes and held her hand over her mouth as she giggled in embarrassment. She was furious. There followed sessions that were almost completely silent except for a few sarcastic comments. She would attempt to turn any question or comment back on the analyst: "You should know, you are the doctor," and similar remarks.

As with Amelia and Beth, I pointed out that this rather dramatic presentation of her anger seemed to replicate her descriptions of her father's behavior. She would acknowledge the identity but did not give up the defense for about six weeks. As subjective material slowly became available, she revealed that the previous winter she had moved to be near my office and she fantasied that I had punished her with my desertion. (I had moved my office during the summer vacation.) She also let me know that during early adolescence she could provoke her father to rages by indulging in such behavior. At those times she felt in complete control. Sometimes she had consciously felt as though she were her father when her mother would try to ingratiate herself or wheedle Claire out of her stormy silence. As long as she could keep it up, she felt no shame or fear and projected her own embarrassed feelings of the supplicant onto her perceived antagonist, in this case the analyst. As the defense began to break down, she would speculate on how uncomfortable it must be for me. She thought that I must feel humiliated and infuriated when I could not control her behavior or thoughts. Here was a clear projection of her own feelings of humiliation. It was only after she gave up the imperious arrogance, which in the end became more of a playful pretense, that I found out that she had not indulged in her binging and bulimia during that period of self-assertion.

Claire's analysis was stormy. She had rather intense, sometimes conscious attachments to her father, whom she associated with her primitive sadistic fantasies. These fantasies were also derived from more primitive maternal introjects, which were accompanied by tremendous guilt and shame, reinforced in part by her fantasied triumph over mother in her oedipal struggle. On a conscious level, the fantasies remained for some time masculine and phallic in nature.

She admitted to having had conscious fantasies of cutting off, or biting off, the penis of almost every man with whom she had been involved, as a punishment for any and all perceived embarrassments. The sadism, extreme masculine envy, and her bulimic anorexia were resolved when she worked through her intense ambivalent fantasied oedipal relationship with her father. She had dreams of overt sexual activity with her father later in the analysis.

Daphne

There is little to say about Daphne, who is in an early phase of treatment, except for the observation that she too has a split-off "masculine" fragment of her personality, which she can call up when she feels vulnerable. Her fantasies of masculinity provide a feeling of power and elation. As yet I do not have material indicating whether or not there is a lessening or relief of symptoms during such periods of perceived control and power.

DISCUSSION

The foregoing clinical material presents a rather dramatic picture of the defensive utilization of partially conscious masculine identifications to avoid feelings of vulnerability and humiliation. These identifications also provided ego-acceptable vehicles for the verbalization and discharge of derivatives of primitive oral aggression. For three of these patients, during the time that they felt justified in maintaining such a stance, there was a remarkable amelioration of the symptoms of bulimia and/or abstinence. In no case, however, did the patient give up her obsessive preoccupation with her perception of her body image, despite her control over other symptoms.

Parenthetically, in these cases an exception was made to the usual practice of avoiding interpretations of sexual, oedipal, or gender confusion early in the treatment of eating disturbances. The analytic material begged for early interpretations of masculine identifications. The patient's acknowledgement of the feeling of confidence and strength in every case led to early discussion of fantasies of penis envy and masculine control. One example is Claire, who rather rapidly disclosed masturbatory fantasies of dancing nude or seminude in front of a group of men and feeling elated as she was able to see her control over their erections. At other times, she consciously fantasized her clitoris as a phallus. Her major pleasure in sexual activity was the demonstration of her control over her partner's penis.

It is important to be cautious of oedipal, sexual, or gender confusion interpretations early in the treatment of patients with marked pregenital regressions. However, when this material presents itself, it must be handled directly.

Amelia, Beth, and Claire were unique also in that they were *consciously* aware early in treatment of the threats they felt from their fathers' physical interests during adolescence; and they were frightened by their abilities to control their fathers with their seductiveness. They frequently handled their shame over this behavior by projections of a general "dirty old man" on the father and on the transference object. Another patient, who was discussed in an earlier book (Hogan 1985c), was certain that if she spoke of her sexual fantasies the analyst would succumb. Still another patient (Hogan 1985c) would go into elaborate fellatio transference fantasies, which soon revealed themselves to be attempts to seduce the analyst as a matter of control. There was no sexual excitement consciously involved. These and other similar projections and fantasied seductions always evolved into bisexual productions. The apparent feminine seduction was experienced as a position of masculine control and was a defense against the unconsciously perceived vulnerability and shame of female sexual excitement and submission.

I am omitting here more primitive determinants that also played a role in the amalgam. The internalized maternal sadistic part-object representation frequently appears as a precursor to the idealized phallic image. The humiliation of wanting a rejecting mother and breast predates and intensifies the shame of sexual sensation and need, with its implied submission and possible rejection.

A similar aspect of the masculine identification that was particularly apparent in the case material above, as well as in other eating-disorder cases, was well described by Sperling. She writes:

Penis envy and the competition with men in these patients is not so much prompted by the wish to please mother as a male as some investigators have assumed . . . but that it resulted from the wish to possess and to control mother sexually, as father does. Father's sexual power and control over mother are attributed by the patient to his having a penis. In all other areas the father and males are usually devalued by the family of such a patient. In the patient's mind the penis becomes the symbol for ultimate control over the mother. [1978, p. 165]

I would add that I had access to the rather extensive notes by Sperling that were the basis for her 1978 publication. Above and beyond the deeper level of penis envy, she called attention to the more superficial fantasy of identification with the father's occasional total control of the mother. This identification with father's power was apparent in the clinical material above. The feeling of control was conscious. The phallic roots appeared only after months of associations in some cases. Parenthetically, the devaluation of the father that Sperling refers to above is frequently part of a shared mother–daughter fantasy of phallic identification.

The patient's rejection of her own sexuality is also seen in the primary symptoms and body image problems of the abstaining or bulimic anorexic. Numerous authors have demonstrated the retreat from a sexually seductive body to a prepubertal figure. The suppression of the menses as a primary neurotic symptom rather than a secondary response to weight loss has been observed repeatedly (Hogan 1985a, Mintz 1985a, Sperling 1978, Thomä 1967, and many others). My own (1985a, p. 123) observations, confirmed by others, disclosed a uniform absence of orgastic response with intercourse and frequently total anesthesia of the vaginal canal, often to the point where the patient is unaware of an inserted penis.

The patient's rejection of her own sexuality is accompanied by gender confusion and masculine fantasies concerning the body image. I have noted the phallic meaning of the breastless sticklike figure (Hogan 1985a,b). Mintz (1985a) has noted the following:

> On an unconscious level the loss of bodily tissue can represent the manifestations of a conflict over psychosexual identity. Many of the girls unconsciously would prefer to be a boy, and their ambivalence about their sexual identity takes the form of the desire to lose body tissue that unconsciously represents the displaced penis. [p. 93]

Ritvo (1986) discussed the conscious desire to avoid the physical identification with ". . . the mature curved female form—the hated mother's body." Countless such references to the bisexual confusion in the body image are available in the psychoanalytic literature. I could add to Mintz's (1985a) observations above by noting that I have had three patients who did not just "unconsciously" wish to be a boy but came into treatment consciously wishing that they were male and feeling that nature and fate had cheated them of the opportunity. Of course, at a later date we discovered that "nature" and "fate" represented the internalized representation of mother.

In regard to acting-out patients professing pride in their femininity, one must note that despite the claim of many of these women that they desire an attractive female body, there are complicated problems of gender identity as they retreat from oedipal temptation. Despite the counterphobic behavior of many of these bulimics as they act out sexual performance (Hogan, 1985a,b,c,d, and Chapter 5 of this volume), they are covering an equally intense fear of sexual excitation. Sexual excitement and desire represent vulnerability and humiliation. Among such bulimics, counterphobic behavior has many determinants. One of the most important is an unconscious masculine identification with the fantasy of control.

This was clearly demonstrated in Claire's pleasure in controlling men's erections.

While in general one concentrates on the masochistic derivatives of aggression in the early interpretations in the psychoanalysis of eating disorders, there are also occasions where early interpretations of difficulties in sexual identity are a necessity when the material presents itself. This is particularly true in transference situations.

It should be emphasized again that while eating disorders present rather dramatic behavioral symptoms, these are only derivative surface demonstrations of complex neurotic disorders. The majority of these patients can be treated with psychoanalysis or psychoanalytic psychotherapy. A mutual discovery by patient and analyst of the lifelong evolution of conflicts and defenses with their resolution, although sometimes trying, is of utmost importance to the patient's ultimate well-being. The resolution of a woman's struggle with sexual identity is no small part of her adjustment to, and pleasure in, the world around her.

SUMMARY

This chapter addressed certain problems of gender confusion and sexual identity in the life histories of abstaining and bulimic anorexic patients.

In all such cases there is a retreat from adolescent oedipal conflicts and sexual impulses to various points of regression and/or fixation. These include profound problems in the experience of sexual identity.

The four cases presented were unique in having apparent split-off areas of masculine identification that were overtly used defensively both in life and in the transference. The uniqueness was also apparent in the availability of the material to consciousness after early interpretation. The discussion of these cases included the defensive, controlling nature of the masculine identifications and the problems of gender identification in the body image conflicts of such patients.

REFERENCES

Bruch, H. (1965). Anorexia nervosa and its differential diagnosis. *Journal of Nervous and Mental Disease* 141:555–566.

_____ (1970). Psychotherapy in primary anorexia nervosa. *Journal of Nervous and Mental Disease* 150:51–67.

_____ (1973). *Eating Disorders: Obesity, Anorexia Nervosa, and the Person Within.* New York: Basic Books.

Fenichel, O. (1945a) Anorexia. In *The Collected Papers of Otto Fenichel,* ed. H. Fenichel, pp. 296–304. New York: Norton, 1954.

_____ (1945b). *The Psychoanalytic Theory of Neurosis.* New York: Norton.

Gero, G. (1953). An equivalent of depression: anorexia. In *Affective Disorders: Psychoanalytic Contributions to their Study,* ed. P. Greenacre, pp. 117–189. New York: International Universities Press.

142   Charles C. Hogan, M.D.

Hogan, C. C. (1985a). Psychodynamics. In *Fear of Being Fat: The Treatment of Anorexia Nervosa and Bulimia,* rev. ed., ed. C. P. Wilson, C. C. Hogan, and I. L. Mintz, pp. 115–128. New York: Jason Aronson.

―――― (1985b). Object relations. In *Fear of Being Fat: The Treatment of Anorexia Nervosa and Bulimia,* rev. ed., ed. C. P. Wilson, C. C. Hogan, and I. L. Mintz, pp. 129–149. New York: Jason Aronson.

―――― (1985c). Transference. In *Fear of Being Fat: The Treatment of Anorexia Nervosa and Bulimia,* rev. ed., ed. C. P. Wilson, C. C. Hogan, and I. L. Mintz, pp. 153–168. New York: Jason Aronson.

―――― (1985d). Technical problems. In *Fear of Being Fat: The Treatment of Anorexia Nervosa and Bulimia,* rev. ed., ed. C. P. Wilson, C. C. Hogan, and I. L. Mintz, pp. 197–216. New York: Jason Aronson.

Masserman, J. H. (1941). Psychodynamics in anorexia nervosa and neurotic vomiting. *Psychoanalytic Quarterly* 10:211–242.

Masterson, J. (1977). Primal anorexia nervosa in the borderline adolescent—an object relations view. In *Borderline Personality Disorders: The Concept, the Syndrome, the Patient,* ed. P. Harticollis, pp. 475–494. New York: International Universities Press.

Mintz, I. L. (1985a). Psychoanalytic description: the clinical picture of anorexia nervosa and bulimia. In *Fear of Being Fat: The Treatment of Anorexia Nervosa and Bulimia,* rev. ed., ed. C. P. Wilson, C. C. Hogan, and I. L. Mintz, pp. 83–114. New York: Jason Aronson.

―――― (1985b). Psychoanalytic therapy of severe anorexia: the case of Jeanette. In *Fear of Being Fat: The Treatment of Anorexia Nervosa and Bulimia,* rev. ed., ed. C. P. Wilson, C. C. Hogan, and I. L. Mintz, pp. 217–244. New York: Jason Aronson.

―――― (1985c). The relationship between self-starvation and amenorrhea. In *Fear of Being Fat: The Treatment of Anorexia Nervosa and Bulimia,* rev. ed., ed. C. P. Wilson, C. C. Hogan, and I. L. Mintz, pp. 335–344. New York: Jason Aronson.

Moulton, R. (1942). Psychosomatic study of anorexia nervosa, including the use of vaginal smears. *Psychosomatic Medicine* 4:62–72.

Ritvo, S. (1977). Adolescence to woman. In *Female Psychology,* ed. H. Blum, pp. 127–137. New York: International Universities Press.

―――― (1986). Psychoanalytic treatment of patients with psychosomatic disorders: eating disorders and female adolescent development, with special reference to disturbances in body image. Discussion Group 12, Midwinter Meeting, American Psychoanalytic Association, New York, December 17.

Schafer, R. (1968). *Aspects of Internalization.* New York: International Universities Press.

Selvini Palazzoli, M. (1978). *Self-Starvation: From Individual to Family Therapy in the Treatment of Anorexia Nervosa.* New York: Jason Aronson.

Sours, J. A. (1974). The anorexia nervosa syndrome. *International Journal of Psycho-Analysis* 55:567–576.

―――― (1980). *Starving to Death in a Sea of Objects, The Anorexia Nervosa Syndrome.* New York: Jason Aronson.

Sperling, M. (1953). Food allergies and conversion hysteria. *Psychoanalytic Quarterly* 22:525–588.

―――― (1968). Acting out behavior and psychosomatic symptoms. *International Journal of Psycho-Analysis* 49:250–253.

―――― (1978). Anorexia nervosa (Part 4). In *Psychosomatic Disorders of Children,* ed. O. Sperling, pp. 129–173. New York: Jason Aronson.

Thomä, H. (1967). *Anorexia Nervosa.* Trans. G. Brydone. New York: International Universities Press.

Volkan, V. D. (1965). The observation of the "little man" phenomenon in a case of anorexia nervosa. *British Journal of Medical Psychology* 38:299–311.

―――― (1976). *Primitive Internalized Object Relations: A Clinical Study of Schizophrenic, Borderline, and Narcissistic Patients.* New York: International Universities Press.

Waller, J. V., Kaufman, M. R., and Deutsch, F. (1940). Anorexia nervosa, a psychosomatic entity. *Psychosomatic Medicine* 2:3–16.

Wilson, C. P. (1985a). The fear of being fat in female psychology. In *Fear of Being Fat: The Treatment of Anorexia Nervosa and Bulimia,* rev. ed., ed. C. P. Wilson, C. C. Hogan, and I. L. Mintz, pp. 9–28. New York: Jason Aronson.

————— (1985b). The family psychological profile and its therapeutic implications. In *Fear of Being Fat: The Treatment of Anorexia Nervosa and Bulimia,* rev. ed., ed. C. P. Wilson, C. C. Hogan, and I. L. Mintz, pp. 29–49. New York: Jason Aronson.

————— (1985c). Dream interpretation. In *Fear of Being Fat: The Treatment of Anorexia Nervosa and Bulimia,* rev. ed., ed. C. P. Wilson, C. C. Hogan, and I. L. Mintz, pp. 245–254. New York: Jason Aronson.

Wilson, C. P., Hogan, C. C., and Mintz, I. L. (1985). *Fear of Being Fat: The Treatment of Anorexia Nervosa and Bulimia.* Rev. ed. New York: Jason Aronson.

PART III

Restrictor Anorexia Nervosa

6

Classical Analysis of a Restrictor Anorexic

Charles C. Hogan, M.D.

The case history discussed in this chapter demonstrates that some anorexic patients can successfully complete a traditional psychoanalytic procedure with few special parameters. This patient illustrates clearly the intensity of the adolescent oedipal conflict following an earlier, more intense infantile oedipal problem continuing into latency. I have noted that anorexic women "defended themselves against intense adolescent oedipal attachments to the father that seemed to be the outgrowth of equally intense infantile attachments" (Hogan 1985, p. 127). Sperling (1978) had previously made similar observations.

Moreover, this case demonstrates the amalgam of oedipal concerns and pregenital regressions. This young woman's sadistic fantasies toward the mother and her overt sadism toward her siblings amply illustrate Sperling's observations that "The unresolved preoedipal fixations to the mother contribute . . . to the intensity of the oedipal conflict in these girls" (1978, p. 166). Fortunately, in this case the pregenital disposition to acting out did not interfere with psychoanalysis.

While concurrent treatment of psychoanalysis of the parents, particularly the mother, is a valuable adjunctive help in many young anorexics, it is not always necessary. These parents refused to cooperate, yet the psychoanalysis proceeded satisfactorily.

It should be emphasized that the overt symptoms dramatized in eating disorders are only superficial manifestations of a serious underlying neurotic illness that should be treated.

CASE HISTORY

Chief Complaint

This 17-year-old patient was referred by her father, a physician, after he diagnosed anorexia nervosa. She weighed 92 lbs. and was five feet, six inches tall. Twenty months previously she had started spontaneous morning vomiting and lost her menstrual periods. She thought she was pregnant but did not confide in anyone. This was apparently pseudo-cyesis.[1] She was afraid to have an abortion but did seriously contemplate suicide. With the return of one period six months later, she realized that her pregnancy was imaginary. At the time treatment began, her weight had decreased from 135 to the 92 pounds and she had been amenorrheic for seven months.

She also complained of very occasional migraine, accompanied not only by nausea and scotoma, but also by marked confusion and motor instability. The first attack had been at the age of 11 when she was scheduled to try out for a class play. She was considered a talented child and accepted in dramatic productions but fell apart and could not even understand the script. The second real migraine was at the end of her junior year in high school when she was expected to take a literature exam; again she fell apart cognitively in spite of the fact that she had been getting straight A's in literature courses. Between these two true migraine events she suffered from severe debilitating headaches about once a year. (It should be noted that once she began analysis, she began to suffer from frequent milder headaches whenever she was dealing with uncomfortable material.)

At the time of the first consultation, she disparaged the severity of her illness. Her only desire was to lose more weight and return to "normal activities."

Family History

Father, age 50, was a physician who was proud of his own academic background, which was heavy in science and mathematics. His father had

---

[1]"Pseudocyesis" is questionable in this case. In classical pseudocyesis the patient is virginal; this patient had had intercourse once with contraception. She had intense conflict over this experience. Four months later she reported abdominal swelling.

been an alcoholic who died in what may have been an alcohol-related accident. The patient's father was a conservative, competitive man, who stressed the importance of athletic endeavors to all of his children. He had little interest in literature or drama but was a compulsive grammatical perfectionist.

He was involved in a seemingly masochistic relationship with his hysterical, possibly paranoid and possibly alcoholic wife, but there was also an apparent enjoyment in his feeling of superiority to her. He would always side with her against the children when she was present but would frequently confide in his children—especially the patient—asking their advice on what to do about his wife's problems or pathology. He frequently discussed hospitalizing her but actually did nothing until late in the patient's treatment. He separated from his wife about a year before the termination of the patient's analysis. The father did, however, support the patient's treatment, often over the rather violent objections of his wife. At one time early in treatment he was referred for psychotherapy but would not follow through.

His particular interest in the patient was apparent. Despite his objections to short skirts, lipstick, and the like, he kept a photograph of the teenage patient in a seductive pose, dressed in a bikini, on the wall of the parental bedroom.

Before his courtship of his present wife, he had been deeply in love with a woman who suffered from anorexia nervosa.

Mother, age 44, had rather severe emotional disturbances but, when not involved in an hysterical, seemingly paranoid and sometimes alcoholic rage, would deny any pathology. Her own father apparently had been violent and perhaps somewhat paranoid.

According to her husband, she had rejected the patient during the child's first two years of life, presumably because she was not a boy. The child had a room on the third floor of the house while her older sister had a crib on the second floor. Though the mother breastfed the older sister, she was unwilling or unable to breastfeed the patient for more than a few weeks. When the children were little, she would go into rages and lock them out of the house for hours at a time. Also she would promise to pick them up at a given time and be hours late. This trait seems to be common in mothers of children with eating disorders.

She had frequent evening rages during which she would complain about how the family mistreated her and, after drinking, she would fall asleep in the living room, either remaining there until morning or making the rounds of the children's rooms early in the morning with complaints, apologies, or protestations of love.

I referred the mother for therapy but she refused to go. Later I referred her to a psychoanalyst in her neighborhood, but she quit after a few sessions because she was sure everything she said was being repeated to me. I found out later that this analyst felt she was paranoid. She insisted that she did not need treatment but merely wanted to know how to help the patient. After two more such failures, one a referral to a psychiatrist and the other to a marriage counselor, she finally was hospitalized for several months as the patient's analysis was reaching its terminal phase.

She was against the patient's entering psychoanalysis and fought her treatment once it began. She continually disparaged therapy and the analyst to the patient, the siblings, her husband, and all of her friends. Despite her alleged shame over her daughter's illness, she spent hours on the phone with her friends, many of whom were parents of her daughter's friends, discussing her daughter's illness, feeling sorry for herself, and asking for advice.

When I first saw the patient, she was completely submissive to her mother. She did most of the household work when she was home, only to hear the mother's complaints about how it was done. The mother tried to maintain control over all of the children by her recitations of her own martyrdom. The patient was the most vulnerable and least rebellious of any of the children.

Older sister, age 19, was an aggressive, beautiful girl who was bulimic. She had severe sexual fears and problems, often confiding in the patient and asking sexual advice.

Before treatment, she dominated my patient. When the patient would try to disassociate herself from the sister, the sister would say: "Don't you love me? Families should love each other." One of the patient's first realizations in treatment was the importance of detaching herself from a rather intense masochistic dependence on this sister, whom she realized she disliked. The sister participated in violence and stealing that went on among the siblings.

Brother, age 15, was the patient's closest friend. He and the patient were in the same bedroom during their early years. There was a great deal of mutual tickling with some overt sexual play. There was also sadistic manipulation by the patient. While the patient was in analysis, the brother ran away from college and the family. He entered a different college in another state, where he supported himself and did well. He said "he had had it." Despite difficulties in school and some acting out, he seemed to be the healthiest of the siblings.

Personal History

There was conflict with the mother during the first two years of life. The patient was evidently very depressed after the birth of the brother but the hostility was displaced to the older sister.

The patient had been a dreamy child, given to a life of fantasy and would lead her brother in theatrical dress-up games. She spent a good deal of time daydreaming and reading. She was an overweight child until the fifth or sixth grade.

During her early childhood, the parents had a maid who was overtly sadistic. She would tie up all the children and beat them, threatening to kill them if they told the parents. The patient was terrified and submissive. The older sister was defiant and would battle, but no one told the parents. After a neighbor complained and the matter came to light, the children verified the complaints. However, the mother did not immediately fire the maid because the maid was black and she felt sorry for her. Fortunately, the maid was so uncomfortable after the discovery that she left.

There was a great deal of violence among the siblings, usually unbeknownst to the parents. The patient once attacked her older sister with scissors, intending to stab her. On another occasion the sister attacked the patient, splitting the skin on her head so that stitches were necessary. The siblings would lock each other in the bathroom and indulge in other hostile acts. While the parents never locked any doors—bedrooms, bathrooms, or others—the children would lock each other up and all became very adept at picking locks.

There was a constant round of clothes stealing between the patient and her older sister, with accompanying rages, tears, and recriminations. The mother would repeatedly purchase expensive clothes for the girls, frequently garments for which they had little use or interest.

The family looked on the patient as "queer" because she read so much. Despite the father's pride in his own academic background, this negative feeling reflected the family's attitude toward anyone interested in reading or literary accomplishment. It was intensely directed toward the patient, particularly after she entered analysis. About age 11, roughly around the time of her first migraine headache, she decided to change herself. She threw herself into athletics, where she soon excelled. Her father was more than proud of her. She lost weight and attempted to suppress her conscious fantasy life, with some success.

It was uncovered in psychoanalysis that from age 7 to 9 she had been frightened by a group of fantasies and dreams about being captured by a pirate, a knight, or a prince and being held prisoner. In various ways she would be loved and taken as a lover by this individual, and in the process she would displace the former lover, wife, or queen. This situation always seemed to involve violence, in which the queen would have her breasts cut off, be decapitated, or suffer some other horrible fate. There was no overt masturbation during these fantasies, but at a later point in the analysis she recalled that she would rub against the sheets, pull her nightgown between her legs, or find some other way to stimulate her genitals. This physical activity continued into early adolescence, but the fantasy life was repressed.

As she was making over her lifestyle at 10 or 11, she gave up crying, found that she did not dream, and stopped reading except for whatever was required by school. Crying did not recur until the second year of analysis. She became a prize-winning swimmer. Her weight decreased and she became quite muscular. From this time on, there were frequent weight fluctuations as she went on diets.

She went through menarche and was terribly ashamed of her breasts and menstrual periods. In contrast, in an earlier period, at age 7, she had fantasized growing up to be amply endowed with voluptuous breasts. After the age of 11 she consciously wanted to shed all evidence of her emerging sexuality.

It was approximately at this time, just before puberty, that she had the migraine described above, which deprived her of a part in her class play. The mother openly accused her of malingering despite her severe disability, which after a few hours forced the mother to obtain medical attention for her.

Within a year or two an event occurred which seemed to take on overdetermined dimensions. Her parents took a West Coast trip and left the children in the care of a young woman. One night a young man broke through a window into the patient's room. What actually happened is still somewhat confused. She recalled having a dream of someone lying on her just before she awakened. As analysis progressed, she recalled that the dream was of the older sister's boyfriend, and various later chains of associations eventually led to the brother and the father. Whether or not the intruder lay upon her is still uncertain. When she awoke, he was bending over her and asking her not to scream. The younger brother was in a bed in the same room, witnessing the event but pretending to be asleep.

The intruder said something about it being an initiation rite and asked to find the way out of the house. She was calm, in an apparent depersonalization, and led him to the front door and let him out. She then awoke the baby-sitter, who was terrified. The police and some relatives came and accused her of making up the story, until it was verified by the younger brother and the broken window screen was examined. An uncle got his shotgun and sat guard through the night, and the next day the parents returned from the West Coast. She was as terrified of the shotgun as she had been of the intruder. When the parents returned, they were angry that their trip had to be cut short.

This experience seemed to be an organizing, overdetermined experience. Dreams repeatedly referred to it. Chains of associations would return to both its gratifying and frightening aspects. At two points during the psychoanalysis she became involved with strange males whom she practically invited into her residence, partially aware that she was inviting rape. In each instance she later felt she was trying to duplicate the earlier experience. Because the initiating dream during the episode was so graphic, the patient felt that the intruder first lay upon her and then became frightened and got off. She condensed fantasies of the sister's boyfriend, her brother, uncle, and father into one experience.

Early in high school she was asked to give an introductory address but refused, despite having a reputation as an excellent speaker. When her parents found this out from other sources, they were furious. The patient recognized during analysis that her refusal was an overt rebellion against her own conscience (superego) and her parents' expectations.

In high school she did exceptionally well academically and athletically. She did indulge rather heavily in drugs and alcohol, often exposing herself unnecessarily to discovery, and she was caught a couple of times. About the time of her pseudocyesis, after coaching her older sister for the same literature exam that she was to take, she had the second migraine experience. Headache, nausea, scotomata, mental confusion, and locomotor instability led to an almost blank paper and a failing grade. She did not complain or excuse herself. She had done so well in the course, however, that after the professor called her in for an explanation, he disregarded the exam and utilized other classroom material to give her an excellent grade.

After two months of treatment, she weighed 100 pounds and her periods returned.

Psychoanalysis

As with most of my other anorexic patients, I placed her on the couch immediately. I explained free association and said that we would look forward to accomplishing it as soon as possible. I made no further demands but did point out obvious inhibitions in her spontaneity and obvious attempts to control both her own productions and me.

Over her parents' objections, I pushed her to attend a local university. She did straight A work there graduating cum laude. During her freshman year she was living at home with her mother, and the analysis was in constant chaos. When she moved to a dormitory at the university, freer of the mother's interference, the analysis calmed down greatly. Still the mother would occasionally call me, often drunk, asking about her daughter's condition.

Early in treatment there was an intense idealization of the analyst. It was not difficult to mobilize the latent aggression toward the mother, who complained about the patient's treatment. The mother continued to refuse treatment for herself. The patient, who had always envied her older sister's ability to fight with the mother, discovered that her mother liked to fight and enjoyed having a child fight back. These fights, which frequently involved physical attacks and mutual threats with the most primitive cursing, opened up some very frightening material for the patient.

The earlier dreams of mutilating a queen or mother figure began to appear again in the analysis. The patient was surprised by sudden conscious fantasies of mutilating mother's breasts. A variety of sadistic and masochistic dreams appeared, some involving castration of her brother, boyfriend, and father. She was working one evening, half asleep, when a fantasy or dream of autocunnilingus came into consciousness, in which she was chewing on her pelvic bones and had the physical sensation of grinding the bone between her jaws. She feared insanity. During that first year there were periods of confusion when she could not remember whether what she recalled was dream or fantasy.

She also began to find herself in neurotic slips of forgetting—keys, pocketbooks, rings, and other items—duplicating earlier irresponsibility before the age of 11 and coinciding with the mother's continual accusations of flightiness—even during those years of conscientious and obsessive control after age 10 or 11.

Her periods were irregular but had returned. She began to free-associate and recall memories and fantasies of smearing feces. She and her siblings had played games of smearing each other with fecal material in early childhood.

During a later phase of analysis we were able to uncover the latent fantasies in an elaborate instantaneous symptom which would occur frequently in her early childhood and was occasionally present during the early period of analysis. It was notably present preceding her two migraine attacks. After a real or an internalized mental confrontation with her mother, she would "white out." Further exploration through dreams and associations revealed a repressed fantasy which occurred as she ostensibly relaxed physically and submitted to mother. In the fantasy, which had variations, she would attack the mother's head or mouth and at times mentally decapitate her. She would "shut her up." Other associations to breasts made me wonder if this did not represent Lewin's (1950) dream screen—the early image of the mother's breast. However, I was unable to confirm this.

After a year and a half of analysis this patient, who had been intermittently depressed, went into a severe depression. This circumstance was a bit different from my experience with other anorexics, who usually had rather profound depressions around the time that their menses returned. This patient had had the return of irregular menses relatively early—two months after entering treatment.

There were a number of suicidal threats from her and much provocative acting out. She came close to an attack or rape after almost inviting an unknown young man into her house at two in the morning. When at the last minute she refused and went to a neighbor, he was enraged and followed her around for several days, obviously threatening and abusive.

While still depressed, she began to have occasional poorly disguised exhibitionistic and sexual transference dreams that she found humiliating. As these were interpreted in the maternal and oedipal contexts, depending on the associations, she began to have frequent overt fellatio fantasies on the couch, which combined her wishes to control mother's breast and to control me through seduction. She would go through elaborate descriptions of approaching me, which I interpreted first as her attempts to control me. When she began to experience embarrassment, I interpreted such material as attempts to excite and seduce me. This led to memories of tickling her brother and to the frustrations with a seductive father.

The patient had made frequent references to pregnancy, including, of course, her pseudocyesis when she thought she was pregnant by her boyfriend. Her associations led back to her fears of looking pregnant when she was overweight. Along with memories of her mother's pregnancy with her younger brother and her feelings of disgust, she began to fantasize having the analyst's child. She would joyfully go on with her elaborations on the future of this idealized mental progeny. However, a series of dreams indicated that this fantasy was covering her fantasy of being a part of me, inseparable and unseparating. I was in a number of roles, but mainly that of a maternal father. With this, she had a series of dreams alluding to anal birth and births by sadistic caesarian sections. She also represented herself as feces being defecated into the toilet or going down the drain.

At the same time as this regressive pregenital fantasy life began to appear, she had a rather marked recurrence of an old symptom. In the shower she would occasionally panic with the fantasy that someone had come into the bathroom and would strangle her. This fantasy had previously been attributed to the mother's uninvited incursions to the bathroom, the invasions of lock-picking siblings, and her fears as she watched the movie *Psycho*. However, at this time she became aware of a pleasurable excitement in the panic and related it to the intruder who came through the window. This led to memories of earlier bathtub masturbation and womb-like fantasies of total enclosure where she was frightened of interruptions. These fantasies went off in two directions: one to vague fantasies of a penis destroying an infant in the womb and to tearing open her mother's pregnant womb, and the other, more adult line of fantasy to sharing the bathtub with an older man who, she agreed, must have been her father.

The symptom cleared and did not return until a transient period before termination, when it was combined with dreams of feces, which she equated with herself, dropping down the bathtub drain. She saw it as a masochistic way of handling her anger at termination. She was nothing more than feces and I was treating her in that manner. She volunteered that she wanted me to sneak up and attack her from behind. It was at this late date in the psychoanalysis that she for the first time associated a strangling attack from the rear to my position behind the couch.

Another line of associations should be mentioned. She elaborated on the womb intrusions and associated to her curiosity about her parents' bedroom, their fights, and their sexual activity. As this material evolved, the depression was clearing and alternating with periods of almost hypomanic excitement. She obtained work as a waitress and worked until early morning while carrying a full academic schedule with straight A's. While she was still dating her former high school boyfriend, who was away at school, she was also frequently dating at her own university and for the first time having sexual experiences with men other than her boyfriend. She became rather aggressively flirtatious and enjoyed the frequent opportunities for dates.

As this hyperactivity returned, she began to worry. She found herself repeating her physical rituals of four to six years earlier. She would run for miles, do push-ups, and so on. During her early years of analysis she had suppressed all such activity, looking on it as pathological. Through dreams and associations she began to equate such activity with masturbation and early physical games with her father. When she was quite small, he had taught her to ski, taken her swimming, and the like. She became increasingly aware of the sensual excitement involved in such activities. She took up swimming again—a pleasure she had also suppressed.

Earlier in the analysis she had at times been aware of her idealization of the male and her envy of his power, and she had even associated her headaches with her envy of the penis and identified her head with that of the penis. She clearly associated her intellectuality with masculinity. Now, however, she recognized that part of the excitement of her renewed physical activity came from an elated fantasy of being masculine. Her sexual fantasies took on a much more aggressive tone and she had conscious fantasies of what it would be like to have orgasm with a penis. At one point she visited her boyfriend and upset him with her repeated questions as to "exactly" how it felt. Such material was interspersed with memories of teasing her younger brother and tickling his genitals—an activity that always upset him and that she accomplished forceably.

Such elated excitement also at times was associated with dreams or fantasies of subduing, seducing, or managing her older sister and mother.

About one year before the termination of analysis the parents separated. The brother had previously left the house and was working his way through a distant college. The older sister had moved into the city. This sister was depressed and failing at jobs. She continually attempted to involve the patient in a hostile, mutually dependent relationship.

With some concern the patient was drawn back into the family's activities, but she handled the aggressive-regressive manipulations with a remarkable maturity. Everyone in the family began to come to her for advice and support. The brother would write only to the patient. Various other members of the family would try to get her to ask her analyst what to do. She gave notice that she would give what help she could but would not be drawn into the chaos. She refused to move back into the family home.

She and her boyfriend decided that they would begin to live together when he was in the city. On his graduation he moved to the South to establish himself in a technical business. The patient obtained an editorial job in the city. We tentatively planned on termination at the end of the next year. She and her boyfriend visited, called, and corresponded during the separation.

In the fall of the last year of analysis there were some of the usual regressive symptoms that accompany termination. She had a recurrence of mild headaches. She had the recurrent fear of attacks in the shower. She was astounded at her feeling that I was deserting her when she herself had decided on the termination date, to which I had agreed. The sexual fantasies and dreams about me reappeared, but she did feel that she was ready to be on her own. She suggested that we continue through February, and I agreed. With some sadness, she left on March 1 rather than January 1 and went south to join her fiancé.

At the time of termination, during her sixth year of psychoanalysis, she was looking forward to a probable marriage and family. At the present time, ten years later, she has both and is asymptomatic.

REFERENCES

Hogan, C. C. (1985). Psychodynamics. In *Fear of Being Fat: The Treatment of Anorexia Nervosa and Bulimia,* rev. ed., ed. C. P. Wilson, C. C. Hogan, and I. L. Mintz, pp. 115–128. New York: Jason Aronson.

Lewin, B. D. (1950). *The Psychodynamics of Elation.* New York: Norton.

Sperling, M. (1978). Anorexia nervosa (Part 4). In *Psychosomatic Disorders in Children,* ed. O. Sperling, pp. 129–173. New York: Jason Aronson.

7

A Comparison between the Analyst's View and the Patient's Diary

Ira L. Mintz, M.D.

INTRODUCTION

The first draft of this chapter was a detailed description of the first three months of treatment. It included the patient's symptomatology, attitudes, and behavior, what she said, what I said, and what I thought was happening. An attempt was made to understand her attitudes, her responses to interpretations, and the effect they had upon the course of treatment. It was with some surprise and curiosity that I learned, eighteen months later, that the patient had kept a diary covering her first five weeks of treatment. Given the opportunity to read the diary, I was able to compare, almost session by session, my impressions of what had transpired with the patient's conscious reactions to many of the sessions. Segments of the diary were subsequently inserted into the paper. As a consequence, I was able to compare what she said, my impression of what took place, what I said, her reaction to it, her written impressions, and finally, my assessment in response to the diary. The diary had unexpectedly produced an additional window into the understanding of the analytic process. It made it possible to view the patient's conscious, private reflections of thoughts and feelings communicated only to herself, with the knowledge that she could be as open and frank as she could tolerate.

It is additionally helpful to see the patient's conscious evaluation of her treatment several hours after the session, when she was in a state of contemplative reflection. It can further clarify and may shed additional light upon how a patient truly feels about her illness, the underlying problems causing it, and the method she feels is most helpful to her in its resolution. While I have frequently noted the anorexic patient's considerable awareness of the factors related to her illness, the underlying meaning of her symptoms, and her conflicts, it was still fascinating to see them spelled out in the diary. Her understanding that she starved and exercised in order to suppress and repress frightening thoughts and impulses is most illuminating. She knew that her fear of being fat was a conscious preoccupation but that underneath there lurked frightening, overwhelming impulses and anxieties. This recognition, spelled out in her diary and also revealed by many other patients, early in treatment, calls into question a form of treatment that concentrates upon nutritional information and preponderant focus upon food and eating and that has the effect of helping the patient hide from her problems instead of solving them.

CASE HISTORY: MARJORIE

The patient, a 19-year-old girl beginning her second year of college, was referred because of a 35-pound weight loss, a starvation type of diet, and amenorrhea. She was 5 feet, 9 inches, had previously weighed 130 pounds, and now weighed 95 pounds. She had been seen in consultation by a local psychiatrist who recommended hospitalization, which the patient refused. The parents were uncertain of what course to follow and sought an additional opinion. The parents were seen first for two visits when they indicated that Marjorie was reluctant to come but felt that she would not object to their coming in for a consultation.

Ordinarily, I should prefer seeing a 19-year-old alone and have little contact with the parents. In cases of anorexia, however, there is such a close tie between patient and parents that it is important for the parents to have at least some initial contact with the therapist in order for them to feel comfortable about turning their daughter over to someone for treatment. When parents are openly resistant or markedly ambivalent about therapy, the patient will often acquiesce to termination of treatment or will identify with the parents' ambivalence and not become fully committed to it. This reaction reflects the anorexic patient's symbiotic attachment to the parent, the inability to separate contributing to the patient's "doing what is expected" without having to be asked. My colleagues and I (Wilson 1985) have not found that initial contact with the parents has had an adverse effect upon the treatment. In addition many of the starving as well as a good number of gorging anorexic patients are reluctant to enter treatment and do so only under parental pressure. It has been found helpful and on occasion essential that the parents briefly see a different therapist in order to help them more fully understand the nature of the illness, what to expect during the course of the treatment, and how to be helpful in facilitating their daughter's recovery rather than unwittingly obstructing it.

The parents stated that Marjorie seemed fine until the previous summer, when they noticed a significant disinterest in eating, a finicky attitude toward food, and a preoccupation with losing weight. Reflecting back, they realized that she had slowly lost 10 pounds during the spring and that increased dieting during the summer had resulted in a total weight loss of 35 pounds. She professed not to be hungry and to feel full but never complained about feeling too fat and, on occasion, had acknowledged that she was thin. There was no distortion in body image acknowledged at this time, and although it is frequently present, I do not feel that it is essential to establish the diagnosis of anorexia, although others have so stated (Bruch 1970, 1973). Every morning she would get on the scale to check her weight and then look at herself in the mirror. She began to drink nothing but diet soda, gave up all meat, and ate mainly lettuce and tomatoes, cottage cheese, and carrots. She ate so many carrots that the palms of her hands began to turn orange. The parents also noticed that, though she had always been shy, she became increasingly withdrawn. Her menstrual period had stopped six months before and had also stopped for three months of the previous summer.

The parents were well educated, poised, and concerned about Marjorie. The father, a minister, was thoughtful and reflective and acknowledged that he enjoyed and was successful in his profession. The mother, a teacher, admitted that at times she was very firm and authoritative with the children. Marjorie was the second of three girls, and the parents were unable to describe any unusual aspects to her development. She was remembered as a normal child believed that she got along well with her two sisters but seemed to have a grudge against the younger one, accusing the parents of favoring her. The youngest child was born with a congenital hip difficulty requiring a good deal of medical care, and the parents admitted that their concern for her may well have been viewed as favoritism by the patient.

The First Interview

The patient was a tall, thin, shy young woman who appeared ill at ease and reluctant to be in the office. In reply to my asking her to tell me a little about what had been going on, she stated that she came to see me because her parents had forced her, that she had already seen a psychiatrist, and that nothing was wrong. After some active questioning, she did talk about her anorexic symptoms and some of her life experiences. She did not speak easily and there were many silences that required my active intervention. She repeated essentially what the parents had described but had a different view of when the anorexia began. She said that in the spring of her senior year in high school she was very conflicted over which of two colleges she should choose. Her choice was one that had an excellent swimming team and was 50 miles from home. The parents felt that the other was better academically, although it was 600 miles away, and they pressured her in that direction. She decided upon the first, however. When the father heard about it, he phoned her at her cousin's house and told her how disappointed he was with her decision. History revealed minimal separation or eating problems in a girl who played reasonably with other children. The family moved a good deal when the children were young because of the father's transfer to a number of different Presbyterian churches. However, in the previous five years the family had lived in the same neighborhood and the children all had established substantial roots in the community. Marjorie's menstrual history had not been remarkable until six months before, when her periods stopped. Menarche began at age 13. Periods were usually regular with occasional irregularities, but not accompanied by depression, tension, or cramps. Marjorie was an excellent athlete and was on the swimming and volleyball teams. Her swimming coach said that she had lost so much weight, he was thinking of benching her. She was upset by this and told us that she was trying to eat but she just felt full. She also admitted that she felt quite tired at times and was no longer well coordinated.

The father stated that Marjorie had always been a thoughtful, considerate girl who, unlike her sister, was rarely argumentative even as a teenager. They always felt that she was the best adjusted of the three because she readily acquiesced to whatever was suggested, without argument or reluctance. He saw her as a perfectionist, who expected a high performance from herself in everything and was distressed if it did not take place. She worked at three part-time jobs (sometimes 55 hours a week) to save money for college, although the parents told her that it was not necessary to do so. She always needed to be busy. The mother interjected that Marjorie was always doing things for people and would frequently clean the entire house without being asked. The mother was also disappointed in her choice of school. This upset her very much, and caused her resolve to wane.

She decided that since her going to the second school would make them happy, it really didn't matter to her. It was in that setting that the anorexia began. I commented, "You must have felt that your wishes weren't important and that you felt obligated to do what others wanted of you." She sat silently as the hour ended. When I suggested the second consultation hour, she stated that it would conflict with her earth science class but that she would cut the class.

I felt tentatively optimistic at that point because, although she stated that she was there against her will, and she needed a good deal of active participation on my part, she did relate and did reveal her perceptions of how the anorexia began. There was some awareness that it was related to the conflict between her and her parents, her separation anxiety about going 600 miles away to the midwest, her problems about aggression, and her defenses of passivity and helplessness.

I indicated in the first session that my feelings were on her side and that I felt that *her* wishes were important. This was essential since these patients have a history of doing what others want of them. She was here because her parents wanted her here, and she feared that I would attempt to control her as she felt her parents did.

Her positive response to my comment was that she did not use the conflicting science course as an obstacle, but decided to cut it in favor of the next session. From that first interview, I indicated that I would not try to control her, that I understood how she felt, and that I would be her ally.

The following is a summary of her diary response to that first session:

> *Friends want to put me in the hospital. I had my first session with Dr. Mintz. He is okay. He said people don't eat to block out problems. . . . It made me begin to realize that I often feel that what I say doesn't matter. I feel that I don't count.*

Increasing Silence

In the second session the patient had great difficulty speaking, and there was a good deal of silence. I said, "Your difficulty in talking is a possible reflection of difficulty in asserting yourself." She acknowledged that it was true and that she had been used to doing what her parents wanted her to do and that she had rarely defied them. I interjected "except by not eating" and attempted to imply in my manner that I could understand that kind of defiance and was not critical of it.

The patient wrote in her diary that her friend . . .

> *Susanna doesn't understand, but I need to go to this doctor. It's getting even harder to eat than before. I think that's because I'm beginning to think about my problems more now, and I have to try even harder than ever to block them out by starving.*

Marked silence persisted in the third session. I suggested, "Eating would result in your being able to speak more easily." In retrospect, my wording was counterproductive. I had meant to say, "Eating would result in having more thoughts in your mind." I had also thought that her fear of her impulses had repressed her thoughts. The diary revealed that frightening thoughts were frequently conscious. Again silence as she watched me intently. I added, "It might be difficult for you to trust someone you don't know well." Silence. After a number of similar comments followed by silence, I remarked, "I wonder if you have difficulty in trusting people because of broken promises." Surprisingly, she agreed and recounted in some detail that her father claimed never to have enough money for her singing lessons, but always had enough money for his liquor. She said, "I had to work to pay for my own singing lessons, although he promised to take care of it. When I reminded him of it, he told me to keep quiet."

"That's why you feel assertion doesn't work," I added, and she agreed. I asked, "Have you ever noticed that when you feel upset, you starve?" She stated, "When I'm upset, if I starve I feel less upset, and if I eat I feel more upset." I interjected that I understood that, and that it was my impression that the upset feelings got absorbed by the starving, but then she had two sets of problems: the original ones, pushed away by the starving, and the new problems produced by the starving. I suggested that she now had the opportunity to talk over things that upset her and to solve them, and then she would not need to starve. So ended the third session, an extra session that she had asked for because one of her classes had been cancelled.

A Tentative Evaluation

It might be helpful at this point to discuss methods, technique, and early goals with this patient. She had been disillusioned by a previous therapist and came for consultation partly because of her passive acquiescence to parental demands. Her silent, suspicious, and withholding behavior was paramount, indirectly, reflecting her hostility and lack of cooperation. My early goal, in speech, attitude, and behavior, was to give her the feeling that there was no authoritative cross-examination, criticism, or allying myself with parents or previous coercive medical attempts to get her to eat. My only comment about eating was to point out that eating would facilitate the emergence of thoughts and feelings.

I attempted to indicate that there were reasons why she did not eat, rather than coercing her into doing so, as she had anticipated. Since not eating in part reflected defiance of authority, to pressure her to eat would encourage her defiance toward me and undermine any possible coopera-tive attitude toward the treatment. Nevertheless, I was aware that I had limited time to obtain her cooperation and interest in treatment so that she would explore her motivations for starving instead of starving. Without specifically saying so, I tried to indicate that I knew that she felt she was faced with overwhelming problems with which I might be able to help her. In the first session I acknowledged her need about school choice, implying that I understood that she had felt controlled and had been overly obedient. It was clear that I did not side with her father's condemnation of her choice. The relationship established in the first session contained enough positive elements to begin to undo her previous negative attitude and to prompt her suggestion that she could cut a class in order to make the second session.

In the second session, along with a great deal of silence, she further acknowledged her difficulties with self-assertion, with her rarely defying her parents. My pointing out her self-starvation as a manifestation of defiance was a deliberate attempt to provide unconscious meaning to her symptoms and to undercut further all the manifold rationalizations that patients provide to justify their starving. It was also done within the framework of her admission of passive obedience, and with my indication that I could understand and accept a healthy element in her indirect defiance.

In the third session an attempt was made to further deal with her profound silence and suspicion, and her fears of betrayal and criticism; she responded by citing a conflict with her father. I mentioned that she might worry that I could also betray any promises I made. Her difficulty in talking was so profound that I chose to interject a question that has pertained to almost every anorexic patient I've seen: the question of whether starving facilitated a repression of conflict. She agreed. Her agreement was made more readily by the fact that she had already acknowledged in her diary, after the second session, that she had to try harder to block out the emerging problems by starving. Also, we had not yet spelled out the specific nature of the conflicts. In essence she agreed to the form of the conflict rather than to its content. That admission was of considerable technical and therapeutic value as one can see in the ensuing few sessions.

Her diary response:

> I saw Dr. Mintz and talked about my parents . . . and how I dealt with them . . . and how I felt that I was unfairly treated. I don't see how speaking out would help. I tried but it just made things worse. It's easier to keep it to myself.
>
> He is still trying to get me to talk and to trust him more. I trust him okay. It's just that it hurts to open up, and I don't feel that it will help. He seems to think it will.
>
> Lately I notice that I'm trying even harder not to eat. I think it is an attempt to keep from talking. No one has ever tried to get me to talk.
>
> Tomorrow I see Dr. Mintz. Even though I feel very withdrawn and depressed, I have some kind of feeling inside me which says that this bubble of anger and pain is going to burst out soon. And for some strange reason I feel that I will be able to eat. I don't know when but something tells me it will be alright.

Marjorie recognized by the third session that starving also facilitates silence by aiding suppression and repression of thoughts and feelings, just as eating liberates conflict and releases upsetting feelings that push toward conscious expression. When the patient feels very frightened and guilty about her thoughts and feelings, she may need to starve and remain silent: an attempt at exercising control over what she eats and what she says. On other occasions, however, controlling the session by silence may permit some eating. Close to hospitalization, a starving emaciated patient may utilize silence to satisfy her need for control over some of her impulses, some control over the analytic hour and over the analyst, or display defiant assertiveness toward the analyst so that she does not have to exercise such intense control over the eating. Under those circumstances, the silence can be viewed as having some current potentially positive qualities that enable the patient to eat a little more and, it is hoped, avoid hospitalization.

Concomitantly, the therapist has the opportunity to permit the patient that degree of control while the pediatrician monitors the physical condition. The patient's silence provides the analyst with the chance to discuss the silence and to give the patient the opportunity to see that he is not angry, threatened, resentful, indifferent, or giving up in response to her uncooperativeness—that her silence is taken in stride, like everything else that emerges during the session. He can speculate about the various reasons for the silence, further clarify the issues previously discussed, consider that she might wish to hear him do the talking while she sits and listens for a change, and acknowledge that there must be certain topics that she is very uncomfortable discussing. All the while, she can see that he is comfortable in the reverse role, as she learns more about him and ultimately learns to trust him and herself more. It is important to recognize, however, that whatever is discussed is directly germane to the treatment dynamically, technically, and therapeutically. Under no circumstance should the patient's silence be dealt with by casual, homey revelations of the therapist's personal life, or any other issues, just to fill up the silence. Ultimately, it can be pointed out that the silence interferes with her understanding herself and getting well.

The patient comments in the diary:

> *I have some kind of feeling inside me which says that this bubble of anger and pain is going to burst out soon. And for some strange reason I feel that I will be able to eat.*

These ideas reflect her early awareness that she has been repressing feelings of aggression and that dealing with the aggression will contribute to resolving her eating difficulties. How prophetic and true. Is there a point to be made that such early insight should be further explored and expanded, rather than diverting her focus on to nutrition counseling and conscious pressuring to eat?

Her diary continued:

> *I just returned from a physical exam. It was hell! ... The worst experience of my life. The questions and lectures were a thousand times worse than the exam. They all think that they understand and they don't. I know it's not a medical problem since seeing Dr. Mintz. It's none of their damn business what goes on in the sessions with him. They feel if I eat, it will all go away, but the problems won't.*

When I reviewed the patient's reactions in her diary, I was a little surprised to see the degree of understanding, cooperation, and hope arising from the first three sessions, although these responses were not communicated to me directly. After the first session she actively considered the possibility that a purpose of the starving might be to block out thoughts and feelings. After the second and third sessions, she became more convinced that her growing willingness to dwell upon upsetting thoughts and feelings resulted in her feeling overwhelmed by turmoil, necessitating starving to decrease her level of tension. Thus one sees in status *nasciendi* the paradoxical situation that progress in psychological treatment evidenced by increasing insight can result in an exacerbation of starving to bind the increasing tension liberated by the patient's facing the conflict. It is therefore important to recognize that at this point in treatment, increased starving may not represent treatment failure so much as increased resistance to facing painful conflict emerging from progress: a situation to be resolved by effective interpretation. This resistance can also be misconstrued as a physiological deficiency interfering with treatment and requiring increased eating and weight gain for its resolution. When the patient is not in treatment, an increase in conflict may result in further decompensation. In treatment, hopefully in a more controlled, insightful, and supportive situation, the patient can be assisted in dealing with the conflict without undue symptomatic regression. The patient in this case was also aware that not eating helped her not to talk. The patient acknowledged, by the second interview, "I need to go to this doctor," and after the third session she expressed a hope that she could get better. Thus it seems evident that it is possible to develop some aspects of a positive transference and a working alliance early in the first few sessions.

A Contract With Parents

The parents were then seen to discuss arrangements for the treatment process, including the fee and three-times-a-week frequency (limited by financial pressures), and to solidify their support and commitment to the therapy. I discussed the general aspects of anorexia, including the importance of not pressuring Marjorie to eat. Unfortunately, it was not feasible for them to seek additional consultations with a colleague because of their financial situation, and I had to be content with the feeling that their current attitudes indicated they would not attempt to subvert the treatment. I did not discuss with them anything Marjorie had said and I told her exactly what had transpired.

Progress, Turmoil, and Regression

In the fifth session we discussed the meeting with her parents. Her diary reports:

> I want to see the doctor, but I hate it when I'm there and after. Afterwards is when it hurts the most. Lately it's so painful. Today we talked about dad's drinking. He says I talk too softly and not enough. But it is so hard. He keeps telling me if I eat, it will be easier to talk. I did talk a little better today.

A strange thing happened on the way home. All of a sudden in the middle of the highway, I started to cry. Something inside me kept growing until I released it in my tears. I got home and I couldn't stop. I ran three miles and my problems seemed to clear up. I'm going to run every day. Just as I control the eating, I'm going to control the running. I'm losing control and I've got to get it back.

The diary revealed an essential psychodynamic constellation: that these patients are filled with inner turmoil, and terrified that it will pour out of them. Starving and not talking aids suppression and repression. Once the patient begins to open up, feelings begin to pour out uncontrollably. The running serves the same purpose as the starving. This point has been confirmed in many anorexic patients (Chapter 15). The control that she feared losing and consciously referred to as loss of control over eating and weight was related unconsciously to loss of control over feelings and impulses, which were displaced onto the eating and weight.

In the sixth session, I attempted to get her to speak after a long period of silence, but to no avail. She had nothing to say. I pointed out the connection between not talking and not eating and how both could represent her control over events and her exercise of independence. She replied suddenly, "When I eat, I'm afraid something terrible will happen . . . something terrible will come out of me . . . about how I feel about people. When I tried to talk about problems with people, they never got solved." I indicated that this didn't mean that we couldn't solve it together. At this point the patient clearly, poignantly, and fearfully indicated again how the starving binds conflict, and the eating facilitates its emergence. This is one of the major reasons why anorexic patients starve and why they resist all blandishments to eat. Her fear of the eruption of aggressive impulses is patently evident.

At the end of the hour she asked about the possibility of an extra session. The diary:

After all that crying at home, when I saw Dr. Mintz I could barely talk at all. I wanted to let things out, but I put the lid on. He saw through it and knew I wasn't letting him in. It is so hard to let people in. He tried to make me realize that the only way to get rid of what is eating away at me and causing my starvation is to talk about it, and ultimately solve my problems. If it doesn't work, I'll have let out all my fears and pains and have no way to control it. I'm so scared. He's right, not eating makes it difficult to talk. I think I'm ready to let the world into my life and take on the fight. The toughest thing I'll ever have to do.

The seventh session continued with my reiterating that she already knew that not eating helped bury the worries and that eating brought them to the surface. I added that running away from her worries damaged her self-confidence and self-esteem and left her feeling unnecessarily helpless and vulnerable. She replied that in the past year she had tried to hide from her worries by exercising constantly, keeping her mind occupied with a number of jobs, and most effectively by starving. She feared that if she spoke about some of her worries, then even more of them would come out. I pointed out that talking about what upset her would enable her to eat. She countered with, "How do I know that?" I suggested that if she had any doubts, she could always try it. Besides, she said, "when I tried to face the worries, they only got worse." I said the fact that she couldn't solve them alone didn't mean that the two of us wouldn't be more successful.

In the eighth session she volunteered that either she would stay sick or she would talk. Additional comments reflected her great anxiety about talking, not wanting to talk, and not wanting to be here in the office with me. Finally with tears spilling down her face, she poured out, "My parents don't understand me, . . . for eight years or longer they always indulged my little sister, they spoil her, and when I object, they yell at me and call me an ingrate. They also accuse me of making my sister act worse when I yell at her."

The diary:

> Yesterday was rough. For the first time I started talking about what really bothered me and I cried. I kept thinking about how I hated to be there, and in a way I don't like Dr. Mintz. I don't know what made me open up. I guess when he asked if I want to get better. I talked about how I felt about no one listening to me at home. How guilty and frustrated I feel about my sister. I never realized how much guilt I kept inside me all these years. He said I starve to punish myself and to keep from achieving goals. Deep down I always felt I've been holding back. Guilty about good grades . . . in doing well in swimming.

The analyst was quite active during these sessions. Being active is almost a necessity in the treatment of these starving patients, where early and at times inexact interpretations are required, in an attempt to forstall hospitalization (Mintz 1985a,c). The therapist cannot afford to wait for the slower emergence of material with these pregenitally fixated, suspicious, apprehensive, and resentful patients. While this patient was bright, her profound difficulty in speaking in general, and discussing personal matters in particular, required the analyst to do a great deal of talking.

It became clearer later, as with other silent patients, that the silence served a number of purposes. It permitted her to find out more about the therapist by watching his behavior and listening to what he said, and it gave her time to consider what she chose to discuss. It also provided her with encouragement to continue the treatment, because his consistent, patient interest and concern in the face of her silent, uncooperative behavior suggested that he might really be interested in helping her and that he might not lose patience in dealing with what she felt were overwhelming difficulties. It should be added, however, that in describing the technique with this patient, I included more of my own comments than the patient's, perhaps giving the erroneous view that I did more talking than actually took place.

In the ninth session the patient was again silent. In view of all that she had said in the previous session, I wondered about her silence. She said, "I was upset for four hours after I left here, and I had to avoid people. I don't want to be upset this way." I pointed out that this reaction was not surprising because she had begun discussing some of her real problems rather than the starving, and that because these problems had been avoided and stored up for so long they were bound to upset her, and might again. Her distress for four hours also suggested the importance of the problems. Further silence. Questioned about her silence in the face of obviously stated problems, she blurted out, "I don't see how talking about my father's drinking will get him to stop, or about my parents' fighting will change it, or even complaining about how they favor my sister will make them stop." I replied that I could understand why those issues distressed her, but I was not sure that those circumstances were her major problems. When she was younger and lived at home, those issues could certainly have preoccupied her and been of more importance. Now, however, living at college and involved in making a new life for herself with issues of school, career choice, friends, a set of standards, ethics, sexuality, marriage, and pregnancy, I wasn't sure that preoccupation with what happened at home was still cogent.

The diary:

> *I was so nervous about going to the session today, but I left feeling a little more confident about life.*

In the next four sessions she acknowledged feeling more optimistic about the treatment, but the marked silence persisted, intermingled with short bursts of very pertinent ideas. She criticized her father also about how badly he treated her sisters, who were so dependent on his judgment. She spoke about all the angry thoughts that she had and how people would criticize her and reject her for them. I indicated that she might feel that way about me. She added that she was furious with her father, mother, and sisters because they all knew that she was unhappy in high school and had no friends because her peers drank and used drugs. Her parents never asked her about how she felt. She was afraid that if she ever got angry at them they wouldn't love her and would ignore her. She told how her father came to the table half drunk, ate, and then coughed up all the food. I asked what would happen if she ate and then threw up all the food at the table. She replied that she would say, "After having to watch you do it all these years, this is what it looks like," and she acknowledged that it would be a hostile act toward her father. I added, "So you do it in secret instead," and noted that the vomiting was an indirect expression of her unhappiness with her family. Further discussions ensued over her wish to assert herself with her parents and her fears of the consequences. These were interpreted as additional fears of criticism by the analyst and an indication that she did not really believe she could speak about anything she chose without adverse consequences.

The diary:

> *I'm scared and I hate to go to the appointment more than anything, but something inside of me keeps pushing me to go. It is as if part of me knows that if I go, I'll get better.*

Following another period of silence, in the fifteenth session, she stated, "I could eat and talk, but then I'd feel overwhelmed by my thoughts . . . the ones that I don't tell you . . . and then I might tell them to my parents and they'd get furious with me." I acknowledged that she still felt that it was too early to tell me all of her thoughts, but I wasn't sure why she felt obliged to tell her parents. I pointed out that young children felt so obligated but that teenagers recognized that they had a right to their own private thoughts.

In these sessions the patient began to reveal crucial, aggressive thoughts and feelings against her parents, along with impulses to assert herself in her own behalf. Guilt for these feelings coexisted with fear of parental retaliation. I was not aware of the intensity of her fears about coming to sessions, nor of the terror set off by her aggressive impulses, until she verbalized the concern about "terrible things coming out of her." I was also surprised about the bursts of optimism associated with increasing insight, as revealed in the diary.

In the fifteenth session she again recognized that she could eat and talk, but would feel overwhelmed by thoughts that she hadn't told me and might tell her parents, who would then become furious with her. Difficulties in dealing with the surfacing of increasing aggression continued. Unable to confide in me, she feared exploding at them with all the attendant consequences. The need to regulate the intensity of the aggression continued through starving, laxatives, vomiting, and running.

Concomitantly, however, the last series of comments in a number of diary statements revealed an increasing level of anxiety, fear, and dislike of the analyst, admixed with a continuous awareness of an increased commitment to the treatment, a developing therapeutic alliance, and an optimism about getting well.

The diary:

> *I'm so terrified. Monday's session was the best ever because I talked, and that night I had a sandwich, and last night I had a salad. But later on I got so scared and my old fears of getting fat and needing to starve returned. Today's session was the worst because I didn't talk at all. I'm so scared I'm regressing. I feel myself going back, and I don't want to. I want to start eating and get strong, but it scares me more than anything. I had to go back to laxatives tonight. But if I don't get some sort of relief from my fears, I won't be able to handle myself. I'm going to run. My biggest fear is getting better.*

The patient again graphically illustrated her awareness that talking resulted in progress, which in turn included an increased ability to eat. At the same time, however, she became filled with turmoil, which frightened her and impelled her to displace conflict and become preoccupied again with a fear of getting fat, and starving. This displacement decreased the conflict, lowered her tension, and reactivated her frantic starving. Progress, therefore, can activate regression. "My biggest fear is getting better." It was not a "fear of getting better," but a fear of having to deal with the problems whose resolution would enable her to get better. Thus she acknowledged her fear of facing her aggressive and sexual impulses. This type of regression in the face of progress is quite common and should always be carefully considered. Her comment, "I'm going to run" appeared overdetermined: to run to decrease the turmoil by exercise, to run from facing her conflicts, and to run from treatment and consider quitting. Fortunately, the third option was not exercised.

Crisis

At this point the patient had been in treatment for almost five weeks, and although a relationship was slowly developing and the patient was becoming increasingly aware of the relationship between conflict and her starving, she was continuing to lose weight. Originally weighing 130 pounds before her anorexia, she began treatment at 95 pounds, and in the initial five weeks she had lost an additional 10 pounds. She was still taking daily laxatives, getting limited nourishment, and would occasionally vomit. Exercising, ostensibly to keep in shape, continued with running, swimming, and calisthenics, although the swimming coach was still contemplating dropping her from the team because of her cachexia. It was clear that someone 5 feet, 9 inches tall and weighing 85 pounds could not continue to lose weight without having to be hospitalized soon.

Some advocates of routine initial hospitalization, or those who provide different forms of treatment, might even consider what had transpired thus far as a treatment failure. While continued weight loss does not always occur in this type of analytic treatment, it is not rare. In addition, when a patient has lost a considerable amount of weight prior to entering treatment, the analyst has limited flexibility in weight or time to stem the downhill course.

It is not sufficient to uncover and attempt to analyze some of the patient's conflicts without consistently linking the conflicts to the patient's need to starve or to keep losing weight. This patient had already dramatically and poignantly expressed that if she ate, "terrible things would happen," and she would be overwhelmed by frightening ideas, feelings, and impulses. As long as she continued to feel that way, starving served as the repository for absorbing and attenuating what she perceived as unbearable turmoil. It was necessary for her to feel that she could bear the tension and begin to cope with the conflicts before she could stop starving.

I was concerned about her physical well-being, particularly since her pediatrician was increasingly reluctant to stand by and do nothing as she continued to lose weight. It was also clear that her extreme passivity, her self-destructive need for attention, and her very punishing superego all suggested the possibility of further decompensation. At the same time, hospitalization was viewed as a last resort, since it would involve forcing her to put on weight by one means or another and so leave her with the feeling that she was again being controlled and not in charge of anything in her life. The weight increase would safeguard her physical well-being but would not solve her problems, and the therapist would face an increasingly suspicious, resentful, and defiant patient even less willing to trust, confide, and work cooperatively. Selvini Palazzoli (1978) also feels that hospitalization should be avoided whenever possible, noting the potential negative consequences.

In the next session I noted that she still seemed to be losing weight and that she had previously mentioned that she still limited her eating, used laxatives, and occasionally vomited. I suggested that since she had acknowledged that she had many problems that upset her, and that eating helped bring them to the surface, for her to not eat reasonably, to continue to lose weight, strength, and health, and to court hospitalization was acting self-destructively. I added the transference interpretation that this behavior was making the task of helping her get better more difficult, and therefore it was also a manifestation of her feelings of resentment toward me. She exploded, "I'm sick of coming here and having you stare at me and keep asking me what's on my mind." I replied that she was really setting me up with that kind of an answer. Where would she expect me to look—at the ceiling? She and I were talking together and it was only natural that we look at each other. At that point her anger vanished and she smiled, in part at the jest, but also in response to my reaction to her hostile outburst. I had taken what she said seriously but without reactive anger or rejection. In addition, by my jest, I had indicated my willingness to accept and tolerate her anger without feeling overwhelmed by it. Her rare angry responses in the past had not been well received by her family.

The transference experience had a number of important reactions upon the patient. The analyst had confronted her directly with her self-destructive behavior, but also with her hostile attitude toward him. Characteristically the patient had not been able to be assertive or aggressive, so one might have expected some type of passive, acquiescent acknowledgement of her "bad" behavior. Instead she blew up and asserted herself, charging that she was both sick of the treatment and resentful at being stared at. It is probable that the increasing buildup of aggressive impulses toward her parents suddenly exploded at me when I made some mention of her feeling of resentment being expressed in the continued starving. It is also suggested that in the intervening sessions a relationship had developed with the analyst in which the patient felt that she could express herself without fearing dire consequences. The previous silence in part served the purpose of providing the patient with the feeling that the analyst might behave differently from other people in her life. His calm, patience, concern, and willingness to deal with her uncooperative silence with questions and statements gradually gave her the feeling that she could trust him more. Another anorexic patient, when asked why she kept being so assertive with the therapist, but was not assertive in her life, replied with a smile, "It's safer."

The analyst's reaction confirmed her conjecture. In response to her outburst, he was not cowed nor unduly distressed, but able to absorb the aggression without undue concern. In general it is important for any hostile, guilt-laden patient to feel that the therapist will not be destroyed by an angry outburst. At the same time it is equally important for the patient to feel that she will not be damaged by a retaliatory response from the therapist. The reaction ranges from feeling demeaned and unimportant if the therapist shrugs off her attack as insignificant, to feeling overwhelmed if the therapist responds with anxiety, anger, resentment, abandonment, or guilt-producing behavior. I had accepted her statement seriously and was willing to discuss it with her.

The use of a jest also served to immediately diffuse the situation by indicating that the analyst was not upset and was able to see some humor in the experience. The use of humor gives these patients the feeling that not everything has dire life-and-death consequences and that the ability to laugh at situations suggests that the situations cannot be as frightening and over-whelming as first perceived. It should be emphasized, however, that the use of jest and humor is not without danger. Since a number of these patients have actually experienced excessive criticism or felt criticized since child-hood, they are very sensitive to that possibility and can misperceive a humorous remark whose purpose is to express concern, understanding, and support, as criticism, sarcasm, or mockery. They can then feel like an object of the analyst's humor or contempt instead of being able to share the humor in an insightful, productive manner. In addition, many anorexic patients tend to project their own critical, punishing conscience onto others, ex-periencing criticism that is exaggerated or does not exist. This complex circumstance requires each therapist to evaluate carefully his capacity to express humor with an attitude and in a manner that ensures that the patient can share the humor rather that be the butt of it. Very careful observation of the patient's demeanor and associations following the remark are in order to try to ascertain its impact. Those therapists who are not comfortable with empathic humor should not use it, since the unwitting expression of sadistic attitudes can outweigh the potential benefits.

I continued that this was a talking treatment and she wasn't talking. She countered, "I have nothing on my mind to say." I reminded her that she had admitted that she starved to avoid thoughts and feelings and that if she chose to eat, she would have plenty to say. I added that she must feel guilty because of all her anger and so she punished herself by starving. Her response was, "What good would it be to tell people how I hate them, so I just keep quiet." I replied that that's what had made her sick in the first place.

In the next session she claimed to have eaten a little more. It was my impression that her beginning to eat more was related to the previous session, in which the analysis of the negative transference resulted in an eruption of hatred toward the analyst. When this outburst was acknowledged and accepted without criticism or rejection, the emergence of further anger was facilitated. My acceptance of her aggression decreased her feelings of guilt and the need to punish herself by starving. Less negative transference permitted a strengthening of the therapeutic alliance and a greater willingness to face her problems in treatment. With this background, she risked eating more.

She also admitted for the first time that she was afraid of sex and of dating, and the way she looked now, no one would ask her out. I emphasized that she was saying that her problem was avoiding sex and she was avoiding food. She volunteered that she would keep trying to eat more. This voluntary attempt at eating bolstered by a limited insight and manifestations of a positive transference is more therapeutic than coercive requirements to eat or be force-fed.

I have described elsewhere (Mintz 1985a,b,c, 1988), as has Sperling (1978), that the unnecessary coercing of a patient to eat often duplicates the childhood traumas of feeling overcontrolled, precipitates the emergence of further pathological passivity, and intensifies the underlying rage, resentment, and negative transference. It therefore clearly interferes with the possibility of analyzing major areas of transference conflict related to being controlled and not listened to, as well as the therapist's authoritarian behavior.

With further reflection, I think that the interpretation of the continued self-destructive behavior and the transference aggression truly illustrated an inexact interpretation. I should have emphasized that I understood how difficult it was for her to bear the tension liberated by every attempt at eating and facing her problems. Progress can set off regression, because the conflict bound up in the symptom is freed up; the patient then frequently feels overwhelmed by anxiety and concludes that she cannot cope with it. I could have implied that while she felt overwhelmed and impelled to starve, I did not feel that she could not cope with her emerging problems. I dealt with an interpretation of her aggressive drives rather than with her ego needs to decrease anxiety. She exploded not just because of transference aggression, but because she felt that I did not clearly understand her, having made just an id rather than an id and ego interpretation.

The patient continued to make progress and began to eat, for although the transference interpretation was inexact, the explosive outburst it set off ultimately had a positive effect, and the patient was further encouraged to face her aggressive and sexual feelings.

Recovery

The diary on the second day following the transference interpretation:

It's 3:00 AM and I just can't fall asleep. I'm surprised I ate a lot at McDonald's last night. Today will be the first time I will eat before I go

*to Dr. Mintz. It scares me because I don't know if I can hide anymore.
I used to feel that not being able to hide anymore would be a defeat.
[Later that night] I made it through the day. I ate more today than I had
all year, and I didn't exercise today, but I wish I did. The session
opened me up more than ever! And it was strange, but when I told him
I was afraid of sex, it was like he was expecting it. I think he knew that
it is a lot of my worry, but I still don't understand why I punish myself.*

*He seems to think I can get well. I don't feel I'm ready. But he still
keeps the thought of the hospital on my mind. He says I'm pretty good
at hiding my feelings and I have to admit that he is 100 percent correct.
He knows I feel pain most of the time. I guess I'm just beginning to
realize how tired, cold, and painful my body has become. Sometimes it
really scares me, especially when I get lightheaded, or get chest pains,
or headaches. Eating at my grandmother's wasn't so bad. I still feel the
food pounding inside of me, but it doesn't hurt as much. I hope I let
myself enjoy life again. I've never stopped appreciating it; I've just
stopped living it.*

The "food pounding inside of me" seems to represent her awareness of
the food as feared-hated introjects. Although the transference interpretation seemed to be the factor that stemmed the downhill course, no mention
was made of this interpretation, her aggressive response to it, or my
reaction. What she focused upon was the consequences of it: her fears that
for the first time she will eat before the session, that she may no longer
need to hide her fears, and that she ate more than she had all year, as well
as the lifting of repressed feelings of fatigue, cold and pain, and anxiety
about physical illness. It seems reasonable to consider that the aggressive
outburst without terrible consequence permitted her to face the further
emergence of underlying conflict, attendant upon eating. It was significant
that this was the last entry in the diary for almost one year when a short
epilogue was added. Earlier in the diary, after a week of not writing, she has
mused, "Perhaps I don't need to write as I get better."

In the nineteenth session she revealed that she was eating more. It is
possible, if the patient frequently volunteers that she is eating more or
gaining weight, that to some degree she may be expressing a compliant
attitude toward the analyst, just as she had behaved toward previous
authority figures. While this would have to be analyzed ultimately, to
prevent a developing negative transference, it should be accepted early in
the treatment, especially when it is necessary to interfere with the downhill course. However, it was not my impression that this patient behaved in
that manner. She spontaneously noted again that after eating, she had the
urge to talk more. "It's not that when I starve I don't have any thoughts,
but they are easier to keep in. When I eat, they come out more easily, and
it's harder to keep them back. When I walk out at the end of a session, I feel
a sense of triumph that I kept the thoughts in for another session." This
would suggest that at times starving has a major effect upon suppression
rather than repression of conflict. This would be in keeping with the

patient's conscious awareness of conflict early in treatment, accounting for her "insight" and concomitantly not dealing with it. I pointed out that she was clearly implying that she knew that she could get better if she faced her problems.

The following session she admitted eating more solid food but plaintively commented, "When I'm this way, no one makes any demands of me. If I got better, I'd have to get all A's and I'd have to win every swimming match I enter." I agreed that it did take the pressure off, but she had to be sick to do it. Body image distortion emerged at this time, although it was not acknowledged in the earliest consultations. She felt that she looked thin to normal after gaining 2 pounds and weighing 87 pounds. I quietly disagreed and stated that she was emaciated and was unable to recognize it. The session ended with her comment that she would eat more.

The following session included a discussion of her not eating and not talking enough as a way of continuing to assert herself. She agreed and added that she was afraid that the more I learned about her, the more information I should have to be able to tell her how to run her life. "People always feel that they know what's best for me."

In the next few sessions her need to control information was discussed further. She admitted that she didn't feel as strongly about it and no longer had a sense of victory walking out and thinking, "I didn't tell him much today." We spoke about her swimming and her recognition that the increasing weight was providing her with more muscle and power. I've noted with athletic anorexics that discussing the need to build muscle tissue to improve athletic ability often has a salutary effect (Mintz 1985b). She agreed that she was swimming faster but that she still tired too easily and could use more muscle. "But then the coach would feel I always have to win," she said.

This patient did not attempt to focus obsessively upon her eating habits, food, or fear of getting fat, unlike many starving anorexic patients. When this does occur, it is helpful to point out the underlying dynamic reasons for the patient's behavior. This pointing out may take the form of analyzing the meaning of the specific behavior from the point of the ego: "You choose not to eat so you can be thin and look like a 12-year-old child, because you are afraid to grow up." The therapist may focus on the behavior to reveal a defensive displacement: "You keep thinking of food and being thin because you feel that it is safer to consider than to think about how helpless you feel in dealing with people." It can be dealt with as resistance: "You know that when you think of starving, all your worries go away and you don't have to talk." It can be examined as a form of negative transference: "As long as you discuss only your diet here, we can never get to your problems. It's your way to control the treatment and complicate any attempt of mine to help you."

As long as the patient continues to focus on her symptoms, the therapist is forced to analyze symptom meaning: drives, defense, resistance, and negative transference. Other than pointing out avoidance of important issues, no attempt should be made to directly pressure the patient into discussing life's problems, since it will be rightfully viewed as an attempt to control what is discussed. Control is an issue about which these patients are exquisitely sensitive. Even if they comply, their doing so fosters their view of the analyst as a controlling parent, and it inhibits the analyst's ability to analyze this conflict and effectively indicate that he is not controlling. Constant analysis of the symptomatic behavior will undermine the patient's emotional investment in the symptomatology and eventually increase her willingness to attempt to deal with her underlying problems.

Increasing trust was evident in Marjorie's revealing the many ways she still distrusted me, and indicating that I still had to be tested. She stated, "I want to eat, and it sounds strange, but if you tell me to eat cake, I would, because I eat if someone tells me to." I told her that I was not going to tell her to eat and control her eating, and if *she* chose to eat, she would. The exchange provoked another of her rare smiles. What the patient was referring to was the anorexic's need for extreme compliance. Actually the anorexic patient may be compliant in almost every way except eating. Her request that I tell her to eat reflected an ambivalent attitude. It was difficult for her to eat and she needed some encouragement. Concomitantly, however, the request contained an aspect of distrust and an additional testing. Even with her request, would I refrain from telling her what to do? Her smile acknowledged my not having fallen into the trap.

From the beginning of treatment she had indicated her difficulty in speaking and had suggested that it was easier to reply to questions. My reaction was to attempt to analyze the reasons for the silence rather than to bypass it with questions. Here, too, the patient was suggesting that the analyst tell her what to talk about, and she would comply and then feel controlled. Later in the treatment this issue was discussed at length. The patient admitted that when she felt upset and angry because she couldn't control what was happening to her in her life, she was more silent in the treatment, displacing her anger and attempting to control the analyst because she could not control external events. This reflected progress in that she attempted to control me rather than regress to control over food.

In one session she spoke about putting on a number of pounds by eating more and said that she felt she was giving up control over her eating and her weight faster than she was achieving control over her relationships with people. I agreed that it may well be so, but that her control over eating was really only symbolic and realistically achieved nothing. She continually vacillated in her attitude, insight, and behavior, all of which required repeated working through.

I'm not sure that I want to get well. Then I'll have all those expectations again. I asserted myself more with my father, who was tactless with my sister, but first I thought of starving instead, but I overcame it. I don't think I should get better [patient had gained 12 pounds]. They'll go back to not listening to me. Now they do listen and ask about how I feel and give me money for things I need. They're still afraid I'll get sick and starve again.

Problems of assertion were prominent and included issues with her roommates, teammates, and friends; she sometimes felt exploited and had great difficulty speaking up and protecting her self-interest.

Problems of silence persisted, requiring repeated analysis. She acknowledged more conscious attitudes about defiance. "I don't feel like talking, just as I don't feel like eating, though I've gained another five pounds and feel stronger." I pointed out that she had described a number of relationships that she felt required increased assertiveness and that I wondered about why she chose to assert herself in the sessions by not talking instead of asserting herself with her girlfriends. She acknowledged with a smile that it was safer. She reverted to feelings that I should not know everything about her because my knowing would increase her vulnerability, to fears that I would be critical, and to fears that she would find out things about herself that she didn't want to know and she would have to starve again.

A competitor treated her with contempt, and the patient felt upset. We discussed the fact that she chose to think of herself as upset and helpless rather than as angry, that she used silence to control her anger, that she did not tell her competitor off, that the incident damaged her self-image, and that by getting stronger she could beat her. She had gained 17 pounds and now weighed 102. The weight gain appeared to be directly related to my repeatedly linking her not eating to her method of avoiding conflict.

Toward the end of the third month the patient revealed more of the conflicts behind her silence, and spoke of how the silence played a role in the transference. It was pointed out that most of her difficulty in talking occurred in the beginning of the sessions, and as the hour progressed she often was able to speak more freely. She acknowledged that she was more tense in the beginning and that she was gradually able to relax more. "It's like a tennis match where it takes time to see how it's going to go and if I'm able to handle it. I'm used to pushing things down that upset me, and you want me to talk about it." I emphasized her resistance to dealing with problems and the fact that she saw me as her opponent in the match, trying to get her to open up, and remarked that in the past she felt good upon leaving and nothing important or upsetting came out. She associated further to her insecurity about facing problems, noting how similar her behavior was to her father's when he avoided issues and drank instead. By contrast she starved.

The patient further illustrated her complex attitude toward the treatment, and toward the therapist. Attempting to get well, she was confronted by some of her intense, conscious fears about her aggressive and sexual conflicts, at the same time recognizing with increasing clarity that she would have to reveal them to herself, and to me, in order to improve. These conflicts terrified her, and at points during their emergence she suffered from hours of intense anxiety. Part of her fought to suppress and repress, just as the healthier part drew her back to the next session. The tennis match truly represented a part of our relationship: adversarial, with my focus on opening up and hers upon closing down. It's worth emphasizing that one does not have a patient wholly dedicated to improving, but rather a patient wanting to get well, to be made well, but often terrified of dealing with the conflicts necessary to achieve wellness. Increasing trust facilitates an expanding therapeutic alliance in which the healthy part of her ego gradually allies itself with the therapist's perspective as both work on conflict resolution.

Marjorie's identification with her father's defenses and similar symptom choice is not uncommon. The similarity between them was well chosen, since it is not uncommon to find anorexic-bulimic patients who cease starving and begin binging, drinking, or using drugs. There is a shift in symptom choice with limited insight, but the ego still feels overwhelmed and chooses to avoid dealing directly with the conflict in favor of an alternate resolution with different symptoms. This occurrence is similar to a shifting of psychosomatic symptoms under a comparable set of circumstances. As ulcerative colitis subsides, it can be replaced by asthma, eczema, migraine, depression, or accident-prone behavior. This phenomenon has been referred to elsewhere (Mintz 1980).

At another point she revealed, "I could eat in a completely normal way right now, but what would I have to fall back on. Then I'd have to face my problems and not run away from or bury them. I can't cope with them successfully. I need to assert myself and I'm afraid I can't. If I do what I want, I'm afraid people won't like me . . . and reject me . . . And besides, whatever I do, I always feel I could do it better. I'm always disappointed in the way I behave." The patient again illustrated her recognition that the starving helps repress conflict, her awareness of difficulty in self-assertion, her typical anorexic perfectionism, and her primitive, punitive conscience, which was never satisfied with her behavior. Nevertheless she volunteered that she was eating more normally than she had been in over a year. She added in a subsequent session, "When I'm silent now, I often have thoughts I don't wish to discuss . . . I don't want to face them, and I don't want to share them with you." She did, however, and they related to conflicts over how to cope with boyfriends. So ended the first three months.

DISCUSSION: INSIGHT, ANXIETY, AND COMMITMENT IN THE EARLY SESSIONS

This patient felt forced into treatment, all the while complaining that there was nothing wrong. There were many long silences beginning in the first session. However, she was still able to reveal the conflict over college choice precipitated by parental control and her acquiescence to it. I pointed out that she must have felt that her wishes were not important. It was in that setting that she accepted a second session even though there was a time it conflicted with a class. My tentative optimism was confirmed by her response in the diary to the first session. Coerced into the consultation, with her perception of "nothing wrong" with her, and considerable suspicious silence and withholding, she was still able to write in the diary, "He's okay, he said people don't eat to block out problems . . . It made me begin to realize that I often feel that what I say doesn't matter." She became involved with treatment in the first session, having accepted one interpretation, "I feel that what I say doesn't matter," and retained another, "People don't eat to block out problems." With the beginning of meaningful involvement, she had chosen to skip a class in favor of a second consultation. This patient's attitude about treatment began to change after the very first session.

In the second session, I suggested that the silence and great difficulty speaking might reflect a problem in self-assertion. Assenting, she added that she was used to acceding to her parent's wishes and had rarely defied them. I added, "except by not eating," as I tried to convey that I was in no way critical of the defiance or the starving, but tried to establish meaning to the starving. Her response in the diary was, "I need to go to this doctor. It's getting harder to eat than before. I think that's because I'm beginning to think about my problems more now, and I have to try even harder than ever to block them out by starving." Her initial awareness was striking in that she recognized that the increased thinking about her problems required that she starve more to repress them. Feeling understood and not criticized, she became even more committed to the treatment, although ambivalence persisted, evident by increasing difficulty in going to the sessions, as well as considerable silence. This silence was also in part to avoid further involvement in treatment and was an attempt to suppress very distressing impulses and feelings.

The diary permits us to recognize that by the second session, a recalcitrant, unwilling patient, who has "nothing wrong" and who is silent most of the two sessions, can at the same time become increasingly committed to a treatment program, begin to utilize interpretations, and experience mounting anxiety from expanding reflections, with impulses to regress by starving, and the healthy part of her ego still can conclude. "I have to see this doctor." The signs of resistance were most evident in the treatment, while the positive signs of commitment, insight, and terror were most evident in the diary.

By the fifth session, as the feelings toward her parents were increasingly mobilized, she began to lose control. She reported in her diary that she began to cry while running and then experienced a release of her problems. She resolved to control the running just as she controlled the eating.

The patient illustrated the eruption of pent-up aggressive feelings, which were perceived as frighteningly uncontrollable and therefore were converted into tears of helplessness. Running and starving were again recognized as methods for repressing and symbolically discharging aggressive drives, in her frantic attempts at regaining control over the hostile impulses. The sixth session further validated the nature of her conflicts as she reported in the session, "When I eat . . . something terrible will come out of me . . . about how I feel about people."

A major contribution of the diary was that it revealed the patient's terror of the treatment and the intense and prolonged anxiety resulting from some of the sessions, those in which she revealed more of her thoughts and feelings. The extent of the turmoil experienced was not revealed directly, in part because the patient must have felt that if she revealed this degree of vulnerability, it might be exploited by the analyst, and she feared his exercise of power and control over her.

The considerable silence was a desperate attempt to contain her almost uncontrollable impulses and feelings, by not exploring them with the analyst but by attempting to suppress and repress them. A superficial conclusion that the silence reflected only resistance, lack of commitment to the treatment, a negative transference, and a flagrant defiance would miss one of its additional crucial components, revealed by the diary. The silence was also derived from her increasing commitment to the treatment, her developing insight, her optimism about the possibility of getting well, and her need to decrease anxiety to tolerable levels. It was this commitment, insight, and optimism that prompted her frightened willingness to retain her thought and feelings in her consciousness and to consider revealing them to the therapist.

Starving and its Relationship to Psychic Equilibrium

Marjorie's understanding of the purpose of her starving was either conscious or certainly very close to conscious awareness. At the same time, however, she initially appeared as a patient coerced into the consultation claiming that there was nothing wrong with her. A large percentage of my patients arrive under these identical conditions. Nevertheless, early exploration with these patients reveals that they have some peripheral awareness that the starving is set off by conflict and that the starving decreases anxiety, or more frequently, they acknowledge it with little surprise when it is suggested to them. A similar situation exists with bulimic patients: they volunteer or acknowledge that the gorging is precipitated by conflict and that it decreases the anxiety; then, like the anorexic patients who return to the starving, they promptly return to the gorging.

Subsequently, the understanding previously alluded to is almost never voluntarily recalled, explored further, or utilized again in the service of attempting to control or avoid future tension or conflict. An open discussion of the past distressing experience is not initiated. If the topic is not reintroduced by the analyst, the patient will ignore it and suppress or repress the previously acknowledged relationship between an external or internal conflict, the development of anxiety, feeling overwhelmed, starving, and the subsequent easing of the conflict. The same sequence exists where binging substitutes for starving. Thus one is confronted with a paradox. A patient under a great deal of pressure to eat normally either starves or secretly binges, while seeming to have some awareness of the cause of her behavior, yet does not voluntarily reveal her understanding. Moreover, she frequently acts as if she were unaware of it and behaves as if there were nothing wrong with her. Concomitantly, a pointing out of the dynamic relationship between crisis, starving, and decreasing anxiety is often accepted without much surprise.

While it may appear that she does not understand the reasons for the starving, or gorging, another alternative is possible: that in spite of the understanding, she still feels that she needs to starve, or gorge, because any attempt at insightfully facing the true problems precipitates such intense anxiety that she feels completely overwhelmed, disorganized, and panicky. Not only is it devastating to confront the problems directly, but the constant tension and anxiety aroused by the conflict may require repeated starving, or binging, for her to achieve a more tolerable level of stress reduction and regain psychic equilibrium. The starver needs to starve, and the gorger needs to gorge, for the same reason. Starving or gorging becomes the major method by which inner turmoil can be regulated. It is therefore not easily renounced without alternative routes of tension reduction available. Surprisingly, this dilemma is clearly acknowledged in Marjorie's diary but was not revealed directly to me, probably out of concern that I might interfere with her ability to continue to use this method. It had become her secret method for feeling better. She did mention her concern that she was giving up the starving and gorging faster than she was gaining alternative control with understanding to control her life.

Progress: A Stimulus for Regression

This patient illustrated the anorexic and bulimic tendency to respond to progress as a stimulus for regression. She clearly displayed an almost fluid shifting between a decision to begin to face conflict, the ensuing anxiety and turmoil that it generated, and then the preoccupation with the symptoms of starving, and exercise, in order to reestablish ego homeostasis, by symptomatic regression.

At the end of the third session the diary reported: "It hurts to open up, and I don't feel that it will help . . . I'm trying harder not to eat. I think it is an attempt to keep from talking . . . I have some kind of feeling inside . . . that this bubble of anger and pain is going to outburst out soon . . . and I feel I will be able to eat . . . and it will be alright."

The patient describes progress in her attempt to deal with problems, states that the emerging anger will enable her to eat, and expresses the feeling that life will improve. Concomitantly, she's trying not to eat to keep from talking and further understand her painful conflicts.

The diary after sessions 15 to 17 described her recognition of progress— that it "was the best [session] ever," that she talked, and that she ate. Simultaneously, she became so frightened and so guilty from her angry accusations toward her parents, that she felt overwhelmed with turmoil. The need to decrease it was accomplished with the return to the fear of getting fat, starving, running, and a silence in the next session to suppress and repress the conflict. As she felt unable to tolerate the ensuing anxiety, regression provided surcease.

A second factor in which progress stimulates regression was described by Marjorie. She was concerned that the healthier she became the more demands would be made upon her by family, friends, and teachers. Parents would expect good grades. The swimming coach would expect her to win the meet. Starving provided a respite, when people would be more considerate of her needs. With her healthy, this secondary gain would be lost.

The third factor is the presence of a strict, punitive superego that requires punishment for preoccupation with and discussions of aggressive and sexual impulses, with all the ramifications arising from the associated fantasies. Any deviation from rigid, puritanical standards is unacceptable and requires punitive suffering, such that progress leading to health, satisfaction, and happiness would also fall into the category requiring punishment. An attempt at modification of strict superego standards should begin early in treatment.

A fourth reason for regression takes place characteristically and primarily in bulimic patients. The anorexic's threat to die is severe enough a punishment to satisfy the primitive dictates of the superego, whereas the bulimic's gorging and vomiting without clear threat of death does not satisfy the superego's primitive, punitive requirements, necessitating repetitive punishing and suffering as an alternative to the threats of death. This self-destructive behavior is elaborated elsewhere (Mintz 1988).

A brief vignette will illustrate. A 25-year-old bulimic patient described a four-year history of anorexia followed by six years of bulimia. Prior to treatment, she was virtually unemployable, exercising six hours a day and gorging and vomiting for two hours. After a year of analysis, all her symptoms cleared. She stopped gorging and vomiting, limited exercising to appropriate time periods, and ate normally, including foods that she had not eaten in ten years. In the midst of this sense of exhilaration, she abruptly quit the analysis, began abusing drugs and alcohol, and associated with disreputable characters unlike previous friends.

The Therapeutic Relationship between Conflict, Starving, and the Decrease of Anxiety

The analyst's pointing out the interrelationship indicates to the patient that he understands the initial insight that is already partially perceived by her but has not yet been utilized. The implication that he will attempt to help her use what she seems to understand can be therapeutic; it provides some degree of hope and encourages the beginning of a working alliance. This chain of events was revealed in Marjorie's diary and might have contributed to the very early positive but unspoken response to the treatment. Conversely, it would also be important for the patient to feel that the therapist understands her well enough so that he would not misuse the information and would not too actively pursue the uncovering of issues that she feels are still too sensitive for her to face. This fear was more clearly evident in the diary than in her discussions in the sessions.

To that end, the long, frequent periods of silence in part represented a slowing down of the uncovering process to a pace that was tolerable and under her control. This could help explain the emergence of periodic concise but very insightful statements in the sessions. It also provided the patient with the time to reflect upon what issues she felt could be revealed, and in what manner. The silence should be recognized as a reflection of a conscious, painful struggle over how to deal with frightening conflict. To view the silence primarily in negative terms of disinterest, defiance, or uncooperativeness would be to ignore those ego functions serving homeostasis and related to her attempts at establishing a tolerable level of functioning in the treatment, maintaining some degree of ego control over her impulses, and being able to choose the content and affects with which she could cope.

Cognizant of this turmoil, the therapist is more able to deal with the silence utilizing it as an opportunity to facilitate development of a therapeutic alliance by illustrating to the patient, both by what he says and by how he behaves, that he is not disappointed, frustrated, or irritated and does not view it as an insurmountable obstacle. This approach is quite different from the response of a therapist who saw a silent patient in the first consultation and told the parents that the daughter was not workable because she did not talk. Conversely, one has to wonder what the effect would be if the therapist focuses exclusively upon eating, diet, and weight. If the patient already partially recognizes that stress causes the need to starve, or to binge, and that the starving or binging decreases the stress and anxiety, then the suggestion for a total nutritional approach appears tangential. The focus upon eating reinforces the symptom rather than analyzing it.

If one concludes that the partial insight is not pursued because to do so precipitously would fill the patient with overwhelming anxiety, then it might be helpful to address that issue. Specifically, one could interpret that facing some of these worries might be very distressing at this time and discussion of certain issues might be postponed. In this way the therapist acknowledges the conflicts without pressuring the patient into talking about them until she is ready, thus reassuring her. The sense of intense anguish in Marjorie's diary would certainly indicate such an approach and clarify to her the past inability to explore what she already knows, since she had previously described attempting to deal with it as a failure. In her case, I might have pointed out to her that I recognized that in certain areas she had been dealing with troubling problems in a careful, thoughtful fashion, which resulted in her most cogent, concise, and insightful statements. It was in great part her decision to reveal her thoughts and feelings that resulted in the almost overpowering anxiety that frightened her and also induced regressive, defensive shifts with thoughts of getting fat, starving, and exercise, all to aid the silence in pushing back the conflict that she had decided to express. It was this expanding dilemma, this progress that increased the ambivalence over opening up, that induced regression. The diary had reported, "I think I'm ready to let the world into my life and take on the fight . . . the toughest thing I'll ever have to do."

The Issue of Control

What was also most striking in an analysis of the patient's diary was her considerable awareness of the meaning of her symptoms: she recognized the presence of aggressive impulses that terrified her and filled her with guilt, and of the almost overwhelming fears that she was out of control in her attempts to contain them. Moreover, she was also aware—as I believe most of my patient's have consciously been aware—that, when she was upset, starving decreased the feeling of distress. This was openly but reluctantly acknowledged by most of my patients.

While starving is a cardinal symptom of anorexia and has multiple symbolic relevance, a number of its determinants have already been mentioned. The recognition of suppressing and repressing conflict is either openly evident to these patients, or so close to consciousness that when the concept is introduced, the patients acknowledge it. To neglect the discussion of this meaning of starving is to avoid a major opportunity to reach out to the patient with a level of understanding that is especially valuable. Such a discussion facilitates an approach to the starving patient that does not pressure her to eat. This helps to avoid having to deal with setting off her anxiety, uncooperativeness, enmity, and desire to terminate treatment because she fears the loss of control. The shift in focus from discussions of why she does not eat is technically and therapeutically important, because it begins to remove the anticipated coercive element from the treatment and helps the patient recognize more fully what she has already partially understood. The patient's profound fear of being controlled cannot be underestimated, particularly since she anticipates an attempt at control from the therapist. Most important, however, is her apprehension that the therapist's goal is to remove her starving, even against her will. The fear is intense because she recognizes how vulnerable she has always been in complying with the wishes and requests of "the other person" in the past. Being able to point out that the starving is being used to push away worries provides a rational for it that is dissociated from her conscious fear of getting fat. Encouraging her to recognize that she feels out of control of problems and therefore she at least needs to control her eating instead adds to her insight. Finally, suggesting that when she deals with her problems and begins to feel in control of the issues in her life she will not need to starve circumvents her fear that the therapist will coerce her to eat.

In addition, if what I'm suggesting is accurate, then to focus upon coercing the patient to eat, without discussing the reasons for the starving, of which she is at least partially aware, is to indicate that the therapist does not understand as much as the patient.

One 16-year-old markedly disturbed bulimic girl demonstrated her fear of control in very poignant fashion. At the beginning of treatment she volunteered, "I'm beginning to like you, but then I'll want to please you . . . and do what you want . . . and then you'll control me . . . so I'm going to quit," and got up and walked out.

The other major component of control is that, dynamically, when these patients are in a starvation state, they unconsciously feel that they have lost control over most of the important issues in their lives. That's why they are starving. The starving with its accompanying control over appetite, food intake, when she eats, what she eats, how much she eats, the arrangement and movement of food around the plate in ritualistic fashion, and her weight to the half pound all facilitates the experience of control. In these obsessional patients, food is dealt with as a compulsive ritual.

One anorexic patient went so far as to ingest a sequence of foods, each having a clearly different color and then attempted to vomit them up, in reverse order, with minimal mixing of the colors. The ability to control the starving can become an all-consuming necessity.

One patient dramatically illustrated this point. Malnourished, and having fainted in the street, she awoke to finding herself in a hospital bed with an intravenous infusion in her arm. With a cry of anguish, she attempted to reach out with the other arm to pull out the needle, while crying out, "That's all I've got." She felt that they were taking away the only source of control left to her, and it was devastating.

Marjorie exclaimed at one point that she was afraid she was giving up control over her starving, and loss of weight, before she had achieved enough understanding and control over the important things in life. She was viewing the progress almost as an exchange of one set of circumstances for another: a titration of change and replacement. And in a sense she was quite correct that the control over starving and weight loss did truly serve a purpose for her. She needed to feel that insight and progress with their accompanying control over her impulses, and her relationships, were essential before she renounced the silence, starving, and exercise with their accompanying but regressive control. There is some validity to this view, and therefore I am not too concerned when the patient temporarily does not gain weight, so long as her physical condition is not medically dangerous.

I find it helpful to be able to point out to the patient that I can understand some of the positive aspects of the starving. This remark is usually quite surprising to a patient who is convinced of the therapist's opposite approach; it helps to dissipate some of the fear and distrust so evident in the beginning of treatment.

I do point out that I see some value in the achievement of control in starving, although the control is symbolic and ultimately dangerous, especially because the patient has not been fully cognizant of how the starving could affect her. I suggest, though, that she might concentrate upon how it affects others. I acknowledge that a previously heavy person subject to ridicule in childhood might well want to be on the thin side, and extra thin just to be on the safe side. I add that starving in the face of pressures by parents and physicians may be an aspect of adolescent rebellion, something that she has been unable to achieve in other times and in other ways. The focus upon exploring, clarifying, analyzing, and understanding without pressure and criticism, establishes a setting for gradual change in the patient's perception of what is expected and a gradual acceptance of the true goal of insight, not just behavioral change. This attitude helps foster a cooperative approach rather than an adversarial one.

THE UNCONSCIOUS MEANING OF STARVING

The unconscious meaning of starving has been described primarily in terms of its ability to decrease anxiety, absorb conflict, and displace onto eating the conscious preoccupations with one's problems. Some of the other determinants of starving are:

1. It can defend against regressed, destructive impulses to destroy by using the teeth (Chapter 14).
2. With further regression, it can defend against primitive cannibalistic impulses (Chapter 14).
3. It can deny dependency cravings symbolized by avoiding the sense of security from ingesting food.
4. It aids in repressing the urge to incorporate or merge with and retain parental imagos or other lost objects.
5. It can symbolize dealing with separation, independence, and ascetic achievement in the service of reestablishing ego equilibrium.
6. It can defend against oral sexual impulses (Mintz 1985c).
7. It can deny oral pregnancy fantasies (Mintz 1985c).
8. It can act out the fantasied starving of an infant in utero (Mintz 1985c).
9. It can resolve conflict over physiological maturation and sexuality by the anorexic's regressing to being preadolescent in physical appearance and unappealing as a sexual object.
10. It can symbolize conflict in psychosexual identity, with the lost tissue representing an unconsciously fantasied series of lost penises (Mintz 1985d).
11. It can serve strict, punitive superego dictates of punishment for forbidden aggressive, sexual, and dependency wishes.
12. It can express a resistance or a negative transference in the treatment.

THE STARVATION CRISIS AND THE ROLE OF "THE OTHER"

When the period of starvation was discussed with Marjorie months later, it became increasingly evident that my concern for her health was well founded. Referring to the early crisis, I asked how long she had contemplated starving. She appeared perplexed at the question and ultimately acknowledged that the issue had never occurred to her. Upon further reflection, she added that she assumed she would have just continued to starve and starve, with no endpoint in mind.

Her focus was not just to starve in order to suppress and repress conflict and to triumph in her control over her appetite instead of her world, but also unconsciously to derive a sense of satisfaction from the fear and anxiety that her starving induced in others. She illustrated a typical anorexic attitude of concern only for how her behavior affected "the other" and a lack of concern for how it affected herself. Without that sense of awareness that she could irreparably damage herself, no self-protective measures could be taken. Her starving that "could control the other" and that others could not prevent could now produce the same sense of apprehension, anxiety, helplessness, and fear in others that she had long been experiencing herself. The control and satisfaction derived from her starving could be perpetuated endlessly and lead to an unrecognized moribund condition.

It was necessary to point out the danger—that she was preoccupied with how her behavior affected others without realizing its dangerous impact upon herself—and as a result she could die by mistake. Sperling (1978) has noted that psychosomatic patients can die from miscalculation. When the weight loss proceeds to the point of physical danger, hospitalization, along with its attendant procedures, is necessary; this has been discussed elsewhere (Mintz 1985a). Routine hospitalization has a potentially negative effect upon the ultimate course of treatment and should be avoided. It can increase feelings of helplessness and lack of control, along with fear and anger toward the hospital personnel, later transferred to the therapist, making the therapy more difficult.

In a considerable number of patients the need to starve is the end product of a long-standing character trait derived from growing up concerned primarily with the well-being of others at their own expense. This takes the form of being too thoughtful, considerate, and helpful, of being obedient and accommodating and not causing any trouble being the perfect child and ultimately so sensitive that requests do not even have to be made. The individual assumes a considerable unconscious burden and develops considerable resentment. With the subsequent development of the anorexia, this character trait becomes modified. Instead of a preoccupation with the need to gratify "the other," it reverses into a need to frustrate "the other." Starving is the outstanding manifestation of this ego shift.

STARVATION AND THE CAPACITY TO THINK

Some researchers feel that a starving patient with considerable weight loss must regain considerable weight in order to be able to think clearly and to be responsive to psychotherapy (Bruch, 1970, 1973, 1978 and Hsu 1986). Garfinkle and colleagues (1982) state, "The effects of starvation must be reversed if the patient is to benefit meaningfully from psychotherapy."

Marjorie's weight went from 130 to 85 pounds, a loss of 30 percent of her body weight. In my experience and that of colleagues, it has not been found that the weight loss interferes with thinking or the ability to utilize analytic treatment. Members of the Psychosomatic Study Group of the Psychoanalytic Association of New York, over a period of twenty-five years of dealing with anorexia nervosa and bulimia, have not found it necessary for a patient to increase her weight as a prerequisite to her working and thinking effectively in analysis or in psychotherapy. A similar attitude has prevailed during the past eight years of intensive research on anorexia and bulimia among the approximately thirty to forty members of the American Psychoanalytic Association, where members are drawn from all parts of the country. This patient illustrated that her capacity to think as well as to experience strong emotions was clearly retained. It was certainly true that the patient did not communicate volubly in the beginning of treatment, but the long periods of silence were not reflective of a problem in thinking or an absence of feeling: quite the reverse. The silence was a consequence of such frightening thoughts and intense feelings that the patient felt overwhelmed by them and so felt it necessary to supress them by all means possible, including silence. It may be that in some cases when a patient is silent and is asked by the therapist what is on her mind, the reply may be "nothing." This less than candid response and defensive attempt at minimizing conflict with its subsequent anxiety could well be misconstrued as the patient's having nothing on her mind.

In the nineteenth session, as Marjorie began to eat more, she spontaneously revealed that it is easier to keep her thoughts in when she starves. She described a sense of triumph after leaving the sessions she "kept the thoughts in for another session." These admissions were revealed after she had begun to eat, and they illustrate her insight.

In addition, however, I also had the opportunity to evaluate, both from the treatment hours and from her diary, that with a 30 percent weight loss, her ability to think clearly and her capacity to experience frighteningly strong emotional reactions were in no manner impaired. Her ability for self-reflection, insight, and thoughtful expression of concepts appeared quite intact. A similar situation was present in the early stage of treatment of a hospitalized 17-year-old girl who lost 50 percent of her weight, dropping from 104 to 53 pounds. Regaining 23 pounds in three months of hospitalization, she regained the remainder and returned to 103 pounds during her course of four to five times a week of psychoanalytic treatment.

Risen (1982) also disagreed with Bruch (1978), who felt that anorexic patients were unable to utilize analytic treatment until there was appropriate weight gain. With a loss of 36 percent of her body weight, his patient amply demonstrated that she was capable of being analyzed: she had the capacity to understand and utilize symbolic representations, to develop a transference, and to benefit from insight in the resolution of her conflicts, at a point before major weight gain.

Epilogue 1

The last entry in the patient's diary.

It's been over a year since I've written. The time has passed so quickly. Within that year, though, I feel I have grown and accomplished more than in all my nineteen years of living. When I read the previous pages, it is as if I'm reading about someone who is so different from me but who I know was once a part of me. Those were the dark days of my life . . . the years I wished never existed but I don't totally regret. My past has brought me closer to who I am.

When I face my problems and accept myself, there is nothing I can't handle. So, those were my feelings and thoughts. If there was a way for me to reach back and rewrite them, I don't know if I would. For it really doesn't matter. All that matters is that I am happy with myself today.

Epilogue 2

The patient completed treatment after four and a half years. During the treatment, her symptoms of starving, preoccupation with food, anorexic food habits, fears of getting fat, laxative use, and vomiting subsided. Menstrual periods returned after the first year. No alternative symptoms appeared to replace the anorexia.

Initially having few friends and being anxious in social situations, she was able to expand her friendships, and her social anxieties subsided. With increasing levels of assertiveness and less fear of exploitation, she developed confidence and self-esteem. Less excessive concern for the well-being of "the other" was replaced by healthy self-interest. Concomitantly, she became comfortable with her femininity and with relating to men. Ultimately, she met a thoughtful, considerate man, and after about a year they married. During the evolving relationship, previous sexual difficulties were further resolved, so that prior to marriage she was orgastic 80 percent of the time.

She also completed college and graduate school and was successfully employed as a bank executive at the time of termination.

SUMMARY

An attempt was made to further clarify the opening phase of analytic technique in the treatment of anorexia nervosa, by evaluation of the patient's response to the session as recorded in her diary, which was examined eighteen months after the beginning of treatment.

The diary revealed three crucial features that were not clearly mentioned by the patient during the course of treatment.

The first was the very early positive reaction to the treatment in spite of the circumstances surrounding its beginning. A patient who felt coerced into treatment, with "nothing wrong," became actively involved in the treatment process during the first three sessions, with the beginning of a positive transference.

The second was the intense degree of anguish that she experienced when contemplating discussing the nature of her conflicts. She truly felt tortured by her self-reflections and her attempts to open up and talk in the sessions. The accompanying return to starving, exercise, and silence as regressive necessities for ego reintegration became palpably understandable in that light, and was not perceived as ineffective treatment.

The third feature was her marked degree of understanding and insight into her conflicts almost from the point of entry into treatment. It is the writer's impression that this degree of insight is not unusual among these patients.

A treatment that avoids the further exploration and clarification of these dynamic issues, but rather places primary focus upon eating and weight gain, may tend to reinforce the symptom rather than analyze it.

The preoccupation with "the other" at the expense of the self, a typical anorexic character trait, was explored during a starvation crisis. The patient's need to starve, with no endpoint in sight, with focus upon its effect on the other person without thoughts of consequence to the self, could produce an illusive sense of satisfaction leading to an unrecognized moribund condition and ultimately death.

A 30 percent loss of body weight revealed no evidence, either from the patient's behavior in treatment or her reflections in the diary, that her thinking capacity or the depth of her emotional experience was in any manner compromised. Her thinking, when she chose to verbalize, was astute, cogent, and incisive, while her range of emotional feelings was broad and intense. This case is similar in this regard to that of other patients and raises the question of whether all patients who starve require nutritional supplements prior to analytic types of treatment. It is possible that a psychological resistance like silence, which needs to be analyzed, may be mistakenly perceived as a physiological defect that requires replenishing.

REFERENCES

Bruch, H. (1970). Psychotherapy in primary anorexia nervosa. *Journal of Nervous and Mental Diseases* 150: 51–67.
_____ (1973). *Eating Disorders: Obesity, Anorexia Nervosa, and the Person Within*. New York: Basic Books.
_____ (1978). *The Golden Cage*. Cambridge, MA: Harvard University Press.

Garfinkle, P., and Gardner, D. (1982). Hospital management. In *Anorexia Nervosa, A Multidimensional Perspective,* pp. 216–257. New York: Bruner/Mazel.

Hogan, C. C. (1988). Eating Disorders. The psychosomatic study group of the Psychoanalytic Association of New York.

Hsu, G. L. K. (1986). The treatment of anorexia nervosa. *American Journal of Psychiatry* 43:573–581.

Mintz, I. L. (1980). Multideterminism in asthmatic disease. *International Journal of Psychotherapy,* vol 8., ed. R. Langs, pp. 593–600. New York: Jason Aronson.

_____ (1985a). An analytic approach to hospital and nursing care. In *Fear of Being Fat: The Treatment of Anorexia Nervosa and Bulimia,* rev. ed., ed. C. P. Wilson, C. C. Hogan, and I. L. Mintz, pp. 315–326. New York: Jason Aronson.

_____ (1985b). Anorexia nervosa and bulimia in males. In *Fear of Being Fat: The Treatment of Anorexia Nervosa and Bulimia,* rev. ed., ed. C. P. Wilson, C. C. Hogan, and I. L. Mintz, pp. 263–304. New York: Jason Aronson.

_____ (1985c). Psychoanalytic therapy of severe anorexia: the case of Jeanette. In *Fear of Being Fat: The Treatment of Anorexia Nervosa and Bulimia,* rev. ed., ed. C. P. Wilson, C. C. Hogan, and I. L. Mintz, pp. 217–244. New York: Jason Aronson.

_____ (1985d). The relationship between self-starvation and amenorrhea. In *Fear of Being Fat: The Treatment of Anorexia Nervosa and Bulimia,* rev. ed., ed. C. P. Wilson, C. C. Hogan, and I. L. Mintz, pp. 335–344. New York: Jason Aronson.

_____ (1988). Self destructive behavior in anorexia and bulimia. In *Bulimia: Psychoanalytic Treatment and Theory,* ed. H. Schwartz, pp. 127–172. Madison, CT: International Universities Press.

Risen, S. (1982). The psychoanalytic treatment of an adolescent with anorexia nervosa. *Psychoanalytic Study of the Child* 37:433–460. New Haven, CT: Yale University Press.

Selvini Palazzoli, M. (1978). Some hints on psychotherapeutic conduct. In *Self Starvation: From Individual to Family Therapy in the Treatment of Anorexia Nervosa,* ed. M. S. Palazzoli, p. 122. Northvale, NJ: Jason Aronson.

Sperling, M. (1978). Anorexia nervosa. In *Psychosomatic Disorders in Childhood,* ed. O. Sperling, pp. 129–173. New York: Jason Aronson.

Wilson, C. P. (1985). The family psychological profile and its therapeutic implications. In *Fear of Being Fat: The Treatment of Anorexia Nervosa and Bulimia,* rev ed., ed. C. P. Wilson, C. C. Hogan, and I. L. Mintz, pp. 29–47. New York: Jason Aronson.

PART IV

Bulimia

8

Analysis of an Adult Male Bulimic

Howard S. Rudominer, M.D.

Bulimia, which literally means *ox hunger*, or a voracious appetite, refers to episodes of binge eating often followed by self-induced vomiting or the excessive use of purges: laxatives, enemas, or diuretics. It is a confusing syndrome that is probably far more prevalent than was formerly thought. Various studies of high school and college students suggest that binge eating is widespread, especially in the female population.

Bulimia often occurs in association with anorexia nervosa, and although it has recently been recognized in England and the United States as a discrete entity, most psychoanalytic investigators still consider bulimia and anorexia nervosa to represent opposite poles of the same disorder. Clinically, they both describe syndromes that can be found in patients ranging from neurotic, borderline, and psychotic to patients with preoedipal and pregenital character disorders.

Two reasons impelled me to write up this case for publication.[1] First is

---

[1]This is a revised version of a case report presented at the discussion group for the psychoanalytic treatment of patients with psychosomatic disorders, fall meeting of the American Psychoanalytic Association, New York, December 1984.

the rarity of finding bulimia in a male, since the male/female ratio is believed to be between 1:10 and 1:20. Second is the virtual absence in the literature of a report on the psychoanalytic treatment of such a patient, although Mintz (1983), Sours (1974, 1980), and Welsh (1983) have offered brief clinical vignettes of male bulimics.

My intent in this chapter is to show that such patients can be analyzed largely by means of a classical approach, although according to Bruch (1973) psychoanalysis is contraindicated with anorexic and bulimic patients. In addition, Sours (1980) feels that bulimics in general have a more guarded prognosis than anorexics and that male bulimics specifically fare worse than females prognostically. To this end I shall present relevant portions of an analysis which began as analytically oriented psychotherapy.

BRIEF SUMMARY OF THE LITERATURE

Stunkard (1959) was the first to identify bulimia as a distinct type of eating disorder while analyzing the eating patterns of obese patients. Since then, the "binge-purge syndrome," as it is often referred to, has been variously labeled in the psychiatric and psychoanalytic literature as "bulimia nervosa" (Russell 1979), "bulimarenia" (Boskind-White and White 1983), "compulsive eating" (Green and Rau 1974, Orbach 1978), "dietary chaos syndrome" (Palmer 1979), the "abnormal normal weight control syndrome" (Crisp 1981), and "fat phobia" (Wilson 1983). Sours (1980) and Wilson (1983) offer extensive reviews of the literature on anorexia nervosa.

The literature on anorexia nervosa can be heuristically separated into three groups. Sperling (1949, 1968) and Jessner and Abse (1960) view binging and food as a concrete representation of the mother-breast of the oral period and purging as the expression of the unconscious, murderous rage toward the introjected, poisonous object-mother. In a parallel fashion, Sugarman (1981) traces bulimia genetically to a developmental arrest in the practicing subphase of the separation-individuation process. Others (e.g., Friedman 1953, Hogan 1983, Schwartz 1986) view binging and purging as a neurotic compromise formation, utilizing the concepts of conflict and defense as representing the patient's unconscious, incestual wishes to impregnate or become impregnated. Hence food is viewed as the paternal phallus, and the conflicts pertaining to it are played out on the phallic-oedipal level. Finally, there are authors who conceptualize bulimia in terms of a Kohutian deficit model (Goodsitt 1985, Swift and Letven, 1984).

CASE ILLUSTRATION

History

A. was a 19-year-old college student when his mother first called. She told me that recently her son had drastically decreased his food intake, had become "depressed and nervous," and insisted on exercising after every meal. An obese and chronically depressed art teacher, she also told me that A., having also been obese most of his life, had lost nearly 100 pounds since joining a health club with his father a year and a half earlier. He had apparently been dieting normally and feeling exhilarated until a few months before, when his symptoms began.

What most impressed me at our initial interview was how much younger than his 19 years A. looked and how crude his diction was in view of his middle-class and educational background. He was undistinguished in appearance, neatly if casually dressed, and of medium height and large frame. A.'s blond, straight, short-cropped hair was combed in a rather boyish style. He was thin but by no means as emaciated as his mother had led me to expect.

A. had two sisters, one five years older, the other eight years older than he. Both were married, had children, and lived within five blocks of A. and his parents. Moreover, both sisters also had had eating problems, the older one having been hospitalized for anorexia nervosa when A. was 12 years old.

A.'s mother encouraged all her children to be dependent on her and demanded unquestioned obedience. His father, a moderately successful, hard-working businessman, liked to plan each hour of his day to the second. Narcissistic, rigid, and sometimes sadistic, he had had periodic fist fights with his eldest daughter during her adolescence and occasionally slapped A. on the head as well.

When A. was in fourth grade, he developed a school phobia that led him to feign diarrhea and vomiting by pouring water into the toilet so he could stay home from school.

In spite of this early school phobia, he managed to do well and was a bright and accomplished student. He was accepted at one of New York City's prestigious high schools, where despite little studying he did moderately well. However, in accordance with his low self-esteem and dependency on his parents, A. chose to attend a mediocre local business college, continued to live at home, and kept his part-time job at the electrical appliance store where he had worked for several years.

A.'s entire family had always been preoccupied with food and eating. Being forced to eat was an unvarying theme throughout his childhood.

A. had always longed for sexual relationships with girls but had felt too fat and intimidated to pursue them. In spite of his withdrawal from heterosexual contact, he nevertheless maintained close relationships with both sexes. He was currently part of a clique of friends in college which functioned for him much like an extended family.

Psychoanalytic Psychotherapy Phase

I initially elected to see A., sitting up, three times a week, because I felt that psychoanalysis might produce in him overwhelming and disorganizing anxiety. His dreams early in treatment centered around his fear that therapy would uncover his intense sexual and aggressive impulses. He guiltily "confessed" to having compulsively masturbated in the past as well as having his dog occasionally lick his anus while he masturbated humping his bed, a disclosure that remained a humiliation to him throughout the therapy and analysis. Whereas I postulated to myself latent homosexual conflicts and unconscious feminine identification in A., his conscious masturbation fantasies were always heterosexual. The patient told me he hoped that when he lost more weight he would become more outgoing with girls. However, much to his dismay, he now found himself devoid of any energy or interest in girls.

Although A.'s family was concerned almost exclusively with his continuing weight loss, A. himself was preoccupied with his future goals in life. His mother wanted him to teach special education. Although he was then majoring in art history, he contemplated a switch to a school where he could major in special education, despite his passion for art. Rather than concentrating on his eating disorder, my initial interventions centered on his fears of becoming an adult and making career choices. This intervention was consoling and comforting to A. and, in part, helped shape an early positive transference and beginning working alliance. He felt understood and grateful that I did not concentrate just on his anorexia, as had his physician, family, and first psychiatrist, whom he left after three sessions because "all he did was take notes on my history."

A. informed me about his recent dancing lessons, his going to a party dressed as a ballerina, his wishing to teach as his mother did, and his sexual difficulties. I privately thought of his possible feminine identification especially with his mother; I found out later that there was a strong identification with one of his sisters as well.[2]

Passive homosexual fears and longing for me in the transference were among the earliest transference paradigms that emerged and led to transient resistances manifested by complaints that the psychotherapy cost too much money and was not really helping him. Derivatives of his unconscious homosexual fantasies and feminine identification filled the hours. He dreamed that while he was having intercourse with a platonic girlfriend in his house, with him lying passively on his back and she on top, his mother walked in and caught them. He associated to his large feminine-looking breasts (see also Falstein et al. 1956) when he was obese. In addition, he had always felt ashamed of his penis, which he believed to be too small.[3] The patient also dreamed that he was sitting in a car with a girl and had to beat up a "black kid" who confronted him and the girl. He was then pursued by a throng of blacks who "ripped down" the gate to his

---

[2]Sperling (1983) has noted an identification with an envied and hated sister as an important dynamic in two of her male patients with anorexia nervosa.

[3]This finding is similar to that in a male anorexic case published by Welsh (1983), although in that case the idea was frankly delusional.

house and attacked him with torches. Although he did not get "torched," he was left with only a burn on his back.

Through his association we discovered that for the past week he had been constipated for the first time in his life and had to give himself a suppository the night before, to no avail. These associations and dreams were overdetermined. I elected to avoid the homosexual transference issues at this early time, concentrating instead on his general fear of the analyst and what might be exposed in the treatment.

During A.'s third month of treatment he became paralyzed and over-whelmed with guilt nearly every time he ate. Consequently, his voracious desire to eat junk food made him feel as if he were "going crazy." He told me that "when I was at my sickest, I actually believed that just talking, thinking, and especially smelling foods could make me gain weight." Upon hearing this, I began to feel uneasy and wondered just how extensive his defects in reality testing were. I intuitively and uncharacteristically told A. not to worry if he gained a few pounds. I remember feeling concerned about his continued weight loss. Although this supportive intervention did temporarily help him to complete his school work, I think it clearly represented a counterreaction due to my own anxiety.

Several weeks later, after continuing to lose weight, A. revealed that he had had his first episode of "pigging out" (his term for binge eating) and enjoyed it without guilt because he thought that I had sanctioned it. A. said he observed me smiling after he had told me what he ate and consequently felt he had pleased me. I pointed out that it was curious that he was just speaking about how his mother just sat and let him eat away, and now he felt that I had done the same. Although I was never sure whether I had in fact smiled, I nevertheless did find his recounting the episode surprising in terms of the enormous quantity of food he had consumed.

As A. gained more insight into the connection between his fear of sexual excitement and his fear of losing control over his eating, genetic material began to emerge relating to his mother's and sisters' nudity. He recalled that his mother and sisters walked around the house wearing only their bras and panties. Bedroom doors always remained open, a finding that conforms with Wilson's (1983) similar observation in all his anorexic families. I think that the dynamics of the "open door policy" relates not only to primal scene exposure and overstimulation, but also to conflicts over separation-individuation, which are ubiquitous in eating-disordered patients. The open doors represent the parents' attempt to discourage the child's growing autonomy and privacy and create the illusion that ev-eryone is merged together in a happy symbiotic orbit.

Over the next several months his bulimia increased in frequency and intensity, as did some other manifestations of his general impulse disorder, such as speeding and passing red lights to get home to finish his binges. After each binge A. became guilt-ridden and ashamed and would usually obsessively promise himself to fast or go on a strict diet.

I focused on helping A. to see the difference between feelings and urges on one hand and action on the other. He began to try to anticipate more and to utilize his signal anxiety and signal guilt to bring his impulses more on a thinking level and less on an action level. Despite the temporary help that these interventions afforded him, he nevertheless continued to be preoccupied with food and the childhood struggles with his parents over their having forced him to eat. For the first time A. began taking laxatives, which over time escalated to larger quantities of both natural and artificial laxatives, sometimes as many as 150 at a time!

After five months of psychotherapy, the dynamics of A.'s bulimia became more understandable as they were brought more into the transference. It became evident that many of his bulimic episodes were preceded by narcissistic humiliation. In one instance he became disappointed and enraged at me for wanting to charge him for several sessions he would miss over his Easter vacation. A. remained in a rage at me over the weekend and for the first time entered a session in the middle of a bulimic episode. He was tense, tearful, and trembling. Because of his core narcissistic pathology, he was disappointed in me and felt empty and depleted. I felt that on one level his bulimia represented a wish to merge with me. On another level his bulimia was the only way he could express his rage at me in the transference. He feared abandonment by me if he expressed his rage directly. I further speculated to myself that for a variety of reasons, including fears of merging and of becoming fat and feminine, this oral introject became dangerous and had to be eliminated anally via laxatives and explosive diarrhea.

After nine months of treatment, A.'s bulimic episodes became like an addiction and occurred at least every other day. He had never developed any other internal or external resources to soothe himself from the mounting tension. Food was the only thing that worked, at least temporarily.

My decision to put him on the couch four times a week, though risky, was based on my conviction that psychoanalysis was the only treatment that could offer him an opportunity to resolve and rework at least part of his severe character pathology, bulimia, and early traumas. Furthermore, I felt that there was an oedipal core with intense castration anxiety underlying A.'s bulimia. The patient was intelligent, highly motivated, insightful, and able to think psychologically. I believed he would now be able to free-associate and form a transference neurosis, and be more capable of a controlled regression in the analytic situation. My greatest concern was in regard to his superego pathology and intense homosexual conflicts, and to whether he would be able to maintain a passive position on the couch without intense anxiety and marked regression.

Psychoanalysis Phase

A. began analysis after eleven months of psychotherapy. Although laxative use had decreased, I soon found out that his stealing from the cash register at the electrical appliance store where he had worked part-time for several years had increased up to $200 a week over the summer break. He related a dream that he had had over the summer in which his father got his middle finger cut off, and although blood was dripping off it, nobody got excited by the sight of it. A. had begun to view his father with less awe and idealization. He now saw him as a castrated man and felt hostile toward him.

Several months into A.'s analysis, important genetic material began to unfold. For the first time he recalled crying when his mother went into the hospital for a mastectomy when he was 5 years old. He was never told of the nature of the operation and only remembered speaking to her on the phone while she was in the hospital. A. never wanted to believe his mother could have had a breast removed. Since the bathroom door was generally left ajar, A. also frequently saw her sitting on the toilet. It took many months of analysis for him to be able to reconstruct his having seen his mother's "amputated" breast while he was growing up and having equated it with her being defective. Moreover, by displacement downward, he viewed women in general as having defective, disgusting, and dangerous vaginas as well. He gradually understood how in part these fantasies led him to feel both fear and rage at women's vaginas. Later I connected this with his premature ejaculation with E., a woman he had begun dating and with whom he had been close friends prior to their sexual relationship.

As his disappointment and rage at his father intensified, his bulimia clearly took on the meaning of serving as a defense against oedipal wishes. A. dreamed that his father "was sick, very sick, as if something was wrong with his stomach. I had a scared feeling in the dream." The day's residue pertained to a hostile exchange with his father at dinner the night before. A. thought his father looked old and tired and was becoming "paranoid," complaining that everyone in the family was picking on him. A. sensed that he was "beating his father out" in the competition for his mother's love. During the sessions he began to display intense anger when openly criticizing his father. A. said that "I get a great deal of satisfaction in seeing him destroy himself. He's no man in my eyes . . . he's not successful."

Over the next few sessions his anger turned into murderous rage as his wish to kill his father became conscious. After another episode of bulimia, I was able to interpret his guilt, need for self-punishment, and fear of retaliation by his father. As A. gained increasing ego control over his binging and the situations that evoked it, further genetic material emerged that corroborated an earlier reconstruction of his mother's depression. During one session when he talked about his urge to eat after an incident with E., who didn't seem enthusiastic to see him, which left him once more feeling devastated and empty, I again reconstructed his mother's lability, chronic depression, and unavailability during his childhood, suggesting that in some way these must have been related to food. A. then vividly recalled watching his mother either mope around the kitchen or put her head down over her hands on the kitchen table. When he asked her what was wrong, she either remained silent or claimed nothing was wrong. At other times she stayed in bed in her room.

Every new painstaking step toward autonomy and integration in the analysis produced anxiety and guilt and led to bouts of binging and purging, a sequence that became frustrating to both of us.

At a time when A. was feeling rejected by his mother, he came in one session and presented a dream in which he was walking someplace filled with spiders. As he backed up, a spider got into his mouth. Through his associations to frightening childhood fantasies of poisonous spiders with long legs, as well as to other frightening images, I felt that his bulimia unconsciously represented a fusion with the breast and the "good" maternal object now that he felt depleted and lonely. It also possibly represented his wish to sadistically devour the depriving split-off "bad" maternal introject. The laxatives and explosive diarrhea represented not only A.'s terror of but also his wish to get pregnant (see also Falstein et al. 1956) and thus identify with his sister and mother. Over several sessions I gradually interpreted that unconsciously the spider represented his mother, whom he needed to feel close to and unconsciously take inside himself by binging whenever he felt humiliated, depressed, or lonely. I further pointed out that because of his rage and dread of his mother, he unconsciously expelled her in the form of his explosive diarrhea. I privately thought that the scary poisonous spider might also symbolize the defective split-off maternal introject who had the mastectomy, since A. stated, "I know I had thought of sex with my mother and my sisters. . . . I feel awful . . . my mother had a mastectomy . . . it was not pleasant to see her in her bra and panties in her room. . . . it was repulsive." With disgust he also recalled seeing one of the cups of his mother's bra stuffed with cotton.

A year into A.'s analysis there was a deepening and intensification of a full-blown workable transference neurosis, although it contained significant preoedipal elements. For the first time A. was able to criticize me directly without fearing retaliation or retribution. In addition, he spoke eloquently of how angry and envious he was of me: that I had and enjoyed everything materially wonderful in the world, had solved all my problems, had married and had children, and lived serenely. This envy was in sharp contrast to his earlier obsession with being like the "macho guys" in his neighborhood. He no longer dressed and talked like a blue-collar worker.

As his relationship with E. progressed, issues over control also became displaced onto her. Now he felt controlled by her assertive and demanding personality. Eating then took on the meaning of being in control, as did his premature ejaculations.

During a session sixteen months into his analysis, after many months of continued bulimia, purging, and other manifestations of his general impulse disorder, I made an intervention that had a surprisingly major mutative effect on him. I was able to show A. that his wish to control could be viewed, in part, as an attempt to master early trauma through repeating it. Similarly, he began to see that his binging was a way of soothing and calming himself from the massive overstimulation from childhood. But now, unlike the way it had been in his childhood, he and not his mother was in charge of how much he ate. No one could tell him what or when to eat. Conversely I also interpreted that his eating represented a regressive attempt to stay close to his mother. These interventions had such a profound effect on A. that his bulimia stopped for six months, and even when it returned again it was short-lived and far less intense.

Just prior to graduation from college, A. abandoned the idea of a career in art or teaching and decided to become a businessman. As we discussed his anxiety over the forthcoming interviews he was setting up with large department stores, oedipal themes once again emerged in full force, especially in his dreams. He began thinking more and more about getting a good job, "making it," and becoming wealthy. He no longer wanted to be like a "macho garbage man." He said that he wanted to "throw it in my father's face if I ever got a job at Bloomingdale's." He came to a session before one of his scheduled interviews feeling like "Mr. X.," and not A, for the first time in his life. He also talked about how lately he was standing up more to E., although he was still fearful of her abandoning him.

Since A. had been an art major in a predominantly business school, he received no job offers but, although mortified, did not resort to his familiar bulimic patterns to deal with this "failure." In fact these rejections led to further exploration of his grandiosity and to improved judgment and reality testing. After much soul searching and turmoil, he decided to work full-time at the electrical appliance store after graduation, with the hope of someday owning his own store. His wedding date was set for May of the following year. A. was now able to pay half of his own modest analytic fee.

He soon began to dislike his job, and over the summer, nearly two years into his analysis, he began binging again and taking laxatives. He held me responsible for his having to continue to work at the store, because working now provided him the insurance coverage for part of his treatment. In addition, he became angry at me because he felt so dependent on me and out of control again, while at the same time feeling controlled by his boss and fiancée. He felt that binging was the only way he could at least gain temporary control. The transference became negative since the summer break, with A. wanting to quit his analysis. He also complained about being a failure and about his boss not appreciating his hard work. I interpreted how he identified with his father in always being dissatisfied with work and always feeling that he gave everything and received little gratitude in return. After several months of his intermittent bulimia, although of much less intensity than before, we finally grew to understand this exacerbation better.

I pointed out that he was blaming me for not being able to leave his job in order to avoid analyzing his own ambivalence and anxiety. A. preconsciously knew that I was not really preventing him from leaving his job, which, parenthetically, was genuinely horrible for him and certainly beneath his potential. After we analyzed his fears about leaving his job as well as his deprived, empty, and hungry feelings with regard to his fantasy that I was getting fed from his insurance company, his bulimia virtually disappeared for the remainder of his analysis.

Over the Christmas holiday A. began to look for an apartment with E. and spent increasing time sleeping at her house. He revealed that he now felt closer to her mother than to his own. He became disappointed and furious at his own parents for not showing any interest in his approaching wedding.

Over the next several months his dissatisfaction at work increased and again he became enraged at me. He came in one session announcing that it was all my fault and everything would be all right if only he would leave analysis. I pointed out that he felt if he left his job for another where he might feel more successful and powerful, then I would punish him and abandon him. It also became clear to A., from a dream, that success for him unconsciously meant surpassing his father and killing him. Soon after this session he did land a more suitable job which opened larger opportunities for him. His anxiety and guilt over leaving his former boss and boss's wife at the store intensified. Even though his boss had often treated him poorly, he still remained an important father figure for A. He had one bout of binging which quickly responded to interpretation. The first session after beginning his new job A. walked into the consultation room dressed in a suit and clutching a leather briefcase. He said confidently: "It's nice working from nine to five. I really feel like an important businessman. My boss took me out to lunch the first day. I got compliments. There is a future here. I'll be doing what the president and vice-president are doing. It will never be boring . . . it all makes me feel very good."

Three days before his wedding, which took place about two months after he began his new job, his anal preoccupation came up for the last time, ushered in by an unusual piece of acting-in. By using too much toilet paper to line the toilet seat in the bathroom, a symptom he had actually given up much earlier in the analysis, he managed to plug up the toilet. In addition, he had, until that day, been constipated since taking the new job almost two months before. Although he knew that the toilet had almost overflowed, he nevertheless said nothing to me when I proceeded to use it just before his session. Much to my chagrin, it suddenly began to overflow, necessitating my running to a different part of the house to get a plunger. As soon as he got onto the couch he said, "I feel guilty because I caused what just happened in your bathroom." This acting-in soon enabled A. to understand his oedipal conflicts in more depth than he had before. He had worried about getting contaminated when he observed a drop of water on the toilet seat.

He also had been feeling more and more that E. in so many ways was just like his mother, such as being critical and controlling. In addition he reported that she would withdraw from him in anger if he spoke to her assertively. Over several weeks he came to see that his fear of contamination was overdetermined. I interpreted his guilt over unconscious masturbation fantasies and his wish to impregnate E. as well as his mother. This fear of contamination also related to a defense against anal aggressive wishes toward E. for controlling him. I also interpreted his unconscious wish to flood-drown me to get out of my control. On another level his action unconsciously represented his oedipal victory, guilt, and fear of retaliation which had intensified when his father had been recently hospitalized for chest pain. A. was both terrified and furious when his father's chest pain turned out to be "nothing" and he felt very critical of his father for his "weakness." Recently A. had truly become the wise and powerful one in the household, to whom everyone came for advice and support, especially his father, who had recently been fired from his job.

At the beginning of a session in June, two and a half years after the start of A.'s analysis, he announced that he definitely made up his mind to stop coming for the summer. A long silence ensued before he told me that he and E. had spent a great deal of money on an apartment, wedding, and honeymoon which had gotten them into debt. E. was a big spender and A. felt too intimidated by her to stop her. Moreover, he no longer wanted his parents to pay for any portion of his treatment. He felt he would get his finances somewhat under control over the summer and then call me to resume his analysis in the fall. I interpreted that he now felt he had a "good mother" in E. and did not need me or the analysis. A. never did return to his analysis after the summer.

I did, however, receive a serendipitous call from A. approximately three years after the end of his analysis asking if I would fill out a form for his life insurance company, since they needed certain information from me relating to his past treatment. I was gratified to find out from him that he was promoted in his job, had moved with his wife to the suburbs away from his parents, was happy, and had had no further bouts of bulimia.

DISCUSSION

Although a number of general principles might be gleaned from the analytic study of a male bulimic, caution should be observed about just how much can be generalized from a single case, especially one that terminated prematurely.

Even though my patient had entered treatment with a three-month history of anorexia nervosa, I am nevertheless considering him to be a bulimic since for most of his three-and-a-half-year treatment he suffered with primary symptoms of bulimia. My patient confirms what Wilson (1983) and Sours (1980) describe as the underlying core conflicts in both disorders, namely the fear of being fat, the need to separate, and the need for control. This last-named conflict seems to be the most ubiquitous and invariable transference paradigm that is evoked in the analysis of such patients (see also Welsh 1983). In A. the fear that I would aggressively uncover his hidden sexual and aggressive impulses was the earliest transference manifestation. Fantasied battles over control manifesting through the transference became the major resistance in A.'s analysis. A.'s stealing, lying, speeding, and addiction to cigarettes correlates with the psychiatric literature on this syndrome, which frequently mentions the close association between bulimia and the impulse and addictive disorders.

Another common transference manifestation with such patients is separation fear, causing feelings of loneliness and emptiness, which become displaced onto the analyst and which can lead to increased binging on weekends (Welsh 1983) and during the analyst's vacation. Moreover, even the slightest break in empathy by the analyst can trigger bulimic episodes because of the patient's marked narcissistic pathology and tendency to defensively split self and object images, leading to a vicious cycle of binging and then purging. The analyst must constantly be vigilant to the exquisite narcissistic vulnerability in such patients.

A.'s feminine identification and his negative oedipal and latent homosexual conflicts (see also Welsh 1983 and Falstein et al. 1956) led to a homosexual transference that I felt should not be interpreted until much later in the analysis, lest serious and potential acting out or quitting occur. Unfortunately, the premature termination of the analysis never permitted me to bring his homosexual longing directly into the transference.

The approach to transference interpretations with these patients varies from analyst to analyst. Wilson (1983) advocates a modified approach early in treatment similar to the techniques that Boyer and Giovacchini (1980) and Kernberg (1975) utilize with borderline, narcissistic, and psychotic personality disorders. To the best of my knowledge, I treated this case through a classical ego psychology approach within the structural and drive defense models. Although some analysts may hold that the initial preparatory phase of psychotherapy itself in my patient was indeed a modification, I feel that basically no special techniques were used. Moreover, I did not go about understanding or interpreting analytic material with the patient in any premeditated manner. Derivatives from all levels of development are evoked in the analysis of bulimic patients and need to be analyzed as they occur. Perhaps the differences here stem from the fact that my patient was more neurotic than borderline, and if I were to treat the more difficult and primitive borderline bulimics, I might also find it useful and necessary to modify the techniques similar to those espoused by Wilson.

Counteractions and countertransference acting out is an ever-present threat for the unwary analyst while analyzing eating-disordered patients. Thomä (1967) observed the countertransference evoked in the anorexic patient. In addition, he delineated a typical countertransferential response to anorexics in which the analyst takes on the role of the overindulgent, infinitely loving mother.

Mintz (1983) underscores the potential negative outcome of being overanxious and phoning a patient and of giving approval when the anorexic patient starts to eat. I would like to stress that this approval can be nonverbal as well. A possible limitation of the case reported relates to my initial counteractions and tacit support of his eating, as well as his periodic phone calls to me during the psychotherapy phase. Whether these could have ever been thoroughly analyzed remains uncertain.

Other common countertransference reactions to bulimics and anorexics in the analytic situation are drowsiness and educative or coercive tactics (Hogan 1983). Flarsheim (1975) reported on the analyst's collusion with his patient's suicidal wishes. He pointed to how the analyst himself replaced the food addiction of the patient in the transference.

It is possible for the analyst's own oral greed and feelings of oral deprivation to be evoked by the bulimic patient, possibly leading the analyst inappropriately to, for example, increase the fee, manipulate insurance coverage, or feel depressed.

Assessing one's own countertransference or counteractions with eating-disordered patients may become difficult at times because of the dire reality of their situation. It is not always easy to decide when setting limits is a necessity to preserve the treatment, or even the patient's life, or when it represents countertransference reactions. For example, I believe that not setting limits for an impulsive patient such as mine in the midst of a bulimic episode, when he frantically sped through stop signs to get home to finish the bulimic episode, would be a far worse technical error than to set limits to protect the patient's life. However, doing so in the form of an interpretation would, of course, be optimal.

I viewed A.'s quitting his analysis, in part, as similar to what is seen in the analyses of some adolescents who eventually equate the analyst with their parents and have to detach themselves to gain their independence. Child and adolescent analysts often speak about "a piece of analysis" with adolescents, who sometimes come back for further analysis during or after college. The analysis did enable A. to reach adolescence and in some ways even early adulthood. He clearly resolved a great deal of his preoedipal pathology, although unfortunately, because of his premature termination, his positive and negative oedipal conflicts were not adequately worked through.

SUMMARY

The basic question has been raised as to whether bulimia is a separate disorder from anorexia nervosa or whether they represent opposite poles of the same syndrome. Diagnostic considerations were elucidated. The underlying central conflicts in both disorders seem to be fear of being fat, the need to separate, and the need for control. The association between bulimia and the addictive and impulse disorders was underscored.

A detailed case was presented to demonstrate that such patients may be able to be analyzed, largely through a classical approach. Derivatives from all levels of development are evoked in the analysis of bulimic patients and must be analyzed as they occur. Analyzing core oedipal conflicts comprised a major portion of the analysis of this patient in addition to analyzing the more typical preoedipal pathology that is found in such eating-disordered patients.

REFERENCES

Boskind-White, M., and White, W. C. (1983). *Bulimarexia: The Binge Purge Cycle.* New York: Norton.

Boyer, L. B., and Giovacchini, P. L. (1980). *Psychoanalytic Treatment of Schizophrenic, Borderline and Characterological Disorders.* New York: Jason Aronson.

Bruch, H. (1973). *Eating Disorders: Obesity, Anorexia Nervosa and the Person Within.* New York: Basic Books.

Crisp, A. H. (1981). Anorexia nervosa at normal body weight! the abnormal normal weight control syndrome. *International Journal of Psychiatry and Medicine* 2:203–233.

Falstein, E., Reinstein, D., and Judas, I. (1956). Anorexia nervosa in the male child. *American Journal of Orthopsychiatry* 26:751–772.

Flarsheim, A. (1975). The therapist's collusion with the patient's wish for suicide. In *Tactics and Technique in Psychoanalytic Therapy,* vol. 2, ed. P. L. Giovacchini, A. Flarsheim, and L. B. Boyer, pp. 155–195. New York: Jason Aronson.

Friedman, L. (1953). Defensive aspects of orality. *International Journal of Psycho-Analysis* 34:304–312.

Goodsitt, A. (1985). Self psychology and the treatment of anorexia nervosa. In *Handbook of Psychotherapy for Anorexia and Bulimia,* ed. D. M. Gerner and P. E. Garfinkel, pp. 55–82. New York: Guilford Press.

Green, R. S., and Rau, J. H. (1974). The use of diphenyl hydantoin in compulsive eating disorders: further studies. In *Anorexia Nervosa,* ed. R. A. Vigersky. New York: Raven Press.

Guiora, A. Z. (1967). A cognitive-behavioral model for the treatment of chronic vomiting. *Journal of Behavioral Medicine* 5:135–141.

Hogan, C. C. (1983). Transference. In *Fear of Being Fat: The Treatment of Anorexia and Bulimia,* ed. C. P. Wilson, C. C. Hogan, and I. L. Mintz, pp. 153–168. New York: Jason Aronson.

Jessner, L., and Abse, D. (1960). Regressive forces in anorexia nervosa. *British Journal of Medical Psychology* 33:301–312.

Kernberg, O. F. (1975). *Borderline Condition and Pathological Narcissism.* New York: Jason Aronson.

Mintz, I. M. (1983). Anorexia nervosa and bulimia in males. In *Fear of Being Fat: The Treatment of Anorexia Nervosa and Bulimia,* ed. C. P. Wilson, C. C. Hogan, and I. L. Mintz, pp. 263–303, New York: Jason Aronson.

Ohrbach, S. (1978). *Fat Is a Feminist Issue.* New York: Berkeley Publishing.

Palmer, R. L. (1979). The dietary chaos syndrome: a useful new term? *British Journal of Medical Psychology* 52:187–190.

Russell, G. (1979). Bulimia nervosa: an ominous variant of anorexia nervosa. *Psychological Medicine* 9:429–448.

Schwartz, H. (in press). Bulimia: psychoanalytic perspectives. *Journal of the American Psychoanalytic Association.*

Sours, J. A. (1974). The anorexia syndrome. *International Journal of Psycho-Analysis* 55:567–576.

——— (1980). *Starving to Death in a Sea of Objects,* New York: Jason Aronson.

Sperling, M. (1949). The role of the mother in psychosomatic disorders in children. *Psychosomatic Medicine* 11:377–385.

——— (1968). Trichotillomania, trichophagy and cyclic vomiting. *International Journal of Psycho-Analysis* 49:682–690.

Stunkard, A. (1959). Eating patterns and obesity. *Psychiatric Quarterly* 1:28–43.

Sugarman, A., and Kurash, C. (1982). The body as a transitional object in bulimia. *International Journal of Eating Disorders* 1:57–67.

Swift, J., and Letven, R. (1984). Bulimia and the basic fault: a psychoanalytic interpretation of the bingeing-vomiting syndrome. *Journal of the American Academy of Child Psychiatry* 23:489–497.

Thomä, H. (1967). *Anorexia Nervosa.* Trans. G. Brydome. New York: International Press.

Welsh, H. (1983). Psychoanalytic therapy: the case of Martin. In *Fear of Being Fat,* ed. C. P. Wilson, C. C. Hogan, and I. L. Mintz. pp. 263–303. Northvale, NJ: Jason Aronson.

Wilson, C. P. (1983a). The fear of being fat in female psychology. In *Fear of Being Fat: The Treatment of Anorexia Nervosa and Bulimia.,* ed. C. P. Wilson, C. C. Hogan, and I. L. Mintz, pp. 21–27. New York: Jason Aronson.

_____ (1983b). The family psychological profile and its therapeutic implications. In *Fear of Being Fat: The Treatment of Anorexia Nervosa and Bulimia,* ed. C. P. Wilson, C. C. Hogan, and I. L. Mintz, pp. 29–47. New York: Jason Aronson.

_____ (1983c). Contrasts in the analysis of bulimics and abstaining anorexics. In *Fear of Being Fat: The Treatment of Anorexia Nervosa and Bulimia,* ed. C. P. Wilson, C. C. Hogan, and I. L. Mintz, pp. 169–193. New York: Jason Aronson.

9

Bulimia, Orality, and the Oedipus Complex in an Adult Female

Kenneth D. Cohen, M.D.

"I did not want to tell you this before; I feel disgusting and dirty when I think of what I do. My life is one of depression and I feel terrible. Each time I do this I feel worse. . . ." These words are from the fourth evaluation interview of a 40-year-old married woman who came for treatment because of severe depression, social anxiety, sexual inhibition, and a general dissatisfaction with life. Following this confession she described episodes of binging during which she purchased huge quantities of candy and cake, ate until she hurt, and then forcibly vomited or used an enema. She did this at times of loneliness, anger, and disappointment. There was an initial pleasure in eating that gave way to a sense of despair with both physical and emotional hurt. Invariably she felt worse after the episode.

Over the years she was able to hide this behavior from everyone, despite episodic weight gain, which had been as much as 50 pounds at one time. This had been totally her secret; now she shared it with me. She was both glad and anxious but wondered what I felt about her. Moreover, she immediately realized that in the future whenever she would binge,

211

someone else would know; she would have to tell me. Another person was now involved in a direct, conscious way. One of the striking aspects of her secret eating was that she had been able, over the years, to convince herself that the eating was totally related to herself and did not involve others. In short, the activity took on for her an objectless meaning. It was purely an action she did to herself.

The denial was striking since it was evident that the patient was aware of the binging as a reaction to painful affects, such as frustration, anger, or fear. Yet she was able to repress the psychological "moment of force" that existed between her and the other person. Thus one of the early tasks of the analysis would be to help the patient become aware of the symptom as something that came about as a result of her interaction with someone else.

In an article Schwartz (1986) presents an excellent review of psychoanalytic writing relevant to the topic of bulimia. Summarizing the trend of the comments made by others, he cites those papers that show the extremely conflicted, ambivalent relationship to mother which reflected the patient's difficulty in effecting a separation from the maternal object. These papers point to the enormous sense of dependency and the unsuccessful attempt on the part of the patient to bring about a separation. The eating in effect becomes a ritual that says, "I take you in and I get rid of you." So the object is never fully assimilated in the psychological sense. He also cites papers that describe two elements clearly related to the oedipal phase of development: symbolic tie to the mother, and phallic oedipal interaction. These two elements proved to be the hallmark of the analytic work with the patient in this report.

The binging represented effort on the part of the patient to retreat from a genital fantasy and become the dependent child to avoid the impact of overt oedipal fantasies. This idea is in keeping with a 1929 paper by Sachs in which he states: "The child–daughter relates to the father in a regressed way using oral mechanisms as the basis for the interaction. This enables the patient to relate to the father." At the same time, according to Sachs, the patient is unable to resolve the attachment, remaining attached to the father but in a way reminiscent of the attachment to the mother. This relationship to the father through an oral mechanism precludes a satisfactory resolution of the Oedipus complex. Moreover, Sachs states that it prevents the evolution of an effective autonomous superego. For this patient there were difficulties in superego function but they were amenable to the analytic process. Relevant to this point is Wilson's (1985) observation that the bulimic patient has a strict superego, but not a punishing one like that of the anorectic.

There is an assumption that the psychopathology of the bulimic is in keeping with the acknowledged psychopathology of the anorectic, namely, that the patient has severe character pathology with perhaps borderline tendencies. Schwartz (1986) cites one writer who felt that eating dysfunction represented an unanalyzable state. Notwithstanding, Schwartz maintains that the issue is whether or not manifestly oral symptoms and fantasies are primary or defensive (p. 455). This statement is quite important. The patient under consideration did react as one might expect a neurotic patient to do, with symptoms of anxiety and depression. Schwartz referred to Sandler and Dare, who stated, "Simply because the disturbance involves oral function, it should not be inferred that the psychopathology . . . originated in early infancy" (p. 444). Fluctuations in moods were intense in the course of the transference evolution. The analysis demonstrated derivatives from every area of psychosexual development which interdigitated at one time or another with aspects of resistance or transference.

BACKGROUND

The patient, the mother of two sons, had a reasonably stable marriage to a hard-driving man given to outbursts of temper, especially toward his wife. The patient reacted to these outbursts with guilt and overt fear, becoming immobilized and unable to carry out the functions of the day. Binging frequently resulted. Moreover, although capable of full sexual satisfaction, she avoided sexual intimacy. Her conscious reason was that her husband was not mindful of her sensitivities. Later it became clear that the major reason centered about the picture of herself as the helpless little girl. In other aspects of her everyday life she seemed to function well, showing interest in her home and the welfare of her children and in related outside activities.

Her early family life was characterized, in her mind, by recollections of herself as the good little girl. She was bright and obedient, never daring to do anything that would bring forth anger. Her father had been devoted to her and spoke to her in terms of adoration and endearment. An older brother was frequently the target of the father's abuse, but the father never spoke harshly to the daughter. Nevertheless, the image of his piercing look and potential violence was a constant reminder of his wrath. This look served as a standard by which she judged men. Early in the analytic work she said to me, "You look very nasty!" It took several months before she was able to associate these comments with the memory of her father's look. He was a man who created intense ambivalence, adoring but capable of evoking strong fear.

When she was between 5 and 7 years old, her father left on what was said to be a business venture. He returned intermittently for brief stays and left just as suddenly. These absences had a traumatic impact on the patient. Several years prior to the analysis the patient's father died; she blamed herself for his death but experienced very little overt grief. This situation eventually resolved itself within the transference when she became aware of her death wishes. The older brother, who was very interested in the patient, became a strong, secondary oedipal object. When she was in her teens, however, he married. His marriage came as a shock, precipitating depression and regression. Binging began some time after that event. It seemed clear that the brother's marriage had revived the recurrent trauma of their father's frequent separations during the oedipal period.

The mother was described as an inadequate, shrinking nonentity constantly preoccupied with herself and her own alleged illnesses. It took a long while before the patient could accept the fact of her mother's limitations. Notwithstanding the mother's shadowy picture, it seemed clear that the patient was overtly identified in a feminine way. She had experienced her menses with little difficulty. There were no prolonged periods of overt menstrual disturbance.

In this regard she resembled some of the patients in Russell's (1979) series in which he described several bulimic patients, among a larger group, who were heavier and did menstruate and were fertile.

Thus the total picture that evolved over several periods of evaluation was one of a severely neurotic woman who had managed to have some degree of stable object ties despite enormous suffering. She was bright and articulate and wanted to get relief from her symptoms. The bulimia represented one aspect of a neurosis—a symptom that should be accessible to the analytic approach.

In this chapter I will describe the nature of the components of the symptom of bulimia and its relationship to various aspects of psychosexual development. The overdetermined nature of the symptom will be demonstrated as having its roots in oral, anal, phallic, and oedipal periods. I will emphasize the close connection between orality and its vicissitudes in the evolution and resolution of the transference oedipal neurosis. Despite the overt psychopathology, the patient's symptom represented efforts on the part of good ego function which proved to be an asset as the patient was able to integrate the work of the analysis to bring about change with accompanied relief of the symptom.

THE EARLY GENESIS OF CONFLICT

Although the patient herself had been breastfed, her mother had admonished her not to do so with *her* children. Nevertheless, the patient did breastfeed successfully. She did not feel a general sense of accomplishment about it, however, although she eventually recognized that it gave her moments of great satisfaction, which were related to her thought that she could not be any different from mother.

Easser (1976) cited a patient who was unable to enjoy her body or her femaleness because of her identification with a mother who disapproved of her (the mother's) own femininity. One might say that to be different is to make the separation from mother. Indeed the patient commented frequently that she was the same and would remain the same. Late in the analysis she was able to come to the conclusion that mother would never change, "but I can."

Sarlin (1981) explores the psychoanalytic ramifications of the reciprocal relationship between mother and child during the feeding process. He comments that the ability to breastfeed does not imply maturity on the part of the mother (p. 640). He cited T. Benedek, who had stated that nurturing encompasses multiple functions and roles beyond nourishment (p. 638). He also quotes Anna Freud, who felt that the infantile attitudes toward feeding reflected one's ability to deal with new experiences or one's tendency to regress to "existing pleasures" (p. 633).

ORALITY AND OEPIDUS

Perhaps the following may serve to explore more fully the meaning of the comfort and pleasure that the patient said she would experience in the symptom.

After she ate, she would at times experience a feeling of lethargy and fatigue which she thought was not unlike a feeling of being drugged. (She was not an abuser of medications.) Her associations to these thoughts were always to some form of comfort followed by punishment.

The meaning of pleasure was not clear until late in the analysis when she began to think of me in a conscious way as mother. She would say that she wanted me to feed her; at times she had the fantasy that I had a breast. This feeling was an extension of an earlier fantasy in which she would become ill and I would come to care for her. This fantasy produced a sense of comfort and pleasure. However, at the same time, she became aware of the erotic feeling that would accompany this sense of comfort. One wondered how these sexual feelings could be related to the oral nature of the fantasies.

Sarlin (1981) noted that Benedek detailed the reciprocal relationship between mother and child during breastfeeding. Benedek used the term "emotional symbiosis" and referred to breastfeeding as "the original primal scene." It was her contention that the primal scene of the phallic-oedipal level is the re-creation of the early primal scene with the mother in which the infant, at the mother's breast, was an active participant in a mutually overtly erotic relationship and not just an outside observer.

The eating and the accompanying feeling that were at the same time erotic and satisfying could be viewed as a re-creation of the feeling tone related to breastfeeding. The patient's mother did in fact breastfeed her. When the patient was confronted by the frustration of the analysis in both the oedipal and oral aspects of the transference, binging then became a source of the lost libidinal gratification of both phases and thereby satisfied the needs of the id insofar as drive is concerned. Then too it kept the superego mollified in that the oedipal situation was not truly satisfied. Moreover, the discomfort she eventually felt certainly took on a quality of punishment.

This aspect of the relationship to mother became more evident in the closing phases of treatment when the patient began to feel the separation from me in the same fashion. She spoke of deep longing and comfort, which in turn were intermingled with the recurrence of the sexual fantasies in which I would succumb to her charms and we would go off together and create a family. It was during this time that she recalled how she sought to change her body image in the course of time to keep herself from being too pretty and too alluring. She could not accept the idea that her body would be attractive. Keeping herself heavy was a means of avoiding this.

Laufer (1982) formulated the understanding that the adolescent may experience a "developmental breakdown." He regarded this as an unconscious rejection of the sexual body. This, he said, resulted in a lack of integration of the physically matured body image as part of the self. This patient struggled with the notion of her own incomplete body. She had masturbation fantasies in which she had a penis.

There was a considerable amount of penis envy in the patient. Her overt submissive attitude was a reaction formation to a strong wish for the paternal phallus. "You men have all the power and that's what I want from you." In one session while talking of this, she reported a dream in which a snake was around her neck. She worried that the snake might starve and she searched for someone to provide it with food. She had been frustrated the night before in her sexual wishes. She felt unfulfilled, was aware of that fact, and said something was missing; she needed "fulfillment." "That's what I need from you," she said. "But I will never get it. Right now I would like to eat it up." When I interpreted that she wanted to get my penis, as she had wanted to get it from father, she responded by saying that eating is a way of filling up: "It gives me a feeling of power." She then recalled a memory from age 4. She was seated in her father's lap. He pulled her close and she felt uncomfortable; she was aware that she was pressing against his penis.

Oral incorporative fantasies in the transference suggest that the patient is utilizing this mode to further the work of the oedipal resolution. Ritvo (1976) stated that aggressive fantasies are a normal aspect of adolescent development but underlie the bulimic and anorectic disturbances. The patient attempts to solve the problem by devouring and incorporating, thereby creating an attachment similar to the one the child had with the mother at the time of feeding. Ritvo states further that the shift from mother to the man has residual persistence of the mother in the man.

Conrad (1965) reviewed aspects of penis envy and obesity and concluded that in the female, the obese body represents the illusory penis fulfilling primary penis envy. He cited Bychowski (1950), who stated that "food functions as a symbolic substitute for the paternal or fraternal phallus. Thus absorption of food represents a partial incorporation of early male objects" (p. 207). Earlier he referred to Lewin, who had observed that when the body represents a phallus, that means the phallus has been orally incorporated. Then, too, Arlow (1953) considered overeating to be an upward displacement of phallic drive. In keeping with this, we can note that this patient's fantasy of masturbating with a penis disappeared shortly after the binging began.

One other aspect of penis envy should be mentioned which this patient illustrates, and that is the tie to the mother. Karme (1981) spoke of the penis as representing a tie to the mother—an umbilical cord, if you will. The patient recorded frequent fantasies of feeling tied to me, and indeed in one dream she spoke of being intertwined by means of a fecal-penis.

We cannot leave the subject of penis envy without observing that vomiting, which is a regular part of the total picture of bulimia, has been understood by Leonard (1944) as a way of symbolically rejecting the phallus, in turn serving to assuage the guilt over the fantasy of castration.

THE OEDIPAL BABY

The wish for the oedipal baby became apparent when the patient brought in a dream of "something hanging upside down." In the course of her associations, she revealed that she had not used the usual method of birth control. Clearly, this was an action that bespoke of her wish for the baby in the transference. The work over several sessions eventually revealed the fantasy that when she ate, she would have a baby. When her menses appeared she saw it as messy and with it the fantasy of the anally delivered baby. She then recalled having a similar thought in childhood.

These thoughts may represent an unconscious denial of the vagina, which then might represent another aspect of penis envy. Kerstenberg (1968) noted a fear of internal genital excitement in females. In response to this, she said, there is a "desexualization of the vagina creating a primitive split between maternality and sexual adjustment," which she says is seen in females who are mildly interested in sex but are truly maternal to their children.

After the work on this issue, the patient came in and said that she had begun to see that her binging was really holding onto the image of the little girl, the one she wanted others to acknowledge. With a note of sadness, yet triumph, she announced that she felt in some way that she now had a choice to make. She no longer could view the binging as something that had an action and impetus all its own, a notion she had reiterated time and again. It was now clear that she had some say over the matter and she felt that it was time to bring things to a close.

TERMINATION

The termination was one of intense feeling which, not unexpectedly, resulted in recurrence of symptoms. The patient felt that she had been cheated, that she did not get what she felt I promised her. I had not given her anything. She then noted with anger that she had not, in fact, become the wife to me. With this came more feeling of how father had seemingly promised her that she would go away with him. When he returned, she always had the fantasy that they would drive away together. Feeling about his death became very intense, and the relationship to the symptom became very clear. She said: "Food is getting what I want. Filling up was for me a way to hold onto father and you, and throwing them up makes him dead again. When I leave you I feel as though you will be dead to me." She recalled her anger at father for leaving, and at her brother for leaving (to get married). This anger was accompanied by a recollection of her oft-stated thought that I might die, as well as her fantasy that if she could not love me, no one would: "You have to die."

Quite some time after the analysis terminated, the patient wrote to me and described the intense mourning she had undergone following the final session. Eventually she felt better, and she commented that she no longer experienced deep depression and had no further episodes of binging.

SUMMARY

A female patient presented with a severe symptom complex that had existed for more than twenty-five years and that included overt symptoms of anxiety and depression together with severe bulimia. Despite the severity, the patient's overall function and capacity for object relations pointed to a neurotic picture. The analysis was undertaken utilizing classical techniques; no parameters were introduced. The symptom of bulimia proved to be multidetermined regressive defense against the oedipal triumph which was couched in oral, cannibalistic terms. This same mechanism was utilized in the effort to overcome penis envy. The patient worked well with the analytic process, experiencing internal change and gradual cessation of the symptom.

REFERENCES

Arlow, J. (1953). Masturbation and symptom formation. *Journal of the American Psychoanalytic Association,* 1:45–58.

Conrad, S. W. (1965). Phallic aspects of obesity. Bulletin, *Philadelphia Association for Psychoanalysis* 15:207–223.

Easser, B. R. (1976). Panel. Psychology of women. *Journal of the American Psychoanalytic Association,* 24:631–645.

Karme, L. (1981). A clinical report of penis envy: its multiple meanings and defensive function. *Journal of the American Psychoanalytic Association,* 29:427–446.

Kerstenberg, J. S. (1968). Outside–inside, male–female. *Journal of the American Psychoanalytic Association,* 16:457–520.

Laufer, M. (1982). The formation and shaping of the oedipus complex: clinical observations and assumptions. *International Journal of Psycho-Analysis* 63:217–226.

Leonard, C. E. (1944). Analysis of a case of functional vomiting and bulimia. *Psychoanalytic Review* 31:1–18.

Ritvo, S. (1976) Panel, Psychology of women. *Journal of the American Psychoanalytic Association,* 24:631–645.

Russell, G. (1979). Bulimia nervoso: an ominous variant of anorexia nervosa. *Psychological Medicine* 9:429–448.

Sachs, H. (1929). One of the motive factors in the formation of the superego in women. *International Journal of Psycho-Analysis* 10:39–50.

Sarlin, C. N. (1981). The role of breast feeding in psychosexual development and the achievement of the genital phase. *Journal of the American Psychoanalytic Association,* 29:631–641.

Schwartz, H. (1986). Bulimia: psychoanalytic perspectives. *Journal of the American Psychoanalytic Association,* 34:439–467.

Wilson, C. P. (1985). Psychodynamic and/or psychopharmacologic treatment of bulimic anorexia nervosa. In *Fear of Being Fat: The Treatment of Anorexia and Bulimia,* rev. ed., ed. C. P. Wilson, C. C. Hogan, and I. L. Mintz, pp. 345–362. New York: Jason Aronson.

PART V

Children

10

The Importance of Aggression in the Early Development of Children with Eating Disorders*

John Hitchcock, M.D.

The psychoanalyses of children with eating disorders indicate that while virtually all aspects of the personality of those afflicted are involved, aggression emerges as the preeminent consideration. The tenacity of the defensive structures which impede, distort, and otherwise alter the experience and expression of aggression suggests that such structures are established very early in life.

Psychoanalytically trained authors (Bruch 1973, Mintz 1983, Sours 1979, Wilson 1983) have speculated that anorectics' problems with aggression originate in infancy. The reported placidity of such patients in their earliest weeks and months of life has prompted the suggestion that there is a congenital deficiency in the aggressive drive (Kramer 1974), although the probability of interference with the expression of aggression has been proposed as more consistent with the observed behaviors. Mintz (1983)

*The author wishes to acknowledge with thanks the many contributions made by Naomi Ragins, M.D., to the formulations in this paper.

found aggression to be a central issue in the five anorexic males he treated psychoanalytically. However, early developmental data were not reported.

Wilson (1985), discussing the metapsychology of persons who develop anorexia, emphasizes the "unremitting pressure of repressed unsublimated aggressive and libidinal drives, conflicts and fantasies" and, further, refers to the genetic influence of "parental conflict about weight and food specifically, and about aggression and libidinal expression generally" (p. 21). The data in this study, while clearly implicating libidinal development at all stages, point to the experience of aggression, and reactions to this experience, as the most powerful premorbid contributor.

Premorbidly, anorectic patients are usually described as having been quiet, accommodating, and compliant infants and children. They tend to shun controversy and conflict and will go to great lengths to do what they perceive is expected of them. Once the disorder is clinically evident, hostile aggression (Parens 1980) is clear in the self-punishing behaviors of extraordinary exercise, dissolution of sexuality, ignoring of the pain of hunger, and self-destructive malnutrition, in some instances resulting in death. These behaviors are object directed in fantasy, and in affect, consciously or unconsciously.

Nondestructive aggression, ostensibly normal in early manifestations in terms of eating and initiation of physical activity, is drawn into the sphere of conflict, as seen in the binge/purge/starvation behaviors and in the compulsion to exercise. Aggression also plays a role in the fantasies, body imagery, and associative thinking of persons with eating disorders in characteristic ways.

The fact that the syndrome of anorexia nervosa is frequently associated with more primitive psychological mechanisms, such as perceptual distortion (apparent absence of awareness of hunger and pain, and distortion of body image), ritualistic exercise, superficial object relationships, preoccupation with control, and the prominence of denial, has led to the exploration of events in infancy and childhood.

Sources of data include the anamnesis, reports by family members, and transference phenomena. Several authors have found the developmental framework advanced by Mahler (1965) to be relevant to their formulations regarding the origins of conflicts in patients with anorexia nervosa. Some have even suggested distortions of subphases or transitions between subphases of the separation-individuation phase of development as specifically pathogenic (Fischer 1986, Mushatt 1978).

While such formulations are of interest from a theoretical point of view, and might serve to inform the construction of a prospective study, this is yet to be accomplished. The preponderance of psychoanalytic thinking is that the ascription of cause of particular behaviors observed at a particular point to specific events occurring earlier in one's life is invalid (see Panel Report 1972, especially Rochlin). The complexities of extra and intrapsychic interactions render any such assumption of causality speculative.

It would seem, however, that the shorter time between generation of the data in question—that is, those from psychoanalyses, from anamnesis, and from observation—the greater the likelihood that significant associations might be found. The psychoanalyses of children offer such a possibility.

Data from the analyses of three children will be considered. Alterations have been introduced in order to protect anonymity. These alterations, however well devised, must have an impact on the presentation, in addition to the effect of the selection of data.

JAMIE

The first analysand, Jamie, was 4 years old when she was brought for her second evaluation for treatment. An earlier evaluation when she was 3, also conducted by a psychoanalyst, resulted in the recommendation that treatment not be undertaken because of evidence of severe parent–child tension, but that consultation be provided to the mother. Jamie was an only child, conceived in the context of parental discord verging on divorce. However, her conception provided a focus for commitment, and her parents continued to regard her as the primary reason for the preservation of their marriage. Mother's pregnancy with Jamie presented no problem, although there was contemporary evidence that mother was intensely ambivalent about the conception. Delivery and neonatal development were entirely normal. There were no reported eating or sleeping problems. In fact, it became apparent that mother could tolerate no indication of distress in Jamie and immediately set about to quiet her cries and still her fussing. Jamie developed a "happy face" very early, and it persisted into adult life, especially when she felt any tension. Concurrently with the dampening of any expression of discomfort, the sense that Jamie was always the best was forcefully inculcated from the beginning.

During Jamie's first weeks and months her mother was never beyond earshot. Although indications of excellent cognitive development and solid musculo-skeletal advances were present, behaviors suggesting differentiating and practicing were meager. Jamie's speech showed interesting bimodal development, with good early vocabulary and articulation. When she began to walk, at about age one, she stopped talking for almost six months. When she again began to speak, she did so in age-appropriate phrases and sentences, but now with a pronounced lateral lisp, which persisted thereafter. Neither Jamie nor her mother could point to any tension between them. Each regarded the other as essentially perfect. Jamie saw herself as a perfect miniature replica of her mother and felt very good about that.

Jamie drew the line when her expectations that she should do whatever was asked of her included going off to school. She quickly learned how to engage the undivided attention of the teacher and to win admiration and praise, but she could not tolerate her peers' taunts and intrusions, and especially the fact that she could not control them, though she tried with all manner of gifts and baubles. She felt troubled at school and so was brought by her parents for a "problem in separating," as they put it, although it was clear that they attributed the problem to the school, whose participants failed to appreciate Jamie's specialness. Jamie's chief complaint was that her mother wouldn't play "love" enough. Love was a game in which she and her mother would embrace and speak of their love for one another.

There were, to be sure, earlier signs that not all was well with Jamie. General delay in her development of independence was clearly evident, although apparently not of concern until the start of school. In addition, Jamie frequently fretted about not feeling well. Such complaints began when she was less than 2 years old. Indications that these complaints were made when she perceived some interference with her mother's availability were downplayed by Jamie and her mother. Yet whenever her mother went out (which, interestingly, she did quite frequently) Jamie developed a headache, ear ache, or stomach ache almost immediately thereafter. When her mother would call on arrival at her destination, which she always did, Jamie would be retching or writhing in pain. Her mother would ask if Jamie wanted her to come home, and Jamie would say "No" in a pitiable tone. "A 'yicky' feeling" was all she could say to describe her experience.

The initial months of analytic work with Jamie were characterized by her entertaining the analyst, being cute, and attempting to discern what might bring her compliments. Eventually, she asked the analyst for help with a task that the analyst felt she could handle quite well, and he wondered at her seeking assistance. Jamie immediately collapsed, fell mute for many minutes, and did not respond when asked what was going on, either at the time or subsequently.

Within a short time she began to develop binge eating and vomiting, ultimately requiring hospitalization. Her eating pattern eventually evolved into one with more restrictor features, although she never lost a significant amount of weight. The analytic work continued throughout, focusing on her denial of her rage at the analyst for his refusal to participate in her efforts to preserve infantile patterns of interaction.

Slow to reveal or even to be aware of fantasies, daydreams, and dreams, as is typical of persons with eating disorders, Jamie gradually began to report dreams in which she could not find her mother as well as dreams of engulfing monsters. These themes were repeated over and over, first with little affect, then with anger increasingly expressed toward her father, followed by outbursts toward her mother that seemed so foreign to her that she would laugh afterward. It was only when these outbursts were directed to the analyst—for not understanding her, for interruptions in the analytic schedule, and for not taking better care of her—that she began to experience a lasting shift in her affective life. In fact, at age 10, after a particularly castigating torrent, she observed that when she felt the anger, she no longer felt the "yicky" feeling. Concurrently, her sense of herself as distinct from her mother was seen in her involvements with friends, her choices of apparel, her activities, and her aspirations.

Jamie's affective life as an infant was always happy, according to her parents. She always smiled in their presence. Even as a toddler, when reporting aches and pains, she would do so with a sorrowful smile. Her parents found nothing noteworthy in this behavior, attributing it to her pleasant disposition. Nursery school teachers were the first to wonder what she might be feeling when they observed her smiling in a state of obvious tension. She never engaged in any behavior suggestive of tantruming.

Beginning at age 4, she would speak of her "yicky" feeling, temporally related to separations from her mother but not causally related in her mind. In fact, the "yicky" feeling was without associated mental content altogether. Episodes of keening began at age 6, also without reported ideational concomitants. Organismic distress, as described by Mahler (1966), best characterized these affective states. By early adolescence there appeared to be a more directed and acknowledged intent to affect another, although she was unable to say what response she sought. Her mother would feel totally helpless at these times, since no amount of holding or cuddling would seem to make a difference.

All of these behaviors were seen in the analytic context, with the addition of an expressionless bland visage when Jamie was unguarded.

A remarkable reaction was noted when Jamie would become engaged in catching objects tossed to her. As the object began its downward arc toward her outstretched hands, she invariably opened her mouth wide, drew her lips back, and bared her teeth until she caught the ball. She was unaware of this behavior and could make no sense of it on inquiry.

When she finally acknowledged her anger and felt it toward the analyst, the "yicky" feeling disappeared.

GERRI

Gerri was 9 years old when she moved to this city. Symptom-free until the move, she developed a tic on starting at her new school. In addition, she showed gross motor choreiform movements which could not be ignored. Gerri was born out of wedlock and never saw her biological father. Her mother, independently wealthy, was a social isolate and kept her infant by her side day and night for the first three years of Gerri's life. She then moved into the home of a divorced man, where his several children also lived. Her mother married this man two years later. It appeared that one reason for their compatibility was that they made few demands on each other; thus mother could continue to devote herself freely to Gerri.

Gerri was slender and tall for her age. In fact, she and her mother shared clothes as well as jewelry. Of significance is the fact that no difficulties were reported in Gerri's early development. Although mother was not happy to be pregnant, she welcomed the thought that motherhood would establish her as independent from her own family of origin. The pregnancy, delivery, and neonatal development were unremarkable. Mother had solid support from her family but undertook the full care of Gerri as soon as she was able.

Gerri was bottle-fed from the outset and had no problems with eating. Sleeping was also problem-free. No autoerotic behaviors were recalled. Motor development, speech, and self-help skills were all well within expected ranges. She was always very active physically but did not endanger herself in any way. Socialization skill acquisition was excellent. Separation experiences were unremarkable, according to Gerri's mother, although it is likely that there was no significant challenge until the time of nursery school. There was some indication that she formed intensely exclusionary relationships with peers, beginning at age 2½. Mother, although never fat, was always dieting. Gerri, thin but never underweight, followed her mother's ups and downs closely. She had become very food conscious by age 6. She was always in motion yet appeared able to relax in spectator situations, and she fell asleep easily. She was always polite to her stepfather and never had anything negative to say about him, although she was rather formal in his presence.

Her own explanation of her tic and arm-flinging behavior focused on the family's move and the loss of her best friend. The arm flinging stopped shortly after analysis began, and the facial ticking diminished until the only vestige was seen when she entered the office at the beginning of the analytic hour. The analytic stance, drawing attention to Gerri's absence of negative affect in situations where she would be expected to be enraged, and where her behavior indicated that she was furious, did not impress her perceptibly. However, she began to escalate her rate of physical activity, always in private, until she was running and dancing many hours a day in increasingly ritualistic patterns. At the same time, her attention to caloric intake intensified, and weight loss soon reached alarming proportions.

She attended her analytic hours regularly, but was withdrawn. At first she could be drawn into talking about her view of her body, revealing her abiding conviction that she was hopelessly fat, but she appeared impervious to the suggestion that she must be very troubled to be abusing herself in this fashion. Her mother was now involved (reinvolved) with her on a moment-to-moment basis, reminiscent of Gerri's infancy and early childhood times. Gerri expressed the idea that for her to be force-fed would be some kind of victory: her mother would have to care for her. Her pediatrician finally gave her an ultimatum, which Gerri ingeniously titrated just to the limit, until the decision was made to intubate her on an outpatient basis. This was done, and she immediately began eating again.

Shortly after she had returned to normal weight, she began to show seductive behaviors in the analytic sessions and to raise questions about the analyst's personal life, denying that she had any interest in the answers. The analyst drew her attention to her body displays and suggested she was having trouble dealing with her feelings for him, especially in terms of her fearing how these feelings might influence her relationship with her mother. Gerri then complained of how much time analysis was taking. She became petulant and negativistic during the sessions. When the analyst wondered if she didn't find him intrusive somehow, over the course of the next several sessions Gerri began a tirade, directed first at the analyst and then at her stepfather, to the extent that her face was contorted, exactly as when she had had the tic, except that the tic had been without ideation or affect. Now she also trembled as well, reminiscent of the choreiform movements she had had. How dare he take her mother from her? How dare he sit next to her (Gerri) on the couch and put his arm around her? He smelled bad. He was thoroughly repulsive. She then began to find fault with her mother for the first time in her life. Her mother was weak. She was bland, indecisive, and dependent. In this context, Gerri was describing an event from her past, referring to an aspect of her mother, and she said, "When we were a baby." She was dumfounded, then saddened by what she took to be the implications of the slip, namely, that her sense of differentiation from her mother rested on an insubstantial foundation. At the same time, and for the first time, she raged and wept over her ineffectual biological father, also to her surprise.

Gerri manifested a phenomenal capacity to lip-read, as we discovered during an analytic session in which she had covered her ears and the analyst spoke quietly. She understood perfectly, and, put to the test with more complex content and no phonation, she could easily comprehend. Since she had never been exposed to hearing-impaired persons, we concluded that the visual vigilance which underlay the development of this remarkable talent must have arisen in situations where the importance of being quiet had been impressed upon her and she strained to observe people from afar, or people who were attempting to communicate without her participation. This discovery had the enormous benefit of impressing upon Gerri the power of early and unremembered events in her life.

Gerri's behavior at home underwent a significant transformation over the next weeks. As much as she railed against her parents at my office, she was more open, involved, and friendly at home.

The subsequent analytic work focused on the issues of her early adolescence, her exhibitionism and the defenses against it, and ultimately her feeling for the analyst as termination approached.

Gerri's mother, like Jamie's, recalled her daughter as having been a contented infant. She was often held and would be tended in anticipation of need, often before any signal from her, according to her mother. A smile was always present. As was the case with Jamie, goods and services were lavished upon Gerri as a basic interactional mode right up to adolescence, and occasionally to her embarrassment, especially in front of peers.

Gerri's smile acquired a "grimacing" dimension in latency, conveying a more biting hostile impression, and grimacing constituted a significant part of the ticking which emerged in the present illness. Angry outbursts were never observed, in infancy or subsequently. It was only after two years of analytic work that her fixed smile gave way to the contorted configuration noted above, in association with anger at her stepfather.

Gerri also displayed the open mouth teeth-bared reaction on catching an object tossed to her, as described with Jamie. Only when her anger was openly expressed and demonstrated in the analytic context did her facial expression convey the range of rich affective life of which she was capable.

ALLISON

Allison was brought for evaluation at age 6, for symptoms of depression and for two instances of impulsive cruelty to animals.

When she was 9 months old, her parents found it necessary to adopt another child, preparations for whom had been underway for some time. Both parents expressed reservations about their parenting abilities. Mother felt herself to be overwhelmed by the responsibilities of infant and child care, although she appeared to be fully competent. Father openly stated that he found small children burdensome and looked forward to the day that they would be grown and off. Yet both parents were warmly involved with their children and supported each other much of the time.

Allison's demeanor was somber from birth. She smiled appropriately but never seemed truly happy. "Competent" was the word used most frequently to describe Allison from her earliest days. She developed skills early or on schedule. She did not appear to be fiercely independent, but quietly and thoroughly mastered tasks and skills so quickly that she seemed to bypass much of the expectable dependency of childhood. Although her parents encouraged these behaviors, they could not recall offering particular rewards. If anything, they were somewhat awed. Eating posed no problems for Allison or for her parents in feeding her. She was a large child, always ate well, and tended to be chubby but not fat.

She rarely cried during her infancy and early childhood. Her parents could not recall needing to comfort her, as they did with her younger sibling quite naturally and often. There were no displays of anger, nor even of displeasure, except for whatever her somber mood might signify. She was always gentle and loving with her younger sibling. Her mother felt she could trust Allison with her sister completely from an early age.

At the first evaluation, Allison had filled the blackboard in the waiting room with hearts and the phrase "I love Mommy" repeated many times. Early in the analytic sessions she showed her envy of her younger sister and her rage at her mother, both smoothly defended with unruffled denial. On one occasion she brought her mother's expensive pen into the session and kept jamming it until it broke. Although frightened, she was at once galvanized into searching for ways to cover the act. Could she reposition the pieces so that the damage would not be noticed? Did the analyst have a pen she could use as a substitute? These possibilities and more were considered without any evidence of guilt, but with a calculated coolness that made the reported episodes of cruelty plausible. She denied having any anger toward her mother. Subsequently, damage was increasingly inflicted on items belonging to the analyst, and even threats to the person of the analyst. However, clear statements as to limits were accepted without hesitation, a reaction suggesting that she found the experience novel. Less easily accepted were suggestions that the behaviors were a reflection of how she felt.

As her anger became intensified, and more focused in dreams, fantasy, and transference, Allison surreptitiously began to eat less and to exercise more regularly. Although she never approached the weight loss that would meet the criteria for an anorexic episode, she had all the other features. In particular, the matter of control was central. As control over her deep sense of rage diminished through the analysis of her defensive reaction formations, she increased the control over her intake, thereby simultaneously directing her aggression toward herself.

Allison's expressions of affect differed from those of Jamie and Gerri. Although she smiled on occasions as an infant, she was almost always serious. She was alert and involved in cognitive ways, but emotionally remote. It was as though "low-keyedness" had become her general state of feeling. No tantrums were recalled. Although hostile destructiveness was evident in certain behaviors, such as cruelty to animals and destruction of property as early as age 3, she was not observed to be angry, nor could she recall feeling angry.

Allison's primary affect during most of her analysis remained blunted, giving the appearance of indifference. Indeed, a frequently stated comment was "I don't care." Dreams of violence were reported in a bland fashion: she took no responsibility for such material. Similarly, she would deny the obvious pleasure she took in flattening a clay creature she had constructed. Repeated attention to the disparities between her reported and observed behaviors and her experiences of affect eventually reduced the gap, as seen, for example, in the tight lips and clenched teeth when she would describe her bitterness about a perceived snub by peers.

While Allison came to appreciate the extent to which she defended herself against awareness of her pervasive rage, it was only on an intellectual level that she could comprehend the fact that the primary target for her rage was her mother. Nonetheless, she was no longer affectively monochromatic, was eating normally, and was much more outgoing.

DISCUSSION

The experience of affect and the development of affective experience appear to have been aberrant from the beginning for the children in this study. Jamie and Gerri were always contented by report, that is, they were recalled as having always been happy in the first two years of life, with overt signs of distress minimal or absent. Jamie began to complain of aches and pains at about 2 years of age, but always with a smile. Allison was recalled as somber from her earliest days, but never as a complainer. None of the children had any tantrum behaviors. Later Jamie developed episodes of crying quietly which, by age 8, intensified to wailing, without any source that she could identify. Yet during their analytic experiences, each child showed a full capacity to feel and express anger. Both the feeling and the expression had been unconscious for these children.

Denial and reaction formation were powerfully developed so early in the lives of these children that only by invoking parental collusion does it seem possible in terms of ego development.

Although each of the children had significant interferences with and aberrations of her development, the central issues were intrapsychic conflict with respect to aggression, and reactions to aggression.

Contemporary independent observational data, in conjunction with the reports of parents in the cases of Jamie and Allison, and parental report alone with Gerri, indicated intense parental ambivalence about the conceptions of these children. The mothers were consciously aware of their efforts to counterbalance their ambivalences by providing perfect parenting. This meant that the perception of stress in the infant, however expectable, must be addressed at once. The normal thrust of nondestructive aggression (Parens 1980), which under optimal conditions propels the infant and young child into and through the subphases of the separation-individuation process, was curtailed, inhibited, and otherwise distorted in these three children because no differentiation was made by parent or child between non-affective destructiveness (defined by Parens [1980] as that activity whereby nourishment can take place), nondestructive aggression, and hostile destructiveness. It is as though all manifestations of the aggressive drive were experienced as hostile destructiveness and therefore as threatening and dangerous. (See Stechler and Halton 1987 for a systems view of this issue.) Precocious and hypertrophied defensive behaviors, especially denial and reaction formation, were observable and demonstrable in each child. Although these characteristic defenses were prominent by at least age 4, precursors could be traced to the first year of life in the form of significant modification and inhibition of the expression of both dimensions of the aggressive drive, namely, assertiveness and the development of intentionality, and hostile aggression (Stechler and Halton 1987).

Aberrations in the experiencing and expression of aggression in the first three years of life of each of these children permeated every stage of psychosexual development, such that the usual stage markers were blurred or absent, as were the markers between subphases of the separation-individuation phase.

Oral aggression, developing usually in the middle of the first year of life, is absent from the spontaneous histories reported by the parents of the three children, and indications of the presence of oral aggression were denied on inquiry. It could be inferred that such indications were diminished or absent, that they were present but not recalled, or both. It would appear that they might have been present and repressed in light of the bare-toothed grimacing observed later in both Jamie and Gerri, in dreams of engulfing monsters, and in the facial ticking and lip-reading, in addition to the oral aggression and sadism entailed in their eating disorders and associated fantasies.

No problems were reported in the development of sphincter control with these children. Compliance was exhibited, with no significant obstinacy and no messing. As was the case with oral aggression, the later emergence of anal-phase behaviors could be seen in the obsessions around food and in compulsive ritualistic bodily activities. Phallic aggression could be understood as contributing to the latter especially.

The presumed tensions involved in early schooling experiences were overtly readily neutralized in Jamie by her ability to transfer her demands and expectations successfully to the teacher, in Gerri by her twinship attachments, and in Allison by her pseudomaturity and remoteness.

None of the children underwent an oedipal experience in any normative sense. In each instance, the father was absent as a force to enhance the development of differentiation and separation between child and mother, with the far-reaching consequence that growth-promoting aggression remained under tightly controlled primitive mechanisms of denial and reaction formation, with the additional pathological manifestations of somatization (Jamie), cruelty to animals (Allison), and archaic interpersonal relationships imposed by reliance on twinning (Gerri).

Latency posed no manifest problem for these children, who were already experienced in the use of reaction formation. Those who were in a position to observe them in greater depth recognized that they had no flexibility along the progression-regression dimension and that there was no evidence that the structure of latency (Sarnoff 1976) was developing. This too has important implications for the reported paucity of fantasy life in persons with eating disorders.

The ultimate challenge to the child predisposed to the development of an eating disorder is adolescence, when physical development and genital sexuality can no longer be denied, short of a distortion of reality of psychotic proportion, which occurs in some instances. From this vantage point, it would seem that the psychoanalytic experience forced Jamie, Gerri, and Allison to confront their infantile attachments in ways that threatened their archaic sense of identity and control. Consistent analytic attention to the defenses against recognition of the power of the aggressive drive, and the powerful infantile origins of these defenses, resulted in pronounced destabilization. It became urgent to demonstrate absolute control over their identities, their bodies, and those around them. Through denial of hunger, they could at the same time forestall further development and prove that no bodily demand, now experienced with genital implications, nor any demand by others could dominate them.

Thus Gerri, whose basic psychopathology was consistent with a borderline personality, underwent a full-blown life-threatening episode of anorexia nervosa; Jamie, inclined to impulsivity, developed a bulimic-anorectic pattern; and Allison, whose psychopathology was more neurotic, manifested all the features of restrictor anorexia except for the extreme weight loss.

McDevitt (1983) notes that early in the practicing subphase the constructive use of aggression provides the impetus for the developmentally essential shift from passivity to activity. It is of interest that none of the children in this study was passive in any sense of the term. In fact, a hallmark of persons with restrictor anorexia is intense physical activity, seen in these children by age 8. It seems likely that this physical hyperactivity, like the denial of hunger, is a desperate effort to compensate for the profound psychological passivity which is evident on deeper examination. McDevitt also mentions the beginning reaction formations evident at this time (early practicing) (1983, p. 277).

Also absent in the children reported here is splitting in which hostile aggression is directed away from mother to the nonmother world, as well as tantruming. Mahler (1971) sees the tantrums of children who have not smoothly negotiated the separation-individuation process as resulting from identification with bad introjects. Instead, in the children in this study, it seems likely that the maternal introjects are narcissistically "laundered" and are experienced as "perfect," not bad. Aggression is directed toward the self in the form of inhibition of the development of independence and, later, overt self-destructive behaviors. The absence of reported or observed autoerotic behaviors in these children is also noteworthy and may be a further reflection of inhibition.

The parents of the children in this study, perhaps because of doubts about their readiness to parent, appear to have needed "perfect" children, that is, children who reflect no deficiencies in parent or child, including "normal" crying, fussing, or negativity.

The psychoanalyst's position must, as always, be one in which the bad mother role is accepted as an integral part of a total relationship. In the case of each child, this position was initially typically unrecognized, then denied and otherwise rendered ineffective, and finally violently rejected by means of the power of an eating disorder. Throughout, steady attention to the underlying rage propelling the child into such self-destructive behaviors eventuated in mobilization of anger toward father, analyst, and mother.

Excessive inhibition and distortion of the expression of aggression in the ways here described in children are also readily recognizable in adults with eating disorders, although more complex and more firmly embedded in defensive/adaptive modes. Many of the features, such as passivity, resistance to regression, and presumed paucity of fantasy, are perceived as mitigating against the recommendation for psychoanalytic treatment. A more thoroughgoing review of the person's experience of aggression may eventuate in the recognition of intrapsychic conflictual elements, and the decision to explore these psychoanalytically.

SUMMARY

Data are presented from the psychoanalyses of three children who developed eating disorders in the course of analysis. Shared features in the early development of these children included evidence of overt and covert ambivalence in the parents about the pregnancies, reported absence of any signs of distress in the newborn infant, consistent compliance on the part of the child, blurring of the expected markers signaling psychosexual stage development and separation-individuation subphase development, and, most notably, the absence of the expression of aggression.

These findings suggest that disturbances in aggression seen in persons with eating disorders can be identified at any age, including infancy, where inhibition even of nondestructive aggression results in stunting of the development of all subphases of the separation-individuation process, while denial and reaction formation are hypertrophied. This stunting leaves the affected person without confidence in the power afforded by successful individuation and channeled aggression. "On the way to object constancy," by which is meant object constancy with respect to libido, neither denotes nor connotes the failure of development of object constancy with respect to aggression. McDevitt (1983) notes that "insofar as hate becomes persistent in the mind during rapprochement, as does love, hate may come to have a quality of constancy similar to, if not comparable with that present in 'libidinal' object constancy." It would appear from the children in this study that it is not only hate, but aggression in its broadest sense, that can undergo adverse development much earlier and can result in a failure of the development of object constancy with respect to aggression.

Object constancy with respect to aggression, upon which depends further movement through anal, phallic, oedipal, and latency stages, is itself dependent upon the experiencing and channeling of aggression in earlier phases. The differentiation and practicing subphases can appear to have been successfully negotiated because of denial and pseudomaturity with respect to locomotion and language development. However, rapprochement experiences, and especially the rapprochement crisis, are vestigial in effect since there was inadequate aggression, or utilization of aggression, to accomplish the necessary antecedent emotional and psychological differentiation of infant/child from mother at the outset.

It is important to note that no attempt is being made to establish causality—for example, that parental ambivalence is the cause of eating disorders. Other factors in the parents not yet identified, other factors in the child not yet identified, and other factors in the interactions between child and animate/inanimate environments may be operative. There are no grounds for closure in considering etiology.

In these children, each of whom developed an eating disorder in the course of analysis, the analysis of aggression appeared to be central to the precipitation of the eating disorder as well as to its resolution.

History from infancy provided by the parents, as well as data provided by independent observers in two of the cases, point to an extraordinary degree of effort to experience the infant as tension-free.

Parens's formulations of the role of nondestructive aggression are cited as useful in tracing the impact of distortions in the experience and expression of aggression on early development.

In addition to cognitive object constancy, and "on the way to libidinal object constancy," the constancy of object and self with respect to aggression has its place.

REFERENCES

Bruch, H. (1973). *Eating Disorders: Obesity, Anorexia Nervosa, and the Person Within*. New York: Basic Books.

Fischer, N. (1986). *Anorexia nervosa and unresolved rapprochement conflicts: a case study*. Paper presented at the meetings of the American Psychoanalytic Association, Washington D.C. May.

Kramer, S. (1974). A discussion of Sour's paper "The anorexia nervosa syndrome." *International Journal of Psycho-Analysis* 55:577–579.

Mahler, M. S. (1965). On the significance of the normal separation-individuation phase. In *Drives, Affects, Behavior*, vol. 2, ed. M. Shur., pp. 161–169. New York: International Universities Press.

———— (1966). Notes on the development of basic moods: the depressive affect. In *The Selected Papers of Margaret S. Mahler*, vol. 2, p. 61. New York: Jason Aronson.

———— (1971). A study of the separation-individuation process and its possible application to borderline phenomena in the psychoanalytic situation. In *The Selected Papers of Margaret S. Mahler*, vol. 2. p. 177. New York: Jason Aronson.

McDevitt, J. B. (1983). The emergence of hostile aggression and its defensive and adaptive modifications during the separation-individuation process. *Journal of the American Psychoanalytic Association* 31 (Supplt):273–300.

Mintz, I. L. (1983). Anorexia nervosa and bulimia in males. In *Fear of Being Fat, The Treatment of Anorexia and Bulimia*, ed. C. P. Wilson, C. C. Hogan, and I. L. Mintz, pp. 263–303. New York: Jason Aronson.

Mushatt, C. (1978). Anorexia nervosa: a psychoanalytic commentary. *International Journal of Psychoanalytic Psychotherapy* 9:257.

Panel Report (1972). The experience of separation-individuation in infancy and its reverberations through the course of life: 1. infancy and childhood. Reported by M. Winestine. *Journal of the American Psychoanalytic Association* 20:135–155.

Parens, H. (1980). An exploration of the relations of instinctual drives and the symbiosis/separation-individuation process. *Journal of the American Psychoanalytic Association* 28:89–114.

Sarnoff, C. (1976). *Latency*. New York: Jason Aronson.

Sours, J. A. (1979). The primary anorexia nervosa syndrome. In *The Basic Handbook of Child Psychiatry*, vol. 2., ed. J. D. Noshpitz, pp. 568–580. New York: Basic Books.

Stechler, G., and Halton, A. (1987). The emergence of assertion and aggression during infancy: a psychoanalytic systems approach. *Journal of the American Psychoanalytic Association* 35:821–838.

Wilson, C. P. (1985). The fear of being fat in female psychology. In *Fear of Being Fat: The Treatment of Anorexia Nervosa and Bulimia*, rev. ed., ed. C. P. Wilson, C. C. Hogan, and I. L. Mintz, pp. 9–27. New York: Jason Aronson.

11

Psychotherapy of a Child with Esophageal Atresia Who Refused to Eat

Christina Sekaer, M.D.

"It takes half an hour to get her to eat one green pea." The exasperation of Emily's parents was evident as they explained that their $5\frac{1}{2}$-year-old girl, born with esophageal atresia, had continued to refuse to eat even following her corrective surgery at age 2. The therapist wondered whether it would be possible to awaken oral pleasure in a child who had never enjoyed eating and, further, how her experience would influence her development. This chapter is concerned with a discussion of Emily, beginning with a brief discussion of the nature of esophageal atresia.

ESOPHAGEAL ATRESIA AND SHAM FEEDING

Esophageal atresia is a congenital defect wherein the esophagus ends with a missing segment between throat and stomach. Esophageal atresia per se does not necessarily cause an eating disorder, although there may be

237

associated neurological impairments in the ability to swallow. There may be a tracheoesophageal fistula (a patent connection from the esophagus to the lungs) either above or below the gap in the esophagus. Surgical treatment with colonic bypass, as it was done on Emily, involves two stages. First, at birth a gastrostomy tube is placed in the stomach to allow feeding, and an opening is made from the throat out the front of the neck to allow drainage of saliva from the mouth (fistulas to the lungs are also closed). In the second stage, done usually between 6 and 24 months, a section of colon is sewn in to fill the gap, the gastrostomy tube is removed, and the drainage opening in the neck is closed. After surgery, the colonic bypass section shows no sequential contractions and no peristalsis; only gravity moves the food (Van der Zee et al. 1981). Aside from the inability to vomit and minor leakage up through the mouth or nose when the individual is lying down, the eating function is potentially normal after repair. Emily's gastrostomy tube was a Foley catheter one-half inch in diameter which emerged from the left side of the abdomen for about 20 inches; an inflatable bubble at the tip, inside the stomach, prevented the tube from slipping out. Colonic bypass, as done on Emily, is a standard procedure still in use, although newer techniques have also been developed (Van der Zee et al. 1981).

Congenital esophageal atresia was first successfully treated surgically in 1941 by C. Haight (Holder and Ashcraft 1970). He noted then that infants fed with a gastrostomy tube must also be given some oral intake at the same time "so they learn to associate chewing and swallowing with appetite satiation" or they would not learn how to eat (p. 461).

Sham feeding was developed to encourage eating and to allow the infant a sense of control. Sham feeding involves slowly putting food into the tube while the infant is sucking and taking fluid orally (which drains out the neck opening). In this way the infant senses control over the input (stopped when he stops sucking) and his sucking motions are coordinated with achieving feelings of fullness. This procedure is effective only for infants willing to suck. In Emily's case, she refused to suck or eat, apparently for emotional reasons.

Cases have been noted (Dowling 1977) in which a gastrostomy tube has continued to be used after repair because of difficulty in learning to swallow, for either emotional or neurological reasons. For Emily, psychotherapy following psychoanalytic principles was applied to resolve use of a gastrostomy tube that was no longer physiologically necessary.

AWAKENING ORAL PLEASURE

Whether it would be possible to awaken oral pleasure in a child who had never enjoyed eating was of concern at the start of the treatment. Oral pleasure, like other sensory experiences, is both a psychological and a physiological phenomenon. One would assume that Emily's oral pleasure could be awakened unless there had been some sort of physiological or psychological critical period of early missed experience.

On a *physiological* level, critical periods have been demonstrated in animals for vision and other functions. Lack of light stimulation during a critical period for a kitten leads to degeneration of cortical visual cells and connections and loss of vision (Hubel and Weisel 1970). In humans, when there is damage to the left-sided language center, language can be learned through use of other areas of the brain such as the corresponding parts of the right brain, depending on the age at which the damage occurs. In general, if the damage occurs before 2 or 3 years of age, the relearned language is likely to be fully fluent; language relearned after damage later in childhood may lack fluency. In an adult, only very rudimentary language can be relearned (Kolb and Whishaw 1980). While this does not exemplify a precise critical period, the principle is the same, that is, of a developing physiological lack of plasticity as neural cells are committed to other specific functions. Regarding Emily, the therapist wondered whether (hypothesized) "oral pleasure" cells or connections had been lost such that oral pleasure would be impossible or could develop only in a partial or stilted way.

Hypothetically one could have similar critical periods in *psychological* development, wherein the lack of certain psychological experiences would lead to an irreversible deficit. For example, an infant whose mother is unable to empathize during the first year may develop apparently irreversible pervasive personality distortions. Perhaps in a similar way Emily would remain unable to enjoy eating because of a lack of psychosocial integration of early positive eating experiences. It is difficult to *prove* irreversibility of the effects of early psychological deficits since infants given poor early mothering sometimes seem to recover if later given good mothering. Even Harlow (Harlow and Mears 1979) modified his assessment of the damage done by emotionally depriving infant monkeys, in the direction that later recovery may be possible.

Clinically it may be difficult to assess which are psychological and which are physiological causes of a given disturbance. Some cases of infants with autistic behavior, for example, have been attributed to psychological causes such as deficient mothering due to unrecognized covert depression in the mother (Call 1978); alternatively, autistic symptoms are attributed to "miswiring" of nerve cells present at birth.

Whichever the etiology, the therapist wondered whether Emily might have suffered a profound deficit due to lack of early oral pleasure which would leave an irreversible gap in her personality and/or brain structure. The therapist felt that oral pleasure could be developed, but she was not sure. Certainly the route for intervention was to attempt to elicit oral pleasure and to remove interfering defenses and conflicts.

ORAL INCORPORATION, PHYSIOLOGICAL AND PSYCHOLOGICAL

Can a child who has never taken food by mouth incorporate relationships with significant others? Oral incorporation as a physiological model is sometimes applied to explain psychological phenomena. Taking in food is compared to taking in aspects of relationships with other persons. Whether this analogy has a concrete validity, any more than, say, Freud's hydraulic model of the libido, is interesting to consider.

Engel and Segal (1956) tried to explore directly both the physiological and psychological aspects of incorporation and the oral organization of early object relations in the unique case of Monica, whose gastrostomy (for esophageal atresia) allowed sampling of gastric HCl. Monica's HCl secretion was compared with observed facial and behavioral indicators of affect. HCl secretion increased with pleasure or anger, and especially so with rage or reunion; it decreased with withdrawal or inactivity. The stomach secretions paralleled behavioral expressions of object cathexes, such as touching, reaching, hitting, and grasping. Engel said that early "relationships with objects in the external world are established . . . with a process of general intaking assimilative organization in which the stomach participates as if the intention is also to ingest the object and digest it" and concludes that early object relations are largely orally organized (p. 396). The physiological marker of incorporation (HCl secretion) paralleled the psychological markers of incorporation (affects and behaviors toward related others). However, this parallel phenomenon does not *prove* an unconscious or subcortical *intent* to ingest or digest the object. Furthermore, the HCl secretion might have occurred in this situation regardless of food having ever been taken into the stomach *by mouth*.

To relate Engel's study to Emily, the point is that virtually no food was taken by Emily by mouth for the first two years of her life. Sham feeding had been unsuccessful. If taking food in by mouth is not needed for gastric secretions to parallel object-related behaviors, then the "oral" (digestive) organization of object relations can occur even without the experience of taking food by mouth; that is, a physical incorporative sensorimotor experience of taking food by mouth is *not* necessary as a foundation for the incorporation of objects.

One might anticipate then that a child like Emily could still develop good object relations if (1) HCl secretion was only an epiphenomenon not causally related to object relations, or (2) HCl secretions are a necessary causally related aspect of object relations, but one for which food ingestion *by mouth* is not necessary. Alternately, if food by mouth *is* necessary for object relations, one would expect Emily to have serious difficulty relating to others. By "necessary," I mean a vital component to integration of a psychological, emotional, and gastric organization of object relations.

This is not to overstress eating by mouth, which is only one aspect of the oral phase of development. Touching, holding, rocking, and other forms of physical closeness as well as visual and vocal contact provide channels for security to grow between an infant and mother. Even so, if a child has not eaten, one might expect to see selected areas of difficulty such as with oral greed or oral aggression. Emily's early oral experiences had been basically unpleasant, with attempts to force food by mouth leading to hysterical gagging or with food simply inserted into the stomach. Her gastric experience was of periodically being filled to the point of painful discomfort without any volitional control.

ORAL INCORPORATION AND LEARNING

Lack of oral experience, besides affecting object relations, might be expected to have a profound impact on learning. Structuring of the outside world and of one's body is significantly related to oral experience. It is well known that infants learn about their world by mouthing objects. They differentiate things from themselves, establish boundaries, and acquire a sensorimotor preverbal, and even preconscious, knowledge of the world as a foundation for later learning.

Meltzoff and Borton (1979) showed that infants selectively look at nipples with the same shape as one placed in their mouth, suggesting that neural wiring exists at birth connecting the infant's mouth sensations with its visual construction of and selective perception of the outer environment. Dowling's infants (1977) with esophageal atresia who lacked early oral experience had difficulty later in areas such as gross motor functions, suggesting that oral motor experience is used as a basis for synthesis of gross body motions.

If early experiences are lacking, deficits in one's learning about the environment may persist. Even a brief period of sensory input may be helpful in allowing synthesis and structuring of one's world. Blind children who had seen for a period of time before going blind are able to continue using a visually based integrated spatial ability to map their environs which children blind from birth do not develop (Rubin 1979, p. 229). Emily did not appear to have had a chance early in infancy to integrate positive experiences of being fed.

Infants also can learn a motivation to act based on the contingency responses to their actions very early in the oral phase (Lewis 1967). For example, they respond to a contingent response to their action (e.g., a light goes on when the infant turns its head) with intense efforts to repeat the act; given random responses to their efforts, they learn not to try (Bower 1982). An infant for whom eating by mouth did not produce satisfaction might learn not to care about eating. Dowling (1980) reports on an infant, Matt, sham-fed from birth, who apparently learned only at 3 months that sucking and eating satisfied his hunger. That is, he learned "a connection between oral activity and pleasurable relief of discomfort." Matt then became intensely motivated toward oral feedings; food given by tube would not satisfy his urge to eat. Dowling contrasts Matt with other esophageal atresia infants who did not develop hunger–satiation rhythms; for these infants, even prolonged periods without feeding did not provoke expressions of hunger.

Infants who have learned not to care about taking in food might also not care about other learning such as taking in knowledge of the world.

242 Christina Sekaer, M.D.

Dowling (1980) discusses the impact of lack of active oral experience on learning in the esophageal atresia infants he studied. They showed subdued initiative in active learning and were better at rote learning. Dowling concluded that the deficient early oral experience led to not "going forth to meet the environment" and that oral experience was extended "from mouth to hand, arm and body, and from nipple to breast, mother, toy and the world at large" (p. 160). Emily was just in kindergarten at the start of therapy. Whether learning difficulties would be significant and what form they would take was of interest.

CASE HISTORY: BACKGROUND

Emily was born with esophageal atresia and had had a gastrostomy tube inserted at birth. Sham feedings were tried but she had no interest in sucking; instead she choked, gagged, rolled up her eyes, and would not swallow. Emily's parents noted that the nursing staff tried forcefully to get Emily to sham-feed and urged them also to be very insistent. Emily was in an incubator for several days after birth, and during this time when the hospital staff tried oral sham feeding, Emily would turn blue, gag, choke, and cry hysterically. This process was repeated on so many occasions that her parents felt a pattern of negative oral experience had been established in the first days of her life. She would gag even at the sight of an approaching spoon. Emily refused to suck a pacifier, her fingers, or anything else. It would seem that an archaic primitive anxiety associated with oral activity became part of a conditioned early core of her personality, preceding the beginnings of her ego and conscious self-awareness (Emde 1983). Following advice from several pediatricians, Emily's parents tried feeding her in spite of the gagging for periods of three weeks at a time.

Emily's motoric developmental milestones were delayed. She did not crawl until 19 months old and walked at 23 months, although she talked at a normal age. At age one, she attended a cerebral palsy nursery, where, her mother said, exercises were done for stimulation because she "did not know where her body was in space." She was awkward in handling her body and seemed to fear movement in space. Mother attempted to make up for the lack of contact around eating with physical contact such as holding Emily, which was enjoyable.

As an additional difficulty, Emily apparently had two petit mal seizures on the day of her birth and first surgery, which were later related to calcium deficiency. She was put on phenobarbital, which was continued until 15 months of age. This medication in all likelihood contributed to her passive behavior. Emily shifted to a much more active approach to the world and to her parents during the latter part of her second year. This marked the point when she was able to relate to them around anal-level issues of interpersonal and bodily control. It also followed the discontinuation of the phenobarbital.

At 22 months a colonic bypass was inserted. Prior to the surgery Emily was "chunky," but she lost 6 pounds during the time of the surgery; afterwards she reportedly "ate well" (for the first time) for two weeks but the pediatrician felt she was not gaining weight fast enough and continued the tube feedings. She stopped eating then and never resumed other than token amounts of food.

Emily's weight continued to remain low as her parents saw several nutritionists. At this time, Emily's parents fed her hourly into the night in an effort to get her to gain weight. In the concern that Emily might lose more weight and die, they filled her as much as possible with the tube, so she often experienced marked discomfort as her stomach would feel "like a rock." Emily learned, at $3\frac{1}{2}$, to say "open the tube" at these times; when it was opened, gastric contents would spurt out, relieving the pressure. She was worked up for failure to thrive and malabsorption of fat at age $3\frac{1}{2}$. Before a definitive diagnosis was made, she was put on a canned formula (via the tube), successfully gained weight, and was maintained only on that for the next three years. A G.I. series done at age 4 was reported normal. In retrospect, her father noted that the nutritionists had frightened them, overstressing the dangers of weight loss.

As she grew older, her parents were advised to try tying her into a high chair. They tried behavior modification techniques, offering all sorts of rewards. They took her to a psychiatrist for hypnosis at about age 4, but they said they felt cheated when they were told that children go into a trance while they play and they are not really hypnotized. They said the psychiatrist simply play-acted feeding dolls with Emily, suggesting she too would eat. Finally they took her to a physical therapist, who did whole body exercises with the idea that the muscle tensions in her mouth, neck, and throat prevented her from swallowing and eating. Only after all of these failed did her mother seek a referral for psychotherapy when Emily was $5\frac{1}{2}$. In retrospect, her mother felt the surgeons and pediatricians had not been helpful in directing them toward treatment for the emotional aspects of Emily's situation.

Emily lived with her parents and two older siblings, who had had no eating problems. There was no family history of congenital deficits. Emily had been born with enlarged cerebral ventricles and other minor signs associated with esophageal atresia which did not appear to cause difficulty.

COURSE OF THERAPY

Presentation of the therapy has been divided into four phases: (1) Introductory (12 months), (2) pre-eating (6 months), (3) pre-op (12 months), and (4) post-tube (24+ months). Emily was seen twice weekly through the first three phases, then once weekly; her parents were seen every two weeks, although usually only her mother attended.

Introductory Phase: $5\frac{1}{2}$ to $6\frac{1}{2}$ Years Old (12 Months)

Overview of Interventions

The provision of a new object for a relationship was the first therapeutic intervention. Emily's need for and readiness to use this relationship as an opportunity for growth and development was indicated by her intense initial involvement. The therapist provided food, discussed Emily's reactions to it, and put *no* pressure on her to eat. Emily was given autonomy in the sessions, which allowed the unfolding of her feelings and ideas. Interpretations included that her love of teasing overrode her wish to grow up as well as warding off her own fears of eating. Her clinging to mother was interpreted as her fear of losing mother because of her anger at mother, which anger was also expressed in the not eating.

Active involvement of Emily's parents in the therapy was essential. Several specific interventions were made with Emily's parents at the start. They were instructed to discontinue *all* efforts to get Emily to eat and instead to tell her that her body needed food and fluid, and if she did not eat by mouth, these would go into the tube but it did not matter which. Similarly, her parents were not to give excessive attention to Emily's talk of the tube (for which all other topics in the past had been dropped). Mother was instructed to fix special foods Emily requested only if she would not get angry if Emily then refused to eat them. Food was stressed as needed for Emily's body rather than as eaten to please mother or father. Regression, especially around oral issues, was encouraged. Rather than pressuring Emily to grow up, her parents were told to tell her that she had a side that wanted to be big and grow up and a side that wanted to be a baby, and that both were acceptable. After a few weeks, mother was instructed not to stay in the waiting room during the sessions, in order to heighten separation issues with Emily.

In this introductory phase a positive relationship with the therapist developed, anger increased directly as the power struggle over food was lessened, bodily tensions relaxed, and material emerged around oral, anal, phallic, oedipal, and separation themes. Emily's defensive use of grandiosity and avoidance became evident.

New Object

Initially Emily was very eager for a relationship with the therapist as a new object, showing intense enthusiasm and excitement. She came eagerly to sessions, wanted to see the therapist daily and to stay forever. In the initial session Emily spent half an hour attempting to tie her shoes. The therapist felt Emily expected her to intervene and, by not doing so, provided Emily with a new experience. Emily identified with the therapist in many ways, calling the objects in the office "mine" (pencils, pocketbook, bookbag) and wearing the therapist's shoes and coat. Emily wished to see the therapist exclusively as hers. She surveyed the people in the waiting room and with exasperation complained, "*Everyone* talks to Christina!!" She was not motivated to discussion and was not consciously experiencing any problems. Questions about her tube or past experiences were met with "shut up!"

At the same time, loyalty to her mother presented a conflict which she dealt with by repeatedly bringing mother into the sessions. At these times, when in mother's presence she often would not hear the therapist and would talk only to mother. She greeted the therapist with a derogatory "Who is *she?*" as though the therapist were a stranger. She feared losing mother, saying to the therapist, "I'm glad you're only my pretend mommy (in a game), because if you were my real mommy . . . I would have no way to get home." She also pointed out similarities between the therapist and her mother.

Control

The issue of control in the form of manipulation, teasing, and power struggles was central from the start. An enormous amount of parental attention and concern had been put daily on Emily's not eating. Emily ate, at the start, cough medicine and bits of onions, garlic, and burnt toast, which seemed related to their not being favored by mother. She chewed gum vigorously and ate occasional bits of junk food or table food. She was deceptive, taking lunch to school, throwing it out, and saying she had eaten it. She had never swigged from a bottle, used a straw, or spit. The therapist felt she could probably eat normally with normal bites but was not certain.

When Emily's parents ceased efforts to get her to eat, Emily, who had been forced, cajoled, and catered to all her life reacted with bewilderment to this new situation. She continued to test control issues repeatedly as the therapy progressed. When mother ignored gagging and choking, Emily would get enraged, saying, "I'm choking! Can't you see?" but soon gave up the behavior. After a few months she began to complain of not wanting the tube feedings either. At the start she ate virtually nothing. She teased, saying she wanted a toasted cheese sandwich and then eating only a crumb. The therapist interpreted her pleasure in teasing, saying that Emily wanted to grow up and be big (by eating), "but you like to tease so very much that you do that instead," at which Emily grinned, laughed with glee, and agreed.

An increase of *direct* expression of anger coincided with the lessening of anger that was expressed in the manipulative interactions around food. Emily enjoyed being increasingly assertive in her new relationship with the therapist, taking a controlling tone in the sessions with the therapist, whom she ordered to do things, "get this," or "pick this up." She became more active and noisy, banging a Chinese checker set loudly so mother heard it from the waiting room; soon she became angrier in sessions and at home. Emily entered into a delayed "terrible twos," with rages and tantrums, self-assertive "no's," and the ability to be verbally "obnoxious" with parents, siblings, and peers. In the first few months of therapy, as she was freer with anger, the tension in her mouth, face, neck, shoulders, and body was alleviated.

Relationship to Food

Emily's relationship to food was a central theme in the sessions from the start. She was indifferent to food, exhibiting no hunger or special preferences. She would taste food and comment "Yum" or "Yuk," both without affect, putting food back after an infinitesimal bite.

Emily did not express a wish to be thin; however, there was a side of her that did not wish to grow up and separate from mother. She did not seem to be afraid to be fat although she confused "dieting" with "dying," at one point noting, "My father is dying; he's getting fatter and fatter." Dieting was done periodically within the family as parents and siblings all struggled to stay within a normal range of weight.

M&M candies, which had by chance been in the drawer during an early visit, took on a special significance. M&M's illustrated many of the issues tied in with food, as Emily would get anxious if she feared the therapist did not have them or enough of them. She would eat tiny bites around the rim and instruct the therapist to do the same. She would have the therapist eat one in about thirty bites and then put hers back, stating, "Mine didn't taste very good." She would eat one over about fifteen minutes, making a gooey mess on her fingers. She would say she "liked" them or at times she "hated" them. She would often take a few with her at the end of the session, more often than not leaving them in the ashtray in the waiting room. She would anxiously ask mother to buy them for her, fearing the stores would not have them. When Emily or the therapist left for a vacation, she uncannily spilled them accidentally on the floor (as though losing the therapist).

Psychosexual Stages

Psychosexual material from all levels emerged simultaneously from the start of therapy. That is, there did not seem to be a sequential unfolding of phases. The absence of oral pleasure in anything, including sucking, mouthing, tasting, and eating, was, from the start of her life, one of the most remarkable aspects of Emily's background. Emily also never played at breastfeeding or bottle-feeding dolls. Efforts were made to encourage regressive oral pleasures (discussed further in the description of the pre-eating phase below).

Inhibition of oral aggression was evident in the physical tension that distorted Emily's mouth and speech, and in her lack of play in which dolls would bite; Emily herself also did not bite in play or in anger. Oral aggression was present in gum-chewing, and she did laugh with glee when her pleasure in chewing gum was pointed out.

Anal themes of messiness, cleaning, and concern with dirt were evident, in addition to control issues. Emily complained of the fuzz from the therapist's wool rug, calling it "yuk" and not wanting it on her pants. Within a few weeks of therapy she made messes, such as with glue on paper, which she had not done before. She cursed, saying "damn it!" and she enjoyed belching (which, because of her unusual esophagus, she was quite good at). She began to have a bowel movement during almost every session. After using the toilet, she would insist mother wipe her; she refused to wash her hands unless they "smelled." She was interested in cleaning and often cleaned the tub, gleefully stating that she was "the maid."

Phallic concerns were evident as (when father was away) she hung a huge bunch of keys on her belt in front. She would boast as to how much "pee" she had made. She also noted how strong she was, a theme later encouraged as a reason for eating.

Castration fears and/or body damage fears related to her surgery were intermingled. She drew an octopus with one leg which turned out to be a penis and then erased the penis. She was very interested in Band-Aids and put one on her knee when the therapist had one on her knee. She didn't like to use torn paper or eat a broken M&M. She was phobic of having her hair cut. Once she went home with an earache and the next session denied she had had a sore ear. She failed a vision test and denied having taken the test. She was fearful of discussing scars and once noted that the therapist had one on her eye just as her mother did. In one dramatic instance she visited a family friend, a woman with a bandaged broken arm, and fled from the room yelling to mother, "What did you do to her?"

Oedipal issues emerged in the second month of therapy as Emily for the first time began a very active questioning of sex differences. She noted her brother had a penis and joked that he did not. She masturbated openly to "make babies" with her teddy bear and said she would marry her father rather than her brother because father was "big so I can get pregnant." She was also very insistent on wanting to sleep with her mother or both parents, using various fears of the dark, the moon, and other things as excuses (not given into), as well as screaming tantrums. She complained that her parents did not kiss as on television. The "baby-making" continued through the first year of therapy and occasionally later.

Defenses

Emily used her defenses, especially of denial grandiosity and omnipotence, extensively and formidably to resist discussion of any areas that she wanted to avoid. "Let's not talk about that," "shut up," not hearing, talking over, "that's boring," and forgetting of issues discussed a few minutes before were expressed frequently, as was running to the bathroom as escape. It was probably not possible to, and was also decided not to, attack these defenses until after the tube was out and overall ego functioning was improved. The therapist felt Emily was progressing toward eating and having the tube out and did not wish to risk disrupting this progress.

248   Christina Sekaer, M.D.

Cognition: Reality Testing, Time Distortion

Cognitive issues which became more central in the third year of therapy were also present from the start. Taking in of knowledge was a conflictual issue similar to taking in of food. Each year Emily just barely maintained her level in class. Her grandiosity and denial (impulsivity, changing the subject, not listening) interfered with learning, as did her anxiety in specific areas. When threatened, she simply insisted her ideas were right: "My brother says I can't make babies with my teddy bear, but I don't care!" Emily made selective cognitive and reality distortions. For example, she would insist that her father was "coming to pick us up" though she knew that he rarely came. Specific areas of cognitive confusion emerged later in therapy such as inside/outside confusion. These difficulties did not constitute a psychotic process nor did she go into psychotic or borderline states.

Other cognitive distortions represented age-appropriate limits in understanding, as when, in a Piagetian storytelling mode, she said air gets into syringes "from California" or when she had difficulty understanding that Foley catheters (her tubes) contained a central channel for fluids to pass through as well as a small parallel channel for filling the bubble at the end with air.

Emily confused and distorted time and used her grandiosity and denial to deal with separations. She would repeatedly mistake the Tuesday–Thursday sessions, saying she came Wednesday or daily. She would ask, "Is time up?" five minutes after the session started and would announce at the end, "You can stay ten minutes more" or simply deny it was time to stop, saying: "No. It's not!"

Transference

Emily would call the therapist "stupid," "dummy," and "idiot" and assumed a role in the transference whereby she knew better than the therapist. She taught the therapist to jump rope, to do math, to draw, to write, and so on. Her view of teaching often was played out with her being the sadistic teacher humiliating the child. Knowledge at these times was something one either had or could be punished for not having. "Do this." "How?" "Just do it and if you don't know how I'll show you." She then punished the therapist for doing it wrong.

Psychological Testing

Emily's parents scheduled periodic psychological testing which delineated areas of delay (especially short- and long-term auditory memory and abstract thinking). Emily was defensive about things she could not do and would discount things she could do as "easy." Speech therapy and resource room were begun at school, and later a private tutor was engaged. The therapist continued to maintain that emotional conflict underlay and could account for some of these deficits.

Separation-Individuation: Separation Anxiety, Clinging, and Ambivalence

Emily's concern with separation was evident at the start. Emily often played separation games wherein the therapist was a child at school crying for her mother. Her lack of object constancy was indicated when the therapist suggested she was crying because she was unable to remember what mother looked like; Emily replied with confirmatory angry negation: "That's because you're so stupid!" At home she was noted to become "hysterical" at brief two- to ten-minute separations from mother on several occasions. In the third month of therapy she was accidentally locked in a closet at home and became hysterical; for about six months after this incident she played locking herself or the therapist in the closet (each would then cry and be let out). When a separation from the therapist was threatened, she taped herself to her on two occasions with 10-foot lengths of tape. When she left sessions, she would typically return to the door twice to say, "Bye." She then would say, with great cheer, a string of separation-related phrases, including "Bye!" "See you soon!" "Have a good day!" As Emily's overt anger and ambivalence at mother increased, she shadowed and clung in typical toddler style—for example, complaining that mother should hold only her hand and not her brother's too. Tantrums became frequent and mother (who was familiar with young children) said Emily "felt like a 2-year-old" for many months.

Transitional Objects

Emily had had an imaginary companion "baby" at age 3 to 5 and would reproach her: "Eat or I'll smack you!" "Eat or you'll go to the hospital!" This she discontinued early in therapy as she expressed anger openly and also could play at being a baby. A transitional object that continued in use was a "rag" she took to bed with her from the age of 22 months. This rag was a blanket Emily had been wrapped in when returned to her parents after painful procedures were done in the treatment room during her hospitalization. Starting at age 6 years she changed this to one of her father's undershirts, which she would stick to her mouth and breathe through as she fell asleep.

Body Image

Emily used her relationship with the therapist to explore issues of body image and mastery. Emily initiated a game of "copy me" with the therapist, mirroring each other's actions, especially facial expressions. She compared her body to mother's, noting that they were both "ladies" or that she did not have "big boobies" like mother. She got into a long period of body mastery games, overcoming her clumsiness to learn to jump rope, Michael Jackson spins, baseball, climbing, headstands, and other games.

Psychodynamic Meanings of the Tube

The meaning of the tube was difficult to explore because of Emily's resistance to free association, fantasy, and symbolic play. Clearly the tube could take on meanings associated with various psychodynamic issues, both limited by her cognitive difficulties and contributing to them. No one theme emerged as primary.

Occasional clues and suggested meanings included, probably most significantly, the tube as an umbilical tie to mother. In addition it was a vagina, in that it got red and needed ointment when her vagina did. At the same time it was a phallic object, which "looks like a snake." She seemed to view it as part of her body, indicating she thought she was born with it. She expressed various attitudes which were not elaborated in word or play: "It will die and go to heaven." "They will fix the hole (in her) with a big stick," she said, pointing to a bar 1 by 20 inches (a pun on "stitch"). The hole would close and it could not be put back in. If it were out, she could die.

The tube was not at all dystonic and she was never teased by peers who would say, "Oh that's Emily; she doesn't eat lunch." Emily wore her tube pinned back inside her shirt so it was barely noticeable. At one point her grandparents had called it dirty and smelly in an unsuccessful effort to make it dystonic. When it came out, she turned pale with fear. This fear was hard to dissociate from her parents' anxiety on these occasions; father in particular was eager to put the tube back in instantly rather than see his daughter anxious or in tears.

Parental Involvement in the Therapy

It was not easy to convince Emily's parents to keep Emily in therapy through the eighteen months before she began to eat; it was necessary to help them to understand that not eating was a symptom and that the underlying issues were progressing. Since Emily's most intense involvement was with mother, and since biweekly meetings were most often attended by mother without father, therapy issues were largely lived through and understood by mother. Mother functioned in many ways as a co-therapist, extending work at home on themes from sessions in addition to discussing relevant material from home with the therapist. In many ways mother facilitated the progress of the therapy, such as implementing the therapist's instruction to cease pushing Emily to eat, or weaning Emily from being wiped by her after bowel movements. Mother was helped to see that her daughter was not weak and sickly but that her "fragile" child was indeed very manipulative, controlling, and provocative. Once realizing this, mother was quickly able to express her anger and to encourage her daughter's anger. When mother first told Emily she was "very angry" with her, Emily stared in disbelief.

Father, while very concerned about his daughter, was less involved with the therapy process and less attuned to the significance of issues (especially control) which underlay the symptom of not eating. It was hard for father to accept not pushing food, since he tended to maintain that food should be somehow forced or pushed or rewarded, especially as months went by and she ate little. He noted that all the prior therapists they had seen had geared them to be active with Emily, whereas now they were told not to act. Father maintained that he had accepted Emily's defects at her birth as "the way it is" and felt no anger. In general, within the family he felt anger was best "swept under the rug." From time to time he tried a practical approach, such as encouraging taste with pictures of things she had tasted, without effect. He continued to feel frustrated at what he saw as the lack of direct progress with eating. Hence six months into the therapy he called to cancel future sessions (leaving one session for termination). A lengthy discussion with him and Emily's mother led to a renewed commitment to the therapy. To his credit, he was willing to go along with the therapy despite his doubts. In retrospect he felt that focusing on family tensions as significant to Emily's not eating was a breakthrough, and that shifting the patterns at home so as not to allow Emily's manipulative behavior to continue was most relevant to her progress.

Pre-eating Phase: $6\frac{1}{2}$ to 7 Years Old (6 Months)

Overview of Interventions

At the start of the second year of therapy the therapist focused on three issues: autonomy, oral pleasure, and body image. Autonomy in eating was stressed at this time with the idea that Emily would not eat until she felt her body was her own. This fundamental step was an essential part of separation from her mother. Hence Emily's parents were told to tell her she must feed herself either by mouth or by pouring formula into the tube so the tube would not serve as a literal tie to mother and so Emily could feel responsible for care of her own body. When doing this became routine, parents were told to use regular table food blenderized rather than formula. As the next step Emily was asked to put her own food in the blender if she did not eat it by mouth. This she did not like but went along with. The therapist continued to interpret that she wanted to eat and grow but preferred to tease over food. Mother was told to point out to Emily when she was teasing. Regulating the amount Emily ate was definitely an area of countertransference, since the therapist was not at all certain that Emily would not starve herself to death if she were given free reign to feed herself only what and when she wanted. It was decided, therefore, that mother and father would regulate the *amount* of food but Emily would be required to feed herself either by mouth or tube, even though giving her total free reign would have made her more autonomous.

Pleasures related to eating and regressive play were encouraged at this time, with the intent of enabling Emily to find her way to whatever oral pleasure she had missed and could still experience. The therapist made

252 Christina Sekaer, M.D.

efforts to support and devise pleasurable experiences in oral activities. Body image was focused on, though Emily had interest only in body surface or action issues. Hence mastery of physical games and interest in her appearance were encouraged. Mother was instructed to encourage her interest in clothes, makeup, and the like.

Other significant material emerged around family tensions and the history of eating issues within Emily's parents' backgrounds. Tubes were provided and tube play occurred throughout this phase. As Emily became more autonomous in control of her tube, she used teasing a lot less. The tube became increasingly dystonic. She discussed fears of choking and could eat normal bites, enjoying food games with the therapist. She learned about her mouth, mastering how to swig, how much fit in it, and so on. Separation fears and psychosexual themes, especially anal, continued.

It was felt that Emily could not accept her body as her own until mother stopped feeding her. As her autonomy and body self developed, Emily began to eat.

Autonomy

Emily went along with putting food into her tube herself. When the shift was first made to table food, Emily watched as mother put it in the blender to become liquid, but when it was time to put it in the tube she ran from the room in a panic, clutching the tube. What was it she thought had been put in her and why was food terrifying? Although what she had thought the formula was was not clarified, it seemed she did not equate it with table food. She then was thrilled to "eat" table food, telling people, for example, "I'm eating scrambled eggs with my tube!" Her parents continued to feed her at night with the tube, against the therapist's advice, and at this point Emily objected if she awoke when feeding was in progress.

With the shift to more autonomy, Emily's use of teasing and manipulation lessened. She still teased in a variety of ways, including around eating, such as holding the tube too low when feeding herself so food would not siphon in, in order to get her mother to sit with her longer. Emily became aware of teasing and began to say, "and I'm not teasing!" For a couple of weeks, as she began to tease less, she had headaches and became forlorn, looking terribly sad or crying. (Father hated to see her cry and tended to give in when she did.) She continued to have angry tantrums, which now took on a desolate, sad quality. Emily enjoyed teasing mother; for example, as she learned the word "full" she told her mother, "Oh, I'm so full!" and then laughed and added, "Just teasing." Constant attempts to reinstate power struggles were aborted as mother "refused to play the game."

Oral Pleasure

The therapist tried to make oral activities and food fun and pleasant irrespective of eating. Emily would still respond to foods with an affectless

"Yum" or "Yuk." A real pleasure in food was not yet evident. For a few sessions Emily used a pacifier to chew and suck. Food grinders were introduced and in sessions she ground up chocolate, licorice, crackers, Tic Tacs, and other items, "cooking" concoctions which were then not eaten. Emily initiated a taste game wherein the therapist and Emily put foods on each other's tongues with eyes closed to guess what they were.

Discussions of how teeth grind up food occurred as she ate tiny crunched-up bits of popcorn. She started a game of "pig," which involved stuffing one's mouth with popcorn bits while making pig snorts, and this usually led to hilarity and great enjoyment.

Emily seemed to remember being force-fed and choking in the past and said, "If you choke, you could die." Discussions of fear of choking if one ate big pieces led to eating whole popcorn and then to seeing how much could fit in one's mouth. She also felt that if she ate dirt or "doo doo" she could die, and she refused brown sugar candies she said looked like "doo doo."

Emily was interested in tube play in a concrete way. Tubes were put into dolls. Tubes were used as necklaces. Food was put in tubes and channeled in and out of containers (she still had no clear comprehension of inside/ outside). Tubes were used to blow bubbles and to suck up fluid or small candies. It became evident that she did not know how to suck on or blow through a straw or swig from a bottle. As she learned, she became daring and had the therapist copy her as she stood on one foot, with an uncapped baby bottle in her mouth, waving her hands in the air, and drank. At home Emily and mother drank from baby bottles a couple of times, as encouraged by the therapist. They also devised contests, such as drinking water, to see whether the tube or mouth were faster (the mouth won).

Gradually, as therapy progressed, she was able to find fun and pleasure in shared oral activities. These activities did *not* lead to verbalized symbolized conscious fantasies.

Parental Intervention

The switch to table food raised issues for Emily's parents; they saw that food volume increased (with air) when blenderized and feared that not enough calories were getting in her. They also disagreed as to what should go into the blender. Should they let Emily choose from whatever was in the refrigerator or should they focus on health foods or greasier caloric foods? Interestingly, no digestive problems ensued. The parents had twice in the past tried withholding tube feedings but each time had panicked when there was a 4-pound weight loss. Exploration of these incidents revealed they had been told by the pediatricians that a 10 percent loss of body weight could spell death. Though Emily's height and weight were below the third percentile, she was normal height for her weight and a 4-pound weight loss did not make her cachectic. The parents felt the surgeons had terrified them on this score and their fear had led to their conscious need to push as many calories as possible. In fact this was the reason feedings had been done so frequently, including hourly into the night even after Emily was asleep.

Discussion of family attitudes regarding food in Emily's mother's and father's backgrounds was helpful. Mother noted she had been thin as a child, anemic and on liver injections, and that her mother would sit with her and sing or tell stories to try to get her to eat. At age 12 she became somewhat overweight and felt that the more her mother then said not to eat the more she would eat! The therapist discussed with her how it might be hard for her to let Emily regulate her own amounts of food.

In the father's family, food was an important issue. He had been a "good eater" as a child. His mother would cook a lot of food which he would eat. As an adult his mother would harp on his being slightly overweight while at the same time feeding him cake, potatoes, and the like. When someone suggested a diet, he said he felt resentful since he did not feel he was overweight.

Emily Starts to Eat

Although the progress in therapy made it seem that Emily would start to eat in the near future, the specific time she chose to start was related to parental pressure. In one parents' session, father was briefly able to acknowledge that some of his anger and frustration at the difficulties (and time and expense) Emily's problems caused were not all directed at the wife or the therapist for not doing enough to resolve Emily's problems quickly, but also were directed in some way at Emily for having the problems. Father felt there had been "no change" (in food intake). He recognized that just to take the tube out might force eating but would lead Emily to distrust. In his frustration, his desire to help his daughter, and his belief in the use of force, he pressed the idea of pushing some food, though the therapist felt doing so might be a little premature. Mother and father together decided to try gently pushing food. The significance of increased parental frustration at this time is not clear. Nevertheless, Emily was able to respond. Each day Emily was asked to drink a glass of milk, *which this time she did.* Two weeks later mother and father called between sessions to announce, "Emily is eating!" She then ate ham, crackers, and Cheese Doodles, large and small pieces, and has continued to eat since.

Emily began by eating "like a 2-year-old," as her mother noted. She wanted mother to help feed her because she was too slow. She lost 2 or 3 pounds, which was not frightening. She would dawdle. She would put only one, and later two, kinds of food on the fork and segregate foods on the plate. She used a spoon for the first time. She would talk baby talk. She would say: "I need help. No, don't help!" Occasionally she held food in her mouth. She would chew and spit food out.

As Emily began to eat, the tube about which she had virtually never before complained became increasingly dystonic. This discomfort was expressed, never directly verbally, but somatically as she complained: "The tube hurts." "The clamp hurts." "The tube itches." But if a suggestion were made to change the tube, Emily went pale with terror.

Body Image: Resistance to Exploration

A third focus at this stage of therapy was Emily's lack of a coherent body image and confused and incoherent understanding of her defect and surgery. Autonomy was relevent here, since it was felt she could not experience her body as her own as long as her mother fed her. She refused to look at or draw pictures of the body, stomach, and so on and would simply not hear related comments and questions. In a rare exception, while she and the therapist drew she insisted babies were in the mothers' stomach (where the food was drawn) "because my mother and father told me and if you don't believe me you can ask them!" (Of course they had not told her this.) Another time the therapist noted how well all the parts of her body worked, except her throat, and her acknowledgement that she had difficulty swallowing was the first verbal acceptance of a problem. Generally her grandiosity and denial were formidable.

Emily was much more receptive to body image issues dealing with the surface of the body. She took an interest in clothes, "party shoes," makeup, nail polish, and showing off physical activities such as jump-rope and baseball. She learned to swim and ride a two-wheeler. She still panicked with any body injury, such as a scrape, being calmed down only after a few minutes of "hysterics." She continued "copy me" games and teaching herself and the therapist to master activities. Many sessions were spent on body mastery, such as jump rope. She was also told that if she still had the tube when she was older, she would feel different from her peers.

Emily seemed to have massive blocks to awareness of her body sensations and especially toward thinking about anything inside. She was very unclear what "hunger," "thirst," and "full" meant. Similarly, she did not understand "inside" and "outside" the body. Body pictures (which she drew rarely) were of one cloacal inside space. She resisted talk of body parts with intense disinterest. "Where does urine or feces come from?" "From the stomach." "Where does food go?" No answer. Tracing her whole body on a large paper, she put a vagina on the side of the abdomen, an oval with a line across it and a dot where the urine came out, and refused to look at it further. Talk about missing parts, and fears about such, were met with "Shut up!" "Let's not talk about that," or simply not hearing.

Separation-Individuation: Humor

Separation fears, while less an issue than at the start, continued. Once, in session angry that mother had gone out for coffee, Emily repeatedly (fifteen times) said "There's my mom!" pointing out the window, and then roared with laughter when the therapist would look and see no one. The therapist continued to interpret her fear of loss of mother linked with her anger at mother for leaving. As further evidence of increasing separation, for the first time Emily began to value privacy both in toileting activities and in not telling others about her tube, which was hidden under her shirt.

Object constancy progressed as Emily could acknowledge and express anger more directly at those she also loved.

Psychosexual Stages

Psychosexually, anal issues predominated. In addition to autonomy and control, discussed above, cleanliness was an ongoing theme. Emily often had a bowel movement during the session. On the toilet she would hold things such as the therapist's keys, beeper, or M&M's. She would tease and yell for mother to wipe her long after mother stopped it. She played at cleaning the bathroom. She got messy with clay. She would mess herself with a marker on her arm and say, "My mom will kill me!" She spent a lot of time writing and erasing.

Post-eating/Pre-op Phase: 7 to 8 Years old (12 Months)

Overview of Interventions

Emily was told it was up to her to set a date for surgery. The tube remained in place unused for 9 months while this issue was dealt with. Eating for her own body rather than for others was stressed. Tube play and doctor play as well as a hospital visit helped prepare for the surgery. Attempts to elicit fantasy play met little success. Emily's play continued to be concrete with some hints of underlying violence. Separation themes and psychosexual material, especially anal, continued to emerge. Work with parents was done to help them allow Emily the necessary autonomy.

Oral Pleasure: Food Intake, End of Tube Feeding

Whether Emily would eat enough was an ongoing concern from the time she started to eat fairly regular meals. It was stressed in sessions and with innumerable repetitions at home that you eat for energy for your body. "If you don't eat lunch, you'll get too tired to swim at the pool." Occasionally she would choose a tube feeding rather than a meal, but this practice quickly stopped. Emily regressed at times; for example, during a week-long viral illness she had her mother feed her (with spoon and fork). Mother used her intuition well in responding to Emily's periodic need to regress.

From discussions early in the therapy, Emily's mother knew it would be difficult to relinquish the control and security of being able to feed Emily via the tube. When Emily lost 3 or 4 pounds because of a virus, her clothes hung on her and she appeared pale. Mother "ran to the closet" for a can of formula but was able to stop herself. This occurred a few weeks after the last tube feeding and marked the end of use of the tube for food. As it turned out, Emily ate enough to maintain her weight and the issue of amount of food was resolved.

Emily continued to tease frequently; for example, she took little pieces of food, upon which mother said "You are doing this to make me mad and it isn't working." Emily said "I see" and ate big pieces. Father still felt that rewards were useful and at one point promised her a bicycle on a given holiday if she ate well for the three weeks preceding it. Emily did eat; then on the holiday, when she got the bicycle, she said to father with pointed sarcasm, "Now I don't have to eat any more!"

In sessions Emily ate a lot. She devised some uniquely relevent games. For example, she had herself and the therapist each eat an end of a two-foot piece of shoestring licorice simultaneously and without hands, approaching closer and closer until one of them broke it. The parallels with her tube as an umbilical tie to mother, eating as it related strongly to separation, and breaking the tube to become separate and independent were all illustrated by this game.

Surgery: Hospital Visits and Setting the Date

Another major issue at this time was to have Emily set a date for her own surgery. The therapist's attitude was that surgery should not be done until Emily insisted the tube be out. Emily tested whether she could decide, stating blandly, for example, "Oh, I think I'll have the tube out when I'm 9" and scrutinizing her mother for her reaction. Mother responded once to Emily's request to see her surgeon by immediately offering to call, whereupon Emily lost interest. Mother was instructed to stay half a step *behind* Emily. The next time Emily suggested calling, mother said "Oh, okay, maybe we'll call tomorrow." After some further testing, Emily followed through and insisted on her calling.

When Emily visited her doctor, she asked many questions and was very assertive, insisting on being told what was to be done and why, saying "It's *my* body," and later raving at what a good doctor he was. Around visits to the doctor she remembered a few things from the past hospitalizations, such as being washed in the sink, swallowing white stuff (barium), and wearing the mask (for anesthesia).

Emily agreed to the doctor's suggestion to arrange a visit to the hospital. She was very positive on her visit, but regressed in play afterwards in session and at home (e.g., making messes and bringing mother again into the bathroom). Following this, Emily then set a date for her surgery.

Meanwhile in sessions Emily continued to play doctor with the tubes in a concrete way. She would put a tube in a doll, with herself and the therapist as the doctors, nurses, or visiting parents. The parents would then be instructed, "Your baby doesn't need the tube because he is eating." An intravenous bag became a source of great hilarity and intense fun as Emily hung it and regulated squirting water into her mouth and throat. This play was felt to be useful as preparation for surgery and as integration of her experiences even though it stayed on a very concrete level.

The timing of the surgery was not optimal in that her father arranged for a family vacation for three weeks prior to the surgery, and the therapist's usual August vacation began one week after the surgery. On return from her family vacation, in the one session before the surgery, Emily was most excited, not about the trip itself but about the amusement park in which funny mirrors made her "fat like Daddy" and he thin like her. She then drew a girl with teeth, for the first time, captioned, "I'll see you when I get back from the hospital." On the morning of the day she went to the hospital for the operation, she fell and scraped both of her knees.

Emily continued to complain of the tube, not per se but through somatic complaints. She put ointment on it. She tried to poke her finger in the hole and poked actively at the bubble inside. But if it came out she was still very fearful. Poking at the tube hole did not appear to be eroticized. The therapist discussed with Emily's parents at length a plan to leave the tube out for a few minutes any time it came out (something that happened every few months). About three months after Emily stopped eating with the tube, they were able to leave it out for fifteen minutes, an achievement they reported with elation.

Fantasies and Dreams about the Tube

Emily's fear at the thought of the tube being out seemed to increase as her wishes to have it out increased and as its being out became a real possibility. As the date of the operation approached, Emily had several dreams, sometimes "scary," that "the tube was out." She would mention these but refuse to elaborate. Once, after the tube was changed, her eating decreased for two to three days until she had a discussion with her mother about whether people die in the hospital; after this she ate again.

She feared that if the tube were out and she did not eat, she could die. She was afraid the tube hole would close instantly or the surgeon would have to put in another one. She was surprised to be told she had not been born with the tube. She looked forward to a bikini without the tube. Mother told her repeatedly that they would still love her just as much without the tube, thinking Emily feared losing her "special" position with respect to her siblings when it was out.

After the tube had been taken out, she joked with her mother, "The tube is coming out!" which got her mother to look, to Emily's great amusement. After the operation she was told not to be too active for a few days to avoid pulling the stitches open and she expressed fear that her stomach would fall out.

Body Image

Body image continued to be worked on. Emily loved action games and showing off, including her "muscles" (which she related to eating well), climbing and tumbling tricks, and hand-slapping games. She expressed concern at minor body damage such as a torn hangnail.

She was extremely resistant to talking about her body insides. She used denial, changing the subject, not listening, "It's boring," and "Let's not look at it," and resisted drawings, picture books, stories the therapist would devise, and other efforts to discuss her confusions and fears about her body. The therapist sensed that, in spite of repeated explanations, Emily did not comprehend many simple facts involving the concepts "inside" and "outside" such as that the tube conveyed food *into* her body. Together they built a three-dimensional folded paper house and the therapist made a paper cutout of smoke to come out of the chimney. Emily had great difficulty inserting the smoke into the chimney, unable to reach inside to pull it in.

Aborted Psychosomatic Equivalents

Just prior to the surgery, Emily also transiently showed bodily complaints which the therapist felt could become psychosomatic substitutes for the tube as a focus for adult anxieties about her. Mother responded to these with minimal attention and they were quickly dropped, though other family members at times expressed anxiety. These complaints included headaches, nausea, stomach aches, dizziness, and coughing.

Separation-Individuation: Humor

Separation continued as an issue and once again Emily often brought mother into sessions. Once Emily left at the end of the session and returned from the waiting room, very sober, to tell the therapist her mother had already gone. When the therapist then found mother to be sitting in the waiting room she roared with laughter. Once also she joked with the therapist that the tube was not in. For a few weeks prior to the surgery Emily lost and mislaid many items such as lunchbox, sweater, and books. At the end of sessions Emily would announce, "We have ten more minutes" and once refused to go, saying the therapist had to get her mother to get her.

Separations were important for mother too. Once when the therapist was twenty minutes late, mother joked that she herself had thought the therapist was "either stuck in traffic or had died." Prior to the operation Emily's parents missed a number of sessions; their not coming was unusual, especially Emily's mother. Mother discussed that it would be quite a change for her if Emily did not need so many appointments (a loss for her).

Transitional Objects

Just prior to the surgery Emily adopted a huge number of toys as objects that *had* to be in bed with her. These included a number of sharp cars and books. When mother said they were too sharp, Emily wrapped them in a plastic bag and slept with them in her arms. Post-op use of these objects diminished, although she still used father's undershirt to fall asleep.

Alexithymia versus Underlying Violent and Paranoid Themes

One might label Emily alexithymic, since she apparently could not fantasize. It was easy to view Emily, on the surface, as a charming, engaging, witty, and cute if somewhat immature child. However, at times her play would almost get into the violent, intense, fearful fantasy material the therapist was convinced was there under the surface.

On one occasion she set up a hospital at *great* length. Suddenly a dog and cat doll fought violently and then the game ended. Interpretation of her fear of the violence led to renewal of the game, an even more violent fight, and then ending the game.

Prior to the operation, in response to a picture drawn of a surgeon operating on a girl, Emily answered the question as to what the girl would like to do to the surgeon by suddenly slashing his throat with a red crayon for blood. (Emily has a surgical scar across her throat and also would never draw a neck on figures.)

These examples provided evidence that bloody and terrifying fantasies lay under the surface. The therapist used such examples with mother to explain that this material would need to be gotten into even after the tube was out.

On rare occasions an underlying paranoid theme emerged. For example, just before the surgery she and the therapist were doctors operating on a doll, telling her they were putting the tube in but winking at each other knowing they were really going to take it out. On another occasion, she insisted she had seen the therapist talking to her teacher about her "eating with her tube" (the therapist had never been to the school nor spoken with the teacher).

Play and Fantasy: Play Remains Concrete

In play Emily continued to be concrete and defensively action oriented. The therapist's interpretations that she was fearful about stories and her imagination were met with obstinate denial. Attempts were made to encourage Emily to draw, tell stories, or fingerpaint to lead into more spontaneous fantasy, to little avail. Fingerpaints led to her coloring the whole page green, blue, yellow, black, and then writing her name in graffiti. In a story in which she was asked to fill in the blank, "The man opened the door and found . . . ," she answered repeatedly "a great big doodyball!" and giggled herself out of breath.

Teasing was still evident; for example, baseball involved a great deal of gleeful laughter as she would try to steal bases, telling the therapist to look at something on the ceiling and then running. There was a quality of an infantile chase game as she would run and have the therapist catch her.

Emily often aborted starts at fantasy play, shifting to a concrete focus. For example, Emily set up a circus wherein "superman" (a female nurse doll) hung on a rope and other people and ladders were set up. But this was diverted to her taking phone orders and names for tickets for half an hour.

Emily's play often had a distinct 2-year-old quality to it. She set up a magic show (she had seen a magician) wherein water would be poured and disappear. In setting it up, she spilled and dumped many toys from one box to another and the theme of filling and emptying seemed predominant. She had an intense transient interest in the Play Doh pusher. She tried to climb into a tiny box (four by five inches). Once, given stacking boxes in the session, she showed intense (transient) interest and found them hard to do. Mother noted that she loved splashing in the tub like a 2-year-old. She noted too that Emily had difficulty sharing things and had frequent "2-year-old tantrums."

Cognitive Difficulties, Time Distortion

Cognitively Emily had difficulty in school and a private tutor was now started. In session, cognitive delays and distortions were noted and were felt to have a strong emotional basis. Concepts such as inside/outside and before/after were not clear. She confused days; she was to see her surgeon "in five days" but when the therapist asked if she meant Monday, she disagreed. Next session the therapist asked if she would see him in three days; she said, "No, in five days." Cognitive issues became central after the tube was out.

Psychological Testing

On psychological testing done at this time Emily's Rorschach yielded sparse minimal responses. She drew a figure with missing neck and legs of different lengths. "Superman" was a sparsley elaborated theme. She could not say how many days were in a week, guessing fifteen, naming the days of the week, then guessing fifteen again rather than counting them. Grandiosity, denial, and avoidance were noted, as well as a vague global view of the world not appropriate for her age.

Transference

In transference the therapist was most often the "stupid" one who could not do school work, made lots of mistakes, and had to ask for help. The therapist continued also to be a "new object," that is, one who allowed Emily to experience herself without the coercion of the long-standing power struggles at home.

Psychosexual Stages

Psychosexually oral pleasure was starting to emerge in eating and enjoyment of food. Anal themes predominated in that her eating and relinquishing the tube were still being disentangled from control and separation-individuation issues. In addition, she played at cleaning the tub, spilling small candies to make a mess, and had bowel movements often during sessions. The hints of underlying violent fantasies were consistent with anal-sadistic material. Phallic issues of mastery and body prowess continued. Oedipal baby-making stopped but she wrote love letters to an older friend of her brother whom she liked.

Gender confusion did *not* emerge as a prominent theme. Although Emily used a female doll as "superman," and once, while viewing a drawing of nude men, boys, women, and girls, pointed to herself as a boy, this was *not* a frequent theme; she seemed strongly identified with her mother as female.

Post-tube Phase 8 to 10+ Years Old (24+ Months)

Overview of Interventions

The main issues focused on in the next two years were body image, cognitive delays, and distortions including school difficulties, lack of independence from mother (this time seen mostly in relation to the school-work), and the continued inability to fantasize or play in a creative manner. In other words, Emily had not yet been able to enter into essential tasks of latency (Sarnoff 1976). With eating no longer an issue, cognitive conflict over learning became a new focus. The therapist interpreted Emily's impulsivity and not taking in of knowledge as being due to her fear and her need for control. Now Emily's general use of grandiosity, avoidance, and denial were focused on as *greatly* interfering with learning. The issue of autonomy also applied to taking in knowledge. Mother's involvement in Emily's schoolwork emerged as parallel to her prior investment in Emily's eating. Work was done with mother to let Emily be responsible for her own thoughts. The therapist also interpreted to mother that further treatment meant further psychological separation from Emily for mother.

Emily's parents decreased session frequency to once per week. This was a compromise between father's view that enough therapy had been done and mother's urging that it continue. The therapist then addressed Emily's humiliation at body damage; this issue led to less resistance to discussing body insides and confusions. The therapist interpreted that Emily's experience of having food put into her, feeling perhaps overly and uncomfortably full, must have made her feel that her insides were "bad" and therefore not to be thought about.

Some progress was made toward the emergence of fantasy play and of underlying violent themes. Some fears were overcome; for example, she got a haircut. A new (and long-missing) theme of oral aggression began to emerge.

Parental Intervention

Prior to the operation the therapist had attempted to make it clear to Emily's parents that a great deal would remain to be done after the tube was out. Father's attitude toward continued therapy, understandable in terms of the time and expense, was that it was not necessary. He told Emily shortly after the surgery that she did not need to continue if she did not want to. She expressed in part *his* attitude by asking why she should go see the therapist because she had no worries. Mother understood more clearly, because of her closer involvement in the process, that there were indications of intense underlying fantasy material that was as yet inaccessible and that was related to the cognitive limits and lack of fantasy play. Pressure built nevertheless to discontinue therapy when at a crucial point Emily had her first very significant dream. She was in a cave with a friend. A man took them, tied them down, shot Emily in the stomach, and then cut her stomach with a knife so that blood and "gush" came out. Mother was thrilled—"this is what you kept telling us was in her"—but then felt pressured by her husband two weeks later to terminate therapy. Again, discussion with both parents led to a renewed commitment to therapy, although at a reduced frequency of once per week. Therapy progressed slowly, but with steady signs of progress.

As eating became no longer an issue, mother shifted to an intense concern with Emily's schoolwork and attempting to have some control over the school's assignment of teachers and tutors. It had been necessary to let Emily control her own body and now it seemed necessary for Emily to control her own thoughts. Although Emily worked hard in school, she took no responsibility for her learning in the sense that regression and defensive blocking were felt as syntonic and large areas of confusion and lack of understanding were cheerfully denied. Mother noted that Emily would come to her "every two minutes" for help with homework, and she was able to let Emily work more on her own.

Cognition

While the therapist felt Emily's cognitive difficulties might have an organic component, clearly there were psychological blocks which needed to be addressed in therapy. Emily's tutor noted her resistance: Emily was unable to learn techniques for more independent learning as well as did more delayed children. At home sometimes Emily would appear "stupid" in a regressive way to get attention, claiming she didn't know how to clean the kitchen, make the bed, or use a knife. With peers she would try to avoid games she could not understand, such as Trivial Pursuit.

Some difficulties responded to interpretation, such as when omnipotence, denial, and avoidance got very much in the way of learning. For example, one day Emily was unable to copy stairs the therapist had drawn, because she continually drew the line in the wrong direction; she got silly, changed the subject, and finally turned the failed drawn stairs into a monster picture. The therapist told Emily she would get to each corner point and then would just go whatever way she pleased rather than copy and hence could not do the stairs. The cause was her omnipotent need to be in control. This exchange was repeated on two successive sessions. Then on the third Emily proudly announced she could draw stairs and did so, explaining casually, "Oh, I just copied yours." In another session Emily could not draw "Pac Man." She drew the pie-piece-shaped mouth with the angle corner out and had great difficulty making a "piece of pie" larger than a given one. Interpretation of her fear and her need for control led to her struggling with it until she got it.

Some of Emily's difficulties were clearly not related to overall intelligence. Her impulsivity and inability to plan ahead or to free herself to consider options was dramatically illustrated when she played checkers with the therapist. She ignored four of her own checkers and insisted there was no possible move because the one she was considering could not move. As another example, Emily was unable to grasp the concept of higher and lower pitch with musical notes.

Some areas of confusion seemed specifically related to dynamic issues, such as the concept of inside/outside. Emily seemed blocked on this concept even beyond her massive resistance to think about the insides of her body. One time she drew a picture of surgery on the throat, noting the skin was cut and then it was sewn up; she appeared baffled when the therapist asked what happened *inside*. Another time she said her operation consisted of a piece of skin taken from her "tush" and sewn onto her neck. Mother reported that "in" and "out" appeared confused, since Emily would put garbage next to and not "in" the pail, or clothes on top of and not "in" the hamper; Emily would then insist she had put them "in."

The memory difficulties and lack of abstract thinking, which had been repeatedly shown in psychological tests, seemed to be related to Emily's massive need to suppress and deny past experiences and current feelings and fantasies. Mother noted that indeed there were times when Emily's memory was excellent.

At home Emily was now organized and not forgetting things, as she had been just before the surgery. She was also more responsible, having a routine of snack, homework, and then play after school, all consistent with a shift into latency. Nevertheless Emily was clearly unable to shift into spontaneous fantasy play and more abstract thinking characteristic of a secure latency. Play themes continued to be concrete; for example, doctors operated on a baby, and mother then took it home.

Cognition: Time Sense

At this point Emily learned, in a normal though delayed way, to tell time. For the first time events she related were put in a context of time and space. Interestingly, simultaneously with this advance she was able to fantasize about time and space. When she was going away for a weekend, she decided to write a letter to the therapist from Virginia but instead wrote it in the session before she left. The letter, displaced in time and space, said: "Here I am in Virginia. The weather has been foggy here for two days. I'm having fun but one of the girls woke me up at 5 A.M. today." Similarly, playing with time, she joked that she would develop breasts like her mother's but not overnight. "Wouldn't it be funny if I woke up tomorrow with big boobies?"

Reality Testing

Part of the lack of move into latency was related to Emily's difficulty distinguishing reality from fantasy on an age-appropriate level when it touched on significant themes. Mother understood this and noted that Emily was unclear, for instance, that television actors who got shot were not really dead. In one session as Emily played with a doll (putting a tube in), she was awestruck by the doll's eyes moving (open/shut) and asked if it was alive. She also watched the plastic peel off as the therapist cut a hole on the doll's abdomen, and asked anxiously if it was really skin.

Emily also entered a period of telling lies. At times these seemed to represent difficulty distinguishing reality from fantasy as she told a friend's mother that a boy she knew had been killed by a car. In fact the boy had had surgery (and was okay) and a friend of her family had been hit by a car (and was okay). Emily's version was more severe and violent, a hint of under-lying aggressive themes in Emily.

Emily would lie to get things, saying, "the teacher said" she needed a certain book or "my mother said" she could walk home alone after school. In reporting on a book for school, Emily changed the story because she didn't like it and made up a happy ending.

Fantasy: Underlying Aggression

Hints of underlying aggression continued to emerge occasionally in Emily's play. In a school test about freedom of the press she answered a fill-in-the-blank, "the mayor is not allowed . . ." with "to kill the people." This answer was apparently related to juxtaposed reading about Indians killing and burning people and leaving dead bodies around, the part she had found the most interesting to study, and it indicated she had a selective memory for violence.

She had a dream that she somersaulted downstairs out of control and all bloody. (She had fallen on the stairs a couple of weeks before.) She wrote scenes from a play about a "cave hole" wherein kids fall in, are scared, and are rescued. She was unwilling to elaborate on these violent themes.

There were also dramatic instances when her ability occasionally to verbalize a fantasy alleviated panic and organized her. Thus one day she scratched her eye climbing a tree. She later complained it hurt, so her mother decided to take her to a hospital. She protested with hysterical crying and panic, yelling, "You can't make me go!" Mother calmly asserted that they were going and Emily then asked, after a thoughtful pause, if they would take her eye out. Having verbalized this fear, she was then calm at the hospital.

Body Image: Fears and Confusions

Emily continued an interest in the surface of her body, dressing up with press-on nails painted red. Mastery continued, such as showing off gulping two and a half glasses of water. She was concerned that she was too short and made a New Year's resolution to eat more to get bigger. Emily also measured "weights" (heights) of herself, the therapist, and her father. For the first time she asked for help from the therapist and from mother to draw a neck, a significant omission in all her prior drawings.

Because of her colonic bypass esophagus, Emily could not vomit; food would leak out her nose at night unless she slept on two pillows. Emily was very confused about body functions like vomiting, which she saw her brother do and seemed to think was "in your chest like coughing." When mother was sick with dry heaves, Emily stared in awe. She noted she was lucky she could not vomit.

On a rare day when she was able to show interest in a book about the body, she let out hints of fantasy: for example, food goes in and "inside there's a little person that eats it." She noted that food goes in "and the stomach eats it." She confused the heart, stomach, and lungs. She then borrowed the book and forgot it at home for three weeks.

Many bits of themes came up without coalescing into a central continuous theme (perhaps in part because of the infrequent sessions), such as discussing that babies are in the mother's stomach and drawing a picture telling how they come out very very slowly. The picture had the vagina off to the side of the body and the focus changed to detail about the nurses and doctors surrounding the mother.

Body Image: Paranoid Theme

She considered getting her ears pierced and played that dolls got their ears pierced. She emphatically denied fear and confusion but wrote a list of what could go wrong. Fantasy material emerged that indicated great cognitive confusion. The list included the possibility that her earlobe could come off so she couldn't hear (her doctor would put on another lobe), that the hole would close and would need to be redone, and even that she would have problems with her stomach because of the ear piercing.

When she went to get her ears pierced, she became afraid at the store and complained that mother was forcing her to do it because she had said "good" when Emily wanted to go. "Well I won't do it!!" said Emily. She seemed to feel that her mother would hurt her and would like doing so. The piercing was put off till another time.

Hair was a big issue. Emily had feared having her hair washed since her early surgery at age 2 when she had been left without mother or father (rare during the twenty-one-day hospitalization) and a nurse had washed her hair in the sink. Emily complained that mother "always hurts me" when she combed her hair. "You like to hurt me," she said. She feared having her hair cut, although she would go to the beauty parlor when mother's hair was done. She feared they would cut her neck with the scissors. She played this out in a session, with the therapist as doctor with big scissors and she as frightened child. With obvious anxiety she lay on the couch with her eyes shut and mouth open, and the therapist clipping with scissors by her mouth to take her tonsils out. At home she cut a chunk of her own hair out and then insisted that mother should cut her hair. Her mother then did so but it came out very choppy. Finally mother "dragged her screaming" to the beauty parlor and she had it washed and cut. She then was very pleased, said it wasn't scary, and was able to shampoo it herself.

Body Image: Narcissistic Injury

The therapist then decided too much of an emphasis had been put on how well her body worked as she had worked on mastery, autonomy, and getting the tube out. The therapist shifted to stressing that indeed her body was different. She had had damage. She had not been in control of what went in and out of her body as an infant. She could not even vomit out what she didn't like. It was stressed how humiliating this must have been, how it hurt her feelings to be not in control and to not have a body that worked right. It was noted that as an infant she had resisted eating by mouth in her angry struggle with her parents but nevertheless food was put in regardless of her feelings. The therapist said that this uncomfortable and uncontrolled feeling inside must have made her insides feel "bad" and therefore not to be thought about. Emily responded to this new tack right away, pouring out a *confusion* of juxtaposed and related responses. She noted that she had had more operations than anyone in her school. She noted that she baby-sat for a 3-year-old whom she rescued from almost eating a Shera doll. She did a fine imitation of a bulimic girl vomiting, which she had seen in a TV movie.

Body Image: Confusion about Insides

She then was able to stick with themes of her body with less resistance (still frequently getting silly, changing the subject, not hearing, but responsive to the therapist's interpreting these defenses). She made a body out of Play Doh which was like a pinched-rim ashtray, adding a head only when the therapist inquired if it could have a head. It was a circle with one cloacal space which she filled with balls of food. She was utterly unable to answer how food got in. She drew "the throat" on paper. She pointed to her neck as the throat and seemed to view it as a hole in the neck. When the therapist put a pinch-pot stomach in her cloacal pinch-pot body, she was unable to say how the food got from the mouth to the stomach. She made a hole through the back of the body to the table as though the food went that way. She dug up into the head and pushed food up there. She tried to thus represent the esophagus, with no success. Finally, she placed the food into the stomach and said "it's 'sposed to go there!" as the answer to *how* it got there. She then listened with stethoscope to her heart and lungs and could not say where they were (since the space was all "stomach").

The therapist felt that educational efforts such as building a Visible Woman kit, drawing diagrams, and looking at pictures of body insides in books had all been obliterated in Emily's mind. The therapist drew a body outline and asked, "Where is the stomach?" Emily indicated a box including the whole trunk. When the therapist said that it couldn't be all that with the lungs and heart still to be fit in, Emily drew a line to bisect the box and said that half was the stomach. She again was unable to say how food got to it. In another session she drew the stomach with the "gut" below; when pressed as to how the food goes *from* the stomach *to* the gut she said, "It packs its bags and goes traveling!" The therapist put a face with mouth on a cardboard tube and she and Emily "fed" it food which fell through the tube. Emily seemed to forget these experiences as she continued to be unable to say how food gets from the mouth to the stomach. The therapist then provided plastic tubing to put bits of food through, in a small Play Doh person, as an esophagus and as a gut to excrete. Emily showed interest and a shaky understanding. After such doll play she drew (prior to a visit to the circus) a clown with chicken pox who says, "I can't clown for you because I have chicken pox; my life is over," as though she was having to acknowledge that a damaged body could not be happy.

Not being clear about inside/outside concepts, Emily also did not seem to view the body as a container. She panicked at a drop of blood on her finger. She told the therapist her theory that blood would keep coming out "unless you wiped it" and seemed to feel one could die from a finger prick. She had no idea of where blood was in the body, how much there was inside, that it would be controlled by the body, or that the skin was indeed a container for the body contents. The issue of how something gets from inside to out was not safe. She would occasionally poke at her belly button and was afraid of anything stuck into her ear; the ear holes were viewed as going into the body insides.

A dramatic contrast to Emily's disinterest in body insides was offered by a 3-year-old child who liked skeletons (from "Ghost Busters" on television). When he discovered the Visible Woman doll, he repeatedly put the skeleton into the transparent body shell and repeated aloud in awe, "Inside! Skeleton inside!" This boy then spent several weeks absorbed in both this doll and pictures in books exploring his new concept. His play showed many creative variations: for example, he put a baby in the woman's stomach and then fed the baby to her by mouth from which it went to inside her skull. He expressed fear that his own skeleton would come out. Emily showed none of this interest.

Aborted Psychosomatic Equivalents

Emily now rarely got sick and missed only one day of school, much less than in the past. She noted "It's 'cuz I have a mother who never lets me stay home sick." No one in the home was pampered when sick.

Emily developed what appeared to be a dramatic psychosomatic symptom: A half hour after noting the eyes of a dead fish in a fish store, she turned extremely pale to the point of appearing gravely ill. She was frightened by this and it took several minutes for her to appear herself again. Mother was even more frightened but suspected, encouraged by the therapist, that the process was in Emily's control. When it happened again, therefore, with no evident physical precipitant, mother simply told her to "snap out of it!" and Emily's pale appearance resolved within a minute.

Psychosexual Stages: Oral Aggression and Incorporation, Oral Pleasure, Oedipal Material

Oral aggression and oral incorporation were new themes. Just prior to going in for surgery Emily had drawn a picture of a girl with teeth. Otherwise oral aggressive themes had been virtually nonexistent. After the tube had been out for a year, more complex oral aggressive and incorporative material began to emerge.

For example, in one session: An alligator puppet visits a dog puppet in the hospital; the alligator eats the dog and then becomes the dog. Then Emily told a dream: A woman from her building was in an elevator with twenty-one ugly black rats. "They were biting us!" (She brushed them off.) People were "buying them to have one." They didn't fear being bitten "because the woman had a thing to toss out to control them." Emily jumped up to get away, fell off the bed, and woke up. She then spoke of a $2\frac{1}{2}$-year-old girl who had fallen down a well, an item on national news for several days. Emily said the girl sang "Winnie the Pooh," which Emily said she had read a long time ago herself. Later it became clear that Emily had no idea how to visualize a hole in the ground twenty feet deep.

Oedipal material included the fact that Emily had a boyfriend her age whom she said she would marry rather than marry father; Emily became enraged when mother and father teased her about him. She wrote letters to her surgeon saying, "I love you" and signed, "Your princess," a term he had long used with her.

Oral pleasure was evident in that eating continued not to be a problem. Emily especially liked swordfish and disliked vegetables. She liked peanut butter, making a mess on her hands. Generally she ate normally for her age, although she remained small.

Separation

The therapist felt Emily had made a great deal of progress toward object constancy, since she was able to relate to the therapist, her mother, and others with a wide range of feelings. Nevertheless separation was still an issue (perhaps related to the unresolved underlying aggressive fantasies).

Emily kept and reread a card the therapist had sent while on vacation and asked if the therapist would come back. She also asked if she would still see the therapist. This concern was in part her picking up father's continued opinion that enough therapy had been done.

Emily became insistent that her mother leave her alone at home "for a long time." Mother finally left her for a few minutes to get the laundry. She returned to find Emily on the phone telling a relative that her mother had been gone "for hours" and she did not know where she had gone and there was only bread and water in the house.

Emily also made a basket to hold a small baby doll. She wrote a note to put on it: "Please take care of my baby. I don't want it any more." She had borrowed this baby and lost it crossing the street outside the therapist's office, where her mother found it.

Death: Ongoing Interest

Emily had a recurrent interest in death, which continued through the treatment. At the start she joked that her grandfather was in heaven playing gin rummy with God and she wanted to telephone him. She had wanted to know why they could not open grandfather's coffin to see him (he had been dead for four years). She got some goldfish and was very interested in their care, concerned not to overfeed them or they could die. She feared that without the tube she would die.

On a visit to a historical town she saw a cemetery for the first time and wanted to know who dug the holes. Then she asked, "Are the people who live here all dead?" Her asking who dug the holes was interesting in view of her concern with "cave holes" and the cave dream.

CONCLUSION

Treatment

Emily's treatment was psychodynamically oriented and focused on individual and family dynamics to deal with reactions built up around her unusual physical disorder. The issues addressed in treatment were derived from the case material, for which there is no direct comparison in the literature. There are, however, many aspects of this case that can be compared with issues in the treatment of anorexia nervosa. Of particular relevance are ego functioning, body awareness, sense of self (Bruch 1973), family dynamics (Minuchin et al. 1978), and other psychodynamic issues (Sperling 1983, Wilson et al. 1983).

Bruch (1973) stresses the anorectic's need to learn about bodily perceptions and to develop autonomy within family dynamics. She describes gross disturbances of body image, including lack of perception of hunger and satiation, distorted sense of body size and proportion, and lack of awareness of inside of the body. She stresses that the anorectic feels "a paralyzing sense of ineffectiveness camouflaged by negativism and defiance" (Bruch 1981). The family contributes to the anorectic's not eating by providing secondary gain and by overprotectiveness, not encouraging or allowing autonomy to develop. With therapy, ego functions are strengthened, the patient acquires an accurate awareness of his or her body size and sensations, he or she develops initiative and responsibility for bodily actions and impulses, and the eating problem resolves. As a patient develops body awareness and autonomy, he or she also develops a sense of self. At this point, according to Bruch, a major part of the treatment is done. The treatment approach described by Bruch applies to Emily's treatment in that a central issue for Emily involved strengthening ego functioning leading to more autonomous care of and feeding of her own body, improved awareness of body sensations such as hunger and fullness, a clearer body image, and a stronger sense of self.

Minuchin and colleagues (1978) focus on family dynamics, especially in the control struggles over eating. Their concern is in altering the family patterns that interfere with eating. Altering family dynamics was an essential part of Emily's treatment as both power struggles and overprotective attitudes had to be changed.

Wilson and colleagues (1983) in accordance with Sperling (1983), Sours (1980), and others, disagree with Bruch in not viewing the ego functioning and body image issues as primary causes of anorexia. Bruch stresses deficit rather than unconscious conflict. Minuchin stresses family dynamics rather than the intrapsychic aspects of the significance for the patient of not eating. But according to Wilson, resolution of issues of body awareness and control over weight do not represent a cure unless underlying psychodynamic conflicts at the core of the personality are also resolved. Leaving such unconscious conflicts unresolved may make the patient vulnerable to resuming anorectic or other symptoms in the future. While Bruch stresses deficits in experience, Wilson views deficits in body awareness and image as due to unconscious conflict; he says that body awareness is split off from consciousness and that interpretation of the conflicts is necessary to change the anorectic's self image.

Emily's treatment addressed both deficit and unconscious conflict. Emily clearly had *deficits* in experience, since she had eaten only minimally and apparently never with enjoyment of taste or the process of eating. Unlike an adult anorectic, who had enjoyed food and then lost interest, Emily had never enjoyed food. But Emily's indifference to food appeared to be based on fears and conflict over taking in food and on the power she derived over her family (and her body) by not eating. She became free to fill in deficits as certain issues were worked through; she could then develop her body image, exploring how big her mouth was (how much popcorn could fit in), how to swig from a bottle, how to suck through a straw, and even how to eat with silverware. Interestingly, her initial exploration of eating (like a 2-year-old's) and initial expressions of anger (delayed "terrible twos") both resembled delayed developmental experiences; these were not educational issues but were free to evolve when conflicts were removed.

Clearly there were areas of *unconscious conflict*. While Emily's subjective experience was of lack of hunger, with therapy she was able to get in touch with her pleasure and anger in teasing and controlling others by not eating, and her fears of autonomy and separation from her mother. Psychosexual themes, which had apparently been held in check, emerged quickly with the lessening of the power struggles. These included oedipal wishes to marry father and have a baby, sexual curiosity, phallic wishes to show off strength and mastery, along with the anal level control issues. The speed of emergence of these issues early in therapy suggests they had been in some way present but not conscious. Oral pleasure appeared slowly, and it is unclear whether some sense of oral pleasure was "split off" or whether oral pleasure developed in a delayed manner.

Oral aggression was the slowest of the psychosexual themes to emerge. Hints of underlying violence were clear in Emily's breaks in play when two animal dolls fought (kicking and biting), in her dream of her stomach being shot open, in her dream of a woman with biting rats, and in other examples. Strongly defended against, these aggressive themes seemed most related to oral (including stomach) aggression and reactions to the trauma of her early surgical experiences. This aggressive material seemed "split off," since it appeared only rarely and briefly and yet vividly. Oral incorporation was also a new theme as the alligator ate the dog and then became the dog, or as food went inside to where "the stomach eats it" or "there's a little person that eats it."

Whether oral pleasure, oral incorporation, and oral aggression were split off or developed to fill a deficit is difficult to prove. It may be that what is split off is a capacity for the development of such themes.

Emily's treatment also dealt with *external conflict* as her family was caught in an intense power struggle with her over eating. Her parents' efforts to use behavior modification, rewarding her for eating, had been futile. Within the family dynamics Emily was seen as a fragile child. Only when the power struggle was made verbally explicit, was understood by Emily's mother, and was interrupted (by stopping efforts to push food) was Emily able to develop autonomy. Mother's increased ability to express anger at Emily (and Emily at mother) helped lessen Emily's fears of separation as well as lessening the need to express anger through the not eating. Externally her environment was thus altered as her parents changed their responses to her.

Obviously there can be multiple meanings to a symptom such as not eating. It is unlikely that Emily would have eaten if therapy had not addressed the unconscious aspects of her enjoyment of teasing, her anger, and her fears of autonomy and separation from mother. For example, Emily may have felt eating by mouth as a threat, a primal early fear of choking and dying, since she gagged and choked early on when attempts were made to feed her. Such early negative experiences could become part of an "affective core" which would underlie further development (Emde 1983). She may have felt that being fed by tube was "bad" because it was unpleasant with sensations of being too full and not having control over input. All of these feelings, along with whatever fantasied meanings they took on, later became repressed and covered with her conscious lack of hunger and indifference to food. Other areas where apparent unconscious conflict and fantasy interfered included acknowledgement of body damage and anger at it (at mother? at the surgeons?) which were hinted at (e.g., in the cave dream) and fear of her own retaliatory fantasies. The lack of resolution of these issues seems related to Emily's inability to think clearly about her own insides, to take in knowledge, to let her thoughts go spontaneously, and to play out themes of oral aggression.

Besides the treatment issues discussed above, a further comparison with anorexia is of interest. Wilson and colleagues (1983) note that although the medical term "anorexia" refers to a lack of interest in and hunger for food, most adults with anorexia nervosa are consciously intensely preoccupied with food and often feel hunger, with which they struggle. They exhibit more a "fear of being fat" than a true anorexia. Emily had no interest in food and did not appear preoccupied with it, *but* her family was certainly intensely invested in her eating; hence with her not eating as a core family problem, Emily could hardly escape being preoccupied with food. While Emily did not appear to fear being fat, she did have an investment in not growing up to separate from her mother.

Could Emily's difficulties be called a psychosomatic disorder? Anorexia nervosa was considered a psychosomatic disorder by Sperling (1983) because of the psychological interference with bodily functions such as menstruation as well as the psychodynamic and family patterns found in anorexia nervosa and other psychosomatic disorders. For a premenstrual child, obviously lack of menses is not yet relevant. However, Emily did in many ways fit a pattern typical for psychosomatic patients. According to Wilson and colleagues (1983), a key issue is control, and the focus becomes control over bodily impulses as well as over other persons. The choice of psychosomatic symptom depends in part on the parents' personalities, a possible physical proclivity toward one organ system, and the patient's intrapsychic structure. Anorexia may interchange with other psychosomatic symptoms. The need for control covers fear of primitive fantasies and wishes that require analysis beyond the control issue. Emily's not eating was a focal point for control of herself and of her parents. Her parents were prone to relating with issues of control and power struggles within the family. Though the choice of symptom was weighted by her physical disorder, she could have chosen other symptoms once the eating issue was resolved, such as her two episodes of turning pale. The eating and control issues needed resolution before underlying fantasy material could be approached.

Alexethymia is a term sometimes applied to psychosomatic patients who appear unable to fantasize. But as Wilson (1983) points out, these patients have intense unconscious fantasies that are split off. Emily seemed to fit this picture, since her concrete manner and minimal spontaneous use of fantasy on the surface seemed to cover underlying violent fantasies that were difficult to get at.

Emily presented a unique anorectic symptom in that she had never shown hunger or interest in food. This could be called a primary anorexia, being present from birth and not acquired. As more effective pediatric treatments are developed for a variety of disorders, more infants are surviving with the experience of having never eaten. It will certainly be of interest to follow oral pleasure and development in these children.

Oral Pleasure

That Emily was able to begin to eat and to enjoy food at age 6 showed she had not experienced an irreversible deficit based on a missed critical period for oral pleasure. Oral pleasure emerged as anxieties and conflicts were dealt with and as she developed a stronger ego in the context of her relationship with the therapist and with her family. The capacity for pleasure in eating had remained intact.

Since eating by mouth is not optional for most human beings, the idea of nonuse leading to loss of the ability to eat or to take pleasure in eating is not often put to a test. For Emily, it seems conflict did not suppress pleasure since the pleasure had never been there, and it seemed to emerge and develop gradually. However pleasure might have been in some way split off. A parallel in splitting of a function from the pleasure in it is often seen in sexual dysfunctions. Here it is not unusual for conflict resolution to lead to a sometimes quite delayed experiencing of genital sexual pleasure.

Oral Incorporation and Object Relations

The fact that Emily was fairly well related to others at age $5\frac{1}{2}$ showed that the physical act of taking in food by mouth was not necessary as a primitive sensorimotor paradigm for later relating to objects. Mother knew Emily needed a substitute for oral pleasure, and she used touch and visual and vocal contact to compensate. Emily's not eating also made her the focus of anxious attention. Even so, she had had a period of apathy and weak relatedness for the first 18 months of her life. She became more related, not over eating, but over issues of control, teasing, and power struggles. Early on she had turned away from food out of primitive preconceptual anxiety (choking to death and presumable associated rage), but then at $1\frac{1}{2}$ to 2 years a passive-aggressive teasing mode of relating developed with intensity and motivation related to her parents. It would thus appear that her relationships in the oral period were weak and passive in spite of the substitution of touch and other modalities. Just as Matt (Dowling 1980) was not motivated to eat until he learned he could control fullness by eating, at which time then he became intensely related and motivated around food, it is possible that not eating caused a delay in Emily's formation of object relations of normal intensity. Emily at first had to be passively fed with no contingent sense of control to motivate her either to eat or to relate to others except in rejecting food by mouth. Then with the anal phase came new channels for relating. Interpersonal control issues provided channels for intense active feelings to be played out with her parents. Brody (1964) noted a similar case in which a child with feeding problems appeared to find a "second chance" to relate in the anal phase. She wrote that passivity set in the oral phase may not be reinforced: "in the anal phase a child may have a second chance to stabilize the balance between active and passive drives" (p. 99).

An alternate explanation for Emily's passivity in the oral phase would be that it was due to the phenobarbital she took from birth to 15 months. Quite likely both the above discussed oral phase issues as well as the phenobarbital contributed to her passivity.

In the course of therapy, Emily did later include, in relating to the therapist and her family, positive oral experiences and the beginnings of oral aggressive themes, including biting, greed, and destructiveness, as she moved toward more mature personality development.

Transitional Objects

Emily's ongoing use of a transitional object suggests less than full resolution of separation issues. Her first transitional object at 22 months, the blanket she was wrapped in and held in by her father after painful hospital treatments, suggests a connection to her father and relief from pain. Her imaginary companion at 4 to 5 years was scolded and threatened with going to the hospital if it did not eat, suggesting identification with the aggressor and a fear of being sent back for more treatment herself. Her shift from the blanket to father's shirt used in falling asleep suggests again security from pain and perhaps also an identification with her father. Her attitude toward her surgeon, writing him letters stressing her love for him, may indicate some reaction formation since she did not express anger at him. Her ongoing use of the transitional object therefore may indicate an ongoing need for safety in the face of split-off fearful and angry feelings resulting from her esophageal atresia and surgical experiences.

Body Image

At the start of therapy Emily did not feel in autonomous control of her body. She was tense and awkward in gross motor activities and oral motor functions. As an infant Emily did not "know where her body was in space," and her early motor milestones were notably delayed. Perhaps her lack of oral experience led to these delays. Meltzoff and Borton (1979) noted that infants relate visual perceptions of the world to oral sensations, thus using mouthing experiences in making sense of the world. Emily's oral motor deficits could have led to delays in visual motor and gross motor functions because of a deficit in basic sensorimotor paradigms for learning. This concept is in keeping with Dowling's (1980) esophageal atresia infants who showed gross motor delays; for example, Paul, who had good mothering and a pacifier but no sham feeding, had marked motor delays. In therapy Emily's body and facial tension relaxed as the power struggles lessened and as she was able to express anger. Then she began to master motoric functions and practiced them intensely and persistently in the context of a positive relationship with the therapist. As conflicts and fears were alleviated and she developed autonomy and responsibility for her own body separate from her mother's, she appeared freed to master her body. She learned to eat big pieces and also discussed fears of choking. She learned gross motor activities such as jump rope and bicycling and also dealt with increased separation and autonomy from her mother. In the course of this progress she became less awkward. Again one could say her early passivity was due to the phenobarbital, but the intensity of her interest in mastery which emerged years after the phenobarbital was stopped seems to indicate an emotional basis.

In therapy Emily also developed her awareness of the surface of her body, dressing up in clothes and makeup and playing "copy me" games, especially with facial expressions. This interest in her appearance progressed without apparent conflict except for her surgical scars, which she continued to view with disinterest.

Emily was not able to and/or willing to conceptualize her own insides. Her understanding of her surgery stayed on the surface: skin taken from her buttock was sewn onto her neck, or a cut made in her neck was then sewn up again. Children at 5 to 10 years of age may not have a clear conception of what is inside their body but they can learn when taught. Intense efforts to teach Emily about her stomach, esophagus, and guts, however, did not alter her view of her insides as a cloacal space which food entered in some mysterious way. Emily's lack of doll-feeding play reflects her avoidance and/or lack of experience with bottle or breastfeeding.

Emily's fear of considering the inside of her body was felt to be related to conflicts over oral aggression and to anxiety related to her body defects and surgery. Her sense of vulnerability was reflected in her weak sense of body boundary; she feared after surgery that her "stomach could fall out" and dreamed she was shot and cut in her stomach. She had no clear images of her body surface (skin) as a reliable containing boundary, so a pinprick could lead to bleeding to death. Her parents had violated her body boundary (of necessity) for six years by simply putting food into her. Emily knew she had had surgery and had multiple scars on her abdomen and throat, yet she was unable to comprehend what had been done to her, not because the concept was too difficult, apparently, but because of fears (of what could be wrong with her) and humiliation and anger (at what had been done to her body). Her confusion in visualizing holes, whether a well in the ground or an esophagus to carry food to her stomach, seemed related to a still unclear unconscious fantasy related to holes and things going into her body without her control.

Besides the above mental aspects of body image, one must consider the possible physiological impact of a missing esophagus on body image. Deficits can occur to specific parts of the body image due to physical injury. For example, a right parietal stroke can cause disowning of a leg such that the stroke victim even tries to throw the "foreign" leg out of his bed (Sacks 1985). As another example, Sacks (1984) vividly describes the experience of a scotoma for his left leg caused by a severe leg injury. Sacks found it hard to imagine his left leg or even "a place where the leg could be." This scotoma resolved only as the leg became reinnervated. It is possible that on a physiological basis a child without an esophagus could not even imagine where it should be or what it should do. Such a child would lack the experience of swallowing, of mapping this experience in subcortical centers as well as cortical centers of experience and memory. There would be no conscious or unconscious memory traces of taking in food, swallowing it, and feeling full. Though scotomas are usually de-scribed for visual fields or parts of the body, one might imagine a scotoma for the experience of swallowing based on nerves that had never been connected to a nonexistent esophageal section. Or the imagined scotoma could exist because of lack of learning due to lack of the sensorimotor experience of swallowing. While such speculations may appear farfetched, they are offered in the interest of stimulating thought about disorders such as Emily's. Modern surgical techniques on infants may introduce a variety of unusual body image problems. Long-term in-depth psychological studies of infants after surgery would help clarify the impact of such surgery on body image and how infants adapt to the changes.

Learning

Emily's esophageal atresia appeared related to some of her difficulties with learning. In a general way, Emily's style of omnipotence, grandiosity, and denial interfered with learning; even when working hard at school-work she would tend to guess impulsively rather than think about prob-lems. Neurologically, it is possible that Emily had some general intellectual limitation associated with enlarged ventricles noted at birth. Also psycho-logically, not learning could reflect an oral mode of conflict over taking in information, a paranoid shutting out of input, or an anal struggle over controlling input of knowledge and taking responsibility for one's auton-omous thoughts, all related to Emily's early tube feedings.

It is interesting to speculate that more specific areas of cognitive difficulty could have a basis in specific missing parts in Emily's brain and early sensorimotor experiences. A deficit in the early experience of swallowing food from mouth to stomach (which she had *never* done until 22 months) might have caused and/or correlated with a lack of mental and/or physiological representation of food going from one place to another. For normally eating children, food disappears as it goes inside, causing one to feel full. It is hard to imagine *not* having had this experience. Emily had great difficulty conceptualizing things being put inside. Conceiv-ably, Emily's lack of sensorimotor experience of taking in food could have caused a failure to learn and integrate concepts such as inside/outside. Her anxiety and fantasies about what went into or was taken out of her body (and her inability to control input or to vomit it out) could further block this learning.

Emily was also confused about causality or *how* things get from point *a* to point *b*. She said food moves to the stomach because "it's supposed to go there." One might speculate that the esophagus in enscribing an early sensorimotor paradigm of objects going from *a* to *b* forms a basis for a child's notion of motion of matter in space. If such is true, the effects of early sensorimotor deficits on cognition could be made up for by later sensorimotor experience (as Emily later did eat by mouth) or by learning in other ways. Blind children who have great difficulty remembering mazes because they cannot "visualize" them are able to learn them better when they can verbally describe them to themselves (Rubin 1979, p. 230).

Emily's confusion about time and her lack of fantasizing about past or future times was part of her general lack of fantasy play. When Emily learned to tell time, after her eating was established, she became able to fantasize, playfully displacing herself and events in space and time. Perhaps a more stable body image allows for a clearer sense of localization in time and place.

Speculations such as these seem worth some thought. While much has been written on learning difficulties in children, little success has been reported in relating specific conceptual difficulties with specific sensori-motor or conflictual issues.

SUMMARY

Though the congenital condition esophageal atresia does not inherently lead to an eating disorder, in the case discussed here Emily refused to eat before and after corrective surgery. Psychotherapy guided by psychoanalytic principles and started at age $5\frac{1}{2}$ allowed resolution of conflicts, fears, and maladaptive family patterns such that Emily began to eat at age 7 and had her gastrostomy tube removed at 8. Issues of control, autonomy, separation, and body image were central. In spite of the absence of positive early oral experience, Emily was able to experience and integrate oral pleasure. Psychodynamic and psychophysiological issues related to early oral experiences, oral incorporation, object relations, and cognitive development were also discussed.

Emily had made significant progress in issues of starting to eat, having her tube removed, developing oral pleasure, mastering gross motor activities with less awkwardness and tension, and developing a more assertive sense of self, more age-appropriate autonomous functioning within her family, and some progress toward autonomy in academic functioning. Still in need of further treatment remained her generalized anxiety and immaturity, her defensive use of denial and impulsivity, her blockage in thinking about her surgery, her difficulty with use of spontaneous fantasy, and further difficulties in learning. One might anticipate also some difficulties with body image as Emily proceeds through the changes of puberty and adolescence.

I have condensed here an enormous amount of case material. Overall a psychoanalytically guided treatment for this child's eating problem proved necessary and productive. The case has been discussed in the hope that it may be of use toward the understanding and treatment of others with eating disorders.

REFERENCES

Bower, T. G. R. (1982). *Development in Infancy.* 2nd ed. San Francisco: Freeman.
Brody, S. (1964). *Passivity: A Study of Its Development and Expression in Boys.* New York:

International Universities Press.

Bruch, H. (1973). *Eating Disorders: Obesity, Anorexia Nervosa, and the Person Within*. New York: Basic Books.

——— (1981). Developmental considerations of anorexia and obesity. *Canadian Journal of Psychiatry* 26:212–217.

Call, J. D. (1978). Follow-up of 20 children with autism treated before the age of 5. Symposium Presentation, Lexington School for the Deaf, New York.

Dowling, S. (1977). Seven infants with esophageal atresia. *Psychoanalytic Study of the Child* 32:215–256. New Haven, CT: Yale University Press.

——— (1980). Going forth to meet the environment: a developmental study of seven infants with esophageal atresia. *Psychosomatic Medicine* 42:153–161.

Emde, R. N. (1983) The prerepresentational self and its affective core. *Psychoanalytic Study of the Child* 38:165–92. New Haven, CT: Yale University Press.

Engel, G. L., and Segal, H. L. (1956). A study of an infant with a gastric fistula: I. Behavior and the rate of total hydrochloric acid secretion. *Psychosomatic Medicine* 18:374–398.

Harlow, H., and Mears, C. (1979). *The Human Model: Primate Perspectives*. New York: Winston.

Holder, T. M., and Ashcraft, K. W. (1970). Esophageal atresia and tracheoesophageal fistula. *Annuals of Thoracic Surgery* 9:445–467.

Hubel, D. H., and Wiesel, T. N. (1970). The period of susceptibility to the physiological effects of unilateral eye closure in kittens. *Journal of Neurophysiology* 206:419–436.

Kolb, B., and Whishaw, I. (1980). *Fundamentals of Human Neuropsychology*. San Francisco: Freeman.

Lewis, M. (1967). *Mother–infant interaction and cognitive development: a developmental construct.* Paper presented at the National Institute of Child Health and Human Development, Symposium on "Issues in Human Development," Philadelphia.

Meltzoff, A. N., and Borton, W. (1979). Intermodal matching by human neonates. *Nature* 282:403–404.

Minuchin, S., Rosman, B. L., and Baker, L. (1978). *Psychosomatic Families: Anorexia Nervosa in Context*. Cambridge, MA: Harvard University Press.

Rubin, I. (1979). Effects of early blindness and deafness on cognition. In *Congenital and Acquired Cognitive Disorders*. ed. R. Katzman, pp. 189–245. New York: Raven Press.

Sacks, O. (1984). *A Leg to Stand On*. New York: Summit Books.

——— (1985). *The Man Who Mistook His Wife for a Hat*. New York: Summit Books.

Sarnoff, C. (1976). *Latency*. New York: Jason Aronson.

Sours, J. (1980). *Starving to Death in a Sea of Objects: The Anorexia Nervosa Syndrome*. New York: Jason Aronson.

Sperling, M. (1983). A reevaluation of classification, concepts, and treatment. In *Fear of Being Fat: The Treatment of Anorexia Nervosa and Bulimia*, ed. C. P. Wilson, C. C. Hogan, and I. L. Mintz, pp. 51–82. New York: Jason Aronson.

Van der Zee, D. C., Zweirstia, R., Koutstrza, G., et al. (1981). Colon interposition as replacement for the esophagus: a follow-up study. *Zeitschrift fur Kinderchirugie* 33:291–97.

Wilson, C. P., Hogan, C. C., and Mintz, I. L., eds. (1983). *Fear of Being Fat: The Treatment of Anorexia Nervosa and Bulimia*. New York: Jason Aronson.

PART VI

Special Topics

12

Onset of Bulimia during Psychoanalysis

Charles R. Keith, M.D.

Case histories of the anorexia bulimic syndrome reported so far in the psychoanalytic literature have involved primarily patients whose symptoms were well established prior to the onset of analysis (Wilson 1985a). This chapter describes the psychoanalysis of a young woman whose bulimic symptoms began during the second year of analytic treatment. The bulimic compromise formation appeared to be stimulated by the deepening transference (Wilson 1986). This transference remained difficult and stormy for the patient until she interrupted analysis during the fifth year of treatment. The patient's general ego functioning had improved considerably over the course of analysis, although the bulimic pattern and its interdigitation with the transference remained incompletely analyzed at interruption.

A further complication was the patient's seeking out and obtaining antidepressant medication at the urging of her mother shortly prior to interruption of treatment. Though the onset of bulimia during analysis appears to be unusual, the volatile transference, interruption of analysis, and the use of antidepressant medications are common issues arising during the analytic treatment of this condition.

Following interruption, the patient made several contacts with the analyst, which culminated in her resumption of treatment at the time this volume was being prepared. Thus this is an account of an ongoing analysis that illustrates many of the central issues, perplexities, and uncertainties faced by the patient and the analyst as they work together to resolve the maladaptive bulimic pattern.

CASE HISTORY

Background

The patient, a white Protestant, was 18 years old, single, and a college freshman when she began analysis. Her chief concerns were severe anxiety and blocking of her thoughts, which made it difficult to function at school.

She was the firstborn child of parents who lived in a large city. The father was a prominent businessman, and the mother was a teacher prior to her leaving work to raise her children. She had a brother, four years her junior, who appeared to have a neurotic performance inhibition that over the years was labeled a "learning disability." These problems culminated in a manic episode at age 20 resulting in a brief hospitalization and lithium therapy. The youngest sibling, born when the patient was 6 years of age, is a severely retarded boy who divided his time between the family and foster care.

Both the patient and her parents perceived her prelatency years as being without undue difficulties until age 6. The parents recall that upon entering school the patient became somewhat of a loner, haughty with her peers and overly concerned about school performance. Most of the patient's earliest memories begin from this period. One was of making cookies with her mother in the kitchen. Later the same cookie mix became one of the primary gorging foods. For the patient, entering first grade was a turning point in her relationship with her mother, which up to this time she had perceived as essentially positive. From the time of her retarded brother's birth when she was 6, the patient experienced her mother as losing interest in doing pleasant activities with her and for her. The patient believes that family photographs showed her becoming a drab, somewhat sad, homely girl after age 6 in contrast to the earlier smiling, well-dressed, happy child.

By age 11 the patient felt "out of it." She described herself as awkward and no longer gaining pleasure from performing well in school. She was no longer needed or wanted for any of the family activities such as caring for the cat and the retarded brother. During the late latency years she masturbated frequently, bringing herself to orgasm. A frequent conscious masturbation fantasy was picturing Zeus ravaging Io while Hera hovered about in a jealous rage. The father was extremely busy in his expanding business and was pictured by the patient as always preoccupied by his work. The struggles developing between mother and daughter at home were experienced by him as burdensome.

When the patient was 12, the parents separated for three years. The patient visited her father regularly at his apartment and felt sorry for him with his spartan surroundings and lonely meals. At home with her mother, the patient developed outbursts of rage and stole from the mother's purse.

At age 13 she felt rejected by a girlfriend, at which point she induced vomiting one time by placing a finger down her throat. She found this "disgusting" and did not repeat it again until during her later analysis.

At age 14 she was taken by her parents to a child analyst who recommended analysis. The parents declined the recommendation, saying they were already burdened by their marital problems and wanted to work those out before considering analysis for her. Psychological testing at that time revealed a full-scale I.Q. of 128 and neurotic-level ego functioning. The analyst saw the patient for once-a-week therapy for the ensuing two years. The analyst noticed the patient's mild weight fluctuations but did not feel at that time that it was an anorectic picture.

When the patient was 15, the parents resumed living together. As life settled down, the analyst again recommended analysis. The parents said they were in favor of it but now the patient declined, saying that she wanted to "go it on her own." At this point the patient stopped psychotherapy. During the psychoanalytic psychotherapy, the analyst had worked primarily with the patient's shyness and aloofness and felt that the therapeutic relationship had been a stabilizing force during a volatile early adolescent period.

The patient's symptoms, particularly social discomfort, decreased considerably at the family's summer resort home, a place she idealized and where she felt more competent and could experience more love and warmth with her mother.

In the tenth grade the patient began to date. The parents surprised her one evening undressing with a boy in her bedroom. The parents immediately drove him to the airport, since he was an out-of-town visitor, and they placed her on severe restrictions for the next year. She felt that for the rest of her high school years she lived under a heavy cloud of guilt and gloom until she left for college. She experienced both intense jealousy and positive feelings toward her next younger brother. A pattern developed through high school and college in which she would become passionately involved, usually with sexual intercourse, with brilliant young men who either were headed for or currently going to Ivy League schools. These relationships ended stormily with the young men saying the patient was "the most difficult girl" they had ever known. Though her school performance was erratic, she made sufficiently high grades to get into the competitive college her mother had attended. The patient never visited this college before enrolling. She chose business as her major, believing that it would be easier than a liberal arts curriculum, which had proved difficult for the mother.

The first six weeks of college were intensely uncomfortable for her, with feelings of depersonalization. She completed assignments three days early to make sure she stayed in control of her academics. Impulsively, she hitched a ride to New England to visit a former boyfriend without telling her parents. While returning to her college, she developed severe anxiety, bought an airplane ticket, and called her parents to say she was coming home. Her father interceded and said she was not coming home; instead she was to get into treatment and thereby learn to function in college. The parents contacted her former therapist, who referred the patient to me.

Initial Phase of Analysis

When I first met the patient, she was an attractive young woman, dressed rather primly in contrast to usual college garb. She appeared to be mildly overweight. In our first session she talked about the need to exercise regularly to keep her body trim. She felt that she had more than the usual concerns about what she was eating. I recalled thinking about anorexia at the time but this material dropped out as the analysis got underway. More striking in these initial hours was the severe blocking of thoughts, making it difficult for her to finish sentences, accompanied by high levels of anxiety which diminished somewhat as she moved into analysis.

She worked out the financial details of the analysis with her parents, since she did not wish them to have direct contact with me. The parents generally respected her wish to be in analysis, supporting it both emotionally and financially until the fifth year of treatment.

She declined to use the couch regularly until the third year of analysis. When I talked of her concerns about using the couch, the patient's usual comment was: "I'm touchy about that subject and uncomfortable with it. I will analyze it later so please don't bring it up. I'll use it when I'm ready."

A prominent theme during the first year of analysis was emerging anger at the parents' secretiveness. The father had had major coronary surgery but did not tell her for fear it would be upsetting and distract her from school work. Another secret revealed that the paternal grandfather committed suicide. The parents had told the patient that he had died of illness. Expression of anger toward the parents in the sessions and direct confrontation with them about secrets helped the patient gain a feeling of separation from them, particularly the mother, and the feeling that she could use the analysis as a place where she could do her own thinking.

She identified "standards" in her mind that felt alive and threatening and that seemed to crush and block her thinking. She linked these standards with fears of her mother, who took on an idealized, powerful, witchlike demeanor in the analytic material. The patient could feel slapping sensations on her hand as she talked about her mother and challenged the cruel standards in her mind. Interestingly, she never had any actual memories of the mother slapping her.

These harsh standards also became connected with her defense of "haughtiness." Particularly painful during the first year of college was her belief that "nice girls don't indulge in childish, silly college activities."

An early transference theme was the need to please me in her continual search to find the right thing to say. This was one factor in the blocking of verbalizations, namely, having to think of each sentence to make sure it sounded right. A full year of analysis was required before her verbalizations could flow more freely. The central interpretation during this first year dealt with identification of the cruel "standards," how they blocked thinking, and how she was externalizing these superego functions onto the analyst. The patient was surprised at the idealization of the mother and her efforts to please these internalized maternal images, since most of the conscious memories of her mother involved stealing from her, raging at her, and the mutual hatred between them.

By the end of the first year of analysis she was more relaxed in the sessions, could wear sloppy college clothes, and was allowing herself to engage in some normal college activities. School grades remained erratic, ranging from an occasional A to F's or incompletes. The emerging pattern was that any success had to be followed by failure.

She asked to increase the frequency of her sessions from four to five times per week and made arrangements to continue in analysis during the summer.

Not only was the analyst seen as a superego figure but there was also idealization. She read *The Impossible Profession* and poured through Brenner's books on analysis. Some of this idealization served a defensive purpose to put me at a distance and not experience me as a sexual transference object. Another prominent transference defense was her acting out and perceiving herself as an obstreperous, exasperating patient who was different from all my other patients, whom she believed were cooperative. This was one of her reasons for not using the couch.

In the second year of analysis she could talk more about her parents and younger brother as real people with troubles of their own. She felt a better sense of separateness from her primary objects. She could also begin to reveal more fantasies about herself, which for a long time were uniformly derogatory. She revealed beliefs that the inside of her body was damaged, as well as her brain, and she felt these beliefs accounted for her always having to look stupid in course work. She read about penis envy, then told of how she always had to pick men who were achievers at prestigious colleges. The hope was that by becoming like them she could perform. She pictured me as being like her boyfriends and believed that by being in analysis she would somehow pick up my strength and make it through college. However, this concept put her in a dangerous position, that of being a man's sexual toy. She became enraged at any gesture on my part that would suggest my appreciation of her as a woman, such as stepping back to let her walk ahead into the office, or offering to open the door for her. During several sessions she stomped out of the office, angrily slamming the door to show me and the world that she was not going to be a man's plaything. My interpretations during this period centered around the theme that her leaving angrily could be protecting us from thoughts and feelings emerging during the sessions. She feared that if she allowed herself to become further involved in the analysis, she might destroy or damage me and the analysis just as she felt she had damaged other people and important activities. She began to touch flowers in my office and finger toys or lumps of clay from the toy table. She became frightened as she touched these objects and wondered if I would become angry and yell at her.

At the fourteen-month period in analysis her mother required surgery and asked the patient to come home for a week to take care of her postsurgically. The patient was exhilarated. It was the first time she could really allow herself to "mother" her own mother, cook meals, and care for the house. She also noticed an urge to cry just before the break in the analysis but quickly assumed her old defense of "being above all that childishness."

Emergence of Oedipal Themes

As we moved into the second year of analysis, the themes gradually shifted from preoedipal concerns with the mother to more oedipal issues. She revealed her favorite childhood story, entitled "The Little Princess," in which a girl whose mother has died wins out over schoolmates with her father's help. She had read the story many times and read it again at this point during analysis. She could calm down and make herself go to sleep at night by telling herself the story. She surprised herself by making an A in a course and then immediately pictured her mother being bored and threatened by her success. She revealed that her mother could make only C's at this university. Now she was outdoing the mother. This revelation gave us the opportunity to rework the superego guilt themes that had been prominent in the first year of analysis. Now the frightening wishes were becoming oedipal.

A childhood memory was recalled. She remembered driving a motor boat up to a dock with her grandfather beside her. Her mother was standing on the dock screaming at her to drive the boat correctly or it would crash. With tears, the patient blurted out the fear that if she were successful she would literally kill her mother or take away what little the mother had in her life then, reminiscent of the preoedipal superego described by Modell (1971). As she became more conscious of competitive urges with her mother, she impulsively tried out for the top sorority on the campus, the one to which her mother belonged. She was not admitted and withdrew from the competition with shame and humiliation. At the same time she broke up with her college boyfriend because of her disgust at being so greedily attached to him.

Onset of the Bulimic Pattern

In the eighteenth month of the analysis, the transference themes were deepening. For the first time memories and thoughts about her father were beginning to enter the material. She was able to express longings for him, then would feel rage at his disinterest. She impulsively acted out this rage and also the ensuing guilt by having another screaming fight with her boyfriend. She was beginning to make more connections in the sessions between emerging wishes toward me and her father and the need to fail either in school or with her boyfriend. She had a vague memory of touching her father's penis at age 5, at which point somebody screamed and terrified her. She then expressed more direct wishes toward me and wondered if I cared about her.

She reported fantasies of preparing a lovely table of food for a man, with a vague baby somewhere about the house. She found these fantasies to be "disgusting and nauseating." There was increased use of such oral terms in describing affective states, which in retrospect should have alerted me to what was about to happen. She announced during one session that she had begun gorging herself and then vomiting out the "disgusting" food. She had done this once during the first year of analysis while visiting an aunt but had not reported it. She found it disgusting, just as she had at age 13, when she tried it and never wanted to do it again. Now suddenly it had become a daily routine because it brought "wonderful" relief from tension and left her calm for several hours or even a day.

There was a sudden preoccupation with her figure as she announced she was losing weight and intended to lose more. Her "flabby" thighs and stomach were "disgusting" to her. She was glad that she discovered vomiting could control the caloric intake from gorging and permit her to lose weight rapidly.

The regressive features of this bulimic pattern were not accompanied by a regression in thought processes. The themes of her associations continued to revolve around oedipal issues. She reported a favorite daydream from age 6 of standing in front of envious female relatives while a man approached and gave her a fond embrace. Now, rather than finding these fantasies to be "bad" or not meeting her "standards," she found them to be nauseating and disgusting, stating that they felt like they were "kicking her in the stomach." Oral terminology seemed to flood the hours.

Once she entered the office a few minutes before the start of the session and looked through a book. She wondered if I would fly into a rage or become angry when I discovered this daring intrusion. She felt she no longer needed to be a parasite upon a man in order to function; she could now "do her own thing" in school and social life. There was a burst of what appeared to be late adolescent independence. She wondered if she really needed analysis. Instead of the old self-portrait of a damaged, malfunctioning girl, she now portrayed herself as a sexy vamp who could make her way in the world. Indeed, she announced to her parents that she was dropping out of school for a year to get a job to support herself. She had always experienced school as submission to someone else. When she went back she wanted to do it because of her own wish to be in school. The parents were dismayed and raised questions about what was going on in the analysis. They threatened to interrupt her analysis by withdrawing financial support. However, the patient took a firm stand, saying that analysis was important and that she wanted to continue and finish. She asked her parents to allow her to have a year working and living in her own apartment, and they reluctantly agreed. The patient plunged into feminist literature and became a Simone de Beauvoir fan.

The daily gorging/vomiting ritual continued. By this time she had left the college dorm and was in her own apartment with a private bathroom. She would spread towels around the toilet, then jump up and down to mix the food in her stomach to ensure that it would all come out. At times the vomiting ritual took almost an hour, after which she would feel exhausted and relieved. Sometimes the vomiting was so violent that she would come to the sessions with conjunctival bleeding and pulled abdominal muscles. At times her description of the vomiting sounded like an orgiastic experience. A few months after the onset of gorging and vomiting she brought her first food into the session, a box of Cheerios, and gobbled it voraciously. She never "dreamed" she would be able to reveal something so private and disgusting to me. She then had a fantasy of my beating her up. She recalled a story read years before of a prostitute who was about to kill a man, with her finger on the trigger of a gun. Just before the explosion, the man grabbed the gun and beat her up. Interpretations centered around the themes of masturbatory and sexual fantasies which were exciting, frightening, and guilt-ridden. The gorging and vomiting seemed to be a regressive defense whose purpose was to keep the fantasies disguised and secret. Much of the affect, including both pleasure and guilty punishment, was being lived out through the gorging/vomiting pattern. She revealed that she had been "dead" sexually since the beginning of analysis or even before; she then felt dizzy in one session, saying that talking about touching herself was very frightening.

At this point in the analysis she was able to talk about her adolescent masturbation struggles, which directly involved her mother. At about age 12 she came to believe that she could achieve orgasm only through use of a vibrator she found in her mother's bedroom. For the next four years she and the mother played a hide-and-seek game in which the mother would hide the vibrator from the daughter and the patient would search, almost ransack the house trying to find it. Then she would attempt to hide it from the mother, who would in turn pry about the patient's bedroom. The mother would retain possession of the vibrator for up to six months at a time, during which the patient would become frantic sexually, feeling that she was somehow prohibited from using her finger as she did during latency. This further increased her rage at the mother, who she felt could now control her masturbatory activities.

The transference continued to deepen. She found herself more and more wanting to look attractive for me and preened before coming to the sessions. She found these urges disgusting and nauseating as she talked about them in the session. A few times she rushed out to the clinic bathroom to vomit. She recalled vague feelings from early latency years of wondering if she was exciting to her father and grandfather, but she checked these feelings by trying to act "neuter." She was becoming more able in the analysis to make these connections on her own.

By this time I was becoming uneasy because the patient had steadily lost 27 pounds. However, she found the thought of becoming severely anorexic unacceptable. She had seen college students and pictures of women with severe anorexia and found them to look morbid and "crazy." In spite of the self-destructive nature of the bulimic pattern, the patient was always able to retain the picture of herself as being an attractive, sexually desirable woman. I felt this ability to be one of the patient's crucial ego strengths, in spite of the opposing beliefs of being damaged and disgusting. She sought out childhood foods to gorge and then vomit. Her only pleasurable sexual activities were fellatio and cunnilingus, and she ascribed this selectivity to the belief that only her mouth was alive and her genitals were dead.

The sexual transference emerged with more vigor as she vomited and lost weight. At times the material seemed to take an alternating pattern of gorging and vomiting followed by a period of calm and expression of sexual transference. Associations indicated that the taking in of food was an all-consuming wish for a love object, whereas the vomiting was the ejection of the love object because it was not acceptable to retain. The content of the transference themes vacillated from the analyst and the father as oedipal love objects to the mother as the wished-for preoedipal love object.

The patient began to delay her vomiting to see what would happen or what would enter her mind. There emerged a sexual fantasy of sitting in a steamy, tropical bar with a low-cut dress while a man sat in front of her, becoming excited and drawn toward her.

The parents wanted to talk with me directly at this point to ask if I would check her weight. The patient again intervened and said she wanted to handle the weight and the analysis herself. In the sessions, she expressed anger at her mother for not feeding the father properly and for not easing the father's worry about his own weight. She felt close to her father as he struggled with his diets. She was thrilled at a newfound ability to write long letters to her parents, describing her feeling states and expressing frustrations with them.

In one vivid session two and a half years into the analysis she related a feeling of being on fire and flying about the room exciting me with her sexual attractiveness. Then she pictured herself as dead, her body burnt up, an ugly piece of charcoal. Then she went back to feeling alive and excited. She felt elated that she could go between these two "selves" and have a feeling of control over them. This was one of the first clear evidences of observing ego and self-analyzing ability. She reported that she was beginning again to experience sexual pleasure in her body and genitals. She had an exciting dream of riding with me in a boat with the front end sticking up in the air. She became giddy as she talked about the dream and spontaneously connected it with her childhood memory of riding in the boat with her grandfather which ended in a confrontation with the mother. However, in this dream there was no confrontation. It was just a pleasurable experience.

She became more tolerant of her mother, picturing her as more of a real person. For the first time she also had early, positive memories involving the mother. The most vivid was of her mother making her a pink dress when she was 3 years old. She loved the dress and wore it often. At age 5 she believed that her mother became burdened with child care so that the clothes she made for her were dowdy and depressing. She linked her taking of clothing articles from her parents' bedroom, a practice that continued into her college years, to her belief that she was never given enough pretty clothes after this age. She had further memories of sadomasochistic sexual play with her next younger brother. They would sit on and suffocate each other with their genitals and buttocks. She recalled at age 7 looking excitedly at her father's *Playboy* magazines. For the first time in the analysis she acknowledged that her father had sexual feelings.

Her tendency to act out impulsively recurred at this time as she arranged some violent sexual activity with an old boyfriend. However, now she could talk about the fantasy she was having during the sexual activity. She imagined that her current boyfriend was standing outside the bedroom door vomiting on the floor because of what was going on with her and the old boyfriend inside the bedroom. I offered an interpretation that she may have been reversing roles; that is, the boyfriend outside the door may have been her standing outside her parents' bedroom door, feeling frightened and nauseated at what she thought was going on inside. The patient rejected this interpretation and, instead, made her own interpretation that engaging in sexual violence in the bedroom, with her current boyfriend outside the door, would make him feel violent. He would then vomit it out. Having gotten rid of all the violence, he would then be able to love her.

With further superego relaxation she could allow herself to become much more demanding of me. She felt angry if she thought I was unresponsive, and she wondered about changes in my voice. She began to express curiosity about my personal life, such as whether I had children or a wife. Up to now this had always been a taboo area for her. She began to fix pleasant meals for herself and her current boyfriend. After having a leisurely meal at a restaurant while reading a book as other college students did, she did not vomit up the meal, saying, "I feel I deserve to eat now."

The gorging/vomiting cycle now occurred every other day instead of daily. The patient attributed this decrease to her ability to talk about her wishes for me and her father, a topic she no longer found so nauseating. Although she was still tempted to use the vomiting to relieve any tension or anxiety, it started to lose its excitement for her. She compared herself to someone who had smoked cigarettes because of a strong emotional need but for whom, after a while, smoking became a "bad" habit, no longer fulfilling its original purpose.

Toward the end of the third year of analysis she returned to school by taking summer sessions to see if she was able to handle studies. To her surprise she found that for the first time she really enjoyed courses, could talk with professors, speak up in class, and concentrate on her homework. Also for the first time she allowed herself to imagine analysis someday being completed. She made a decision to use the couch regularly, saying that she could finally give up her old provocative "bad girl" façade.

Upon her return to school, she drifted away from her most recent boyfriend. I sensed this happened because of the continuing deepening of the transference and her belief that in order to do school work she could not be "tied" to a man.

She moved back into a campus dormitory to share a room with a female roommate. She felt doing this was a step toward gaining control of her gorging/vomiting pattern since she would no longer have a private bathroom. For the first time, she could become involved in a friendship with a roommate. They spent long hours talking about personal issues, with the patient often using insights gained in analysis to help her roommate.

This surge forward ran into immediate difficulty when the mother again threatened to end analysis, stating that the patient was becoming "too dependent on it." Several months of struggle culminated in the mother's agreeing to support analysis until the patient was graduated, at which time the insurance benefits would end.

The patient utilized this struggle with her mother to gain further independence but also as a defense against transference feelings. When the mother finally agreed to continue support of the analysis, the patient suddenly announced her wishes to terminate, as happened in early adolescence with her first analyst. Interpretations intensified around the patient's wishes to stop analysis as a defense against feelings toward the analyst and whom he represents. For the first time, she brought business assignments and worked on them in sessions. She stated she was doing homework because she was now bored with the sessions. It was obvious that she also wanted to show the analyst how complicated her work was and how well she was now doing academically.

As the turmoil over stopping analysis receded, sexual wishes concerning a man, particularly the analyst, were openly verbalized but still were experienced as humiliating and nauseating. Gorging and vomiting cycles were now reported as occurring every four days.

She brought her long-standing college boyfriend into the session one day and announced their intentions to marry immediately. Somewhat startled, I wondered if she and her boyfriend might consider a delay to allow the patient the opportunity to analyze the issue of marriage and what it meant for her now. Part of the decision to marry seemed to be an attempt to defuse and act out the intensifying transference. This particular boyfriend had been a key figure from the early days of analysis since his own issues appeared to play into the patient's old masochistic need for a sadistic, punitive love relationship. They agreed to a delay, and afterwards she became enraged at me for interfering like mother.

Following this tumultuous period, the patient experienced a spurt of ego growth. There was increased tolerance for her parents and their difficulties. She could talk about the parents' love for each other and the fact that she had to get on with her own life. However, this realization brought renewed fears as to whether her own cravings for a man would devour and destroy him. She stated: "If I delay my eating and vomiting and bring the feelings in here instead, it will be like releasing wild horses. Maybe I won't be able to control them." She then said, "If I were to say I love you, would you humiliate me?"

This more direct verbalization of wishes and their attendant concerns brought another cycle of the gorging and vomiting. This time it was accompanied by scratching and pinching minuscule pimples on her face. However, she was better able to contain the surge of wishes and their punishments in the sessions, since she received a top grade for the first time and felt even more excited about career opportunities. In the sessions she could now have fantasies of marrying and having a baby some day, whereas formerly she had always pictured herself as killing a baby from neglect and ineptitude.

With additional relaxation of superego strictures, she was able to write down a sexual fantasy of several years' duration and bring it into the hour for me to read. She was never able to verbalize this fantasy directly.

The fantasy consisted of her using a dildo on her mother, who initially experienced pain and discomfort that gradually gave way to gratification. Her father watched this scene in pleasure and pride. She then submitted to the father in sexual intercourse, during which the dildo was abandoned and the father assumed the active penetrating role. She was embarrassed about revealing this fantasy but also pleased that she could. She wrote down this story in flowing, descriptive language. She connected this with her growing ability to write personal letters and themes for her courses.

She now portrayed the gorging and vomiting as the price she must pay for her relationship with the analyst. She felt that any love relationship can only be maintained through suffering and degradation as symbolized by the degrading gorging/vomiting.

She reported a dream in which she inserted a tube into her insides to clean out "twenty-two years of shit" while her father stood by approvingly. Her first association to the dream was, "Is it all right to think of you wanting me?" She now hated the gorging/vomiting, picturing it as an unacceptable part of herself.

The analysis was now at the four-and-a-half-year point. The patient was about to receive her college degree and was interviewing for jobs in the area to permit continuation of analysis. She had made many gains in her ability to maintain self-esteem, tolerate frustration, and be more consistent in her work and relationships with lovers, colleagues, and authority figures. However, the bulimic vomiting cycle continued to occur every three or four days, although its increasing dystonicity raised hopes that it could be brought productively into the analysis.

The parents announced that they would definitely no longer financially support the analysis following the patient's graduation. The patient offered to pay for part of the analysis with future wages. Failing to persuade them, she requested that I meet with the parents. She declined my invitation to sit in with us. I felt in a difficult position. The parents requested a meeting to discuss the continuation of the analysis. I decided to meet with them because the patient had done considerable analytic work concerning her relationship with them and had achieved considerable late adolescent independence. She was more comfortable with verbalization and working on transference issues. It was hoped that whatever concerns might arise could be sufficiently analyzed. The patient had taken a job with a company whose insurance paid only a small part of the fee. At the time she accepted this job, she believed that her parents would continue to pay for a portion of the fees.

The parents changed their minds and agreed to support the analysis. During our meeting the father appeared somewhat depressed. However, within a few weeks they again reversed their decision, stating it was time for their daughter to become independent of them and analysis.

The patient thereupon experienced an array of emotions, including relief and pleasure at being "cut loose" by her parents, excitement at beginning her first full-time job, fears about putting the analysis in jeopardy, and anger at me for not offering a reduced fee, yet simultaneously saying a lower fee would not be acceptable. She vacillated between the possibility of appealing to her parents again for financial help, reducing the sessions from five to two sessions per week, or ending treatment altogether since it represented her "childish" past.

To complicate matters, the patient insisted upon a trial of antidepressant medications, having read material sent by her mother concerning the efficacy of drug therapy for bulimia. For some time her mother had been promulgating the use of antidepressants. Earlier suggestions of drug use had been vehemently rejected by the patient as interference with her autonomy and submission to the mother's domination. Now, however, she swung around to identifying with her mother on this issue. There was also evidence that with interruption in the wind, a medication might be a reassuring part-object similar to the taking of an article of clothing from the mother when returning to college from vacation. In general, I had always taken the position that she had the capacity to analyze and master the bulimic compromise formation through her analytic abilities and ego strength. The patient had been able to use this stance to ward off the mother's intrusion. Now, however, my analytic position was viewed as a maternal thwarting of her desires for medication. After considerable analytic work, the patient continued to wish for medication and asked for a referral to a psychiatrist for drug therapy. She expected me to say "no" and was surprised when I reminded her that this was her decision and that she was continuing to picture me as being like her mother, standing in the way of what she wished. Attempts to connect her wish for medication with her concerns about the possible interruption of analysis and the emerging oedipal transference that had been so prominent a short time before were in general unsuccessful.

The patient was placed on 150 mg. of imipramine per day by a psychiatrist. There was no reported change in her bulimic symptom, which continued every three to four days. However, she reported feeling somewhat calmer in contrast to her often turbulent affects. Meanwhile, in spite of initial anxiety, she performed well at work. Unanticipated apartment, car, and clothing expenses made it difficult for her to pay for the three sessions per week, the frequency agreed upon when the parents withdrew financial support.

In spite of this turmoil, she continued to have periods of good analytic work, punctuated by increasing concerns about ending analysis. The patient decided she wanted to be independent of analysis just as she had become more independent of her parents. She was adamant that this wish to end analysis not be within the sphere of our analytic scrutiny. She realized that analysis was not completed and was somewhat discouraged about the persistent bulimic symptom. I continued to express interest in analyzing these issues, at the same time acknowledging how difficult it was at this particular time to look at the many issues that were making her wish to interrupt the analysis.

Then one day she arrived angrily saying that this would be her last session for the time being and that she did not want any lengthy good-byes. She stated that it was her style to leave in anger because it was too painful to say good-bye.

Follow-Up

For the ensuing year the patient sent brief letters to me telling about how her job was progressing and how the bulimic symptom was faring. One letter told that the imipramine was ineffective so she was switched to phenelzine, which brought about a "miraculous" cessation of the bulimia.

Twelve months after interruption she asked for an appointment, stating that she still had sexual difficulties and wanted to work them out through further analysis. She had become involved with a new lover who was pushing for marriage. To her consternation, this deepening relationship had brought back her urges to gorge in spite of high levels of phenelzine (105 mg. daily). However, she felt the phenelzine allowed her to control the vomiting, and the result of retaining the gorged food was a sudden weight gain of 30 pounds. One of her long-standing beliefs about the vomiting was that it was only secondary to gorging, that is, a quick way to get rid of the excess calories and a control of large weight gains. She requested a return to treatment.

In her early return sessions she thought again of being in a room with a man, fixing a meal for him, with a cat or a baby in the background. This was one of the principle transference fantasies in the earlier analysis and it made an immediate reappearance. She seemed more tolerant of these thoughts and did not complain of feeling nauseated about them. Upon resumption of treatment, the patient now faces the central issue of further resolving the transference with its orally tinged oedipal wishes and their accompanying fears of loss of love and superego guilt, all of which result in the maladaptive, defensive, regressive symptom of gorging and vomiting. In addition, there is now the task of working through her nascent psychological dependency on the medication. Also related to the drug dependency issue is whether she will be able to achieve true ego mastery over these impulses without the affect-dampening of the medication (Wilson 1986, Wilson 1985a, Yager 1985).

DISCUSSION

The anamnestic data so far and the pattern of the bulimia's emergence during treatment suggest that the gorging/vomiting complex was present but for the most part latent until puberty. Prior to puberty, the patient's perceived loss of her mother during the oedipal phase and at the time of her retarded brother's birth was handled by defenses of inhibition, haughtiness, moderate asceticism, and denial of depressive affect. Struggles within herself over the rage at the perceived loss of the mother's care led to a constricted, unhappy latency period, leaving her ill-prepared for pubertal developmental tasks.

Following the loss of one of her few girlfriends during puberty, there was a regressive oral acting out of the conflictual issues over loss through an attempt at gorging and vomiting. Though this activity was apparently not repeated until analysis at age 18, there occurred other acting out of conflicts, particularly with her mother, such as the living out of the masturbatory fantasy involving the ownership and use of the vibrator. Blos (1966) has noted that the early adolescent phase is characterized generally by a shift toward acting rather than internal verbalization in the mastery of separation-individuation and oedipal issues which recrudesce at puberty. The acting out can be in the service of developmental progression. However, with this patient much of the acting was not sufficiently progressive and instead locked her into a developmental stalemate with both the external real mother and the internal infantile maternal imago (Ritvo 1984).

Her efforts to move toward the oedipal father and appropriate heterosexual adolescent relationships were repeatedly thwarted by fears of loss of love, guilt, and punishment at the hands of the threatening preoedipal and oedipal maternal introjects. The father's depressive trends and the parents' marital turmoil during the patient's early adolescent years further complicated these developmental efforts.

A period of psychoanalytic psychotherapy during early adolescence helped to stabilize her ego functioning and prevent further regression. It was probably fortunate that her therapist was a woman analyst whose neutral stance could mitigate the patient's fears of the witchlike internalized mother. Also crucial were the patient's basic ego strengths built in part upon positive internalizations of the mother.

298   Charles R. Keith, M.D.

By the time the patient began analysis at age 18, there was little evidence of any general forward movement in her adolescent developmental lines. In many ways she appeared still locked into the pubertal struggle with mother with only unsuccessful thrusts toward late adolescence independence, pleasurable mastery of work tasks, and achievement of stable heterosexual relationships. The principle benefit of analysis so far has been the partial freeing up of some of the adolescent developmental process so that the patient can work more productively, attain more stable love relationships, and have a firmer sense of autonomy and independence from the parents.

Thorny issues remain, however, particularly the continued propensity to act out rather than verbalize the wishes, fears, guilts, and defenses involved in the gorging/vomiting (Sperling 1967). What verbalizations and dystonicity she can produce concerning the bulimia in the analytic sessions still have insufficient carryover into her outside life, where she experiences the urges as "taking over." Ritvo (1984) has noted that the eating rituals and practices carried out with the readily available body and mouth make it more difficult for the adolescent with an eating disorder to bring the conflicts into the transference.

One might speculate that the phenelzine could provide the patient with more affect control, which would then allow more verbalization and ego control over the bulimia. So far there is little clinical evidence that this has happened. Though she reported at one time that there was a "miraculous" cessation of the bulimia, the respite proved fragile and broke down as she became intimate with a lover and returned to treatment. Any discussion of the effect of antidepressant medication is complicated by the fact that when the patient is upset she typically reduces the phenelzine dosage or stops the medication entirely, reflecting the old struggles with her mother. When the dosage is sufficient to stop the bulimia, she feels "estranged" and "iffy," a feeling resulting in further wishes to reduce or discontinue the medication.

From a psychobiological perspective, the history of affect disorder, at least in the male side of the family, suggests a possible diathesis toward affect disregulation. Clearly, she has a long-standing difficulty regulating her emotional life. Her old defenses of constriction and haughtiness were always prone to break down, with resulting temper tantrums and affect storms. However, this affectivity may have also been a positive factor, since it usually occurred in the presence of a love object and represented, in part, a strong, albeit stormy, thrust toward the object. Furthermore, the rages and angry depressions were punctuated by intense surges of loving feelings and positive wishes. She has always had and continues to have many men who are genuinely in love with her.

In discussing a case such as this, the question may arise as to whether she is a borderline individual requiring the necessary technical modifications or whether she functions at a neurotic level requiring usual analytic techniques. There are differing definitions of "borderline," but the patient's impulsivity, acting out, affectivity, and tendency to split maternal images into good and bad suggest commonly accepted borderline features. However, some hold to the view, as does this author, that for a diagnosis of the borderline condition there must be some evidence of ego weakness, specifically momentary losses of reality testing. No loss of reality testing has been discerned. Even during the most stormy periods of analysis, when she raged, slammed the office door, and threw objects in the office, she maintained a clear perception of the analyst's role and the importance of his neutral position. She once stated: "No matter how awful I am, don't come off your position with me. If you did, you'd no longer be the analyst and my treatment would have to end." Anorexic-bulimic symptomatology occurs in individuals with a wide range of ego functioning from higher-level neurotic through borderline to psychotic levels (Risen 1982). This patient has always appeared to function within the more severely neurotic portion of the spectrum.

A corollary of this impression of neurotic level functioning has been the patient's perception of her role vis-à-vis the parents, both inside and outside the analysis. The entanglements and separation-individuation difficulties with her parents, particularly the mother, along with the mother's ambivalence toward her daughter's independence, resulting in eventual withdrawal of support of treatment, are by now well-documented clinical phenomena in the anorexic-bulimic syndrome (Wilson 1985b). However, from the beginning of analysis the patient has always believed and perceived that her difficulties were not being "caused" by a parent but were primarily within herself and were her ultimate responsibility to resolve.

The central neurotogenic and therapeutic issue which stands out above all others so far in the analysis is the patient's sadistic, savage superego (Schwartz 1986). The superego beliefs are experienced by the patient as almost literal personae within her mind, demanding punishment and suffering for each forward step (negative therapeutic reaction). Interpretation and modification of the degradation and suffering demanded by the superego beliefs, as lived out in the gorging/vomiting, remain a central therapeutic task, since they block the expression of the underlying libidinal and aggressive wishes represented within the bulimic symptom.

REFERENCES

Blos, P. (1966). The concept of acting out in relation to the adolescent process. In *A Developmental Approach to Problems of Acting Out,* ed. E. N. Rexford, pp. 118–136. New York: International Universities Press.

Modell, A. H. (1971). The origin of certain forms of pre-oedipal guilt and the implications for a psychoanalytic theory of affects. *International Journal of Psycho-Analysis* 52:337–346.

Risen, S. E. (1982). The psychoanalytic treatment of an adolescent with anorexia nervosa. *Psychoanalytic Study of the Child* 37:433–460. New Haven, CT: Yale University Press.

Ritvo, S. (1984). The image and uses of the body in psychic conflict—with special reference to eating disorders in adolescence. *Psychoanalytic Study of the Child* 39:449–470. New Haven, CT: Yale University Press.

300   Charles R. Keith, M.D.

Schwartz, H. J. (1986). Bulimia: psychoanalytic perspectives. *Journal of the American Psychoanalytic Association* 34:439–462.
Sperling, M. (1967). Transference neurosis in patients with psychosomatic disorders. *Psychoanalytic Quarterly* 36:342–355.
Wilson C. P. (1968). Psychosomatic asthma and acting out: a case of bronchial asthma that developed de novo in the terminal phase of analysis. *International Journal of Psycho-Analysis* 49:330–333.
_____ (1985a). Psychodynamic and/or psychopharmacologic treatment of bulimic anorexia nervosa. In *Fear of Being Fat: The Treatment of Anorexia Nervosa and Bulimia,* rev. ed., ed. C. P. Wilson, C. C. Hogan, and I. L. Mintz, pp. 345–362. New York: Jason Aronson.
_____ (1985b). The family psychological profile and its therapeutic implications. In *Fear of Being Fat: The Treatment of Anorexia Nervosa and Bulimia,* rev. ed., ed. C. P. Wilson, C. G. Hogan, and I. L. Mintz, pp. 29–47. New York: Jason Aronson.
_____ (1986). The psychoanalytic psychotherapy of bulimic anorexia nervosa. In *Adolescent Psychiatry,* Vol. 13, ed. S. C. Feinstein, pp. 274–314. Chicago: University of Chicago Press.
Yager, J. (1985). The outpatient treatment of bulimia. *Bulletin of the Menninger Clinic* 49:203–226.

13

Anorexia Nervosa as an Expression of Ego-Defective Development

Cecil Mushatt, M.D.

Wilson (1982–1983), showing the primitive roots of the concerns of normal women about their body weight and appearance, has succeeded in providing us with a very important contribution to the psychoanalytic study of anorexia nervosa. The main focus here will be on certain aspects of the psychodynamic understanding of anorexia nervosa that bear on Dr. Wilson's paper. Dr. Wilson has given a very extensive clinical picture of the varied presenting issues in anorexia. His examples in the main, like those given by Sperling (1978), emphasize the part played by sexual conflict in the etiology of the illness. Sperling (1978) takes the position that anorexia nervosa is "a specific pathological outcome of unresolved oedipal conflicts in a female, who by her preoedipal relationship with her mother is predisposed to this particular reaction under certain precipitating circumstances" (p. 165). Wilson (1982–1983) places less emphasis on oedipal conflict and shows correctly that the illness can be derived from any level of psychosexual development. Earlier contributions (e.g., Waller et al. 1964) link sexual fantasies, especially pregnancy fantasies, with the precipitation of anorexia nervosa. Masserman (1941) and Leonard (1944) describe conflicts over assuming a female role as central.

Primary emphasis on sexual conflicts is a limiting and narrow view of the problem. These conflicts belong within a much broader model. Savitt (1980) points out that anorexia nervosa, like obesity, involves separation-individuation conflicts. Wilson refers to this concept, but he does not emphasize it to the extent that it should be as central to the development of illness. Anorexia nervosa is an expression of defective ego development arising from varying degrees of failure to resolve the separation-individuation processes and of failure to develop a sense of individuality. This determines the character of disturbances in object relationships. The more serious the symptoms of the illness, the more intense or primitive is the symbiotic level of functioning; although mild symptoms do not necessarily mean the opposite. Stating this in the reverse, the greater the impairment of the sense of separation of self from object, the more severe are the symptoms likely to be. This can be said of all psychosomatic illnesses, but it can be seen in very blatant form in anorexia nervosa.

The more defective the ego is in terms of separation of self from object, the more pronounced are primitive elements in the instinctual life and strivings and the less developed is control over transformation and sublimation of the instincts. Control in these circumstances demands the erection of massive defensive maneuvers. Ego defects result in persistence and intensification of pregenital and aggressive strivings. Such intensification of primitive strivings may in turn aggravate the defects in the ego. From this point of view, it is difficult to accept Sperling's (1978) view that anorexia nervosa is an "impulse disorder." Failure in instinctual maturation is here secondary to failure in ego development. The disruption of the process of separation-individuation also creates difficulties in establishing an integrated sense of sexual identity. In persons with ego defects, sexualization of all aspects of interpersonal relationships is fostered by the intensification of the need for sensory stimulation (e.g., by touch, fantasy of touch, vision, and oral fantasies and activities) to help maintain a sense of contact with the environment. This in turn intensifies the need for defensive formations.

The apparent predominance of sexual and aggressive conflicts and fantasies can best be understood within this framework. For example, focus on sexual and aggressive fantasies as ends in themselves can often lead to interminable analysis and failure of resolution. Understanding and translation of such conflicts into terms of ego strivings, developmental efforts toward resolution of the problems involved in separation-individuation, often will make for significant maturational development and relief of anorexic symptoms.

Wilson's emphasis on the fear of being fat rather than on the reluctance to eat and the desire to be thin in patients with anorexia and in normal women is very significant. This may seem at first sight a relatively unimportant distinction, but it is very valuable for the orientation that it induces toward the patient. It helps to focus on some of the major sources of conflict in anorexics, namely the fear of their voraciousness and insatiability, and with this of the intensity of their narcissism; with these are the patients' fear of destructiveness associated with such fantasies and the intolerance of the resulting archaic guilt that bedevils the lives of anorexic patients. These fears and fantasies can be understood as derived from the fear of separation, the fear of the destructive effect of separation on the object (mother and also father and siblings), and the rage over the apparent insoluble dilemma in regard to the struggle to achieve a sense of separateness.

On the more symbiotic level of functioning, there is heightening of ambivalence and, as was already mentioned, sexualization of all aspects of interpersonal relationships and difficulty in differentiating unconsciously between concrete and symbolic, between primary and secondary process. The fear of loss of control over impulses, referred to by Wilson (1982–1983), can be understood as a fear of loss of control over sexual appetite and aggression as expressions of the struggle to resolve the separation-individuation impasse, as well as the fear of loss of control over the desire for closeness. The desire for closeness unconsciously is equated with total merging with or total incorporation of the object.

The achievement of separation involves renunciation of old ambivalent identifications and taking in of new ones as a form of restitution for the loss and as a form of reunion. In their primitive thinking, the more impaired patients unconsciously equate incorporation and identification with destruction of the object in part or whole, and renunciation of identifications and separation also with destruction of the object. Here one sees how an intolerable impasse in development can arise with an enormous burden of guilt. Wilson (1982–1983) describes in some detail the family climate of patients who develop anorexia. Briefly, the environment is one in which the mother and father are unable to tolerate separation and strivings on the part of the child for growth. They infantilize the child and induce guilt over any effort toward independent behavior, while at the same time expecting perfection in behavior and achievement and control. Thus they create intolerable ambivalence, hostility, and guilt. The growing child unconsciously recognizes and identifies with the parents' fear of separation and unconsciously responds to the strong love–hate conflicts in the parents.

Several papers (Mushatt 1954, 1959, 1972, 1975) describe the manner in which bodily functions can express the separation-individuation process and the loss-destruction-restitution conflict. One example comes from the case of a young man, who, though not anorexic, for a long time ate only frugally on the excuse of lack of finances. He had had a symbiotic attachment to both parents and had found going to school as a child very difficult, and later it was extremely difficult for him to leave home to go to college. He was constantly preoccupied with his bowel functions. To pass even one day without a bowel movement made him very anxious, while he also felt unable to defecate or urinate in public toilets. He would hold back both until he could reach the privacy of his own home. At the same time, he was alarmed by stories of violence and rape and was afraid he would be attacked and raped anally by men. He was especially afraid that his wife would be attacked and raped. These fears justified for him his own rage toward men and his fantasies of attacking them anally. At the same time he came to recognize his own rage toward his wife for having "lured" him away from his mother. Both sets of fantasies were usually followed by longing to return home to his mother and father for safety.

Significant resolution of his projections of his fear of rape of himself and his wife and of his own hostile feelings was achieved by repeated analysis of his longings to return home to his mother and father. There came through the fantasy and his longing to be in bed with his parents, lying between them, with his father's penis in his rectum, and his own penis in his mother's rectum—a blissful state of complete union and sole possession of both parents. Threat of disruption of this blissful state aroused intense resentment and hostility in him. This material soon led to his remarking, on discussing his problem about "constipation," that defecating gave him a feeling of independence, a feeling of letting go of both his mother and father. These insights were now related to hitherto unconscious transference fantasies and were quickly followed by marked diminution in his preoccupation with newspaper reports of violence and rape and with his bowel activities. He was freed to pursue his career with much less conflict and to develop a more peaceful relationship with his wife. This example is significant because of the occurrence of constipation in anorectic patients, to which both Wilson (1982–1983) and Sperling (1978) make reference. Defecation can be expressive not only of riddance and destruction of the object but of separation, while constipation can express the holding onto introjected objects and retention of attachments (Mushatt 1980).

Preoccupation with violence and rape reappeared much later in this patient and was clearly related to primal scene fantasies. Primal scene fantasies and especially fantasies aroused by exposure to primal scene, reinforce regression to or fixation in a symbiotic position and interfere with the process of individuation. Furthermore, this patient's symptom of constipation was directly related to fantasies about violence. On later analysis, the primitive fantasy of the explosive destructive power of feces came through. Constipation to him represented a defense against the fantasy of destroying his parents by defecating on them. At the same time it expressed a desire to hold back his feces until he could possess even greater destructive power. In his adolescence, he lived out this fantasy symbolically by behavior endlessly provocative and troublesome for his parents.

Menstruation and amenorrhea can be approached in the same way in terms of their symbolic representations. In addition to arousing conflicts over pregnancy, castration fears, absence of a penis, and overdestructive fantasies, the bleeding can represent loss and separation: loss of a part of oneself, loss of the child in oneself, and separation from a childhood attachment to the mother. It can represent identification with the mother as a mature woman with loss of the image of oneself as a child. Amenorrhea can symbolize the retention of the image of oneself as a child, retention of childhood attachments, and denial of maturation. Menstruation can symbolize a sense of deprivation in human relationships. Depression over menstruation is often described as a reflection of disappointment at not being pregnant. In the more symbiotic type of woman, pregnancy can often internally symbolize, through identification with the fetus, the realization of the fantasy of symbiotic reunion of the child with the mother, and in this sense menstruation can symbolize the disruption of such a fantasy and the unconscious realization and confrontation of the reality of separation from the mother.

The symbolic equation of food and human objects is seen in its simplest form in an adult female patient's remark when examining her episodes of excessive eating: "I need a mother to take care of me, so I stuff myself with food, to be a mother to myself. I'd like you to take me in your arms, and let's pretend I am a baby and you are my mother." An alcoholic woman discussing the fact that she had innumerable friends throughout the country said, "My father hoarded food during the war [actual World War and "war" at home with his wife]; I hoard people."

The case of a young man with peptic ulcer and severe anorexia is a further example (Mushatt 1959). For him food and individuals in whole or in part became identical. Compulsive searching for companions took the place of meals, and when he did have companions at meal time, he could not eat because of his conscious and preconscious oral incorporative fantasies. Sharing a meal is a normal expression of friendship. It can be seen as an expression of a readiness for mutual identification, sharing each other with one another. Fear of overeating and thereby becoming fat can conceal not only hostile feelings but the effort to defend against narcissistic longings, entitlement, and the desire to have everything for oneself, and to restrain oneself against excessive closeness or possessiveness.

A man who complained especially of bouts of nausea, after announcing that he had undertaken a plan to reduce weight, went on to describe frequent dinner scenes with his large family. He told how when he noticed any member of his family eating slowly, he would ask, "Are you going to finish your meal?" On a recent such occasion, one son replied, "I think you want my dinner for yourself." The patient immediately recognized his fantasy of sweeping all the filled plates toward himself with his arms and eating all the food himself. This fantasy was a very vivid reflection of his *narcissistic entitlement* (Murray 1964). He had wanted children, wanted them close to him, but resented giving anything of himself to them, while expecting their complete devotion to him. He was jealous of them and the better circumstances in which they grew up. It is not surprising that all the children were very hostile to him but at the same time found it hard to live their lives independent of the father.

Food and its symbolic relationship to the task of separation from mother and father and to narcissistic entitlement can be seen again in the sequence of associations of a young married woman who had sought treatment for a variety of problems. For some time she had been feeling depressed over the departure of a close woman friend to a distant city to take a new job. In addition, she had been concerned about her mother, relatively recently widowed. The patient herself was still grieving over the death of her father. Her mother at this point lived at a considerable distance from the patient, making it difficult to visit. Her mother was now contemplating moving to the West Coast. The patient feared that she would not be able to see her mother if she moved. At the same time she felt torn between having her mother come to live closer to her and the desire to maintain some distance from her mother for the sake of her marriage. At times she felt tempted to have her mother come to live with her and her husband.

In one session the patient began by saying that she had decided to go on a diet. She felt that she was too fat (she would by no means be considered "fat"); it made her unattractive and set her apart from her women friends, who were all much thinner. She did not want to diet; she liked to eat, especially between meals. "I am naughty to be eating so much," she said, and then went on to give other examples of her sense of entitlement since childhood, which she called her "naughtiness," adding that she liked to do things like a defiant, naughty child. One of the recent "naughty" things she had done was to drive too fast on a trip to a reunion with her friend who had moved. The reunion had been a source of great pleasure to her. Then later in the session she stated that she had reached a compromise solution about her mother. Her husband had agreed that her mother could come to visit with her in their home and then spend a lengthy vacation within easy driving distance, so that the patient could visit with her mother either on weekdays or on weekends. She felt pleased with the arrangement and abruptly said, "The time is up and I can leave now." She had completed the circle from her concern about being fat and her love of eating to her expected reunion with her mother, and relief from guilt over the separation and over visiting her friend instead of her mother. In her next session, several days later, the patient was depressed, and there came through her profound sense of guilt toward her mother, especially over the fact that she was living in more affluent circumstances than her mother, and over all her naughtiness in relation to her mother. Finally she said: "I feel so guilty. I feel I can't care any more what I do, so I ate a lot today. But then I feel guilty over eating so much."

In the final remarks of this woman, there is the hint of the various physical symptoms seen in anorexia, especially the anorexia itself, that can find symbolic expression in various areas of the personality. Another woman, whose male friend had to move to a distant town because of his job, described how she now did not feel interested in eating since she had been alone. With her boyfriend present she could always eat a hearty meal, but now that she was alone, when she came home from work in the early evening, she would often go to sleep instead of preparing dinner, and on awakening several hours later she would be content with a meager snack. She now, as rarely occurred, reminded the therapist of her anorexia in adolescence and told of how her mother would often say, "You can always do without . . ." Then she remarked: "I think of looking for a new apartment, for new furniture, for new clothes, but eh! I can't stand it. I'd rather be outside doing anything but being in a store." This patient was not given to bulimia or extravagance in any form, but in other anorexics one often sees the expression of bulimia followed by vomiting in terms of what for them is extravagant spending of money on themselves and indulgence in pleasurable activities, both followed by extreme guilt and subsequent self-denial.

The stronger the fixation at or regression to a symbiotic position or partially symbiotic position, the stronger are narcissistic elements. Greater degrees of ambivalence, primitive aggression, pregenital sexual problems, archaic guilt, and magical thinking, and greater difficulty in sustaining new identifications that can undo the loss of older, more ambivalent identifications with key family figures, go with such a developmental position. All of this accounts, to a great extent, for the difficulty in treating such patients. The importance of the degree of narcissistic organization and the extreme sense of guilt enhanced by the unconscious demands of entitlement experienced by anorexics must be emphasized. In the more severe cases, it is easy to recognize the expectations of perfection, omnipotence and omniscience, the desire for complete subservience of the mother and the world—that is, complete control over key persons, internally represented by desire for control over the self and one's body, and the demand to be the one and only, worshipped by all. The intensity of these narcissistic expectations, and the continuing disappointment in achieving them, arouse a profound sense of inadequacy and helplessness, which promotes further intensification of the desire for infantilization. The resulting depression mobilizes rage and guilt. The degree of reaction to the failure to realize entitlement fantasies can be a measure of the degree of blurring of the boundaries between self and the outside world, a measure of the depth of symbiotic attachment. There are instances when the rejection of food expresses the fantasy of omnipotence and invulnerability because of the unconscious fantasy of complete union with the mother. Because of the symbiotic fantasy, there is no need to eat. To eat food is to acknowledge the fact of separation and of one's mortal being. One patient would fly into a rage at the sight of a funeral. It confronted her with her own mortal nature and the need to eat to live.

Not eating is frequently regarded as an expression of hostile rejection of the mother and father, and, as Wilson (1982–1983) points out, it causes suffering for the parents not only externally through worry and guilt, but by unconscious starvation of the introjected parents. However, the appearance of rejection of the parent can mask the fantasy of relentless attachment to the parent. In the more symbiotic patient, the line between love and hate can be blurred. The symptom, with its symbolic representations, can express both. Rejection of dependency on the analyst, rejection of identification with him in the analytic task, and, through that, rejection of the analyst's interpretations and help through understanding should not always be interpreted as hostile behavior. There are times when such behavior in anorexics is due to unconscious concern for the welfare of the therapist, determined by the unconscious equation of incorporation and identification with destruction in part or in whole of the therapist (Mushatt 1975, 1980).

As was indicated earlier, many of these observations are by no means exclusive or specific to anorexia nervosa, but in cases of anorexia one sees these elements in an extreme form. As Wilson indicates, anorexia may be precipitated by and expressive of conflicts from all levels of development, but when it occurs in patients with more mature egos, a significant measure of failure in earlier levels is requisite. The more integrated the ego organization, the more obscure and circumscribed are the primitive elements, and the more the latter are seen in highly derivative form. In the normal woman, the fear of being fat can be understood as derived from unresolved aspects of the more primitive conflicts outlined above, especially from the eternal struggle to solve the separation-individuation conflicts. Overeating, obesity, or relative overweight can be seen as reflecting unconsciously an individual's dependency and infantile longings for attachment, as well as reflecting narcissistic longings that are accompanied by shame, anger, and guilt. Guilt over narcissistic strivings and hostility can be relieved by fasting or token fasting, that is, by constraint and restriction of diet. To eat or not-to-eat can reflect the eternal conflict between love and hate in relationships, as well as conflict over unconscious desire to control sexual and aggressive appetites.

SUMMARY

The view is presented that primary emphasis on sexual conflicts, especially oedipal, as causative psychological factors in anorexia nervosa is a limiting approach to the problem. The symptomatology and sexual and aggressive conflicts and fantasies, with the accompanying defenses, can best be understood within the framework of the process of separation of self from object and the seemingly insoluble dilemma in regard to the struggle to achieve a sense of separateness and individuality. This has its effects on the development of the body image, with its internalized symbolic representations of the environment, and through the body image on the ego, superego, and instinctual life. Anorexia nervosa is an expression of ego-defective development arising from varying degrees of failure to resolve the process of developing a sense of individuality. There result primitive aggression, archaic guilt, and great difficulties in establishing an integrated sense of sexual identity. Sexualization of all aspects of interpersonal relationships is fostered by intensification of the need for sensory stimulation, such as by touch, the fantasy of touch, vision, and oral fantasies and activities. This leads to intensification of defenses against overt sexual expression on all levels, as well as against primitive aggressive fantasies and guilt. The symbolic significance of various symptoms in anorexia nervosa is discussed.*

---

*This chapter is reprinted with permission of the International Journal of Psychoanalytic Psychotherapy.

REFERENCES

Leonard, C. E. (1944). An analysis of a case of functional vomiting and bulimia. *Psychoanalytic Review* 31:1–18. Quoted by Sperling, M. (1978).

Masserman, J. H. (1941). Psychodynamisms in anorexia nervosa and neurotic vomiting. *Psychoanalytic Quarterly* 10:211–242. Quoted by Sperling M. (1978).

Murray, J. M. (1964). Narcissism and the ego ideal. *Journal of the American Psychoanalytic Association* 12:477–511.

Mushatt, C. (1954). Psychological aspects of non-specific ulcerative colitis. In *Recent Developments in Psychosomatic Medicine,* ed. E. D. Wittkower and R. A. Cleghorn. Philadelphia: Lippincott.

_____ (1959). Loss of sensory perception determining choice of symptom. In *On the Mysterious Leap from the Mind to the Body: A Workshop Study on the Theory of Conversion,* ed. F. Deutsch, pp. 201–234. New York: International Universities Press.

_____ (1972). Grief and anniversary reactions in a man of sixty-two. *International Journal of Psychoanalytic Psychotherapy* 1:83–106.

_____ (1975). Mind-body-environment: toward understanding the impact of loss on psyche and soma. *Psychoanalytic Quarterly* 44:81–106.

_____ (1980). Melitta Sperling memorial lecture. Presented at Psychoanalytic Association of New York, February 25.

Savitt, R. (1980). Discussion of "On the Fear of Being Fat in Female Psychology and Anorexia Nervosa," by C. P. Wilson. *Psychoanalytic Association of New York Bulletin* 17:809.

Sperling, M. (1978). Anorexia nervosa, In *Psychosomatic Disorders in Childhood,* pp. 131–173. New York: Jason Aronson.

Waller, J. V., Kaufman, M. R., and Deutsch, F. (1964). Anorexia nervosa: a psychosomatic entity. In *Evolution of Psychosomatic Concepts: Anorexia Nervosa, A Paradigm,* ed. M. R. Kaufman and M. Heiman, pp. 145–276. New York: International Universities Press.

Wilson, C. P. (1982–1983). The fear of being fat and anorexia nervosa. *International Journal of Psychoanalytic Psychotherapy* 9:233–256.

14

The Unconscious Role of Teeth in Anorexia and Bulimia: the Lizard Phenomenon

Ira L. Mintz, M.D.

HISTORICAL REVIEW

Cannibalistic behavior and fantasy have a long if not illustrious history. Frazer (1959) has detailed a plethora of overt cannibalistic behaviors in diverse tribes around the world. He described the Jagas, an Angolan tribe, who put all their babies to death during forced, conquering marches in order not to slow down the women. The tribe would then eat their captives and adopt the adolescent children of the parents whom they had eaten.

He illustrated the incorporative quality of thinking in savage people, who believed that eating the flesh of an animal or man provided them with the physical, intellectual, and psychological qualities of the consumed object.

Osiris, god of the Egyptians, encouraged their renunciation of savagery and cannibalism.

Some North American Indian tribes believed that consuming the flesh of a particular animal provided the Indian with the outstanding physical attributes of that animal; for example, venison provided swiftness and intelligence. Indians in Ecuador would eat the flesh of the bird, monkey, and deer to assure agility.

Caribs avoided eating pigs, out of fear of developing small eyes. Bushmen avoided timidity by not eating a jackal's heart but did consume the heart of the brave leopard. Carrying the idea further, different tribes ate the body parts and blood of dead men to incorporate their bravery, strength, wisdom, and other qualities. The human heart is particularly imbued with courage and virtue. After enemies and other victims are killed, the killer often consumes their hearts. The Sioux Indians would eat the powdered heart of a courageous enemy in order to absorb his valor. The headhunters of the Celebes would eat their victims' brains and drink their blood to increase their bravery. Indians of the Orinoco region used to toast and powder the hearts of their enemies and drink the liquid to increase their bravery before battle. Ancient Mexican priests would smear their bodies with an ointment made from the ashes of poisonous snakes, spiders, and scorpions to increase their bravery, and then set the mixture before the God as a divine food. They apparently felt that the power derived from the reptiles could be absorbed through the skin as well as by ingestion.

Cannibalistic themes emerge also in painting and sculpture. One of Goya's black paintings at the Prado, painted during a period of turmoil, is that of a man eating a child. The famous water fountain figures of Berne, Switzerland, except for the Zahringer fountain, were created in the second quarter of the sixteenth century by Hans Gieng. One of these, the *Kindlifresser,* is that of a man holding three children in one arm while consuming the fourth.

Fairy tales contain cannibalistic themes: "Little Red Riding Hood and the Wolf," "The Gingerbread Boy and the Fox," and "Hansel and Gretel and the Witch." In addition, contemporary theater has its cannibalistic productions, such as *Sweeney Todd* and *The Little Shop of Horrors.*

Finally we have overt cannibalistic behavior to stave off starvation. Freud's first attempt in 1912–1913 to understand the formation of primitive societies concluded that the leader of the group was killed and eaten by his sons. In a more current paper, Schlossman (1991), utilizing mythology, religion, and archaeological studies, analyzes the changes that may have taken place beginning with prehistoric man and continuing through biblical times. He notes the evidence of cannibalism in France with bones dated from 4000 B.C.

In his paper, Mahon (1981) compares the many references to animals in literature with the paucity of animal references in psychoanalytic literature. Starting with Freud's cases of Little Hans, The Wolf Man, and The Rat Man, he lists references in Ferenczi, Abraham, Heiman, Pearson, Volkan, Kupferman, and Shengold. The thrust of Mahon's developmental study is to point out the importance of pets in the unfolding world of the infant-child's object relatedness. He postulates that beyond the infant's primary relationship to the mother, which merges into Winnicott's world of transitional objects, is another stage of the child's relatedness to animals.

The animal "can be fed, toilet trained, beaten, killed and mourned." The choice of the animal "reveals much about the instinctual needs, the psychic structures and the developmental tensions of the child." Relating to animals permits the child to expand the nature and quality of his or her relationship beyond the transitional object.

Freud's Rat Man (1909, p. 165) described the incident that precipitated his entry into analysis: a conversation with a cruel captain who described a bound prisoner whose buttocks were exposed to a group of rats that "bored their way" into his anus. Shengold (1967, p. 403) emphasizes that Freud's case illustrates "that the rat can stand for subject or object of any stage of libidinal development, but is particularly associated with eating and being eaten, and with anal erogeneity."

Shengold (1963, 1967, 1971) deals with patients' regressive cannibalistic preoccupations as a consequence of overstimulation in childhood by seduction and being beaten by psychotic parents. He feels that the patient in repetition compulsion fashion (1967) relives the earlier trauma:

> I try to show the importance of fixation on, and regression to, the cannibalistic level of libido development, with concomitant mal development and regression of the ego. . . . I view the image of the rat as a kind of hallmark indicating cannibalism. The omnivorous destructiveness, murder, and cannibalism directed against members of its own species, and perhaps above all the remarkable teeth of the rat, have established it as one of the chief cannibalistic imagos (others are spider, wolf, snake, vampire, sphinx, witch). [p. 403]

I should certainly concur and add shark, lizard, dragon, piranha, and gerbil, illustrated by the subsequent case material.

Shengold's (1971) paper further amplifies the psychodynamic relevance of the rat as the symbolic carrier of issues related to infantile experience, oral and anal sadistic drives, cannibalistic impulses, and castration anxiety, and examines the role of teeth in both the rat and the developing infant.

Schwartz (1988), in his review of the literature on the meaning of food, notes Janet's 1906 report of a 22-year-old woman suffering from "boulimia" who "wished to run or to ride horseback the whole day." He adds that Sours (1980) and Risen (1982) mentioned that their women patients with eating disorders were "horse-crazy." Schowalter (1983), studying the unconscious meaning of horses, mentioned that his patient was bulimic. In studying the unconscious psychodynamic meaning of the horse, Schwartz (1988) refers to the additional work of A. Freud, Fraiberg, Pearson, Glover and Mendell, and Hendrick, in which the adolescent girl attempts to undo castration anxiety by using the horse as a restitutive phallus, which facilitates identification with the father and also serves as an external primary regulator of self-esteem. This concept was further confirmed by Thomä (1967) in the study of his anorexic patients and by Blos (1974).

Oliner (1988) described a case of a woman who was a compulsive overeater. She was unable to eat the meat that she cooked, because she saw it change from the raw to the cooked state, so she and her husband ate different foods. At that time she mentioned a dream in which "a rat was gnawing at her dress." Oliner concluded that there were unconscious cannibalistic fantasies preventing the patient from eating the meat and referred to Shengold's concept of the rat as related to cannibalism, anal penetration, and dirt. She mentioned another overeating patient who, as a child, would rush from the flushed toilet because of a fear of mice coming out of the toilet.

Gesensway (1988) described a bulimic patient with a fear of spiders that he felt reflected her childhood view of her own genitals: "She regarded her own vulva as a shameful wound: slimy, wet and creepy, yet the source from which babies came. Babies, like spiders, emerge and crawl, having been buried alive, and like her baby siblings, were objects of destructive aggression. Babies were at first like cancers, slimy, wet, and creepy, growing inside making the belly distent." He concluded that the patient's fear of "spiders represented her forbidden wishes for her father's penis-baby as well as her oral aggression (the black widow) against her mother and mother's babies" (p. 317).

Sperling (1971) discussed eight cases in her paper on spider phobias and fantasies: three children, two adolescents, and three adults. She felt that although the cases differed clinically, there were particular genetic and dynamic similarities of considerable relevance. "All these patients experienced maternal rejection in their childhood together with a high degree of overstimulation particularly in the visual spheres. . . . The mother's identification of the child with an unconsciously hated and rejected part of herself is an important genetic factor in the development of psychosis in the child" (p. 490).

Sperling concluded that the use of the spider symbol occurred at points of great turmoil when the patients experienced overwhelming anxiety and concomitant concern over ego dissolution. Preoccupation with the spider prevented flooding by uncontrollable pregenital fantasies and impulses. Moreover, she felt that unless the spider core were analyzed, the underlying fantasies would continue to threaten psychic equilibrium. While she agreed with other clinicians that the spider symbolizes the "orally devouring and anally castrating mother," and that the major conflicts of these patients evolve about their sexual identifications, she emphasized that the patient's view of the mother is a consequence of her "own denied oral and anal-sadistic impulses."

In considering symptom choice, Sperling felt that the spider reflected an anal-sadistic fixation in a preponderantly hostile but overattached relationship to the mother. In support of this thesis she cited one patient's intense separation anxiety from the mother, culminating in a severe anxiety attack during which she experienced a giant spider attempting to engulf her with its many legs so that she could not free herself. Anal birth fantasies in which the baby-fetus was discarded as worthless feces contributed to an additional component of the spider choice. In addition, since the satisfying achievement of sphincter and impulse control is so important during the anal stage of development, the rejection from and hostility toward the mother impaired this potentially gratifying experience, with the frustration projected on to the spider-mother. The spider also reflects the patient's devalued self-image and guilt for her own perceived disgusting and hostile feelings.

In another paper, Sperling (1968) described a patient with a terrible fear that insects would fly into her mouth. Pulling out her hair and eating it would result in the sensation of swallowing live insects, which symbolized sperm, feces, and intense dependence upon her mother.

Rudominer (1984) reported a dream of a male anorexic who described how "a spider jumped into his mouth." Barkin's anorexic patient also described a fantasy about being eaten by maggots (1989).

Wilson (1985b) reported a 16-year-old anorexic girl who dreamed, "A man was a vampire in the house with me and another woman. He wanted to kill us or suck our blood" (p. 251). Associations led to two previous repetitive dreams of a "stone cottage with a lake" and "a stone castle by a lake." Wilson interpreted that the stone symbols represented teeth and oral drives and that the patient "projected her devouring impulses onto men and the analyst . . . when threatened by separation" (p. 251).

He also described another anorexic woman's dream that she "was aware of rats and mice running under the couch." Associations were to other dreams of rats that Wilson felt "reflected fears of being bitten and being entered anally."

Hogan (1985) described an anorexic woman's conflict over childbirth, which initiated a bout of colitis and a dream of her cat giving anal birth to bloody kittens. Associations were made to her disliked sister.

THE LIZARD PHENOMENON IN MALE ANOREXIA

Eric

The first case is presented because the patient's symptoms, behavior, and dynamic conflicts most clearly illustrate the theme of the "lizard phenomenon" in his plethora of animal identifications. It also clarifies the position of the animal symbolism in the genetic origin and unconscious preoccupations of his anorexia along with manifest cannibalistic conflicts.

Eric was a 10-year-old boy referred by his pediatrician after a physical workup because of an increasingly severe diet over ten weeks during which his weight plummeted from 80 to 55 pounds. His mother reported that he had appeared unhappy during his Christmas vacation and became irritable and morose. Following vacation he stopped eating almost all food and would pick at whatever was on his plate, moving it about rather than eating it. He renounced all the foods that he had previously enjoyed, now preferring diet soda, salad, and typical low-calorie foods. At the same time, however, the mother astutely noted that he became unduly preoccupied with food, although he said that he didn't like food anymore. He constantly asked what they were having to eat and compulsively rummaged through the refrigerator and kitchen cabinets. The mother added that Eric watched everything the family ate, "every morsel that goes into our mouths, almost as if he'd like to eat but something is holding him back." He would often attempt to get his little sister to eat more, to the degree that the mother would insist that he stop trying to force-feed her.

The mother also recognized a personality change. He became tense, fidgety, and irritable, and his restlessness was marked. It appeared that he could not remain still. He was almost unable to sit. He watched television standing up and kept pacing restlessly from one room to another. The teacher reported that he disturbed the class by moving his feet up and down as he sat at his desk. He used to love sports, and before he got too weak he exercised constantly. However, although avoiding sports and exercise, "just when you thought that he had no strength left" he would ride the mother's exercise bicycle.

The father interjected that Eric had become very withdrawn and no longer spent time with his friends. Instead he returned home after school and just hung about the house with a very forlorn expression. He was no longer spontaneous, and when asked questions about his day, he would respond with, "I don't know." The mother added that he also developed the habit of following her all over the house. After eating at McDonalds, he began demanding milk shakes. "For the past weeks, that's all that he ate. He has four milk shakes at seven P.M. and then goes to bed and doesn't eat or drink again for twenty-four hours. Not a drop of food or water passes his lips."

Prior to the present illness, the parents felt that he was well adjusted. He had a number of friends, got good grades, and was well thought of by the teachers. He was developing into a good athlete, played basketball with his friends, and was beginning to enjoy tennis with his father. He became interested in chess at a young age and frequently was able to beat his father and older brother. He got along well with his older brother, but not with his sister, who was three years younger. She was very competitive, provocative, and headstrong. She was very well coordinated and repeatedly challenged him both in athletics and in other circumstances. Often she would tease him and openly provoke a fight. Prior to the development of the anorexia he would accept the challenge, and in the ensuing melee she was often sent off crying. Since the onset of anorexia, however, he avoided fighting, passively submitting to her bullying.

In the second interview the mother spontaneously commented that, although she never remembered any feeding difficulties, about eight months prior to the starving, Eric told her that he felt too fat. The mother replied that he tended to be heavy the way *she* was, while his sister and brother were thin like the father.

The conversation occurred at a time when the father's sister became pregnant with her first child. Although this aunt lived in a different state, her husband was a traveling salesman and would often drive her to the patient's home to stay for a few days while he was out of town. Eric's starving seemed to begin just after his aunt gave birth to a little girl.

Eric was born and spent his first four years in California, where the father was a lawyer for a large corporation. Then he was transferred to the East, where the family resided in a small suburban community. The mother preferred the East, where she was near her family and especially her three sisters, with whom she was very close. The father had to make periodic business trips to California, which set off separation anxieties in Eric with fears that the plane might crash.

When seen in consultation, Eric was a taller-than-average 10-year-old with stylish black hair that hung over one eye and a somewhat noticeable scar on his chin from a bicycle accident. His outstanding characteristic, in addition to his weight loss, was a profound sense of sadness that contributed to his forlorn appearance. He replied to questions or comments briefly and in a monotonous, almost inaudible tone. He agreed that he wasn't eating, had no interest in eating, and felt full whenever he ate. He added that when he ate now he began to "feel weird inside" and "the food moves about" in his stomach. He acknowledged that he had lost 25 pounds. He denied feeling thin, but his subsequent associations were that he always felt cold no matter what he wore, and he frequently felt tired. His major worry seemed to be that he would not do well in school, although most of his grades were A. He volunteered that he resented doing so much homework. He acknowledged that he had a lot of friends but hadn't seen them very much recently because he wasn't interested in being with them or in playing sports. He also mentioned that prior to Christmas, he had had no difficulty eating and used to enjoy food, often taking two or three helpings.

In the second session he asked permission to stand because he needed to walk back and forth, and if he couldn't, he had to walk in place. Otherwise he got unpleasant tingling sensations in his upper thighs. He even had to walk in place while he sat at his desk in school. This walking began after he started starving, and he couldn't stop or the tingling would get worse. At that point, he began to cry. Sometimes when he was tired at the end of the day, he couldn't walk, and the tingling got worse and he didn't know what to do. He did not initially ask me for permission to stand up and walk because he was afraid that I would get angry with him. Again I was struck by his sadness.

A detailed description of the actual treatment is described elsewhere (Mintz 1985c), but it is of dynamic and technical interest to view here the emergence of the aggressive fantasies. Brief aspects of the treatment process will be provided. In these cases, particularly where great weight loss has occurred with the spectre of hospitalization looming ahead, an active interpretative approach is vital.

When he spoke about eating nothing but milk shakes, I pointed out that not eating could make him sick. In response to his feeling that I was pressuring him, I told him that I would not pressure him to eat, but if he was like other children with this illness, he had other problems that he was covering up and was focusing on not eating instead. We discussed his choice of just drinking milk and I pointed out that babies drink only milk. He added that his little cousin was born in December. We spoke more about babies, and I suggested that he might be afraid of growing up and wished to remain little.

In the first seven sessions he was guarded, defensive, accusatory, and plaintive. He feared that I would pressure him to eat, would yell at him (though I spoke softly), and would pressure him to talk when he had nothing to say. I said that he had difficulty talking because he kept his thoughts inside and did not trust me. He then commented that it all began when he heard that his aunt was pregnant and he began to think of being fat. The starving started just after she gave birth.

In sessions 9 through 15 he talked about how babies are made and discussed his little sister. Subsequent sessions facilitated the release of a great deal of repressed hatred toward the sister, resulting in a dramatic improvement in his appearance, the alleviation of his depression, and aggressive behavior toward his sister. Following a number of discussions about his hatred toward his sister he began a session with the comment that he had so many ideas that he didn't know which one I'd like to hear about.

It was at this time that he spoke at great length about his interest in lizards, especially those with teeth, and in snakes that eat live mice. It was my impression that a developing therapeutic alliance, emerging trust, feeling better, being able to verbalize his destructive impulses, and a newly developing relatively positive transference all contributed to the emergence of these fantasies. This was the first session in which there was no pacing or walking about.

The following week, in discussing further his resentment toward his sister, I commented that the birth of his little cousin probably reminded him of how annoyed he must have been when his little sister was born. Referring to the new cousin he commented, "You can't pick her up and throw" and stopped. I interjected, "and throw her. That's what you might have wanted to do with your baby sister." He spoke about how his sister once climbed into the clothes dryer and closed the door, suggesting his additional impulse to return her to where she came from. In a subsequent session he revealed that his worst thought about his sister was his fear of killing her and then getting punished. A week later he remembered that at age 8 he had thought of getting a knife and stabbing her in the heart. During another session he remembered wishing that she were dead.

His comment about feeling full associated with the food moving around in his stomach and feeling "weird inside" suggested his unconsciously identifying with being pregnant, the disturbance it created to his sense of masculine identity, and the anger towards his sister for being born.

In the third month he described the movie *Pete and the Dragon,* in which Pete was made a slave by his parents. Pete had an invisible dragon that protected him from the cruelty of his parents and from his mean teacher. I added that it might be nice if a boy had a dragon that protected him and that maybe he wished to have a strong friend instead of being strong himself. He replied that he had been trying to get a pet iguana like the giant komodo lizard, which was 15 feet long and ate deer and buffalo. He drew a picture of the lizard with its mouth full of alligator-like teeth and a picture of a pet iguana as its miniature prototype.

In one session during an outpouring of talk about babies, Eric corrected, or was more open about, his knowledge of their birth. He spoke about a television program on which a baby died from a cord around its neck, and he knew that babies begin with a penis into the vagina and not by a seed. He also knew all about the umbilical cord, and he saw that his little cousin had the end of it drying up. From a television program he also heard about circumcision and how the end of the penis is cut off. He wondered recently if he were growing an extra knee, but his father said that it was just his muscle. He also read about a person who had three legs, he saw a picture of a horse with three eyes, and he knew of a museum that had a cow with five legs.

The patient seemed to be dealing with his castration anxiety and with compensatory attempts at coping with it. It is not unreasonable to consider that the sight of his little girl cousin's absence of a penis initiated castration threats, which were then reinforced by the upward view of the remains of the umbilical cord: a displaced, drying up, withering penile stump. He was already bewildered over threats to his masculine identity, through his identification with the aunt-mother during her pregnancy, and filled with death starving wishes toward the little cousin-sister, with anticipation of retaliatory castration-death, and these conflicts each played a role in the ultimate coalescing of a self-destructive starvation syndrome. In it, he attempted unconsciously to clarify his own identity and, concomitantly, identify with the sister in his attempt to starve and kill her.

The misperception that he was growing an extra knee-penis and that all kinds of animals can have extra limb-penises represented a fantasied restitutive attempt to cope with castration anxieties. The muscle tissue in his body, unconsciously viewed by him as a symbolic penis and lost or dried up by starvation, reflected his ambivalent attitude about whether his identification was masculine or feminine. The starving and the loss of tissue-penises can represent a flight from a masculine identity, while at the same time the loss of fat can be viewed as an attempt to rid himself of an inner picture of being pregnant and feminine. Thus the tissue can represent aspects of both masculine and feminine identities, depending upon how the ego views it at different points in time and in consonance with other aspects of life experience and the inner sense of self. What is also interesting is that anorexic women have the same kinds of unconscious perceptions about their body tissue (Mintz 1985a).

In the fourth month he described increasing manifestations of his oral destructiveness. He reported an avid interest in biology and would spend many hours in the library perusing books on lizards, rodents, and biting insects. He was particularly fascinated by the surge of rat movies, including *Willard,* in which a boy befriended rats, who then became his friends and allies. He recounted with some sense of sadistic glee how the rats would eat and destroy anyone who mocked the boy or stood in his way. He identified further with the boy in the movie by searching for rats after rainstorms and, seeing a number of them coming out of storm sewers, attempting to get close to them, almost as if he were attempting to emulate the boy in the movie and make them his allies. He described the movie *Ben,* about a leader of the rats, friendly with a boy; Ben along with thousands of other rats attack, destroy, and eat people alive. He also reported a third movie in which a special food grew 10-foot-tall giant rats.

In another session Eric spoke about visiting a farm and seeing how the farmer caught rats in traps. He remembered seeing the rats with their necks cut and their tongues hanging out. I pointed out that after he spoke about what a pest his sister was, he spoke about how the rats got killed. "My sister is a rat," he responded. Two sessions later he reported a Dracula movie in which the vampire bit the girl three times in the neck, after which he could control her. I wondered aloud that if the vampire could control the girl by biting her in the neck, maybe he thought that it might also work with his sister. He replied that you couldn't control her no matter what you did.

In the fifth month he spent two or three weeks discussing his preoccupation with sharks. He had spent one whole Saturday in the library reading about sharks and their feeding frenzies, during which they eat everything in sight. "A fisherman was bitten by a shark . . . and sharks like to eat dolphin babies . . . my friend's little cousin bites people and they call him 'Jaws III.' . . . the piranha fish that ate a man's leg . . . a tribe of Indians cuts the enemies' heads off . . . When I went fishing, we cut the fish up for bait . . . and I cut out the insides of the fish and cut out the eyes. . . . Once I cut one fish open and found pink and white eggs . . . I felt sick to my stomach." Preoccupied with destructive, cannibalistic impulses and fantasies, it seemed apparent that the fishing trip facilitated the emergence of these murderous impulses to rip open his mother and kill his sister and that the fish eggs represented these babies. The erupting guilt resulted in the described squeamish feelings, which ultimately led to the starvation and the eating difficulties. Subsequently he described the movie *Jaws,* in which a diver found a man's head with one eye missing. Here he identified with the destructive shark by ripping open the fish and cutting out the eyes. He then described a whole series of frightening dreams, one of which was, "I am being sawed up and I wake up scared." His aggression is denied and projected into the mechanical shark (the saw) and he becomes its victim.

He then confidentially reported a series of cannibal dreams and revealed that he had experienced them over a number of years. "I'm on an island with a girl and we watch cannibals chasing someone and throw a spear at him pinning him to the tree. They pull him apart and roast the parts of his body on a spit." He obliged by drawing a picture of the dream: a man's head, arm, and leg skewered by the spit and being roasted over the fire. He associated to a picture he saw of a pig being roasted over the fire about two months before his anorexia began.

Another dream: "I am with a girlfriend and the boat gets turned over and we end up on an island where cannibals cut people's heads off . . . and put them in a pot and boil and eat them.''

In another hour he revealed that he had had such dreams since the second grade, sometimes as many as three or four a week. Thus we see that while the overt manifestations of his illness began with an eating disorder at the age of 10, the seeds of the conflict were clearly present at least four years earlier. With this perspective one can view the anorexic illness as the culmination and decompensation of a long-standing conflict in which the physical illness is the surface manifestation rather than a suddenly erupting new disease.

Discussion

The patient was now beginning the sixth month of treatment. We had already discussed and explored certain dynamics of his anorexia: ideas about oral impregnation, his self-image in which he needed to be weak in order to minimize the impact of his aggressive impulses, his concern that being heavy would link him too closely with his mother and a feminine identification, his aggressive and murderous impulses toward his sister, his wish to remain a little boy, a baby drinking only milk, and his defiant not eating in response to being forced to clean his plate or be punished. These discussions had resulted in a great deal of improvement. He renounced his passivity and reaction formations toward his sister and schoolmates, he recovered from his depression, and he returned to an active play, school, and sports life. He put on 20 pounds and was unconcerned about the increase in body tissue. His restless pacing ceased.

Still he ate not a morsel of food nor drank an ounce of water. He drank only his milk shakes.

The treatment was progressing satisfactorily. Appropriate and necessary character changes had taken place, but the resolution of the crucial factor of cannibalism was essential to his resumption of eating regular food with the use of his teeth. It was because of that essential feature that I was especially careful not to make a premature interpretation about his oral sadistic impulses, for fear that his discussions about them would cease. Weeks passed as he progressed from descriptions of a desired alliance with a fantasied dragon, which was miniaturized into an iguana, to his interests in rats and snakes with the beginnings of eating live animals and humans, to his preoccupation with sharks, and finally to the actual cannibalistic preoccupations in story and in dream.

Once the sequences of associations progressed to cannibalistic dreams, I felt that it was appropriate to interpret his cannibalistic destructiveness. In a session discussing the cannibals, I noted that I thought I understood more of his eating trouble. I stated that he had been talking about how people eat sheep and other animals, and at the same time talking about how cannibals eat people. I thought that, in the back of his mind, his idea about eating meat and regular food made him feel somewhat like a cannibal and that was why he did not eat it. He reacted with perplexity and denial. "Why would I want to eat people?" I told him that he felt so angry with his sister at times that he said that he wished her dead or thought about sticking a knife into her. Maybe in the back of his mind he also thought of destroying her by eating her. While the perplexity and the denial continued, his questioning and statements indicated that the ideas had made some connection: "I wouldn't do that because if I began to cook her, people would see the smoke from the fire (as on the cannibal island) and they would find out. Besides, my father is a lawyer and he knows judges who send you to prison. I wouldn't know where to bury the bones. They would dig them up, and then I'd go to jail." I acknowledged that the situation as he described it did indeed present him with a great dilemma and that not wanting to give in to his impulse to eat her resulted in his inability to eat all meat and other food.

The next morning Eric's mother called to say that Eric had eaten his first meal in six months.

Herbert

Herbert was a 14-year-old boy referred by his uncle, a local surgeon, because of a chronic pattern of bizarre eating habits resulting in an emaciated state. The parents in consultation, described eating difficulties beginning in his first year of life. Currently Herbert was 5 feet, 8 inches and weighed 92 pounds. The father, a forceful-appearing corporate executive, stated that Herbert's difficulties had been present for so long that he and his wife had gotten used to them, but currently they were concerned about his emaciated appearance. While the father dominated the conversation, the mother timidly added comments to amplify the father's description, but she never contradicted him.

The mother said that she was concerned because Herbert had no friends. Children would come over to play with his three younger brothers but never with him. He would play with the more timid boys, or an occasional girl who visited. The father added gruffly that he could not interest the patient in sports from the time he was little, no matter how hard the father tried. His younger brothers, ages 11, 9, and 6, were better coordinated, better athletes and more sports oriented. Herbert's interests were drawing, painting, chess, jewelry making, and raising tropical fish and hamsters. He occasionally rode his bike or took a walk.

The mother volunteered that Herbert had not been a problem at school. He was reserved and obedient, did his work, and tried to stay out of trouble. Grades were usually B's; some teachers felt that he was not working up to his abilities. The mother noted that he had no friends in school. When he was 7 to 8, the children used to pick on him and call him names, and he would come home crying. Once a bully took his new camera and Herbert just let him have it, not even reporting the incident to the teacher or to his mother.

The mother reported that Herbert was an unplanned pregnancy, but she was delighted and the pregnancy and delivery were uneventful. He was breast-fed for seven months as were the other three children. "They took everything out of me, and I lost 15 pounds. I loved it." Four months after Herbert was born, the mother returned to law school. After she graduated, the family moved around quite a bit because of the father's transfers to different corporate offices.

At age 2, Herbert was enrolled in nursery school. All the teachers commented about his strange eating habits: he had specific preferences of the food he would touch and the way it had to be prepared. He managed by bringing dry cereal for his own snack. During his first few years he was thin, but the pediatrician did not seem concerned.

The father mentioned that Herbert was a bed wetter until the age of 6 and remembered the mother's persistent attempts to get Herbert to eat—telling him to eat this for mother and that for father. As he got older he would reply that he couldn't eat the food or he would vomit. Gradually the mother renounced her attempts at getting Herbert to eat.

The mother remembered that he had tics of the eye and head from ages 2 to 4. At 7, while attempting to ride a bicycle, he fell and broke his left wrist. The mother recalled he was a happy and affectionate infant and child. He still enjoyed hugging and kissing his mother and father, and occasionally his brothers. The father stated that Herbert never liked aggressive boys and thought that might have played a role in his lack of friends. The younger brothers didn't seem to mind aggressive play. The mother noted that Herbert spent a great deal of time alone in his room, reading, painting, and redecorating the room over and over. "He does pretty paintings and gives them to me for birthday gifts." The mother stated that the family was not unduly modest, and the boys walked into her room occasionally while she was dressing.

The mother's comment about breast-feeding was interesting. "They took everything out of me, and I lost 15 pounds. I loved it. He always loved milk." Since she was of normal body build and weight loss was not desirable, this comment suggests her need to deny how she really felt, by use of defensive reaction formation. It is reasonable to wonder, if the nursing experience was so gratifying, why Herbert would develop a severe and continuing eating disorder so early. There is also a suggestion of Herbert's identification with the mother's reaction formations with his still hugging and kissing his mother and father, given the emergence of the subsequent material. The mother also appeared contented with the boy's sensitive, gentle, artistic behavior and seemed to encourage it, as is evidenced by his bringing the paintings to her as gifts. The father, by contrast, appeared annoyed by Herbert's lack of assertiveness and masculinity. Disharmony between the parents could have seeped into their attitudes toward the children.

In the second interview the parents acknowledged that their marriage had been a poor one, with much friction and three separations. In marital counseling in Chicago it had been suggested that some of the husband's resentment was a result of his wife's professional status as a lawyer and her financial independence.

In reply to questions, the mother stated that Herbert did not seem to be afraid of getting fat, and there was no history of obesity in the family.

Toward the end of the interview the father said that he had been an athlete and that Herbert's passivity infuriated him. The father usually felt calm but at times he could get so angry that he could not control himself. The mother added that when Herbert was just over one year of age and cried, the father would lose his temper and hit him, but this occurred infrequently.

In consultation, Herbert was a tall, very thin, graceful-appearing 14-year-old who spoke in a soft, controlled fashion. He sat alert, silent, waiting, but was responsive to questions.

"I just don't like to eat regular food . . . The taste bothers me . . . swallowing it is difficult . . . I gag on foods . . . I don't like the taste of steak or roast beef . . . don't like any meat but white meat or chicken and turkey . . . any veins and I gag and don't eat it . . . I stopped eating hard-boiled eggs, cheese, butter, and hot dogs. I like Fritos but not pretzels. I like soft bacon but not crisp . . . pancakes but not crunchy edges . . . cold cereal but without milk. I like fruits and cantaloupe but not watermelon. I don't like the crisp edges of french fries. I drink lo cal soda, and skim milk, and punch, and grapefruit juice, and orange juice without pulp. I like ice cream but only Carvel. I eat vanilla cake, and only the inside of the cake . . . I eat certain kinds of chocolate, but only if I mix it with Puffed Rice. I don't eat in restaurants, or at home when anyone is in the kitchen."

He added, "Every year a different teacher tries to get me to eat." Looking directly at me, "This year a guidance teacher is trying to get me to eat, but I just avoid him. My father wants me to eat and gets mad when I don't so I eat a little to get him to stop bothering me. My three brothers all call me skinny. I am thin. I wouldn't mind 115 pounds but I feel healthy." He made no attempt to increase his weight. In reply he stated that he weighed himself two to three times a month, and never looked at his body in the mirror except at his head.

After consultations with Herbert, I saw the parents and in a general way described some of the dynamic reasons why a boy might not wish to eat. They agreed that probably he had shifted his involvement with people into his involvement with food, where he exercised great control, and that he probably was being defiant by not eating.

They agreed to his entering analysis, and they raised a problem. Because they felt he was an underachiever, they told him that they were enrolling him in a private school in New York, even though they lived in an affluent community with a good school system. He responded with a temper tantrum, screaming that he hated them and that he did not want to go. They had never seen him react that way before. When I suggested that if he felt coerced, his defiance could increase with more starving and complications in beginning treatment. They decided to continue him at the local public school.

It was my impression that Herbert had a chronic, severe eating disorder that did not correspond to the typical anorexic syndrome in males, but that he had some clinical and dynamic features in common with these anorexics and in time the clinical picture might more closely resemble that of the typical anorexic. He was extremely compulsive about his eating habits. Also, there was no preoccupation with looking at himself in the mirror, especially at his abdomen and thighs, behavior typical of male and female anorexics, and no distortion in body image. He knew that he was thin and allegedly did not mind putting on weight. The typical need to exercise, so prominent in the male anorexic, was also missing. He did not illustrate the usual gross restlessness of the male anorexic except for repeated bursts of rapid fingers and foot movements. His inordinate need to control his eating behavior was clear, as was his signaling to me in the first interview that any effort of mine to coerce him into eating would be met with a struggle and attempt to leave treatment.

In the following session he was very talkative and introduced a theme that persisted and was elaborated upon for the next three months. An avid reader, he digested many science fiction books, all with similar type stories: "There was this man who can control other people by his thinking. His daughter can make fires occur just by thinking them and she can destroy any building by burning it down." He also mentioned a series of other books featuring waves of destructiveness.

It was evident early on that Herbert was concerned that I would attempt to pressure him to eat, as did "guidance counselor," or this man "who can control people by his thinking," or his father. It was important for him to know that I would neither pressure him to eat nor attempt to control him.

In the next hour he stated that he ate very little food, even if he liked the food; he made indirect allusions to a fear of getting fat, although he denied it directly and did not have a history of previous obesity. Two sessions later he remembered that between the ages of 4 and 6 he had had many nightmares of monsters coming out of the ground and destroying people. He recalled repetitive dreams about a witch that terrified him because she would cut his hands off. He began to sleep with his hands under the pillow and continued to do so, reassuring all that he wasn't doing anything with them anywhere else. He then associated to a story about his grandfather, who had no legs because of diabetes, and of two uncles who both had a stroke. He spoke of three of the family's dogs and four of their cats all having died. He looked sad and fearful as he mentioned that a neighbor's 11-year-old girl had died of leukemia.

Herbert's early nightmares of monsters coming out of the ground and killing people, followed by other repetitive dreams of a witch who would cut his hands off, and then a series of castration associations suggest both his underlying aggressive impulses as the monster, and his retaliatory castration fears by the witch.

He jumped repeatedly when the phone rang in the office. He associated to his fear of intruders as a child and to the noises on the stairs of the big old house they had previously lived in.

In the ninth session he described how fussy he was about the choice and preparation of his food. While his current weight was 90 pounds, he really would have preferred to be 130 to 140 pounds because he knew he was thin. He voluntarily acknowledged that he had an eating problem, that he did not know why, but that he would like to be rid of it.

In the tenth session he described an intense preoccupation with a series of science fiction books in which one planet comes close to another and invades it with "threads," wormlike organisms that devour everything in sight, killing people and penetrating the ground. (This was the opposite of his childhood nightmares of monsters coming out of the ground.) In defense, the people on the invaded planet hatch dragon eggs and, by feeding the little dragons, "impress them," that is, fuse their minds with the minds of the dragons, who then do what the people want them to. The people feed the dragons large turkeys, but when they want the dragons to kill the threads, they feed them fire stones. The male dragons then breathe fire and kill the threads, with the boys riding the dragons and guiding them to the attack.

How closely the boys riding the powerful dragons who destroy the threatening "threads" resemble Eric, who allies himself with the hordes of rats who devour and destroy all opposing enemies. The turkey-eating dragons seem to be projections of the patient, just as the rats, lizards, and Dracula represented Eric's projections.

I commented that eating seemed to be important in the story because it was mentioned three times: the "threads" that killed and ate everything, feeding the dragons turkeys to make them become your friend, and feeding fire stones to kill the threads. He quietly assented, and the hour ended.

In the next session he continued: Only the queen dragon produces eggs, but she can't breathe fire; the girl who rides her, gets her own flame-thrower to kill the threads. I wondered out loud whether it was coincidental that he was wearing a turkey T-shirt, since he had just talked about feeding turkeys to the dragons so they could grow. He demurred with the comment that it was a gift from his grandmother.

He then associated to having written a story at the age 7 "of all the children being snowflakes falling from the sky, and when some of the other children opened their mouths and let the flakes fall on their tongues, the snowflakes were eaten." I acknowledged that it was a creative story but chose to interpret nothing out of concern that it would shut off his associations. The linkage between the fire-breathing dragons, with their tongues, and the children melting the snowflakes seemed apparent. There did appear to be an increasing correlation between the eating conflict and aggression, with the animals seen as both protective and destructive extensions of the self.

The story is notable for its defensive, reaction-formation motif, which in a sense parallels Herbert's overt character traits and behavior. Like the delicate snowflakes falling and melting on the children's tongues, Herbert too, is gentle and delicate, passive and unassertive, interested in drawing and painting and eschewing all overt aggression or hostility. Restless behavior is also delicate. Associative linkages, far removed from conscious awareness, reveal him to be the boy riding the dragon to destroy the invaders, and also identify him with the destructive threads.

Herbert's intense preoccupation with the war between the planets seemed to reflect his conflict over aggression, his multiple identifications, cannibalistic impulses, anal sadism, and primitive superego punishment. "Threads" from an invading planet kill all the people and penetrate the ground, a much-multiplied symbol of the Rat Man's fearful anal preoccupation (Freud 1909).

For protection, people raise and train dragons, who obey them because the dragons' minds become fused with theirs. This fantasy emerged early in the transference with his concern that I could control him with my thinking, the way he wanted to control the dragons with his. With Herbert, fear of loss of control is more than a need to regain a realistic relationship with people, or a loss of control over angry impulses; it appears to involve primitive intense aggressive impulses with their attendant primitive consequences. Reaction formations help contain the aggression. Associations are linked to boys riding fire-breathing dragons, feeding them fire stones, eating the threads, cannibalism and fusion.

The turkey-eating dragon seemed to be an ambivalent and important symbol for Herbert. White-meat turkey and chicken were the only meat he consumed, a fact suggesting both aggressive destruction of the turkey and identification with it. Wearing a turkey T-shirt reinforces his identification. It is not clear whether the same masochistic attire was requested when he arrived at a subsequent session wearing a T-shirt with gaping shark's jaws under a logo "Feed Me," a gift from his mother. As with the turkey symbolism, here again he is the subject (shark), as well as object (shark food). Being viewed as a "turkey" can have derogatory implications reflecting his feelings of contempt for his passivity on one level, while reassuring him that he need not fear an eruption of fire-breathing draconian revenge. A melding of the dragon and the turkey might yield an acceptable compromise.

In the next session he stated that he had been introduced to monsters when he was 5 years old, when his mother read *The Hobbit* to him. Another hour revealed displaced resentment to the father as he described how mean his uncle was, subsequently associating to his father's criticizing him and buying him books that he did not enjoy reading. When the teacher told him to write a story on anything, he couldn't; he wanted to be told what to do. He said that it was a problem to start each session without any direction from me. After this discussion, it was easier for him to begin and he seemed more at ease.

In another session he reported that he didn't like swimming and never learned how. He had some thoughts, though, that if he were ever in a boat and it turned over, the situation could be dangerous. This thought spawned memories of a series of frightening dreams.

"I'm underwater and I tried to bring up a treasure, but I couldn't get back to the surface."

"Someone is chasing someone."

"Statues are staring at me and moving."

There are numbers of "falling-off-cliff" dreams in which he hits the bottom and wakes up with a start. And there are dreams in which he awakens startled and doesn't know why.

In a later hour he described TV programs in which a man took advantage of a woman. In one he brutalized the woman and she killed him. In another the daughter killed the father. The next hours he returned to science fiction stories in which a monster killed and ate people. He frequently reported the same theme: a woman was able to set fires with her mind and destroy the entire town. In a different session he reported a horror movie in which pets and people who were buried came alive again, and so did a son, who came back so weird that he had to be killed.

In subsequent sessions he brought in a series of his drawings of various kinds of dragons that he had copied from books that he had read. He spoke in detail about stories of demons, magicians, warriors, and of people who cast spells. I wondered if it was to control them, and he agreed. He told stories about prehistoric people who used signs to communicate, and about later people who were able to talk. In one story a girl's family was killed in an earthquake, and after she was saved, she learned to hunt small animals. He had earlier mentioned that at 5 years of age he had dressed up as a girl on Halloween. He remembered that from ages 5 to 9 he was very interested in dinosaurs; he knew all the names and types, and what they did in their pursuit of food, and who killed whom.

On a day when I commented about his thin jacket on a cold day, he revealed that it was his mother's and then launched into considerable criticism of his father and his attitude about clothing, restaurants, and grades. He concluded with the statement that his father was not satisfied unless Herbert was perfect. The father would comment, "What kind of a son do I have who won't wear the new suit and jacket that I gave him?" The patient always chose to sit in the car or at home and read rather than spend time with his father. It seemed that his voracious appetite for reading partly served as an excuse to withdraw and avoid a relationship with his father and with his peers. He was, however, appearing more animated in the sessions.

In another session, he reported on a trilogy that he had read: A girl defies her sick father by running away and marrying and having four children. Her husband dies, and she returns home to find that her father will leave her his money only if she has no children. She hides her children in the attic and agrees with the conniving grandmother to slowly poison them by feeding them cookies laced with arsenic. When the youngest child succumbs and dies, the other three children run away. In another book, germs are released and kill everyone in the world.

I wondered about his voracious reading habits, and whether reading so much interfered with his opportunity to make and play with friends. This he denied, although the parental history had contradicted him. Herbert finished a book every day and a half. He always read in the waiting room, although he waited for only a few minutes. One sensed his need to "devour" books, a symbolic displacement from his repressed cannibalistic impulses to incorporate and destroy people. Just as most anorexics are compulsively concerned with food, weight, exercise, and academics as means of exercising aspects of ego control, Herbert appeared to be compulsively concerned with food, weight, and reading as attempts at ego mastery over substitute objects.

Another book absorbed most of three sessions. Visitors appear from space and appear nice and look human, but they are lizard people underneath, who eat people and animals alive . . . They kidnapped 500,000 people to take away and eat . . . They have long tongues that they use to inject poison into people. They look human with normal skin, but when you rub off the skin, there are scales underneath the skin . . . The people on earth had to find some way to kill the lizard people. The story was amplified in the next session: The lizard people arrived in a space ship that hovered over the earth and sucked up all the water, turning California into a desert . . . They ate rodents, animals, and the fresh meat of humans . . . They also used a conversion chamber to completely force people into doing what they wanted. Here the lizard people inject poison with their tongues, in contrast to Eric's Dracula, who sucks blood out of people to kill them.

Discussion

Herbert clearly is both subject and object, similar to Shengold's description of his patients. He appears normal on the outside, but if you peel away the skin, you find the destructive cannibalistic lizard underneath. The lizards that suck up all the water to destroy the land reveal the intensity of the destructive aggressive component to sucking. This is most evident in Eric's Dracula vampire fantasies, Shengold's patients, and others. Wilson (Chapter 1) describes a dream of a 16-year-old bulimic-anorexic girl in which "a man was a vampire . . . and wanted to kill us and suck our blood." This identification with the sucking destroyer was also dramatically illustrated in the fantasies of a 12-year-old girl with anorexia and asthma (Mintz 1989), in which violent sucking machines, projections of her unconscious destructive impulses during asthmatic attacks and her denied gorging impulses, destroyed whole populations. Other projections of her sucking impulses were to tornados, volcanos, and earthquakes. Destructive aspects of sucking are not fully recognized in patients with anorexia and with asthma in spite of the latter's obvious inability to suck in air.

A number of sessions revealed Herbert's passivity and repressed aggressive conflicts. At age 6 he was bullied by a fat boy every day after school. The patient passively accepted this. Finally the mother had to walk Herbert home and scold the tormentor. About a year before treatment Herbert found that boys were stealing from his gym locker. He hid, saw the transgressors open his locker, and then walked away, doing and saying nothing. The next day when one of the boys teased him, "I suddenly hit him in the head with the locker." He made the slip three times, with my pointing out his repressed urge to hit him over the head with the locker and Herbert denying it. Finally he was able to say, "I hit him in the eye with the lock and gave him a black eye, and the boy never bothered me afterward." I wondered if he might not wish to be strong and drop lockers on people's heads. When others picked on him, he still ignored them and never told his parents. He denied all conscious revenge fantasies or retaliating dreams but one, in which "A boy insulted me through the ventilator and I had the urge to throw water through it." His associations were not helpful.

In another session he spoke about superwoman, who has great strength and power. A machine with the type of toothed jaws seen in earth-moving machines was chasing someone to pick him up in its mouth. This displacement of human jaws to the inanimate was also present in the dream of Eric, who was being cut up by a saw reflecting the same mechanism. Bad people were sucked out of the world and eaten. A subsequent hour revealed Herbert's sadistic cannibalistic preoccupations with his pets: "The cats tried to knock over the bird cage and eat the birds, and almost did, but the bird died of fright . . . One cat tried to get at the fish with its paw . . . A woman next door had a hundred cats in her yard . . . and she fed them . . . The cars killed some as they crossed the street . . . She also fed pigeons in the yard and the cats killed the pigeons and ate part of them . . . Then the lawn mowers (teeth) cut up the rest of the pigeons' bodies . . . and you could see parts of the bodies on the grass."

At the next session, at which he wore the shark "Feed Me" T-shirt, he described a play that he had just seen about a man-eating plant that initially thrived on blood and ultimately ate four people. Someone in the play wanted to take cuttings to propagate the plant widely. The plant said, "We can eat everyone and control the world." This statement is of particular relevance since it provides an additional dynamic understanding of the relationship between eating and relating to people.

It had been clear in the clinical picture of innumerable patients that the conflict over eating represented a displacement from a more important and overwhelming dilemma about helplessness in dealing with events and people and a feeling of being out of control. Controlling food and weight in the most exquisite manner served as a substitute for the inability to control people. Here we see that not only does the eating serve the aggressive impulse to destroy people, but in addition, by destroying everyone in opposition, the patient regains control over the world of objects. The magnitude of the destruction contributes to the intensity of the guilt and the severity of the punishment, although the strict superego broaches no deviation from perfection without retribution.

The next hour followed a weekend visit to the Baltimore aquarium and a long commentary about sharks. Herbert added again that he couldn't swim and didn't wish to learn, especially in the ocean because of the sharks, the octopi, and the barracuda. (Eric had voiced the same fear.)

The first four months of treatment ended.

Marshall

Marshall was an 18-year-old high school senior, referred by his uncle, a dermatologist, after the family requested his help. One morning after an argument with his brother, Marshall broke down sobbing and confessed to his parents that he was sick: He had been eating and vomiting for five years and recently recognized that he could not stop. The parents were shocked and immediately contacted the uncle, who referred him for consultation. Marshall was five feet, nine inches, weighing 120 pounds. He appeared agitated, sad, and apprehensive.

At the first interview, during the Christmas vacation, he volunteered the following information. The gorging and vomiting had begun five years before, after a fight with his younger brother during the brother's birthday party. He had been chastised by the parents in front of the company. He remembered feeling upset, going into the kitchen, and eating half a cold chicken until he was so full that he felt like vomiting. He vomited to rid himself of the stuffed feeling, and he had been doing it in secret ever since. He did not remember being troubled about it until about two months before, when he tried to stop and could not. He had decided to stop because the eating and vomiting had increased, often to three times a day, and his stomach hurt. His attempts to stop, however, resulted only in severe headaches. When he realized that he was unable to stop, he became frightened.

A member of the cross-country track team throughout high school, the patient now felt obligated to run more frequently and for longer distances than the coach prescribed. As a result the coach criticized him. To make things worse, two weeks before his confession to his family, he had forced himself to stop vomiting. The result was that he then felt it necessary to run twice the previous distance and was averaging 100 miles a week; further-more, he was bicycling daily and secretly doing calisthenics twice a day in his bedroom. Since he stopped the vomiting, he also developed severe restlessness and insomnia. He would awaken every hour throughout the night. Not vomiting, and fearful of gaining weight from the gorging, he felt that exercising to burn off the calories was his only recourse. It was not clear whether this was a fully conscious decision, or whether he felt impelled to do so and justified his reasons for it. He added that he also fasted for twenty-four hours whenever he felt he had overeaten the previous day.

In general he ate little breakfast and lunch and gorged by himself in the late evening. He did not experience feelings of hunger but enjoyed the taste of food if it was prepared by him to his exact specifications. Since cessation of vomiting, he dreamed about doing it every single night. He also volunteered that he was totally preoccupied with thoughts about food. Prior to falling asleep he would spend one or two hours deciding what foods he would have the next day and how he would prepare them. If unable to carry out his plan, he would be furious. Thus ended the first consultation.

In consultations with the parent, they revealed how shocked they felt when the patient confessed his gorging and vomiting practices. The mother knew that Marshall always was fussy about food, but she viewed it as part of his perfectionist personality: he placed undue emphasis on cleanliness, showering, and his clothes, and since adolescence he had brushed his teeth five times a day. She was unable to remember that he had any eating disturbance as an infant, nor was he prone to preoccupation with food. He was a hyperactive child, however, and they had considered using sedation at night but did not. The father remembered that he was well coordinated and enjoyed playing ball. During adolescence he was a better than average athlete, although the father thought that he might have been accident prone because of numerous bruises and occasional minor fractures. He also had frequent respiratory infections with high fevers.

In the previous few months the parents had noticed that Marshall was drinking beer excessively and on two occasions seemed drunk. There was also a temper outburst in an argument with his brother during which he threw a plate on the floor.

The father was a local minister and the mother had recently returned to teaching high school science. A 21-year-old sister seemed to have developed unremarkably, and a brother, two years younger than the patient, had asthma. Both parents were in favor of Marshall's treatment because of his obvious distress.

As the first month of analysis unfolded, the patient expressed surprise that he was able to speak almost continuously four times a week. Since he had no friends, he rarely spoke to anyone for more than a few minutes. He talked a great deal about his compulsive, perfectionistic eating habits. I pointed out that the eating behavior seemed to reflect his need to be in control of food, since so many other areas of his life appeared out of control. The control issue emerged immediately in the transference and continued throughout the course of the analysis. Somatic symptoms appeared, especially headaches, which are not uncommon in anorexics, and they were interpreted as manifestations of resistance to facing thoughts and feelings, and defiant attempts to cope with what he felt was my attempt to control him. I repeatedly stated that I had no interest in controlling him or in trying to run his life. In a dramatic way he was able to see that thinking of food was a method of covering up what really bothered him and permitted him to avoid thoughts about his future. In one session, when I was speaking about his problem of having no friends, he said that while I was speaking he was thinking of what kind of fruit he was going to buy at the market, because it upset him to realize that he had no friends. "I don't want to think about it."

Concerns over control and competitiveness were evident in much of his behavior. In the third week he volunteered that he had stopped eating breakfast and lunch and now ate only dinner. I remarked that his talking tended to bring problems to the surface, and his increased attempt at starvation was an attempt to counter the emerging thoughts and feelings by burying them further. Although his attempt to battle with me by increasing the starving was not interpreted at that point, his subsequent associations brought it to the fore nevertheless. "I wait here to see who talks first. If you do, then I win. Then I look you in the eye, and if you turn away, then I win." I pointed out his concern about being controlled and his competition with me. In the following session he stated that he ate breakfast that morning but then got a terrible headache. I indicated that the headache was a substitute for painful thoughts. He added: "I'm concentrating more and more on thoughts about eating since I've been coming here, but I know that I have problems with friends. I even have to control the entrance door at school and the elevator door in the hall." I said that he was controlling what goes in and what goes out just as he did food, and he replied, "I don't listen to what you say, I think of food; I don't want the headaches or to be upset all day." At this point he became momentarily tearful.

In the third week he reported his first dream: "I thought of a recurrent dream to tell you. I was moving all the books from my father's library one by one and bringing them into my room. When they were all there, I had to move them all back." He associated to how hard his father had to work to become successful, and how many people at church had asked the patient what he was planning to do with his life. He really didn't know. During the next week he described a series of episodes, some disguised and some obvious, which indicated that he felt his brother was both thoughtless and inconsiderate and that he resented him tremendously.

At the next session he reported the following dream: "I was at a big party. The tables were full of food. I began to eat and eat. Suddenly a rat hidden in the food jumped into my mouth. I grabbed it by the throat and pulled it out. Then I began to vomit up one rat after the other until I vomited up eight or ten. I felt disgusted. Then I began vomiting up coins, toothpicks, and pencils. I felt very weak."

He associated the coins to the money it took to get to my office and the coins for the parking meter. He used toothpicks to keep his mouth clean. I observed that he was concerned about having a foul mouth, and he agreed but without seeing the link to aggressive outburst. The pencils reminded him of school and his concern over his future. The party reminded him of a recent family party, where, as usual, his brother acted obnoxious and spoiled. The rats reminded him of the pet hamsters he used to have as a child. He thought that they were rodents because they used their teeth a great deal. One got out and ate a hole in the cellar door. They had babies all the time and he used to worry that the babies would die. "If I think of rats in my mouth, maybe that's why I brush my teeth so often."

In the next hour he associated further to the dream, with the hamsters reminding him of other pets. He had a tropical fish tank and he would spend hours feeding the fish and watching them. He observed that you can't get close to a fish, but also if it dies you can always get others. He then spoke about a friend he had when he was little. He moved away. After that he played ball with other kids, but he never had any as friends.

In the next hour he reported an upsetting event. He had bought three apples that day, planning to eat them that evening. After finishing one, he returned to the refrigerator and found that his brother had taken one. He was suddenly filled with rage and with thoughts of killing his brother. He did not remember ever experiencing that degree of anger before: now he knew why people killed. He shook for an hour, and afterwards he became nauseated, developed a headache, and cried. He continued, "It's as if the apples were children." Responding to his awareness that there was still one apple left, he explained, "If a mother has an injured child, she worries about losing it, even if she has another living child." It was clear that the food represented people and additional determinants: his identification with the mother, hatred toward the brother for taking his food, loss of the food-friend, and the gorging representing frantic attempts at incorporating longed-for objects as well as destroying hated ones. Schlossman (1979) has reported an anorexic girl who collected little containers of food in the refrigerator, giving each of the containers names of people she knew. I pointed out the displacement of his concerns with people to the preoccupation with food, the need to control the food as a substitute for his perceived inability to control people, and his concern over his violent temper. He associated to other recent episodes when, as he now realized, he was angry with his brother. He concluded the session with the comment that since starting the analysis, he had been crying frequently and that he had never cried before.

The next hour he reported the following dream: "I'm at the pulpit of a church. The minister is killed with an ice pick. I catch him, put him on the floor, put on his robes, and continue preaching without telling anyone that he is dead." The dream reminded him of a repetitive dream that he had for more than eight years: "I was walking through the grounds of a castle past the guards and up to a king. I stab him and he falls, and I sit on his throne." He recognized that both dreams revealed his anger and his competitive drives: to be king, to be the authority, and to replace the boss—his father. He spoke about how demeaned he felt being bossed about and running errands for everyone. At the end of the session he remembered that the minister in the dream was black and that the dream occurred two days after Martin Luther King was assassinated. (Eric also reported long-standing repetitive dreams of stabbing his sister.)

A number of sessions later he referred to the rat dream again. When he was 10 years old he visited his aunt and uncle in Arizona. They had a big barbecue with a whole stuffed pig with an apple in its mouth. "You could eat as much food as you wanted, and I ate too much and I threw up. I never saw a whole animal before with the head attached." He again associated to angry feelings toward his brother, whom he often thought of as a pig in the ways that he behaved.

Discussion

Marshall's rat dream illustrated his repressed, aggressive conflict. The outpouring of rats symbolized his cannibalistic impulses that he feared would pour out of him and destroy the hated objects, especially his father and younger brother. Disgust at his unconscious identification with the filth and habits of the rats contributed to his constant need to keep his mouth clean by brushing as well as to cleanse it of dirty, violent thoughts, feelings, and foods. Since he could not sit still, it was a great effort to remain at the table during meals. He avoided the movies and the theater for the same reason. I was one of the ambivalently cathected introjects that he wished to eject because I symbolized the authoritarian father and also was responsible for attempts to help him uncover thoughts and feelings that he desperately needed to avoid by binging, vomiting, and exercising. The party in the dream reminded him of a family party where his hated brother acted spoiled. Unconsciously associating childhood to the brother as a rat, he spoke of the rodents of childhood, the hamsters and his emphasis on their teeth, which could destroy and eat right through a cellar door. Some of the toothpicks in the dream might stand for wood-shaving residuals of hamster destructiveness.

The hamster-rat also stood for the hated brother, the hamster babies that he feared-wished would die. When he fed his tropical fish, he must have noted their cannibalistic propensities: the young babies are frequently gobbled up, a fate he unconsciously reserved for his brother. An additional determinant to the fish was the negative aspect, that he couldn't get close to them (make close friends), but was balanced by the positive feature that they were easy to replace. It is clear that he was unconsciously talking about friendship; his next association was to his childhood friend who moved away (died). I had to call him once to change an appointment and the following session he reported, with mixed feelings, that it was the first telephone call he had received in years. Friendship had been irreparably damaged by his having unconsciously associated potential friends with his hated brother, and so kept peers at a distance. He was the cold fish.

His brother's eating one of "his" apples filled him with such fury that the rage almost overwhelmed him. The panic he felt that he would lose complete control was still evident in the next session when he reported the incident. This certainly highlights the intense problem that anorexic and bulimic patients have with aggression. I cannot think of a single case where aggressive conflict was not of major importance. Kramer's (1974) suggestion that these patients may lack aggression is therefore puzzling. Hogan

(1985) also emphasizes the importance of aggression. Repressed hostility is intense.

Sadistic feelings of rage toward the father were also abundant. While the two dreams in which he stabs the minister-king and replaces him have oedipal relevance, oral and anal sadistic levels predominate.

It is worth noting that 14-year-old Herbert also raised hamster and tropical fish and experienced some of the same identifications as a child that contributed to an isolated, friendless early adolescence surrounded by dragons and lizards and his cannibalistic preoccupations.

THE LIZARD PHENOMENON IN WOMEN

Eleanor

Eleanor was a 15-year-old anorexic girl, who was born and raised in southern California. The youngest of three children, she was her father's favorite. After a stormy marriage, the father obtained a divorce and received custody of Eleanor, because of the alcoholic mother's neglect during long and frequent periods of intoxication. Two older brother, ages 22 and 19, both with alcohol problems, remained in California but did not live with the mother. The older brother dropped out of college during a period of drug usage requiring hospitalization. The father, a lawyer reared in the South, was the oldest of three brothers: the only one able to rise out of his economically deprived environment and achieve a college education. While the father had a close, supportive relationship with Eleanor, there was minimal contact with his sons. The mother would occasionally write to Eleanor or would see her on infrequent visits to the East, a contact that produced ambivalent feelings of resentment, guilt, and remorse in Eleanor.

A year into treatment, Eleanor announced that her father was seeing a divorced woman lawyer and seemed to like her. While intellectually happy for her father, emotionally she resented the intrusion into their lives and felt that she would forfeit attention by sharing her father's affections with "an intruder." After the father began seeing Norma regularly, Eleanor launched into a tirade against her. As she reintroduced the topic of her father's girlfriend, she began to pull at the tissue of her thighs, echoing a recurrent complaint: "I feel fat . . . I still feel fat. I keep thinking of my father and Norma."

Norma, who was with a large metropolitan law firm, worked long hours and often encouraged the father to have dinner with her in the city rather than returning home to the suburbs. On some occasions, concerned about Eleanor's feelings, she would suggest that the three of them eat out together. This thoughtfulness did not placate Eleanor, who complained bitterly that she and her father used to eat home together. "Now that bitch makes us eat out all the time. It's not home anymore. I don't deserve this.

She doesn't belong. She's turning my life upside down. He's my father! . . . You know, I need to find a decent person that I can get involved with and who will love me, but that's too far off . . . It's hard to wait.''

A discussion followed that led to my suggesting that she might fear rejection if she does finds a worthwhile person, who will get to know her and find out that she isn't decent. This interpretation, which may appear premature, was made because of her previously demonstrated strict, punitive conscience, and the frequency of these feelings in so many anorexic and bulimic patients. She countered with an initial denial and then with an association: "No, I'm decent, intelligent, and thoughtful . . . I just had a thought . . . of a little furry animal coming out of my mouth, and I push it back in . . . a little gerbil. Isn't that the animal that kills snakes? No, I can't remember which one kills boa constrictors with its teeth. My friend had one when I was little. Well, anyhow, it's a mean, vicious, little animal that you can't trust . . . I know that I'm talking about myself, but I'm not that way. . . . Ugh, it's disgusting.''

I suggested that the idea of the gerbil—the mean, vicious little animal— occurred to her after I mentioned that she might feel that a decent guy might not be interested in her if he found out that deep inside she wasn't a worthwhile person. Then she spoke about the hidden part of her, the part inside, the mean little gerbil trying to get out, and she partially recognized that part of herself. During the ensuing discussion, when thinking of the little animal inside, she also spoke about rats and mice and then of maggots eating meat.

It was as if my pointing out her fear of a mean streak inside her crystalized the infantile, sadistic core in the form of the destructive gerbil-rat-maggot-person, which is disgusting and must be shunned. It is also plausible that the fantasy contains the unconscious attempt to rid herself of the vicious, sadistic core by extruding it and cleansing herself, as well as an attempt to deny its existence by pushing it back inside. The remark, "Ugh, it's disgusting,'' was a response to her perceived internalized dirty, vicious gerbil-rat introject.

In the beginning of the session, angry, resentful, and feeling overwhelmed by her father's increasing preoccupation with another woman, Eleanor attempted to avoid dealing with the conflict through the typical anorexic defense of displacing it onto her concern over her fat thighs and her feeling fat. The displacement failed, however, as is evident by the reemerged thought, "I keep thinking about my father and Norma.'' Her fear that she could not get better as long as the situation between her father and Norma persisted was a consequence of unconscious recognition that the jealousy spawned a level of overwhelming rage that filled her with guilt and the need to suffer. These feelings forced her to conclude that she was such a terrible person that no decent person would remain with her. Having this pointed out resulted in the emergence of the hateful introject.

The patient presented oedipal conflict in a preoedipal regressive oral sadistic and anal fashion similar to Shengold's and Sperling's patients.

A year later Eleanor reported her fear of moray eels, vicious creatures

338 Ira L. Mintz, M.D.

that one encounters when snorkeling around rocks. Mean and vicious, with teeth that can tear and rip at your flesh, she was describing a frightening projection of her own denied cannibalistic impulses, akin to the previous gerbil-rat-maggot introjects. "They could rip the flesh off your body with their teeth," she said. "Then the sharks would come for the blood and eat you. That's why I don't like to swim near fish and have them nibble at me." Here, obvious cannibalistic projections are associatively linked to the eels that rip at you, sharks that eat you, and the little fish that nibble at you.

The projection was further clarified a few months later when she mentioned that she playfully bit a boyfriend's back with her teeth. Spontaneously elaborating further, she added that she had long enjoyed biting people on their necks, just as the vampire does. Thus we see that the gerbil coming out of her not only serves to rid her of the aggressive biting impulses; it also, like the projected moray eel, represents both her conscious biting behavior and its unconscious aggressive cannibalistic determinants.

Concomitantly, we do have data to suggest that the gerbil coming out of Eleanor's mouth is similar to the rats pouring out of Marshall's mouth in his dream. Marshall almost wore his gums down in his compulsive tooth brushing, in an attempt to clean out his "foul" mouth and rid himself of the presence of the destructive, dirty introject. Eleanor's similar passion for cleanliness and need for innumerable showers contained suggestions of the same conflict.

Florence

Florence, a 15-year-old anorexic girl, an only child, had been in psychotherapy for about two years. Her father was born in England, and in his late teens moved to Canada with his family. There he met his wife, an executive in an international company, and they made their home in Toronto. He received a promotion from his company, and was transferred to head a division in New York. Florence was very attached to a friend, one of few in Toronto, and was distressed at moving. Five months after the move, when the parents noted her increasing withdrawal and difficulty in making new friends, the anorexia began.

Two years into her treatment, she arrived at the session upset because her mathematics teacher had been severely injured in an automobile accident. She reported the following dream: "Henry Anderson, my math teacher, was dead . . . and he was being eaten by maggots. I thought that I'd stay and get eaten by maggots too, and I knew we'd be together. A huge maggot was eating at my elbow, and I got very upset."

She associated to the feelings of disgust about the maggots, and to her worry that her teacher might die. She then spoke about a strict uncle of hers and about her father, whom she often missed because he did a great deal of traveling. Having previously spoken about her attachment to her mother, who suffered from migraine and excema, she then complained about her parents' excessive demands upon her and her rising resentment about these demands. "But as much as I argue with my parents, I'll end up doing what they want me to do and be devoured and controlled by them."

Here the patient illustrated conflicts over separation and aggression. The feared loss of her teacher by death or separation, which symbolized her unconscious conflict with her parents, was dealt with in the dream with her also being eaten and destroyed so that she could rejoin the lost love object, pay for her aggression, and be together inside the maggots inside mother earth where the maggots live. Her association to being "devoured" and controlled by her parents illustrated her ambivalence toward them. Depression and unconscious suicidal thoughts following ambivalent feelings about death wishes toward them reveal the hostility and the resulting guilt as well as the extreme separation anxiety and need for reunion inside the maggots. Denied, projected cannibalistic anger toward the parents is evident in her comment about feeling "devoured" by them.

I am indebted to Dr. L. Chiorazzi for the preceding case history, and for the one that follows.

Katherine

Katherine was a 17-year-old high school senior who had been in psychotherapy for a year for anorexia that began at age 15. The youngest of four children of bright but poorly educated working-class parents, she worked after school to minimize the financial burden of her treatment. The father, owner of a plumbing concern, managed reasonably well but invariably complained of financial burdens. The mother, while overtly supportive, unwittingly undermined the treatment at every opportunity.

While passive and compliant in most situations, she had dreams and memories filled with carnivorous animals. Growing up in Colorado, she remembered as a child being preoccupied with and destroying anthills wherever she could find them. Angry at her parents as an 8-year-old, she remembered taking three gerbils, throwing them against the wall until she had killed them, and then hiding the bodies and telling her parents that they escaped from the cage.

She also remembered being frightened about thinking of taking a knife and killing her little brother. She reported a childhood dream of her three gerbils dying of starvation because she forgot to feed them.

Six months into treatment she dreamed of "being a little girl who found a puppy and wanted to feed it milk but was afraid her parents would get angry, so she drowned it in a bag in the river."

Visiting a pet store to buy fish, she watched the hamsters stuff food into their pouches and thought about their eating each other. Her childhood fantasies, dreams, and behavior reveal her killing and starving gerbils, ants, and turtles, which probably represented her hated little brother. Her impulses to kill her little brother with a knife were identical to Eric's fantasies about killing his little sister, and Marshall's killing his father and brother. The hidden, cannibalistic impulses were revealed in the displacement to the hamsters' eating each other. In treatment, the dream of being the little girl who wanted to feed the puppy, but drowned it instead, suggested her ambivalent behavior toward the brother and the wish to return him to his earlier unborn state.

ADDITIONAL SUPPORTIVE DATA

The following brief clinical vignettes provide additional supportive evidence of the frequent presence of tooth-prominent animals in dreams, fantasies, associations, and preoccupations, and play a major role in anorexic conflict: a reflection of using the teeth to bite, its denial through abstinence (starving), losing control (gorging) and ultimately cannibalism, and its displaced symbolic representation in the form of knives and cutting machines.

A 16-year-old patient with a history of marked obesity followed by a mixed anorexic-bulimic pattern reported that she kept having rat dreams. Relatively early in the treatment, she described four of them:

1. A rat was on my arm. I was afraid of being bitten.
2. I was seeing rats all over the room and trying to get rid of them with a broom.
3. Rats were under the bed and I was afraid of being bitten.
4. Rats were all around.

Her associations were to her mother constantly calling her a "BRAT." This possible unconscious interchange between her and her mother was not commented upon.

In order that the reader not immediately conclude that this possible connection is reaching too far, I should point out that on the next page, I report that a mother, in consultation, commenting on her bulimic daughter, described her eating habits as "shredding food like a rat." My experience with these patients indicates that there is a very close unconscious relationship between these anorexic and bulimic patients and their parents, especially the mother.

An additional association of this patient was that when she was little, she used to be afraid of rats and raccoons under her bed. Additional clarifying associations were not forthcoming at that time. After a number of months of treatment, however, it became increasingly evident that the patient behaved in a very helpless and passive manner and was almost totally unable to assert herself in any fashion. This defensive lack of assertion and her passivity covered a great deal of aggression and hostility and contributed to her unconscious need not to use her mouth in talking. Her aggressive components were further highlighted in the "toothbrush" vignette described in Chapter 15.

A mother seen in consultation described her bulimic daughter's eating habits . . . "picking at and shredding food like a rat picked it over—just like a rat." The mother was extremely reluctant to permit the patient to enter analytic treatment because she was afraid that the daughter would become too dependent upon the analyst and not continue to be close to and confide in her. Furthermore, as she herself was in once-a-week therapy and felt overwhelmed by the stress, she was certain that her daughter would not be able to cope with it either. The symbiotic relationship precluded her recognizing that the daughter's relationship to the treatment might differ from her own. The unduly close relationship between her and her daughter facilitated her unconsciously recognizing the underlying carnivorous quality to her daughter's eating patterns.

In another case, having been abused as a young child, an anorexic teenager's father had long vowed that he would never permit his children to suffer the way he did. Devoted and loving toward his children, he unwittingly overindulged them. At one point he referred to his mother's behavior toward him as "crocodiles eating their young." His unconscious perception of the mother's primitive orality was similar to the above mother's awareness of the daughter's "rat-like" behavior.

Hogan (1985) described a patient who had castrative wishes toward men. Another anorexic patient had a fantasy of dismembering her mother. He also mentioned, in a personal communication (1990), two anorexic cousins who would fight by attacking each other with scissors. A patient of mine described a fantasy of attacking a boyfriend with a knife and, another time, of using a pair of scissors. The replacement of the knife by the scissors can symbolize a condensation of the teeth and the upper and lower jaws. Another patient spoke contemptuously about her passive boyfriend: "I want to chew him up and spit him out."

I am indebted to Freiman (1989), who described three of his anorexic patients' knife and symbolic teeth preoccupations. The first was a 20-year-old woman who recalled a repeated childhood fantasy that soothed her before falling asleep. It was set off by watching a workman excavate earth in her backyard using a crane. These fantasies were similar to the fantasy described by Herbert earlier in this chapter. The fantasy was of the tooth-edged crane coming down and scooping up the hated little brother and throwing him into the earth.

A second patient, after seeing Hitchcock's movie *Psycho,* developed the fantasy of taking a knife and ripping at the father while he was taking a shower. She also had cannibalistic fantasies of devouring the father's genitals and becoming pregnant by him. Freiman's third anorexic patient reported her fantasy of wanting to put her hated brother's penis in her mother's food slicing machine.

Shaw (1984) reported a case of a 24-year-old bulimic woman with multiple knife fantasies: being raped and stabbing the attacker in the chest with a knife; a repeated fantasy of stabbing her mother in the stomach, associating to her mother's being pregnant with her hated brother; and cutting herself with a bread-slicing machine. One of my anorexic patients actually did cut her finger in a bread-slicing machine (Chapter 15). The accident suggests an unconscious symptomatic act of being cannibalized, since the multiple knives of the slicing machine can represent the thirty-two teeth-knives of the mouth.

Chiorazzi (1985) described a dream of an anorexic teenager: "I had metal in my mouth. I took it out. Then I noticed that my boyfriend wanted to kiss me, but he had metal in his mouth. He began to kiss me, and the metal began cutting up my throat. I woke up terrified." The teeth-knives are suggested in the manifest content of the dream.

One anorexic teenaged patient in the early stages of her illness reported an argument with her boyfriend during which she got so angry that she took a knife and cut her own arm. It was quite evident who the true victim really was.

Risen (1982) connected his patient's urge to rip and tear her mother apart with the inhibited use of her teeth. The patient replied that her mother felt that the analyst should be "cut up." I told her I get "cut up" enough. Both the patient, her mother, and most other anorexics seem to use knife symbolism to express strong aggressive feelings. Later the patient stated, ". . . It's like killing her, stabbing her."

Link (1990) described a 24-year-old bulimic who fantasied that her husband might stab her in the back with a knife. Another of her bulimic patients fantasied a disembodied knife stabbing her in the back and felt impelled to sleep on her back to feel comfortable.

Another colleague described a bulimic patient's fantasy of wanting to cut off all the testicles of the male workers in the large corporation where she worked. Subsequent associations were to animals with prominent teeth and to her own teeth.

DISCUSSION: THE UNCONSCIOUS SIGNIFICANCE OF TOOTH-PROMINENT ANIMALS

I have emphasized the importance and meaning of the widespread clinical evidence of tooth-prominent animals in the dreams, fantasies, and behavior, in childhood and adult life, of anorexic and bulimic patients. These animals merge with fantasied dragons and vampires, in whom the teeth serve the same unconscious purpose. Vampires, in addition to biting, add the element of aggressive sucking. The preoccupation with these animals, in the form of either identification or projection, represents an attempt to deal primarily with the patient's aggressive impulses. In that sense, the denial of the aggression, and the projection of the aggressive impulses onto the animal, with subsequent fear of them, represents a phobic resolution of conflict. Wilson (1985a) described the anorexic's fear of being fat as a fat phobia. He also points out (1989) that "stone symbolizes teeth and masks conflicts about oral sadistic cannibalistic incorporation of the breast (mother)" (p. 142). These destructive impulses are dealt with by anorexic patients through denial and repression of their impulses to eat. Thus they are able unconsciously to reassure themselves that they can control the aggressive use of their mouth, through starving, weight loss, and malnutrition courting death. This self-punitive behavior is a somatic equivalent of a depression. Conversely, in the beginning of the process of getting well, a patient will typically begin to become more assertive, verbalize, and act out aggression instead of starving and being depressed.

The bulimic patient, by contrast, is unable to control aggressive impulses as effectively, tending impulsively and self-destructively to act out hostility with drinking, stealing, drug use, promiscuity, and antisocial behavior (Mintz 1988a). Bulimic patients who gorge and destroy the food are unconsciously acting out hostility against ambivalently cathected "food-people," shredding the food in the same manner that they would like to shred the people.

The aggressive conflict at its more primitive level represents a split-off part of the ego because of the identification with voracious, tearing animals, and it is a manifestation of early cannibalistic impulses, with the patient dealing with the desire to destroy and eat the hated object or its parts (Mintz 1988a, Wilson 1985b and others). Signs of this conflict are revealed in the anorexic's typical aversion to red meat, whose association is so close to human flesh that it is totally avoided in the patient's diet. Bulimics reveal in their eating patterns other clues that indicate the nature of their aggressive conflicts as well as the underlying primitive connotations. The patient who gorges often demonstrates indiscriminate food choice during bouts of bulimic binging. Most graphic is the appearance of insatiable, frenetic wolfing down of endless quantities of all kinds of food. The need for the food can become so desperate that the individual will search out any source, which in extreme cases can include pillaging the garbage can in the kitchen or even in the street. The bulimic while binging appears in many ways similar to rats, sharks, and other vicious carnivores in their eating habits. The main difference seems to be that the animals may eat voraciously until they are satiated; the bulimic does not eat to the point of food satiation, but rather until the fury toward the hated object is satiated. Thus the bulimic eats until aggressive discharge is spent, and this need to satisfy voracious aggressive impulses contributes to the patient's fear of blowing up and getting fat.

The emphasis here on the anorexic and bulimic patient's aggressive conflicts is not meant to suggest that the behavior is solely a result of aggressive conflict. Other conflicts are also recognized and have been described elsewhere (Wilson et al. 1985a). Major conflict is related to dependency needs: fusion, attachment, separation, individuation, loss, and death. A third group is related to sexual conflict: puberty, sexual identity, adolescent body change, menstruation, sexual behavior, pregnancy, delivery, and motherhood.

Knife Symbolism

A symbolic displacement of the identification with tooth-prominent animals, with their destructive ripping, tearing impulses, is evident in the frequent knife-wielding fantasies of these patients. These fantasies reveal impulses to act out with the knife in the same ripping, tearing fashion, thus emulating the animal's behavior. The clinical material is replete with illustrations that the knife represents the tooth and that the patient behaves as if he or she is walking about with thirty-two sharp knives in his or her mouth.

Three of the six patients I have presented here in the detailed cases were preoccupied with stabbing impulses. Ten-year-old Eric had thoughts of stabbing his sister for two years. Marshall had dreams of stabbing his minister-king-father and brother, and Katherine was frightened about stabbing her little brother. Eric provided the clearest clue to the symbolic meaning of the knife. When he described the shark that he thought bit out the man's eye, he then described his identification with the shark as he cut out the fish's eye with his knife (teeth). This was followed by his association to a dream where, in retaliation, "he is being sawed up" (by displaced mechanical teeth-jaws), and he awakened frightened. Associating further, he reported repetitive dreams of cannibals who spear the victim (knife him), then skewer him (with a long knife), followed by dreams about cutting off people's heads and eating them. It was my impression that tooth symbolism was prominent in the expression of Eric's cannibalistic impulses. The knife can stand for a single tooth or teeth. We can also see in Herbert the tendency to externalize a part of the body onto an inanimate object; this patient described an earth-moving machine with upper- and lower-teeth that picked up people in its mouth.

Shengold (1967, 1971) also emphasized the preoccupation with and importance of teeth in his "Rat People," and Klein (1933) pointed out that the infant experienced the fear of being eaten from projecting oral-sadistic impulses onto the mother. Simmel (1944) suggested that the infant's identification with food set off cannibalistic fear. Shengold (1971) added, "With the teeth painfully forcing their way through the mucosa of the gum, the infant can be said to bite himself (and experience being bitten) before he can bite anything else" (p. 283).

Further Tooth Symbolism

Sperling (1978a) described a 7-year-old boy with severe ulcerative colitis, for whom animals represented attempts at dealing with sadistic aggressive impulses. She also noted that while it was common for patients with ulcerative colitis to have anorexia, the true anorexia syndrome emerged in some of the adolescent girls with concomitant ulcerative colitis, so that these ulcerative colitis patients have relevance to anorexic conflict. Overstimulated by having seen repeated parental intercourse, her child-patient acted out his sadistic conflict in play analysis and in nightmares and also revealed the conflict in repeated dreams of animals: "I was sleeping and saw a big rat coming towards me. I got very frightened and started to run away . . . and I climbed up a tree. The big rat with the big mouth . . . started to climb up after me and wanted to eat me up" (p. 146). He awoke with fear and diarrhea, which was connected to his devouring, destructive impulses. Another time: "I dreamed I was a pig. A man chopped off his neck. They wanted to eat it, but the pig was still walking with his head chopped off."

Eric described a feast where a whole pig dominated the meal. He also identified with the pig, as he had identified with lizards, rats, piranhas, sharks, and cannibals. Marshall also reported memories of seeing a whole roasted pig, with emphasis on the head. Both of these occurred around the time the patients developed their anorexic illness.

Pigs and humans are the only animals that are omnivorous, eating both plant and animal. Schlossman (1983) described the importance of swine in Egyptian mythology; the pig was viewed as a cannibalistic figure, epitomizing the people's fear that the God Set would eat them. The Egyptians buried their dead in shallow sand graves, where pigs would uncover and devour the bodies. Schlossman also felt that the Hebrews' prohibition against eating pigs arose from an unconscious hostile, cannibalistic impulse against the father from unresolved oedipal conflict.

Sperling (1978b) also reported the case of a 7-year-old girl with all the typical symptoms of anorexia except amenorrhea, the onset of the symptoms following the birth of a brother the year before. She also became afraid of cats and was paranoid toward her mother. "Oral impregnation and anal birth fantasies dominated her fantasy life. She had strong cannibalistic impulses which had to be repressed, leading to an inhibition of biting and chewing. She had wishes to eat something "alive" (p. 143). These wishes expressed her fantasy of the baby getting into the mother's belly and being swallowed alive. These repressed impulses were, in part, externalized and projected onto cats as manifested in the cat phobia."

Eric's anorexia also followed the birth of a girl cousin from his mother's sister, which reawakened memories of the birth of his own hated sister. Eric's cannibalistic fantasies ultimately emerged as his impulse to kill, cook, and eat his rival for parental affection. His attempt to repress his cannibalistic impulses took the form of displacing them onto the sharks, lizards, piranha, rats, and vampires. Concomitantly, however, his voracious appetite for eating and destroying his sister was in part satisfied by his interest, gratification, and thirst for endless knowledge and his devouring information about the eating patterns of these tooth-filled reptiles, resulting in hours of research in the library about their habits, including his satisfying discovery of the shark's "feeding frenzies."

At the same time, however, repression of his own impulses to destroy and cannibalize with his teeth required not only that he not eat meat, but that he eat no food at all except milk shakes. In this way he reassured himself that he was a toothless baby, totally unable to cannibalize, and left to suck at the nipple-straw of the milk shake, which replaced eating the hated rival sister. He relived the role of the "toothless baby" on a rigid feeding schedule. (He had to have his milk shakes at home at 7:00 P.M. exactly, or he would fast totally for the next twenty-four). Doing this permitted him to be the baby again, in an attempt to regain the oral feeding from the mother when he felt deprived by the hated sister's birth.

346   Ira L. Mintz, M.D.

Starving also provided him with a great deal of attention and concern, which he was able to regulate and control by a threat to starve. It also caused him punishment for his hostility from his strict, archaic superego. In addition, the rigid control over choice of food, time, and quantity reassured him that he could control his destructive impulses and also feel in control of a part of his body in place of his world in disarray. How similar is he to Sperling's patient with illness precipitated by the birth of the hated rival and the inhibition of biting and aggression covering up the oral and sadistic conflicts.

Once Eric began to eat, he ate all foods normally, including meats and complete meals, in contrast to most anorexics, whose eating patterns change gradually. He noted that as he ate meat, he experienced funny feelings in his teeth, suggesting that their use set off internal discomfort from probable unconscious cannibalistic linkages.

The mother of an anorexic daughter described bring abused physically and psychologically by very disturbed parents. (Shengold described similar histories with his patients.) She also experienced repeated terrifying childhood dreams that her parents turned into wolves. At age 14 she saw a movie about people from another planet burrowing into the earth. When earthlings fell into the hole, they would inject someone in the neck and turn him into a terrible person. "I used to look at my parents' necks to see the marks," she recalled.

Teresa, a 28-year-old bulimic patient who had a four-year history of binging and vomiting, revealed a childhood history of nightmares almost every night for about two years.

I'd wake up and see snakes or spiders, tons of them covering the room and walls. Then the room was on fire, and I couldn't get out. I'd scream and call my parents. I don't remember the dream itself, just the aftermath. Sometimes there was water on the floor, or I'd awaken afraid. I'd see the snakes. I'd almost hear the sound of fire. Snakes were all intertwined on the floor. Centipedes and spiders were on the wall . . . fire or water on the ground . . . deep and black.

I learned to swim but I wouldn't go swimming in the ocean at night because I was afraid of eels and sharks. I'd rather swim in a pool. We had a new baby brother when I was 7 years old. My mother had wanted another baby for a long time; so did my father. My mother had two previous miscarriages . . . When we moved to another home because my father was transferred, I didn't want to go. I'd lose all my friends. The new house in another city was big, because my father was promoted. It scared me . . . I think that my nightmares stopped at age 9. Then my stomach began to bother me and it has, on and off, for years.

The nightmares seem to be related to the hostile feelings that the patient had to the birth of her brother. The snakes, spiders, and sharks represent her projected identifications, very similar to those of the other patients, especially Eric, and Sperling's patient, whose illness was precipitated by the birth of a sibling. Additional confirmatory evidence is suggested by the fear of the deep, black water, from which the hated, sibling-shark can retaliate with the same cannibalistic retaliatory behavior projected onto it, and from which the hated sibling can emerge.

Here we see a modification of the clinical picture, with similar underlying psychodynamics. Eric and Sperling's patient both developed anorexia in childhood after the birth of a sibling. Teresa described a two-year period of nightmares at age 7, following the sister's birth. Teresa's hostile reaction to the sibling's birth set off the nightmares about snakes, spiders, and subsequent fear of sharks, all of which represented a phobic resolution to the conflict instead of an anorexic solution. Her nightmares subsided with the subsequent development of a long-standing shark phobia and stomach symptoms: different symptomatic solutions to the same underlying conflict. In her middle twenties, her underlying unresolved, aggressive conflict ultimately resurfaced with the bulimic symptoms.

It is particularly illuminating, for our understanding of the psychodynamics of anorexic illness, to be able to compare the coping with aggressive conflict in childhood in Eric's and Sperling's patient's anorexia, and the temporary resolution provided by Teresa's nightmares. The nightmares were replaced by the shark phobia and the stomach symptoms, and years later by the crystalizing out of the bulimic illness. Hitchcock (Chapter 10) describes three girls in analysis, ages 4, 6, and 9, perpetual smilers who developed anorexia-bulimia during treatment. The 4-year-old reported dreams of "engulfing monsters." She demonstrated interesting behavior when attempting to catch a ball. "As the object began its downward arc toward her outstretched hands, she invariably opened her mouth wide, drew her lips back, and bared her teeth until she caught the ball." He suggests that the animal-like behavior with bared teeth represented an unconscious identification with a tooth-bearing animal, in circumstances that did not require the use of the mouth, and that the lips-drawn, bared-teeth expression reflected the emergence of a regressed aggressive posture.

Validation of these manifestations of repressed aggressive conflict was evident when the analysis of one child's hostility resulted in the replacement of her perpetual smile with a hostile grimace, and the other child developed a tightening of the lips and clenched teeth.

Herbert, the 14-year-old boy discussed earlier, demonstrated a similar type identification, evident in his story at age 7 of the children being snowflakes falling from the sky: when some of the other children opened their mouths and let the flakes fall on their tongues, the snowflake children were eaten. The cannibalistic theme is expressed, colored by his typical reaction formations, with aggressive conflict reflected in gentle, delicate fashion. However, the associative linkages, far removed from conscious awareness, reveal him to be the boy riding the dragon and destroying the invaders. A cannibalistic theme was evident both in the behavior of the child playing ball and in Herbert's story.

Sperling (1978b) emphasizes the primary role of sexual conflict in anorexia while minimizing the importance of aggressive conflict: "Anorexia nervosa is a specific outcome of an unsuccessful attempt at solution of an unconscious sexual conflict concerning sexual identity (p. 168)." While it is true that sexual conflict can and frequently does play a major role in most anorexic patients, it is my impression that the preponderant conflict feeding the anorexic syndrome is aggressive conflict.

My colleagues and I (Mintz 1985b) have felt that the therapeutic approach to treating these patients involves dealing first with self-destructive conflict and punitive superego attitudes, and then approaching externalized aspects of aggression when superego guilt is modified and able to tolerate the aggression. Analysis of sexual conflict should usually follow analysis of aggressive conflict. Using this approach, one can often see the subsiding of anorexic symptoms before much of the sexual conflict is dealt with, and in some cases with its hardly being dealt with at all.

Sucking Symbolism

Sucking is usually considered to be related to oral drive, nutrition, early infant–mother relationship, dependency, and security. Sucking as a sign of aggressive drive discharge is less frequently mentioned.

Fourteen-year-old Herbert's preoccupations suggest that his need to repress and deny his aggressive cannibalistic impulses was so strong that at times it required regression back to sucking, which then symbolized aggressive, cannibalistic discharge. His description of the lizard people who inject people with poison and eat them also includes the following: "The lizard people arrived in a space ship that hovered over the earth, and sucked up all the water, turning California into a desert . . . They ate rodents, animals, and the fresh meat of humans." Thus we see the juxtaposition of sucking up the water and creating a desert by destroying the land linked to the cannibalistic destruction of people. Most notable in this regard, historically, was the mother's remark during the initial consultation: "He was breastfed for seven months, as were the other three. They took everything out of me and I lost 15 pounds. I loved it. He always loved milk." Clearly she felt "sucked dry" just like a desert, while reaction formation obscured her true feelings and suggested conflict over breast-feeding and nurturing.

His memory, between ages 4 and 6, of monsters coming out of the ground and destroying people served as the anlage for his later adolescent thoughts of the monsters going into the ground and destroying people. Additional aggressive conflict surrounded the terrifying dreams of the witch who cut off his hands, along with a whole series of castration memories. The persistence of the conflict was well illustrated in his current need still to sleep with his hands under the pillow so that they would not be cut off. Here too is the prominence of knives. This conflict and the aggression that it generated in Herbert contributed to his early and prolonged eating disorder. The description of the early voracious, aggressively perceived sucking led into later denial of voracious eating impulses. Herbert became an exquisitely picky eater, denying his cannibalism, demonstrating his control over his impulses with extremely careful choosing of food, and projecting his own conflict into his cannibalistic fantasies of dragons, monsters, demons, and dinosaurs. Both Herbert and Eric had a voracious appetite for devouring an endless series of books on cannibalism, suggesting an identification as the cannibalism and the cannibalized. The infant's concept of being eaten was referred to by Simmel (1944) and by Shengold (1967, 1971).

Eric's resolution of similar conflict was almost identical in his identification with cannibalistic animals. Whereas Herbert's destructive sucking impulses were projected onto the planet people when he was an adolescent, and onto the killing monsters coming out of the ground in his childhood dreams, Eric projected onto vampires that suck, and he became an "infant vampire" that sucked only milk shakes. Concomitantly, he did not eat a piece of food or drink a drop of water for six months. His jealousy of and hatred for his little sister was much more flagrant than Herbert's, with his anorexic decompensation following the birth of his girl cousin. At the time, I had neglected to inquire of his mother whether he had observed his new born cousin sucking at the breast or bottle prior to his shift from his typical anorexic diet to just milk shakes.

While Eric's sucking up of his milk shakes can represent a denial of the existence of his teeth and the concomitant aggressive impulses toward his "cousin-sister," through regressive helplessness, the return of the repressed may take the form of a destructive sucking up of the milk. Aggressively sucking up the mother's milk is eating a part of the mother's body (cannibalism) and leaving the breast-body-bottle as arid as the desert. This idea is also present in Herbert's fantasy, as well as in his mother's perception of the nursing experience. Eric's, Herbert's, and Eleanor's fantasy of the vampire sucking falls into the same category. Interestingly, the vampire fantasy presents the fusion of the biting and the sucking impulses. The vampire bites and then sucks.

A 12-year-old girl with symptoms of anorexia (Mintz 1989) developed symptoms of asthma at 18 months of age following the birth of her brother. Anorexic cannibalistic fantasies took the form of jokes: "How do you get out from under a pile of babies? Eat your way out." While destructive sucking was prominent in this girl's asthmatic fantasy life, with whole towns being sucked up and destroyed by the sucking wind of tornadoes, the fantasies might also be relevant in the evolution of her anorexic syndrome.

In asthma and anorexia, the violent sucking in of the air-milk-mother may be present and indicative of aggressive conflict towards the ambivalently cathected introject. In asthma, the unconscious impulse to aggressively suck in and destroy the introject is denied and repressed, as is the aggressive impulse to explode out with an outpouring of air-wind to destroy the object (Mintz 1988b). The conflict may be expressed symbolically in the asthmatic's inability to inhale and exhale air containing these dangerous impulses and dangerous introjects. In anorexia, the ambivalently cathected air-milk-mother can be ingested and destroyed through feeding (breast milk = mother's body) or, once ingested, can destroy from within. The conscious need to lose weight by not eating or by vomiting and purging covers the unconscious need to avoid ingesting and destroying the introject or, once it is ingested, eliminating the danger from within by vomiting or purging. From the aspect of the ego, the asthmatic's inability to breathe and the anorexic's inability to eat are attempts to contain the aggression and control the air-food-object, as well as superego punishment for the aggression.

In normal development as well as in anorexia and asthma, libidinal and dependency needs may be satisfied by inhaling of the loved object in the warm air as the air-milk-mother. In the same manner, the irresistible urge to gorge also serves the need to internalize the sought-after object. It is also possible that during nursing, the close proximity of the mother's face and breathing bathes the infant's face in a rhythmical movement of air, further predisposing a fusion of the gastrointestinal and respiratory systems and causing the infant to associate the movement of the warm air against the face with the presence of the mother, mother's milk, and dependency needs. A validating vignette was provided by the mother of a 10-month-old infant. The baby's aunt initiated a game by blowing on the baby's face, prompting him to respond with a sucking-in-movement of the lips followed by laughing during repeated play. The bathing of the infant's face with air was reminiscent enough of the breast-feeding, and it prompted him to initiate sucking movements and a happy response. An anorexic patient described the sense of satisfaction she achieved when inhaling the warm air of cigarette smoke or the warm air during a hot shower. Once out of the warm shower into the cooler bathroom, she felt rejected.

It appears plausible that during nursing the infant ingests part of the mother's body as milk and inhales part of her body as her exhaled air, so that eating and breathing are both associated with oral incorporation of the air-milk-mother. This early cathexis of the gastrointestinal and respiratory systems with an ambivalent relationship to the mother predisposes them to the expression of later conflict in the form of asthma and anorexia.

SUMMARY

A review of a large number of anorexic and bulimic patients reveals that a considerable number are preoccupied with all kinds of tooth-prominent animals and their symbolic representations. These animals emerged in play, dreams, fantasies, and behavior. An identification with these animals was evident, as was a projected phobic representation of the aggressive conflict.

Subsequently the clinical material demonstrated that the "animal-patient's teeth" was the primary aggressive weapon, represented symbolically by a knife, and that the patient, in the frequent use of the knife in dreams and fantasy, was aggressively using his or her "knife-teeth": the patient's teeth represented thirty-two knives.

Unconscious identification with these rapacious, ripping, and devouring animals, at the most primitive level, represented impulses to attack, kill, and devour the object or its parts. This suggests that these unconscious impulses and fantasies are much more common than is reported, and they indicate a broader based underlying cannibalistic preoccupation in these patients. Vigorous sucking is a less-recognized but relevant component in aggressive conflict in both anorexia and asthma, as the patient attempts to deal with the ambivalently cathected introjects, with conflict over retaining or expelling them. The early source of this conflict may arise during the infant's nursing, when it cannibalistically ingests part of the mother's body as milk and inhales part of her body from her exhaled air. Finally, I am indebted to Green (1990) and Friedman (1990) for pointing out that Marc Blitzstein's adaptation of Brecht's lyrics in the *Three Penny Opera* compare Mac the Knife's behavior to that of the shark.

The shark has pretty teeth, dear
And he shows them gleaming white.
Just a jackknife has MacHeath, dear
But he keeps it out of sight.
When the shark bites with his teeth, dear
Scarlet billows start to spread.
Fancy gloves wears MacHeath, dear
So there's not a trace of red.

REFERENCES

Barkin, L. (1989). Paper presented at the psychoanalytic study group to the Psychoanalytic Association of New York.

Blos, P. (1974) The genealogy of the ego ideal. *The Psychoanalytic Study of the Child* 29:43–88. New Haven, CT: Yale University Press.

Chiorazzi, L. (1985). Personal communication.

Frazer, J. (1959). *The New Golden Bough*. New York: Criterion Books.

Freiman, G. (1989). Personal communication.

Freud, S. (1909). A case of obsession neurosis. *Standard Edition* 10:20.

_____ (1912–1913). Totem and taboo. *Standard Edition* 13:1–164.

Friedman, S. (1990). Personal communication.

Gensensway, D. (1988). A psychoanalytic study of bulimia in pregnancy. In *Bulimia: Psychoanalytic Treatment and Theory*, ed. H. Schwartz, pp. 299–345. Madison, CT: International Universities Press.

Green, A. (1990). Personal communication.

Hogan, C. (1984). Personal communication.

_____ (1985). Psychodynamics. In *Fear of Being Fat: The Treatment of Anorexia Nervosa and Bulimia*, rev. ed., ed. C. P. Wilson, C. C. Hogan, and I. L. Mintz, pp. 115–128. New York: Jason Aronson.

Kestenberg, J. (1975). Attunement and clashing in mother–child interaction. In *Children and Parents: Psychoanalytic Studies in Development*, pp. 157–170. New York: Jason Aronson.

Klein, M. (1933). Early development of conscience in the child. In *Contributions to Psychoanalysis*. London: Hogarth Press, 1948.

Kramer, S. (1974). Discussion of J. Sour's paper, "The anorexia nervosa syndrome," *International Journal of Psycho-Analysis* 55:577–579.

Link, D. (1990). Personal communication.

Mahon, E. (1981). *The secondary worlds of childhood*. Paper presented at meeting of the Association for Psychoanalytic Medicine, New York, NY.

Mintz, I. (1985a). The relationship between self-starvation and amenorrhea. In *Fear of Being Fat: The Treatment of Anorexia Nervosa and Bulimia*, rev. ed., ed C. P. Wilson, C. C. Hogan, and I. L. Mintz, pp. 335–344, New York: Jason Aronson.

――― (1985b). The clinical picture of anorexia nervosa and bulimia. In *Fear of Being Fat: The Treatment of Anorexia Nervosa and Bulimia*, rev. ed, ed. C. P. Wilson, C. C. Hogan, and I. L. Mintz, pp. 83–114. New York: Jason Aronson.

――― (1985c). Anorexia and bulimia in males. In *Fear of Being Fat: The Treatment of Anorexia Nervosa and Bulimia*, rev. ed., ed. C. P. Wilson, C. C. Hogan, and I. L. Mintz, pp. 263–303. New York: Jason Aronson.

――― (1988a). Self-destructive behavior in anorexia and bulimia. In *Bulimia: Psychoanalytic Treatment and Theory*, ed. H. Schwartz, pp. 127–172. Madison, CT: International Universities Press.

――― (1988b). *The clinical and theoretical association between anorexia nervosa and bronchial asthma*. Paper presented at the meeting of the New Jersey Psychoanalytic Society, Hackensack (NJ) Medical Center.

――― (1989). The analytic treatment of a case of anorexia and severe asthma in a twelve-year-old girl. In *Psychosomatic Symptoms: Psychodynamic Treatment of the Underlying Personality Disorder*, ed. C. P. Wilson and I. L. Mintz, pp. 251–308. Northvale, NJ: Jason Aronson.

Oliner, M. (1988). Anal components in overeating. In *Bulimia: Psychoanalytic Treatment and Theory*, ed., H. Schwartz, pp. 227–253. Madison, CT: International Universities Press.

Risen, S. (1982). The psychoanalytic treatment of an adolescent with anorexia nervosa. In *Psychoanalytic Study of the Child* 37:433–460. New Haven, CT: Yale University Press.

Rudominer, H. (1984). Psychoanalysis of a male bulimic patient. Discussion group on psychosomatic diseases. Winter meeting American Psychoanalytic Association, New York, NY.

Shaw, N. (1984). Personal communication.

Schlossman, H. (1979). Personal communication.

――― (1983). Swine in myth and religion. *American Imago* 40:35–49.

――― (1991). *Human sacrifice and cannibalism*. Paper presented at the New Jersey Psychoanalytic Society, Hackensack (NJ) Medical Center, September.

Schowalter, J. (1983). Some meanings of being a horsewoman. *Psychoanalytic Study of the Child* 38:501–517. New Haven, CT: Yale University Press.

Shengold, L. (1963). The parent as a sphinx. *Journal of the American Psychoanalytic Association* 11:725–751.

――― (1967). The effects of overstimulation: rat people. *International Journal of Psycho-Analysis* 48:403–415.

――― (1971). More about rats and rat people. *International Journal of Psycho-Analysis* 52:277–288.

Schwartz, H. (1988). Psychoanalytic perspectivies. In *Bulimia: Psychoanalytic Treatment and Theory*, ed. H. Schwartz, pp. 31–53. Madison, CT: International Universities Press.

Simmel, E. (1944). Self-preservation and the death instinct. *Psychoanalytic Quarterly* 13:160–185.

Sours, J. (1980). *Starving to Death in a Sea of Objects*. New York: Jason Aronson.

Sperling, M. (1968). Trichotillomania, trichophagia, and cyclic vomiting. *International Journal of Psycho-Analysis* 49:682–690.

――― (1971). Spider phobias and spider fantasies: a clinical contribution to the study of symbol and symbol choice. *Journal of the American Psychoanalytic Association* 19:472–498.

――― (1978a). Psychoanalytic study of ulcerative colitis in children. In *Psychosomatic Disorders in Childhood*, ed. O. Sperling, pp. 77–98. New York: Jason Aronson.

――― (1978b). Case histories of anorexia nervosa. In *Psychosomatic Disorders of Childhood*, ed. O. Sperling, pp 139–156. New York: Jason Aronson.

Thomä, H. ed. (1967). *Anorexia Nervosa*. New York: International Universities Press.

Wilson, C. P. (1967). Stone as a symbol of teeth. *Psychoanalytic Quarterly* 36:418–425.

_____ (1971). On the limits of the effectiveness of psychoanalysis: early ego and somatic disturbances. *Journal of the American Psychoanalytic Association* 19:552–564.

_____ (1981). Sand symbolism: the primary dream representation of the Isakower phenomenon and of smoking addiction. In *Clinical Psychoanalysis,* ed S. Orgel and B. D. Fine, pp. 45–55. New York: Jason Aronson.

_____ (1985a). The fear of being fat in female psychology. In *Fear of Being Fat: The Treatment of Anorexia Nervosa and Bulimia,* rev. ed., ed. C. P. Wilson, C. C. Hogan, and I. L. Mintz, pp. 9–28. New York: Jason Aronson.

_____ (1985b). Dream interpretation. In *Fear of Being Fat: The Treatment of Anorexia Nervosa and Bulimia,* rev. ed., ed. C. P. Wilson, C. C., Hogan, and I. L. Mintz, pp. 245–254. New York: Jason Aronson.

_____ (1989). Dream interpretation. In *Psychosomatic Symptoms: Psychodynamic Treatment of the Underlying Personality Disorder,* ed. C. P. Wilson and I. L. Mintz, pp. 133–145. Northvale, NJ: Jason Aronson.

15

Clinical Vignettes

Ira L. Mintz

THE RELATIONSHIP BETWEEN ANOREXIA-BULIMIA AND EXERCISE

As our population has become increasingly health conscious, exercise—and particularly running—has become a national pastime. Thousands of runners enter endless races, while millions of joggers pursue their individual running goals. Anorexic and bulimic patients form a dramatic and little recognized segment of this group. Their dedication and preoccupation with running and exercise form an integral part of the clinical syndrome. A bulimic teenage girl has provided additional understanding into the nature of this picture.

Mary

The distressed parents of a 14-year-old girl described their concern about their daughter's changed behavior over the previous six months: a sudden

355

drop in grades with no interest in studying, socializing with an undesirable peer group, coming home drunk on a number of occasions, and their finding marijuana in her room. They had hesitated to intervene until Mary's aunt found a letter to Mary's cousin admitting that she was bulimic with gorging and vomiting. Confronted with the letter, Mary tearfully admitted that she had been bulimic intermittently for a number of months. The father, an ophthalmologist, and the mother, a lawyer, then sought help.

Salient features in Mary's history were the development of asthma at age 4, which was moderately severe until age 10 and then occurred infrequently during her adolescence. Her father and grandfather also had a history of asthma. No anorexia was evident in any of the four children, but the oldest was obese. Both parents were overweight and had been preoccupied with food all their lives. During latency, Mary exhibited separation anxiety with symptoms of crying at the beginning of first and second grades. At age 10 she was unwilling to sleep at her friends' homes but always encouraged them to sleep at hers. Signed up for sleep-away camp that summer, she was unable to go.

Relevant aspects of the parents' life revealed indifference and neglect by their own parents. The mother's two brothers were both alcoholic, while the father's sister suffered from a severe hearing defect from neglected repeated otitis media, as well as polio in childhood, which left a limp.

Mary was the youngest child with four older brothers, all outstanding athletes. Also an excellent athlete, she concentrated on basketball, tennis, and running. Receiving considerable recognition from her parents and friends for her athletic prowess, she appeared to enjoy sports. While she did not appear accident prone, she experienced two accidents in the sixteen months preceding the consultation. The father reported that she tripped while playing basketball, fracturing her elbow. A year later in the finals of a basketball tournament she landed awkwardly, fracturing her ankle and again requiring a cast.

Interviewed, Mary was an attractive, short-haired blonde, petite young woman, 5 feet, 2 inches, weighing 111 pounds. She was in consultation at her parents' request but was nevertheless pleasant and cooperative. She became tearful, however, as she recounted her parents' complaints of her friends' behavior, her own poor grades, and the drinking and marijuana smoking. At this point she also volunteered that she had been having an affair with a boy at school for the previous three months, which was initiated one evening when she was inebriated. In a question about her eating habits, she replied: "It probably began when I broke my elbow, because when I was in a cast, I couldn't run. When I can run, I can eat and not put on weight. Now I have to use willpower to decide how little I can eat and not put on weight. If I have a salad or fruit, it's all right, but if I have just one cookie, I feel guilty." (Just one cookie?) "Yes, and when I went back to sports, the guilt stayed with me. I couldn't eat any junk food at all." I commented that feeling guilty over one cookie suggested a pretty strict conscience. She replied, "It was a question of control: that I'd have the willpower not to eat one cookie."

This exchange appeared quite revealing. First it suggested that the injury that prevented running interfered with her perceived ability to control her weight consciously and seemed to be the stimulus setting off her fear of being fat. As a consequence, she became more conscious of and preoccupied with food. One might say that this sequence was quite natural and understandable, representing perfectly reasonable thinking without psychic conflict. More carefully scrutiny, however, reveals a different possibility. "If I have just one cookie, I feel guilty" suggests not only a very strict conscience, typical of anorexia and bulimia, but also an unreasonable and unrealistic quality to the statement, of which the patient was quite aware. She later acknowledged that a single cookie would not make her fat. This awareness emerged in her statement, "It was a question of control: that I'd have the willpower not to eat one cookie." The conscious use of willpower to control her impulses to eat may represent a symbolic displacement from her unconscious fear that she could not adequately control her aggressive and sexual impulses, or her relationships to external objects displaced onto the need to control food and weight.

In the second consultation it became more plausible that the preoccupation with food, the increasing fear of being fat, and the gorging and vomiting crystallized out of the first accident, from the resultant immobility, and subsided with the returning ability to exercise. The bulimia recurred following the second injury. The second episode, which also required initial bed rest, a leg cast, and limitation of movement, again resulted in increased eating symptoms. In this second consultation, however, a number of weeks post-injury, she was becoming increasingly mobile and active even with her crutches. She had insisted upon visiting a local Nautilus club, where she engaged in almost daily vigorous exercise of almost all the muscles of her body excluding the casted leg.

"I'm feeling better. I'm able to be more casual about food and weight these past few days. I just don't pay as much attention to it as I did before." I wondered aloud why that might have happened. "I can get around better on the crutches and I'm not restricted to home. I went to the tennis matches and even saw a golf tournament and walked the whole course. The Nautilus exercise makes me feel good. I can exercise the other parts of my body. That's why I feel better—the exercise."

In the third consultation with the parents, the father volunteered that he thought both accidents may have occurred because of Mary's very aggressive play in both basketball games; "She's the most aggressive player on the team."

In the third consultation with Mary, she commented that she was back to helping coach Little League basketball, was exercising two hours a day, and hadn't had any thoughts about food or paid undue attention to what she was eating. The possibility that this latest behavior might reflect a typical flight into health becomes less feasible when one considers her reflective comment in that session. She had been wondering why she started the eating and vomiting, wanted to find out, and consented to coming for treatment prior to my spelling out the conditions. I subsequently saw her weekly for about a dozen sessions while she worked out and moderated the rebellious, out-of-control behavior described earlier.

A colleague with whom I discussed Mary's symptoms wondered whether the anorexic behavior, which I attributed to the inability to run or exercise, might be a consequence of an emerging phobic response to the presence of the cast. This was conceivable since we know that during the course of treating anorexia or bulimia, it is not uncommon to see the subsiding anorexic symptoms replaced by a phobia. A developing phobia in response to the anxiety set off by the cast was certainly a valid consideration. However, a careful evaluation of the patient's reaction to her cast appeared to rule out that possibility. She was aware of no anxiety, inner tension, feelings of being trapped, or any need to rid herself of the cast. On the contrary, she volunteered feeling quite comfortable with the cast and voiced no pressuring impatience for its removal. To her knowledge, the exercising seemed to be the only factor in her anorexia. Its absence disturbed her greatly. The ability to exercise again was what seemed to restore her equilibrium. She stated that once she was able to exercise, even with the cast remaining, she felt more comfortable and reexperienced a sense of control over her weight, and her preoccupations with food and dieting disappeared.

Discussion

In an article exploring the relationship between obligatory running and anorexia, Yates and colleagues (1983) attempted to delineate common ground between the two phenomena. The term "obligatory running" was used to describe those runners who ran 50 or more miles a week. They noted that the emergence of 31 million runners in the United States coincided with the explosive incidence of anorexic illness. They found that the childhood development, character structure, thinking, and preoccupation with food of the runners was similar to those of the anorexics. In addition, they stated that when the runners experienced emotional distress, they needed to increase their levels of running markedly, and they feared any situation that would interfere with their running. Schlossman (1989) described a patient who stated that whenever he felt very angry, he had to run and run until he ultimately felt better and more intact. Kaminer (1989) reported a patient who stated that if he could not exercise, he began to eat more and developed anxiety about getting fat. Levine (1989) described a very athletic teenage girl whose bulimia was precipitated by a knee injury, which prevented her being able to exercise. Sacks (1979) felt that fast running was an effective means of discharging aggression. Yates's term, "obligatory running" was an excellent one because it recognized the "need" to run in contrast to the more popular but superficial concept of a "desire" to run. Obligatory runners got upset, anxious, and depressed when they could not run.

While exercise has been recognized as an integral component of the anorexic-bulimic syndrome, it has usually been viewed as a conscious means of regulating weight levels and of controlling the individual's fear of being fat. Its unconscious role of mediating aggressive drive discharge and increased ego control over a component of the environment has been minimized. From this perspective, we can consider that different types of exercise, especially running, can serve to drain off intolerable levels of aggressive build-up and attempt to reestablish more acceptable levels of ego homeostasis, preventing overt anorexic decompensation. It then appears reasonable that when Mary fractured her elbow and was unable to exercise, she decompensated with gorging and vomiting. As she regained the capacity to discharge aggression with exercise, the bulimic symptoms abated. A subsequent fracture impeding her ability to exercise again resulted in a decompensation with gorging and vomiting, which again subsided with reemerging ability to exercise.

In support of Yates's data, a 20-year-old man in analysis for bulimia Mintz (1985e), who initially reported "loving" to run, ultimately acknowledged that he "had" to run. The possibility that he would be unable to run because of physical injury resulted in anxiety bordering on panic. His concern was intensified with his emerging awareness of many aspects of self-destructive behavior, including running in the dark so that he could not see the ground clearly, landing on rocks and in holes and twisting his ankle, or accelerating on pebbly curves and slipping and falling. He reported that an early achievement in the analysis was his cessation of self-destructive running patterns, which eased his anxiety about injury and permitted him the increased confidence that he would be able to continue his running unimpeded. Since self-destructive thinking and behavior are so characteristic of the anorexic-bulimic syndromes, and obligatory runners have typical anorexic character traits, one wonders whether the large number of injuries suffered by runners is in part a consequence of self-destructive behavior, illustrated by the case of Mary and the numerous injuries reported by Yates.

Prior to treatment, my patient, who had a history of gorging and vomiting, was accustomed to running about 50 miles a week. He decided to stop the vomiting abruptly by exercising great willpower. At that point, however, he suddenly felt forced to double his running and found that he had to run over 100 miles a week. It appeared that one of the functions of vomiting was to discharge aggression, and when this outlet was blocked, the patient felt it necessary to use another means of aggressive discharge. This phenomenon is not unusual, since during the course of treatment we frequently see that one symptom can be replaced by another. When insight interferes with the use of one psychosomatic symptom, yet the underlying unconscious conflict is still not fully resolved, another symptom may take its place (Mintz 1980–1981).

At another point, after revealing his intense anger at his aunt, he reported that the only way he was able to remain at the dinner table with her, during her visits from Florida, was to run 40 minutes to decrease his anger prior to coming into dinner. It is well accepted that aggressive conflict is a major problem in anorexia-bulimia: in my mind, the major conflict. A 19-year-old insightful anorexic woman (see Chapter 7), after the fifth session of her treatment, wrote the following in her diary:

A strange thing happened on the way driving home [from treatment]. All of a sudden, in the middle of the highway, I started to cry. Something inside me kept growing until I released it in my tears. I got home and I couldn't stop. I ran three miles and my problems seemed to clear up. I'm going to run every day. Just as I control the eating, I'm going to control the running. I'm losing control, and I've got to get it back.

Around the same time, she had noted that over the past year she had tried to hide from her worries by exercising constantly, keeping her mind occupied with a number of jobs and, most effectively, by starving.

It is of interest to note that the patient was spontaneously aware over the year prior to starting treatment that starving was the most effective method of suppressing conflict: that unconsciously feared loss of control over aggressive and sexual impulses and dependent yearnings were controlled by displacing the conflicts onto controlling her impulse to eat, by starving. Demonstrating to herself that being able symbolically to control her appetite reassured her that she could control aggressive and sexual impulses and dependency feelings that threatened to erupt and overwhelm her. In addition, controlling her eating provided her with the symbolic illusion that she was in control of her external world without having to face recognizing that it was in chaos.

A teenage anorexic began to run for the first time following a suicide attempt, commenting that the running "got the anger out." Running before the visit of a disliked uncle, she remarked how relaxed she then felt in his presence. I have found this recognition in a considerable percentage of patients. With so many patients aware that starving suppresses conflict, one has to question the effectiveness of an approach that suggests that the patient does not know what to eat and that encourages the patient to seek the help of a nutritionist to supervise meal planning. To focus on eating when starving is a displacement from the real conflict is to collude with the patient in focusing upon the wrong issue.

A corollary that would follow, one also reported by many patients, is that eating liberates conflict. Thomas, a 16-year-old anorexic patient (Mintz 1985e), at one point reported that nothing bothered him and that he had no problems and therefore nothing to say. When he complained of nothing to discuss, I suggested that he had fewer conscious worries because he starved and therefore buried them. If he ate, the worries would emerge. Accepting what he perceived as a challenge, he ate that night. The next session he reported having worries on his mind all night, to the degree that he was unable to study for an exam and was also unable to sleep.

In the case of the patient who kept the diary (see Chapter 7), it was clear that the conflicts were close to the surface and pushing into consciousness, as is illustrated by her comment, "Something inside me kept growing until

I released it in my tears. . . . I ran three miles and my problems seemed to clear up.'' She realized that the running also dissipated her fears but did not recognize that running was a mechanism that discharged aggression. This point became patently clear in the following session when she commented, "When I eat, I'm afraid something terrible will happen. . . . something terrible will come out of me . . . about how I feel about people." The initial rupturing forth of aggression had been replaced by tears of helplessness. Later reflection had modified her perspective with increasing awareness of the anger. Without her understanding the dynamics, however, it had been clear to her that the running was the antidote to the experience of conflict.

One can also clearly see the defensive value of the symptom: starving and running serve to suppress and repress upsetting thoughts, feelings, and anxieties that she feels will overwhelm her ability to cope. In essence, she controlled her impulses by starving, and she discharged her impulses by running. Her comment, "I'm going to run every day" is a declaration that at one level, she is unwilling to face her problems and that the treatment represents a threat, in attempting to uncover what she is desperately trying to hide. If the patient has doubts about being able to deal with problems with analytic help and understanding, how can she be expected to face them with no understanding at all, such as by being coerced to eat. Ideally, if there is no medical emergency, no attempt should be made to interfere with the patient's eating or exercising at this stage of reliance upon the treatment. Her continued control over eating and running can permit her to modulate the amount of anxiety and conflict that she experiences until increasing understanding resolves the conflicts and the symptoms subside.

The importance of exercise was further highlighted in the opening phase of treatment in a 16-year-old anorexic boy (Mintz 1989b). I learned that he also had asthma, severe enough to cause marked wheezing just from walking slowly. With this history it was somewhat surprising to learn that he was running unimpeded as a member of his high school cross-country track team. I was told not to inform his internist that he was on the track team, because no one was going to interfere with his running. In an imploring, plaintive voice, he threatened that he had to run or he would die. Here we see what appears to be a physiological inconsistency: severe exercise, which typically precipitates asthmatic attacks in asthma-prone individuals, has no effect upon this boy, yet very mild exercise in the form of slow walking is associated with wheezing. The observation begs for a psychological explanation rather than a physiological one. This physiological inconsistency may not be as rare as it appears, however. A 12-year-old severely asthmatic girl (Mintz 1989b) on occasion revealed a similar experience. Unable to walk up stairs without marked wheezing, she was still able to ski vigorously without ill effect. She too was anorexic. It may be that this condition is more common in patients with both asthma and anorexia where the intense need of the anorexic to exercise overrides any physiological tendency to precipitate asthmatic attacks. We know that strong emotional investment in an experience can interfere with physiological reactions (Deutsch 1987).

Summary

A case of a 14-year-old bulimic girl was presented in which bulimic symptoms developed and subsided at two distinct points of time correlated with two fracture injuries which required casting and interfered with running and exercise. On both occasions, the inability to run and exercise precipitated bulimic symptoms which promptly cleared with the resumption of exercise although the patient still remained in a cast.

It is suggested that some individuals potentially vulnerable to anorexia and bulimia may unconsciously prevent its emergence by running and exercising, thereby facilitating aggressive discharge and replacing passive helplessness with regained ego mastery and the avoidance of psychological decompensation.

GUM-CHEWING IN ANOREXIA NERVOSA AND BULIMIA

Intensive gum-chewing in starving anorexic patients is a very common phenomenon. One patient reported chewing 125 sticks a day; another, 65. In some cases, a considerable amount of the daily caloric intake is derived from sugar in the gum. At 15 calories a stick, 100 sticks would yield 1,500 calories. The fact that gum is chewed so intensively suggests that its choice is overdetermined.

The patient will say that she enjoys chewing gum because of its sweet taste. Sweet candylike taste is reminiscent of child and adolescent enjoyment of candy, a return to the relationship with mother and, ultimately, unconsciously, to nursing. Another patient described that "gum-chewing is like eating all the time and keeping my mouth busy." In a subsequent session she reported that one day when she decided not to chew gum, she got so tense that she didn't know what to do and ended up eating everything in sight, even food that she didn't like. Gum-chewing was an alternative to gorging and weight gain. On another occasion she stated that a number of girls at school treated her nastily; when she had the impulse to blow up at them, she grabbed for her gum and chewed and chewed, and the hatred subsided. This behavior was the equivalent of gorging with food, with the same discharge of aggression. An important component of the constant chewing was the use of her teeth.

Preoccupations with the teeth are present in a high percentage of starving anorexic patients and are related to the destruction of food, which unconsciously stands for people. Schlossman (1979) described an anorexic patient who would keep containers of food in the refrigerator labeled with people's names. The need to destroy through the use of the teeth is evident in the fantasies of starving anorexic patients. Burton (1991) described an anorexic girl who had difficulty eating string beans because they reminded her of dead bodies.

The unconscious preoccupation with teeth is clearly illustrated in the behavior of a 10-year-old anorexic boy (Mintz, Chapter 14) whose denial of his impulses to use his teeth was illustrated in his diet of milk shakes. For six months not a drop of food or water entered his mouth—only milk shakes. At the same time, his behavior and fantasy life were filled with preoccupations with teeth. He became totally absorbed with stories and thoughts of dragons, iguanas, lizards, sharks, and rats, wherein he identified with the animals who used their teeth to ravenously destroy people. These fantasies ultimately led to dreams and fantasies of the killing, cooking, and eating of his hated sister. He defended against these unconscious cannibalistic impulses by acting out a role of being a toothless baby able only to drink milk. Similar unconscious fantasies lie behind the typical anorexic's inability to use the teeth and eat meat, a food most closely associated with human flesh and, ultimately, with the unconscious fantasy of cannibalism and the destruction of the person. The 10-year-old boy described "strange feelings" in his teeth as he began to recover from anorexia and chew and eat meat.

Because of an ambivalent dilemma resulting from unresolved aggressive and dependency conflict, in which the patient has impulses to destroy because of the aggression and at the same time needs to preserve the person because of the dependency, gum plays a particularly unique role. It is the only food substance that can be chewed endlessly and not be totally destroyed. It therefore permits the patient to "chew out," attack, and destroy the ambivalently cathected object and at the same time be able to preserve it. The endless gum-chewing symbolically reenacts this process over and over. Binging with food, by contrast, destroys the object. Finally, the strict, punitive, primitive conscience that exacts retribution in the form of starving for the expression of anger is also assuaged, because the object remains preserved even after the destructive attack.

THE UNCONSCIOUS MEANING OF LAXATIVE USE IN ANOREXIA AND BULIMIA

Laxative use in anorexia and bulimia is a commonly recognized phenomenon. It is justified consciously by the patient to rid herself of constipation or to hasten the passage of food out of the intestine, in order to avoid her major dread: the fear of getting fat. Alternate means of dealing with the fear of getting fat are interfering with intake by starving and interfering with digestion by vomiting.

Hogan (1985) commented upon the problem of constipation and laxative use in anorexic patients. Emphasizing the obsessive-compulsive traits in these patients, he pointed out the importance of anal withholding and defiance and noted that the excessive use of laxatives was not primarily an attempt to rid the patient of constipation. He indicated that the stool represented internalized objects. One patient called her laxatives "little parents." Another referred to her "turds" as mother or fetuses.

Relationship of Laxative Use to Object Loss

A very distressed anorexic-bulimic 16-year-old girl had symptoms of starvation, gorging, and vomiting and used laxatives and diuretics heavily. The laxatives and diuretics had caused considerable physiological abnormality, requiring past hospitalizations. She described a past average use of sixty laxatives at one time. "When 60 didn't 'hurt,' I mean work, I tried 120. I'd recover in a day or two, and then I'd do it again." Her slip indicated the unconscious meaning behind the excessive laxative usage. Consciously justified to avoid weight gain, unconsciously they were used to "hurt" her insides, to produce pain, and to satisfy the strong inner requirements symbolized by their usage.

This was a girl who had been badly hurt. After a five-year chronic illness, her mother died of a brain tumor, two years before her anorexia began. The hurt that she felt at the loss of her mother was passively endured and experienced as an overwhelming trauma over which she had no control. Incorporation of the lost mother was symbolically represented by the stool within her. The passively endured, painful loss of the mother, over which she realistically had no control, was actively re-created by the use of the excessive laxatives, whereby she herself caused the pain and was also able to control and stop it as the effect of the laxatives spent themselves. Through the use of the repetition compulsion, the patient attempted to turn a passively experienced traumatic loss into an actively induced, but controlled, experience in the service of ego mastery. The loss of the diarrhea stool stood for the loss of the mother and ultimately the reunion with the lost mother in death, with this and other self-destructive behavior. Finally, the need to so badly damage her internal organs, by starving, gorging, vomiting, diarrhea, and electrolyte imbalance, represented a violent attack upon herself. Her anger was turned inward because of the guilt she felt for unconscious hatred toward the mother for leaving her in death. The laxative shredding the fragmented stool reflected part of this anger at the incorporated "mother-stool."

An additional confirming feature was the patient's statement that the excessive laxative use began the previous August, at around the third anniversary of the mother's death.

Gorging is the most prominent pathological feature that ultimately predisposes the patient to vomiting or laxative use. As with most other anorexic and bulimic patients, gorging most frequently results when a patient perceives a distressing experience as overwhelming, concludes that she cannot cope with it, and feels that the anxiety and distress require immediate relief. The gorging usually results in a decrease in anxiety and turmoil, as the patient displaces her conscious concern on to the binging and its repercussions, just as the anorexic, filled with anxiety and conflict, displaces her worry on to the starving and to food preoccupations, with similar reduction in anxiety. Thus, in both syndromes, anxiety reduction takes place at the price of repressed symptomatic solution, a further devaluated ego that accepts the belief that it cannot cope with conflict, and a regressed feeling of control over symbolic rather than realistic experience. Still, it is the relief of anxiety that makes it so difficult for these patients to renounce the gorging. In addition, the gorging represents the destruction of "food-people," and the discharge of aggression also decreases tension. During the actual binging, the patient does not report feeling well but notices a decrease in the conflict, which is replaced by all-consuming thoughts about the binging, guilt for it, and a frightening fear of getting fat.

In many of these patients the current painful experience sets off increasing feelings of rejection, isolation, and loneliness, with the perception of unendurable pain, leading to an almost irresistible impulse of binge. The gorging with food additionally symbolizes a sudden desperate attempt to undo the empty feelings of loss and loneliness, with the food regressively fulfilling symbolized experiences of love, attention, closeness, nurturing, and mother.

Relationship of Laxative Use to Aggressive Conflict

A 15-year-old bulimic girl suffering with severe constipation, gorging, and use of large numbers of laxatives provided the opportunity to clarify further the underlying meaning of laxative use. During the treatment it became increasingly clear that the stool unconsciously stood for many important people in her life: father, mother, sisters, brother, a baby, the babyish part of herself, the analyst, food, a penis, a boyfriend, and a vicious little animal. These ambivalently cathected introjects were sources of fear, love, and hatred.

Hatred toward the object, with the need to destroy it, or fears of being destroyed by it, required expulsion of the stool. Destruction of the hated internalized part of the self (the vicious little animal) also necessitated destruction of the stool. From time to time the patient would speak of her tremendous feelings of rage toward these introjects and of the impulses to destroy them. It was within this context that the laxative use became more understandable.

The patient would use not one or two laxatives to clear up the constipation, but fifty, sixty, or ninety. Then she would recoil in pain, cramps, and misery and need to remain in bed for twenty-four to thirty-six hours to recover. When confronted with the fact that constipated patients manage for years on only one or two laxatives, she rationalized by pointing out her severe condition. In one association, however, she indicated that she felt much better if the evacuated stool were shredded, not whole. It became evident that shredding the "stool-person" served to destroy it further. The excessive amount of laxatives was used to unconsciously kill the feared-hated person within her.

A corroborative association preceded the shredding fantasy by a number of days. During a vacation she became involved with a boyfriend, the son of family friends. She expressed frustration with his unreliable behavior, which set off episodes of gorging. Describing the incident after returning from the weekend, she bemoaned his not calling her. Becoming increasingly resentful and agitated, she finally exploded, "I'm so furious with him that I'd like to take a knife and chop him up into little pieces." The expression of conscious anger by "chopping him up" seemed to represent an externalization of the unconscious impulse to chop up the "food-boyfriend" with her "teeth choppers," since his frustrating behavior caused intense rage. To stab him was not enough. Excessive laxative use unconsciously reflected a chemical shredding of the stool in the bowel, in contrast to binging, which represented both a mechanical shredding of the food and a chemical shredding with digestive enzymes in the mouth.

The fantasy further validates an interesting link between the use of the knife as a weapon and the use of the teeth in destructive cannibalistic biting. Knife fantasies in anorexic and bulimic patients are further illustrated in Chapter 14, where the knife unconsciously represents a tooth in the regressive use of biting to destroy the ambivalently cathected introject. Here we see the direct, conscious expression of aggression (by chopping him up with a knife), the unconscious expression of aggression with the internalization of the conflict (by gorging and cannibalistically destroying the introject with the teeth), the denial of the same impulse (by starving), and finally, a repetition of the destruction of the internalized object (by shredding the "stool boyfriend" in the bowel with laxatives).

Relationship of Laxative Use to Sexual Conflict

Jeanette, an 18-year-old anorexic patient discussed elsewhere (Mintz 1985c), at one point revealed that the previous year she had been involved in a sexual relationship with a boy and was terrified that she had become pregnant. Starving episodes were associated with those memories, her thought being that she would starve herself and in the process starve her baby and thereby abort the pregnancy. Every morning she stood in front of her mirror staring at her abdomen, increasingly pleased at seeing its marked concavity and thinking that she just couldn't be pregnant with an abdomen looking like that. I wondered whether her daily viewing of her abdomen was necessary because of her fear that, as the pregnancy developed, it would gradually make its appearance rising out of the pelvis. She did not reply.

Subsequently there were bursts of gorging, followed by purging with fifty laxatives. At one session she stated that she realized the binging pushed away the worry that she was pregnant, and she worried that she was afraid of becoming fat instead. She did not recognize the conscious fear of becoming fat as her previous fear of pregnancy. In a later session, however, as she recognized that the diarrhea stool represented the destroyed baby, she began to discuss her terrible fear of childbirth; she recalled that when she saw a movie on childbirth, she became so nauseated that she had to stop looking at it. She remembered her fear of "being torn open" by the child during the delivery. Hogan (1985) has described the relationship between constipation, laxative use, and fears of childbirth. Early in treatment she had spoken about not wanting children without explaining that feeling. Additional associations at this time were to long-standing preoccupations with pregnancy fantasies dating back to early adolescence. She felt revulsed by the tremendous weight gain evidenced by some pregnant women, and then admitted that her binging was associated with fantasies of being pregnant and fat.

Jeanette's anorexic-bulimic syndrome revealed multidetermined aspects of sexual conflict. First, the anorexic starving indicated the first attempt to starve the ambivalently valued fetus and precipitate an abortion. Second, while this view was not revealed by this patient, another patient did volunteer that she viewed gorging as oral rape and impregnation (Mintz 1985b). Third, the purging with excessive laxative use represented a chemical shredding of the "stool-fetus": in a sense, a second level attempt at the destruction of the introjected ambivalently cathected fetus. Vomiting, the alternative to purging, indicated a similar explosive ejection of the shredded fetus, from the mouth instead of the anus. Finally, purging also related to her terror of childbirth and the fear of being ripped open during delivery. Shredding and liquifying the "stool fetus" decreased this "birth" conflict.

Summary

Three cases of anorexia or bulimia were presented to illustrate varying unconscious motives for excessive laxative usage. The conflicts involved object loss, aggression, and sexuality. While each case focused upon one of these conflicts for clarity and brevity, varying admixtures of aggressive, sexual, and dependency conflict were present in each situation.

LIVING ON THE EDGE

Esther

In treatment for three years and no longer emaciated, Esther, a 17-year-old anorexic girl, reported that she liked to be "on the edge." Asked to amplify, she stated that she no longer wanted to be emaciated, and in fact now felt disgusted by its appearance, but she did derive great satisfaction in being quite thin, finding it beautiful and exciting. Some models were so thin that she found them repulsive, but most thin models were beautiful and had attractive bodies. That's the way she preferred to be. Both fellows and girls would admire her.

In the beginning of her treatment, at five feet, three inches, weighing 80 pounds, she became aware that one of the reactions to her emaciation was that all her friends, relatives, and teachers paid attention to her, worried about her, extended themselves to be thoughtful and compassionate, and strictly avoided doing anything to upset her, all without her having to say anything.

Concomitantly, she also reported that people did not act sharply toward her nor behave mean or nasty. After further exploration, she acknowledged that the reason for their considerate behavior was that they did not want her to get sick and make them feel guilty. As further confirmation, she had noticed that the man in the luncheonette seemed to make her larger portions of food than he did the other diners.

These discussions ultimately led to her elaborating on her dependency problems. Acrimonious parental divorce when the patient was 8 years of age exposed her to a great deal of their fighting, irregular visitation from the father, and overprotective, infantilizing behavior from the mother, all contributing to her inordinate need for attention. Her "waiflike" status evoked the concern that her unresolved dependency needs required.

Living with her and her mother were two brothers, eight and ten years older, from the mother's previous marriage. The free and open attitudes from that marriage persisted, with minimal modesty about nudity and bowel habits, reported by Wilson (1985a). The older brothers would consistently walk around in their underwear, and frequently nude. The patient also walked around in her underwear. During her parents' marriage, vacations to French Caribbean Islands exposed her to nude beaches. She remembered, as a child of 5, looking at dressed men and wondering where in their trousers their penises were.

Sexual attitudes and behavior ultimately revealed in treatment revolved around Esther's fear of losing control of her sexual impulses. She mentioned that at age 12, because she was physically well developed, she began dating an 18-year-old. While she did not have intercourse, the intimacy went beyond what she recognized as her choice. Frightened, she broke off the relationship after three months. Because of her physical development and her attractiveness, she was very popular with boys and had difficulty fending off their advances. The advent of her anorexic emaciation was followed by a rapid drop-off of sexual interest by her male classmates. Repressed fears about her sexual conflicts in the beginning of treatment resulted in her vociferous complaining about the boys no longer being interested in her.

In the third year of treatment, with her weight stabilized at about 92 pounds, she still voiced concern about being unattractively heavy, although she acknowledged that she knew she would not be fat at 105 pounds. It was then that she elaborated further on how important it was for her to be attractively thin but not emaciated. Earlier discussions had revealed that part of her disgust for other girls' emaciation was related to her jealous, competitive reactions to the attention and concern it drew to them, at what she felt was her expense. She petulantly complained, "What right do they have getting my symptoms?"

Discussion

Esther's need to be "on the edge" seemed to have two major determinants. Unresolved dependency conflicts required an inordinate degree of attention. She acknowledged that her father's inconsistent and flagging interest in her well-being appeared to be reestablished by his worry about her possible exacerbation of anorexic illness, and that her thinness upset him. While her mother's excessive infantilizing and overconcern consciously annoyed her, the underlying attention was still gratifying. Most openly admitted, however, was the attitude of her friends. While she seemed well, they indirectly indicated, by their solicitous behavior, that she might slip back. Consequently, they were more consistently attentive and considerate and thought twice about upsetting her. Their worry and concern was not as acute as it was during the starving, but was under the surface, yet visible to her.

The other factor in her being "on the edge" was her sexuality. She was unconsciously terrified about being unable to control her sexual impulses. Discussion about it, ultimately resulted in her consciously admitting that to lose control and be exploited by men truly frightened her, setting off great feelings of guilt as well as need for punishment. Her episodic gorging contained elements of destroying the "food man" in the mouth, and the excessive laxative use destroying the "stool man" in the colon. Even older men would make passes at her. While she disclaimed the transference reference, she did volunteer that she did not know what I was like outside the office and I might be a nut like some psychiatrists who take advantage of their patients and have sex with them.

In a reflective moment she added that while she really thought her thinness was beautiful, the loss of feminine curves might well turn off some guys who otherwise might feel compelled to pressure her intensely and persistently. She amplified that the thinness can be associated with fragility, which could discourage boys. While she felt beautiful on the surface, unconsciously her thinness served to gratify persisting dependency needs and to minimize sexual pressures from men and intense sexual impulses of her own. Kelly, another anorexic girl described identical attitudes.

Summary

A vignette is presented to illustrate the unconscious attitudes underlying an anorexic girl's persistent wish to be thin, but not cachectic: "on the edge." The secondary anorexic gains regarding dependency needs and sexual conflict are preserved, but with less intensity. Aggressive discharge is manifested in the gorging and in the laxative use to destroy the ambivalently cathected introjects.

It is suggested that many chronically thin anorexic patients, who no longer starve but are excessively thin, may also reflect a decrease in conflict but not a complete resolution.

AN ANOREXIC PERSPECTIVE ON TOOTHBRUSH SWALLOWING IN ANOREXIA AND BULIMIA

Roberta

A 16-year-old bulimic patient reported in the second session that she had been about 50 pounds overweight for a number of years. Attempting to diet, she lost the 50 pounds but kept on dieting. As she got thinner, she felt that she was being pressured to eat. At 5 feet, 1 inch, weighing 110 pounds, she felt satisfied with her weight, but her parents wanted her to gain more. Because of her compliance, she began to eat, but in order not to put on the expected weight, she started to vomit by putting her finger down her throat . . . She noted that whenever she felt upset, if she ate and vomited, she felt better. She had been eating and vomiting almost daily for the past six months, but then had to stop. When asked why, she said that she stopped "when I swallowed the toothbrush. I used to use my finger all the time, but then it didn't work anymore, so I used a toothbrush to be able to put it further down my throat so that I could gag and vomit. It finally slipped. . . . I passed it in three weeks, but now I swallowed a second one. . . . I had to tell my mother, so I told her that a carrot got stuck in my throat and as I tried to get it out, I swallowed the toothbrush."

She added that she felt more grouchy and tense because she had to eat more due to the parents' and internist's pressure. "They say that I have a large bone structure and could use the extra weight. Everyone in my family is heavy. . . . When I get mad at something, I have the urge to eat and vomit. . . . If I don't vomit, I'll put on weight. If I stop eating and vomiting with the toothbrush, I have to chew gum. Then I eat ten packs of gum each day. My doctor told me, 'If that toothbrush gets caught, you're on your way to the grave.' "

In the third session she reported that she had swallowed a third toothbrush, and the two were still there. At my request, she brought in the X-rays, which showed the two toothbrushes with the brushes up, sitting in the stomach. Although they could be removed with the gastroscope, patience was suggested, and in the next three weeks she vomited one up and passed the other.

She volunteered in that session that when things upset her, she gorges, "and then the worry goes away." In a subsequent session she reported that thinking about her problems got her so upset, that she just had to gorge, and then, preoccupied with the consequences, "I forget what I was worried about." The early understanding of the dynamic meaning of starving and gorging by these patients is further explored in Chapters 7 and 14.

In the seventh session she anxiously revealed that she had almost cut off her left third finger in a bread-slicing machine. The boss in the bakery where she worked on weekends began speaking to her, and in order to listen carefully, she paid little attention to slicing the bread. Associations were to how difficult it was for her to assert herself with people, and how overconcerned she was about criticism and how she anticipated it.

A month later the issue of the toothbrushes came up again. She commented that she just had to gorge and vomit to get rid of her worries and anxieties. At the same time, however, she felt increased pressure from the parents and physician to desist. She was afraid not to comply, yet equally fearful of putting on weight, with the accompanying memories of mockery when she was heavy, and so her dilemma increased. She took diuretics for five days to see whether the increasing weight was due to water retention. Frustrated at this approach, and experiencing increasing inner turmoil, she revealed that she thought that if she swallowed the toothbrush, her parents would get so worried that they would stop yelling at her when she ate and vomited. "When I told them, they said 'Oh my God!' . . . and then I felt a sense of relief."

Discussion

There should be caution in totally accepting the patient's conscious explanation for swallowing the toothbrushes without considering unconscious determinants. The self-destructive gorging and vomiting served the purpose of absorbing intrapsychic conflict. In a considerable number of these patients, forcibly interfering with this "necessary" symptomatic choice of conflict resolution can result in alternate, even more desperate symptom choice. (Selvini Palazzoli 1978) The intense level of conflict experienced by many of these patients is poignantly described in detail by Marjorie in the sessions and especially in her diary (Chapter 7). With great insight, at one point she anxiously reflected that curbing the starving, with its accompanying loss of control over eating, was proceeding more rapidly than the developing insight and its compensatory control of her relationships with people. One desperate patient, in the hospital after fainting in the street, and noting the intravenous fluids entering her arm, desperately attempted to pull out the needle with the plaintive cry, "That's all I've got."

This does not mean, however, that any of these patients should be permitted to die from medical neglect, but rather that the intervention should be predicated upon clear-cut medical criteria, rather than a dubious protocol that recommends that all these patients require hospitalization or a return to relatively normal weight levels in order for the patient to be amenable to therapy. Coercive feeding, when not essential, will usually make the patient much more difficult to treat, because it deprives them of all sense of control, even overeating. Criteria for hospitalization, the purpose it achieves, and the methods used are described elsewhere (Mintz 1985a).

Additional determinants in Roberta's need to swallow toothbrushes were not clearly established with any great degree of certainty. However, on the basis of the general knowledge of these patients' inner conflicts, and the unconscious meanings of their symptoms (Bruch 1973, Hogan 1985, Mintz 1985b, Schwartz 1988, Sours 1974, Sperling 1978a, Thomä 1967, Wilson 1985, and others), certain tentative speculations can be considered.

We do know, for example, that unconscious fantasies of oral impregnation are very common in these patients and that one of the determinants behind the inability to eat and swallow is a reflection of the conflict over the impulse for fellatio, as well as the need to defend against it by not eating and choking and by the specific avoidance of eating meat. The patient's conscious explanation of losing a piece of carrot in her throat as an excuse to the mother suggests that the carrot unconsciously represented the penis and the repressed fellatio fantasy.

Reporting that she almost got her finger "accidentally" cut off in the bread-slicing machine can be associatively linked to the unconscious impulse to aggressively bite off the penis, with the accompanying guilt, requiring a retaliatory punishment in kind with the loss of the "finger-penis." Here the finger symbolizing the penis is again reinforced.

Each of the attempts at vomiting by putting her finger into the back of her throat can be viewed as acting out a symbolic fellatio fantasy. This type of fantasy was clearly established by a patient who described her attempts at vomiting by putting her finger down her throat. Her associations were to viewing the finger as a penis, bruising her uvula with her fingernail so that it bled as a defloration, and the spasmodic contractions of the throat and esophagus during vomiting as an orgiastic equivalent (Mintz 1985b).

The meaning of the slicing machine is similar to that of the frequent knife fantasies of anorexic and bulimic patients, which are not unusual in patients dealing with aggressive conflict and are described by other anorexic and bulimic patients in more detail in Chapter 14.

Finally the presence of ambivalently cathected introjects in the throat, stomach, and colon of anorexic patients is described in Chapter 14. These internalized objects, usually associated with repressed aggressive, sexual, and dependency conflicts, are often unconsciously perceived as violent, dirty, and disgusting, and such patients fear rejection and abandonment when friends get to know her well enough to recognize these reprehensible traits. They must, therefore, be cleaned out in order to be acceptable. One patient, who described a dream of a series of rats pouring out of his throat and felt repelled by it, connected his inordinate need to compulsively and vigorously brush his teeth to an attempt to get the dirty sensations out of his throat (Chapter 14). Roberta's swallowing the toothbrushes can similarly be considered an unconscious attempt to clean out the dirty, forbidden thoughts and impulses inside her intestinal tract.

Summary

A case history is described of a 16-year-old bulimic patient who swallowed three toothbrushes. While her conscious reason was to frighten the parents so that they would cease pressuring her to stop gorging and vomiting, additional possible unconscious determinants were explored. These included unconscious fellatio fantasies, self-destructive acting out, by almost getting her finger cut off, and needing to clean out the dirty, internalized ambivalently cathected introjects.

It was also suggested that the forcible removal of these symptoms, whose purpose was to absorb intrapsychic conflict, can sometimes result in other symptoms or acting out that can be more dangerous than the original symptoms.

MENSTRUATING IN ANOREXIA AS A DEFENSE AGAINST SELF-DESTRUCTIVE ACTING OUT

The patient was a 22-year-old anorexic woman who had been in analytic treatment for three years, during which time her conflict increasingly became expressed by binging and excess laxative use. Rejected in childhood, she responded to any later perceived rejection with depression, alternating with binging and excessive laxative use, both of which she increasingly came to recognize as self-destructive behavior.

At the beginning of treatment she was amenorrheic, assuming, on the basis of what she had read, that the amenorrhea was caused by weight loss. Exploring further, however, she acknowledged that she did not want her period, had never wanted it, and since she was not planning to become pregnant now or maybe ever, she saw no use for it. Moreover, she felt repelled by it, seeing it as disgusting, embarrassing, inconvenient, painful, interfering, and unesthetic. During the course of treatment, as her various feelings and attitudes about femininity were explored and clarified, her attitude changed. Concomitant with the change, her periods reappeared, at first infrequent and scant, accompanied by ambivalent feelings about their return. For months they were regular, until she regressed, feeling repelled by them, and again they disappeared. By the middle of the second year she felt strongly that she wanted her periods, volunteering that their presence established her sense of mature desired femininity. She stated, with a sense of conviction, "I know I'm going to get my period." At this time she felt convinced that its presence or absence was under her control. Psychological control over menstrual or bowel bleeding has been described elsewhere. (Mintz 1985d, 1989a).

By the third year, she had improved considerably in her capacity to tolerate frustration, to control her need for immediate gratification, to avoid precipitous intense relationships, and to deal with rejection in interpersonal relationships. She felt more in control and felt less of a necessity for symbolic binging. For a while she avoided relationships with men in order to avoid self-destructive encounters. With considerable care, she subsequently permitted a very gradual development of a relationship with a thoughtful and considerate man, who equally appeared comfortable with the slowly evolving experience. She felt satisfied, confident, and proud of her behavior and noted that the absence of her previous promiscuity was a particular source of satisfaction, now recognizing that it had resulted in severe self-condemnation, marked depression, binging, and laxative usage.

One day she was shocked to hear that her boyfriend had been consistently approached by his previous girlfriend, with whom he had had an intense two-year relationship. He acknowledged that he liked the patient but he had unresolved feelings for his previous girlfriend and wanted to reestablish the earlier relationship.

Bewildered by ambivalent feelings, the patient experienced intense turmoil. She attempted to cope with strong feelings of rejection, reawakened from earlier life experience. The rejection also set off bursts of anger toward him, which she tried to deal with by recognizing that part of her could understand his reactions. He had known the girlfriend for a number of years and had known the patient for a relatively short time. The ability to accept this conclusion was tempered by inner unrealistic narcissistic attitudes that she was a very "special" person, different from others, and how could he do this to her.

I discussed this attitude with her, pointing out that she could certainly continue to view herself as a bright, talented, and worthwhile person, but why did she need to feel that she was "special" and different from others. She replied that she had had a terrible childhood and had suffered a great deal, and consequently she felt that she shouldn't have to suffer any more: she was "special," and fate required that she should be treated well, and different from others. I added that while I could understand how she could arrive at that conclusion, it was still unrealistic, and accepting that idealized concept of how people should treat her would make it difficult for her to cope with life's frustrations and disappointments. She would consequently suffer more from them. It would also leave her increasingly vulnerable to past traumatic experiences and complicate her perspective in dealing with them. She was no longer helpless and unable to deal with adversity. Wilson (1990) emphasized this issue, pointing out the importance of analyzing the "little princess" internal image, which predisposes the patient to inability to deal with frustrations and disappointment, and predisposes her to self-destructive acting out.

Concomitant with the feelings of rejection, anger, and being someone special, she felt bolstered by the recognition that this had been the healthiest relationship ever: she had not acted impulsively, or promiscuously developed a precipitous, intensely intimate relationship for which she could now later flagellate herself. She felt no guilt or self-condemnation. Nevertheless, it was not an easy time. Temporarily, she lost control, with binging and the use of sixty laxatives, resulting in the usual terrible cramps, diarrhea, and infirmity. Previous insight into the meaning of her gorging and excessive laxative use did not prevent the acting out. A week later, however, with mixed feelings, she noted that the gorging did not provide the satisfaction that she once achieved from it. The acting out no longer decreased anxiety and tension feelings of relief. She still thought about the events and was distressed by them. Her insight into the meaning of the symptomatic experience interfered with the symptom's capacity to absorb the conflict. She reported going out with friends and drinking excessively as a means of pushing away her turmoil. She volunteered that she was now binging with alcohol instead of food, but without the need to damage herself with laxative use. At the same time, she felt satisfied that she was exercising a degree of control by still working effectively in graduate school and limiting the drinking to weekends. It was pointed out that the drinking undermined her self-confidence, suggesting to herself that she could not face and resolve the conflict.

She then announced that she had decided to have a sexual encounter with a casual pickup just to have an orgasm. It was just sex, no relationship; she did not plan to see the man again. In spite of my suggesting that previous, similar behavior had resulted in great self-condemnation, guilt, and depression, or binging and laxative use, she persisted in contemplating that course of action.

At the following session she stated that she had decided against a sexual pickup. "Besides I got my period today." I acknowledged her using her insight and wondered about her juxtaposing her decision against a pickup with getting her period. After some silence, I said that she had amply demonstrated over many months that she had control over the onset of her periods. If she truly did not want her period, it would not have happened. This she readily accepted. I added that her conscious decision not to act out promiscuously was reinforced unconsciously by her permitting the arrival of her period. She was using her menstruation to augment her self-control over her impulses.

BINGING INSIDE AND OUTSIDE AS THE DISPLACEMENT OF DEPENDENCY CONFLICT

Binging attacks are usually precipitated by anxiety, tension, and conflict. The typical conflicts that set off the binging are related to aggressive, sexual, and dependency problems. Different symbolic manifestations of the binging can express these disparate difficulties.

Where the aggressive conflict predominates, the active destroying of the food by the teeth stands for symbolic attack upon the "food-people." A consequence of the binging is often laxative use, whereby the "stool-people" are again shredded and destroyed in an attempt to deal with these ambivalently cathected introjects (vignette 3 in this chapter). Sexual conflicts are also dealt with through binging, which can take the form of fellatio and oral impregnation fantasies. There is sometimes subsequent vomiting of the ingested food, initiated by putting the finger down the throat. Vomiting under these circumstances has been described by patients as displaced rape, defloration, and coitus, with the finger representing a penis. Semideliberate scratching of the back of the throat to induce bleeding of the uvula is followed by the convulsive reverse peristalsis, with vomiting representing orgasm (Mintz 1985b).

Dependency conflict, the focus of this vignette, can also be represented by gorging. One patient described the impulse to binge whenever she felt rejected. Aside from the resentment evoked by the rejection, she experienced a longing for the lost object. Feeling worthless, devalued, and empty, inside, she noted that the gorging filled the emptiness and provided a sense of warmth and security. Dependency conflicts were paramount in the life of this patient, who had suffered from feelings of maternal rejection in infancy and childhood.

This patient's mother was also bulimic, but her behavior was less obvious. It is not uncommon to find that the parents of anorexic and bulimic patients also have subclinical manifestations of the same illness. The patient recognized that when the mother appeared concerned or distressed, at times she would begin to eat. The eating, though not reaching the intensity of a voracious ingesting of food, was characterized by rapid, endless taking in of large quantities of food, almost without selectivity, which would continue until the mother felt so engorged that she could not eat another morsel. This would be followed by quasi-fasting for the next twenty-four to thirty-six hours, until the sense of bloating gradually subsided. This stress-induced gorging would take place every few weeks over a period of years, with no one acknowledging its morbid peculiarities.

As the patient understood more about her own binging and was able to recognize excessive alcohol consumption as another form of binging, she reported that her mother also seemed to binge on clothing. She realized that on some occasions when the mother got upset, instead of eating she would go on a buying spree for several days, purchasing tremendous quantities of clothing from many stores, ultimately keeping a great deal, and returning the remainder. With these buying binges recurring under subsequent periods of stress, the mother had thousands of dollars of clothing filling the closets.

Binging and filling the inside of one's body with food is symbolically reproducing the early sense of nursing and feeding from which the infant derives the feelings of love, warmth, and security reminiscent of being fed by the mother. Binging with clothing reflects a displacement of the same inner needs from the inside to the outside of the body. The external clothing provides the needed warmth and security.

A conflict can be displaced from the outside of the body to the inside and then, during the course of treatment, again projected back to the outside, but displaced from the original location. An asthmatic patient's unconscious impulses to choke someone can be denied, repressed, and regressively emerge with an asthmatic attack. With treatment, the asthmatic attack within the bronchi is now projected to the outside of the body, with the patient's complaint of feeling that her finger is being choked by her ring (Mintz 1989b). A sexual conflict can be displaced from the vagina to the throat in asthma (Karol 1989) or from the vagina to the rectum in ulcerative colitis (Sperling 1978b).

I make this point to illustrate that binging on clothing as an alternative form of bulimic behavior is compatible with other forms of displacement phenomena. In these cases, in the face of rejection the bulimic patient can attempt to recapture the lost object and fill the void inside with clothing outside. This behavior is analogous to bulimic gratification of the impulse to suck by binging with food, alcohol, drugs, or stealing.

REFERENCES

Bruch, H. (1973). Primary anorexia nervosa. *Eating Disorders, Obesity, Anorexia Nervosa, and the Person Within.* New York: Basic Books.

Burton, A. (1990). Floor discussion, meeting of the New Jersey Psychoanalytic meeting, September, in, Hackensack Medical Center. Hackensack, NJ

Deutsch, L. (1987). Reflections on the psychoanalytic treatment of patients with bronchial asthma. *Psychoanalytic Study of the Child.* 42:239–260. New Haven, CT: Yale University Press.

Hogan, C. (1985). Psychodynamics. In *Fear of Being Fat: The Treatment of Anorexia Nervosa and Bulimia,* rev. ed., ed. C. P. Wilson, C. C. Hogan, and I. L. Mintz, pp. 115–128. New York: Jason Aronson.

Kaminer, H. (1989). Floor discussion, department of Psychiatry meeting, Hackensack Medical Center. Hackensack, NJ, June 22.

Karol, C. (1989). The role of primal scene in masochism and asthma. In *Psychosomatic Symptoms: The Psychodynamic Treatment of the Underlying Personality Disorder,* ed. C. P. Wilson and I. L. Mintz, pp. 309–326. Northvale, NJ: Jason Aronson.

Levine, A. (1989). Personal communication.

Mintz, I. L. (1980–1981). Multideterminism in asthmatic disease. *International Journal of Psychoanalytic Psychotherapy* 8:593–600.

———— (1985a). An analytic approach to hospital and nursing care. In *Fear of Being Fat: The Treatment of Anorexia Nervosa and Bulimia,* rev. ed., ed. C. P. Wilson, C. C. Hogan, and I. L. Mintz, pp. 315–326, New York: Jason Aronson.

———— (1985b). Psychoanalytic description: the clinical picture of anorexia nervosa and bulimia. In *Fear of Being Fat: The Treatment of Anorexia Nervosa and Bulimia,* rev. ed., ed. C. P. Wilson, C. C. Hogan, and I. L. Mintz, pp. 83–114. New York: Jason Aronson.

———— (1985c). Psychoanalytic therapy of severe anorexia: the case of Jeanette. In *Fear of Being Fat: The Treatment of Anorexia Nervosa and Bulimia,* rev. ed., ed. C. P. Wilson, C. C. Hogan, and I. L. Mintz, pp. 217–244. New York: Jason Aronson.

———— (1985d). The relationship between self-starvation and amenorrhea. In *Fear of Being Fat: The Treatment of Anorexia Nervosa and Bulimia,* rev. ed., ed. C. P. Wilson, C. C. Hogan, and I. L. Mintz, pp. 335–344. New York: Jason Aronson.

———— (1985e). Anorexia and bulimia in males. In *Fear of Being Fat: The Treatment of Anorexia Nervosa and Bulimia,* rev. ed., ed. C. P. Wilson, C. C. Hogan, and I. L. Mintz, pp. 263–303. New York: Jason Aronson.

———— (1989b). Treatment of a case of anorexia and severe asthma. In *Psychosomatic Symptoms: The Psychodynamic Treatment of the Underlying Personality Disorder,* ed. C. P. Wilson and I. L. Mintz, pp. 251–308. Northvale, NJ: Jason Aronson.

Mintz, I. L. and Wilson, C. P. (1989a). Varieties of somatization. In *Psychosomatic Symptoms: Psychodynamic Treatment of the Underlying Personality Disorder,* ed. C. P. Wilson and I. L. Mintz, pp. 171–210. Northvale, NJ: Jason Aronson.

Sacks, M. H. (1979). A psychodynamic overview of sport. *Psychiatric Annals* 9:127–133.

Schlossman, H. (1979). Personal communication.

———— (1989). Floor discussion, Department of Psychiatry meeting, June, Hackensack Medical Center, Hackensack, NJ.

Schwartz, H. (1988). Bulimia: Psychoanalytic Perspectives. In *Bulimia: Psychoanalytic*

Treatment and Theory, ed. H. Schwartz, pp. 31–54. Madison, CT: International Universities Press.

Selvini Palazzoli, M. (1978). Some hints on psychotherapeutic conduct. In *Self-Starvation: From Individual to Family Therapy in the Treatment of Anorexia Nervosa,* ed. M. S. Palazzoli, p. 122. New York: Jason Aronson.

Sours, J. A. (1974). The Anorexia Nervosa Syndrome. *International Journal of Psycho-Analysis* 55:567–576.

Sperling, M. (1978a). Anorexia nervosa (part 4). In *Psychosomatic Disorders in Childhood,* ed. O. Sperling, pp. 129–173. New York: Jason Aronson.

———— (1978b). Psychoanalytic study of ulcerative colitis in children. In *Psychosomatic Disorders in Childhood,* ed. O. Sperling, pp. 77–98. New York: Jason Aronson.

Thomä, H. (1967). Psychogenesis and psychosomatics of anorexia nervosa. In *Anorexia Nervosa,* ed. H. Thomä, pp. 234–314. New York: International Press.

Wilson, C. P. (1985a). Psychological profile and its therapeutic implications. In *Fear of Being Fat: The Treatment of Anorexia Nervosa and Bulimia,* rev. ed., ed. C. P. Wilson, C. C. Hogan, and I. L. Mintz, pp. 29–50. New York: Jason Aronson.

———— (1985b). Contrasts in the analysis of bulimic and abstaining anorexics. In *Fear of Being Fat: The Treatment of Anorexia Nervosa and Bulimia,* rev. ed., ed. C. P. Wilson, C. C. Hogan, and I. L. Mintz, pp. 169–196. New York: Jason Aronson.

———— (1990). On beginning analysis with eating disorders. In *On Beginning Analysis,* ed. T. J. Jacobs and A. Rothstein, pp. 243–260. Madison, CT: International Universities Press.

Yates, A., Leehey, K. and Shisslak, C. M. (1983). Running—an analogue of anorexia? *New England Journal of Medicine* 308: 251–255.

16

A Psychodevelopmental Perspective on Rumination

Barton J. Blinder, M.D.

Rumination is an uncommon disorder consisting of the postprandial regurgitation and subsequent reswallowing of partially digested food. It may occur at any stage of life from earliest infancy (usually after three months of age) to later adulthood. Although rumination has long been underrecognized by the medical community as a distinct and sometimes fatal disorder, its recent association with other psychiatric disorders (e.g., bulimia, anorexia nervosa, and depression) in adolescents and adults has brought greater attention to the severity of its consequences (Blinder 1991, Blinder et al. 1988).

There are notable medical complications such as aspiration pneumonia, electrolyte abnormalities, and dehydration (Herbst 1983). Medical disorders in infants and adults such as gastroesophageal reflux and hiatal hernia have also been reported (Grybowski 1983, Herbst et al. 1971). It is also considered in the differential diagnosis of vomiting (Fleischer 1979) and failure to thrive (Sheagran et al. 1980) in infants and young children. From latency through adulthood, rumination may have an apparently benign

379

course (Blinder 1986, Levine et al. 1983). However, rumination has recently been associated with bulimia (Blinder 1983, Fairburn and Cooper 1984), anorexia nervosa, and depression (Levine et al. 1983). As early as 1907 it was reported to be associated with a restrictive eating disorder, as evidenced by Brockbank's (1907) case study of a 15-year-old female ruminator who was thin and "ate but little."

In the most recent *Diagnostic and Statistical Manual of Mental Disorders* (DSM–III–R 1987) rumination is designated as a disorder of infancy (307.53). The infant shows "a characteristic position of straining and arching the back with sucking tongue movements and the gaining of satisfaction" (DSM–III–R, p. 72). Diagnostic criteria include repeated regurgitation without nausea or associated gastrointestinal illness for at least one month following a period of normal functioning. There may be weight loss or failure to make expected weight gain (DSM–III–R 1987).

Rumination may be underreported, since only severe cases with medical complications (malnutrition, electrolyte disturbances, hiatus hernia) are likely to be referred to a gastroenterologist. Minor cases are likely to be treated by parents or primary physicians. Because rumination in adolescents and adults is embarrassing, patients often conceal the problem when giving medical histories. Furthermore, primary physicians are often unacquainted with the disorder. Rumination in anorexia nervosa and bulimia may also be underreported because of omission in the systematic medical history and the reluctance of patients to volunteer specific clinical information.

The course of rumination may depend on the severity of complications and the age of the patient. Mortality has been as high as 25 to 40 percent in infants (Kanner 1957). The infant may show manifest hyperphagia followed by postingestive regurgitation leading to progressive malnutrition. In the adolescent, bulimia and affective disorder may be present (Fairburn and Cooper 1984). Rumination in adults has been reported in association with gastric carcinoma (Long 1929) and anemia (Djaldetti et al. 1962, Geffen 1966). Medical complications occur more frequently in the retarded (Danford and Huber 1981), with a mortality rate of 12 to 20 percent (Rast et al. 1981).

DEVELOPMENTAL AND PSYCHOSTRUCTURAL FACTORS

Infancy and Early Childhood

Lourie (1954) describes a ruminating child, five months of age, overstimulated because of the behavior of his tense and fearful mother, who was inappropriately "constantly doing something with the baby." Substitute care by a nurse was effective in abolishing rumination, despite the presence of mild esophageal dilatation as an organic factor.

In another case Lourie describes the behavior of a foster mother who kept a 9-month-old baby "in a small back bedroom," limiting his contact with siblings. In this case, understimulation produced an irritable child who, in addition to ruminating, stimulated himself with rhythmic rocking movements. The child was hypersensitive to sound and touch, frustrating his foster mother. When she attempted to soothe him physically, he reacted by avoidance (which unfortunately contributed to her continued neglect). However, when he was placed in another home, with increased stimulation, he ceased ruminating.

In yet another case, rumination was precipitated by an object loss. A male of 11 months developed rumination after the departure of his father. Prior to this time the mother had been depressed as a result of separation from her own mother. The child lost interest in his mother and in eating and appeared to be depressed.

Infants admitted to a neonatal intensive care unit, who subsequently develop rumination (Sheagran et al. 1980) may be physically overstimulated because of high noise levels and multiple procedures, and *affectively understimulated* because of lack of a consistent nurturing figure.

Lourie (1954) feels that such infants lack basic trust in their maternal objects. This lack of trust in turn causes a failure of appropriate attachment and fulfillment of the infant's dependency needs. The infant's immature ego is overwhelmed by external and internal conditions, and regression from a previous adequate level of object relations occurs (Fenichel 1945).

Additionally, Lourie believes that these infants use denial as a proto-defense mechanism to adjust to their overwhelming situation. Rumination as a *pseudo-feeding* may substitute hallucinatory wish fulfillment for the inadequately available maternal object (Ferenczi 1950). The infants then react to overwhelming environmental overstimulation or understimulation by seeming voluntarily to feed themselves. Through the rumination, they reexperience, a self-directed pleasurable habit which replaces the inadequate maternal–infant relationship (Gaddini 1969). Thus rumination in infants may be conceptualized as a defensive habit pattern that, once started, for whatever reason, becomes a self-reinforcing behavior which is difficult to arrest (Chatoor and Dickson 1984).

Erotization of the esophagus and an ecstatic pleasurable feeling during rumination, followed by a marked diminished tension, have also been described (Cameron 1925, Richmond et al. 1958). Prenatal libidinization of the act of deglutition and of the esophageal interior related to the swallowing of amniotic fluid in utero has been proposed by Milakovic (1967). *These primitive oral behaviors may be models for the development of early human object relationship which subsequently act through reciprocity and attunement to alter ingestion from a primitive bidirectional oral flux in utero toward unidirectional competence in the postnatal period. Thus both psychostructural and maturational factors derived from the earliest experiential roots are implicated.*

Lourie (1954) suggests that the infant's response to an inadequate love object is similar to the reaction noted by Spitz and Wolf (1946) in infants with anaclitic depression. However, rumination has not been described in institutional infants who have no primary caretaker (Spitz and Wolf 1946).

This suggests that infants need to have developed a partial object attachment in order to develop rumination. Some degree of psychic structuralization would appear to be a crucial element in the perpetuation of clinically significant rumination.

Reciprocity between mother and infant implies sensitivity and attunement of the mother to her child's individuality, rhythm, communications, and reciprocal ability to initiate and maintain communication needs. This mutual "fitting together" of mother and infant is crucial for true psychobiologic reciprocity. A temperamental mismatch due to the baby's heightened sensitivities (to sound, touch, or noise) and mother's impatience may occur (Bergman and Escalona 1949). Failure of reciprocity may result in rumination. Disturbed mothers may be emotionally unavailable to develop reciprocity with their child (Gaddini 1969, Gaddini and Gaddini 1959, Kreisler 1967, Lourie 1954, Richmond et al. 1958). Many authors have commented on the presence of maternal psychopathology in conjunction with infant rumination (Gaddini and Gaddini 1959, Hollowell and Gardner 1965, Lourie 1954, Menking et al. 1969, Richmond et al. 1958).

The *developmental structuralist* approach to understanding infant–mother interactions implicates a maladaptive caregiver who is unavailable, depressed, abusive, and hypo- or hyperstimulating. Etiologic factors can thus be defined in terms of either an infant *developmental diagnosis* (such as a disorder of attachment or homeostasis), a *symptom diagnosis* (such as eating disturbance which may include rumination), or as a function of maladaptive caregiving. For example, a mother might not be able to recognize her baby's attempts at autonomy and its needs for attachment, basic trust, curiosity, and communication. She may be insensitive to her child's signals to be fed, she may feed him on a rigid schedule, or she may feed him too fast, not allowing him the freedom to obtain food autonomously. She may also feed him in error when he signals for other physiologic or psychologic needs (Greenspan and Lourie 1981).

Gaddini (1969) noted that the mothers of ruminators were generally rejecting, irritable, and ambivalent, especially toward unplanned babies. These mothers were described as "immature, inadequate personalities who are anxious and had disturbed object relations." Communication of anxiety interrupts expected cycles of tension reduction (oral satisfaction, satiety-fullness, and sleep) that contribute to the regularity of first-stage object constancy. Auto-stimulation and the need to reexperience the object may be determinants of the structure and repetition of the ruminatory act.

How does this functional model become converted to a parallel intrapsychic model? The failure of reality (i.e., absent, ineffective, or affectively depriving mother) stimulates fantasy "in such a way as to give rise to a physical experience imitative of that gratifying fusion which is no longer to be experienced in reality" (Gaddini 1969). The syndrome of infantile rumination may be defined as a psychophysical complex response to a state of oral frustration of an absolute type. It tends in practice to obtain a reduction of the tension aroused by the serious frustrations of the oral area and, to such an end, aims at regaining through a physical imitative reproduction the gratification that had previously been experienced (Gaddini 1969).

From a study of six children with rumination (age three to eight months), Gaddini and Gaddini (1959) note serious frustration of oral activities and traumatic weaning. In all the cases the relationship of mother to child was "decidedly pathological." Rumination occurred at variable intervals after meals—in some instances immediately after meals, and in others up to an hour and a half later. This study contrasts with other studies (Blinder 1983, Blinder et al. 1986) of adult and adolescent rumination where the return of food to the mouth occurs in a seemingly obligatory manner (as demonstrated by radionuclide gastrography) commencing at the end of a meal and continuing with excursions of diminishing frequency and intensity over a period of one to two hours. Gaddini (1969) describes the ruminatory behavior confirming Cameron's (1925) emphasis on a coanaesthetic (internal stimuli) direction of attention.

Ruminating infants have been described as passive and oversensitive to deprivation, with the ruminating act seeming to relieve inner tension in an infant distressed by deprivation or overstimulation (Lourie 1954). Rumination, considered as a habit disorder, has been observed in children with repetitive self-stimulatory behavior such as head banging, body rocking, genital and fecal play, and finger- and thumb-sucking (Richmond et al. 1958). This self-reinforcing habit can become so potent that the infant, preferring self-soothing through rumination, may become affectively unavailable and resistant to its mother's attempt to intervene (Chatoor et al. 1984).

Latency

Rumination in latency-age children who are not retarded is rarely reported. Brockbank (1907) discussed two children, ages 3 (female) and 6 (male), who imitated a ruminant housekeeper, and a 7-year old male who imitated his ruminant foster mother. Griffin (1977) described rumination in a 7-year old male who had no accompanying gastrointestinal abnormality and whose physical development was normal. His birth was unplanned and he sustained a partial maternal object loss at five months of age when his mother returned to work. The patient was lovingly and competently cared for by his maternal grandmother until age eighteen months, when his mother moved with him to another city, after which he rarely saw his grandmother. The child thereby suffered a second significant object loss in the critical practice-rapprochement-phase transition of the separation-individuation sequence (Mahler 1975). After separation from his grandmother, his appetite decreased and he began to ruminate. His parents later described him as an easily agitated, overanxious child whose rumination was exacerbated by their demands, especially those of the father, who would not tolerate his son's oppositional behavior. Significant separation coinciding with anal-phase development (at age eighteen months) may

have resulted in a developmental arrest accentuating the patient's oppositional passive-aggressive behavior. Rumination, occurring after the object
loss of the grandmother, suggests an association with depressed affect and
abrupt termination of attentive rewarding stimulation.

Another 7-year-old has been reported with vomiting and reflux dating
from six months of age (Chatoor and Dickson 1984). Although an upper
gastrointestinal series did not reveal reflux, at thirteen months a Nissen
fundoplication surgery was performed. During the surgery, no evidence of
esophagitis or gastric outlet obstruction was seen. At 6, the boy was
described as agitated, irritable, and tense. His rumination was associated
with physical or emotional excitement and occurred most often when
someone in authority was angry at him or when he was unable to express
anger. His parents refused psychiatric treatment, preferring to return him
to his original surgeon, who performed a second Nissen fundoplication.
This resulted in his inability to swallow solid food and necessitated surgical
dilation of an esophageal stricture. It is suggested that treatment of his
conflicts, centering around aggression, might have abolished his rumination and spared him unnecessary traumatic surgical intervention.

Levine et al. (1983) described a 7-year-old male who had ruminated since
birth with presenting complaints of halitosis and a positive family history
of rumination. The family resisted psychiatric investigation or treatment.
There are also reports of adults with milder forms of rumination, who have
ruminated throughout life, passing through latency and adolescence with
no apparent medical or psychiatric problem (Blinder et al. 1986, Brockbank 1907, Levine et al. 1983).

Adolescence

Except for reports of mentally retarded individuals, current literature
contains few cases of rumination in adolescence. Brockbank (1907) may
have described the first adolescent with rumination and a restrictive eating
disorder when he reported a 15-year-old female who "ate but little."
Cauwels (1983) and Fairburn and Cooper (1984) have documented rumination in adolescent bulimic eating-disorder patients. Levine et al. (1983)
described three adolescent ruminators aged 15 (female), 14 (female), and
15 (male). They had no associated gastrointestinal complaints, and their
barium studies were normal. The two females had ruminated since birth,
and the male for four years; there was no family history of rumination in
any of the cases. Geffen (1966) described a 17-year-old male with iron
deficiency anemia, which was a secondary symptom to bleeding from
esophagitis. This boy's involuntary lifelong rumination was associated
with "nervousness and tension."

Rumination may be precipitated by object loss in adolescence. A 13-year-
old female was hospitalized after losing 5 pounds and complaining of
heartburn. This weight loss coincided with increased marital strife between
her father and stepmother. Her developmental history revealed no manifest eating problems as an infant or young child. When she was 9 years old,

her natural mother died and her father became severely depressed and reclusive. The mother died of lymphoma, which caused anorexia and vomiting with rapid deterioration and death in six months. The child developed involuntary postprandial rumination soon after her father's remarriage the next year. The patient conveyed a deep sadness, passivity, and overcompliance. She apparently identified with her dead mother's terminal vomiting episodes in an attempt to compensate for the further loss accentuated by her father's remarriage. The patient also showed over-concern with thinness and spoke of feeling powerless in her family and a victim of an overwhelming course of events. She managed her distress by rumination.

The author has treated two adolescents whose manifest symptoms were depression and a ruminatory disorder:

Case 1

Merle, a 14-year-old female, developed postprandial rumination as a symptom in association with marked depressive affect, withdrawal, and oppositional behavior, within two months following the suicide of her college-aged brother. Her grief was masked by an intense desire to be with her girlfriends. She felt extreme underlying guilt at both her survivorship and her secret knowledge of her brother's depression and suicidal thoughts (which she had not revealed to her parents before his death). She experienced the rumination both as a sense of loss of control (a shock she related to the onset of her menses, which even with her foreknowledge came as a remarkable surprise) and as a punishment (if the food kept coming up, she would lose weight and eventually die). Her parents, in their own deep grief and even more profound guilt, were virtually affectively unavailable to Merle.

Merle began a provocative, hostile, and seductive interaction with her father (representing an intensification and reactivation of the more displaced and vicariously experienced incestuous fantasies and desires related to her lost brother). The frustration of her genital wishes toward her father may have led to a regressed oral mode of relating to him. After several months of psychotherapy, Merle's depression lifted gradually (along with the abrupt cessation of the ruminatory behavior). Continuing treatment of the parents and family sessions revealed earlier concerns about the father's ill health: a moderately severe neurologic disorder, one symptom of which had been difficulty swallowing.

Case 2

Janice, a 16-year-old high school honor student, was seen initially for ruminatory behavior of three years' duration along with episodes of depressed mood. The symptoms arose at the time of her parents divorce. An only child, Janice had sought out friends and school activities (leadership, athletics, scholarship) for the gratification denied by a rather dismal home atmosphere. Her father was a driven executive experiencing cycles of success and financial failure and removed from his wife. The affective unavailability and periodic incompetence of her chronically depressed and alcoholic mother led to role reversal, with Janice "caring" for her mother, feeding her, putting her to bed, cleaning, and shopping for the household. Eating and ruminating became a "companion" to long hours of studying and being alone while her mother was often in a semi-stuperous state, unattentive and unavailable.

As she yielded her private indulgent world up to treatment and elaborated her fantasies, Janice at first lashed out at the therapist for infringing on her retreat. Rage toward her mother, emerging from the reaction formations of the caring "maternal" child, was soon followed by Janice's awareness of her growing intense heterosexual interests. She held on to the ruminatory behavior even as her mood gradually lifted. Therapeutic focus involved her disappointment with her father and the elements of sadistic anger which he often displaced toward her in ventilating his frustrations with his wife over the years. The rumination became more compartmentalized, devoid of former gratification, and gradually decreased in frequency over a period of two years.

Adulthood

Adult rumination is often a chronic disorder (Levine et al. 1983), except when associated with bulimia (Fairburn and Cooper 1984). The individual episode is postprandial, without nausea, effortless, and predominantly involuntary. It may occur after a hastily eaten meal, causing embarrassment, or it may appear seemingly voluntary and pleasurable (Brown 1968, Levine et al. 1983, Long 1929). The symptomatic presence of active ruminatory behavior varies, lasting from as little as six months to a lifetime (Brockbank 1907, Levine et al. 1983). Patients may complain of food returning to the mouth, belching, precordial distress (possibly due to esophagitis), indigestion, halitosis, and excessive dental difficulties.

There were no structured psychiatric evaluations or uniformity of diagnostic criteria in ruminators noted in the literature until Levine et al. (1983) evaluated nine patients with both a psychiatric interview and questionnaire. The interviews revealed a family psychiatric history of disturbed relationships in four of the patients. Three patients had psychiatric histories (overdose, anorexia nervosa, brief reactive depression). Seven of the patients had personalities described as anxious, five as obsessional, and six as sensitive. Four of five adult patients had psychosexual and marital problems. However, on current formal mental status examination, only one of the nine patients had current psychiatric symptoms (in the form of anxiety state). The questionnaire data revealed that mild traits of anxiety, hysteria, and neuroticism were present. In only one patient did symptoms interfere with psychosocial functioning, and the group revealed no evidence of a current psychiatric illness. The authors concluded that substantive psychiatric disorder was absent in this group of patients. However, the findings are suggestive of affective spectrum disorder (depression, anorexia nervosa, overdose) in three of five adults and a significant family history of psychiatric disorder in four of eight of the patients whose family history was accessible. An instrument such as the SADS (Spitzer and Endicott 1978) might have been a more significant diagnostic tool for detecting psychiatric disorder in the adult ruminator group studies.

Fairburn and Cooper (1984) report rumination (with a duration of at least twelve months) in seven of thirty-five female patients with a diagnosis of bulimia. Three patients had postprandial effortless regurgitation on a daily basis. Food was reswallowed or regurgitated. The patients complained of loss of control of eating, and shame about their rumination. All patients had disturbed eating habits, abnormal attitudes toward body and shape, and high psychiatric co-morbidities. In the subgroup of bulimic ruminators, a history of both anorexia nervosa and psychiatric treatment for an eating disorder was more prevalent than among the bulimic nonruminators. The habit by itself was difficult to stop, but successful treatment of the bulimia led to cessation of the rumination.

Blinder (1983) reported a subgroup of normal-weight bulimic patients with primary ruminatory behavior antedating bulimic symptoms. The patients were more likely to be polyphagic during binge episodes rather than demonstrating the more usual specific carbohydrate preference. Ruminatory behavior shifted to regurgitation during adolescence to aid them in weight control. The patients often did not show the pattern of impulsive behavior, affective disturbance, or family history of alcoholism seen in other patients diagnosed as bulimic.

There may be two adult subgroups of ruminators: one group having minimal psychiatric problems, and the second group with either an associated eating disorder (such as anorexia nervosa or bulimia) or associated anxiety, affective, or marital/familial psychiatric disturbance. Since patients are reticent about their illness, a diagnosis of psychiatric disturbance may be underreported.

The only report of psychoanalytic treatment (a 20-year-old male with rumination) emphasized unconscious anger toward authority figures, who were aggressively ejected (representationally) by the ruminatory behavior. Interpretation of unconscious conflict led to cessation of this behavior (Philippopoulus 1973). Ruminatory behavior in this context was part of a conversion process linked to affective expression associated with torment, competitiveness, and destructive wishes toward internalized object representations.

TREATMENT

Infants and Children in a Hospital Milieu

Since rumination in infants and young children may be life threatening, a multidisciplinary approach is mandatory. The primary physician must

388   Barton J. Blinder, M.D.

decide whether hospitalization is indicated. The decision may be based on the chronicity of the rumination or the presence of significant medical complications (e.g., failure to thrive, dehydration, electrolyte abnormalities) or gastrointestinal disturbances (e.g., hiatal hernia). Hospitalization may also be indicated when the primary caretaker's ability is severely compromised. Since rumination often occurs in multiproblem families, careful evaluation of the child's psychosocial situation is important.

Although many authors have stressed deficient mother–infant interactions (Gaddini and Gaddini 1959, Lourie 1954, Richmond et al. 1958), some reports (Chatoor et al. 1984, Levine et al. 1983) have noted on occasion a positive relationship between the mother and the infant. Rumination, without severe weight loss or other physiologic alterations, in the context of a supportive family may respond to outpatient treatment.

Hospitalization of the child is often a terrifying experience for the mother (Gaddini and Gaddini 1959), who may feel guilty, inadequate, and responsible for her infant's problem. She should be encouraged to ventilate her fears and frustration that her child is not getting well immediately and to understand that there are medical and psychological reasons for the rumination. A physiologic description of reflux may be helpful.

The staff's observations of the temperament of the mother and child and the degree of reciprocity should be recorded. A two- to three-hour home visit is suggested to determine the interactive relationship of mother and child, preferably during a sleep and waking cycle. Levy (1981) also offers an excellent review of mother–infant relations during feeding with specific target questions such as: Is the baby allowed active participation in feeding? Are the foods well presented? Who decides when feeding will end?

A more structured interview with the child's mother, father, or other primary caretaker is also crucial. The mother's own developmental and personal psychiatric history may contain determinants of current conflictural attitudes and behavior toward the infant. The mother's relationship with her own mother and her siblings, her feelings during pregnancy and postpartum period, and the feeding history need to be explored. Deficits and gaps in the mother's history of the nurturant relationship with her own mother are often revealing. Memories of deprivation, competition, and ambivalence may be reactivated, along with identification with a withholding mother of childhood.

Rumination can be attributed to a baby who has a problem with homeostasis and withdrawing into a maladaptive habit. The mother should be told she is both an expert with her child and an important colleague in the treatment process. Her feelings about the rumination, associated failure to thrive, techniques that have been helpful in reducing the rumination, or what events have precipitated it should be explored. The mother's possible fragile self-esteem and her frustration and feelings of incompetence should be acknowledged and countered by her being designated an important colleague in the child's treatment.

In the hospital, the baby should be placed near the nursing station to increase the child's visual and auditory stimulation. There should be a specific nurse on each shift who will give primary care to the child. Frequently an involved social worker will be able to pick an empathic nurse who will be emotionally available during an eight-hour shift to spend much of her time with the baby. In the case of one child who was not interested in people, a relationship was started by a nurse who interested him with bright colored clothing and jewelry. These visual and auditory stimuli, combined with the crib rocking, initiated the attachment process. In another infant, who had withdrawn from any social contact, placement in a crib with another baby was helpful in starting an object attachment. Later, holding both children on a nurse's knee reinforced the attachment process.

The nurse acts as a substitute (surrogate) mother with whom the baby can develop attachment (Lourie 1954). Later the mother will become more involved with feeding and the child will transfer its attachment and thus restore object relationship with its mother. The mother will need to recognize her child's strivings for autonomy and its need to be a stimulated and active participant in the feeding process. Feeding should terminate when the child is finished, and rigid schedules should be abandoned. The mother may need to stimulate the infant by increasing her eye contact, vocalizing, and smiling during feeding. She may have to work through any of her own uncomfortable feelings that may have been present during the feeding process (Levy 1981).

The next therapeutic task will be interruption of the rumination. The child's unique rumination pattern should be recorded (for example, whether it occurs when the baby is alone or occurs when the mother pushes the baby away). The nurse who is aware of this pattern should be present to interrupt the possible anxiety-producing situation or frustration that may precipitate rumination.

The last therapeutic task focuses on the relinquishing of maladaptive rumination and self-stimulatory patterns. The goal for the baby is to develop external object satisfaction by using a combination of negative and positive social reinforcers. As the child ruminates, the nurse will say "no," gently touch the mouth, and place the baby down. In two minutes she will check the baby, and if rumination has ceased she will again play with him or her. Ideally, the nurse will be able to play with and stimulate the baby during her entire shift, thus providing positive social reinforcement. At times the child may be turned around and remain close to the nurse. This type of reinforcement may be more effective than the aversive behavioral techniques of squirting lemon juice and pepper sauce during rumination (Singh 1979).

Treatment after Leaving the Hospital

Although rumination frequently will cease, problems in the family may exist after discharge. A number of reports of continued maternal depression have been described (Chatoor et al. 1984, Gaddini and Gaddini 1959,

Lourie 1954, Richmond et al. 1958). Therefore a long-term goal may include individual treatment for a depressed mother. As part of discharge planning, home visits and increased support from friends and family are advised. If the child continues to ruminate, placement outside the home may be necessary.

THEORIES OF RUMINATION

Behavioral

Behavioral theory describes rumination as a habit pattern. Reinforcements enhance and maintain the specific behavior, which eventually becomes temporally linked to its consequences. Positive reinforcement, such as attention and holding of food, increases the frequency of antecedent behavior. The reduction or removal of an undesirable event, such as electroshock, also increases the likelihood of an antecedent behavior. Behavioral theories focusing on the maintenance of rumination (Lavigne and Burns 1981, Winton and Singh 1983) suggest that rumination is an operant behavior maintained by its specific consequences and describe it as a learned habit that can be extinguished by appropriate chronologic manipulation of events (Starin and Fugua 1987).

Association with Affective Disturbance

Infants and children with rumination have been described as appearing sad and withdrawn (Chatoor et al. 1984, Chatoor and Dickson 1984, Gaddini and Gaddini 1959, Lourie 1954). Several reports (Gaddini and Gaddini 1959, Hollowell and Gardner 1965, Lourie 1954, Richmond et al. 1958) describe the affective unavailability of the mother to her child due to attitudes of rejection toward an unwanted infant and concurrent maternal depression. This conceptualization also underlies Lourie's (1954) notion of the understimulation of infants with a ruminatory disorder. He notes both passivity and diminished affective signaling of needs in such infants. This behavior could foster and accentuate parental confusion in responding to the child's actual needs and lead to frustration, helplessness, and depression in the caregiver. Lourie also notes these children to be markedly rejection-sensitive, a trait also observed in adult atypical depression (Liebowitz and Quitkin 1984).

There is a subgroup of children for whom object loss is a manifest onset condition for the appearance of ruminatory behavior (Flanagan 1977). Protest, despair, and withdrawal in reaction to object loss may be a developmentally specific clinical feature in the symptom complex of rumination.

Observations linking ruminatory behavior in adults with depressive symptoms, anorexia nervosa, and bulimia have been recently reported (Blinder 1983, Fairburn and Cooper 1984, Levine et al. 1983). *Maternal affective disorder may jointly contribute both a genetic predisposition to the infant and an affective deprivational impact. A lack of adequate maternal affective availability may contribute to increased risk for the infant of both mood vulnerability and ruminatory disorder. There may also be a subgroup of infants and children with rumination who have an affective disturbance, rejection sensitivity, passivity, and increased incidence of psychiatric disorders.*

Biological Determinants

Proponents of a biological etiology view rumination as a consequence of gastroesophageal reflux and diminished lower esophageal sphincter pressure. However, there may be two subgroups of ruminators: one with significant gastrointestinal structural problems (reflux or hiatus hernia) and another with no significant gastrointestinal problems. In the former, the psychological context may provoke a response that exceeds a threshold for manifest symptoms; in the latter a deprivational or affective disturbance may be the primary determinant of a complex neurobiologic functional disorder (e.g., depression, rumination) (Blinder 1986).

Geffen (1966) posited that rumination occurs from an increased pleuroperitoneal gradient across the diaphragm with simultaneous relaxation of the cricopharyngeal and lower esophageal sphincters. Rapid gastric peristalsis with a covert contraction of the abdominal musculature further increases this pressure gradient. Incompetence of the lower esophageal sphincter, secondary to hiatus hernia, exacerbates this process. Herbst and colleagues (1971) also suggest that the abnormal findings associated with rumination should be viewed as part of an extended syndrome of gastroesophageal reflux.

The role of neuropeptides (including opioids) in mediating rumination in the CNS and peripherally in the gastrointestinal tract remains to be precisely defined (Blinder et al. 1986). The neuropeptides that elevate the lower esophageal sphincter pressure (LESP) are gastrin and motilin. Neuropeptides that decrease LESP are glucagon, secretin, cholecystokinin, and vasoactive intestinal peptide (VIP, considered the primary inhibitory gut neurotransmitter).

Opioid-containing neurons innervate the circular smooth muscle of the lower esophageal sphincter. Opioids diminish acetylcholine release, produce transient smooth circular muscle contraction, and block inhibitory transmission in circular muscle. Herman and Panksepp (1978) note the following:

It is conceivable that a brain circuit for separation distress represents an evolutionary elaboration of an endorphin-based pain network. Part of the distribution of opiate receptors in the mammalian brain overlap with tradi-

392   Barton J. Blinder, M.D.

tional pain pathways and the extension of opiate receptors into the limbic system suggests an additional affective role for endorphins. It is likely that a variety of affective processes are controlled by these limbic endorphin circuits. . . . one function of these systems is to modulate emotions arising from social variables. . . . attachment may simply represent an endogenous cellular addiction process in which an infant becomes physiologically dependent upon its mother for endorphin stimulation. [p. 219]

Blinder and colleagues (1986) have shown that an opioid agonist (paragoric) totally inhibited postingestive rumination, suggesting either a central or peripheral opioid mechanism controlling rumination which resulted from opioid receptor insensitivity or a reduction in endorphinergic neurotransmission.

Chatoor and colleagues (1984), acknowledging the foregoing finding and noting the hypothesis of Panksepp (Herman and Panksepp 1978) suggesting that attachment behavior is mediated by endogenous opioids, hypothesize that deficiency of attachment and the occurrence of separation may diminish endogenous opioid activity, thereby provoking rumination behavior in infancy. Subsequently the rumination activity may act as a compensatory mechanism increasing endogenous opioid levels, creating a type of self-stimulating addiction. Adjunctive autoerotic behaviors in infancy, which persist after loss and detachment, may entail a similar mechanism (Spitz and Wolf 1946).

The foregoing observations provide the first stages of a database to formulate a stable hypothesis bridging the gap between psychodevelopmental events and neurobiologic determinants.

SUMMARY

Rumination is an uncommon disorder occurring from infancy through adult life. It consists of regurgitating and then reswallowing partially digested food. Rumination may result in considerable morbidity in infants and young children. Adult ruminators may have a benign course with embarrassing involuntary reflux or may have an associated eating disorder (bulimia or anorexia nervosa) or depression.

Biologic theories of etiology associate rumination with gastroesophageal reflux, hiatus hernia, and delayed gastric emptying. Psychological theories discuss infants who have severe failure to thrive and often appear depressed. Severe dysynchrony between mother and infant, and maternal psychopathology consisting of anxiety, depression, and the inability to adequately nurture the child may be present. Behavioral theory discusses the self-reinforcing aspect of the ruminatory behavior. Theories of neuropeptide and opioid regulation posit central and peripheral deficits of endorphinergic neurotransmission and receptor sensitivity. There may be an endorphinergic deficit that appears in response to disruption of attachment, resulting in the appearance of rumination.

Therapy approaches include biologic treatment of reflux, psychological treatment of the infant–mother dysynchrony (with the use of substitute caretakers), and behavioral treatment, using both aversive stimuli and positive reinforcement. Rumination may also be considered an affective disorder variant. Since rumination may have either a biological- or a psychological-predominant context, a multidisciplinary approach to diagnosis and treatment, with use of various treatment modalities, is imperative to treat this disorder comprehensively and effectively.

REFERENCES

Bergman, P., and Escalona, S. K. (1949). Unusual sensitivities in very young children. *Psychoanalytic Study of the Child* 3/4:333–352. New York: International Universities Press.

———— (1986). Rumination: a benign disorder? *International Journal of Eating Disorders* 5:385–386.

———— (1991). Eating disorders in psychiatric illness. *Clinics in Applied Nutrition* 1:68–80.

Blinder, B. J., Bain, N., and Simpson, R. (1986). Adult rumination: evidence of an opioid neurotransmission mechanism. *American Journal of Psychiatry* 143:255.

Blinder, R. J., Goodman, S. L., and Goldstein, R. eds. (1988). Rumination: a critical review of diagnosis and treatment. In *The Eating Disorders: Medical and Psychological Bases of Diagnosis and Treatment,* ed. B. J. Blinder, B. F. Chaitin, and R. Goldstein, pp. 315–330. New York: PMA.

Brockbank, E. M. (1907). Merycism or rumination in man. *British Medical Journal* 1:421–427.

Brown, W. R. (1968). Rumination in the adult. *Gastroenterology* 54:933–939.

Cameron, J. C. (1925). Lumeian lectures: on some forms of vomiting in infancy. *British Medical Journal* 1:872.

Cauwels, J. M., ed. (1983). *Bulimia: The Binge-Purge Compulsion.* New York: Doubleday.

Chatoor, I., and Dickson, L. (1984). Rumination: a maladaptive attempt at self-regulation in infants and children. *Clinical Proceedings Childrens Hospital National Medical Center* 40:107–116.

Chatoor, I., Dickson, L., and Einhorn, A. (1984). Rumination and treatment. *Pediatric Annals* 13:924–929.

Danford, D. E., and Huber, A. M. (1981). Eating dysfunctions in an institutionalized mentally retarded population. *Appetite* 2:281–292.

Djaldetti, M., Pinkhas, J., and de Vries, A. (1962). Rumination and cardioesophageal relaxation associated with pernicious anemia. *Gastroenterology* 43:685–688.

Fairburn, C. G., and Cooper, P. J. (1984). Rumination in bulimia nervosa. *British Medical Journal* 288:826–827.

Fenichel, O. (1945). *Psychoanalytic Theory of Neurosis,* pp. 65–84, 375–386. New York: Norton.

Ferenczi, S. (1950). Stages in the development of the sense of reality. In *Sex in Psychoanalysis,* pp. 213–239. New York: Basic Books.

Flanagan C. H. (1977). Rumination in infancy past and present. *Journal American Academy of Child Psychiatry* 16:140–149.

Fleischer, D. R. (1979). Infant rumination syndrome. *American Journal of Diseases of Children* 133:266–269.

Gaddini, E. (1969). On imitation. *International Journal of Psycho-Analysis* 50:475–484.

Gaddini, R. D., and Gaddini, E. (1959). Rumination in infancy. In *Dynamic Psychopathology in Childhood,* ed. J. Jessner and E. Pavenstedt. New York: Grune & Stratton.

Geffen, N. (1966). Rumination in man. *American Journal of Digestive Disorders* 11:963–972.

394   Barton J. Blinder, M.D.

Greenspan, S., and Lourie, R. S. (1981). Developmental structuralist approach to the classification of adaptive and pathologic personality organization: infancy and early childhood. *American Journal of Psychiatry* 138:725–735.

Griffin, J. B., Jr. (1977). Rumination in a 7-year-old child. *Southern Medical Journal* 70:243–245.

Gryboski, J. D. (1983). Gastroesophageal reflux. In *Gastrointestinal Problems in the Infant,* 2nd ed., ed. J. D. Gryboski, W. A. Walker. Philadelphia: Saunders.

Herbst, J. J. (1983). Diagnosis and treatment of gastroesophageal reflux in children. *Pediatric Review* 5:75–79.

Herbst, J. J., Friedland, G. W., and Zboralske, F. F. (1971). Hiatal hernia and rumination in infants and children. Journal of Pediatrics 78:261–265.

Herman, B. H., and Panksepp, J. (1978). Effects of morphine and naloxone on separation distress and approach attachment. *Pharmacology, Biochemistry and Behavior* 9:213–220.

Hollowell, J. G., and Gardner, L. T. (1965). Rumination and growth failure in male fraternal twins: association with disturbed family environment. *Pediatrics* 36:565–570.

Kanner, L. (1957). Rumination. In *Child Psychiatry,* 3rd ed., pp. 484–487. Springfield, IL: Charles C. Thomas.

Kreisler, L. (1967). Psychosomatic conditions in pediatrics. *Psychiatrie de L'Enfant* 9:89–222, 1966; Excerpta Medica 20:8 #2578.

Lavigne, J. V., and Burns, W. F. (1981). Rumination in infancy: recent behavioral approaches. *International Journal of Eating Disorders* 1:70–82.

Levine, D. F., Wingate, D. L., and Pfeffer, J. M. (1983). Habitual rumination: a benign disorder. *British Medical Journal* 287:255–256.

Levy, R. (1981). Mother–infant relations in the feeding situation. In *Textbook of Gastroenterology and Nutrition in Infancy,* ed. E. Lebanthal. New York: Raven Press.

Liebowitz, M. R., and Quitkin, F. M. (1984). Psychopharmacologic validation of atypical depression. *Journal of Clinical Psychiatry* 45:22–25.

Long, C. F. (1929). Rumination in man. *American Journal of Medical Science* 178:814–822.

Lourie, R. S. (1954). Experience with therapy of psychosomatic problems in infants. In *Psychopathology of Childhood,* ed. P. H. Hoch and J. Zubin. New York: Grune & Stratton.

Mahler, M. (1975). *Psychological Birth of the Human Infant.* New York: Basic Books.

Menking, M., Wagnitz, J. G., Burton, J. J., et al. (1969). Rumination: a near fatal psychiatric disease of infancy. *New England Journal of Medicine* 280:802–804.

Milakovic, I. (1967). Hypothesis of a prenatal deglutative state in libidinal development. *International Journal of Psycho-Analysis* 48:76–78.

Philippopoulus, G. S. (1973). The analysis of a case of merycism. In *Topics on Psychosomatic Research. Psychotherapy and Psychosomatic.* 22:354–371.

Rast, J., Johnston, J. M., Drum, C., et al. (1981). The relation of food quantity to rumination behavior. *Journal of Applied Behavioral Analysis* 14:121–130.

Richmond, J. B., Eddy, E., and Green, M. (1958). Rumination: a psychosomatic syndrome of infancy. *Pediatrics* 22:49–55.

Sheagran, T. G., Mangurten, H. H., Brea, F., et al. (1980). Rumination: a new complication of neonatal intensive care. *Pediatrics* 66:551–555.

Singh, N. N. (1979). Aversive control of rumination in the mentally retarded. *Journal Practical Approach to Development Handbook* 3:2–6.

Spitz, R. A., and Wolf, K. M. (1946). Anaclitic depression: an inquiry into the genesis of psychiatric conditions in early infancy. *Psychoanalytic Study of the Child* 2:313–324. New York: International Universities Press.

Spitzer, R., and Endicott, J. (1978). Schedule for affective disorders and schizophrenia. New York: New York Psychiatric Institute.

Starin, S. P., and Fugua, R. W. (1987). Rumination and vomiting in the developmentally disabled. *Research in Developmental Disabilities* 8:575–605.

Winton, A. S. W., and Singh, N. N. (1983). Rumination in pediatric populations: a behavioral analysis. *Journal of American Academy of Child Psychiatry* 22:269–275.

17

Epilogue

C. Philip Wilson, M.D.

The problem of psychoanalytic cure in patients with severe preoedipal psychopathology is complex. The results with the eating disorders are related to those of psychosomatic disorders in general because the same patient may suffer from an eating disorder and another psychosomatic symptom. One could hope that when the apparent preoedipal and oedipal conflicts that cause and are masked by eating disorder symptoms are resolved, along with the eating disorder symptoms themselves, the fear-of-being-fat, obsession-with-being-thin body image will be resolved. In our experience, there was a significant but varying decathexis of the pathological fat-phobic body image in successfully treated cases, as was true of the cases in our *Fear of Being Fat* (Wilson et al. 1985). However, in two cured cases that returned years later, some body-image pathology was still present. The analysis of these women's inhibitions of self-assertion and aggression especially their oral-sadistic, cannibalistic-incorporative conflicts and impulses, particularly in relation to their children, their mothers, and their lovers or spouses, was crucial for the resolution of this residual body-image pathology.

The analysis and psychotherapy of forty-four restrictor and bulimic anorexics were recently described by Hogan, Mintz, Sperling, and me (Wilson et al. 1985). I have worked analytically with twenty-four restrictor and bulimic cases and have seen many more in consultation and supervision. Three cases who completed their treatment are illustrative. One adolescent, who alternately abstained, gorged, and vomited, resolved her conflicts in a year's analysis. She was neither amenorrheic nor dangerously underweight. The treatment prevented the development of phobic fear of being fat (anorexia nervosa). Both the second and third cases abstained, gorged, and vomited, but they did not use laxatives. Neither brought her weight down to dangerous levels. Diagnostically, they suffered from mixed neuroses with severe preoedipal conflicts. Both patients, unlike the typical restrictor anorexic, had an abundant psychosexual fantasy life and had masturbated in childhood.

Experienced analysts have expressed doubts to me about the possibility of analyzing any anorexic. Cases that I have analyzed and supervised, however, have experienced a full resolution of their fear-of-being-fat body image and their obsession with being thin. I reported (1988) on a twenty-two-year follow-up of a case of severe regressive, restrictor anorexia nervosa. The patient had been successfully analyzed with a complete resolution of her psychoticlike fear-of-being-fat, obsession-with-being-thin, body-image pathology. She married, had two children, a boy and a girl, and evidenced healthy interpersonal and career functioning. I likewise have a fifteen-year follow-up of a case of a chronic severely ill bulimic anorexic who achieved structural change, symptom resolution, and major improvement in her body-image pathology. She married, had a healthy child and was successful in her career as a bank executive.

Thus long-term follow-up studies showed that these patients were able to face and master the conflicts of self-fulfillment in a career, pregnancy, childbirth, and motherhood. If the restrictor or bulimic anorexic process can be analyzed in *status nascendi,* the prognosis may be favorable. The difficulties encountered in the treatment of chronic restrictor and bulimic anorexics are explicated in our publications (Wilson et al. 1985). Of course, statements about prognosis must be qualified by the psychodynamic diagnosis of the individual case and by the presenting situation. Obviously, if the addicted restrictor or bulimic is seen when acutely alcoholic or under the influence of drugs, all the technical problems involved in the management and treatment of such cases confront the therapist.

My colleagues and I do not follow up our cases by questionnaires and the like. For patients who have the most serious problems, final separation from the analyst may be achieved only long after office visits have stopped. One patient graphically expressed this conflict when she told me that I would know when *she was through with me* the year I did not receive a Christmas card from her. For seven years I received a card or letter from the patient telling me how she was doing, about her children, activities, and husband. There has been no communication from her for six years, which indicates that she has separated from me and indeed is through with me, that is, has matured.

In our psychosomatic volume, Silverman (1989) describes the analysis of a 10-year-old girl with a complete resolution of her restrictor anorexia nervosa in a six-year follow-up. Her severe asthma attacks were resolved but she still had occasional wheezing. Mintz (1989) in the same volume reports a seven-year follow-up of a 12-year-old girl with a complete resolution of her subclinical restrictor anorexia nervosa and severe asthma. Like Silverman's patient, she still had occasional wheezing in conflictual situations. Mintz noted that he had seen twelve cases of asthma and anorexia nervosa in adolescent girls. Either the asthma was present until adolescence, when it was replaced by anorexia nervosa, or the two symptoms occurred simultaneously. Gonzalez (1988), in his comprehensive chapter on bulimia and adolescence, reports a one-year follow-up of the three-year analysis of a 16-year-old girl with symptom resolution, the two-year analysis of a 16-year-old girl who at termination had rare bulimic episodes, the one-year analysis of an 18-year-old girl with control of symptoms and clearing of depression, and a two-year follow-up on the three-year analysis of a 14-year-old girl with symptom resolution. Risen (1982) reported on the successful analysis of a 14½-year-old girl.

I have supervised the psychodynamic treatment (analysis or psychotherapy) of twenty-two eating disorder cases, fourteen bulimic and six restrictor anorexics, one atypical eating disorder, a patient who was fat phobic and bulimic but did not vomit or purge, and one superobese patient. Among refractory cases was a superobese woman who mastered her bulimic gorging, vomiting, and kleptomania in twice-a-week psychotherapy and an alcoholic bulimic male college student who resolved his alcoholism and eating disorder in analytic psychotherapy. Cohen and Rudominer in this volume detail successful results with two bulimic cases.

At a panel on compulsive eating, obesity, and related phenomena (Reiser 1988), I reported on the analytic treatment of six obese patients. Five of them had successful results, achieving structural change, symptom resolution, and normal weight. The refractory case terminated prematurely at the time that psychosexual conflicts were emerging. Rowland (1988) at the same panel reported successful analytic psychotherapeutic results in a superobese man. This 420-pound man was able to take off 230 pounds, to face the dieter's depression, and to marry. Another patient was a 360-pound man who lost 50 pounds in eight months of psychotherapy. Mintz reported on the analysis of three obese patients at this panel, and Barkin described the treatment of a 400-pound man.

Galenson (1987) reported on the psychodynamic treatment of the mother of four anorexic failure-to-thrive infants that resulted in a cure of the babies' eating disorders. Blinder (1988) detailed the psychodynamic treatment of a mother who was a bulimic anorexic and whose new baby was anorexic: the resolution of pathological maternal attitudes about eating resulted in a cure of the child's eating disorder. These cases are confirmatory of Sperling's (1978) analysis of a 2-year-old anorexic and the mother and Blum's (1991) analysis of an infantile eating disorder in statu nascendi. I reported a case (Wilson 1982, Wilson et al. 1985) in which the analysis of the mother's fear-of-being-fat complex and her pathological relation to her daughter resulted in a clearing of developing anorexia (fat phobia) in the 12-year-old daughter.

EATING-DISORDER EQUIVALENTS

Because of the ineffective and inconsistent ego functioning of eating-disorder patients (who basically suffer from an impulse disorder), abrupt changes in behavior (acting out), neurotic or severe regressive symptoms, or different manifestations of psychosomatic disease can be caused by changes in the level of stress or in patterns of defense, in shifting intensity of drives, and in alternating levels of ego integration and regression as well as changes in object relations (Mintz 1980, Sperling 1968, Wilson 1968, 1980b, Wilson et al. 1985). At different times, for reasons that are overdetermined, the conflicts that compose the underlying personality disorder can be expressed in different illnesses. Depression, anxiety, neurosis, or other psychosomatic symptoms may precede the development of an eating disorder or may appear after symptoms subside.

More than thirty years ago Gero (1953) described anorexia as a depressive equivalent and Sperling (1959) emphasized that psychosomatic symptoms in general were depressive equivalents. Restrictor and bulimic anorexia nervosa have been reported as alternating with stiff neck (Wilson et al. 1985), ulcerative colitis (Sperling 1983, Tucker 1952), migraine (Hogan 1985), asthma (Mintz 1985), celiac disease (Ferrara and Fontana 1966), and masturbation (Wilson 1986b). Eating-disorder symptoms are frequently replaced by or alternate with spastic colitis, headache, neurodermatitis, and ulcers.

Eating-disorder equivalents are an aspect of the more general problem of psychosomatic equivalents (Wilson and Mintz 1989). I have seen psoriasis replaced by asthma (Wilson 1968), migraine by ulcerative colitis and then by migraine, obesity by hypertension, and ulcers by globus hystericus (Wilson 1981). A patient of Mintz (1980) developed in sequence: ulcerative colitis, asthma, depression, self-destructive acting out, migraine, noninfectious monoarthular arthritis of the knee, angioneurotic edema, eczema, and nasorhinitis.

I regard the eating disorders as impulse disorders, and the first phase of analysis involves the interpretation of such defenses as denial, rationalization, withholding, lying, projection, and projective identification so that the patient can become aware of the split-off narcissistic aspects of his or her personality disorder, particularly in the dyadic transference. As the underlying conflicts are analyzed, the eating-disorder behavior becomes ego alien and abrupt processes of internalization can occur.

INTERNALIZATION AND SUPEREGO FORMATION

My research confirms Blum's (1985) observations that the superego is never fully independent of the original objects throughout childhood and adolescence, and the child continues to interact with the postoedipal parents (as well as with peers). The individual, his original objects, and surroundings are all different from what they were in childhood. To my mind, the superego has a far greater legacy than "as heir to the Oedipus complex" (Freud 1923, pp. 48–49). In addition to the preoedipal roots of the superego, the internalization and consolidation of parental relationships, authority, attitudes, and values continue beyond the oedipal phase through preadult life. Cognitively, the child can gradually make more subtle moral discriminations and more abstract moral judgments, distinguishing his own moral code from that of parents and others. The parents are at first idealized, as are their standards and values. The child's first "morality" is conformity and blind obedience to the parents' authority and appraisal. Initially, externalized authority and global introjections give way to more selective, enduring identifications. A. Freud (1936) stated (p. 119), "True morality begins when the internalized criticism, now embodied in the standard exacted by the superego, coincides with the ego's perception of its own fault."

THE HEALING OF THE SPLIT IN THE EGO AND ITS TRANSFERENCE MANIFESTATIONS

When eating-disorder symptoms subside in analysis, the split in the ego (Wilson et al. 1985) has been partially resolved and abrupt processes of internalization may occur in the context of the development of the superego. No matter what the age of the eating-disordered patient, a delayed adolescent maturational process occurs in analysis. However, as Ms. A.'s dream (presented later in the chapter) so graphically illustrates, revived archaic superego introjects can emerge, coexisting with new superego developmental elements. Thus dream images of a mother, policewoman, and priest, and the confusion of the analyst with the priest, illustrate the working through of superego conflicts in the analysis. In this developing dynamic process, the patient can abruptly project the archaic superego introject onto the analyst (projective identification).

I described the appearance of asthma de novo in analysis (1968, 1980b) as a manifestation of processes of abrupt internalization and superego formation in an obese patient with a severe impulse disorder. The dynamics involved in the development of asthma in this case shed light on similar processes that occur in the analysis of eating-disordered patients when asthma and other symptoms develop.

Case History

Jane, a 25-year-old obese woman, came to analysis with intense oral conflict. She was a chain-smoking alcoholic who drank herself into a stupor every evening after work and was severely depressed and suicidal. She lost one job after another. Behind a façade of helpless, childlike behavior was overwhelming oral greed. Denial and exhibitionism had characterized her neurotic parents' behavior as she was growing up. Her wealthy socialite mother was an alcoholic whose drinking was denied completely by the family. The father, a very successful businessman, insisted that the family was poor, and they lived in a rent-controlled building in an impoverished area. A compulsive man, he did daily exercises in the nude in a ritualistic fashion in front of his wife, son, and daughter. These exercises, which were preceded by a large glass of water and followed by copious urination, was one of the patient's earliest memories. He also kept binoculars on the living room windowsill so that he could look at certain exhibitionistic women in nearby apartments.

A second analysis confirmed my 1968 hypothesis that transference caused by a precipitous superego formation played a significant role in the asthma de novo. Also clearly demonstrated was the pathological effect that perverse sexual and toilet behavior had upon the patient's psychosexual development.

The patient developed asthma in the analysis as the expression of a final wish to control and defeat the analyst by being sick and forcing a termination of treatment. As the patient later admitted, she wanted to marry her big lover because on the surface he looked healthy but she knew that she could control him. She wanted to defeat me since I had come to stand for the end of her acting out.

In the working through of unresolved oedipal conflicts in the transference neurosis, the most regressive narcissistic drives struggled for expression. A new and strict superego forced an internalization of incorporative impulses that had formerly been externalized in her acting-out, overeating, and addictions. Displacement upward had already been established in the symptom of stream weeping. This weeping had expressed a wish to get sympathy and pity; however, as Greenacre (1945) points out, such tears are crocodile tears, masking intense oral-sadistic incorporative drives. This patient wanted to devour with the eyes. The tears also variously symbolized urine, semen, and saliva. This symptom had been successfully interpreted many times in the analysis. At the time of the development of asthma, there had been marked improvement in the patient's ability to let herself cry and to tolerate affects. All her oral sadism was internalized and expressed by way of respiratory incorporation. Many times previously in analysis she had expressed wishes to kill, bite, and devour me, and at other times to kill herself in order to placate her primitive superego.

The patient's psoriasis, which had expressed preoedipal exhibitionistic drives, cleared up prior to the development of the asthma, which was now the last somatic outlet for this neurotic exhibitionism. A physical illness, pneumonia, which occurred at the height of the oedipal period, provided a channel (somatic compliance) for the expression of symptoms when oedipal conflicts were revived and worked through in analysis.

Unanalyzed transference played a crucial role in the precipitation of the asthma. What took me by surprise was the sudden internalization of conflict that was occurring in the process of new superego formation.[1] The asthma was a manifestation of this structural change. Many different conflicts were interpreted during the two years that she had asthma, but I would like to emphasize the interpretation of the overly strict superego. An example of such an interpretation occurred at the time of her third asthmatic attack. The patient reported that she had been walking to work and had the thought that I (the analyst) was really trying to help her; then she suddenly got asthma. In the session I pointed out to her that once she admitted to my doing anything for her, she had to do everything to please me, she had to be perfect; her only recourse was to be sick and asthmatic.

The dynamics in this case can be contrasted with those observed in another case. A male patient had been enuretic up to the age of 5, when (following a tonsillectomy) the enuresis cleared but he developed severe bronchial asthma, which did not subside until he left his home (mother) to go to college. In this case, the development of asthma clearly represented an identification with the father, who had been an asthmatic for many years. Urinary fantasies were prominent in this case. The patient always utilized condoms in his sexual affairs. Analysis revealed that following intercourse, which was usually effected with a partially full bladder, he would urinate into the condom, ostensibly to find out if there were any leaks in the rubber. Unconsciously, urine and ejaculation were equated, and his repressed wish was to drown (impregnate) the woman with urine. The man's asthmatic attacks were a talion punishment for this sadistic infantile wish: he was drowned for wanting to drown someone. In this man's case, as in the case study above, an overly strict superego was present while the patient had asthma. Polymorphous perverse impulses emerged as analysis progressed, and acting out became a serious problem. The course of analysis was the reverse of that in the asthma de novo case in that he started with the strict superego and asthma, which she developed in termination.

The following clinical material from two patients illustrates (1) the replacement of eating-disorder symptoms by a psychosomatic symptom, asthma, and (2) the replacement of eating-disorder symptoms by structural changes in the underlying personality disorder.

Ms. A.: Asthma as an Eating-Disorder Equivalent

A 25-year-old lawyer, Ms. A. came to analysis for symptoms of chronic bulimic, fat-phobic anorexia nervosa. An intelligent young woman, she

---

[1]Later analysis revealed that it was the idealized oedipal father, me in the transference, whom she wanted to marry, not the reality husband. These fantasies and feelings had been withheld.

dated the onset of her symptoms to her first year away at college, when she felt homesick and depressed. She initially went on a diet and lost 30 pounds over two months. However, she could not maintain the diet and began gorging, vomiting, and taking large quantities of laxatives (Dulcolax). She had three to five bulimic episodes a day.

Developmental

The patient was born and brought up in Los Angeles; she had an amnesia for large periods of her childhood development. She recalled nightmares at the time of her second brother's birth when she was 4 years old and school phobia during the first grade at age 6. She had a habit of nail-biting that cleared up "more or less" in adolescence. She was, on the surface, a very well-behaved little girl. She had two younger brothers, one who was born when she was a year old and another when she was 4. She knew that her mother was sick during the pregnancies, with symptoms of nausea and vomiting. When she was 12, her parents divorced. The divorce was a shock to the patient, since the parents had kept their many years of quarreling from the children. As in many anorexic homes, the dominant force was the mother, a hypermoral, religious woman whose only "vice" was smoking. The father smoked cigarettes, had a boisterous sense of humor, and enjoyed social drinking. He was looked down on and seen as "the spoiler." His considerable success in the insurance business was also deprecated. After the divorce, the father remarried within a year and moved into a house two blocks from the patient's home. She saw a lot of her father, his new wife (a divorcée), and their little girl, who was five years younger than the patient.

The parents' behavior correlated with the bulimic-anorexic psychological profile (Wilson 1980a, 1983, 1985, 1986, Wilson et al. 1985): perfectionism, repression of emotions, infantile decision-making for the child, parental dieting and fears of being fat, sexual and toilet exhibitionism that was denied (the father wore boxer shorts at home and the patient had many memories of seeing his genitals half-revealed).

The patient had been unconsciously chosen by the mother for the development of anorexia. Contributing to this choice was the fact that the patient was the first child and the only female. The patient knew that her mother had felt guilty about her sons' births, though she felt they were favored as males. "Mother felt she had to atone to me because I was no longer the only child."

Psychosexual Development

The patient did not "know much about sexual matters." The mother was a strict Catholic, the father a "lapsed Baptist," and the patient went to church and confession until adolescence, when she came to the conclusion that religion made no sense and became an agnostic. She was not prepared for pubertal changes and menstrual periods, which were late, at 14 years of age. She did not date until the third year of college. Her boyfriend, a classmate, was Jewish, and in their senior year she moved in with him. They talked of marriage, but she was afraid of her parents' objections because of the difference in religious background.

At the time of referral, the patient was functioning in a law firm with great difficulty. She was depressed and tried to relieve the depression by prodigious eating, which set in motion self-induced vomiting to expiate, and the taking of laxatives, up to 100 Dulcolax a day. She had been on antidepressant medication and in both group and individual therapy once or twice a week for many years. She gained some insight into her conflicts, but no improvement in her symptoms. She came for consultation through a friend of hers who had resolved her neurosis and eating disorder by analysis. My evaluation at this time was of a mixed neurosis. She began four-times-a-week analytic therapy.

Course of Therapy

For the first year she was seen vis-à-vis. I interpreted her defenses against admitting to her anger toward and mistrust of her previous therapy, other doctors she had seen, and me. For a time she called me on weekends, depressed and crying, and I interpreted the primitive preoedipal need to control me totally, to have my exclusive love and attention in the context of dreams and associative material. At this phase of therapy, her masochism was interpreted in the context of the harsh demands of her archaic superego and the guilt she experienced over admitting to any conflict. Next, defenses against aggressive conflicts and impulses were interpreted.

Six months into the third year of analysis the patient evidenced a "flight into health." Her episodes of bulimia stopped, and she curtailed her use of Dulcolax to one or two a day. She reported improvement in her sexual relations with her boyfriend. At her job, she received a promotion, she was assigned to work on an important case with a senior lawyer, and her salary was doubled. She began an exercise program. Most significant of all, her periods returned, although they were irregular. To the patient and external world, these healthy changes seemed remarkable; however, she began to develop increasingly severe episodes of bronchial asthma. She had had minimal asthma in early adolescence, and tests showed her to be allergic to dust and molds. The following material documents the replacement of bulimic symptoms by asthma.

The patient began a session reporting that she awoke with asthmatic wheezing after the following dream:

> I made a serious factual mistake in a letter to a client. There was a bulimic woman who went out of control and began ravenously eating a box of chocolates. My mother and a policewoman came into the room and began screaming at the woman to stop gorging. Then I was walking down a deserted waterfront area, crying and feeling lonely. Next I was talking to a priest about how lonely I was. The priest was confused with my analyst.

Associations: When I first began to gorge and vomit, my mother once caught me doing it and yelled at me. The bulimic woman in the dream must be part of me that would like to gorge and vomit again, the way I used to do when anyone left me or anything bothered me. Last night I felt depressed and cried. I have been crying on and off in recent days and have not told you about it. Last night I was angry about the time analysis takes and the money I pay you. When I used to go to confession, the priest would absolve me of guilt if I confessed; you don't do that. You confront me with my problems and my conflicts in asserting myself. I guess I saw mother and sometimes must see you like a policewoman. I know you aren't and you tell me about my strict, perfectionistic conscience. I guess that may be the policewoman inside me. Sometimes I can't believe the things that analysis uncovers; that it is healthy to assert myself. The mistake in the letter to the client is my obsession with being perfect, that I have to endlessly check and recheck my work. The senior partner the other day told me I worry too much, that people make mistakes and we are only human. It is not that I just recheck my work. I have a law clerk working for me and I do her work for her. I even make her reprints of law opinions she should look up for herself. She has not learned to use our law library yet because I baby her so much. She teases me and calls me "Mamma X" for always taking care of her.

My interpretation to the patient was to remind her that I had told her I was not going to see her for sessions the following week and that she had not mentioned her feelings about separation; she wished that I was a priest (mother) who would always be there for her, that I would have no one else to love except her, and that I would have no self-interest, not cancel sessions, and not charge her. The patient confirmed the interpretation, saying: "It is funny, I forgot about the canceled sessions. I must be angry with you and want to go on vacation myself. I am sick and tired working the way I do."

Two weeks later the patient reported a dream in which she was a little girl in bed with her mother. She began to choke as gas filled the room. She thought someone left the oven gas jets on. She was afraid of dying.

Associations: She awoke from the dream wheezing from an asthma attack. She thought of the previous evening when she and her boyfriend had gone to a dinner party at her mother's; that evening mother was "full of gas"—she never stopped talking about herself and her wonderful work as an interior decorator. One thing that had always really bothered the patient about mother was her cigarette smoking. "Mother was so hyper-moral; she had no vices except smoking. Mother had a perfect figure and often said that if she stopped smoking she would gain weight." When the patient was 14 years old, she tried smoking secretly in her room, but mother caught her and screamed at her to stop, saying it was bad enough that she herself had the habit. After that, the patient went on a diet: it was the beginning of her eating disorder. More thoughts about the dream were that smokers gas people, make nonsmokers ill, by smoking. "Mother must know this; how could she smoke like that at her own dinner party?" Once when the patient was young, a baby-sitter made herself a cup of coffee and left the gas on, and the patient, who was asleep, woke up choking on the gas that leaked into her room. She remembered the sitter rushing into the room and frantically opening the windows. Her final thought was that the gas in the dream was mother's cigarette smoke, that she must have choked on the smoke as a little girl. Mother's fingers were always yellow with nicotine stains. An interpretation was made that the patient was choked to death by asthma as a punishment for her anger at her mother and that there was a talion wish to poison mother with gas (smoke) as she felt poisoned by mother.

The analysis of the sadomasochistic conflicts that were repressed and internalized in the psychosomatic symptoms resulted in a clearing of the patient's asthma. Space does not permit detailing the analysis of the underlying personality disorder in this patient. In the majority of analyzed cases of asthma, the primary fixations are at the anal level (Sperling 1963; Wilson 1982). However, the fantasies repressed and internalized in asthma are specific for the individual case, but not for asthma in general. Oral fixations and fantasies appear in every case. Analytic technique in such cases has been described by my colleagues and myself (Karol 1980; Mintz 1980; Wilson 1980a; Wilson and Mintz 1989).

Ms. R.: Overly Aggressive Behavior Replacing Eating-Disorder Symptoms

A 38-year-old married woman, Ms. R., came for consultations because of marital conflicts. She felt that she was in some way provoking her husband, who complained that she was bitchy. Ms. R. had been born and brought up in a suburb of Chicago. In childhood she had been enuretic and a thumb-sucker until age 9. Her mother was the perfect "chicken soup mother" who did everything for her children. The patient was the youngest of three children. A sister, two years older, was married and had two children. Her brother, four years older, was also married with one child. Ms. R. had been the baby, a special, lovely little princess, a role that she was teased about but that she not so secretly enjoyed.

She was a very well-behaved girl and did well in school. She started ballet lessons in her early years, and the family thought she would become a ballet star, but in adolescence she broke her ankle practicing and gave up formal ballet, although she continued with daily exercise, jogging, and aerobics. She was inhibited about sexual matters and upset and shy at the development of precocious puberty at 9 years of age. She thought that her first menstrual bleeding was a hemorrhage and was ashamed of the development of her breasts. She achieved excellent marks in high school and college.

She married the first man who really dated her, a medical student at a university near the women's college she attended. Shortly after marriage she developed symptoms of bulimic anorexia nervosa, and after four years of hiding her symptoms from her husband, a successful surgeon, she came to me for consultation. I referred her to a colleague for analysis. She was in analysis for four years and her bulimic symptoms cleared; however, she terminated analysis prematurely against the advice of the analyst, who told her that she had not worked through her resentment and anger with men. For a time following termination, she did well. She had a child, a healthy little boy, and she was promoted to senior editor in a publishing firm. However, she had increasingly severe and painful quarrels with her husband. Although she was completely free of her bulimic symptoms, her fear of being fat and her obsession with a thin body image, although less intense, still preoccupied her. The following clinical material illustrates the structural shift that replaced the bulimic symptoms in this patient.

In the second week of therapy the patient reported a dream of an operation in which some flesh was removed. Her associations were to a fight that she had had with her husband after she bought a book entitled, *How to Take 20 Pounds Off Your Man* (Simon & Schuster, 1985). Her thoughts were that her husband was 20 pounds overweight and did not exercise regularly. He became angry when she brought up the book and suggested that he join a health club. She thought of how much she enjoyed her aerobics class. She realized her husband worked long hours in the hospital and knew that she should not nag him about his weight, but she could not help it. She knew that her nagging had something to do with their not having had sex for two weeks. Her association to the dream was the thought that surgeons should be able to remove fat from people's bodies by operations. The interpretation was made that the patient still had the process in her that demanded instant perfection of herself and her husband, and that it would be in her best interests not to pressure her husband about losing weight because she had not fully analyzed her fear-of-being-fat complex. Her reply was that she knew I was right, that her husband repeatedly told her that he was not that much overweight, that she had a thing about weight, and that she turned him off by talking about weight.

Two weeks later the patient reported another dream of a woman's body with a weird sort of penis attached to it. The patient's associations were to missing her husband, who was away at a medical convention. She knew her husband was faithful to her, but she was jealous of the women doctors he would be with at the meeting. She recalled how angry her mother used to be with father when he came back from business trips. Father "confessed" to mother that he was unfaithful to her. As a little girl, the patient knew that father and mother quarreled behind closed doors, but she could never think of her parents divorcing, even though when she got older, her mother told her of their quarrels. She remembered father in the bathroom urinating; his genitals looked so strange. She could not recall whether she saw his testicles or not. The patient ruefully said about the dream, "I must want my husband to be a female with a penis."

The interpretation was made that the patient unconsciously confused her husband with her father and that she was expressing anger (castrating him) that she could not express to father when she was a child. The patient burst into tears and said that over the past weekend she had been depressed and missed her mother. A further interpretation was made of her wanting me and her husband to mother her.

It is not possible here to go further into this woman's analysis; of course, her dreams had many other meanings. Her unresolved penis envy and problems in separation-individuation were central themes. The one dynamic to be emphasized here is the defense of identification with the aggressor. An emerging identification with her father's strict superego enabled her to master her bulimic symptoms (her acting-out impulses). As she talked of her "bitchy," controlling loss of temper with her husband and me in the transference, many memories emerged of her father's rigid, perfectionistic, moralistic demands and his outbursts of righteous anger. At meals, for example, he would snap at her about her overeating and table manners, just as she did with her husband.

This case illustrates another problem with these patients; just when major changes occur in symptom resolution, the patients may terminate abruptly before working through their conflicts. In this case, as the patient came to understand the conflicts underlying her neurosis and was able to analyze them in the transference neurosis, the marital quarrels decreased in frequency and a healthy sexual relationship developed with her husband.

Discussion of Clinical Cases

In Ms. A.'s clinical material we can see that her eating disorder behavior, which is represented in the dream as the bulimic female who gorges and vomits, has become ego alien. When a patient dreams of a symptom, the patient is on the way to giving it up. Likewise, the patient was becoming aware of her identification with masochistic aspects of her mother's behavior. Ms. A.'s developing insight into her archaic, punishing superego is expressed in the appearance of the policewoman in the dream and particularly the wish that the analyst were a priest. All these and other conflicts were lines of interpretation that had been repeatedly interpreted in analysis. The point must be reemphasized, however, that insight and structural change can lead to sudden internalization, and the alternate psychosomatic symptom that emerges should be analyzed like any other symptom formation in the course of analysis. The follow-up dream of being gassed shows that further sadomasochistic impulses and fantasies, which are recurrent conflicts in asthma (Wilson 1980b), were being worked through in the analysis.

In the second case we can see what developed when Ms. R. terminated her first analysis prematurely because her bulimic symptoms had cleared. In her bulimic phase she had been submissive to her husband; she recalled, for example, that one time when she was angry at her husband's going out to play golf and leaving her alone on a Saturday, she ate a whole box of chocolate cookies, vomited into the cardboard container they came in, and then put it in a drawer and "forgot" about it. Her husband found the "smelly" box a week later and "almost lost his temper" with her. Now when her husband left her for male activities, instead of gorging and vomiting she became bitchy and critical. For a time she was flooded with narcissistic fantasies that her husband should be able to work long hours as a physician but also make the beds, do the dishes, and baby-sit with their child while she went out and did what she wanted. She wanted to resume every premarital pleasure that she had enjoyed: ballet lessons, horseback riding, and travel. Her dream of the woman with the penis reflected her magical wishes of her husband, that he be a magical mother with a breast-phallus. They also reflected her wishes for a penis herself.

THE WISH FOR THE BREAST AND CHANGES IN THE SENSE OF TIME IN THE ANALYSIS OF AN IMPULSE DISORDER MASKED BY EATING-DISORDER SYMPTOMS

A profound distortion of the sense of time was displayed by a young man who suffered from a severe impulse disorder. His symptoms included obesity and hypertension, phobias, hypochondriacal fears, addiction to alcohol and cigarettes, nail-biting, and flesh picking and tearing. At a point in his analysis when profound structural changes and improvements had been effected, the patient became aware that he still drained off his polymorphous perverse, sadomasochistic impulses in his "habit" of chewing and picking at the flesh around his cuticles until bleeding occurred. In his struggle to master this habit, he reported the following dreams:

1. My mother was cured of cancer and gave me a hug. She reached for my penis and brushed the pubic hair.

2. Your wife, who is confused with my mother, is propped up in bed with pillows. I am aware of lots of children who, apparently, are yours. One of them has an intravenous feeding. I storm out in a rage, saying, what is the point of this?

3. I dreamed that I dreamed I had a nosebleed and then I really woke up to find I did not have a nosebleed.

4. I looked at my watch and realized that I had lost a day. I thought I was going a little crazy, like an amnesia. It was as if a guy hit me and I was knocked out for twenty-four hours.

The patient's associations were to black prostitutes and to a play, *The Virgin and the Gypsy*. He recalled erotic fantasies about his mother, who developed tuberculosis and spent a year in bed when he was 12 years old. He further associated to his oedipal rivalry with his father and me in the transference, which confronted him with castration fear. He responded to the fear by a feminine identification, which was expressed by nosebleeds that he induced in childhood by nose picking. These nosebleeds for him expressed a wish to menstruate in rivalry with his mother for his father's love. These associations, of course, are but a small sampling of what emerged in the analysis. I select them here in order to focus on the patient's sense of time.

One dream wish was to lose time. He achieved this in his flesh chewing and picking, by which he denied his mother's death. (She had in reality died of cancer when he was 24.) The flesh of his finger represented for him the maternal breast at which he was eternally sucking, biting, and chewing. He would occasionally bite off bits of flesh and chew and swallow them. He said that he had it made, because the flesh of his fingers always regrew. In the transference he did not want to give up the analyst-mother by finally analyzing his sadomasochistic habit.

This patient's sense of time prior to analysis had been profoundly impaired. A college dropout, he lived on impulse, with no ambition, that is, no plans for time future. Discrimination of time past from time present was constantly blurred by his addiction and his nail-biting and finger chewing. With these habits he also denied castration fear and any acceptance of his own or other people's death. At the point in analysis when he dreamed of losing time, he was now finally facing reality, competing, and tolerating affects such as fear, anxiety, anger, and love, which he had been avoiding in his addictions and habits. The wish to destroy expressed the wish to be at mother's breast again to achieve the timelessness of the early oral phase.

ANALYTIC CURE, BODY IMAGE, AND EATING-DISORDER EQUIVALENTS

Unless the eating-disordered patient's pathological fear-of-being fat body image is resolved, one cannot say that there has been a "cure" (Wilson 1982, Wilson et al. 1985). The conscious fear of being fat masks unconscious preoedipal and oedipal conflicts. In the case of Ms. A., during the times that she was asthmatic, there was a decathexis of the conscious fear of being fat and obsession with being thin, but the unconscious fear-of-being-fat complex and distorted body image were not basically changed.

In the case of Ms. R., although her bulimic symptoms had been cleared in the first analysis, there was still a disturbed body image. She was no longer intensely fat phobic, but she was still afraid of being fat and wanted to keep her figure on the thin side—not thin to a skeletal level, but thin in the sense that she wanted to have a muscular body with no flab. Although she was no longer extremely compulsive about exercise, she was still overly preoccupied with it; she jogged, did isometric exercises, and went to a health club as often as she could. Body-phallus conflicts still had to be analyzed.

During the alcoholic phase of Jane's analysis, the asthma de novo case had a very disturbed body image. She consciously hated her obese body and her psoriatic lesions that were even on her breasts. When she developed impulse control and a functioning superego, she was able to give up her addictions to food, cigarettes, and alcohol. However, she *developed a fear-of-being-fat body image*. She exercised regularly and was very careful about her figure, keeping her weight 4 or 5 pounds under normal. Further analysis was needed to resolve this body-image pathology.

All three of these women controlled the frequency, intensity, and quality of their sexual relationships by controlling their weight. When they took off a few pounds, their lovers would unconsciously react to the castrating meaning of this behavior and become upset or angry. These women avoided being curvaceous and sexy, which they knew would arouse a man. The deepest fear of the eating disorder patient is of losing control. Likewise, drugs may clear eating-disorder symptoms but they do not resolve the underlying body-image pathology.

SUMMARY

Some follow-up data were presented and the point made that while there are many successfully analyzed cases, if eating-disorder symptoms clear before there has been sufficient change in the underlying neurosis and the object relations, symptom equivalents may emerge that include self-destructive acting out; an alternate addictive disorder such as obesity, alcoholism, or drug addition; alternate psychosomatic symptom formation; neurotic symptom formation; or severe regressive symptom formation. Clinical material was presented from the analyses of an alcoholic woman whose obesity and addictions were replaced by asthma de novo, from a woman with bulimia and asthma whose asthmatic symptoms replaced the bulimia, and from another bulimic case where the eating-disorder symptoms were resolved but a neurotic character development ensued characterized by ego alien "bitchy" behavior. Material from the analysis of an obese man was presented to demonstrate how he used nail-biting and cuticle chewing to achieve the timelessness of the oral phase and carry out the fantasy of being at mother's breast.

REFERENCES

Barkin L. (1988). Discussion at the Panel on Compulsive Eating, Obesity and Related Phenomena. Reported by L.W. Reiser. *Journal of the American Psychoanalytic Association,* 1:171.

Blinder, B. J. (1988). The psychoanalytic treatment of a mother whose new baby was anorexic, with a resolution of pathological maternal attitudes about eating which resulted in a cure of the baby's eating disorder. Psychosomatic Discussion Group of the American Psychoanalytic Association, C. P. Wilson, Chairman. New York, December 5.

Blum, H. P. (1985). Superego formation, adolescent transformation, and the adult neurosis. *Journal of the American Psychoanalytic Association,* 33:887–909.

———— (1991). *Dyadic Psychopathology and Infantile Eating Disorder, Psychoanalytic Study and Inferences: An Infantile Eating Disorder in Statu Nascendi.* Presented at a meeting of the Long Island Psychoanalytic Society, June 5.

Ferrara, A., and Fontana, V. J. (1966). Celiac disease and anorexia nervosa. *New York State Journal of Medicine* 66:1000–1009.

Freud, A. (1936). The Ego and the Mechanisms of Defense. Writings, 2 New York: International Universities Press.

Freud, S. (1923). The ego and the id. *Standard Edition* 22:66–67.

Galenson, E. (1987). Personal communication, November 16.

Gero, G. (1953). An equivalent of depression: anorexia. In *Affective Disorders: Psychoanalytic Contributions to Their Study*, ed. P. Greenacre, pp. 117–189. New York: International Universities Press.

Gonzalez, R. G. (1988). Bulimia and adolescence: individual psychoanalytic treatment. In *Bulimia: Psychoanalytic Treatment and Theory*, ed. H. J. Schwartz, pp. 399–441. Madison, CT: International Universities Press.

Greenacre, P. (1945). Pathological weeping. *Psychoanalytic Quarterly* 3:359–367.

Hogan, C. C. (1985). Psychodynamics. In *Fear of Being Fat: The Treatment of Anorexia Nervosa and Bulimia*, rev. ed., ed. C. P. Wilson, C. C. Hogan, and I. L. Mintz, pp. 115–128. New York: Jason Aronson.

Karol, C. (1980). The role of primal scene and masochism in asthma. *International Journal of Psychoanalytic Psychotherapy*, 8:577–592.

Mintz, I. L. (1980). Multideterminism in asthmatic disease. *International Journal of Psychoanalytic Psychotherapy*, 8:593–600.

_____ (1985). Anorexia nervosa and bulimia in males. In *Fear of Being Fat: The Treatment of Anorexia Nervosa and Bulimia*, ed. C. P. Wilson, C. C. Hogan, and I. L. Mintz, rev. ed., pp. 263–304. New York: Jason Aronson.

_____ (1988). The Fear of Being Fat in Normal, Obese, Starving and Gorging Individuals. Presentation to the Panel on Compulsive Eating, Obesity and Related Phenomena. Reported by L. W. Reiser *Journal of the American Psychoanalytic Association* 1:165–166.

_____ (1989). *Psychosomatic Symptoms: Psychodynamic Treatment of the Underlying Personality Disorder* (ed. with C. P. Wilson). Northvale, NJ: Jason Aronson.

Reiser, L. W. (1988). Panel report: compulsive eating, obesity, and related phenomena. *Journal of the American Psychoanalytic Association*, 1:63–71.

Risen, S. E. (1982). The psychoanalytic treatment of an adolescent with anorexia nervosa. *Psychoanalytic Study of the Child* 37:433–459. New Haven, CT: Yale University Press.

Rowland, C. V. Jr. (1988). Compulsive eating and depression. Presentation to the Panel on Compulsive Eating, Obesity, and Related Phenomena. Reported by L. W. Reiser *Journal of the American Psychoanalytic Association* 1:166–167.

Silverman, M. A. (1989). Power, control, and the threat to die in a case of asthma and anorexia nervosa. In *Psychosomatic Symptoms: Psychodynamic Treatment of the Underlying Personality Disorder*, ed. C. P. Wilson and I. L. Mintz, pp. 351–364. Northvale, NJ: Jason Aronson.

Sperling, M. (1959). Equivalents of depression in children. *Journal of the Hillside Hospital* 8:138–148.

_____ (1963). Psychoanalytic study of bronchial asthma in children. In *The Asthmatic Child: Psychoanalytic Approach to Problems and Treatment*, ed. H. Scheer, pp. 138–155. New York: Harper and Row.

_____ (1968). Acting out behavior and psychosomatic symptoms: clinical and theoretical aspects. *International Journal of Psycho-Analysis*, 49:250–253.

_____ (1978). *Psychosomatic Disorders in Childhood*. New York: Jason Aronson.

Tucker, W. I. (1952). Lobotomy case histories: ulcerative colitis and anorexia nervosa. In *Anorexia Nervosa*, ed. J. E. Meyer and H. Feldman, pp. 51–59. Stuttgart: Georg Thieme.

Wilson, C. P. (1968). Psychosomatic asthma and acting out: a case of bronchial asthma that developed de novo in the terminal phase of analysis. *International Journal of Psycho-Analysis*, 49:330–335.

_____ (1980a). The family psychological profile of anorexia nervosa patients. *Journal of the Medical Society of New Jersey*, 77:341–344.

_____ (1980b). Parental overstimulation in asthma. *International Journal of Psychoanalytic Psychotherapy*, 8:601–621.

_____ (1981). Sand symbolism: the primary dream representation of the Isakower phenomenon and of smoking addictions. In *Clinical Psychoanalysis*, ed. S. Orgel and B. D. Fine, pp. 45–55. New York: Jason Aronson.

_____ (1982). Fifteen-year follow-up of a case of ulcerative colitis. Case presentation to the

412   C. Philip Wilson, M.D.

Psychoanalytic Discussion Group of the Psychoanalytic Association of New York, February 14, New York.

———— (1983). Fat phobia as a diagnostic term to replace a medical misnomer: anorexia nervosa. Meeting of the American Academy of Child Psychiatry, October, San Francisco.

———— (1985). Obesity: personality structure and psychoanalytic treatment. Panel on Compulsive Eating: Obesity and Related Phenomena. Pietro Castelnuovo-Tedesco, Chairman. Winter Meeting of the American Psychoanalytic Association, December 11, New York.

———— (1986a). The psychoanalytic psychotherapy of bulimic anorexia nervosa. In *Adolescent Psychiatry,* ed. S. Feinstein, pp. 274–314. Chicago: University of Chicago Press.

———— (1986b). A discussion of E. Levin's paper, Bulimia as a masturbatory equivalent. *Jefferson Journal of Psychiatry,* 3:24–35 (1985) and 4:77–87 (1986).

———— (1988). Long-term follow-up of a case of restrictor anorexia nervosa. Case presentation to the Psychosomatic Discussion Group of the Psychoanalytic Association of New York, January.

———— Hogan, C. C., and Mintz (1983). *Fear of Being Fat: The Treatment of Anorexia Nervosa and Bulimia.* Rev. ed. New York: Jason Aronson.

———— and Mintz, I. L. (1989). *Psychosomatic Symptoms: Psychodynamic Treatment of the Underlying Personality Disorder,* pp. 20–26. Northvale, NJ: Jason Aronson.

Index

developmental/psychostructural
factors in, 380–387
adolescence, 384–386
adulthood, 386–387
infancy and early childhood,
380–383
latency, 383–384
overview of, 379–380
theories of, 390–392
treatment of, 387–390
Russell, D., 27
Russell, G., 196, 214

Sachs, H., 212
Sachs, O., 83
Sacks, M. H., 358
Sacks, O., 276
Sadomasochism
adolescent crisis and, 116
interpretation technique, 60–61
restrictor anorexia, 44–45
sexual identifications and, 131,
133
Sadomasochistic oral-incorporative
states, obesity and, 88
Sandler, J., 213
Sand symbols
obesity and, 87–88
oral-phase symbols, 19–23
Sarlin, C. N., 214, 215
Sarnoff, C., 20, 233
Savitt, R. A., 16, 29, 82, 89, 92,
94, 302
Schafer, R., 129–130
Schiebel, S., 89
Schlossman, H., 312, 345, 358,
362
Schowalter, J., 313
Schutze, G., 65
Schwartz, H. J., 19, 29, 62, 196,
212, 213, 299, 313, 372
Searles, H. F., 58
Segal, H. L., 240
Sekaer, C., 7
Selvini Palazzoli, M., 29, 61, 120,
130, 171, 371

Separation anxiety, esophageal
atresia, 249
Separation-individuation
brain and, 391–392
bulimia and, 215–216
bulimia onset during
psychoanalysis, 297
childhood eating disorders and,
227
eating disorders and, 23, 25
ego-defective development and,
303
ego functioning and, 30–31
esophageal atresia and, 249,
255–256, 259, 269–270
Sex differences
anorexia nervosa and, 17
eating disorders and, 111–112
Sexual conflict
binging behavior and, 375–377
laxative use and, 366–367
Sexual identifications, 129–143
clinical case examples, 132–138
discussion of, 138–141
overview of, 129–130
pregenital determinants in eating
disorders, 131–132
Sexuality
social factors and, 122
women and, 122
Sham feeding, esophageal atresia
and, 237–238
Shaw, N., 341
Sheagran, T. G., 379, 381
Shengold, L. L., 26, 313, 344, 346,
349
Siblings, parental psychopathology
and, 26
Silence
denial defense and, 59
patient's diary/analyst's view
compared, 161–162
Silverman, M. A., 18, 25n2, 59n8,
397
Simmel, E., 344, 349
Sims, E. A. H., 68, 82n1
Singh, N. N., 389, 390